ORACLE
HOW-TO

THE DEFINITIVE PROBLEM-SOLVER FOR ORACLE DEVELOPERS AND DATABASE ADMINISTRATORS

Waite Group Press™
A Division of
Sams Publishing
Corte Madera, CA

Edward Honour

Publisher: Mitchell Waite
Associate Publisher: Charles Drucker

Acquisitions Manager: Jill Pisoni

Editorial Director: John Crudo
Project Editor: Lisa H. Goldstein
Developmental Editor: Russ Jacobs
Technical Editors: Greg Costanzo, Steve Schifflet
Copy Editor: Michelle Goodman/Creative Solutions

Production Director: Julianne Ososke
Production Manager: Cecile Kaufman
Production Editor: Mark Nigara
Senior Designer: Sestina Quarequio
Designer: Jil Weil
Cover Illustration: Cathleen Toelke
Illustrations: Steve Adams, Clint Lahnen, Casey Price, Marvin Van Tiem
Production: Chris Barrick, Elizabeth Deeter, Ayanna Lacey, Paula Lowell, Mark Walchle

Printed in the United States of America
97 98 99 • 10 9 8 7 6 5 4 3

*Library of Congress Cataloging-in-Publication Data
Honour, Edward, 1963-
    Oracle how-to / Edward Honour.
        p.   cm.
    Includes index.
    ISBN 1-57169-048-4
    1. Oracle (Computer file)   2. SQL (Computer program language)
I. Title.
QA76.9.D3H655   1996
005.75'65--dc20   96-34501
                                                                              CIP

DEDICATION

To my parents, Edward and Carolyn, and my wife Terri

ABOUT THE AUTHOR

Edward Honour assists organizations in effectively designing, developing, and managing solutions using Oracle products. He has worked with Oracle products since 1989 and has participated in the design and development of several large-scale client/server applications for a variety of industries. Prior to forming his consulting practice, he was the director of information systems for a nationwide food service company based in Chicago, where he was responsible for the development and implementation of large-scale, mission-critical Oracle applications.

Ed lives with his wife in Schaumburg, Illinois and is a principal of Software Dynamics Ltd. He can be reached on the Internet at ehonour@msn.com, or by visiting the Software Dynamics Web site at http://www.sdcnet.com/.

TABLE OF CONTENTS

CONTENTS

ACKNOWLEDGMENTS

Thanks to Mohammed Jamal and Tony Catalano for their expert analysis of the chapters as I developed them. Their insight was critical to the development and presentation of the topics covered in this book.

Thanks to the following people for posing the tough technical questions and identifying the requirements on which this book is based: Maggie Keane, Paul Reyes, Tom Keane, Debbie Vaisnor, Stan Brown, John Wiff, Brian Michael, Andrew Marshall, Avery Cohen, Rob O'Neal, Chandra Dorsey, and Tammy Henry.

I would like to acknowledge the dedicated people at Waite Group Press for producing the final product ahead of our original schedule. A special thanks to Lisa Goldstein, the project editor, for keeping the project on track, keeping a smile, and shortening deadlines.

INTRODUCTION

The Oracle Relational Database Management System (RDBMS) is the most popular relational database in the world. It is an extremely powerful, flexible, and complex system. Oracle can be used for applications ranging from small single-user systems, to applications supporting thousands of concurrent users. There are a variety of roles for computer professionals supporting Oracle and a full range of Oracle tools to support them. Application developers build new applications using Oracle's Developer 2000, PL/SQL, and most recently, Oracle WebServer. Oracle's Designer 2000 is a highly sophisticated CASE tool used to design and generate sophisticated applications and support structured methodologies. Oracle database administrators support the complex Oracle architecture, providing a reliable, highly tuned database for the users of Oracle applications. Oracle architects design databases to support the enterprise. Oracle is suited for every task, from a single database system, to a distributed system using snapshots and replication, to a clustered or massively parallel system using Oracle Parallel Server. This book provides real-world answers to the issues faced by computer professionals using Oracle.

Oracle How-To is divided into 20 chapters, each covering an integral part of the Oracle database and tools.

Chapter 1, SQL*Plus: This chapter covers SQL*Plus and provides tips for using this fundamental tool of the Oracle system. SQL*Plus provides the most direct access to Oracle, and using it effectively will improve your productivity with Oracle.

Chapter 2, User Accounts and Roles: This chapter covers the creation and management of user accounts and roles. Each user of the Oracle system must be assigned a user account for connecting to the database. Privileges can be granted directly to user accounts or indirectly through roles.

Chapter 3, Security: This chapter provides techniques used to implement security for your Oracle database. It uses many of the techniques presented in Chapter 2 and expands them to provide useful security techniques.

Chapter 4, Tables: Tables are the fundamental storage object of data within Oracle. This chapter presents techniques related to the creation and management of tables within the Oracle database.

Chapter 5, Views: Views can be used to present data in a format independent of the actual data storage. This chapter presents techniques related to the creation and management of views within Oracle.

Chapter 6, Sequences: Sequences, which are a powerful feature of Oracle, generate unique numbers within the database. This chapter presents tips and techniques related to the creation, management, and use of sequences.

Chapter 7, Synonyms: A synonym is an alias for a database object and is important within multiuser applications. This chapter covers tips and techniques related to the management and effective use of synonyms.

Chapter 8, Manipulating Data: This chapter presents powerful techniques for manipulating data within the database. Topics are presented relating to the creation, modification, and removal of data in the database.

Chapter 9, Querying Data: This chapter presents powerful techniques for retrieving data from the database. Oracle is a powerful database capable of using many sophisticated methods to retrieve data.

Chapter 10, Dates, Text, and Numbers: This chapter presents the Oracle functions used to manipulate dates, text, and numbers. Oracle provides a variety of built-in functions used to manipulate values in the database.

Chapter 11, Distributed Databases: The days of a single large database handling all database requirements are over. This chapter presents tips and techniques related to the distribution of data over multiple Oracle databases. The management of database links and snapshots are presented in this chapter.

Chapter 12, PL/SQL: This chapter covers PL/SQL, the procedural language of Oracle. The advanced features of PL/SQL are presented within the chapter topics. Entire books are devoted to the techniques presented in this one chapter. By studying the code shown in Chapter 12, you will gain a thorough understanding of PL/SQL.

Chapter 13, Procedures, Functions, and Packages: This chapter covers some of the most powerful features of the Oracle database. Stored procedures, functions, and packages allow applications to use the database server for processing application-related code. The techniques presented in this chapter will help you develop powerful stored procedures, functions, and packages.

Chapter 14, Built-In Packages: This chapter presents techniques using the powerful built-in packages that come with Oracle. In this chapter, you will learn how built-in stored packages provided by Oracle can perform many of the tasks you would normally expect to code.

Chapter 15, Database Triggers: This chapter presents topics related to the creation and management of database triggers. Database triggers allow the business rules of the database to be enforced at the database level.

Chapter 16, Application Tuning: This chapter presents techniques used to improve the performance of applications running on the Oracle database. Even the most well-designed applications may have performance problems that can be resolved using the techniques contained in this chapter.

Chapter 17, Database Tuning: This chapter presents techniques used to improve the performance of all applications running on the Oracle database. Although the topics presented in this chapter are geared toward the Database Administrator, they give application developers a good foundation for performing Oracle database tuning.

Chapter 18, Oracle Objects for OLE: This chapter presents Oracle Objects for OLE, which extends the functionality of the Oracle database to any development tool supporting OLE automation.

Chapter 19, Building Web Applications with Oracle WebServer: This chapter provides techniques for developing intranet and Internet applications using Oracle WebServer. The Web is quickly becoming an integral part of enterprise computing, and Oracle's Web products will have a major impact on the industry.

Chapter 20, Administering WebServer: This chapter provides tips and techniques for administering Oracle WebServer. Oracle WebServer is administered though Web documents using any browser. The techniques presented in this chapter are important to effectively manage a WebServer environment.

Appendix A, Handling Error Messages: This appendix provides solutions for the most common error messages encountered when developing and supporting Oracle applications. This appendix takes you directly to the cause and solution of error messages you are sure to encounter when developing and maintaining applications using Oracle.

Appendix B, Tools on the Accompanying CD: The accompanying CD contains products from Oracle Corporation and products developed by the author. This appendix provides information for getting the most out of the contents of the accompanying CD.

Who Is This Book Intended For?

This book is intended for beginning, intermediate, and advanced Oracle developers and database administrators. The book is meant to solve problems occurring in the normal development of applications for the Oracle database. Many of the How-Tos contained in this book provide a foundation of knowledge that will help to solve other problems as they occur. The topics covered in the book range from the very basic to the very advanced. When developing or supporting applications for Oracle, you will come across the full spectrum of problems covered in this book. Specific examples of programming problems and techniques for all levels are given.

Installing Examples Found on the CD

All of the files used within the book can be found on the accompanying CD-ROM. SQL*Plus is used throughout the book to demonstrate most of the techniques. Each example is contained in a SQL file in the \SAMPLES\CHAPxx directory and is in the format CHxx-xx.sql. When working with a chapter, you should copy the contents of the directory into the SQL*Plus working directory. If you do not wish to copy the files from the CD-ROM, specify the full path of the directory on the CD-ROM when using the GET or START command within SQL*Plus.

Appendix B contains information about the other software products contained on the CD-ROM.

Typographical Conventions Used

Most of the examples within the book use SQL*Plus to demonstrate a solution to a problem. Because SQL*Plus is an interactive environment, the following typographical conventions are used.

Information entered by the user is presented in `normal computer type`. Information displayed by SQL*Plus is printed in **`boldface computer type`**.

CHAPTER 1
SQL*PLUS

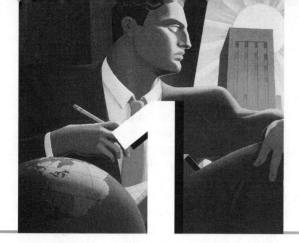

SQL*PLUS

How do I...

SQL*Plus is one of the most powerful tools used in developing applications for the Oracle database. SQL*Plus provides the most direct access to Oracle. Although it may seem that SQL*Plus is not user-friendly like graphical query tools, SQL*Plus provides a great deal of flexibility and runs on all platforms supporting Oracle. Unlike most graphical query tools, SQL*Plus can be used to manipulate data and create database objects.

SQL*Plus plays an important role in application development. It is a powerful prototyping tool that you can use to develop and test SQL statements before integrating them into your application. A working knowledge of SQL*Plus is strongly recommended for any developer using Oracle. In this chapter, you will learn how to make SQL*Plus an integral part of your development process. You will see examples of how SQL*Plus can help you develop Oracle applications efficiently.

1.1   Save SQL statements to a file

The more you work with Oracle, the easier it becomes to develop powerful SQL statements. But how can you avoid retyping the same SQL statement every time you need it? SQL*Plus lets you save SQL statements to files so they are available the next time you need them. This How-To guides you through the task of saving SQL statements to files.

1.2   Run a SQL*Plus command file

SQL*Plus can be used for many tasks, and most tasks consist of more than one step. SQL*Plus allows you to save a series of SQL, PL/SQL, and SQL*Plus commands in a file and run them as a single statement. SQL*Plus command files can be nested to create a complex sequence of events. This How-To explores how to create and run SQL*Plus command files.

1.3   Connect to SQL*Plus as another user

Within an Oracle environment, a developer needs to connect to different user accounts and databases. When maintaining a system, you often need to connect to the database with a different user account. This How-To explains connecting to a database from within SQL*Plus and connecting to a different database on the network.

1.4   Edit a statement using SQL*Plus

Nobody is a perfect typist, and the longer your SQL statement becomes, the more likely you are to make a mistake. SQL*Plus contains editing functions that allow you to edit the SQL statement you are working on. If you are familiar with Microsoft Windows-based editors, the SQL*Plus editing functions may seem like a trip back to the Dark Ages. But with a little practice, your speed at editing SQL statements will increase dramatically. This How-To takes you through the basic editing commands needed in the SQL*Plus environment.

1.5   Repeat my last SQL statement

It is amazing how often it is necessary to repeat the same SQL statement. SQL*Plus allows you to repeat the last SQL statement without retyping it. SQL statements can be retrieved from files and executed repeatedly. This How-To covers repeating statements and executing a statement from the SQL buffer.

1.6   Save query results to a file

It is often necessary to save the results of a query to a file. The output of a query can be edited, printed, merged into a word processing document, or even run as a SQL script. In most cases, a report is just query results saved to a file and printed. Saving output to a file is the first step to developing reports with SQL*Plus. This How-To explores the method used to write the results of a query to a file.

1.7   View and modify SQL*Plus system variables

Within SQL*Plus, system variables control the behavior of the SQL*Plus environment. In many ways, changing system variables is like executing commands. Changing the values of system variables changes the way SQL*Plus behaves when executing statements and retrieving records. In this How-To, you will learn to view and modify SQL*Plus system variables.

1.8   Format a report using SQL*Plus

SQL*Plus commands and system variables allow you to format a report within SQL*Plus. You can create titles, change column headings, break on column changes, and even calculate totals. By using the formatting capabilities of SQL*Plus, you can create reports quickly and have greater control over the output of your queries. This How-To takes you through the different steps of formatting a report in SQL*Plus.

1.9   Create user-defined variables in my SQL scripts

User-defined variables give SQL*Plus a new level of flexibility. Developers can create variables that can be defined in SQL scripts or accepted from the user. This How-To explores creating user-defined variables in SQL*Plus and defining the values of the variables dynamically.

1.10   Log SQL script progress to a file

Scripts can be created to perform many of the regular tasks in your organization. But what happens if a script fails or some undesired results occur? You can save the feedback SQL*Plus provides when executing a statement, just as you would when writing the results of a query to a file. This How-To covers the techniques used to log the progress of a SQL*Plus command file as it is executed.

1.11   Use SQL*Plus to create SQL statements

Almost everything you need to know about your Oracle database can be queried through SQL*Plus. Since SQL*Plus can write query output to files and command files can be executed by SQL*Plus, SQL*Plus can be used to create SQL statements. This How-To explores using queries to create SQL statements, which is the foundation for many other techniques discussed in the book.

1.12   Select columns of the LONG datatype

The LONG datatype stores large amounts of text in a single column. Unfortunately, it is difficult for many tools like SQL*Plus to handle the LONG datatype. Some common data dictionary views used throughout this book contain LONG datatype columns. This How-To shows you how to query LONG datatype columns using SQL*Plus.

1.13   Time the execution speed of a query

How long does it take? This is a common question you should ask about any new query or data management SQL statement. The first step to tuning a query is identifying performance problems. This How-To explores two methods for timing queries and presents examples for using each method.

1.14   Kill a user's session using SQL*Plus

Is it possible to kill a user's session with SQL*Plus? Although the Session Manager is perfectly capable of performing this task, you may not always want to leave SQL*Plus in order to kill a session. This How-To demonstrates the power of SQL*Plus by using it to query the active sessions on the database and terminate a user's session.

COMPLEXITY
BEGINNING

1.1   How do I...
Save SQL statements to a file?

Problem

I often need to execute SQL statements more than once. When I write a long SQL statement or a SQL statement that I need to run repeatedly, I want to save it to a file so I can run it later. How do I save a SQL statement to a file?

Technique

The SQL*Plus SAVE command is used to save the SQL statement currently in the SQL buffer to a file. The SQL buffer contains the most recent SQL statement entered into SQL*Plus or retrieved from a file. As soon as SQL*Plus recognizes a statement as a SQL statement, it replaces the current statement in the SQL buffer with the new statement. Think of the SQL buffer as the Windows Clipboard for SQL*Plus. The SQL buffer can be saved to a file with the SAVE command, retrieved from a file with the GET command, and edited with a variety of SQL*Plus commands. How-To 1.4 explores editing the contents of the SQL buffer in great detail.

The syntax of the SAVE command is

```
SAVCE] filenameC.extJ CCRECATE]|REPCLACE]|APPCEND]]
```

Characters and options shown in brackets [ ] are optional. Options separated with the pipe symbol | are exclusive. The default action of the SAVE command is to create a new file. If the file exists, the REPLACE or APPEND keyword is required. By default, SQL*Plus will save the file with the .SQL extension to identify it as a SQL*Plus file. If you want it saved with a different extension, you can specify one when you execute the SAVE command.

> **NOTE**
>
> The SUFFIX system variable can be modified to change the default extension from .SQL to another value. For more information on setting system variables, see How-To 1.7.

Steps

1. Enter the SQL statement you wish to save. Do not to end the statement with a semicolon. If the SQL statement is terminated with a semicolon, SQL*Plus will attempt to execute it.

```
SQL> SELECT EMPNO, ENAME
2    FROM EMP
3    ORDER BY EMPNO
4
```

Unlike a SQL*Plus command, SQL statements can span multiple lines without a line continuation character. The line continuation character for SQL*Plus commands is the dash -. You can begin a new line by pressing ENTER. SQL*Plus automatically numbers the lines as they are entered. If ENTER is pressed on an empty line, SQL*Plus returns to the SQL prompt. The SQL statement entered remains in the SQL buffer until it is cleared, replaced with another SQL statement, or SQL*Plus is exited.

2. Save the file with the SAVE command. If successful, SQL*Plus will notify you that the file was created.

```
SQL> SAVE EMPQRY
Created file EMPQRY
```

The file is automatically created in the current working directory with the .SQL extension. You can specify a complete path including a different extension for the file. If the file already exists, an error message will be returned. Figure 1-1 shows SQL*Plus displaying the error message.

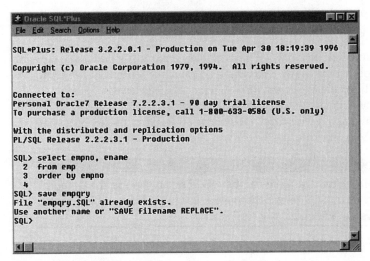

Figure 1-1 SQL*Plus with an error message
trying to create a file

3. Because a SQL*Plus command file can contain multiple SQL statements, the APPEND option allows you to add the contents of the SQL buffer to the end of an existing file. Save the contents of the SQL buffer to the same file with the SAVE command and the APPEND option.

```
SQL> SAVE EMPQRY APPEND
Appended file to empqry
```

If the file does not exist when an attempt to append to it is made, the file will be created.

How It Works

The SQL*Plus SAVE command is a SQL*Plus command (not a SQL statement). Executing it does not replace the contents of the SQL buffer. If the SAVE command is executed against Oracle using a different tool, an error will occur. Step 1 creates a SQL statement but does not execute it. Step 2 saves the contents of the SQL buffer created in Step 1 to a file using the SAVE command. Step 3 appends the contents of the SQL buffer to the end of an existing file by including the APPEND option with the SAVE command.

Comments

When statements are entered into the SQL buffer, SQL*Plus expects only SQL or PL/SQL statements. SQL*Plus commands will not be saved in the SQL buffer. If you want the SQL script to contain formatting statements use the INPUT command, which places all statements in the SQL buffer and does not analyze the statements as they are entered. Do not put a semicolon at the end of the SQL statement when using the INPUT command or an error will occur.

COMPLEXITY
BEGINNING

1.2 How do I...
Run a SQL*Plus command file?

Problem

I know I can load a SQL statement into the SQL buffer from the disk using the GET command. I want to run a SQL*Plus command file from SQL*Plus without loading it into the SQL buffer first. This is important because my SQL*Plus command files contain formatting commands and multiple SQL statements. How do I run a SQL command file?

Technique

The START command executes a SQL*Plus command file. The START command can be substituted with the @ symbol, and the commands are interchangeable. When a START command is executed, each statement in the file is executed in order. Errors occurring in the file are displayed, and the file continues to run. SQL*Plus command files can be nested. START commands can be part of SQL*Plus command files to run the contents of other files. The technique of nesting command files can be used to set system variables as the result of queries, shown in How-To 1.9.

Steps

1. CHP1-1.sql on the accompanying CD is a SQL*Plus command file. It can be executed to create or replace the sample tables used throughout this chapter. The contents of the file show the structure of a SQL*Plus command file.

```
SET TERMOUT OFF
SPOOL CHP1-1.LOG
DROP TABLE DEPT1_1;
DROP TABLE EMP1_1;
CREATE TABLE DEPT1_1 (
```

continued on next page

continued from previous page

```
    DEPTNO    NUMBER(6),
    DNAME     VARCHAR2(30));
CREATE TABLE EMP1_1 (
    EMPNO     NUMBER(6),
    ENAME     VARCHAR2(30),
    SALARY    NUMBER(12,2),
    DEPTNO    NUMBER(6));
INSERT INTO DEPT1_1
    VALUES (1, 'MARKETING');
INSERT INTO DEPT1_1
    VALUES (2, 'SALES');
INSERT INTO DEPT1_1
    VALUES (3, 'ACCOUNTING');
INSERT INTO EMP1_1
    VALUES (1, 'SMITH, JOHN', 24000,1);
INSERT INTO EMP1_1
    VALUES (2, 'JONES, MARY', 42000,1);
INSERT INTO EMP1_1
    VALUES (3, 'BROWN, BILL', 36000,2);
INSERT INTO EMP1_1
    VALUES (4, 'CONWAY, JIM', 52000,3);
INSERT INTO EMP1_1
    VALUES (5, 'HENRY, JOHN', 22000,3);
INSERT INTO EMP1_1
    VALUES (6, 'SMITH, GARY', 43000,2);
INSERT INTO EMP1_1
    VALUES (7, 'BLACK, WILMA', 44000,2);
INSERT INTO EMP1_1
    VALUES (8, 'GREEN, JOHN', 33000,2);
INSERT INTO EMP1_1
    VALUES (9, 'JONHSON, MARY', 55000,3);
INSERT INTO EMP1_1
    VALUES (10, 'KELLY, JOHN', 20000,2);
COMMIT;
SPOOL OFF
SET TERMOUT ON
```

The first command is a SQL*Plus command that suppresses the output of the statements when a script runs using the START command. The second line writes the output generated by the statements to the file specified with the SPOOL command. For more information about creating output files, see How-Tos 1.6 and 1.10. The two DROP TABLE statements remove the sample tables if they already exist. The CREATE TABLE statements build the sample tables, and the INSERT statements add data to the tables. For more information on creating and modifying tables, see Chapter 4, Tables. The COMMIT statement saves the transactions to the database. The SPOOL OFF statement stops the writing of the file, and the final statement resets the TERMOUT system variable to ON.

2. Execute CHP1-1.sql by using the START command. You must be connected to a database and have the privileges required to create tables. Chapter 2, User Accounts and Roles, covers the creation of user accounts and How-To 1.3 covers the process of connecting to different user accounts.

```
SQL>   START CHP1-1
SQL>
```

Because the output of the file is suppressed with the first line of the file, no information is in SQL*Plus when the file runs.

How It Works

The START command substituted with the @ symbol runs a file which can contain SQL, PL/SQL, and SQL*Plus commands. The statements and commands in the file are executed by SQL*Plus as if they were typed into SQL*Plus in order. If you were to take a SQL*Plus command file and enter each line, it would behave exactly as if running the file. The command file CHP1-1.sql contains SQL statements and SQL*Plus commands. The first line writes the output of the script to file CHP1-1.LOG. The next two lines remove the sample tables if they exist. If they do not exist, errors will be displayed; however, they can be ignored. The two CREATE TABLE statements create two sample tables. The INSERT statements put sample data into the tables. The COMMIT statement saves the transactions to the database, and the last command closes the output file.

Comments

When you are working with long SQL*Plus scripts, it is often easier to develop the script using a text editor like Windows Notepad and run it with the START command. Although SQL*Plus has text editing capabilities, they can be difficult to use when working with large statements. If you run CHP1-1.sql, you must be connected to an Oracle database and have privileges to create tables. If you are not sure what database access you have within your organization, contact your database administrator.

COMPLEXITY
BEGINNING

1.3 How do I...
Connect to SQL*Plus as another user?

Problem

When working in SQL*Plus, I use a couple of different database accounts. I also connect to different databases within my network. If I leave SQL*Plus, I will be prompted for a user account when I return. Unfortunately, this is too time consuming. How do I change user accounts or databases in SQL*Plus?

Technique

The CONNECT command, abbreviated CON, is used to connect to a database. Each user has a user account and password for each database to which he or she has access. Before allowing access to the database SQL*Plus will require a user account and password, which must be supplied with the CONNECT command. The syntax of the CONNECT command is shown here:

```
CONN[ECT] [USERNAME][/PASSWORD][@database]
```

The username and password can either be supplied on the same line as the CONNECT command, or SQL*Plus will prompt for them. Each computer has a default database to which it will attempt to connect if no database name is supplied with the CONNECT command. In environments with only one database, all users connect to the same default database.

Steps

1. Run SQL*Plus and connect as any user account. Connect as the WAITE user account by executing the CONNECT command. The WAITE user account is created with the installation script provided on the accompanying CD. If you have not created the WAITE user account, do so by running the INSTALL.sql file contained in the \SAMPLES directory on the CD.

```
SQL> CONNECT WAITE/PRESS
Connected.
```

If the user account or password is not valid for the default database, an error will occur. Figure 1-2 shows the error message displayed when an invalid logon is attempted.

An invalid attempt to connect to another user account or database will disconnect your current SQL*Plus session. In order to execute any database access statements, you must reconnect to the database.

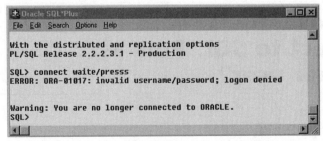

Figure 1-2 Invalid connection error message

2. Entering a password on the command line is fine if you are working at home or no one is around you, but you may want to avoid someone reading your password. If the password is not entered on the command line, SQL*Plus will prompt for it. Execute a CONNECT command without specifying a password.

```
SQL>   CONNECT WAITE
Enter password: *****
```

SQL*Plus prompts for a password when it is not specified. When the password is entered, it will not be readable.

3. In a distributed system, there can be more than one database. Each database is identified by a unique name. To connect to a database other than the default database, specify a database name in the CONNECT command. Either of the following statements can be used to connect to a remote database.

```
SQL>   CONNECT WAITE/PRESS@other_database
```

```
SQL>   CONNECT WAITE@other_database
```

The user account and password must be valid for the remote database.

4. The DISCONNECT command, abbreviated DISC, is used to disconnect from the database. Execute the DISCONNECT command to log out of the database.

```
SQL> disconnect
Disconnected from Personal Oracle7 Release 7.2.2.3.1 - 90 day trial license
To purchase a production license, call 1-800-633-0586 (U.S. only)

With the distributed and replication options
PL/SQL Release 2.2.2.3.1 - Production
SQL>
```

Once you have executed the DISCONNECT command, no SQL or PL/SQL statements can be executed on the database. In order to reestablish a connection, execute the CONNECT command.

How It Works

The CONNECT statement, abbreviated CON, is used to connect to a database; the DISCONNECT statement, abbreviated DISC, is used to disconnect the current connection. A database can be selected with the database specification after the @ symbol. If a database is not specified, SQL*Plus assumes it is connecting to the default database. Step 1 connects as a user account specifying a user name and password on the command line. Step 2 uses the CONNECT command without supplying a password. When a password is not specified, you are prompted to enter a password. Step 3 presents the options for connecting to a database that is not the default database, and Step 4 presents the DISCONNECT command to disconnect from the database. Exiting SQL*Plus automatically disconnects the session from the database.

Comments

Connecting and disconnecting from a database are common operations. The default database for your computer should be the one used most often. If you plan to walk away from your computer, you should always disconnect your session to prevent someone else from using your account.

COMPLEXITY
INTERMEDIATE

1.4 How do I...
Edit a statement using SQL*Plus?

Problem

Unfortunately, I am not perfect when I type statements in SQL*Plus. Retyping a statement every time I make a mistake is time-consuming, not to mention annoying. I need to be able to edit a SQL statement in SQL*Plus. How do I do this?

Technique

For simple changes like the misspelling of a word or the addition of a little more code, SQL*Plus provides text editing capabilities. Although it is possible to use SQL*Plus to create complex scripts, editors such as Windows Notepad are preferable for editing long SQL statements. The EDIT command within SQL*Plus executes the default editor for your operating system. In Windows, Notepad is executed and the current statement is displayed. Table 1-1 shows the editing commands used in SQL*Plus.

SQL*PLUS EDIT COMMANDS		DEFINITION
APPEND	A	Adds text at the end of a line
CHANGE /old/new	C	Changes line
CLEAR BUFFER	CL BUFF	Deletes all lines from the buffer
DEL		Deletes the current line
INPUT	I	Adds one or more lines
LIST	L	Lists all lines in the SQL buffer

Table 1-1 SQL*Plus edit commands

Steps

1. Run SQL*Plus and connect as the WAITE user account. Load CHP1-2.sql into the SQL buffer with the GET command. The file contains a fairly long query which will be edited for practice. Figure 1-3 shows the execution of a GET command in SQL*Plus.

The contents of the file are automatically listed when loaded with the GET command. The listing of the file contents can be suppressed by supplying the NOLIST clause after the filename.

2. Launch the default editor for your operating system by entering the EDIT command. If you are making more complex changes to the file, the EDIT command is the easiest way. Figure 1-4 shows the contents of the SQL buffer loaded into Windows Notepad for editing.

Once you have made the necessary changes to the statement, save the changes and exit the editor to return to SQL*Plus. The changes made in the editor will be loaded into SQL*Plus automatically.

3. List the lines in the SQL buffer. The LIST command is used to list the lines in the SQL buffer. The command is abbreviated with the letter L.

```
SQL> L
  1  SELECT
  2    DEPT1_1.DEPTNO, DEPT1_1.DNAME,
  3    EMP1_1.EMPNO, EMP1_1.ENAME, EMP1_1.SALARY
  4    FROM DEPT1_1, EMP1_1
  5  WHERE
  6    EMP1_1.DEPTNO = DEPT1_1.DEPTNO
  7    ORDER BY DEPT1_1.DEPTNO,
  8*   EMP1_1.EMPNO
```

The asterisk on line 8 identifies it as the current line. If a CHANGE or DEL command is executed without specifying a line, it will be executed on the current line.

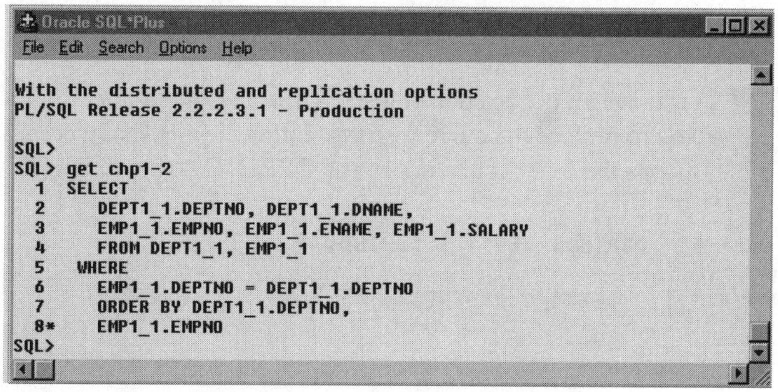

Figure 1-3 The SQL*Plus GET command

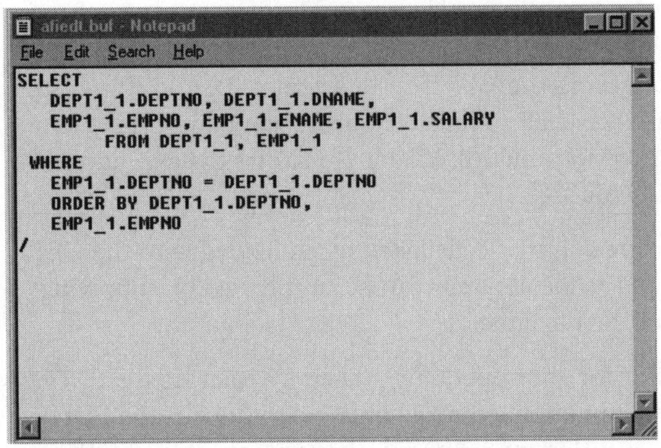

Figure 1-4 The contents of the SQL buffer
being edited in Windows Notepad

4. Use the LIST command and specify a line number to display the line and
make it the current one.

```
SQL>   L 1
  1*   SELECT
```

The line listed will become the current line of the buffer. If you want to edit
a line in the buffer, use this technique to make it current.

5. Change text using the CHANGE command. The CHANGE command,
abbreviated by the letter C, is used to change the first occurrence of a text
string within the current line. You must first use the LIST command with a
line number in order to change a line to the current line.

```
SQL>   L 2
  2*   DEPT1_1.DEPTNO, DEPT1_1.DNAME,

SQL> C/DNAME/DEPTNO
  2* DEPT1_1.DEPTNO, DEPT1_1.DEPTNO,
```

If the line contains two occurrences of a string you wish to change, the
CHANGE command must be issued twice.

6. To remove an occurrence of a string from within a line, do not specify a
string to replace the current string. Enter the CHANGE command, which
removes the first occurrence of the DEPTNO string in line 2.

```
SQL>   L 2
  2*   DEPT1_1.DEPTNO, DEPT1_1.DEPTNO,
SQL> C/deptno/
  2*   DEPT1_1., DEPT1_1.DEPTNO,
```

7. Delete lines from the SQL buffer using the DEL command. Entering the DEL command alone removes the current line, making the previous line the new current line.

```
SQL> DEL
SQL>
SQL> LIST
  1   SELECT
  2     DEPT1_1.DEPTNO, DEPT1_1.DNAME,
  3     EMP1_1.EMPNO, EMP1_1.ENAME, EMP1_1.SALARY
  4     FROM DEPT1_1, EMP1_1
  5   WHERE
  6     EMP1_1.DEPTNO = DEPT1_1.DEPTNO
  7*    ORDER BY DEPT1_1.DEPTNO,
```

8. A line number can be specified with the DEL command to delete a specific line. When a line is deleted, the other line numbers are renumbered if necessary to keep the line numbers sequential. Delete line 5 by including the line number with the DEL command.

```
SQL> DEL 5
SQL>
SQL> LIST
  1   SELECT
  2     DEPT1_1.DEPTNO, DEPT1_1.DNAME,
  3     EMP1_1.EMPNO, EMP1_1.ENAME, EMP1_1.SALARY
  4     FROM DEPT1_1, EMP1_1
  5     EMP1_1.DEPTNO = DEPT1_1.DEPTNO
  6*    ORDER BY DEPT1_1.DEPTNO,
```

9. Use the CLEAR BUFFER command to delete all the lines from the SQL buffer.

```
SQL> CLEAR BUFFER
buffer cleared

SQL> LIST
No lines in SQL buffer.
```

How It Works

SQL*Plus contains a variety of editing commands that allow the statements in the SQL buffer to be modified. Step 1 loads a query into the SQL buffer using the GET command. Only statements in the SQL buffer can be edited using the SQL*Plus editing commands. Step 2 uses the EDIT command to launch the default editor for your system and prepare the contents of the SQL buffer for editing. When the editor is closed, the modified contents of the SQL buffer are returned to SQL*Plus and displayed. Steps 3 and 4 use the LIST command, abbreviated with the letter L to list the contents of the SQL buffer. The LIST command can be used to list the entire buffer, a single line, or a range of lines. Steps 5 and 6 present the CHANGE command used to change lines within the SQL buffer. Steps 7 and 8 show how lines can be deleted from the SQL buffer with the DEL command. Step 9 presents the CLEAR BUFFER command used to remove the entire contents of the SQL buffer.

Comments

SQL*Plus contains a complete set of editing commands, but they are by no means user-friendly. Whenever possible, use a text editor like Windows Notepad to edit SQL statements. When working with multiple commands, you should use a text editor since SQL*Plus allows you to only edit the statements in the SQL buffer.

COMPLEXITY
BEGINNING

1.5 How do I...
Repeat my last SQL statement?

Problem

Sometimes I run the same SQL statement repeatedly. I do not want to retype the statement every time I run it. I know that the last SQL or PL/SQL statement remains in the SQL buffer after it runs. How do I repeat my last SQL statement?

Technique

Every time a SQL or PL/SQL statement is executed in SQL*Plus, it remains in the SQL buffer until it is replaced by another statement or SQL*Plus is exited. The forward slash, /, executes the command in the buffer.

Steps

1. Enter and execute a SQL statement like the one shown in Figure 1-5. In order to run a SQL statement when it is entered, terminate it with a semicolon. CHP1-1.sql, referred to in How-To 1.2, creates the DEPT1_1 table and loads sample data. If this table does not exist on your system, refer to How-To 1.2 and execute CHP1-1.sql. Figure 1-5 shows a query of the DEPT1_1 table and its results.

Execute the query shown in Figure 1-5. After the statement is executed, it remains in the SQL buffer. To view the contents of the SQL buffer, use the LIST command.

```
SQL> L
  1  SELECT
  2     DEPTNO,
```

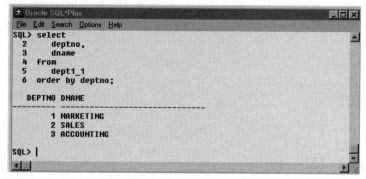

Figure 1-5 A simple query of the sample table
created by CHP1-1.sql

```
3        DNAME
4     FROM
5        DEPT1_1
6*   ORDER BY DEPTNO;
```

2. The slash executes the statement currently in the SQL buffer. Execute the statement by entering a slash.

```
SQL> /

DEPTNO DNAME
------ ----------------
     1 MARKETING
     2 SALES
     3 ACCOUNTING
```

If the SQL buffer is empty, attempting to run a statement will return an error message. Execute the CLEAR BUFFER command to remove the current statement from the SQL buffer and attempt to execute the command in the buffer.

```
SQL>  CLEAR BUFFER
buffer cleared
SQL> /
Nothing in SQL buffer to run.
SQL>
```

3. Load CHP1-3.sql into the SQL buffer with the GET command. Once the statement is in the SQL buffer, it can be executed by typing a slash at the SQL prompt.

```
SQL> GET CHP1-3
  1   SELECT
  2      DEPT1_1.DNAME
  3   FROM DEPT1_1
  4*    ORDER BY DEPT1_1.DEPTNO
```

4. Execute the statement in the SQL buffer. Because the SQL statement loaded from the file is in the SQL buffer, it can be executed by entering a slash.

```
SQL> /

DNAME
--------------------
MARKETING
ACCOUNTING
SALES
```

How It Works

Entering a slash at the SQL prompt executes the SQL statement in the SQL buffer. It does not matter if it is the last statement executed, a statement just entered, or a statement retrieved from a file. This is one of the most used commands in SQL*Plus. Step 1 executes a simple query of the DEPT1_1 table. Step 2 executes the same query presented in Step 1 by entering a slash. Steps 3 and 4 load a SQL statement from a file using the GET command and execute the command by entering a slash.

Comments

Only SQL statements and PL/SQL blocks of code can be executed using this method. SQL*Plus commands such as DESCRIBE or SET cannot be repeated. At first you may find it annoying that SQL*Plus does not repeat SQL*Plus commands, but you will soon realize that retyping a SQL*Plus command is much easier than retyping a long SQL statement. This is a very useful technique when you have a SQL statement that needs to be run repeatedly. How-To 1.10 uses this technique with substitution variables to make repeated queries or SQL statements more efficient.

COMPLEXITY
BEGINNING

1.6 How do I...
Save query results to a file?

Problem

Sometimes I run large queries that return many rows. I need to write the results of my query to a file so that I can edit and print the results. How do I save the results of a query to a file?

Technique

One of the most powerful features of SQL*Plus is its ability to write query results and the feedback from SQL statements to a file. Query results can be written to files to produce reports, be imported into spreadsheets, or run as command files. The results of long running SQL*Plus scripts can be written to output files and checked later to ensure successful execution. The SPOOL command writes SQL*Plus output to a file. The syntax of the command is

```
SPO[OL] [file_name[.ext]|OFF|OUT]
```

If the full path of the output file is not specified, it is written to your working directory. If an extension is not specified, the extension .LST is appended to the filename. The SPOOL OFF command is used to stop the writing of output and close the file. The SPOOL OUT command stops the writing of the output and sends the output directly to the default printer. This is useful when creating reports with SQL*Plus.

Steps

1. CHP1-4.sql, shown in Figure 1-6, contains a SQL script which includes the SPOOL command to save the results of a query to a file. The query contained in the file references a table created in How-To 1.2 by CHP1-1.sql. If you have not executed CHP1-1.sql to create the sample tables, run the file first using the START command.

The first line of the file contains the SPOOL command which writes the output of the subsequent statements to the file C:\TESTFILE.LST. The following three lines contain a simple query of the DEPT1_1 table created by CHP1-1.sql. The SPOOL OFF command closes the output file. Execute CHP1-4.sql with the START command.

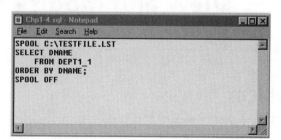

Figure 1-6 CHP1-4.sql contains a SQL script that writes its output to a file

```
SQL>   START CHP1-4

DNAME
--------------------
MARKETING
ACCOUNTING
SALES
```

When the SQL file is executed, the SPOOL and SPOOL OFF commands do not generate any output; however, they write the results of the query to the file.

How It Works

The SPOOL command is used within SQL*Plus to write the output generated to a file. CHP1-4.sql demonstrates the process. The first line opens the file C:\TESTFILE.LST and instructs SQL*Plus to write a copy of all output to this file. Until spooling is stopped, all statements entered or displayed on the screen will be written to the file. The last statement, SPOOL OFF, stops the spooling of the file and closes the file.

Comments

Writing the output of a query to a file is the basis for developing reports using SQL*Plus. The SPOOL command is an easy way to redirect output from SQL*Plus to a file. Many of the How-Tos throughout the book use the SPOOL command. How-To 1.10 uses the SPOOL command to log the output from a batch script to a file.

COMPLEXITY
BEGINNING

1.7 How do I...
View and modify SQL*Plus system variables?

Problem

I know there are many SQL*Plus system variables and that these variables control the behavior of SQL*Plus. I often need to see the value of a variable and, if necessary, change it. How do I view and modify the values of the SQL*Plus system variables?

Technique

The SHOW command is used to view the values of SQL*Plus system variables. The ALL keyword makes SQL*Plus show the value of all 68 system variables. System variables are changed with the SET command. Any system variable can be changed, and it will retain its new value throughout the SQL*Plus session.

Steps

1. View the values of the system variables by executing the SHOW ALL command. The trailing portion of the output is shown in Figure 1-7.

2. Display the value of a single system variable by replacing the ALL keyword with the name of the variable to display.

```
SQL>  SHOW FLUSH
flush ON
```

3. Change the value of the FLUSH system variable with the SET command. The FLUSH system variable can have the values ON or OFF. To change the value to OFF, execute the SET command specifying the system variable and the new value.

```
SQL>  SET FLUSH OFF
SQL>
```

How It Works

The SHOW and SET commands are the two commands used to maintain SQL*Plus system variables. Most system variables are restricted to specific values. If an attempt is made to change a system variable to an invalid value, an error is returned. Step 1 uses the SHOW ALL command to display all 68 system variables. Step 2

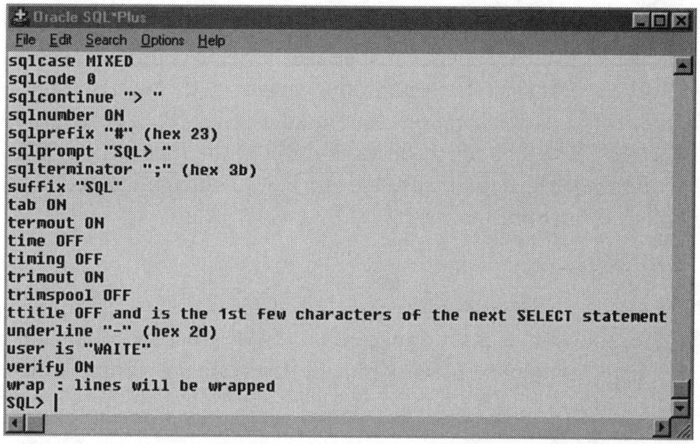

Figure 1-7 The results of SHOW ALL in SQL*Plus

specifies a single system variable to display using the SHOW command. Step 3 uses the SET command to change the value of a system variable.

Comments

When the values of SQL*Plus system variables are changed, they are only changed for the duration of the current session. If SQL*Plus is exited, all the system variables will return to their default settings the next time SQL*Plus is started. If there are certain settings you would like changed every time SQL*Plus is used, they can be placed in a file and executed with the START command.

COMPLEXITY
ADVANCED

1.8 How do I...
Format a report using SQL*Plus?

Problem

I am often called upon to develop quick reports for top management. The query portion of the report is the most complicated part. I need to format the output of the query so it can be printed as a report. I know SQL*Plus has many report formatting functions. What are they and how do I use them?

Technique

SQL*Plus can be used as a reporting tool. SQL*Plus contains a complete set of formatting commands. System variables can be set to control the behavior of SQL*Plus while the report runs. In this section, we will go through the steps required to format a report. Since a report generated in SQL*Plus contains many SQL*Plus statements, it will be much easier to develop the report using Windows Notepad. Although SQL*Plus can be used to edit a SQL statement, I do not recommend it for complicated scripts.

Steps

1. Run SQL*Plus and connect as the WAITE user account. Execute CHP1-1.sql, using the START command to create the sample tables used in this How-To.

```
SQL> START CHP1-1
SQL>
```

2. Launch Windows Notepad and create the SQL statement that is the basis for the report. The SQL statement shown in Figure 1-8 is the basis for the report presented in this How-To.

Save the file to the working directory of SQL*Plus. Use the START command to run the SQL command file. Figure 1-9 displays the unformatted output of CHP5-1.sql in SQL*Plus.

Because no formatting commands have been executed, the output is unacceptable as a report. The next step will format the columns of the report.

3. Change the column headings to descriptions that are more meaningful to the user. Column headings are formatted in SQL*Plus using the COLUMN command. Insert these lines at the beginning of the file.

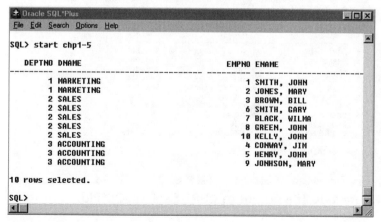

```
Chp1-5.sql - Notepad
File  Edit  Search  Help
SELECT DEPT1_1.DEPTNO,
       DEPT1_1.DNAME,
       EMP1_1.EMPNO,
       EMP1_1.ENAME,
       EMP1_1.SALARY
FROM DEPT1_1, EMP1_1
WHERE
       EMP1_1.DEPTNO = DEPT1_1.DEPTNO
ORDER BY
       DEPT1_1.DEPTNO,
       EMP1_1.EMPNO;
```

Figure 1-8 CHP1-5.sql contains the query that is the basis for the report

```
Oracle SQL*Plus
File  Edit  Search  Options  Help
SQL> start chp1-5

  DEPTNO DNAME                           EMPNO ENAME
--------- ------------------------    --------- ------------------------
        1 MARKETING                           1 SMITH, JOHN
        1 MARKETING                           2 JONES, MARY
        2 SALES                               3 BROWN, BILL
        2 SALES                               6 SMITH, GARY
        2 SALES                               7 BLACK, WILMA
        2 SALES                               8 GREEN, JOHN
        2 SALES                              10 KELLY, JOHN
        3 ACCOUNTING                          4 CONWAY, JIM
        3 ACCOUNTING                          5 HENRY, JOHN
        3 ACCOUNTING                          9 JONHSON, MARY

10 rows selected.

SQL>
```

Figure 1-9 The unformatted output of CHP1-5.sql

```
COLUMN DEPTNO FORMAT 9999 HEADING "Dept"
COLUMN DNAME FORMAT A15 HEADING "Department|Name"
COLUMN EMPNO FORMAT 9999 HEADING " "
COLUMN ENAME FORMAT A15 HEADING "Employee|Name" TRUNCATE
COLUMN SALARY FORMAT $999,999 HEADING "Salary"
```

CHP1-6.sql shows the script as it should look after this step. Carefully note the different formats a column can have. DEPTNO and EMPNO are formatted as four digit numbers; SALARY is formatted as money containing a dollar sign and commas. DNAME and ENAME are formatted as 15-character text strings. The TRUNCATE clause at the end of the COLUMN command for the ENAME column truncates the output if it is longer than 15 characters; otherwise the output would be wrapped within a 15-character column. The Employee|Name heading contains the heading separator character. This causes the heading to be printed as

Employee
Name

You can view the current value of the heading separator character with the command SHOW HEADSEP.

4. Save the file and run it with the START command. Figure 1-10 shows the output of CHP1-6.sql with formatted columns.

The output is starting to look very much like a report. In the next step, a title is added to the beginning and end of each page, and the row count at the end of the query is removed.

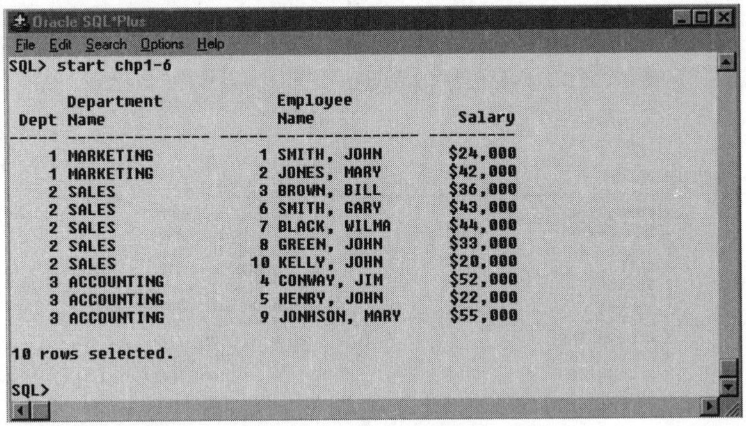

Figure 1-10 The output of CHP1-6.sql in SQL*Plus

5. Add the commands to provide a title for the report. CHP1-7.sql contains the script as it should look after this step. title can be printed at the bottom or top of each page by using the BTITLE and TTITLE commands, respectively. The following commands are added to the beginning of the file to create a top and bottom title.

```
TTITLE CENTER 'Employee Salary Report' SKIP 1 LINE
BTITLE LEFT 'Page: ' format 999 sql.pno
SET LINESIZE 80
SET FEEDBACK OFF
```

The TTITLE command creates a title for the top of each page. The SKIP 1 LINE clause makes the report skip one line after printing the title. The CENTER clause centers the title based on the width of the line represented by the LINESIZE system variable. If the title requires multiple lines, they are appended to the TTITLE command. For example,

```
TTITLE CENTER 'Salary Report' SKIP 1 LINE LEFT 'CHAP1-SQL'
```

centers the Salary Report line, skips one line, and left-justifies CHAP1-SQL on the next line. The BTITLE command creates a title for the bottom of each page. The sql.pno variable used in this statement always represents the current page number. The SET LINESIZE 80 command sets the width of the line to 80 characters. The SET FEEDBACK OFF command eliminates the row count from the end of the query.

6. Save the file and run the script to generate the report as it looks after the previous step. Figure 1-11 shows the output of CHP1-7.sql after the titles are created for the report.

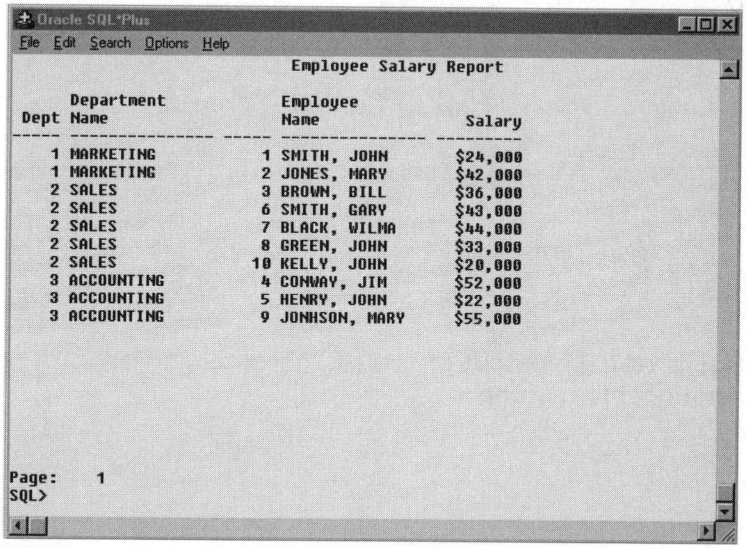

Figure 1-11 The output of CHP1-7.sql containing titles and formatted output

The output of the query is beginning to look like a report. In the next step, common data will be grouped together to give the report a more pleasing look.

7. Add the lines required to group repeating values within SQL*Plus. In the query, data is ordered by DEPTNO and DNAME. In the output of the query, there is repeating DEPTNO and DNAME data. The BREAK command groups together repeating occurrences of values. Adding the following statements to the file, groups the output on the DEPTNO and DNAME fields. CHP1-8.sql shows how the script should look after this step.

```
BREAK ON DEPTNO ON DNAME ON REPORT SKIP 1
```

The SKIP 1 clause leaves a blank line in the report after each grouping. You can vary the number of lines skipped or change the number to SKIP 1 PAGE in order to move to the top of a new page after each data group.

8. Save the file and run the report to show the results after the last step. Figure 1-12 shows the output of CHP1-8.sql within SQL*Plus.

In the next step, the salaries will be totaled for each of the departments and a grand total will be calculated for the report.

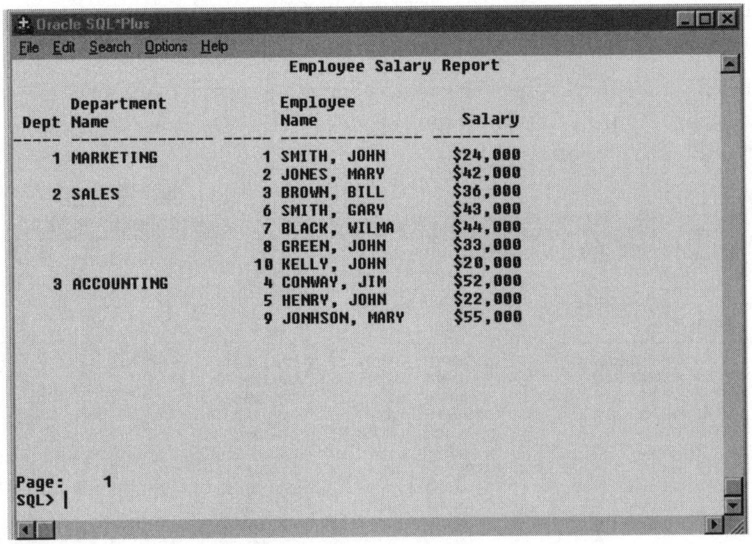

Figure 1-12 The output of CHP1-8.sql containing additional formatting

9. Add the lines required to provide totals and subtotals. The COMPUTE command allows calculations to be created for grouped data. The following statement calculates the sum of the SALARY column for each distinct occurrence of DEPTNO and generates a grand total for the report. CHP1-9.sql file contains the final results of this operation.

```
COMPUTE SUM OF SALARY ON DEPTNO REPORT
```

10. Save the file and run the report. Figure 1-13 shows the final output of this process.

In addition to calculating the sum of columns, the group calculations shown in Table 1-2 can be performed.

COMPUTE CLAUSE	RESULTS
AVG	Average
COUNT	Count - not NULL columns only
MAX	The largest value
MIN	The smallest value
STD	The standard deviation
SUM	The sum
VAR	The variance
NUM	Count - including NULL columns

Table 1-2 Compute functions

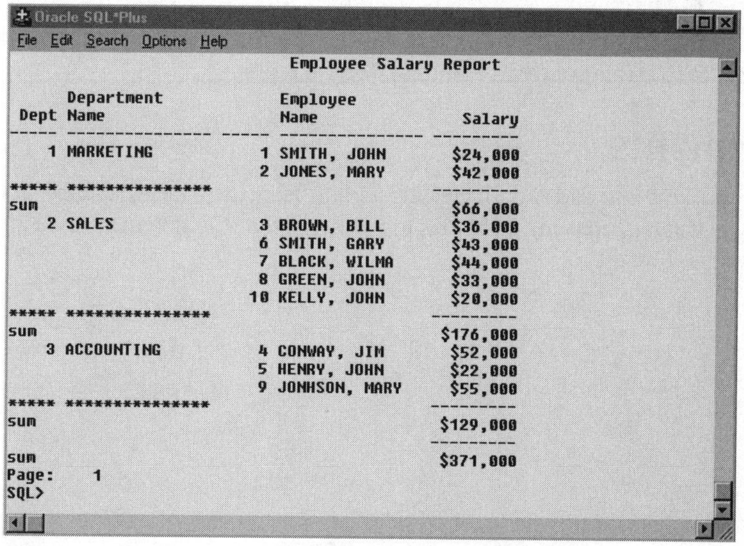

```
                               Employee Salary Report

      Department                  Employee
 Dept Name                        Name                 Salary
----- --------------- ----- --------------- ---------
    1 MARKETING           1 SMITH, JOHN       $24,000
                          2 JONES, MARY       $42,000
***** ***************                       ---------
sum                                           $66,000
    2 SALES               3 BROWN, BILL       $36,000
                          6 SMITH, GARY       $43,000
                          7 BLACK, WILMA      $44,000
                          8 GREEN, JOHN       $33,000
                         10 KELLY, JOHN       $20,000
***** ***************                       ---------
sum                                          $176,000
    3 ACCOUNTING          4 CONWAY, JIM       $52,000
                          5 HENRY, JOHN       $22,000
                          9 JONHSON, MARY     $55,000
***** ***************                       ---------
sum                                          $129,000
                                            ---------
sum                                          $371,000
Page:     1
SQL>
```

Figure 1-13 Running CHP1-9.sql shows the results of the report creation process

How It Works

A report created with SQL*Plus can be a large query formatted using SQL*Plus commands and controlled with system variables. Table 1-3 contains the commands used most often in formatting reports.

COMMAND	DEFINITION
break on	Controls where spaces are placed between sections and where to break for subtotals and totals.
btitle	Sets the bottom title for each page of the report.
column	Sets the heading and format of a column.
compute	Makes SQL*Plus compute a variety of totals.
remark	Identifies the words that follow as comments.
save	Saves the contents of the SQL buffer to a file.
set linesize	Sets the width of a line in characters for the report.
set newpage	Sets the number of lines between pages of a report.
spool	Tells SQL*Plus to write output to a file.
start	Tells SQL*Plus to execute a file.
ttitle	Sets the title for each page of the report.

Table 1-3 Report formatting commands

Step 1 creates the sample tables which are queried in the How-To. Step 2 presents a query which is formatted in the How-To. Steps 3 and 4 use the COLUMN command to format the columns retrieved by the query. Steps 5 and 6 use the TTITLE and BTITLE commands to create titles for the report. Steps 7 and 8 use the BREAK command to group common data together. Steps 9 and 10 use the COMPUTE command to create subtotals and totals for the report.

Comments

SQL*Plus is a valid tool for creating reports using the Oracle database. In many cases, you will end up using SQL*Plus to prototype the SQL statement used in your report writer.

COMPLEXITY
INTERMEDIATE

1.9 How do I...
Create user-defined variables in my SQL scripts?

Problem

In many cases, I do not know the information I want to use in my SQL scripts but can get the information at runtime. I need to create my own user-defined variables that I can reference throughout my script. I want to be able to use them like substitution variables, but in other ways too. How do I do this?

Technique

User-defined variables can be created in SQL*Plus using the DEFINE command. The DEFINE command creates a user-defined variable for the life of the SQL*Plus session. When a user-defined variable is created, any references to it are replaced with the value of the variable. The format of the DEFINE command is

`DEFINE VARIABLE = text`

The ACCEPT command works like the DEFINE command, except the execution of the script is halted and the user is prompted to enter a value for the variable. Once the value is entered, the execution of the script continues at the line following the statement. The format of the ACCEPT command is

`ACCEPT VARIABLE`

Once a user-defined variable has been created using either of these methods, it can be used throughout the SQL*Plus session by prefixing the variable name with an ampersand (&). The user will not be prompted for the value of the variable again, even if it is used as a substitution variable.

Steps

1. CHP1-10.sql shown in Figure 1-14 uses a complex method for defining user-defined variables.

The first line of the script sets the HEADING system variable to OFF to suppress the output of the headings generated by the query. The SPOOL statement contained in the second line opens a temporary file which is later

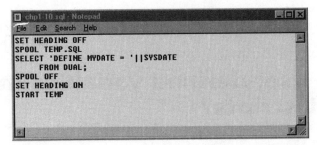

Figure 1-14 CHP1-10.sql creates a user-defined
variable from a query

executed. Lines 3 and 4 create a DEFINE statement using the result of a
query of the DUAL table to dynamically generate a statement. The SPOOL
OFF statement in line 5 terminates the creation of the temporary file. The
SET HEADING ON statement restores the headings for subsequent queries.
The last statement executes the temporary file using the START command.
Once the DEFINE statement is executed, the variable can be used in other
statements. Execute CHP1-9.sql using the START command.

```
SQL>   START CHP1-10

DEFINE MYDATE = 01-FEB-95
```

When this script is executed, the net result is that the MYDATE user-
defined variable gets populated with the results of a query. The statement
shown in the output of the query is executed by the START command in
the last line of the script.

2. Use the MYDATE user-defined variable in a statement. Any reference to
&MYDATE in a SQL statement or SQL*Plus command will be replaced
with a string containing a system date.

```
SQL>   SELECT '&MYDATE' FROM DUAL;

_01-FEB-9
-----

01-FEB-95
```

How It Works

The first step creates a query which outputs a DEFINE command to a temporary
file. The first line of CHP1-10.sql turns the column headings off for the next few statements. The second line uses the SPOOL command to create a file called TEMP.sql.
The two lines that follow are a query returning the literal value DEFINE MYDATE
= concatenated with the current system date. The SPOOL OFF command stops output to the TEMP.sql file and closes the file. The command START TEMP runs the

temporary command file to define the MYDATE user variable. Since user-defined variables exist for the life of the SQL*Plus session, when Step 2 is executed the user is not prompted for a value for &MYDATE.

Comments

This technique is useful for creating titles in reports or output files based on the system date or other output from a query. User-defined variables add flexibility to SQL*Plus command files. A command file can include variables set at runtime or previously defined. Whenever possible, you should exploit the value of user-defined variables.

COMPLEXITY
INTERMEDIATE

1.10 How do I...
Log SQL script progress to a file?

Problem

I use SQL*Plus to execute many regular processes. I do not watch the execution of the scripts every time I run them. I need a method to write the output from SQL*Plus to a file as the scripts run. This way I can view the file later to ensure that everything ran correctly. How can I log SQL*Plus script progress to a file?

Technique

The same technique used to write the output of a query to a file is used to log the progress of a SQL*Plus script. The SPOOL command writes all SQL*Plus feedback to the specified file. SPOOL OFF terminates the spooling operation. The ECHO system variable is set to ON, causing SQL*Plus to display all commands executed from a file.

Steps

1. Run the CHP1-11.sql file on the accompanying disk. This file contains a sample SQL script that logs its execution to a file. The contents of the script are shown in Figure 1-15.

The SPOOL command in line 1 writes the output of all subsequent statements to the output file specified in the command. The next six statements contained in the file will generate output that is written to the output file. The SPOOL OFF statement in the last line stops the output of the file. Run the file using the START command.

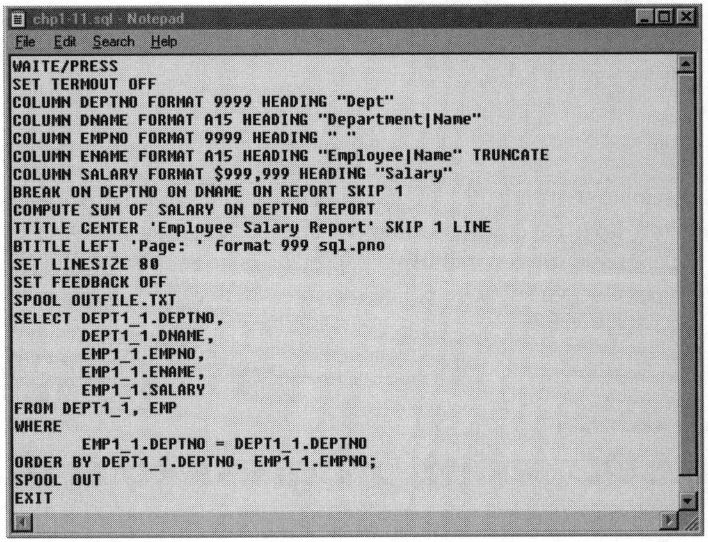


```
WAITE/PRESS
SET TERMOUT OFF
COLUMN DEPTNO FORMAT 9999 HEADING "Dept"
COLUMN DNAME FORMAT A15 HEADING "Department|Name"
COLUMN EMPNO FORMAT 9999 HEADING " "
COLUMN ENAME FORMAT A15 HEADING "Employee|Name" TRUNCATE
COLUMN SALARY FORMAT $999,999 HEADING "Salary"
BREAK ON DEPTNO ON DNAME ON REPORT SKIP 1
COMPUTE SUM OF SALARY ON DEPTNO REPORT
TTITLE CENTER 'Employee Salary Report' SKIP 1 LINE
BTITLE LEFT 'Page: ' format 999 sql.pno
SET LINESIZE 80
SET FEEDBACK OFF
SPOOL OUTFILE.TXT
SELECT DEPT1_1.DEPTNO,
       DEPT1_1.DNAME,
       EMP1_1.EMPNO,
       EMP1_1.ENAME,
       EMP1_1.SALARY
FROM DEPT1_1, EMP
WHERE
       EMP1_1.DEPTNO = DEPT1_1.DEPTNO
ORDER BY DEPT1_1.DEPTNO, EMP1_1.EMPNO;
SPOOL OUT
EXIT
```

Figure 1-15 CHP1-11.sql contains a SQL script that logs its execution to a file

```
SQL>  START CHP1-11

Table created.

1 row created.

1 row created.

1 row created.

Commit complete.
```

This output of the operation is not very descriptive. If an error were to occur on one or more of the statements, it would be very difficult to track down its location.

2. Run CHP1-12.sql. This file employs a SET ECHO ON command before any of the other statements are executed. The SET ECHO ON command is the key to logging the progress of the script. It causes SQL*Plus to repeat the command before it is executed.

```
SQL>  START CHP1-12

SQL> CREATE TABLE DEPT1_12 (
  2    DEPTNO       NUMBER(8),
  3    DNAME        VARCHAR2(30));
```

```
Table created.

SQL> INSERT INTO DEPT1_12 (DEPTNO, DNAME)
  2    VALUES(1, MARKETING );

1 row created.

SQL> INSERT INTO DEPT1_12 (DEPTNO, DNAME)
  2    VALUES(2, SALES );

1 row created.

SQL> INSERT INTO DEPT1_12 (DEPTNO, DNAME)
  2    VALUES(3, ACCOUNTING );

1 row created.

SQL> COMMIT;

Commit complete.

SQL> SET ECHO OFF
```

Because each of the statements is displayed before execution, if one of them failed it would be very easy to track down the location of the error.

How It Works

The ECHO system variable displays all statements executed from a command file before execution. Writing this output creates a log file which can be analyzed later. The TERMOUT system variable can be used to turn off terminal output. This will cause the log file to be written without displaying data to the screen. Step 1 executes a script that logs its progress without setting the ECHO system varaiable to ON. Step 2 executes a similar script that logs its progress to a file and displays its progress by setting the ECHO system variable to ON.

Comments

It is important to log the results of SQL scripts that run at night or in batch processes. If one or more SQL statements failed within a script, you would have no way of knowing a problem occurred without logging the results to a file. Set the TERMOUT system variable to OFF for all batch commands. Displaying output to the screen can slow down the execution of the command file.

1.11 How do I...
Use SQL*Plus to create SQL statements?

Problem

I need to run a SQL statement for each table in the database. It is a great deal of work to type in a statement for each table. I know that I can save the results of a query to a file and that I can run a file. Is there any way for me to create SQL statements within SQL*Plus?

Technique

The data dictionary contains just about everything you ever wanted to know about the structure of your database. Oracle allows you to concatenate text using the concatenation operator. By concatenating the keywords required by the statement you wish to create to the query output, you can build a series of SQL statements based on a query. Since any string can be concatenated with the results of a query, the output of the query can be forced into the format of a SQL statement.

Steps

1. Run SQL*Plus and connect as the WAITE user account or a user account that owns tables. Remove the column headings. A heading can be suppressed by setting the HEADING system variable to OFF.

```
SQL> SET HEADING OFF
SQL>
```

2. Remove the row count feedback by setting the FEEDBACK system variable to OFF. The FEEDBACK variable controls the row count displayed at the end of a query. The extra line of information will cause an error in the SQL script. Execute a SET command to turn row feedback off.

```
SQL>   SET FEEDBACK OFF
SQL>
```

3. Widen the output line. SQL*Plus attempts to make it easier to read the output of a query by wrapping the lines. When creating a SQL statement with a query, the default line length may be too small. The LINESIZE system variable determines the length of a line. The maximum value of LINESIZE is operating system dependent. In Microsoft Windows, the maximum value is 32,000.

```
SQL>  SET LINESIZE 132
SQL>
```

4. Construct the query that creates SQL statements. To do this, concatenate the keywords the statement requires to the table name as it is retrieved from the database. Figure 1-16 shows a query and its results. Run the query once to check for syntax errors before writing the output to a file. Running the statement verifies the output.

Because there are no column headings and no row count, the output is a sequence of SQL statements without the undesirable statements.

5. Write the output to a file. The SPOOL command is used to create the output file.

```
SQL>  SPOOL CMDS.SQL
SQL>
```

SQL*Plus commands, query results, and SQL*Plus feedback are written to the CMDS.SQL file. Once spooling begins, only statements that produce SQL statements are desired. Be sure to execute all necessary SQL*Plus commands prior to executing the SPOOL command. Unfortunately, there will be a couple of undesired lines since the slash and the SPOOL OFF commands are written to the file. These lines will create runtime errors, which can be ignored. Or, you use any text editor to remove the unwanted lines from the file.

6. Execute the SQL statement. This time when the query is executed, the results will be written to the CMDS.SQL file.

```
SQL>  /
```

7. Stop writing to the file by executing the SPOOL OFF command. SPOOL OFF stops the spooling operation and closes the output file.

```
SQL>  SPOOL OFF
```

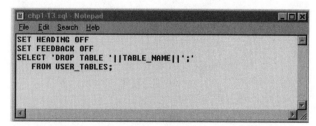

Figure 1-16 CHP1-13.sql contains a query to create SQL statements

A file that runs like a SQL*Plus command file is created. Figure 1-17 shows the results of the operation.

How It Works

Every SQL statement begins with keywords, such as SELECT COUNT(*) FROM, DROP TABLE, or INSERT INTO, and ends with a semicolon. The string concatenation function (||) allows static text to be combined with the query output to create a SQL statement. The ability of SQL*Plus to write query output to a text file and execute the file allows you to dynamically build SQL scripts as the output from a query. Step 1 suppresses the headings usually displayed by the query. Step 2 suppresses the row count feedback which is displayed at the end of a query. Step 3 widens the length of the line to ensure that the output fits on a single line. Step 4 creates and runs a query to create the desired SQL statements. Step 5 begins writing the output of the query to a file. Step 6 runs the query, and Step 7 ends the spooling process.

Comments

Using SQL*Plus to create SQL commands is a very useful feature. If you look to this technique whenever you need to execute a large number of statements on the database, you will increase your productivity greatly. This technique will be used in many places throughout the book.

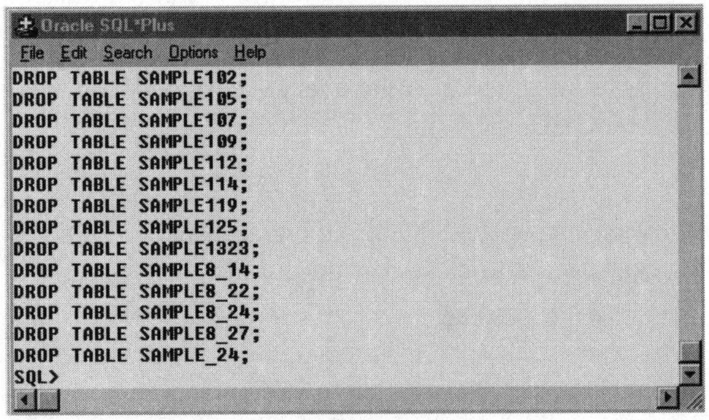

Figure 1-17 The results of the query

1.12 How do I...
Select columns of the LONG datatype?

Problem

When I query data dictionary views which have columns of the LONG datatype, the data gets truncated. I cannot see a large portion of the LONG columns when they are retrieved. How can I select columns of the LONG datatype?

Technique

An example of a common query which uses LONG data returns the SELECT statement of a view from the data dictionary. The LONG system variable in SQL*Plus identifies how many characters of a LONG column SQL*Plus will display. The default value is 80 characters. Since a system variable controls this behavior, the SET command is used to change it. Because of memory size restrictions, it is sometimes necessary to retrieve LONG data in sections. The LONGCHUNKSIZE system variable identifies the amount of data in characters retrieved at one time. The MAXDATA system variable defines the maximum amount of data in bytes that can be retrieved per row.

Steps

1. Load CHP1-14.sql into the SQL buffer with the GET command. The file contains a query that returns data of the LONG datatype from the data dictionary.

```
SQL> GET CHP1-14
  1    SELECT TEXT
  2    FROM
  3        ALL_VIEWS
  4    WHERE
  5*       VIEW_NAME = _ALL_TAB_PRIVS
```

2. Execute the statement. Since the TEXT column is of the LONG datatype, it will be truncated to the length contained in the LONG system variable.

```
SQL>  /

TEXT
-------------------------
select ur.name, ue.name, u.name, o.name, tpm.name,
decode(oa.option$, 1, _YES ,
```

A large amount of the data was truncated when the column was retrieved, because the value of the LONG system variable limits the amount of data returned by the query. In the next step, the amount of data displayed will be increased by specifying a larger value for the LONG system variable.

3. Increase the value of the LONG system variable. Keep in mind that if you make the LONG system variable too large, you will need to increase the value of MAXDATA when SQL*Plus attempts to return more data than the value specified by MAXDATA .

```
SQL> SET LONG 2000
SQL>
```

Once the new value has been specified for the LONG system variable, the query will return more data for each column of the LONG datatype.

4. Execute the query again. This time the entire contents of the column will be displayed.

```
SQL>  /
TEXT
-------------------------------
select ur.name, ue.name, u.name, o.name, tpm.name,
decode(oa.option$, 1, _YES , _NO )
from sys.objauth$ oa, sys.obj$ o,
sys.user$ u, sys.user$ ur, sys.user$ ue,
table_privilege_map tpm
where oa.obj# = o.obj#
and oa.grantor# = ur.user#
and oa.grantee# = ue.user#
and oa.col# is null
and u.user# = o.owner#
and oa.privilege# = tpm.privilege
and (oa.grantor# = userenv(_SCHEMAID ) or
oa.grantee# in (select kzsrorol from x$kzsro) or
o.owner# = userenv(_SCHEMAID ))
```

The value of the LONG system variable has a dramatic effect on the results of the query and must be specified in order to see the entire value of the column.

How It Works

The LONG system variable is modified using the SET command just like any other system variable. Data in LONG columns is truncated to the size contained in this variable. Steps 1 and 2 execute a query of a data dictionary view containing a LONG column. Since the value of the data in the column is larger than the default value of the LONG system variable, data was truncated. Although the data was not entirely displayed, no error was returned when the query was executed. It is possible to create statements that appear to work when querying LONG columns but do not produce the desired results. Step 3 increases the amount of data displayed by increasing the value of the LONG system variable. Step 4 shows the effect the new value has on the results of the query.

Comments

When developing applications, the LONG datatype can be useful, but only use it if you need to. Manipulating LONG data can be tricky, and it places restrictions on the actions that can be performed in SQL*Plus. For example, you cannot insert the value of a LONG column into another table through SQL*Plus.

COMPLEXITY
INTERMEDIATE

1.13 How do I...
Time the execution speed of a query?

Problem

When I write SQL statements, I like to test the execution speed of the statements. When I make changes to a statement, I want to see the impact the change had on performance. How can I time the execution speed of a SQL statement in SQL*Plus?

Technique

There are two methods for timing the execution of SQL statements within SQL*Plus. The performance of a single query can be timed by setting the value of the TIMING system variable to ON. The SQL*Plus TIMING command allows you to set multiple timers and time groups of statements. The TIMING command allows you to give each timer a name and view timing information individually. The command SET TIMING ON sets the SQL*Plus system variable ON and causes SQL*Plus to time the duration of each SQL statement, as long as the TIMING variable is set to ON. The command SET TIMING OFF ends the timing of individual statements. The TIM-ING command has various keywords which control the use of the command. The syntax of the TIMING command is shown here:

```
TIMING START TIMERNAME
```

A timer is created with the name specified on the command line.

1. Execute the SET command to change the TIMING system variable to ON to begin timing individual statements.

```
SQL> SET TIMING ON
SQL>
```

Once the TIMING variable is set to ON, each statement displayed will be followed with the timing results from the statement.

2. Execute a statement which you would like timed. In this example, a constant from the DUAL table will be retrieved and the query timed.

```
SQL> SELECT 'X' FROM DUAL;

'
-
X

real:  390
```

This shows that the query took 390 milliseconds to complete. The 390 milliseconds is elapsed time. It does not account for system load or CPU usage of the query.

3. Turn off the TIMING system variable with another SET command. The OFF keyword causes SQL*Plus to stop timing statements.

```
SQL> SET TIMING OFF
SQL>
```

4. The TIMING system variable is good for timing individual statements, but it is not good for timing the execution of an entire script. Use the TIMING command to create a timer with a name.

```
SQL> TIMING START MYTIMER
SQL>
```

This command starts a timer named MYTIMER. It is possible to start multiple timers by starting another timer before stopping the first timer. Each statement run will not display timing results. The TIMING SHOW command must be used to display elapsed time since the timer was started.

5. View the current value of the timer by using the TIMING SHOW command.

```
SQL> TIMING SHOW MYTIMER
timing for MYTIMER:
  real:  22410
```

The TIMING SHOW command leaves the timer running. The amount of time elapsed since the timer was started can be displayed at different points within the script without stopping the timer.

6. Stop the timer by using the TIMING STOP command.

```
SQL> TIMING STOP MYTIMER
timing for MYTIMER:
  real:  44230
```

The TIMING STOP command shows the value of the timer when it is stopped. The timing results show elapsed time since the timer was started. It does not show how much of the CPU or other resources were used. After the timer has been stopped it can no longer be referenced. If you attempt to execute a TIMING SHOW command for the timer, an error message will be displayed. The TIMING command should be used for timing an entire script or a set of statements. The first command of the script starts the timer, and the last command stops it. A sample script file is displayed in Figure 1-18.

The first statement creates a timer named MYTIMER with the TIMING START command. The timer keeps a running execution time until the TIMING STOP command in the last statement stops it. The TIMING SHOW command is used to display the value of the timer at a point within the script. The command displays the current value of the timer but does not stop or reset it.

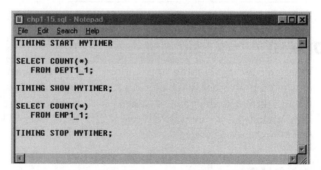

Figure 1-18 CHP1-15.sql is a sample script using timers

How It Works

The SQL*Plus TIMING system variable causes SQL*Plus to return the amount of time each query takes to execute. Step 1 sets the value of the TIMING system variable to ON. This times the execution of Step 2. The time displayed in Step 2 is real time, not the amount of CPU or other resources used. Step 3 sets the value of the TIMING system variable to OFF to stop the timing of statements. When timing multiple statements, use the TIMING command. It operates the like the TIMING system variable, but lets timers operate over multiple SQL statements and multiple timers run at once. Step 4 starts a timer with the TIMING START command. The timer keeps time until Step 6 stops it. Step 5 uses the TIMING SHOW command to display the amount of elapsed time since the timer began. Step 6 uses the TIMING STOP command to end the execution of the timer.

Comments

There are many factors that can effect execution time. These techniques allow you to compare execution times fairly accurately. Keep in mind that the amount of time a statement takes to run can be affected by outside factors, such as other processes running on the system. It is always good practice to keep timing statistics for batch scripts or nightly processes. This will give you an indication of how performance changes over time.

COMPLEXITY
ADVANCED

1.14 How do I...
Kill a user's session using SQL*Plus?

Problem

When we are developing applications, we have occurrences of runaway and unwanted processes. When a query runs for an unacceptable amount of time, we want to terminate the process. When I get a call from a user or developer wanting a session killed, I do not want to leave SQL*Plus. How can I kill a user's session using SQL*Plus?

Technique

In order to kill a user's session using SQL*Plus, you must be connected to the database as a user with the ALTER SYSTEM privilege. The SYS and SYSTEM users have this privilege by default. The V$SESSION view contains information about sessions connected to the database. Figure 1-19 shows the description of the V$SESSION view in SQL*Plus.

The V$SESSION view can be queried to find out what sessions a user has running on the database. The ALTER SYSTEM KILL USER statement is used to terminate a user's session through SQL*Plus. It requires the session identifier (SID) and the process serial number as part of the command.

Steps

1. Run SQL*Plus and connect as the SYS or SYSTEM user account. Load CHP1-14.sql into the SQL buffer with the GET command. The file contains a SQL statement which can be used to determine session information for a user. The USERNAME column identifies which user owns the session. Determine the session ID and serial number for the session to be killed.

```
SQL> GET CHP1-16
  1  SELECT SID, SERIAL#, STATUS
  2    FROM V$SESSION
  3*   WHERE USERNAME = _WAITE
```

Line 1 returns the session ID, serial number, and status of the session. Line 2 specifies the V$SESSION data dictionary view as the source of the query. Line 3 causes records to be returned only for the WAITE user account.

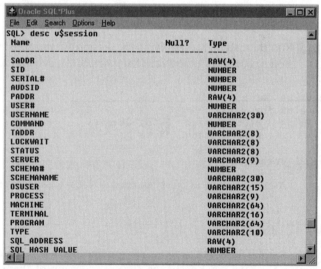

Figure 1-19 The V$SESSION data dictionary view

2. Run the query to return the active connections.

```
SQL> /

    SID   SERIAL# STATUS
 ----- ----- ----
      9         3 ACTIVE
     11        26 INACTIVE
```

The output from the query gives the information needed in the next step to kill the process.

Notice that the STATUS column was queried. This column is important since a user can have more than one session, and only the right one should be terminated. A common example of multiple sessions is when Oracle Reports creates a separate session any time a report is run.

3. Load CHP1-17.sql into the SQL buffer. The ALTER SYSTEM statement contained in the file contains the KILL SESSION keywords to kill an Oracle session.

```
SQL> GET CHP1-17
  1   ALTER SYSTEM
  2*     KILL SESSION _&sid,&serial
```

Line 1 contains the ALTER SYSTEM keywords that are required to kill an Oracle session through SQL*Plus. Line 2 contains the KILL SESSION option and specifes the session ID and serial number with the &SID and &SERIAL substitution variables.

4. Run the statement supplying the session ID and serial number of the session to be killed for the &SID and &SERIAL substitution variables.

```
SQL> /
Enter value for sid: 11
Enter value for serial: 26
old   2:     kill session _&sid, &serial
new   2:     kill session _11,26

System Altered
```

Once the statement has been executed, the session is terminated.

How It Works

The V$SESSION view is a virtual performance view. It is constantly changing as the dynamics of the system change. There are many of these views which can be queried at any time. Many performance monitoring tools regularly query these views to provide online monitoring of the system. The ALTER SYSTEM statement allows a user with the ALTER SYSTEM privilege to make changes to the system immediately. As soon as this statement is executed, the user's session will be killed. Steps 1 and 2 query the V$SESSION view to get information about the session to be killed.

The SID and SERIAL# columns are required to kill a session with the ALTER SYS-TEM statement. Steps 3 and 4 execute an ALTER SYSTEM statement to kill the session.

Comments

Unwanted or runaway sessions can steal CPU and other system resources from your system. Terminating processes through SQL*Plus is one of the ways to keep them from robbing your system of performance. It is important to develop a strategy for monitoring process utilization and performance. The V$ views allow you to create your own programs for monitoring database resources.

CHAPTER 2
USER ACCOUNTS AND ROLES

USER ACCOUNTS AND ROLES

How do I...

2.1   **Create a new user account?**

2.2   **Create a new role?**

2.3   **Grant and revoke privileges to user accounts and roles?**

2.4   **Determine the active user account?**

2.5   **Modify user defaults and profiles?**

2.6   **Restrict a user account's disk space?**

2.7   **Determine the privileges granted to a role?**

2.8   **Determine the privileges granted to a user account?**

What good is an application if nobody can use it? The management of user accounts and roles is fundamental to the development and maintenance of multi-user database applications. Each person using an Oracle database must have a user account. Users should not share accounts, and each user account should have a password to protect the database from unauthorized access. A *privilege* is the permission to perform a task on the database or access another user's database object. A *system privilege* allows the user to perform an action, such as create a session or create a table. An *object privilege* allows the user to access a specific object such as a table, view, or stored procedure. Within an organization, people perform different functions. A *role* is a

51

group of related privileges which can be granted to user accounts as a single privilege. The structure of roles within Oracle allows database security to be modeled around the organization. A role can be defined at a high level, such as a person using system, or at a more detailed level, such as an accountant, payroll clerk, or supervisor. Within a production system, user accounts and roles are usually managed by the database administrator. The examples presented in this chapter can be found on the accompanying CD-ROM in the \SAMPLES\CHAP2 directory.

2.1 Create a new user account

Users are the reason applications are developed. Creating user accounts is a fundamental task in delivering a new application. This How-To takes you through the steps of creating a new Oracle user account.

2.2 Create a new role

A role defines a group of related privileges. Roles assign user accounts a collection of privileges in a single step. Instead of granting user accounts access to each object individually, user accounts can be granted access to a role defining the complete set of privileges. This How-To takes you through the process of creating a new role.

2.3 Grant and revoke privileges to user accounts and roles

Once a user account is created, it needs to be granted access to the database and the objects required by the application. Privileges can be granted directly to the user account or indirectly through database roles. This How-To takes you through the process of granting and revoking privileges to user accounts and roles.

2.4 Determine the active user account

In order to enforce any security model within an application, it is necessary to identify the user account connected to the database. This How-To takes you through the methods available to determine the user of an application.

2.5 Modify user defaults and profiles

User account defaults and profiles define the default location of database objects and the quantity of usable database resources. This How-To covers the management of user defaults and the creation and assignment of user profiles.

2.6 Restrict a user account's disk space

Disk space is a limited resource. In environments where users or developers can create their own data objects, it is important to restrict the amount of disk space a user account's objects can occupy. This How-To explores the method used to restrict a user account's disk space.

2.7 Determine the privileges granted to a role

Granting a role to a user account gives the user account all privileges assigned to that role. This How-To covers the task of determining which system and object privileges are assigned to a role and provides SQL statements to determine these privileges.

2.8 Determine the privileges granted to a user account

As part of maintaining user accounts, it is necessary to determine which privileges have been granted to them. User accounts can be granted privileges directly or through roles. This How-To shows methods for identifying the privileges and roles granted to a user account.

COMPLEXITY
BEGINNING

2.1 How do I...
Create a new user account?

Problem

After developing my application, I need to create user accounts for the people who will use it. I also want to create user accounts within our development environment to test my application with different sets of privileges. How do I create a new user account in Oracle?

Technique

The CREATE USER statement is used to create a new user account in an Oracle database. User accounts can be created by using SQL*Plus. This How-To focuses on using SQL*Plus to create user accounts, since it is portable across all database platforms. In this How-To, we will create user accounts which will appear throughout the examples in this chapter and in Chapter 3. The syntax of the CREATE USER statement is shown in Figure 2-1.

The CREATE USER statement is a SQL statement and ends with a semicolon. The DEFAULT TABLESPACE clause identifies where objects created by the user account will reside if a tablespace is not specified in the CREATE statement. The TEMPORARY TABLESPACE clause identifies where temporary data will reside when required by operations performed by the user account. The QUOTA clause, which can occur many times within the statement, specifies the amount of disk space the user account's objects can occupy in a given tablespace. The PROFILE clause identifies the profile the user account uses to control resources available, such as the number of concurrent sessions and the maximum CPU time per call.

```
                      CREATE USER Syntax

         CREATE USER username
           {[IDENTIFIED BY password] |
                  DEFAULT TABLESPACE tablespace |
                  TEMPORARY TABLESPACE tablespace |
                  QUOTA integer ON tablespace
                  PROFILE profile }
```

Figure 2-1 CREATE USER syntax

Steps

1. Run SQL*Plus and connect as the WAITE user account created by the installation script. Load CHP2-1.sql into the SQL buffer. The file contains a CREATE USER statement to create a new user account.

```
SQL> GET CHP2-1
  1   CREATE USER FRED
  2*        IDENTIFIED BY NEWUSER
```

Line 1 contains the CREATE USER keywords and specifies the name of the new user account. The IDENTIFIED BY clause contained in line 2 specifies the password required when the user account connects to the database. Since no modifying clauses are specified, the user account is created with default properties. Although the user account is created, it has no permission to do anything with the database. How-To 1.3 covers the granting of privileges to user accounts.

2. Execute the statement to create the user account.

```
SQL> /
```

```
User Created.
```

3. Load CHP2-2.sql into the SQL buffer. The file contains a DROP USER statement to remove the user account FRED from the system.

```
SQL> GET CHP2-2
  1* DROP USER FRED
```

Line 1 contains the DROP USER keywords and specifies the user account to be removed. If the user account owns database objects, the CASCADE clause must be specified in order to remove all the user account's objects from the database.

4. Run the statement to remove the user account.

```
SQL>   /

User dropped.
```

How It Works

The CREATE USER statement is used to create new user accounts in the database. Executing the CREATE USER statement does not create an account that can use an application or even connect to the database. The user account must be granted system privileges to use the system and object privileges to access database objects. The DROP USER statement is used to remove a user account from the system. If the user account owns objects, the CASCADE clause must be included to remove the objects owned by the user account. A user account cannot be removed if objects remain. Steps 1 and 2 create a new user account, and Steps 3 and 4 remove the account.

Comments

The SQL*Plus method for creating user accounts is important since it is portable across all platforms. If you are creating a large number of user accounts, you may find it easier to create the statements in Windows Notepad or another text editor and run all the statements as a single script. How-To 2.2 covers the creation of roles. Roles define a group of related privileges. When creating a new user account, keep in mind that it has no privileges until they are granted. Privileges can be granted directly to a user account or indirectly through roles. How-To 2.3 covers the granting and revoking of privileges. The file CHP2-1.sql contains all the statements required to build the user accounts used in this chapter. The examples later in this chapter and in Chapter 3 assume these user accounts exist.

COMPLEXITY
BEGINNING

2.2   How do I...
Create a new role?

Problem

In my application, I have groups of users who perform related functions. The number of people using my application is very large. I do not want to grant privileges on all of the database objects to so many people. How do I create a new role to represent a group of users?

Technique

Database roles should be created to represent related groups of privileges within the database. The CREATE ROLE statement is used to create a new role. The syntax of the CREATE ROLE statement is shown in Figure 2-2.

The IDENTIFIED BY clause defines a password for the role. When a role contains a password, the password must be supplied when enabling the role. When a new role is created, it has no privileges. Privileges must be granted to the role in order for the role to have any effect on a user account. The CONNECT, RESOURCE, and DBA roles are provided by Oracle to supply different levels of access. User accounts with the CONNECT role have access to the database but cannot create their own objects. They can access other user account's objects to which they have been granted permission. User accounts with the RESOURCE role can create their own database objects. The DBA role gives the user account very powerful privileges: complete access to the database and the ability to grant privileges to other user accounts.

Steps

1. Run SQL*Plus and connect as the WAITE user account. Load CHP2-3.sql into the SQL buffer. The file contains a CREATE ROLE statement to create a new role.

```
SQL> GET CHP2-3
  1  CREATE ROLE IS_DEV
```

The CREATE ROLE keywords are required to create a new role. A name must be specified for the role when it is created. Once the role has been created, it must be granted privileges to be of any use. How-To 2.3 covers the processes of granting privileges to roles.

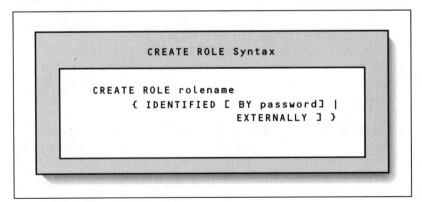

```
              CREATE ROLE Syntax

   CREATE ROLE rolename
           { IDENTIFIED [ BY password] |
                         EXTERNALLY ] }
```

Figure 2-2 CREATE ROLE syntax

2. Execute the statement to create the role.

```
SQL>  /

Role Created
```

3. Load CHP2-4.sql into the SQL buffer. The file contains a CREATE ROLE statement which creates a new role protected with a password.

```
SQL> GET CHP2-4
  1   CREATE ROLE ID_ADM
  2*     IDENTIFIED BY SECURE
```

Line 1 contains the CREATE ROLE keywords to create a new role and specify the name of the role. The IDENTIFIED BY clause in line 2 specifies an optional password which must be provided when the role is enabled.

4. Execute the statement to create the role.

```
SQL>  /

Role Created
```

5. Load CHP2-5.sql into the SQL buffer. The file contains a DROP ROLE statement to remove the role created in Steps 1 and 2.

```
SQL> GET CHP2-5
  1* DROP ROLE IS_DEV
```

The DROP ROLE keywords presented in line 1 are required to remove a role from the database. The role to be removed must be specified in the statement.

6. Run the statement to remove the role.

```
SQL> /

Role dropped.
```

When a role is removed, all user accounts that were granted the role immediately lose their privileges.

How It Works

The CREATE ROLE statement is used to create a new role in the database. Steps 1 and 2 create a new role using the CREATE ROLE statement. Steps 3 and 4 create a role containing a password which must be specified when the role is enabled. The IDENTIFIED BY clause creates a password for a role. Steps 5 and 6 present the DROP ROLE statement, which is used to remove an existing role. When a role is removed, the privileges provided by the role are removed immediately from the user account granted the role privileges.

Comments

Roles play a major part in the development of an organizational security model. In the early releases of Oracle, the CONNECT, RESOURCE, and DBA roles were used to administer security to user accounts. Access to tables and views was granted to each user account individually or to the PUBLIC user group, which allowed all user accounts access to the data. Roles increase the security capabilities of Oracle and reduce the maintenance required by the system administrator. A security model should be developed using roles that effectively protect your database.

COMPLEXITY
INTERMEDIATE

2.3 How do I...
Grant and revoke privileges to user accounts and roles?

Problem

When I create a new user account or role, I need to grant it privileges. If I do not grant privileges to my user accounts, they cannot use my applications. If I do not grant privileges to my roles, granting them to a user account is useless. How do I grant privileges to a user account or role?

Technique

Privileges are granted to user accounts and roles with the GRANT statement. The syntax of the GRANT statement is shown in Figure 2-3.

One or more privileges or roles can be granted to one or more user accounts with a single statement. The PUBLIC keyword specifies that all user accounts receive the privilege. The WITH ADMIN OPTION clause specifies that the grantee can grant this privilege to another user account or role. Privileges are removed from a user account or role with the REVOKE command. The syntax of the REVOKE command is shown in Figure 2-4.

If a privilege is revoked from a user account, the user account loses the privilege immediately. If a privilege is revoked from a role, user accounts with access to the role lose the role's privileges immediately.

```
                        GRANT Syntax

        GRANT { privilege | ALL}
            ON object
            TO { user | role | PUBLIC }
            [ WITH GRANT OPTION ]
```

Figure 2-3 The syntax of the GRANT statement

```
                        REVOKE Syntax

        REVOKE { privilege | ALL }
            [ ON object ]
            FROM { user | role | PUBLIC }
```

Figure 2-4 The syntax of the REVOKE statement

Steps

1. Run SQL*Plus and connect as the WAITE user account. CHP2-6.sql, shown in Figure 2-5, creates the sample user account and role which will be used throughout this How-To.

The CREATE USER statement creates the SMITH user account, which is granted privileges in the following steps. The CREATE ROLE statement creates the GENERAL role, which is granted privileges and granted to the user account. The DEPT2_6 table is created in order to have an object which can be granted privileges in the example statements. Run the SQL script to create the objects.

```
SQL>  START CHP2-6

User created.

Role created.

Table created.
```

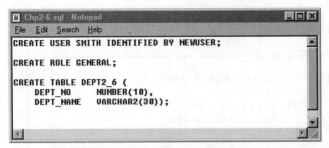

```
Chp2-6.sql - Notepad
File  Edit  Search  Help
CREATE USER SMITH IDENTIFIED BY NEWUSER;

CREATE ROLE GENERAL;

CREATE TABLE DEPT2_6 (
    DEPT_NO      NUMBER(10),
    DEPT_NAME    VARCHAR2(30));
```

Figure 2-5 CHP2-6.sql creates the objects
used in How-To 2.3

2. Load CHP2-7.sql into the SQL buffer. The GRANT statement contained in
the file grants CREATE SESSION and ALTER SESSION privileges to the
sample role.

```
SQL> GET CHP2-7
  1  GRANT CREATE SESSION,
  2*     ALTER SESSION TO GENERAL
```

Line 1 contains the GRANT keyword, used to grant privileges to a user
account or role. The CREATE SESSION and ALTER SESSION system privileges are granted to the GENERAL role, which was created in step 1. Any
user account granted this role can connect to the database after this statement is executed.

3. Run the statement to grant the privileges.

```
SQL>  /
```

```
Grant succeeded.
```

4. Load CHP2-8.sql into the SQL buffer. The statement in the file grants the
CONNECT, RESOURCE, and DBA privileges to the SMITH user account
created in step 1.

```
SQL> GET CHP2-8
  1  GRANT
  2      CONNECT, RESOURCE, DBA
  3* TO SMITH
```

Line 1 contains the GRANT keyword. Lines 2 and 3 specify that the CON-
NECT, RESOURCE, and DBA default roles will be granted directly to the
SMITH user account.

5. Run the statement to grant the privileges.

```
SQL>  /
```

```
Grant succeeded.
```

6. Load CHP2-9.sql into the SQL buffer. The GRANT statement contained in the file grants SELECT, INSERT, UPDATE, and DELETE privileges on the DEPT2_3 created in Step 1 to the TECHIE role created in Step 1.

```
SQL> GET CHP2-9
  1   GRANT SELECT, INSERT, UPDATE, DELETE
  2      ON DEPT2_6 TO
  3*  GENERAL
```

Line 1 contains the GRANT keyword and specifies that SELECT, INSERT, UPDATE, and DELETE privileges will be granted on the object. Line 2 specifies that the privileges are granted on the DEPT2_6 table created in Step 1. Line 3 specifies that the GENERAL role is the recipient of the privileges.

7. Run the statement to grant the privileges.

```
SQL>  /
```

```
Grant succeeded.
```

8. Load CHP2-10.sql into the SQL buffer. The GRANT statement contained in the file grants the GENERAL role to the SMITH user account.

```
SQL> GET CHP2-10
  1   GRANT GENERAL
  2*     TO SMITH
```

This statement grants the GENERAL role created in Step 1 to the SMITH user account created in Step 1. When the statement is executed, any privileges granted to the GENERAL role will be available to the SMITH user account.

9. Run the statement to grant the privileges.

```
SQL> /
```

```
Grant succeeded.
```

How It Works

The GRANT statement is used to give privileges to user accounts or roles. Object or system privileges can be granted to user accounts or roles. Role privileges can be granted to user accounts or other roles. Step 1 creates a user account, role, and table which are used throughout this How-To. Steps 2 and 3 grant the GENERAL role CREATE SESSION and ALTER SESSION privileges. User accounts granted this role can connect to the database. Steps 4 and 5 grant the CONNECT, RESOURCE, and DBA roles to the SMITH user account, effectively giving the user account complete control of the database. Steps 6 and 7 grant SELECT, INSERT, UPDATE, and

DELETE privileges to the GENERAL role for the DEPT2_6 table. Steps 8 and 9 grant
the GENERAL role to the SMITH user account.

Comments

Privileges can be granted to a user account or role. It is easier to create roles and grant
each privilege once to the role than to each user account individually. If a database
object is removed and then re-created, all grants to the object must be re-created.
If the privileges are granted to each user account individually, grants must be reis-
sued for each user account.

COMPLEXITY
BEGINNING

2.4 How do I...
Determine the active user account?

Problem

In my programs, I need to be able to determine who holds the active user account.
In order for my application to control the user's access to different screens and reports,
the application must know who each user account is. How do I determine the active
user account?

Technique

Oracle makes the user account name available through the USER pseudo-column.
A *pseudo-column* is a column that can be included in a query but is not part of any
table. The USER pseudo-column can be queried from a dummy table called DUAL.
The DUAL table contains one record, and its primary use is to let users access
pseudo-columns and make the database perform calculations. The USER pseudo-
column can be referenced directly in PL/SQL. USER is treated like a read-only constant
in PL/SQL.

Steps

1. Run SQL*Plus and connect as the WAITE user account. Load CHP2-11.sql
into the SQL buffer with the GET command. The statement queries the
USER pseudo-column from DUAL.

```
SQL> GET CHP2-11
  1* SELECT USER FROM DUAL
```

The USER pseudo-column can be included in a query to return the connected user account. Line 1 queries the USER pseudo-column from the DUAL system table.

2. Execute the query to view the current user account.

```
SQL> /

USER
-----------------------------------
WAITE
```

3. Load CHP2-12.sql into the SQL buffer. The PL/SQL block contained in the file uses the USER pseudo-column. Unlike SQL, PL/SQL allows access to the USER pseudo-column without including it in a query.

```
SQL> GET CHP2-12
  1  DECLARE
  2      X VARCHAR2(10);
  3  BEGIN
  4      X := USER;
  5      DBMS_OUTPUT.PUT_LINE('The value of X is '||X);
  6* END;
```

Lines 1 and 2 contain the declarative section of the PL/SQL block, which is used to define variables for the modules. Line 4 assigns the value of the USER pseudo-column to the variable X created in line 2. Line 5 displays the variable by using the DBMS_OUTPUT.PUT_LINE procedure.

4. Set the SERVEROUTPUT system variable to ON to display output from the DBMS_OUTPUT.PUT_LINE procedure in SQL*Plus and run the PL/SQL statement.

```
SQL>  /
The value of X is WAITE

PL/SQL procedure successfully completed.
```

How It Works

Steps 1 and 2 use the USER pseudo-column as part of a query from the DUAL table to display the connected user account in SQL*Plus. Steps 3 and 4 show how to use the USER pseudo-column within a PL/SQL module.

Comments

The USER pseudo-column is an easy way to determine the active user account. It can be queried as part of any SELECT statement or used in PL/SQL code.

2.5 How do I...
Modify user defaults and profiles?

Problem

When I create user accounts in the database, they have some high limits on the amount of CPU time they can use and the number of sessions to which they can connect. When a user or developer creates a table, it is created in an undesirable location. How can I modify the user defaults and session profiles?

Technique

The PROFILE clause in the CREATE USER and ALTER USER statements allows a profile to be specified for user accounts. A profile restricts the use of database resources for user accounts assigned to it. The CREATE PROFILE statement creates a new profile. The syntax of the CREATE PROFILE statement is shown in Figure 2-6.

```
                      CREATE PROFILE Syntax

CREATE PROFILE profile LIMIT
    { SESSION_PER_USER { integer | UNLIMITED | DEFAULT } |
      CPU_PER_SESSION { integer | UNLIMITED | DEFAULT } |
    CPU_PER_CALL {integer | UNLIMITED | DEFAULT } |
    CONNECT_TIME {integer | UNLIMITED | DEFAULT } |
    IDLE_TIME {integer | UNLIMITED | DEFAULT }
    LOGICAL_READS_PER_SESSION
          {integer | UNLIMITED | DEFAULT } |
    LOGICAL_READS_PER_CALL
          {integer | UNLIMITED | DEFAULT }|
    COMPOSITE_LIMIT { integer | UNLIMITED | DEFAULT } |
    IDLE_TIME { integer | UNLIMITED | DEFAULT } |
    PRIVATE_SGA { integer } }
```

Figure 2-6 The syntax of the CREATE PROFILE statement

Once a profile has been created, it can be assigned to new user accounts with the PROFILE clause of the CREATE USER statement. It can also be assigned to existing user accounts by executing an ALTER USER statement.

The default tablespace specifies where data objects will be created when the location is not specified in a CREATE statement. The temporary tablespace specifies the tablespace used when temporary storage is required by an operation the user account executes. The ALTER USER statement is used to change the default tablespace and the temporary tablespace of a user account. The syntax of the ALTER USER statement is shown in Figure 2-7.

Steps

1. Run SQL*Plus and connect as the WAITE user account. The CREATE PROFILE privilege is required to perform this step. Any user account with the DBA role has this privilege. Load CHP2-13.sql into the SQL buffer with the GET command. The statement contained in CHP2-13.sql creates a profile restricting the number of concurrent sessions a user account can have connected to the database. Since no other parameters are specified, they are assumed to be the default.

```
SQL>   GET CHP2-13
  1    CREATE PROFILE WAITE_PROFILE
  2*       LIMIT SESSIONS_PER_USER 4
```

Line 1 contains the CREATE PROFILE keywords and specifies the name of the profile to be created. Line 2 limits the number of sessions per user account to four.

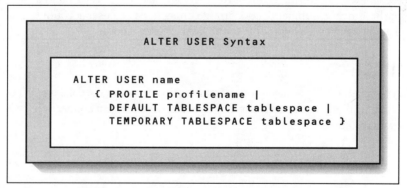

Figure 2-7 The syntax of the ALTER USER statement

2. Run the statement from the SQL buffer.

```
SQL> /
```

Profile created.

3. Load CHP2-14.sql into the SQL buffer. The file contains an ALTER USER statement to assign the new profile to the WAITE user account.

```
SQL> GET CHP2-14
  1   ALTER USER WAITE
  2*      PROFILE WAITE_PROFILE
```

Line 1 contains the ALTER USER keywords, and line 2 contains the PROFILE clause to specify a new profile.

4. Execute the statement to modify the user account.

```
SQL> /
```

User Altered

The WAITE user account is limited to four concurrent sessions by the profile.

How It Works

A profile limits resources allocated to a user account. A profile is somewhat like a role since it groups user accounts into defined categories. A profile can be created by any user account with the CREATE PROFILE privilege and is assigned to a user account with a CREATE USER or ALTER USER statement. Steps 1 and 2 create a profile limiting the number of concurrent connections of a user account to four. Steps 3 and 4 assign the new profile to the WAITE user account.

Comments

A profile should be created for users and developers within the database. When developing applications, a developer may have many concurrent connections, which can drain resources.

COMPLEXITY
INTERMEDIATE

2.6 How do I...
Restrict a user account's disk space?

Problem

Some developers in my organization like to create huge tables when they test their applications. Since we have a limited amount of space in the database, I need to limit the amount of disk space a user account can occupy. How can I restrict a user account's disk space?

Technique

The QUOTA clause of the ALTER USER statement is used to restrict the disk space of an existing user account. The disk space can be restricted for a new user account by specifying a QUOTA clause in the CREATE USER statement. A user account is restricted storage by tablespace.

Steps

1. Run SQL*Plus and connect to the database as the WAITE user account. CHP2-15.sql shown in Figure 2-8 contains three ALTER USER statements to restrict disk usage in the SYSTEM tablespace.

The three CREATE USER statements create the user accounts that will be restricted by the ALTER USER statements. The user account WILMA is restricted to 10 megabytes, BETTY to 500 kilobytes, and BARNEY to 100,000 bytes in the SYSTEM tablespace.

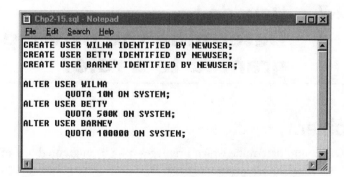

Figure 2-8 CHP2-15.sql creates three user accounts and restricts their disk usage

2. Execute CHP2-15.sql to create the user accounts and restrict their disk space.

```
SQL>   START CHP2-15
User created.

User created.

User created.

User altered.

User altered.

User altered.
```

How It Works

The QUOTA clause of the CREATE USER and ALTER USER statements limits the amount of disk space a user account's objects can occupy. The first three statements in CHP2-15 create user accounts that will be restricted by the following statements. The first ALTER USER account restricts the WILMA user account to 10 megabytes represented with the statement 10M. The user account BETTY is restricted to 500 kilobytes, represented by 500K. If M or K is not specified, the statement interprets the value in bytes. The BARNEY user account is restricted to 100,000 bytes.

Comments

Creating disk quotas is mainly an issue for developers and users running decision support applications that create summary tables. The UNLIMITED TABLESPACE privilege gives a user account unlimited space within all tablespaces and ignores the quotas placed on the user account.

COMPLEXITY
INTERMEDIATE

2.7   How do I...
Determine the privileges granted to a role?

Problem

I want to determine which privileges have been granted to a role. This will let me see if the role requires more privileges or is the right role to grant a user account. How do I determine which privileges have been granted to a role?

Technique

The ROLE_TAB_PRIVS data dictionary view contains the object privileges granted to a role. The ROLE_ROLE_PRIVS view contains the roles granted to another role, and the ROLE_SYS_PRIVS view contains system privileges granted to a role. Determining the privileges granted to a role can become complicated when role grants become nested. If roles have not been granted other roles, it is easy to determine the privileges granting a role provides. Figure 2-9 shows the description of the data dictionary views within SQL*Plus.

Steps

1. Run SQL*Plus and connect as the WAITE user account. CHP2-16.sql, shown in Figure 2-10, creates a table and two roles which are used throughout this How-To.

The first statement creates the WAITRESS role, and the second statement creates the BARTENDER role. The CREATE TABLE statement creates a table with privileges on it granted in the first GRANT statement. The second GRANT statement grants the CONNECT default role to the BARTENDER role. Run the file to create the sample roles.

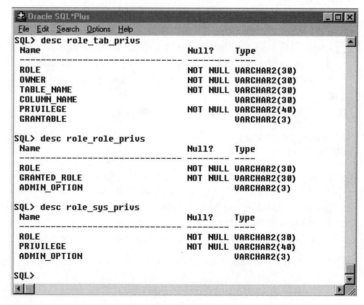

Figure 2-9 Role privilege data dictionary views

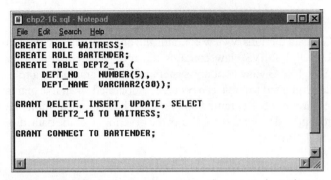

Figure 2-10 CHP2-16.sql creates the sample roles and objects used in How-To 2.7

```
SQL> START CHP2-16

Role created.

Role created.

Table created.

Grant complete.

Grant complete.
```

2. Load CHP2-17.sql into the SQL buffer. The file contains a query used to determine the object privileges granted to a role. The ROLE_TAB_PRIVS view contains all the object privileges granted to roles.

```
SQL> GET CHP2-17
  1   SELECT OWNER||'.'||TABLE_NAME OBJECT,
  2      PRIVILEGE FROM
  3      ROLE_TAB_PRIVS
  4* WHERE ROLE = '&ROLE'
```

Line 1 concatenates the OWNER and TABLE_NAME columns to return the object in the format in which it is usually used. Line 2 returns the privilege granted to the object. Line 3 specifies the ROLE_TAB_PRIVS data dictionary view as the source of the query. Line 4 causes information for the role specified by the &ROLE substitution variable to be returned.

3. Format the output of the column using the COLUMN command. Execute the query for the WAITRESS role created in Step 1 by replacing the &ROLE substitution variable with WAITRESS.

```
SQL>   COLUMN OBJECT FORMAT A30
SQL>   COLUMN PRIVILEGE FORMAT A30
SQL>   /
Enter value for 1: WAITRESS
```

```
old    4:      where role = '&ROLE'
new    4:      where role = 'WAITRESS'

OBJECT                              PRIVILEGE
-------------------------------     -------------------------------
WAITE.DEPT2_16                      DELETE
WAITE.DEPT2_16                      INSERT
WAITE.DEPT2_16                      SELECT
WAITE.DEPT2_16                      UPDATE
```

4. Load CHP2-18.sql into the SQL buffer. The file contains a query which identifies roles granted to a role.

```
SQL>   GET CHP2-18
  1    SELECT GRANTED_ROLE
  2        FROM ROLE_ROLE_PRIVS
  3*   WHERE ROLE = '&ROLE'
```

Lines 1 and 2 return the GRANTED_ROLE column from the ROLE_ROLE_PRIVS. Line 3 causes information to be returned for the role specified by the &ROLE substitution variable. The ROLE_ROLE_PRIVS view returns roles which have been granted to other roles.

5. Execute the script for the BARTENDER role to view roles granted to this role. Replace the &ROLE substitution variable with BARTENDER.

```
SQL>   /
Enter value for role: BARTENDER
old    3:      where role = '&role'
new    5:      where role = 'BARTENDER'

GRANTED_ROLE
-------------------------------
CONNECT
```

6. Load CHP2-19.sql into the SQL buffer. The file contains a query that identifies system privileges granted to a role.

```
SQL>   GET CHP2-19
  1    SELECT PRIVILEGE, ADMIN_OPTION
  2    FROM
  3        ROLE_SYS_PRIVS
  4    WHERE
  5*       ROLE = '&ROLE'
```

Line 1 returns the PRIVILEGE and ADMIN_OPTION columns. The ADMIN_OPTION contains YES if the privilege can be granted by users of the role to other user accounts and roles. Line 3 specifies the ROLE_SYS_PRIVS data dictionary view as the source of the query. Line 5 returns information for the role specified by the &ROLE substitution variable.

7. Execute the statement for the CONNECT system role by specifying CONNECT as the &ROLE substitution variable.

```
Enter value for role: CONNECT
old    5:      role = '&role'
new    5:      role = 'CONNECT'

PRIVILEGE                                    ADM
-------------------------------------------  ---
ALTER SESSION                                NO
CREATE CLUSTER                               NO
CREATE DATABASE LINK                         NO
CREATE SEQUENCE                              NO
CREATE SESSION                               NO
CREATE SYNONYM                               NO
CREATE TABLE                                 NO
CREATE VIEW                                  NO

8 rows selected.
```

How It Works

The ROLE_TAB_PRIVS data dictionary view contains object privileges granted to a role. ROLE_SYS_PRIVS contains system privileges granted to the role, and ROLE_ROLE_PRIVS contains other roles granted to a role. Steps 1 and 2 list the object privileges granted to a role by querying the ROLE_TAB_PRIVS view. Steps 3 and 4 list the roles granted to a role by querying the ROLE_ROLE_PRIVS view. Step 5 queries ROLE_SYS_PRIVS to determine the system privileges granted to the role.

Comments

To determine the privileges granted to a role, take all the system and object privileges granted directly to it and add the privileges provided by other roles. The data dictionary is the source for information regarding privileges and roles. How-To 2.8 goes into detail about determining the privileges granted to a user account.

COMPLEXITY
INTERMEDIATE

2.8 How do I...
Determine the privileges granted to a user account?

Problem

I want to be able to determine what privileges have been granted to a user account. Since a user account's privileges are the sum of its directly granted privileges and its role privileges, it's hard to tell if a user account has a specific privilege. How do I determine which privileges have been granted to a user account?

Technique

The DBA_TAB_PRIVS view contains object privileges granted directly to user accounts. The DBA_ROLE_PRIVS view contains the roles granted to user accounts, and the DBA_SYS_PRIVS view contains system privileges granted to user accounts. The ROLE_TAB_PRIVS and ROLE_SYS_PRIVS views used in the previous How-To can be used with the other views to calculate the effective privileges of a user account. Figure 2-11 describes the data dictionary views within SQL*Plus.

```
Oracle SQL*Plus                                          _ | □ | X
File  Edit  Search  Options  Help
SQL> desc dba_tab_privs
Name                                  Null?     Type

GRANTEE                               NOT NULL  VARCHAR2(30)
OWNER                                 NOT NULL  VARCHAR2(30)
TABLE_NAME                            NOT NULL  VARCHAR2(30)
GRANTOR                               NOT NULL  VARCHAR2(30)
PRIVILEGE                             NOT NULL  VARCHAR2(40)
GRANTABLE                                       VARCHAR2(3)

SQL> desc dba_role_privs
Name                                  Null?     Type

GRANTEE                                         VARCHAR2(30)
GRANTED_ROLE                          NOT NULL  VARCHAR2(30)
ADMIN_OPTION                                    VARCHAR2(3)
DEFAULT_ROLE                                    VARCHAR2(3)

SQL> desc dba_sys_privs
Name                                  Null?     Type

GRANTEE                               NOT NULL  VARCHAR2(30)
PRIVILEGE                             NOT NULL  VARCHAR2(40)
ADMIN_OPTION                                    VARCHAR2(3)

SQL> |
```

Figure 2-11 User privileges' data dictionary views

Steps

1. Run SQL*Plus and connect as the WAITE user account. CHP2-20.sql, shown in Figure 2-12, creates the sample user accounts and roles used throughout this How-To.

The first statement creates the TERRI user account with a CREATE USER statement. The second statement creates the ROOFER role, and the third statement creates the DEPT2_20 table. The first GRANT statement grants all privileges on the DEPT2_20 table to the TERRI user account. The second GRANT statement grants the CONNECT and RESOURCE default roles, along with the ROOFER role, to the TERRI user account. Run the file to create the sample objects.

```
SQL> START CHP2-20

User created.

Role created.

Table created.

Grant succeeded.

Grant succeeded.
```

2. Load CHP2-21.sql into the SQL buffer. The file contains a query used to determine the system privileges granted directly to a user.

```
SQL>    GET CHP2-21
  1     SELECT PRIVILEGE, ADMIN_OPTION
  2         FROM SYS.DBA_SYS_PRIVS
  3*    WHERE GRANTEE = '&GRANTEE'
```

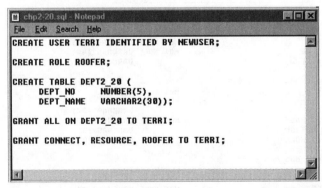

Figure 2-12 CHP2-20.sql creates the sample objects used throughout this How-To

Line 1 returns the PRIVILEGE granted to the user account, along with the ADMIN_OPTION column. Line 2 specifies the SYS.DBA_SYS_PRIVS data dictionary view as the source of the query. Line 3 returns data for the user account specified by the &GRANTEE substitution variable.

3. Execute the query for the TERRI user account, and replace the &GRANTEE substitution variable with TERRI.

```
SQL>  /
Enter value for 1: TERRI

PRIVILEGE                                       ADM
----------------------------------------------- ---
UNLIMITED TABLESPACE                            NO
```

The only system privileges granted to TERRI are from the CONNECT and RESOURCE system roles. This produces only the UNLIMITED TABLE-SPACE privilege in the DBA_SYS_PRIVS view. This does not accurately represent TERRI's system privileges. The ROLE_SYS_PRIVS view must be included in the query to show system privileges granted through roles.

4. Load CHP2-22.sql into the SQL buffer with the GET command. The file contains a statement that queries privileges from both the DBA_SYS_PRIVS and ROLE_SYS_PRIVS views. The DBA_ROLE_PRIVS view is used to determine which roles the user account has been granted.

```
SQL>  GET CHP2-22
  1    SELECT PRIVILEGE, ADMIN_OPTION
  2    FROM
  3      DBA_SYS_PRIVS
  4    WHERE
  5      GRANTEE = '&GRANTEE'
  6    UNION
  7    SELECT PRIVILEGE, ROLE_SYS_PRIVS.ADMIN_OPTION
  8      FROM
  9    ROLE_SYS_PRIVS, DBA_ROLE_PRIVS
 10    WHERE
 11      ROLE_SYS_PRIVS.ROLE = DBA_ROLE_PRIVS.GRANTED_ROLE AND
 12      DBA_ROLE_PRIVS.GRANTEE = '&GRANTEE'
 13*   ORDER BY 1
```

Lines 1 through 5 return the system privileges granted directly to a user account by querying the DBA_SYS_PRIVS data dictionary view. Lines 7 through 12 return system privileges granted to the user account through roles. The UNION operator in line 6 connects the two queries to generate a single result.

5. Execute the statement for the TERRI user account by replacing the
&GRANTEE substitution variable with TERRI. Since the system privileges
provided by the CONNECT and RESOURCE roles are displayed, the output of the query is more useful in determining the privileges of the user
account. Figure 2-13 shows the execution of this step in SQL*Plus.

6. Load the file CHP2-23.sql into the SQL buffer. The file contains a query
used to determine the roles granted to a user account. The
DBA_ROLE_PRIVS view contains roles granted to user accounts. The
DBA_ROLE_PRIVS view was used in Step 4 to determine the system privileges provided to a user account through a role.

```
SQL>  GET CHP2-23
  1     SELECT GRANTED_ROLE, DEFAULT_ROLE
  2         FROM DBA_ROLE_PRIVS
  3*   WHERE GRANTEE = '&GRANTEE'
```

Line 1 returns the role granted to the user account and its status as a default
role. If a role is a default role, it is enabled automatically when the user
account connects to the database. Line 2 specifies the DBA_ROLE_PRIVS
data dictionary view as the source of the query. Line 3 specifies the user
account granted access to the role with the &GRANTEE substitution
variable.

```
PRIVILEGE                           ADM
---------------------------------   ---
ALTER SESSION                       NO
CREATE CLUSTER                      NO
CREATE DATABASE LINK                NO
CREATE PROCEDURE                    NO
CREATE SEQUENCE                     NO
CREATE SESSION                      NO
CREATE SYNONYM                      NO
CREATE TABLE                        NO
CREATE TRIGGER                      NO
CREATE VIEW                         NO
UNLIMITED TABLESPACE                NO

11 rows selected.

SQL> |
```

Figure 2-13 The system privileges granted to
a user account

7. Execute the query for the TERRI user account by specifying TERRI for the substitution variable.

```
SQL>  /
Enter value for 1: TERRI

GRANTED_ROLE                     DEF
------------------------------   ---
CONNECT                          YES
RESOURCE                         YES
ROOFER                           YES
```

8. Load CHP2-24.sql into the SQL buffer. The file contains a query used to determine the object privileges granted directly to a user account. The DBA_TAB_PRIVS view contains all object privileges granted directly to user accounts.

```
SQL>  GET CHP2-24
 1    SELECT OWNER||'.'||TABLE_NAME OBJECT,
 2       PRIVILEGE FROM
 3       DBA_TAB_PRIVS
 4*      WHERE GRANTEE = '&GRANTEE'
```

Line 1 concatenates the owner of the object and the object name to return the object in the format most often used to represent it. Line 2 returns the privilege granted to the object. Line 3 specifies the DBA_TAB_PRIVS data dictionary view as the source of the query. Line 4 specifies the user account granted the privileges with the &GRANTEE substitution variable.

9. Execute the query for the TERRI user account by replacing the &GRANTEE substitution variable with TERRI. The TERRI user account has been granted privileges directly on the table, so the DBA_TAB_PRIVS view contains data for the user account. If all object privileges were granted to the user account through roles, the query would return no rows.

```
SQL>  /
Enter value for 1: TERRI

OBJECT                           PRIVILEGE
------------------------------   ----------------------------
WAITE.DEPT2_20                   DELETE
WAITE.DEPT2_20                   INDEX
WAITE.DEPT2_20                   INSERT
WAITE.DEPT2_20                   SELECT
WAITE.DEPT2_20                   UPDATE
WAITE.DEPT2_20                   REFERENCES
WAITE.DEPT2_20                   ALTER

7 rows selected.
```

10. Load CHP2-25.sql into the SQL buffer with the GET command. This file contains a query used to determine object privileges granted to the user account through roles.

```
SQL>    GET CHP2-25
  1     SELECT RP.OWNER||'.'||RP.TABLE_NAME, PRIVILEGE
  2     FROM
  3          ROLE_TAB_PRIVS RP, DBA_ROLE_PRIVS DP
  4     WHERE
  5          RP.ROLE = DP.GRANTED_ROLE AND
  6          DP.GRANTEE = '&GRANTEE'
```

Line 1 returns the owner and table name on which the user account was granted privileges through a role. ROLE_TAB_PRIVS and DBA_ROLE_PRIVS views are specified in line 3 as the source of the query. The WHERE clause in lines 4 through 6 joins the views and returns only records specified by the &GRANTEE substitution variable.

11. Execute the query for the TERRI user account by replacing the &GRANTEE substitution variable in both locations with TERRI. The user account's privileges are listed one per row, making the output difficult to read. CHP2-26.sql, shown in the next step, formats the data as an easy-to-read report.

```
SQL> /
Enter value for grantee: TERRI
old    6:        DP.GRANTEE = '&GRANTEE'
new    6:        DP.GRANTEE = 'TERRI'
Enter value for grantee: TERRI
old   12:        UP.GRANTEE = '&GRANTEE'
new   12:        UP.GRANTEE = 'TERRI'

no rows selected
```

12. CHP2-26.sql contains a SQL*Plus report to print all privileges granted directly or indirectly to a user account. The report can be run by executing a START command.

```
COLUMN OBJECT FORMAT A20 HEADING 'OBJECT/PRIV'
COLUMN PRIVILEGE FORMAT A10
COLUMN A FORMAT A6 HEADING ' ' TRUNCATE
COLUMN B FORMAT A6 HEADING ' ' TRUNCATE
COLUMN C FORMAT A6 HEADING ' ' TRUNCATE
COLUMN D FORMAT A6 HEADING ' ' TRUNCATE
COLUMN E FORMAT A6 HEADING ' ' TRUNCATE
COLUMN F FORMAT A6 HEADING ' ' TRUNCATE
COLUMN G FORMAT A6 HEADING ' ' TRUNCATE
SELECT PRIVILEGE OBJECT,
   DECODE(ADMIN_OPTION,'YES','ADMIN',NULL) A,
   NULL B, NULL C, NULL D, NULL E, NULL F, NULL G
```

```
FROM
   DBA_SYS_PRIVS
WHERE
   GRANTEE = '&&GRANTEE'
UNION
   SELECT PRIVILEGE OBJECT,
   DECODE(ROLE_SYS_PRIVS.ADMIN_OPTION,'YES','ADMIN',NULL) A,
      NULL B, NULL C, NULL D, NULL E, NULL F, NULL G
FROM
     ROLE_SYS_PRIVS, DBA_ROLE_PRIVS
     WHERE
       ROLE_SYS_PRIVS.ROLE = DBA_ROLE_PRIVS.GRANTED_ROLE AND
       DBA_ROLE_PRIVS.GRANTEE = '&&GRANTEE'
UNION
SELECT   RP.OWNER||'.'||RP.TABLE_NAME OBJECT,
        DECODE(SUM(DECODE(PRIVILEGE,'ALTER',1,0)),1,'ALTER',NULL) A,
        DECODE(SUM(DECODE(PRIVILEGE,'INDEX',1,0)),1,'INDEX',NULL) B,
        DECODE(SUM(DECODE(PRIVILEGE,'SELECT',1,0)),1,'SELECT',NULL) C,
        DECODE(SUM(DECODE(PRIVILEGE,'ALTER',1,0)),1,'INSERT',NULL) D,
        DECODE(SUM(DECODE(PRIVILEGE,'UPDATE',1,0)),1,'UPDATE',NULL) E,
        DECODE(SUM(DECODE(PRIVILEGE,'DELETE',1,0)),1,'DELETE',NULL) F,
DECODE(SUM(DECODE(PRIVILEGE,'REFERENCE',1,0)),1,'REFERENCE',NULL) G
  FROM
        ROLE_TAB_PRIVS RP, DBA_ROLE_PRIVS DP
 WHERE
    RP.ROLE = DP.GRANTED_ROLE AND
    DP.GRANTEE = '&&GRANTEE'
    GROUP BY RP.OWNER, RP.TABLE_NAME
UNION
 SELECT
UP.OWNER||'.'||UP.TABLE_NAME,
    DECODE(SUM(DECODE(PRIVILEGE,'ALTER',1,0)),1,'ALTER',NULL) A,
    DECODE(SUM(DECODE(PRIVILEGE,'INDEX',1,0)),1,'INDEX',NULL) B,
    DECODE(SUM(DECODE(PRIVILEGE,'SELECT',1,0)),1,'SELECT',NULL) C,
    DECODE(SUM(DECODE(PRIVILEGE,'ALTER',1,0)),1,'INSERT',NULL) D,
    DECODE(SUM(DECODE(PRIVILEGE,'UPDATE',1,0)),1,'UPDATE',NULL) E,
    DECODE(SUM(DECODE(PRIVILEGE,'DELETE',1,0)),1,'DELETE',NULL) F,
   DECODE(SUM(DECODE(PRIVILEGE,'DELETE',1,0)),1,'REFERENCE',NULL) G
  FROM
    DBA_TAB_PRIVS UP
  WHERE
    UP.GRANTEE = '&&GRANTEE'
  GROUP BY UP.OWNER, UP.TABLE_NAME
  ORDER BY 1;
```

Run the report for the TERRI user account. Figure 2-14 shows the results of the operation in SQL*Plus.

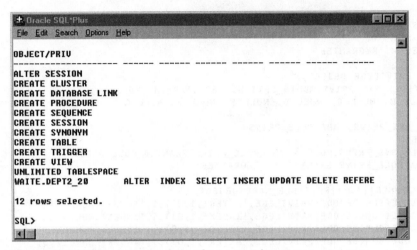

```
 Oracle SQL*Plus                                              _ □ ×
File  Edit  Search  Options  Help

OBJECT/PRIV
-------------------- ------ ------ ------ ------ ------ ------ ------
ALTER SESSION
CREATE CLUSTER
CREATE DATABASE LINK
CREATE PROCEDURE
CREATE SEQUENCE
CREATE SESSION
CREATE SYNONYM
CREATE TABLE
CREATE TRIGGER
CREATE VIEW
UNLIMITED TABLESPACE
WAITE.DEPT2_20        ALTER  INDEX  SELECT INSERT UPDATE DELETE REFERE

12 rows selected.

SQL>
```

Figure 2-14 The output of the formatted query
contained in CHP2-26.sql

How It Works

Step 1 creates the user account, role, and table used throughout this How-To. Steps 2 and 3 list the system roles granted directly to a user account by querying DBA_SYS_PRIVS. The query used in steps 4 and 5 includes the system privileges provided by roles granted to the user account. Steps 6 and 7 list the roles granted to a user account. Steps 8 and 9 list the object privileges granted directly to a user account by querying DBA_TAB_PRIVS. Steps 10 and 11 include object privileges granted to the user account through roles. Step 12 presents and runs the CHP2-26.sql file, which displays a report of all privileges granted to a user account either directly or through roles.

Comments

The data dictionary views provide information about privileges granted to a user account. Most of the views used in this How-To are DBA views. There is a complete set of corresponding USER views that allow a user account to query its own privileges. USER_TAB_PRIVS contains the object privileges granted to the connected user account. USER_ROLE_PRIVS contains roles granted to the user account, and USER_SYS_PRIVS contains system privileges granted to a user account.

CHAPTER 3
SECURITY

SECURITY

How do I...

3.1   **Determine a user's roles at runtime?**

3.2   **Remove a default role from a user?**

3.3   **Enable a password-protected role?**

3.4   **Enable a role without disabling other active roles?**

3.5   **Encrypt and decrypt data?**

3.6   **Restrict access from ad hoc query tools?**

3.7   **Restrict a specific program from modifying data?**

Security is a major issue in the development of multi-user Oracle applications. Advances in technology have created tools which can access Oracle databases in more sophisticated ways. With ad hoc query tools becoming easier to use, it is important to ensure that only approved applications can query and modify data. This chapter explores topics related to enhancing security within your Oracle applications. The examples in this chapter use the user accounts and roles created in Chapter 2, User Accounts and Roles. CHP2-1.sql creates the user accounts and CHP2-2.sql creates the roles.

3.1   Determine a user's roles at runtime

Roles granted to user accounts can be enabled or disabled at runtime. An application can use the status of database roles at runtime to determine which screens and reports to provide the user. This How-To explains the method used to determine roles enabled at runtime using SQL and PL/SQL.

3.2   Remove a default role from a user

When a role is granted to a user account, it is a default role unless otherwise specified. Password-protected roles do not require a password if they are a default role. In order to use password-protected roles fully, they must not be default roles. This How-To explains the method for making roles non-default.

3.3   Enable a password-protected role

Password-protected roles must be enabled at runtime in order for the application to use the privileges they provide. The method for enabling a password-protected role depends on the environment being used. This How-To explains the methods for enabling roles in SQL*Plus and PL/SQL.

3.4   Enable a role without disabling other active roles

When a role is enabled, all currently enabled roles become disabled for the session at hand. This can cause problems within your application if it depends on the privileges provided by the other roles. This How-To explores methods for enabling a password-protected role while keeping the other roles enabled.

3.5   Encrypt and decrypt data

It is sometimes necessary to store sensitive information, such as a password, in a table. Encrypting data when it is inserted into the table and decrypting it when it is retrieved helps protect sensitive information. This How-To provides a method for encrypting data which can be later stored in the database and decrypting the encrypted data. The technique presented in this How-To makes use of the TRANSLATE function to convert text contained in a string.

3.6   Restrict access from ad hoc query tools

Ad hoc query tools pose a complicated problem in an Oracle environment. It is sometimes necessary to restrict users from data used in their applications. Do you really want your payroll clerks running ad hoc queries against your payroll data with Microsoft Access? This How-To explores the process of protecting sensitive data from ad-hoc query tools.

3.7   Restrict a specific program from modifying data

In some cases it is important to limit certain programs from modifying data. This is possible by checking the name of the program in the V$SESSION data dictionary view before letting data modification occur. This How-To provides a technique to restrict the access of a specific tool.

COMPLEXITY
BEGINNING

3.1   How do I...
Determine a user's roles at runtime?

Problem

When my application is running, I need to know what roles are enabled. From How-To 2.8, I know how to get the roles granted to a user account, but I need to determine whether a specific role is enabled at runtime. I need to do this in SQL*Plus and PL/SQL. How do I determine which user account's roles are enabled at runtime?

Technique

The SESSION_ROLES data dictionary view contains the roles enabled for a user account at runtime. Figure 3-1 shows the description of the SESSION_ROLES view in SQL*Plus. Within PL/SQL, the IS_ROLE_ENABLED function from the DBMS_SESSION package returns TRUE if a role is enabled, FALSE if not.

The ROLE column contains the name of the enabled role. One record exists in the view for each role currently enabled in the system.

Steps (SQL*Plus)

1. Run SQL*Plus and connect as the WAITE user account. Load CHP3-1.sql into the SQL buffer. The file contains a statement querying the SESSION_ROLES data dictionary view. SESSION_ROLES provides role information for the current session only. It cannot be queried for another user account's session.

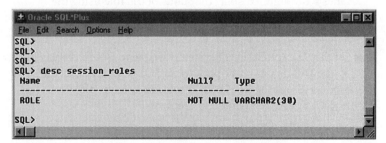

Figure 3-1 The SESSION_ROLES data dictionary view

```
SQL>   GET CHP3-1
  1    SELECT ROLE
  2*       FROM SESSION_ROLES
```

2. Execute the query. The WAITE user account was granted CONNECT, RESOURCE, and DBA privileges when the installation script created it. Since these are all default roles, the query will return all three roles.

```
SQL>   /

ROLE
--------------------------------
CONNECT
DBA
RESOURCE
```

Steps (PL/SQL)

1. Run SQL*Plus and connect as the WAITE user account. Load CHP3-2.sql into the SQL buffer. The file contains PL/SQL code using the IS_ROLE_ENABLED function to determine if a specific role is enabled. As long as the query is not part of a stored procedure, the SESSION_ROLES view can be used in a PL/SQL script.

```
SQL>   GET CHP3-2
  1    DECLARE
  2       A BOOLEAN;
  3    BEGIN
  4       A := DBMS_SESSION.IS_ROLE_ENABLED('RESOURCE');
  5       IF A THEN
  6           DBMS_OUTPUT.PUT_LINE('ROLE IS ENABLED');
  7       ELSE
  8           DBMS_OUTPUT.PUT_LINE('ROLE IS NOT ENABLED');
  9       END IF;
 10*   END;
```

Line 2 declares a boolean variable to hold the value returned by the function in line 4. Line 4 uses the IS_ROLE_ENABLED function from the DBMS_SESSION package to determine the status of the RESOURCE role. Lines 5 through 9 display the status of the role using the DBMS_OUTPUT.PUT_LINE procedure. For more information about displaying information from within PL/SQL modules, see How-To 12.4.

2. Set the SERVEROUTPUT system variable to ON to display output created by the DBMS_OUTPUT package in SQL*Plus and execute the PL/SQL module. Since the RESOURCE role is a default role, the IS_ROLE_ENABLED function returns TRUE.

```
SQL>   SET SERVEROUTPUT ON
SQL>   /

ROLE IS ENABLED

PL/SQL Statement Executed Sucessfully.
```

How It Works

The SESSION_ROLES data dictionary view contains all of the enabled roles for a session. SQL*Plus Steps 1 and 2 query this view directly. PL/SQL Steps 1 and 2 determine whether a specific role is enabled within PL/SQL by executing the IS_ROLE_ENABLED function contained in the DBMS_SESSION package. For more information about built-in packages, see Chapter 14, Built-In Packages.

Comments

Whenever possible, use roles to control access to screens and reports in your applications. The first event in your application can execute the IS_ROLE_ENABLED function from the DBMS_SESSION package to determine whether a role is enabled. If the role is enabled, activate the screens and reports related to the role.

COMPLEXITY
BEGINNING

3.2 How do I...
Remove a default role from a user?

Problem

When I grant a password protected role to a user account, it is created as a default role for the account. Since it is a default role, it is enabled at runtime automatically and does not require a password. How do I remove a role as a default role from a user?

Technique

The DEFAULT ROLE clause of the ALTER USER statement is used to specify the default roles for a user account. The syntax of the ALTER USER statement as it pertains to the DEFAULT ROLE clause is shown in Figure 3-2.

```
                    ALTER  USER  Syntax


          ALTER  USER  name
              { DEFAULT  ROLE  rolename  |
                ALL  |
                ALL  EXCEPT  rolename  |
                NONE  }
```

Figure 3-2 The ALTER USER statement to set default roles

The ALTER USER keywords begin the statement and a valid user name must be specified. The DEFAULT ROLE clause is required to specify the operation performed by the ALTER USER statement. A list of default roles can be specified separated by commas; or ALL or NONE can be specified. The ALL EXCEPT clause allows one or more specific roles to be excluded.

Steps

1. Run SQL*Plus and connect as the WAITE user account. CHP3-3.sql, shown in Figure 3-3, creates the user account and role used in upcoming examples.

The CREATE USER statement contained in line 1 creates a user account named RICHARD. Line 2 uses the CREATE ROLE statement to create a role named DEVELOPER. The last line uses the GRANT statement to give the RICHARD user account access to the DEVELOPER role and the CONNECT role. The role is automatically a default role when granted to the user account. For more information about creating user accounts and roles, see Chapter 2, User Accounts and Roles. Run the statement to create the sample user account and role.

```
SQL>   START CHP3-3

User created.

Role created.

Grant succeeded.
```

2. Load CHP3-4.sql into the SQL buffer. The file contains an ALTER USER statement that excludes the DEVELOPER role from the list of default roles.

```
SQL>   GET CHP3-4
    1    ALTER USER RICHARD
    2        DEFAULT ROLE
    3*       ALL EXCEPT DEVELOPER
```

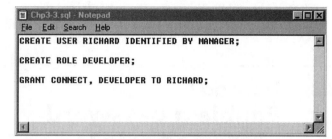

Figure 3-3 CHP3-3.sql creates the user account
and role used in How-To 3.2

Lines 1 and 2 specify the ALTER USER statement containing the DEFAULT
ROLE clause. The ALL EXCEPT clause in line 3 specifies that the DEVEL-
OPER role not be a default role, but all other roles granted to the user
account are.

3. Execute the statement to alter the user account.

```
SQL>  /

User Altered.
```

The DEVELOPER role is disabled for the RICHARD user account when it
connects to the database. All other roles granted to this account will be
default roles and are enabled when the user connects to the database.
Modifications to the user account will take place the next time the user connects to the database. If the user account is currently connected, the active
session is not modified with the new list of default roles.

How It Works

The ALTER USER statement is used with the DEFAULT ROLE clause to specify the
roles enabled automatically when the user account connects to the database. Step
1 creates a user account and role used to demonstrate the process. Steps 2 and 3 use
the ALTER USER statement with the DEFAULT ROLE and the ALL EXCEPT clauses to set all roles except DEVELOPER as default roles. Since the DEVELOPER and
CONNECT roles were granted to the user account in Step 1, the account will automatically enable only the CONNECT role when the user connects to the database.
The MARKETING role will not be returned in a query of the SESSION_ROLES view
when the RICHARD user account connects to the database.

Comments

Do not forget to make password-protected roles non-default. If the password-
protected role is a default role, it will provide no security to the database because

it will always be enabled. When granting new password-protected roles to user accounts, do not forget to use the ALTER USER statement to remove the role as default.

COMPLEXITY
INTERMEDIATE

3.3 How do I...
Enable a password-protected role?

Problem

Within my application, I want to enable a password-protected role at runtime. I need to enable a role from within PL/SQL or SQL*Plus. Since the user accounts employing this role do not have it specified as default, the role's privileges will not be available to the session until the role is enabled. How do I enable a password-protected role?

Technique

The SET ROLE statement is used to enable a password-protected role. The syntax of the SET ROLE statement is shown in Figure 3-4.

The SET ROLE keywords are required to begin the statement. One or more roles can be enabled with a single statement by separating them with commas. If the role is password protected, the IDENTIFIED BY clause must be provided with the role's password. The ALL keyword allows you to enable all the roles for the user account, and the ALL EXCEPT clause allows you to exclude one or more roles from being enabled.

Unfortunately, the SET ROLE statement cannot be executed from within PL/SQL, making it almost worthless within applications. Oracle provides the built-in package DBMS_SESSION to execute certain session commands, such as SET ROLE, through

```
                    SET ROLE Syntax

    SET ROLE
        { rolename \ {IDENTIFIED BY password] \
          ALL \
          ALL EXCEPT rolename }
```

Figure 3-4 The SET ROLE statement

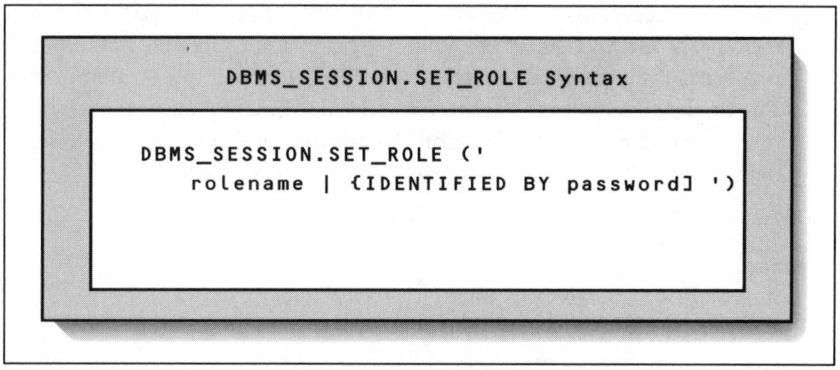

```
                DBMS_SESSION.SET_ROLE Syntax

    DBMS_SESSION.SET_ROLE ('
        rolename | [IDENTIFIED BY password] ')
```

Figure 3-5 The DBMS_SESSION.SET_ROLE procedure

PL/SQL. This package can be executed by any development tool supporting Oracle stored procedures, such as Visual Basic, Developer 2000, or Delphi. The SET_ROLE procedure in the DBMS_SESSION package is used to set a role through PL/SQL. The syntax of the statement is shown in Figure 3-5.

The names of all of the roles to be enabled must be specified within single quotes in the procedure call. If the role is password protected, the IDENTIFIED BY clause and password must be specified with the role.

Steps

1. Run SQL*Plus and connect as the WAITE user account. CHP3-5.sql, shown in Figure 3-6, creates a user account and two roles used in the later steps.

The CREATE USER statement contained in line 1 creates the LISA user account, which will be granted access to a password protected role. The CREATE ROLE statement in line 2 creates the SALES role that is not password protected. The next CREATE ROLE statement creates the HELPDESK

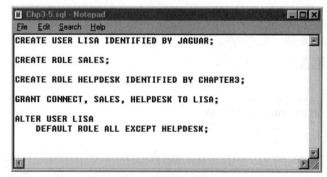

```
CREATE USER LISA IDENTIFIED BY JAGUAR;

CREATE ROLE SALES;

CREATE ROLE HELPDESK IDENTIFIED BY CHAPTER3;

GRANT CONNECT, SALES, HELPDESK TO LISA;

ALTER USER LISA
    DEFAULT ROLE ALL EXCEPT HELPDESK;
```

Figure 3-6 CHP3-5.sql creates the sample user accounts and roles used in How-To 3.3

role, which contains an IDENTIFIED BY clause to make it password protected. The GRANT statement in line 4 grants the CONNECT system role, in addition to the two new roles, to the LISA user account created in line 1. The final statement in the script uses the ALTER USER statement to make the password-protected role a non-default role, and the other two roles default. Run the statement to create the user account and roles.

```
SQL>   START CHP3-5

User created.

Role created.

Role created.

Grant Succeeded.

User altered.
```

2. Connect to the LISA user account created in step 1 using the CONNECT command, and load CHP3-1.sql into the SQL buffer. CHP3-1.sql is used throughout the chapter to determine the roles enabled during a session.

```
SQL>   CONNECT LISA/JAGUAR

Connected.

SQL>   GET CHP3-1
  1    SELECT ROLE
  2*      FROM SESSION_ROLES
```

For more information about the CONNECT command, see How-To 1.3.

3. Execute the query to view the roles enabled for the session. Since the HELPDESK role is not a default role, only the CONNECT and SALES roles will appear in the list.

```
SQL>   /

ROLE
-------------------------------
CONNECT
SALES
```

4. Load CHP3-6.sql into the SQL buffer. The SET ROLE statement contained in the file enables the HELPDESK role created in Step 1.

```
SQL>   GET CHP3-6
  1    SET ROLE HELPDESK
  2*      IDENTIFIED BY CHAPTER3;
```

Line 1 contains the SET ROLE statement used to enable a role during a session. The name of the HELPDESK role is supplied on the line to specify the role to be enabled. Line 2 contains the IDENTIFIED BY clause required to supply the role's password to the database.

5. Run the statement to enable the role.

```
SQL>  /

Role Set.
```

Once the role is enabled, the privileges provided by the role will be available to the current session, and the role will be listed in the SESSION_ROLES data dictionary view. The CONNECT and SALES roles, which were enabled until this step, are disabled by the statement. How-To 3.4 covers the process used to enable a role without disabling the previously enabled roles.

6. Load CHP3-7.sql into the SQL buffer. The file contains a PL/SQL module which executes the SET_ROLE procedure from the DBMS_SESSION package to enable the password-protected role.

```
SQL>  GET CHP3-7
  1   BEGIN
  2      DBMS_SESSION.SET_ROLE('HELPDESK IDENTIFIED BY CHAPTER3');
  3*  END;
```

The SET ROLE procedure in the DBMS_SESSION package allows PL/SQL statements to execute a SET ROLE statement. Executing the SET ROLE statement directly in PL/SQL causes an error.

7. Execute the PL/SQL module to enable the role.

```
SQL>  /

PL/SQL procedure successfully completed.
```

The statements presented in steps 4 and 6 perform the same action. The PL/SQL version of the technique must be used in applications, since the SET ROLE statement cannot be executed in PL/SQL.

How It Works

The SET ROLE statement is used within SQL*Plus to enable one or more roles. In PL/SQL, the DBMS_SESSION.SET_ROLE procedure performs the same task. Step 1 creates a user account and two roles. The HELPDESK role is password protected and requires a password to be enabled. Both roles are granted to the new user account, and the HELPDESK role is removed as a default role. Steps 2 and 3 connect to the new user account and execute a query of the SESSION_ROLES data dictionary view to display the enabled roles. Since the HELPDESK role is not a default role, it is not contained in the list. Steps 4 and 5 enable the password-protected role within SQL*Plus using the SET ROLE statement. Steps 6 and 7 perform the same task within PL/SQL by using the DBMS_SESSION.SET_ROLE procedure.

Comments

Executing DBMS_SESSION.SET_ROLE within a PL/SQL block is the most common way of enabling a role within an application. This procedure cannot be used within a stored procedure because it is not allowed by Oracle. The procedure must be executed from within your application and not within a stored procedure.

COMPLEXITY
ADVANCED

3.4 How do I...
Enable a role without disabling other active roles?

Problem

When I use the SET ROLE command or the SET_ROLE procedure from the DBMS_SESSION package to enable a role as shown in How-To 3.3, all of the currently enabled roles are disabled. I need to leave the current roles active when I enable a new role. How do I enable a role without disabling the other roles?

Technique

The SET ROLE statement allows multiple roles to be enabled within a single statement. All currently enabled roles must be listed in the statement in order for them to remain active. In SQL*Plus, this means you must query the SESSION_ROLES table first and execute a single SET ROLE statement. In PL/SQL, you can query the USER_ROLES view to list all roles the user account has been granted and execute the IS_ROLE_ENABLED function from the DBMS_SESSION package. Once you have determined all of the enabled roles, a single DBMS_SESSION.SET_ROLE statement can be executed.

Steps

1. Run SQL*Plus and connect as the WAITE user account. CHP3-8.sql, shown in Figure 3-7, creates a user account and two roles used in this How-To.

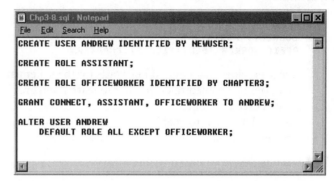

Figure 3-7 CHP3-8.sql creates the sample objects used in How-To 3.4

The CREATE USER statement creates a new user which demonstrates the techniques shown in this How-To. The ASSISTANT role created in the second statement is not password protected. The OFFICEWORKER role created with the second CREATE ROLE statement contains the IDENTIFIED BY clause to create a password. The GRANT statement gives the new user account the two new roles and the CONNECT role. The ALTER USER statement makes the OFFICEWORKER role a non-default role. Run the file to generate the sample environment.

```
SQL>   START CHP3-8

User created.

Role created.

Role created.

Grant complete.

User altered.
```

When the ANDREW user account connects to the database, the CONNECT and ASSISTANT roles will be enabled automatically. Since the OFFICE-WORKER role is not a default role, it must be manually enabled for each session.

2. Connect as the ANDREW user account using the CONNECT command and load CHP3-9.sql into the SQL buffer. The SET ROLE statement contained in the file enables the OFFICEWORKER role and leaves the other roles enabled.

```
SQL> CONNECT ANDREW/NEWUSER

Connected.
```

continued on next page

continued from previous page

```
SQL> GET CHP3-9
  1   SET ROLE
  2       CONNECT, ASSISTANT,
  3*      OFFICEWORKER IDENTIFIED BY CHAPTER3
```

Line 1 provides the required keywords for the statement. Line 2 specifies the currently enabled roles in order to leave them enabled when the statement is executed. Line 3 specifies the OFFICEWORKER role with its password, in order to enable it. The roles listed in the statement must be separated with commas.

3. Execute the statement to enable the role.

```
SQL>/
Role Set.
```

The statement leaves the CONNECT and ASSISTANT roles enabled and enables the OFFICEWORKER role. If the two currently enabled roles had not been listed in the SET ROLE statement, they would have been disabled.

4. Load CHP3-1.sql into the SQL buffer to query the enabled roles.

```
SQL>  GET CHP3-1
  1   SELECT ROLE
  2*     FROM SESSION_ROLES
```

5. Execute the query. All three roles will be listed since they were all specified in the SET ROLE statement in Step 2.

```
SQL>  /

ROLE
--------------------------------
CONNECT
ASSISTANT
OFFICEWORKER
```

The technique shown in the previous steps works when you know the names of all the currently enabled roles. The technique shown in the following steps can be used within PL/SQL without knowing which roles are enabled.

6. Reconnect as the ANDREW user account to reset the default roles as the enabled roles, and load CHP3-10.sql into the SQL buffer. The file contains PL/SQL code to enable the OFFICEWORKER role and all other enabled roles.

```
SQL> GET CHP3-10
  1   DECLARE
  2   CURSOR C1 IS
  3       SELECT GRANTED_ROLE
  4       FROM USER_ROLE_PRIVS;
  5   TMP VARCHAR2(100);
```

```
6   ISENABLED BOOLEAN;
7   BEGIN
8       TMP := 'OFFICEWORKER IDENTIFIED BY CHAPTER3';
7       FOR I IN C1 LOOP
8           ISENABLED := DBMS_SESSION.IS_ROLE_ENABLED(I.GRANTED_ROLE);
9           IF ISENABLED AND I.GRANTED_ROLE != 'MARKETING' THEN
10              TMP := TMP||', '||I.GRANTED_ROLE;
11          END IF;
12      END LOOP;
13      DBMS_SESSION.SET_ROLE(TMP);
14* END;
```

Lines 2 through 4 declare a cursor to retrieve all roles granted to the user account. For more information about PL/SQL and cursors, see Chapter 12, PL/SQL. Line 8 puts the statement required to enable the OFFICEWORKER role into the TMP variable. Lines 7 through 12 loop through each role queried to determine whether the role is enabled. Line 8 uses the DBMS_SESSION.IS_ROLE_ENABLED function to determine whether each role is enabled. If it is, the role name is concatenated to the TMP variable to create a string containing all roles to be enabled. Line 13 enables the roles by executing the DBMS_SESSION.SET_ROLE procedure.

7. Execute the PL/SQL block to enable the role.

```
SQL>  /
```

```
PL/SQL procedure successfully completed.
```

8. Load CHP3-1.sql into the SQL buffer to view the enabled roles. When the previous step was executed, the PL/SQL block did the work of identifying which roles to include in the SET ROLE statement.

```
SQL>  GET CHP3-1
  1   SELECT ROLE
  2*     FROM SESSION_ROLES
```

9. Execute the query to display the enabled roles.

```
SQL>  /
```

```
ROLE
-------------------------------
OFFICEWORKER
ASSISTANT
CONNECT
```

The CONNECT and ASSISTANT roles remain enabled, and the OFFICE-WORKER role was enabled by the PL/SQL module.

How It Works

In order to enable a role without disabling the currently enabled ones, all of the roles must be included in the SET ROLE statement. In SQL*Plus, you can query the SESSION_ROLES data dictionary view to list the roles already enabled. Within PL/SQL, you can dynamically create the parameter to which DBMS_SESSION.SET_ROLE is passed by querying data dictionary views. Step 1 creates user accounts and roles used to demonstrate the technique. Two roles are created, one of which is password protected. Steps 2 and 3 use the SET ROLE statement within SQL*Plus to enable the password-protected role and leave the existing roles enabled. The currently enabled roles will remain so if they are listed within the SET ROLE statement. Steps 4 and 5 query the SESSION_ROLES view to display the results of the operation. Steps 6 and 7 present a PL/SQL block which enables the password-protected role and queries the data dictionary to list the currently enabled roles. The currently enabled roles are passed to the DBMS_SESSION.SET_ROLE procedure, along with the new role, in order to keep the roles enabled.

Comments

If the role being enabled contains all of the privileges of the other active roles, it is not necessary to specify all of the roles in the SET ROLE statement. Unfortunately, it is difficult to ensure that all privileges provided by the currently enabled roles exist in the role being enabled.

COMPLEXITY
ADVANCED

3.5   How do I...
Encrypt and decrypt data?

Problem

In some of my more sensitive applications, I need to store a password in the database. Although I take other security precautions, I want to encrypt the password to provide an extra level of security. How do I encrypt and decrypt a password stored in a table?

Technique

The TRANSLATE function is used to replace characters in a string with corresponding characters from another string. The function call

```
X := TRANSLATE('ED','ABCDEFGHI','RSTUVWXYZ')
```

will return VU to the variable X. The letter E is the fifth letter in the second parameter and is replaced by the fifth letter in the third parameter, V. The letter D is the fourth letter in the second parameter, so it is replaced by the fourth letter in the third parameter, U. This function allows you to replace characters in a string with values from a key you create. In the PL/SQL procedures presented in this How-To, the use of the TRANSLATE function will be expanded to generate encrypted data that is hard to decode.

Steps

1. Run SQL*Plus and connect as the WAITE user account. Load CHP3-11.sql into the SQL buffer. The file contains a statement to create a stored function which is passed a string and returns an encrypted string.

```
SQL> GET CHP3-11
  1   CREATE OR REPLACE FUNCTION ENCRYPT(INPASS IN VARCHAR2)
  2         RETURN VARCHAR2 AS
  3    STRING_IN  VARCHAR2(78);
  4    STRING_OUT VARCHAR2(39);
  5    OFFSET NUMBER(2);
  6    OUTPASS VARCHAR(30);
  7   BEGIN
  8      OFFSET := TO_NUMBER(TO_CHAR(SYSDATE,'SS')) MOD 39;
  9      STRING_IN  := 'YN8K1JOZVURB3MDETS5GPL27AXWIHQ94C6FO#$_';
 10      STRING_OUT := '_$#ABCDEFGHIJKLMNOPQRSTUVWXYZ0123456789';
 11      OUTPASS := SUBSTR(STRING_IN,OFFSET,1);
 12      STRING_IN := STRING_IN||STRING_IN;
 13      STRING_IN := SUBSTR(STRING_IN,OFFSET,39);
 14      OUTPASS := OUTPASS||TRANSLATE(UPPER(INPASS),
 15                          STRING_IN,STRING_OUT);
 16      RETURN OUTPASS;
 17* END;
```

Lines 1 and 2 contain the CREATE OR REPLACE function keywords which specify that a single parameter is passed to the function and that it returns a string. Lines 3 through 6 contain the declarative section of the function and define the variables used in the function. Lines 7 through 17 contain the executable section of the function. Line 8 generates a semi-random number between 0 and 38 by selecting the seconds from the system time. This number is used to create a different encrypted value each time the function is run. Line 9 sets the STRING_IN variable to a *key* string containing each of the letters of the alphabet, the numbers 0 through 9, and the underscore (_), percent sign (%), and dollar sign ($) characters. When implementing your own encryption routine, create your own unique key that includes these characters. Line 10 sets the STRING_OUT variable to each of the letters, numbers, and symbols that are possible in the decrypted value. Line 11 creates a single character key which tells the decryption routine what offset was calculated in line 8. Lines 12 and 13 rotate the key by the value of the offset, creating a new key. This ensures that the password cannot be decrypted easily. Line 14 uses the TRANSLATE function to replace each character in the password with a character from the key. The password is concatenated with the offset character and returned by line 16.

2. Run the statement to create the stored function.

```
SQL>  /
```

Function created.

3. Load CHP3-12.sql into the SQL buffer. The file contains PL/SQL code to encrypt a string and display the encrypted result.

```
SQL> GET CHP3-12
  1   DECLARE
  2       X VARCHAR2(40);
  3   BEGIN
  4       X := ENCRYPT('HELLO');
  5       DBMS_OUTPUT.PUT_LINE('Encrypted: '||X);
  6   END;
```

The string HELLO is encrypted in line 4 with a call to the ENCRYPT function. Line 5 displays the encrypted data using the PUT_LINE procedure from the DBMS_SESSION package.

4. Set the SERVEROUTPUT system variable to ON to display the output from the PL/SQL statement and execute the PL/SQL statement.

```
SQL>  SET SERVEROUTPUT ON
SQL>  /
```

Encrypted: #2PVV9

PL/SQL procedure successfully completed.

Each time you run the statement, you will get a different encrypted result. The encryption function uses the seconds in the system time to choose the encryption offset. The first character of the encrypted string represents the offset used.

5. Load CHP3-13.sql into the SQL buffer. The file contains the stored function to decrypt a string which was encrypted using the ENCRYPT function.

```
SQL> GET CHP3-13
  1   CREATE OR REPLACE FUNCTION DECRYPT(OUTPASS IN VARCHAR2)
  2          RETURN VARCHAR2 AS
  3     STRING_IN  VARCHAR2(78);
  4     STRING_OUT VARCHAR2(39);
  5     OFFSET NUMBER(2);
  6     INPASS VARCHAR2(30);
  7   BEGIN
  8     STRING_IN  :=   'YN8K1JOZVURB3MDETS5GPL27AXWIHQ94C6FO#$_';
  9     STRING_OUT := '_$#ABCDEFGHIJKLMNOPQRSTUVWXYZ0123456789';
 10     OFFSET := INSTR(STRING_IN,SUBSTR(OUTPASS,1,1));
 11     STRING_IN := STRING_IN||STRING_IN;
 12     STRING_IN := SUBSTR(STRING_IN,OFFSET,39);
 13     INPASS := TRANSLATE(UPPER(SUBSTR(OUTPASS,2)),
```

```
14                    STRING_OUT,STRING_IN);
15    RETURN INPASS;
16* END;
```

Lines 1 and 2 provide the keywords required to create the DECRYPT function and specifies that it receives one parameter and returns a string. Lines 3 through 6 contain the declarative section of the function and define the variable used within the function. Lines 7 through 16 contain the executable section of the function. Line 8 defines the STRING_IN variable with the same key used in the ENCRYPT function. Line 10 determines the offset created by the ENCRYPT function by determining the location of the first character of the encrypted password in the key. Lines 11 and 12 rotate the key to the same position the ENCRYPT function did when it encrypted the password. Lines 13 and 14 decrypt the password by using the TRANSLATE function to reverse the encryption. Line 15 returns the decrypted password.

6. Run the statement to create the DECRYPT function.

```
SQL>  /

Function Created.
```

7. Load CHP3-14.sql into the SQL buffer. The file contains PL/SQL code to decrypt the password encrypted in Step 6. Run the statement to display the results.

```
SQL> GET CHP3-14
  1  DECLARE
  2     X VARCHAR2(30);
  3  BEGIN
  4     X := DECRYPT('#2PVV9');
  5     DBMS_OUTPUT.PUT_LINE(X);
  6* END;
```

Line 2 defines a variable which is used to hold the value decrypted by the function. Line 4 calls the DECRYPT function with the encrypted string displayed in Step 6. Line 5 displays the decrypted data using the DBMS_OUTPUT.PUT_LINE procedure.

8. Run the statement to decrypt the procedure.

```
SQL> /
HELLO

PL/SQL procedure successfully completed.
```

How It Works

The TRANSLATE function returns a string which has values replaced by the corresponding characters in another string and can be used with PL/SQL to encrypt and decrypt data. Steps 1 and 2 create a stored function which passes a string as a parameter and returns it encrypted. A semi-random number is generated from the seconds in the system time to create an offset causing a different encrypted value to be created each time the function runs. A key string is used in the function to replace letters in the string with an alternate character. Steps 3 and 4 test the encryption function. Steps 5 and 6 create a function that decrypts a string encrypted by the function created in Step 3. It passes the encrypted string as a parameter and returns it decrypted. The same key is used in the decryption function to convert the characters in the encrypted string back to their original values. Steps 7 and 8 test the function created in Steps 5 and 6 by decrypting the data encrypted in Steps 3 and 4.

Comments

The encryption methods presented in this How-To will deter people from reading the encrypted data, and it will be very difficult to break the key. If security is a major issue within your organization, Oracle provides additional security products for Oracle7.

COMPLEXITY
ADVANCED

3.6 How do I...
Restrict access from ad hoc query tools?

Problem

Within my application, I control what information the users can view. With the availability of easy-to-use ad hoc query tools, the users of my applications can query data from the database. I cannot remove their user accounts since they are valid users of the application. How do I restrict access from ad hoc query tools?

Technique

This How-To uses the topics covered in the rest of this chapter to present a method for restricting access from ad hoc query tools. Access can be restricted at two levels. Ad hoc tools can be restricted from modifying data or totally restricted from viewing data. Password protected roles are the key to restricting the access of ad hoc query tools. Applications using the tables must embed a SET ROLE statement or call the DBMS_SESSION.SET_ROLE procedure after connecting to the database. The password of the role must be kept secret from the users of the application. Without the password of the role and the method for enabling it, users will have restricted access to the data.

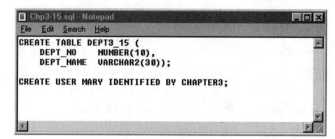

Figure 3-8 CHP3-15.sql creates the sample table and user account employed in How-To 3.6

Steps

1. Run SQL*Plus and connect as the WAITE user account. CHP3-15.sql, shown in Figure 3-8, creates a sample table that will be restricted by the technique presented in this How-To.

Run the file to create the sample table.

```
SQL>   START CHP3-15

Table created.

User created.
```

2. Create the roles which control access to the data. If ad hoc query tools are only restricted from modifying data, create two roles. The first will be a default role with SELECT privileges. Users can query information without enabling additional roles. A second role provides all of the privileges required to use the approved applications. The second role will be a non-default, password-protected role. It must be enabled by the application to be used. If ad hoc query tools are totally restricted from the data, only create the password-protected role.

```
SQL>   CREATE ROLE SELECT_ROLE;

Role Created.

SQL>   CREATE ROLE UPDATE_ROLE IDENTIFIED BY SECURE;

Role Created.
```

3. Grant privileges on the database objects to the roles.

```
SQL>   GRANT SELECT ON DEPT3_15 TO SELECT_ROLE;

Grant succeeded.
```

continued on next page

continued from previous page

```
SQL>   GRANT SELECT, INSERT, UPDATE, DELETE
  2>          ON DEPT3_15 TO UPDATE_ROLE;
```

Role Created.

4. Grant the role privileges to the users of the application. If two roles were created in Step 2, grant both roles to the users.

```
SQL>   GRANT SELECT_ROLE, UPDATE_ROLE TO MARY;
```

Grant Succeeded.

5. Remove the role with all privileges from the user account's default roles. This forces the user to enable the role to use it.

```
SQL>   ALTER USER MARY
  2>       DEFAULT ROLE ALL EXCEPT UPDATE_ROLE;
```

6. Insert program code to enable the role into applications allowed to modify data. Use the techniques presented in How-To 3.3 and How-To 3.4 to enable password-protected roles at runtime.

How It Works

Step 1 creates a sample user account and table used throughout this How-To. Step 2 creates the roles used to restrict access to the database. Step 3 grants the privileges required on the database objects to the roles created in Step 2. Step 4 grants the users of the system the role privileges. Step 5 removes the password-protected role as the default from system users. Step 6 is where code would be inserted into applications which need to use the restricted table. The DBMS_SESSION.SET_ROLE procedure is used within applications to enable password-protected roles.

Comments

Password-protected roles can be used to restrict access from ad hoc query tools. They can be used to disable INSERT, UPDATE, and DELETE privileges or to disable all privileges. When SELECT privileges are restricted through password-protected roles, side effects can occur. You must be very careful how you develop your applications when restricting the SELECT privilege through roles. Some development tools look at the database before running their first statement. For example, Oracle Reports interprets the code in PL/SQL formatting triggers before executing the first statement of code. The SET ROLE procedure must be run before this occurs. Unfortunately, it cannot. If you are restricting SELECT privileges with the roles, you cannot use PL/SQL format triggers in Oracle Reports.

COMPLEXITY
ADVANCED

3.7 How do I...
Restrict a specific program from modifying data?

Problem

In our production environment, I want to restrict specific tools from modifying data. One tool I want to limit is SQL*Plus. Although we control security through roles and no user should be able to use SQL*Plus to modify data, I want the added security. How do I restrict a specific program from modifying data?

Technique

Database triggers can be put on tables which execute before the insertion, update, or deletion of data. These triggers can be used to prevent a user from modifying data with a specific tool by analyzing the PROGRAM column of the V$SESSION view. The V$SESSION view contains information about all sessions connected to the database. Figure 3-9 shows the description of the V$SESSION view within SQL*Plus.

```
Oracle SQL*Plus                                          _ □ ✕
File  Edit  Search  Options  Help
SQL> desc v$session
 Name                             Null?    Type
 -------------------------------- -------- ----
 SADDR                                     RAW(4)
 SID                                       NUMBER
 SERIAL#                                   NUMBER
 AUDSID                                    NUMBER
 PADDR                                     RAW(4)
 USER#                                     NUMBER
 USERNAME                                  VARCHAR2(30)
 COMMAND                                   NUMBER
 TADDR                                     VARCHAR2(8)
 LOCKWAIT                                  VARCHAR2(8)
 STATUS                                    VARCHAR2(8)
 SERVER                                    VARCHAR2(9)
 SCHEMA#                                   NUMBER
 SCHEMANAME                                VARCHAR2(30)
 OSUSER                                    VARCHAR2(15)
 PROCESS                                   VARCHAR2(9)
 MACHINE                                   VARCHAR2(64)
 TERMINAL                                  VARCHAR2(16)
 PROGRAM                                   VARCHAR2(64)
 TYPE                                      VARCHAR2(10)
 SQL_ADDRESS                               RAW(4)
 SQL_HASH_VALUE                            NUMBER
 MODULE                                    VARCHAR2(48)
 MODULE_HASH                               NUMBER
```

Figure 3-9 The V$SESSION view in SQL*Plus

The SID column contains the session ID. The USERNAME column contains the user account connected to the database, and the PROGRAM column contains the name of the program the user is running. A database trigger can check the PROGRAM column for the record representing the current session to ensure that the program manipulating data is not a restricted program. The DBMS_SESSION.UNIQUE_ SESSION_ID function is used to return a unique session ID for a connection to the database. The value returned by the function can be converted to the format of the SID column in the V$SESSION view to identify the connected session.

Steps

1. Run SQL*Plus and connect as the SYS user account. In order for a stored procedure to be created referencing an object, the owner of the stored procedure must have privileges granted directly to the object. The privileges cannot be granted through a role. Execute a GRANT statement to give the WAITE user account SELECT privileges on V_$SESSION. V_$SESSION is the object referenced by the V$SESSION view.

SQL>   GRANT SELECT ON V_$SESSION TO WAITE;

Grant Succeeded.

2. Connect as the WAITE user account. CHP3-16.sql, shown in Figure 3-10, creates a sample table which will be restricted using this technique.

The DEPT3_16 table will be protected from updates by the database triggers shown in the following steps. Run the file to create the table.

SQL>   START CHP3-16

Table created.

3. Load CHP3-17.sql into the SQL buffer. The file contains a PL/SQL module which uses the DBMS_SESSION.UNIQUE_SESSION_ID function to return an identifier representing the connected session.

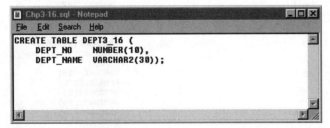

Figure 3-10 CHP3-16.sql creates the sample table used in How-To 3.7

```
SQL> GET CHP3-17
  1  DECLARE
  2    X VARCHAR2(40);
  3    Y NUMBER;
  4  BEGIN
  5    X := DBMS_SESSION.UNIQUE_SESSION_ID;
  6    SELECT DECODE(SUBSTR(X,1,1),'A',10,'B',11,'C',
  7             12,'D',13,'E',14,'F',15, TO_NUMBER(SUBSTR(X,1,1))) +
  8          (DECODE(SUBSTR(X,2,1),'A',10,'B',11,'C',
  9             12,'D',13,'E',14,'F',15, TO_NUMBER(SUBSTR(X,2,1))) * 16) +
 10          (DECODE(SUBSTR(X,3,1),'A',10,'B',11,'C',
 11             12,'D',13,'E',14,'F',15, TO_NUMBER(SUBSTR(X,3,1))) * 256)
 12    INTO Y FROM DUAL;
 13    DBMS_OUTPUT.PUT_LINE(X||', '||TO_CHAR(Y));
 14* END;
```

The value returned by the function is not in the same format as the SID column in the V$SESSION view. Lines 1 through 3 contain the declarative section of the PL/SQL block to define the variables used in the block. Line 5 uses the DBMS_SESSION.UNIQUE_SESSION_ID function to return a unique identifier into the X variable. The first three characters in the identifier are a hexadecimal representation of the SID value contained in the V$SESSION view. Lines 6 through 12 calculate the value of the SID by converting the characters to the hexadecimal representation working left to right. The DECODE function is used to convert the alphabetic values to their numeric representation. Line 13 displays the value returned by the function and the calculated SID value.

4. Set the SERVEROUTPUT system variable to ON and run the statement from the SQL buffer.

```
SQL> SET SERVEROUTPUT ON
SQL> /
CA00AE200000, 172
```

The value returned by the DBMS_SESSION.UNIQUE_SESSION_ID is translated to the number 172 in the PL/SQL module. The converted number can be used to query the current session from the V$SESSION view.

5. Load CHP3-18.sql into the SQL buffer. The file creates a stored function which identifies whether SQL*Plus is executing an INSERT, UPDATE, or DELETE statement on the database.

```
SQL> GET CHP3-18
  1  CREATE OR REPLACE FUNCTION STOP_UPDATE
  2          RETURN BOOLEAN AS
  3    USID VARCHAR2(20);
  4    SSID NUMBER(5);
  5    CNT NUMBER(3);
  6  BEGIN
  7    USID := DBMS_SESSION.UNIQUE_SESSION_ID;
```

continued on next page

continued from previous page

```
 8      SELECT DECODE(SUBSTR(X,1,1),'A',10,'B',11,'C',
 9             12,'D',13,'E',14,'F',15, TO_NUMBER(SUBSTR(X,1,1))) +
10         (DECODE(SUBSTR(X,2,1),'A',10,'B',11,'C',
11             12,'D',13,'E',14,'F',15, TO_NUMBER(SUBSTR(X,2,1))) * 16) +
12         (DECODE(SUBSTR(X,3,1),'A',10,'B',11,'C',
13             12,'D',13,'E',14,'F',15, TO_NUMBER(SUBSTR(X,3,1))) * 256)
14       INTO SSID FROM DUAL;
15      SELECT COUNT(*) INTO CNT
16         FROM V$SESSION
17      WHERE
18         SID = SSID AND
19         PROGRAM = 'SQL*Plus 3.2';
20      IF CNT > 0 Then
21         RETURN TRUE;
22      ELSE
23         RETURN FALSE;
24      END IF;
25* END;
```

The STOP_UPDATE function returns TRUE if the statement is executed from SQL*Plus, FALSE if not. Lines 1 and 2 provide the required keywords to create the stored function. Lines 3 through 5 define the variables used within the function. Lines 6 through 14 use the technique presented in the previous steps to calculate the session ID (SID). Lines 15 through 19 execute a query which returns 1 if the current session is executing SQL*Plus, 0 if not. Since no SQL*Plus processes are allowed to execute a restricted action, lines 11 through 15 check the value and return TRUE if the count is greater than 0, FALSE if not.

6. Run the command to create the stored procedure.

```
SQL> /
```

```
Procedure Created.
```

7. Load CHP3-19.sql into the command buffer. The file contains a statement to create a BEFORE INSERT trigger on the DEPT3_16 table. The trigger is fired before a record is inserted into the table.

```
SQL> GET CHP3-19
 1   CREATE OR REPLACE TRIGGER BI_DEPT3_16 BEFORE INSERT
 2           ON DEPT3_16
 3   BEGIN
 4       IF STOP_UPDATE THEN
 5         RAISE_APPLICATION_ERROR(-20001,
 6               'INVALID OPERATION FOR THIS TOOL');
 7       END IF;
 8* END;
```

Line 1 provides the required keyword to create a BEFORE INSERT trigger on the DEPT3_16 table and specifies its name. Lines 3 through 8 contain the executable section of the trigger. Line 4 executes the STOP_UPDATE function created in the previous steps. If the value returned from the function is TRUE, Line 5 executes a RAISE_APPLICATION_ERROR procedure to stop the execution of the trigger and return an error.

8. Execute the statement to create the trigger.

```
SQL>  /
```

```
Trigger Created.
```

Once the trigger is created, any attempt to insert a record into the DEPT3_16 table with SQL*Plus version 3.2 will fail. The trigger can be modified to restrict any application from modifying data.

9. Attempt to insert a record into the database. Since the operation is performed using SQL*Plus, the database trigger and the STOP_UPDATE function will cause the operation to fail and the ORA-20001 error to be returned. SQL*Plus, the database trigger and the STOP_UPDATE function will cause the operation to fail and the ORA-20001 error to be returned.

How It Works

Step 1 grants the required privilege on the V_$SESSION view to the WAITE user account. In order to create the stored function in Steps 5 and 6, SELECT privileges are required directly on the base object used by V$SESSION. Step 2 creates the sample table restricted by the process presented in this How-To. Steps 3 and 4 use the DBMS_SESSION.UNIQUE_SESSION_ID function to return a unique session identifier and convert its value to the format of the SID column in the V$SESSION view. Steps 5 and 6 create a stored function which checks the V$SESSION view to determine whether the source of the operation is SQL*Plus. Steps 7 and 8 create a BEFORE INSERT trigger which executes before a row is inserted into the sample table created in Step 1. The trigger calls the stored function to determine whether the operation should be terminated. If the stored function returns TRUE, an error is returned to SQL*Plus and the operation is terminated.

Comments

Database triggers can provide an extra level of security. The method shown in this How-To is not without cost. The trigger and stored function is executed every time a record is inserted into the table. If the table is heavily used, this can create substantial overhead. To completely protect the table, a BEFORE INSERT, BEFORE UPDATE, and BEFORE DELETE trigger must be created on the table.

CHAPTER 4
TABLES

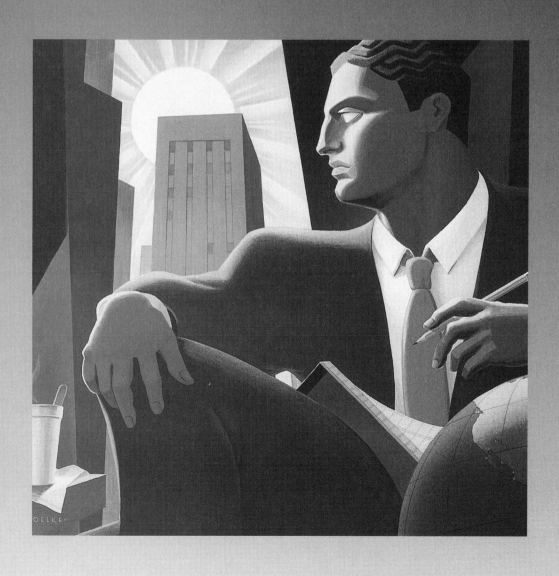

TABLES

How do I...

Tables are the fundamental data storage objects within a relational database. Without tables, your applications would have no need for Oracle or any relational database. This chapter covers the creation, removal, and manipulation of tables within Oracle. Most likely, the Data Definition Language (DDL) statements used to manipulate production database tables in your organization are maintained and executed by the database administrator. Techniques used to design and build tables are important to both application developers and database administrators. The relationships between tables and the business rules governing these relationships can be enforced by Oracle by using constraints. *Constraints* move much of the work away from the applications and to the database.

4.1 Determine which tables are available

Applications can contain many tables, and user accounts can be granted privileges on tables owned by other user accounts. This How-To explains the methods used to determine the tables available to a user account. It also presents a method to view comments about tables in the data dictionary.

4.2 Put comments on a table and its columns

Comments can be stored in the data dictionary to describe tables and their columns. Comments should always be stored in the data dictionary to provide a central repository for information about the schema. The better the database is documented, the easier future maintenance of the applications will be. This How-To covers the process of creating comments on tables and columns.

4.3 Create a table from another table

Tables can be created from a query of one or more other tables or views. The table can be populated with data when it is created. This How-To covers the methods used to create a table as the result of a query.

4.4 Remove all tables owned by a user account

During development and maintenance processes, it may be necessary to drop all tables owned by a user account. This How-To develops a process and provides scripts which let you drop all tables for a user account without typing DROP TABLE statements.

4.5 Re-create CREATE TABLE statements

After a table has been altered a few times, the original scripts used to create it may look nothing like the table in production. The best way to re-create the scripts needed to rebuild a table is to query the data dictionary. This How-To covers the task of building CREATE TABLE statements from the data dictionary using SQL*Plus.

4.6 Determine the space available in the database

Determining the space available in the database is an important data administration task. When new applications are developed and new tables created, you must find a location in the database to put the tables and you must be sure you have enough room. This How-To provides the process and queries used to determine the space available in the database.

4.7 Use check constraints to validate data

Check constraints allow the database to perform important validation tasks. Adding a CHECK constraint to a table ensures that applications will not create invalid data in the table. It also lets the database perform some of the work the application normally would do. This How-To takes you through the different methods used to create check constraints.

4.8   Create default values in a table

Default values can be specified for columns within a table. If a value for a column is not specified when a record is inserted, the column will default to the value specified. This How-To explains the process of creating default values.

4.9   Create a primary key on a table

A *primary key* is the set of columns which uniquely identifies the rows in a table. The task of creating a primary key is essential to enforcing referential integrity at the database level. Creating a primary key establishes a unique index on the table, which can increase the performance of applications using the table. This How-To covers the process of creating a primary key on a table.

4.10   Enforce referential integrity

Referential integrity constraints within Oracle are used to enforce the business rules specified in the data model. It is critical that the data in the database follow the rules developed when the database was designed. This How-To covers the topic of creating referential integrity constraints within Oracle.

4.11   Enable and disable constraints

Constraints enforce rules within the database. There are times, such as during database maintenance or batch operations, that constraints can be temporarily violated. Constraints can be disabled and enabled to let batch operations and system maintenance be performed. This How-To explains how constraints are enabled and disabled.

COMPLEXITY
BEGINNING

4.1   How do I...
Determine which tables are available?

Problem

I need an easy way to determine the names of all the tables available when creating my application. I have access to a large number of tables and I cannot always remember their names. How can I determine the names of the tables I have available?

Technique

The tables available to a user account can be queried from the data dictionary. The USER_TABLES data dictionary view contains all tables owned by the user account connected to the database. The ALL_TABLES view contains all tables for which the connected user account has privileges. Figure 4-1 shows the columns in the ALL_TABLES data dictionary view.

TThe OWNER column contains the name of the user account whose schema contains the table. The TABLE_NAME column contains the name of the table. When a table from another user account's schema is referenced, both the owner and table name must be provided unless a synonym is used.

Steps

1. Connect to SQL*Plus as the WAITE user account. The WAITE user account was created by the installation script provided on the accompanying CD-ROM. If the WAITE user account has not been created, run INSTALL.SQL from the \SAMPLES directory on the CD. If you do not create this account, you can use any account with CREATE TABLE privileges. Load CHP4-1.sql in the SQL buffer. The query contained in the file returns all tables owned by the connected user account.

```
SQL> GET CHP4-1
  1  SELECT TABLE_NAME
  2    FROM USER_TABLES
  3* ORDER BY TABLE_NAME
```

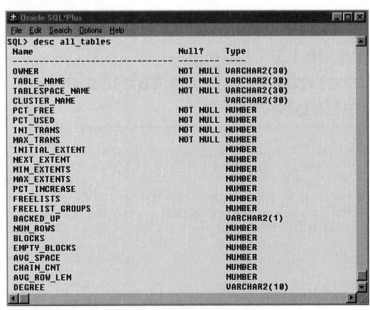

Figure 4-1 ALL_TABLES data dictionary view

Line 1 contains the TABLE_NAME column in the select list of the query. Line 2 specifies the USER_TABLES data dictionary view as the source of the query. The ORDER BY clause in line 3 returns the results ordered by TABLE_NAME.

2. Execute the query to view the tables owned by the WAITE user account. The tables shown as the results of the query were created by CHP1-1.sql in Chapter 1. Your results may vary depending on the tables you have created for the WAITE user account.

```
SQL>  /

TABLE_NAME
-------------------------------
DEPT1_1
EMP1_1
```

3. Load CHP4-2.sql into the SQL buffer. The file contains a query of the ALL_TABLES data dictionary view to return all tables that the connected user account owns or has privileges to use. The OWNER column is included in the select list in order to determine which user account owns the table.

```
SQL> GET CHP4-2
  1   SELECT OWNER, TABLE_NAME
  2    FROM ALL_TABLES
  3* ORDER BY OWNER, TABLE_NAME
```

Line 1 contains the select list of the query. The OWNER and TABLE_NAME columns are returned by the query. Line 2 specifies the ALL_TABLES data dictionary view as the source of the query. The ORDER BY clause contained in line 3 orders the output by OWNER and TABLE_NAME.

4. Execute the query. Since the WAITE user account was granted the DBA role by the installation script, every table in the database will be included in the query. The output of the query has been abbreviated in order to conserve space.

```
SQL>  /

OWNER                           TABLE_NAME
-------------------------------  -------------------------------
SYS                             TRIGGER$
SYS                             UET$
SYS                             UNDO$
SYS                             USER$
SYS                             VIEW$
SYS                             _default_auditing_options_
WAITE                           DEPARTMENT
WAITE                           EMPLOYEE

8 rows selected.
```

A user account can have < privileges on many tables. Since the name of a table does not always fully describe its use, comments can be placed on a table. The ALL_TAB_COMMENTS view contains the table comments. The ALL_COL_COMMENTS view contains the comments on individual columns. Figure 4-2 shows the columns contained in the ALL_TAB_COMMENTS and ALL_COL_COMMENTS views.

5. Load CHP4-3.sql into the SQL buffer. The file contains a query of the ALL_TAB_COMMENTS and ALL_TABLES data dictionary views to return the names of the tables that <the user account has privileges on and any comments on the table.

```
SQL> GET CHP4-3
  1   SELECT A.OWNER, A.TABLE_NAME, B.COMMENTS
  2   FROM
  3    ALL_TAB_COMMENTS B, ALL_TABLES A
  4   WHERE
  5    A.TABLE_NAME = B.TABLE_NAME AND
  6    A.OWNER = B.OWNER
  7* ORDER BY A.OWNER, A.TABLE_NAME
```

A row exists in the ALL_TAB_COMMENTS view for every table in the ALL_TABLES view, even if the table has no comment. Line 1 specifies the select list of the query and returns the owner of the table, its name, and any comments placed on the table. The FROM clause in lines 2 and 3 specifies the source tables of the query. The WHERE clause in lines 4 through 6 joins the TABLE_NAME column in the ALL_TABLE view with the same column in the ALL_TAB_COMMENTS view and the OWNER columns of the two views.

6. Format the columns to make the query more readable with the COLUMN command, and execute the query.

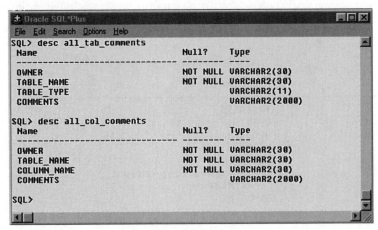

Figure 4-2 Comments data dictionary views

```
SQL>   SET COLUMN OWNER FORMAT A10
SQL>   SET COLUMN TABLE_NAME FORMAT A20
SQL>   SET COLUMN COMMENT FORMAT A45
SQL>   /

OWNER         TABLE_NAME              COMMENTS
----------    --------------------    ---------------------------------------------
SYS           TRIGGER$
SYS           UET$
SYS           UNDO$
SYS           USER$
SYS           VIEW$
SYS           _default_auditing_
              options_
WAITE         DEPT1_1
WAITE         EMP1_1

8 rows selected.
```

The tables created so far do not contain any comments. How-To 4.2 covers the technique used to place comments on a table.

How It Works

The USER_TABLES and ALL_TABLES data dictionary views contain information about the tables to which a user account has access. The USER_TABLES view contains information about the tables in the user account's schema. The ALL_TABLES view contains all tables on which the user account has privileges. Steps 1 and 2 query the TABLE_NAME column from the USER_TABLES view to show all tables owned by the current user account. Steps 3 and 4 show all tables the user account owns in addition to the tables to which it has been granted privileges. The ALL_TABLES view is queried in Steps 3 and 4. Steps 5 and 6 show all the tables queried in Steps 3 and 4 and include the comments on the table. The ALL_TAB_COMMENTS data dictionary view contains table comments placed on the table. The ALL_TAB_COMMENTS view is joined to the ALL_TABLES view to produce the query results in Steps 5 and 6.

Comments

If you own all of the tables you work with, the USER_TABLES view is the fastest way to determine the names of the tables. The USER_TABLES view only contains tables owned by the connected user account.

4.2 How do I...
Put comments on a table and its columns?

Problem

With the large number of tables used in our applications and the number of developers working in our organization, it is important that we document tables and columns contained in the database. The last step of How-To 4.1 showed how to query comments from the data dictionary. How do I put comments on tables and their columns?

Technique

The COMMENT statement is used to create comments on tables and columns. The comments are stored in the data dictionary and can be queried through the ALL_TAB_COMMENTS and ALL_COL_COMMENTS data dictionary views. Figure 4-3 shows the syntax of the COMMENT statement.

If the user account connected to the database is not the owner of the table, the user account must have the COMMENT ANY TABLE system privilege in order to put a comment on the table.

Steps

1. Run SQL*Plus and connect to the WAITE user account. CHP4-4.sql, shown in Figure 4-4, creates a sample table that is used throughout this How-To.

```
                    COMMENT Syntax

COMMENT ON
    { TABLE table |
      COLUMN table.column }
      IS 'text'
```

Figure 4-3 COMMENT statement syntax

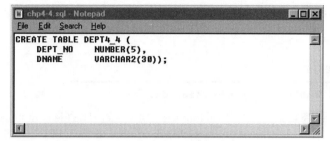

Figure 4-4 CHP4-4.sql creates the sample table used in How-To 4.2

Run the file to create the sample table.

```
SQL> START CHP4-4
```

Table created.

> **2.** Load CHP4-5.sql into the SQL buffer. The file contains a statement to put a comment on the DEPT4_4 table created in the previous step.

```
SQL> GET CHP4-5
  1  COMMENT ON TABLE DEPT4_4 IS
  2* 'Departments in the Organization.'
```

> The COMMENT statement is used to put a comment on either a table or a column. Line 1 presents the required keywords and identifies the DEPT4_4 table as the recipient of the comment. Line 2 specifies the comment placed on the table.

> **3.** Execute the statement to create the comment.

```
SQL> /
```

Comment created.

> **4.** Load CHP4-6.sql into the SQL buffer. The file contains a query to view the comment created in the previous step.

```
SQL> GET CHP4-6
  1  SELECT COMMENTS
  2   FROM USER_TAB_COMMENTS
  3* WHERE TABLE_NAME = 'DEPT4_4'
```

> The query returns the COMMENTS column from the USER_COMMENTS data dictionary view. The WHERE clause in line 3 only returns records for the sample table created in Step 1.

5. Execute the query to view the comment created in Steps 2 and 3.

```
SQL>   /

COMMENTS
------------------------------------------------
Departments in the Organization.
```

6. Load CHP4-7.sql into the SQL buffer. The file contains a statement to create a comment on the DNAME column of the DEPT4_4 table.

```
SQL>   GET CHP4-7
1    COMMMENT ON COLUMN DEPT4_4.DNAME IS
2     'The name of the department.'
```

Line 1 contains the COMMENT keywords and specifies the table and column name receiving the comment. Both the table and column name must be specified in the statement. If the table name is not included, the COMMENT statement will fail.

7. Execute the statement to create the comment on the column.

```
SQL>   /

Comment created.
```

8. Load CHP4-8.sql into the SQL buffer. The file contains a statement to query the comment created in Steps 6 and 7.

```
SQL>   GET CHP4-8
1    SELECT COMMENTS
2     FROM USER_COL_COMMENTS
3    WHERE
4     TABLE_NAME = 'DEPT4_4' AND
5     COLUMN_NAME = 'DNAME'
```

Line 1 specifies that the COMMENTS column is returned by the query. The FROM clause in line 2 specifies the USER_COL_COMMENTS data dictionary view as the source of the query. The WHERE clause in lines 3 through 5 returns records for the DNAME column of the sample table created in Step 1.

9. Execute the statement to view the comment.

```
SQL>   /

COMMENTS
------------------------------------------------
The name of the department
```

How It Works

Step 1 creates the sample table DEPT4_4, commented in later steps in this How-To. Steps 2 and 3 create a comment on the DEPT4_4 table using the COMMENT statement. The comment is stored in the COM$ table owned by the SYS user account and can be queried through the ALL_TAB_COMMENTS and USER_TAB_COMMENTS data dictionary views. Steps 4 and 5 query the comment created in steps 2 and 3 using the USER_TAB_COMMENTS data dictionary view. Steps 6 and 7 create a comment on the DNAME column of the DEPT4_4 table. Column comments are also stored in the COM$ table, but are queried from the ALL_COL_COMMENTS and USER_COL_COMMENTS views. Steps 8 and 9 query the comments created using the USER_COL_COMMENTS view.

Comments

It is important to document the tables and columns in your database. Create comments on tables and columns in order to improve the maintainability of your database and applications. Table and column comments can be used within your application by querying the data dictionary views.

COMPLEXITY
INTERMEDIATE

4.3 How do I...
Create a table from another table?

Problem

When developing applications, I like to make a backup of a table before making untested operations on the table. To do this, I want to create a new table from the existing table and make a copy of all of the rows. In our production environment, we want to create summary tables which are complicated queries of other tables. How do I create a table as a query from another table?

Technique

The CREATE TABLE statement is used to create new tables. The CREATE TABLE statement allows a query to be specified as the source of the columns and rows for the table. If the query used in the CREATE TABLE statement returns rows, the rows are inserted into the new table when it is created. If the query does not return rows, the table is created containing no rows. Complex queries can be used to create a table. A column alias is required if Oracle cannot create a valid column name from the column in the query.

Steps

1. Connect to SQL*Plus as the WAITE user account. CHP4-9.sql, shown in Figure 4-5, creates the sample tables used in this How-To and populates them with data.

The DEPT4_9 table is created by the CREATE TABLE statement and populated with one record. In the steps that follow, a new table will be created by querying the sample table. The EMP4_9 table is created and populated with three records. The final example in the How-To creates a new table by joining the DEPT4_9 and EMP4_9 table. Run the file to create the sample table and populate it with data.

```
SQL> START CHP4-9

Table Created.

Table Created.

1 row created.

1 row created.

1 row created.

1 row created.

1 row created.

Commit complete.
```

2. Load CHP4-10.sql into the SQL buffer. The file contains a CREATE TABLE statement that makes a new table as a query of the table created in Step 1.

```
CREATE TABLE DEPT4_9 (
     DEPTNO     NUMBER(5),
     DNAME      VARCHAR2(30));

CREATE TABLE EMP4_9 (
     EMPNO      NUMBER(5),
     DEPTNO     NUMBER(5));

INSERT INTO DEPT4_9 VALUES (1,'SALES');
INSERT INTO EMP4_9 VALUES (1,1);
INSERT INTO EMP4_9 VALUES (2,1);
INSERT INTO EMP4_9 VALUES (3,1);
COMMIT;
```

Figure 4-5 CHP4-9.sql creates the sample tables used in How-To 4.3

```
SQL> GET CHP4-10
 1   CREATE TABLE NDEPT4_9
 2*  AS SELECT * FROM DEPT4_9
```

> The CREATE TABLE keywords presented in line 1 are used to create a new table in the database. The table name, NDEPT4_9, is specified in line 1. Line 2 contains a query that specifies the columns to be created and the initial data populated in the table.

3. Execute the statement to create the new table.

```
SQL> /
```

Table Created.

> The table is created, but Oracle does not tell you how many rows were inserted. In order to get the number of rows, COUNT(*) can be queried from the new table.

4. Load CHP4-11.sql into the SQL buffer. The file contains a statement to create a new table with the same columns as the original table, but with none of the data.

```
SQL> GET CHP4-11
 1   CREATE TABLE N2DEPT4_
 2    AS SELECT * FROM DEPT4_9
 3* WHERE 1 = 0
```

> Line 1 contains the CREATE TABLE keywords used to create a new table. The query contained in lines 2 and 3 define the columns for the new table, but the WHERE clause in line 3 doesn't create any records in the table.

5. Execute the statement to create the new table.

```
SQL> /
```

Table Created.

6. Load CHP4-12.sql into the SQL buffer. The file contains a query to create summary data from multiple tables.

```
SQL> GET CHP4-12
 1   CREATE TABLE N3DEPT4_9 AS
 2    SELECT D.DEPTNO, D.DNAME,
 3    COUNT(*) NO_EMPLOYEES
 4    FROM
 5    DEPT4_9 D, EMP4_9 E
 6    WHERE
 7    D.DEPTNO = E.DEPTNO
 8    GROUP BY
 9*   D.DEPT_NO, DNAME
```

Line 1 contains the required keywords and specifies the name of the new table. The query contained in lines 2 through 3 defines the columns of the new table and creates the initial records. Lines 2 and 3 define the columns returned by the query and created in the new table. An alias is required on all calculated fields so that a valid column name can be created. The NO_EMPLOYEES alias in line 3 tells the CREATE TABLE statement what to name the column. Functions such as COUNT are reserved words and cannot be used as the column name in the new table. Lines 4 and 5 contain the FROM clause and specify the two sample tables created in step 1 as the source of the query. The WHERE clause in lines 6 and 7 joins the two tables used in the query. The GROUP BY clause in lines 8 and 9 is required by the COUNT function specified in line 3.

7. Execute the statement to create the new table.

```
SQL> /
```

Table Created.

8. Describe the new table using the SQL*Plus DESCRIBE statement. The columns created in the new table will have the datatypes of the source table. The datatype of calculated fields will have a datatype based on the operator used in the SELECT statement. The description of the new table is shown in Figure 4-6.

9. Load CHP4-13.sql into the SQL buffer. The file contains a statement to create a table with custom storage parameters and tablespace information.

```
SQL> GET CHP4-13
  1   CREATE TABLE N4DEPT4_9
  2     STORAGE (
  3       INITIAL 1M
  4       NEXT 1M)
  6     AS SELECT * FROM DEPT4_9
```

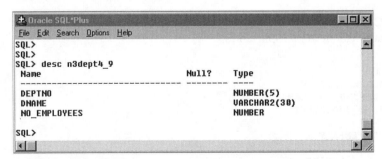

```
SQL>
SQL>
SQL> desc n3dept4_9
 Name                             Null?    Type
 -------------------------------- -------- ----
 DEPTNO                                    NUMBER(5)
 DNAME                                     VARCHAR2(30)
 NO_EMPLOYEES                              NUMBER

SQL>
```

Figure 4-6 The description of the table created by a multiple table query

Line 1 defines the new table created by the statement with the CREATE TABLE keywords. Lines 2 through 5 contain custom storage parameters which define how the table will be created in the database. The INITIAL clause specifies how much storage is allocated when the table is first created. The NEXT clause specifies how much storage will be allocated when the first allocated storage is used. Line 5 contains the query used to create the table.

10. Run the statement to create the table. The table is created with the storage parameters defined by the STORAGE clause.

```
SQL>  /

Table created.
```

How It Works

Step 1 creates the sample tables used by this How-To. Steps 2 and 3 create a new table with all of the columns and data from the DEPT4_9 table created in Step 1. The CREATE TABLE statement includes an AS SELECT clause to create the new table from the results of the query. Steps 4 and 5 create a new table as a query without moving any data into the table. The WHERE 1 = 0 clause in the SELECT statement ensures that no rows will be returned by the query, but still creates the table. Steps 6 and 7 create a new table as a complex query from multiple tables. An alias is required for all calculated fields to give the column a name in the new table. Step 8 describes the table created in the previous two steps using the DESCRIBE command. The data type of the calculated column is the result type of the expression. Steps 9 and 10 create a new table as a query containing a STORAGE clause. The STORAGE clause is usually at the end of the CREATE TABLE statement, unless the table is created from a query.

Comments

Creating a table as a query from one or more additional tables or views is a very useful technique. It can be used to create summary tables which can dramatically improve the performance of summary data queries. The Parallel Query Option in Oracle7 dramatically improves the performance of CREATE TABLE statements with SELECT clauses on multiprocessor computers.

COMPLEXITY
ADVANCED

4.4 How do I...
Remove all tables owned by a user account?

Problem

I often need to remove a large number of tables or all the tables for a given user account. When developing applications, we create many tables in our own schema for development purposes. It seems like too much work to identify and remove each table individually. How can I make the task of removing all tables from a user account easier?

Technique

The USER_TABLES view contains all the tables owned by the user account connected to the database. The ALL_TABLES view contains all tables to which the user account has access. To remove the tables owned by a user account, use the USER_TABLES view to build a DROP TABLE statement for each table. Figure 4-7 shows the description of the USERS_TABLE data dictionary view in SQL*Plus.

```
± Oracle SQL*Plus                                          _ □ ×
File  Edit  Search  Options  Help
SQL> desc user_tables
 Name                             Null?    Type
 -------------------------------- -------- ----
 TABLE_NAME                       NOT NULL VARCHAR2(30)
 TABLESPACE_NAME                  NOT NULL VARCHAR2(30)
 CLUSTER_NAME                              VARCHAR2(30)
 PCT_FREE                         NOT NULL NUMBER
 PCT_USED                         NOT NULL NUMBER
 INI_TRANS                        NOT NULL NUMBER
 MAX_TRANS                        NOT NULL NUMBER
 INITIAL_EXTENT                            NUMBER
 NEXT_EXTENT                               NUMBER
 MIN_EXTENTS                               NUMBER
 MAX_EXTENTS                               NUMBER
 PCT_INCREASE                              NUMBER
 FREELISTS                                 NUMBER
 FREELIST_GROUPS                           NUMBER
 BACKED_UP                                 VARCHAR2(1)
 NUM_ROWS                                  NUMBER
 BLOCKS                                    NUMBER
 EMPTY_BLOCKS                              NUMBER
 AVG_SPACE                                 NUMBER
 CHAIN_CNT                                 NUMBER
 AVG_ROW_LEN                               NUMBER
 DEGREE                                    VARCHAR2(10)
```

Figure 4-7 The USER_TABLES data dictionary view

This How-To will use the procedures described in Chapter 1, SQL*Plus, to create a SQL script using SQL*Plus.

Steps

1. Run SQL*Plus and connect as the user account whose tables you wish to remove. Set the SQL*Plus system variables that control column headings and row feedback to OFF.

```
SQL>   set heading off
SQL>   set feedback off
```

Setting the HEADING system variable to OFF removes the column headings from the beginning of the output. Setting the FEEDBACK variable to OFF suppresses the record count at the end of the query.

2. Load CHP4-14.sql into the SQL buffer. The file generates a DROP TABLE statement for each table contained in the USER_TABLES view. It does this by concatenating the keywords required for each statement to the table name as it is retrieved from the database.

```
SQL> GET CHP4-14
  1   SELECT 'DROP TABLE '||TABLE_NAME||';'
  2    FROM
  3*  USER_TABLES
```

Line 1 concatenates the DROP TABLE keywords to the name of the table returned from the data dictionary. Do not forget the trailing space after DROP TABLE. Forgetting the space creates statements that generate errors. A semicolon is concatenated to the end of each line to execute the statements at the same time as the output of the query and SQL script. Lines 2 and 3 contain the FROM clause of the query and specify the USER_TABLES data dictionary view as the source of the query.

3. Spool a file that will contain the SQL script and execute the statement. The DROP TABLE statements are written to the file to be executed in a later step.

```
SQL>   SPOOL DROPS.sql
SQL>   /

DROP TABLE DEPT4_4;
DROP TABLE DEPT4_9;
DROP TABLE NDEPT4_9;
DROP TABLE N2DEPT4_9;
```

The records returned by the query depend on the tables existing in the user account's schema where you run the query.

4. Stop spooling. The SPOOL OFF command stops the spooling operation and closes the output file.

```
SQL> SPOOL OFF
```

5. The DROPS.SQL file contains the statements required to drop all tables owned by the user account. The first line of the script will generate an error that can be ignored, because executing the query creates an unwanted line. That act of executing the statement creates SQL> / as the first line of the output file. You can remove this line by editing the file with Windows Notepad before running the file. Run the file to drop all tables with the START command.

```
SQL>   START DROPS.SQL

Table Dropped.

Table Dropped.

Table Dropped.

Table Dropped.

Table Dropped.
```

How It Works

Step 1 turns off the HEADING and FEEDBACK system variables to eliminate unwanted lines from the output of the query. Step 2 creates a statement to build DROP TABLE statements. Every DROP TABLE statement begins with the keywords DROP TABLE and ends with a semicolon. The string concatenation function (||) allows these two pieces of static text to be concatenated with the tablename as it is retrieved from the data dictionary. Step 3 executes a SPOOL statement that begins writing the output of the query to a file and runs the statement created in Step 2 to create a script file. Step 5 ends the spooling of the output file, closing the file. Step 5 also runs the output file to drop the tables.

Comments

If your database contains foreign key constraints, you may need to run the script repeatedly or disable the constraints before running the script. If a table is referenced as a foreign key of another table, it cannot be dropped as long as the referencing table exists. Running the script repeatedly will delete the child tables in the first passes and the parent tables in subsequent passes.

COMPLEXITY
ADVANCED

4.5 How do I...
Re-create CREATE TABLE statements?

Problem

I need a SQL script to re-create one or more tables. I do not have any of the original statements used to create the tables. I know I can use the DESCRIBE command in SQL*Plus to list all the columns in the table, but I have many tables and the output of the DESCRIBE statement does not look like a CREATE TABLE statement. How can I generate scripts to re-create these tables?

Technique

The data dictionary view USER_TABLES contains all of the tables owned by a user account. The USER_TAB_COLUMNS data dictionary view contains each of the columns in the table. Unless the CREATE TABLE statement requires tablespace and storage information, only columns from the USER_TAB_COLUMNS view are needed. Figure 4-8 shows the columns in the USER_TAB_COLUMNS data dictionary view.

The TABLE_NAME column contains the name of the table to which the column belongs. The COLUMN_NAME column contains the name of the column as it was defined when the table was created. The DATA_TYPE column contains the datatype of the column.

```
Oracle SQL*Plus
File  Edit  Search  Options  Help
SQL>
SQL> desc user_tab_columns
 Name                            Null?    Type
 ------------------------------- -------- ----
 TABLE_NAME                      NOT NULL VARCHAR2(30)
 COLUMN_NAME                     NOT NULL VARCHAR2(30)
 DATA_TYPE                                VARCHAR2(9)
 DATA_LENGTH                     NOT NULL NUMBER
 DATA_PRECISION                           NUMBER
 DATA_SCALE                               NUMBER
 NULLABLE                                 VARCHAR2(1)
 COLUMN_ID                       NOT NULL NUMBER
 DEFAULT_LENGTH                           NUMBER
 DATA_DEFAULT                             LONG
 NUM_DISTINCT                             NUMBER
 LOW_VALUE                                RAW(32)
 HIGH_VALUE                               RAW(32)
 DENSITY                                  NUMBER

SQL>
```

Figure 4-8 The USER_TAB_COLUMNS view

Steps

1. Run SQL*Plus and connect as the WAITE user account. CHP4-15.sql, shown in Figure 4-9, contains a CREATE TABLE statement that will be rebuilt in this How-To.

Run the file to create the sample table.

```
SQL> START CHP4-15
```

Table created.

2. Turn off the heading and trailing statements and widen the length of the output line by setting the SQL*Plus environment variables.

```
SQL> SET HEADING OFF
SQL> SET LINESIZE 132
SQL> SET FEEDBACK OFF
```

The SET HEADING OFF command removes any column headings from the output generated by the query. The SET LINESIZE 132 command ensures that the output generated by the query does not wrap to multiple lines for a single row. The SET FEEDBACK OFF command suppresses the row counter that displays the number of rows returned by the query and the end of the output.

3. Load CHP4-16.sql into the SQL buffer. This file contains a statement to query some of the column information for the table we are trying to re-create.

```
SQL> GET CHP4-16
  1  SELECT
  2   COLUMN_ID,
  3   COLUMN_NAME,
  4   DATA_TYPE
  5  FROM
  6   USER_TAB_COLUMNS
  7  WHERE TABLE_NAME = 'DEPT4_15'
  8* ORDER BY COLUMN_ID
```

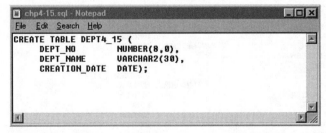

Figure 4-9 CHP4-15.sql contains the sample table used in How-To 4.5

Lines 1 through 4 contain the columns returned by the query. The TABLE_NAME column contains the name of the table. COLUMN_ID represents the order of the column in the table. COLUMN_NAME contains the name of the column. DATA_TYPE contains the data type of the column. Lines 5 and 6 contain the FROM clause of the query, specifying the USER_TAB_COLUMNS data dictionary view as the source of the query. The WHERE clause in line 8 returns records for the sample table created in Step 1. The ORDER BY clause in line 8 organizes the records in the order of the columns in the table.

4. Run the statement to display the results of the query.

```
SQL>   /

1    DEPT_NO                     NUMBER
2    DEPT_NAME                   VARCHAR2
3    CREATION_DATE               DATE
```

This query looks somewhat like the SQL*Plus DESCRIBE statement. In the next step, the data will be formatted to look more like a SQL statement.

5. Load CHP4-17.sql into the SQL buffer. The file contains a statement to begin formatting the output to look like a SQL statement.

```
SQL> GET CHP4-17
  1    SELECT DECODE(COLUMN_ID,1,'CREATE TABLE '||
  2       TABLE_NAME||' (', '    '),
  3     COLUMN_NAME,
  4     DATA_TYPE
  5    FROM USER_TAB_COLUMNS
  6     WHERE TABLE_NAME = 'DEPT4_15'
  7    ORDER BY COLUMN_ID
```

Lines 1 and 2 use the DECODE function to concatenate the CREATE TABLE keywords and the tablename to the beginning of the first output line. The COLUMN_ID field represents the order of the columns in the table. The DECODE function works like an in-line IF statement. If COLUMN_ID = 1, then display the keywords; otherwise, display a blank space.

6. Run the query to display the output from the previous step.

```
SQL>   /

    CREATE TABLE DEPT4_15 (    DEPT_NO                     NUMBER
                DEPT_NAME                   VARCHAR2
                CREATION_DATE               DATE
```

The results are starting to look like a DDL statement. The CREATE TABLE keywords and the name of the table are only displayed on the first line of output.

7. Load CHP4-18.sql into the SQL buffer. The query contained in this file handles the different data types possible in a table. The CHAR, VARCHAR2, and NUMBER data types require a length, scale, or precision modifier. All other data types do not require any more information. The DECODE function is used to put the correct modifiers with the data type. In Step 8, this statement will be combined with the statement created in the previous steps.

```
SQL> GET CHP4-18
  1  SELECT DATA_TYPE||DECODE(DATA_TYPE,
  2  'VARCHAR2','('||TO_CHAR(DATA_LENGTH)||')',
  3  'NUMBER','('||TO_CHAR(DATA_PRECISION)||
  4                   ','||TO_CHAR(DATA_SCALE)||')',
  5  'CHAR','('||TO_CHAR(DATA_LENGTH)
  6     ||')')
  7  FROM USER_TAB_COLUMNS
  8  WHERE TABLE_NAME = 'DEPT4_15'
  9* ORDER BY COLUMN_ID
```

Lines 1 through 6 create a single column of output, creating the datatype of a column with the proper length, scale, and precision. Line 2 handles the VARCHAR2 datatype by concatenating the DATA_LENGTH column to the datatype. Lines 3 and 4 handle the NUMBER datatype by concatenating the DATA_PRECISION and DATA_SCALE columns to the datatype. Line 5 handles the CHAR datatype by concatenating the DATA_LENGTH column to the datatype.

8. Run the statement to view the output from the previous step.

```
SQL>  /

NUMBER(8,0)
VARCHAR2(40)
DATE
```

Using the DECODE function to handle the possible data types generated is an important part of the statement. The query created in this step replaces the DATA_TYPE column in the previous query

9. CHP4-19.sql, shown in Figure 4-10, contains a combination of the two queries. When the queries are combined, the column name in the statement becomes long. To make the statement more readable, the columns are aliased and formatted in SQL*Plus.

Run the file using the START command.

```
SQL>   START CHP4-19

CREATE TABLE DEPT4_15 (       DEPT_NO         NUMBER(8,0),
                              DEPT_NAME       VARCHAR2(40),
                              CREATION_DATE        DATE,
```

```
chp4-19.sql - Notepad
File  Edit  Search  Help
COLUMN A FORMAT A30
COLUMN B FORMAT A20
COLUMN C FORMAT A20
SELECT DECODE(COLUMN_ID,1,'CREATE TABLE '||TABLE_NAME||' (',' ') A,
       COLUMN_NAME B,
       DATA_TYPE||DECODE(DATA_TYPE, 'VARCHAR2',
                '('||TO_CHAR(DATA_LENGTH),
       'NUMBER','('||TO_CHAR(DATA_PRECISION)||
                ','||TO_CHAR(DATA_SCALE),
       'CHAR','('||TO_CHAR(DATA_LENGTH))||')'||', ' C
FROM USER_TAB_COLUMNS
WHERE TABLE_NAME = 'DEPT4_15'
ORDER BY COLUMN_ID;
```

Figure 4-10 CHP4-19.sql builds the basis of
a CREATE TABLE statement

Note that the ending parenthesis and the semicolon are missing. Although
this looks easy to correct, it is the most complicated part of the process. A
parenthesis and semicolon must be placed only after the last column of the
table. The last column in the table is the column with the largest
COLUMN_ID. The steps that follow will correct this problem.

10. Load CHP4-20.sql into the SQL buffer. The file contains a query of
USER_TAB_COLUMNS, which returns the highest numbered column in
the table.

```
SQL> GET CHP4-20
  1   SELECT MAX(COLUMN_ID)
  2    FROM
  3   USER_TAB_COLUMNS
  4    WHERE
  5* TABLE_NAME = 'DEPT4_15'
```

The query returns the value required, but it must be used as part of a
DECODE statement within the query. The MAX function is a GROUP function. It works on all rows of the query and returns a single value. The query
used to build the CREATE TABLE statements must return one row for each
column in the table. This is not consistent with the use of a group function.
To get around the problem, the table must be joined with itself, executing a
GROUP statement on only one instance of the table. The next step shows a
simplified version of this concept.

11. Load CHP4-21.sql into the SQL buffer. The file contains a query that joins a
table with itself to execute a group by function as part of a multi-row query.

```
SQL> GET CHP4-21
  1   SELECT MAX(T2.COLUMN_ID), T1.COLUMN_ID
```

continued on next page

continued from previous page

```
2    FROM
3    USER_TAB_COLUMNS T1, USER_TAB_COLUMNS T2
4    WHERE
5     T1.TABLE_NAME = T2.TABLE_NAME
6     AND T1.TABLE_NAME = 'DEPT4_15'
7     GROUP BY T1.COLUMN_ID
8*   ORDER BY T1.COLUMN_ID
```

Line 1 selects the largest COLUMN_ID column from one instance of the table and the COLUMN_ID value from the other. Line 3 contains the same table twice in the FROM clause. The first instance of the table has the alias T1 and the second has T2. Oracle will treat them as two separate tables. Line 5 joins the two instances of the table together using the TABLE_NAME column. Line 6 forces the query to run for only the DEPT4_15 table. Line 7 contains a GROUP BY clause which is required to group data by the T1 instance of the table.

12. Execute the query to show a group by result on each line.

```
SQL>  /

              3         1
              3         2
              3         3
```

A number now exists that can be compared with the current COLUMN_ID to determine whether it is the last column in the table.

13. CHP4-22.sql, shown in Figure 4-11, contains a SQL statement recreating a CREATE TABLE statement for a single table.

```
📄 chp4-22.sql - Notepad                                      _ □ ×
File   Edit   Search   Help
SELECT DECODE(T1.COLUMN_ID,1,'CREATE TABLE '||T1.TABLE_NAME||
             ' ('','  ') A,
         T1.COLUMN_NAME B,
         T1.DATA_TYPE||DECODE(T1.DATA_TYPE, 'VARCHAR2',
             '('||TO_CHAR(T1.DATA_LENGTH)||')',
         'NUMBER','('||TO_CHAR(T1.DATA_PRECISION)||
             ','||TO_CHAR(T1.DATA_SCALE)||')',
         'CHAR','('||TO_CHAR(T1.DATA_LENGTH)||')')||
                  DECODE(T1.COLUMN_ID,
MAX(T2.COLUMN_ID), ');',',') C
FROM USER_TAB_COLUMNS T1, USER_TAB_COLUMNS T2
WHERE
     T1.TABLE_NAME = T2.TABLE_NAME AND
     T1.TABLE_NAME = 'DEPT4_15'
GROUP BY T1.COLUMN_ID, T1.TABLE_NAME, T1.DATA_TYPE,
         T1.DATA_LENGTH, T1.DATA_SCALE, T1.COLUMN_NAME,
         T1.DATA_PRECISION
ORDER BY T1.COLUMN_ID;
```

Figure 4-11 CHP4-22.sql rebuilds a CREATE TABLE statement for a single table

14. Execute the query using the START command.

```
SQL>    START CHP4-22

CREATE TABLE DEPT4_15 (          DEPT_NO            NUMBER(8,0),
                                 DEPT_NAME          VARCHAR2(40),
                                 CREATION_DATE      DATE);
```

How It Works

Step 1 sets the HEADING and FEEDBACK system variables to OFF to remove unwanted heading and trailing statements from the query results. Steps 2 and 3 query the column name and data type from the USER_TAB_COLUMNS view. The view contains all columns for tables owned by the current user account. Steps 4 and 5 use the DECODE function to format the query by concatenating the CREATE TABLE keywords to the beginning of the first column. Steps 6 and 7 use the DECODE function to create the scale and precision modifier for each of the columns. Step 8 uses the results from the prior steps to create a query with results very much like a CREATE TABLE statement. After these steps, a closing parenthesis and semicolon are all that is needed by the statement. Steps 9 through 11 present the method for joining a table to itself to determine the last column of the table. Step 12 puts this all together to create a final query.

Comments

It is not necessary to rewrite this script every time you need to recreate a table, or even type it in once. The accompanying CD-ROM contains SQL scripts that can be used to re-create CREATE TABLE statements. SQL*Plus is a powerful tool for managing your database. Looking to the data dictionary and SQL*Plus to solve this type of problem saves you many hours. Re-creating CREATE TABLE statements would be a very tedious job if done manually.

COMPLEXITY
INTERMEDIATE

4.6 How do I...
Determine the space available in the database?

Problem

When I create a new table, I need to know whether I have room for it in the database and must determine in which tablespace to put the table. I want to calculate the amount of space available in each tablespace. I also want to know the largest amount of contiguous free space in each tablespace. How do I determine the space available in the database?

Technique

The DBA_FREE_SPACE data dictionary view contains the free extents within the database. A *free extent* is an area in the database available to hold new data. Figure 4-12 shows the columns contained in the DBA_FREE_SPACE view.

The sum of either the BYTES or BLOCKS columns can be used to determine the total free space in a tablespace or the entire database. The largest block of contiguous free space can be identified by querying the MAX of either the BYTES or BLOCKS columns.

Steps

1. Run SQL*Plus and connect as the WAITE user account. Load CHP4-23.sql into the SQL buffer. The file contains a query of the DBA_FREE_SPACE view, which calculates the total amount of free space within each tablespace.

```
SQL> GET CHP4-23
  1   SELECT TABLESPACE_NAME,
  2    SUM(BLOCKS),
  3    SUM(BYTES)
  4   FROM
  5    SYS.DBA_FREE_SPACE
  6   GROUP BY TABLESPACE_NAME
  7*  ORDER BY TABLESPACE_NAME
```

Line 1 queries the TABLESPACE_NAME column from the table. Lines 2 and 3 use the SUM function to calculate the sum of the BYTES and BLOCKS columns for each tablespace. Line 5 specifies that the SYS.DBA_FREE_SPACE data dictionary view is the source of the query. Since the TABLESPACE_NAME column is not a group expression, a GROUP BY clause is required in line 6.

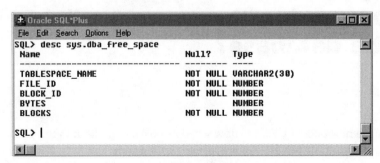

Figure 4-12 The SYS.DBA_FREE_SPACE view

2. Execute the query.

```
SQL>  /

TABLESPACE_NAME                      SUM(BLOCKS)  SUM(BYTES)
------------------------------------ ------------ ----------
ROLLBACK_DATA                        6011         12310528
SYSTEM                               5974         12234752
TEMPORARY_DATA                       3522         7213056
```

3. Load CHP4-24.sql into the SQL buffer. The file contains a query that returns the largest block of contiguous free space in each tablespace along with the total amount of free space.

```
SQL> GET CHP4-24
  1  SELECT TABLESPACE_NAME,
  2    SUM(BYTES),
  3    MAX(BYTES)
  4  FROM
  5    SYS.DBA_FREE_SPACE
  6  GROUP BY TABLESPACE_NAME
  7* ORDER BY TABLESPACE_NAME
```

Line 1 returns the name of each tablespace where data is stored. Line 2 uses the SUM function to calculate the total amount of free space in each tablespace. Line 3 uses the MAX function to determine the largest extent in each tablespace. The value returned by line 3 is the maximum size of a new table in the tablespace. The GROUP BY clause in line 6 is required since the TABLESPACE_NAME column is not a group function and the SUM and MAX functions are.

4. Execute the query to show information about each tablespace.

```
TABLESPACE_NAME                      SUM(BYTES)  MAX(BYTES)
------------------------------------ ----------  ----------
ROLLBACK_DATA                        12310528    3981312
SYSTEM                               12234752    5107712
TEMPORARY_DATA                       7213056     5117952
```

How It Works

Steps 1 and 2 query the SYS.DBA_FREE_SPACE data dictionary view to retrieve the number of blocks and bytes free in each tablespace. The SUM of the BLOCKS and BYTES columns are grouped using the GROUP BY clause in the query. Steps 3 and 4 change the query slightly to view the number of bytes in the largest free extent in each tablespace. The MAX function is used to retrieve the largest value in the BYTES column for each tablespace.

Comments

Calculating the free space in the database is a fairly easy task. A table can be as large as the largest amount of space free in one of the tablespaces. The largest size of the initial extent for a table is the size of the largest free extent.

COMPLEXITY
INTERMEDIATE

4.7 How do I...
Use check constraints to validate data?

Problem

In our systems, we want to ensure that the values in some columns fall within allowable ranges. Our applications can verify the values within the data, but I want to ensure that no invalid data can be created. I have heard that check constraints allow the database to validate data. How do I use check constraints to validate data?

Technique

When a table is created using the CREATE TABLE statement, a CHECK clause can be specified after a column. The syntax is

```
CREATE TABLE tablename (
 columnname datatype CHECK (expression));
```

A CHECK clause can also be created for existing tables. The ALTER TABLE statement allows check constraints to be created for a table.

Steps

1. Run SQL*Plus and connect as the WAITE user account. Load CHP4-25.sql into the SQL buffer. The file contains a statement to create a table with a check constraint.

```
SQL> GET CHP4-25
 1   CREATE TABLE CHK4_25 (
 2    CHK_NU      NUMBER(8),
 3    CHK_DSC     VARCHAR2(30),
 4    CHK_DOLLARS NUMBER(10,2),
 5*   CHK_COUNT   NUMBER(5) CHECK (CHK_COUNT > 5))
```

Line 1 contains the CREATE TABLE keywords used to create a new table. Lines 2 through 5 define the columns which make up the table. The

CHECK clause in line 5 requires that the value of the CHK_COUNT column be greater than 5 for a record to be created. Check constraints can be viewed by querying the USER_CONSTRAINTS data dictionary view.

2. Run the statement to create the table. When the table is created, a constraint will be added to the USER_CONSTRAINTS data dictionary view and given a name generated by the database.

```
SQL>  /
```

Table Created.

3. Load CHP4-26.sql into the SQL buffer. The file contains an ALTER TABLE statement to add a check constraint to the table created in Steps 1 and 2.

```
SQL> GET CHP4-26
 1   ALTER TABLE CHK4_25
 2     ADD CONSTRAINT CHK_CHK1
 3*      CHECK (CHK_DOLLARS >= 0)
```

Line 1 contains the ALTER TABLE keywords used to modify a table. Line 2 contains the ADD CONSTRAINT clause used to add a new constraint to a table. Line 3 adds a check constraint at the table level using the CHECK clause. The expression within parentheses must evaluate to TRUE for a record to be inserted. The syntax used in this step is required since column constraints cannot be added with the MODIFY clause of the ALTER TABLE statement.

4. Execute the statement to create the check constraint.

```
SQL>  /
```

Table altered.

5. Load CHP4-27.sql into the SQL buffer. The INSERT statement contained in the file attempts to insert an invalid row into the table. The statement will fail because the value of the CHK_DOLLARS column is negative.

```
SQL> GET CHP4-27
 1   INSERT INTO CHK4_25
 2    (CHK_NO, CHK_DSC, CHK_COUNT, CHK_DOLLARS)
 3   VALUES
 4*   (1, 'TEST CHECK', 10, -4)
```

The VALUES clause in lines 3 and 4 attempts to insert a negative value into the CHK_DOLLARS column of the CHK4_25 table.

6. Execute the statement to attempt the invalid operation.

```
SQL> /

insert into chktab1 (chk_no, chk_dsc, chk_dollars (1, '
    *
ERROR at line 1:
ORA-02290: check constraint (WAITE.CHK_CHK1) violated
```

How It Works

Steps 1 and 2 create a table with a check constraint. A check constraint can be created for columns within a CREATE TABLE statement. Steps 3 and 4 create a check constraint on an existing table using an ALTER TABLE statement with an ADD CONSTRAINT clause. The constraint must be added at the table level, since check constraints cannot be created on columns with the ALTER TABLE statement. Steps 5 and 6 attempt to insert an invalid row into the table. The error message displayed in Step 5 contains the constraint name created when the constraint was added.

Comments

Any time data rules can be handled with check constraints, you should use them. Check constraints force the database to do some of the work your applications normally would do. If an application fails to check for invalid values, you can be assured that the database will catch the error.

COMPLEXITY
INTERMEDIATE

4.8 How do I...
Create default values in a table?

Problem

When a user does not specify a value for some of the columns in a table, I want the value of the columns to default to specific values. How do I create default values in a table?

Technique

When defining a column using the CREATE TABLE or ALTER TABLE statements, you can specify a default value for a column by using a DEFAULT clause. Whenever a row is inserted into the table without the column specified, the default value will be inserted into the column.

Steps

1. Run SQL*Plus and connect as the WAITE user account. Load CHP4-28.sql into the SQL buffer. The file contains a CREATE TABLE statement that creates a table with two default columns.

```
SQL> GET CHP4-28
  1   CREATE TABLE CREDIT4_28 (
  2    CUST_ID      NUMBER(10)    NOT NULL,
  3    DEPT_NO      NUMBER(10),
  4    EFF_DATE     DATE DEFAULT SYSDATE,
  5*   CREDIT_LIMIT  NUMBER(12,2) DEFAULT 10000)
```

The EFF_DATE column will default to the system date and the CREDIT_LIMIT column will default to 10,000. Since the CUST_ID is specified with a NOT NULL constraint, a value must be provided for every record.

2. Run the statement to create the table.

```
SQL>  /
```

```
Table created.
```

3. Load CHP4-29.sql into the SQL buffer. The file contains an ALTER TABLE statement to create a default value for the DEPT_NO column.

```
SQL> GET CHP4-29
  1   ALTER TABLE CREDIT4_28
  2*  MODIFY (DEPT_NO NUMBER(10) DEFAULT 1)
```

A default value can be specified for a column in the MODIFY clause of an ALTER TABLE statement. Line 2 presents the MODIFY clause to add a default value to the CREDIT4_28 table. If the table contains NULL data, it will not be converted to the default.

4. Execute the statement to create the default value for the column.

```
SQL>  /
```

```
Table altered.
```

How It Works

Steps 1 and 2 create a table with a DEFAULT clause for two columns. A default expression cannot contain references to other columns and must be of the same datatype as the column. Steps 3 and 4 create a default value for an existing column in a table with the ALTER TABLE statement.

Comments

Default values should be used whenever you know the column should default to a specific value. The default values can be created with the table or added later. The datatype of the default value created must match the datatype of the column. The column must also be long enough to hold the value created. A DEFAULT expression cannot contain references to other columns. The default values can be created with the table or added later. The datatype of the default value created must match datatype of the column. The column must also be long enough to hold the value created. A DEFAULT expression cannot contain references to other columns.

COMPLEXITY
BEGINNING

4.9 How do I...
Create a primary key on a table?

Problem

In my data model, I have defined a primary key for all of my tables. I want to create primary keys in the database to enforce uniqueness. How do I create a primary key on a table?

Technique

A *primary key* constraint can be created with the table as part of a CREATE TABLE statement, or later using the ALTER TABLE statement. Within a CREATE TABLE statement, the PRIMARY KEY clause is used to define the columns contained in the primary key. The columns that are part of the primary key must contain NOT NULL constraints. Within an ALTER TABLE statement, a primary key can be created with the ADD PRIMARY KEY clause or the ADD CONSTRAINT...PRIMARY KEY clause. If the table contains data, the columns that are part of the primary key must not contain NULL data.

Steps

1. Run SQL*Plus and connect as the WAITE user account. Load CHP4-30.sql into the SQL buffer. The file contains a CREATE TABLE statement which creates a table with a primary key. Although it is a good idea to create a primary key for every table, doing so is optional.

```
SQL> GET CHP4-30
  1  CREATE TABLE CUST4_30 (
  2    COMPANY_ID        NUMBER(10) NOT NULL,
  3    CUST_ID           NUMBER(10) NOT NULL,
```

```
 4    ADDRESS            VARCHAR2(60),
 5    ADDRESS2           VARCHAR2(60),
 6    CITY               VARCHAR2(30),
 7    STATE              VARCHAR2(2),
 8    ZIP                VARCHAR2(5),
 9    ZIP4               VARCHAR2(4),
10*   PRIMARY KEY (COMPANY_ID, CUST_ID))
```

Line 1 contains the CREATE TABLE keywords used to create a new table. Lines 2 through 9 identify the columns that make up the table. Line 10 defines the primary key as a concatenated key containing two columns. Note that line 9 was terminated with a comma. The COMPANY_ID column in line 2 and the CUST_ID column in line 3 are part of the primary key, so they are declared as NOT NULL.

2. Execute the statement to create the table and primary key.

```
SQL>  /
```

Table created.

3. Load CHP4-31.sql into the SQL buffer. The file presents an ALTER TABLE statement to create a named constraint.

```
SQL> GET CHP4-31
 1   ALTER TABLE CUST4_30
 2     ADD CONSTRAINT PKEY_CUST
 3*    PRIMARY KEY (COMPANY_ID, CUST_ID)
```

Line 1 contains the ALTER TABLE keywords and specifies table CUST4_30 to be modified. The ADD CONSTRAINT clause contained in line 2 is used to add a constraint to the table and specify its name. Line 3 identifies the constraint as a primary key constraint and identifies the columns contained in the key. The COMPANY_ID and CUST_NO columns will make up the primary key of the table.

How It Works

Steps 1 and 2 create a primary key on a table when it is created with the CREATE TABLE statement. The primary key is specified by the PRIMARY KEY clause of the statement. The columns that are part of the primary key must be declared as NOT NULL, or the NOT NULL constraint will be created automatically. The statement would fail if the primary key columns contained NULL data. Step 3 presents a statement used create a primary key on an existing table. The ALTER TABLE statement is used with the ADD CONSTRAINT clause to create a primary key with a specified name. The columns that are made part of the primary key will have NOT NULL constraints added automatically if they do not already exist. A unique index is created on the primary key columns.

Comments

The columns within a primary key cannot be NULL. Creating a primary key on a table will create NOT NULL constraints on the columns included in the key. The LONG and LONG RAW datatypes cannot be included in a primary key. A primary key can contain 16 columns at most. A unique index is created on the columns contained in the primary key.

COMPLEXITY
INTERMEDIATE

4.10 How do I...
Enforce referential integrity?

Problem

We have many applications updating the same sets of data. I want to ensure that the business rules governing the relationships between data in tables is enforced. It is important that no application can create data that violates the data relationships in our data model. Each application currently checks to ensure that new data and changes to existing data are valid. Unfortunately, if there is a bug in one of the applications, it is very difficult to determine which application created the bad data. How do I enforce referential integrity at the database level?

Technique

Declarative referential integrity is a feature of Oracle which ensures that the data in a database fits the data model. Referential integrity is enforced by using a combination of primary keys and foreign keys. A *primary key* is a set of columns that uniquely identifies a row in a table. A primary key can be created in the CREATE TABLE statement or added later with an ALTER TABLE statement. The primary key ensures that each row in the table is unique. How-To 4.9 covered the creation of primary keys. A *foreign key* defines the columns in a table that must exist as the primary key in another table. A foreign key constraint can be created in the CREATE TABLE statement or added later with an ALTER TABLE statement.

Steps

1. Run SQL*Plus and connect as the WAITE user account. The file CHP4-32.sql, shown in Figure 4-13, contains the statements to create the two sample tables used in this How-To. The TAB_NO column in the RITAB1 table is the primary key for the table and will be referenced by the same field in the RITAB2 table.

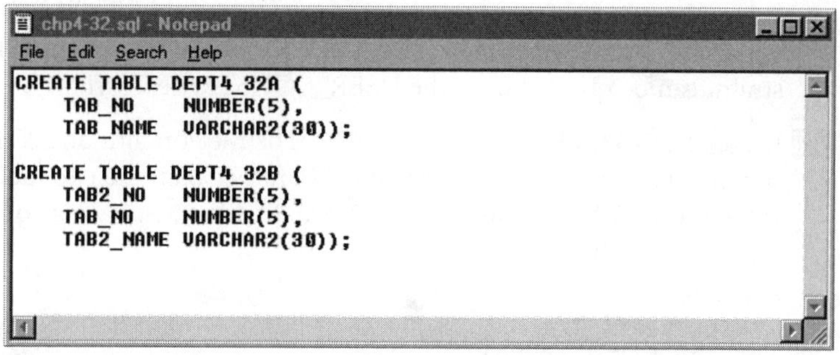


```
CREATE TABLE DEPT4_32A (
    TAB_NO     NUMBER(5),
    TAB_NAME   VARCHAR2(30));

CREATE TABLE DEPT4_32B (
    TAB2_NO    NUMBER(5),
    TAB_NO     NUMBER(5),
    TAB2_NAME  VARCHAR2(30));
```

Figure 4-13 CHP4-32.sql creates the sample table used in How-To 4.10

The DEPT4_32A and DEPT4_32B tables created in the script will be related by the common TAB_NO column. In the steps that follow, a primary key will be placed on the DEPT4_32A table and a foreign key will be created on the DEPT4_32B table. Run the file to create the two files.

```
SQL>  START CHP4-32

Table created.

Table created.

Table altered.

Table altered.
```

2. Load CHP4-33.sql into the SQL buffer. The file contains an ALTER TABLE statement to create a primary key on the DEPT4_32A table.

```
SQL> GET CHP4-33
 1  ALTER TABLE DEPT4_32A
 2    ADD PRIMARY KEY
 3*     (TAB_NO)
```

Line 1 contains the ALTER_TABLE keywords and specifies that table DEPT4_32A be altered. The ADD PRIMARY key clause in line 2 creates a primary key on the TAB_NO column of the table. The data in the TAB_NO column must be unique or else the statement will fail. Since there is no data in the table, the statement will be successful.

3. Run the statement to create the primary key.

```
SQL>  /

Table altered.
```

When the primary key is created, a unique index is placed on the table which can been seen in the USER_INDEXES view. The primary key constraint can be queried from the USER_CONSTRAINTS view.

4. Load CHP4-34.sql into the SQL buffer. The file contains an ALTER TABLE statement to create a foreign key constraint between the two tables. Any value for the TAB_NO field in the RITAB2 table must have a corresponding record in the RITAB1 table.

```
SQL> GET CHP4-34
1   ALTER TABLE DEPT4_32B
2     ADD FOREIGN KEY (TAB_NO)
3     REFERENCES
4*      DEPT4_32A (TAB_NO)
```

Line 1 contains the ALTER TABLE keywords and specifies the name of the table altered. Line 2 contains the ADD FOREIGN KEY clause to create a foreign key on the TAB_NO column of the table. Lines 3 and 4 make the foreign key reference the TAB_NO column on the DEPT4_32A table.

5. Run the statement to create the foreign key.

```
SQL>  /

Table altered.
```

The foreign key constraint can be queried from the USER_CONSTRAINTS data dictionary view. The constraint will be enabled automatically.

6. Load CHP4-35.sql into the SQL buffer. The file contains an INSERT statement to attempt to insert a row into the RITAB2 table.

```
SQL> GET CHP4-35
1   INSERT INTO DEPT4_32B
2*    VALUES(0,0,'TEST')
```

7. Run the statement to insert the record. Since there is no corresponding record in the DEPT4_32A table, the statement will fail.

```
SQL>  /

insert into dept4_32a values (0,0,'TEST')
               *
ERROR at line 1:
ORA-02291: integrity constraint (WAITE.SYS_C00370) violated - parent key
not found
```

The name of the constraint violated is displayed in the error message. In order for the statement to succeed, the constraint must be disabled. How-To 4.11 explores the topic of disabling constraints.

How It Works

Step 1 creates the tables used throughout this How-To. Steps 2 and 3 create a primary key on the DEPT4_34A table created in Step 1. A primary key must exist on the child table in order for a foreign key to be created. Steps 4 and 5 create a foreign key on the DEPT4_34A table, which references the DEPT4_34B table. In order for a record to be created in the DEPT4_34A table, there must be a corresponding record in the DEPT4_34B table. Steps 6 and 7 attempt to insert an invalid record into the DEPT4_34B table.

Comments

Referential integrity helps ensure that data is valid, regardless of its source. Before Oracle 7, applications had to ensure that data integrity existed. As an application became larger or multiple applications accessed the same data, it became difficult to track down the cause of invalid data when it occurred. By using referential integrity constraints, applications are prevented from creating invalid data.

COMPLEXITY
BEGINNING

4.11 How do I...
Enable and disable constraints?

Problem

In order to manipulate data in some batch processing functions within our organization, I need to disable constraints. Without disabling the constraints, programs cannot perform any tasks that violate referential integrity, even temporarily. After the batch processes have completed, I need to enable the constraints. How do I enable and disable constraints?

Technique

The ALTER TABLE statement is used to enable and disable constraints. You must know the name of the constraint in order to enable or disable it. The USER_CONSTRAINTS data dictionary view contains information about constraints on tables owned by the current user account. Figure 4-14 shows the description of the USER_CONSTRAINTS view in SQL*Plus.

In order to enable or disable a constraint, the user account must be the owner of the table or have the ALTER ANY TABLE privilege.

Steps

1. Run SQL*Plus and connect as the WAITE user account. CHP4-36.sql, shown in Figure 4-15, creates the sample table used in this How-To.

```
Oracle SQL*Plus
File Edit Search Options Help

SQL> desc user_constraints
 Name                            Null?    Type
 ------------------------------- -------- ----
 OWNER                           NOT NULL VARCHAR2(30)
 CONSTRAINT_NAME                 NOT NULL VARCHAR2(30)
 CONSTRAINT_TYPE                          VARCHAR2(1)
 TABLE_NAME                      NOT NULL VARCHAR2(30)
 SEARCH_CONDITION                         LONG
 R_OWNER                                  VARCHAR2(30)
 R_CONSTRAINT_NAME                        VARCHAR2(30)
 DELETE_RULE                              VARCHAR2(9)
 STATUS                                   VARCHAR2(8)

SQL>
```

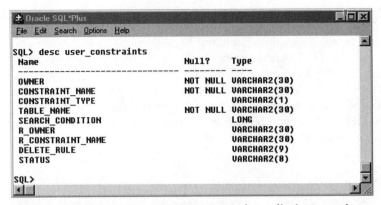

Figure 4-14 The USER_CONSTRAINTS data dictionary view

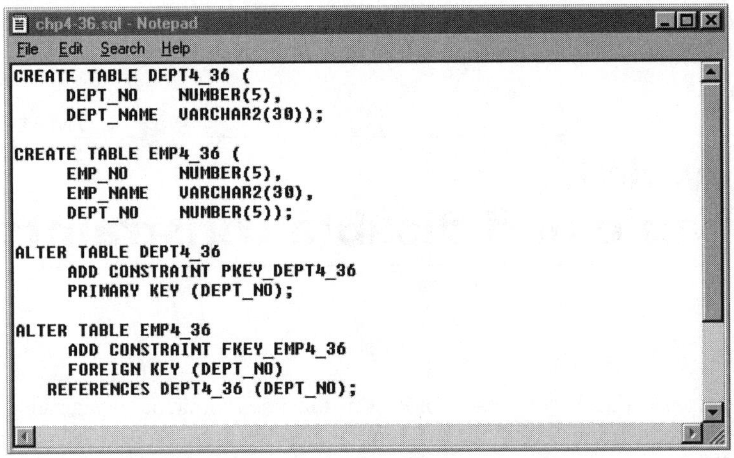

```
chp4-36.sql - Notepad
File Edit Search Help
CREATE TABLE DEPT4_36 (
     DEPT_NO     NUMBER(5),
     DEPT_NAME   VARCHAR2(30));

CREATE TABLE EMP4_36 (
     EMP_NO      NUMBER(5),
     EMP_NAME    VARCHAR2(30),
     DEPT_NO     NUMBER(5));

ALTER TABLE DEPT4_36
     ADD CONSTRAINT PKEY_DEPT4_36
     PRIMARY KEY (DEPT_NO);

ALTER TABLE EMP4_36
     ADD CONSTRAINT FKEY_EMP4_36
     FOREIGN KEY (DEPT_NO)
   REFERENCES DEPT4_36 (DEPT_NO);
```

Figure 4-15 CHP4-36 creates the sample tables used in How-To 4.11

2. Load CHP4-37.sql into the SQL buffer. The file contains a query that returns information about the constraints on tables owned by the user account.

```
SQL> GET CHP4-37
  1  SELECT
  2   TABLE_NAME,
  3   CONSTRAINT_NAME,
  4   STATUS
  5  FROM
  6*  USER_CONSTRAINTS
```

The STATUS column contains ENABLED if the constraint is enabled, DISABLED if not. The CONSTRAINT_NAME column contains the unique

name of the constraint. If a name is not provided when a constraint is created, a name is generated by the database. The ALL_CONSTRAINTS view could be used in place of USER_CONSTRAINTS. ALL_CONSTRAINTS contains the constraints on all tables on which the user account has privileges.

3. Run the statement. Neither of the two constraints shown were given a name by the user when created. Constraint names created by the system begin with SYS_C.

```
SQL>    /
```

TABLE_NAME	CONSTRAINT_NAME	STATUS
DEPT4_36	PKEY_DEPT4_36	ENABLED
EMP4_36	FKEY_EMP4_36	ENABLED

Both constraints are enabled as shown in the STATUS column. When a new constraint is created, its status defaults to enabled. Load CHP4-38.sql into the SQL buffer. The file contains an ALTER TABLE statement to disable the constraint on the DEPT4_36 table. The name of the constraint was obtained from the query in the previous step.

```
SQL> GET CHP4-38
  1   ALTER TABLE EMP4_36
  2   DISABLE CONSTRAINT
  3*     FKEY_EMP4_36
```

The DISABLE CONSTRAINT clause instructs Oracle to disable the constraint specified in line 3. If the constraint is already disabled, the statement will not return an error.

4. Run the statement to disable the constraint.

```
SQL>    /
```

```
Table altered.
```

After a constraint is disabled, the database does not check to ensure that an operation follows the rules of the constraint. If an operation is performed that violates a disabled constraint, the data must be corrected before the constraint can be enabled or an error will occur.

5. Load CHP4-37.sql into the SQL buffer. This is the same file used in Step 1 to view the status of the constraints.

```
SQL>    GET CHP4-37
  1   SELECT
  2     TABLE_NAME,
  3     CONSTRAINT_NAME,
```

continued on next page

continued from previous page

```
4    STATUS
5    FROM
6*   USER_CONSTRAINTS
```

6. Run the statement to view the status of the constraints. The constraint SYS_C00368 will be shown as disabled since it was disabled in Steps 3 and 4. When a constraint is disabled, it cannot be used to create new constraints. For example, a foreign key constraint requires a primary key constraint on the child table. If the primary key constraint on the child table has been disabled, the foreign key cannot be created.

```
SQL> /
```

TABLE_NAME	CONSTRAINT_NAME	STATUS
DEPT4_36	PKEY_DEPT4_36	ENABLED
EMP4_36	FKEY_EMP4_36	DISABLED

7. Load CHP4-39.sql into the SQL buffer. The file contains an ALTER TABLE statement to enable the constraint that was disabled in Steps 3 and 4.

```
SQL> GET CHP4-39
  1    ALTER TABLE EMP4_36
  2    ENABLE CONSTRAINT
  3*     FKEY_EMP4_36
```

8. Run the statement to enable the constraint. Enabling the constraint changes the STATUS column in the USER_CONSTRAINTS and ALL_CONSTRAINTS views to ENABLED.

```
SQL> /

Table altered.
```

How It Works

Steps 1 and 2 query the constraint name and status from the USER_CONSTRAINTS data dictionary view. Steps 3 and 4 execute an ALTER TABLE statement with a DISABLE CONSTRAINT clause to disable a constraint. Steps 5 and 6 view the constraint status after being disabled by querying the USER_CONSTRAINTS view. Steps 7 and 8 enable the constraint that was disabled in the prior steps by using an ALTER TABLE statement with the ENABLE CONSTRAINT clause.

Comments

> **NOTE**
>
> Constraints should be used whenever possible to ensure data integrity. Constraints can cause problems in batch processes or during system maintenance because they will not allow some operations to be performed. Disabling a constraint makes it possible to violate the rules of the constraint if necessary. The data in the tables affected by the constraint must be valid before the constraint is enabled. Oracle will not allow the constraint to be enabled if the data in the table violates the constraint.

CHAPTER 5
VIEWS

VIEWS

How do I...

A *view* is a logical table based on a query. Views themselves do not store data, but present data from other sources. To an application, a view looks and acts like a table. Data can be queried from a view, and in many cases data can be inserted, updated, and deleted through a view. Views can be used to present data in a different format than how it is actually stored in the underlying tables. Views simplify the presentation of data by hiding the actual structure of the base tables. Views can secure data at the row level by presenting a restricted subset of the underlying table to the user.

5.1   Determine the views available

The views available to a user can be queried from the data dictionary through the USER_VIEWS and ALL_VIEWS data dictionary views. Since it is possible to have many views available, an easy method to determine the views available is presented in this How-To.

5.2   Re-create CREATE VIEW statements

It is often necessary to re-create the CREATE VIEW statements that were used to create views. As we have done throughout the book, SQL*Plus and the data dictionary are used to re-create DDL statements with a complex query of the data dictionary. This How-To presents the queries used to rebuild CREATE VIEW statements from the data dictionary.

5.3   Determine whether a view can be updated

A view's data can be manipulated if the structure of the view meets certain criteria. A view cannot be updated if it joins tables, uses a DISTINCT operator, or contains a GROUP BY clause or group functions. This How-To presents SQL and PL/SQL statements to quickly determine if a view is updatable, without analyzing the structure of the view.

5.4   Simulate a cross-tab query using a view

A cross-tab query in Microsoft Access presents data from multiple rows on a single line. This type of query is useful for presenting data, such as monthly summary data, in a spreadsheet type format. This How-To presents a method to create a view that displays multiple records as a single record.

5.5   Restrict access to data using views

One of the most common uses of views is to restrict access to data from users. Users can have different views of the same data. A subset of the data in the base table can be shown by including a WHERE clause in the view, which restricts data that is based on the user account's name or privileges. This How-To presents methods for restricting access to data using views.

5.6   Restrict insert of data into a view

If a user is unable to query a row from a view, he or she should be restricted from inserting that same row into the view. The WITH CHECK OPTION clause in the CREATE VIEW statement can be used to restrict the insert or update of view data. This How-To presents the method for restricting the insert or update of data in a view.

5.7   Create a view with errors

A view can be created even if the SELECT statement used in the view contains errors. This can be useful during system maintenance or database creation if you want to create the view before the base tables are created. The view can be recompiled later to remove the errors. This How-To shows the method for creating views with the FORCE option and manually recompiling views.

5.8 Simplify privilege maintenance using views

Privileges can be granted to views without being granted to the underlying base tables. If data management operations can be performed on a view, user accounts with privileges on the view can modify data in the base table through the view. Maintaining privileges on a view is easier than on a table because a view can be replaced without losing the privileges granted to it. This How-To presents methods to simplify the maintenance of privileges by using views.

COMPLEXITY
BEGINNING

5.1 How do I...
Determine the views available?

Problem

We have many views in our organization. I cannot always remember the names of the views to which I have access. Within our decision support applications, I want to present a list of the views a user has available to display data. How do I list the views available to a user account?

Technique

The USER_VIEWS data dictionary view contains views owned by the user account connected to the database. The ALL_VIEWS data dictionary view contains the views which a user account owns or has been granted privileges on. Either view can be queried to list the views available. Figure 5-1 shows the columns available in the ALL_VIEWS data dictionary view.

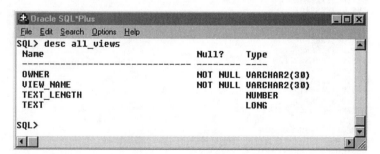

Figure 5-1 ALL_VIEWS data dictionary view

The OWNER column contains the owner of the view, and the VIEW_NAME column contains the view's name. The TEXT column contains the query used to generate the records returned by the view.

Steps

1. Run SQL*Plus and connect as the WAITE user account. Load CHP5.1.sql into the SQL buffer. The file contains a query to list the views available to the user account.

```
SQL> GET CHP5.1
 1 SELECT OWNER||'.'||VIEW_NAME
 2 FROM
 3* ALL_VIEWS
```

Line 1 concatenates the owner of the view with the name of the view to present the output in the owner.objectname format.

2. Run the statement to list the views. Since the WAITE user account was granted the DBA role by the installation script, every view in the database is listed. The results of the query are shown in Figure 5-2.

How It Works

The ALL_VIEWS data dictionary view contains information about the views to which a user account has access. Steps 1 and 2 query the ALL_VIEWS data dictionary view to list all views to which the WAITE user account has been granted access. The OWNER and VIEW_NAME columns are concatenated to return a single column. If you wish

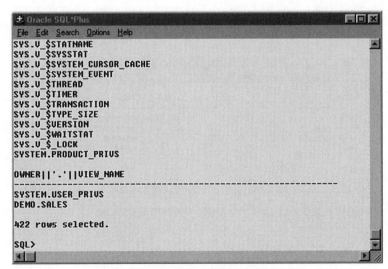

Figure 5-2 A query of the ALL_VIEWS data dictionary view

to list only the views owned by the connected user account, use the USER_VIEWS data dictionary view.

Comments

Views can be used in many places, just like tables. Retrieving a list of available views is a fairly easy process. If you are developing an application which needs to include a list of view names, you can include the data dictionary views in your application.

COMPLEXITY
INTERMEDIATE

5.2 How do I...
Re-create CREATE VIEW statements?

Problem

I need to re-create the CREATE VIEW statements used to develop some of the views in our system. I know that we use SQL*Plus and the data dictionary to rebuild other DDL statements throughout this book. How do I re-create CREATE VIEW statements using the data dictionary?

Technique

The query used to rebuild CREATE VIEW statements uses the ALL_VIEWS data dictionary view. The TEXT column contains the query used by the view to return rows. The TEXT column is of the LONG datatype, which makes it harder to work with in SQL*Plus. Many operators and functions cannot be used with columns of the LONG datatype.

Steps

1. Run SQL*Plus and connect as the WAITE user account. CHP5.2.sql, shown in Figure 5-3, depicts a query of the TEXT column in the ALL_VIEWS data dictionary view.

The first three commands set SQL*Plus system variables to turn the heading off, set the long data display to 2,000 characters, and turn feedback off. This formats the output of the query and removes the query heading and the feedback displayed when the query completes. Line 4 suppresses the verification of substitution variables. The query retrieves the TEXT column from the ALL_VIEWS data dictionary view.

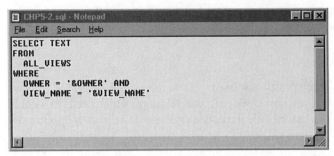

Figure 5-3 CHP5.2.sql queries the TEXT column of
the ALL_VIEWS data dictionary view

2. Run CHP5.2.sql. Substitute the &OWNER substitution variable with SYS
and the &VIEW_NAME substitution variable with DBA_CONSTRAINTS.

```
SQL>   START CHP5.2
Enter value for owner: SYS
Enter value for view_name: DBA_CONSTRAINTS

select ou.name, oc.name,
decode(c.type, 1, 'C', 2, 'P', 3, 'U',
4, 'R', 5, 'V',7,'C', '?'),
o.name, c.condition, ru.name, rc.name,
decode(c.type, 4,
decode(c.refact, 1, 'CASCADE', 'NO ACTION'), NULL),
decode(c.type, 5, 'ENABLED',
decode(c.enabled, NULL, 'DISABLED','ENABLED'))
from sys.con$ oc, sys.con$ rc, sys.user$ ou, sys.user$ ru,
sys.obj$ o, sys.cdef$ c
where oc.owner# = ou.user#
and oc.con# = c.con#
and c.obj# = o.obj#
and c.rcon# = rc.con#(+)
and rc.owner# = ru.user#(+)
```

3. The CHP5.3.sql file, shown in Figure 5-4, includes the CREATE OR
REPLACE VIEW keywords. The keywords are not concatenated to the
TEXT column because the column is of the LONG datatype. LONG

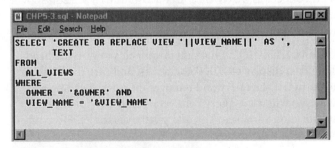

Figure 5-4 A SQL script to return
CREATE VIEW statements

columns cannot be concatenated to other columns and cannot use any of
the character functions.

4. Spool the output of the query and run CHP5.3.sql. Replace the &OWNER
substitution variable with SYS and the &VIEW_NAME substitution variable
with DBA_CONSTRAINTS.

```
SQL>   SPOOL VIEWS1.sql
SQL>   START CHP5.3
Enter value for owner: SYS
Enter value for view_name: DBA_CONSTRAINTS

CREATE OR REPLACE TABLE DBA_CONSTRAINTS AS
select ou.name, oc.name,
decode(c.type, 1, 'C', 2, 'P', 3, 'U',
4, 'R', 5, 'V',7,'C', '?'),
o.name, c.condition, ru.name, rc.name,
decode(c.type, 4,
decode(c.refact, 1, 'CASCADE', 'NO ACTION'), NULL),
decode(c.type, 5, 'ENABLED',
decode(c.enabled, NULL, 'DISABLED','ENABLED'))
from sys.con$ oc, sys.con$ rc, sys.user$ ou, sys.user$ ru,
sys.obj$ o, sys.cdef$ c
where oc.owner# = ou.user#
and oc.con# = c.con#
and c.obj# = o.obj#
and c.rcon# = rc.con#(+)
and rc.owner# = ru.user#(+)
```

5. Stop spooling the output file. The output file contains a CREATE OR
REPLACE VIEW statement which can build the view.

```
SQL> SPOOL OFF
SQL>
```

Once the output file is closed, it can be run as a SQL*Plus command file to
rebuild the view queried from the data dictionary.

How It Works

A CREATE VIEW statement can be rebuilt by querying the ALL_VIEWS data dictionary view. Steps 1 and 2 return the query used by a view from the ALL_VIEWS
data dictionary view. The value of the LONG system variable was changed in
order to display the entire value of the LONG column. Steps 3 and 4 build a CRE-
ATE OR REPLACE VIEW statement by adding the keywords to the query. Step 5 spools
the output to a file which can run as an SQL script and runs the query to build the
statements.

Comments

Once again, the data dictionary is used to rebuild a DDL statement. The LONG column in the ALL_TABLES view causes some problems in SQL*Plus. The LONG system

variable in SQL*Plus is used to set the size of long data queried from the view. The LONG datatype prevents many operations from being performed on the column.

COMPLEXITY
ADVANCED

5.3 How do I...
Determine whether a view can be updated?

Problem

We use views to make querying data easier. I know many views can be updated, but I need a method to determine which ones they are. How do I determine if a view can be updated?

Technique

A view cannot be updated if it joins tables, uses a DISTINCT operator, or contains a GROUP BY clause or group functions. You could use the TEXT column in the ALL_VIEWS data dictionary view to determine if any of these limitations exist in the query. An easier way to determine if the view can be updated is to perform a data management operation and trap the error if it occurs.

Steps

1. Run SQL*Plus and connect as the WAITE user account. CHP5.4.sql, shown in Figure 5-5, contains the statements used to build two tables and two views that will test the code segment developed in this How-To.

The two tables, TAB5_4A and TAB5_4B, are the source tables for the two views. The first view, VIEW5_4A, selects all of the columns from the TAB5_4A table and can be updated. The second view, VIEW5_4B, joins the two sample tables and cannot be updated due to the join condition.

2. Run the statement to create the tables and views.

```
SQL>   START CHP5.4

Table created.

Table created.

View created.

View created.
```

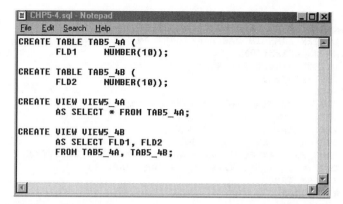

Figure 5-5 CHP5.4.sql creates the sample objects used in How-To 5.3

3. Load CHP5.5.sql into the SQL buffer. The file contains an INSERT statement that tests if a data management statement can be performed on a view. Since the INSERT statement uses a query of the view, it is not necessary to know the structure of the view. The technique shown in this step will test all views.

```
SQL> GET CHP5.5
 1  INSERT INTO VIEW5_4B
 2   SELECT * FROM VIEW5_4B
 3*  WHERE 1 = 0
```

Line 1 specifies that records are inserted into VIEW5_4B. Line 2 specifies that the records inserted are also queried from VIEW5_4B. The WHERE clause in line 3 doesn't insert any rows, since 1 is never equal to 0. If an INSERT statement cannot be executed on the view, an error will occur when the statement is run.

4. Run the statement to attempt to insert a record into the view.

```
SQL>  /
insert into view5_4b select * from view5_4b
*
ERROR at line 1:
ORA-01732: data manipulation operation not legal on this view
```

The Oracle error ORA-01732 is returned when a data manipulation operation is attempted on a view where it is not allowed.

5. Load CHP5.6.sql into the SQL buffer. The statement in the file creates a stored function to determine if a data manipulation operation can be performed on a view. For more information about the creation of stored functions, see Chapter 13.

```
SQL>  GET CHP5.6
 1 CREATE OR REPLACE FUNCTION CHECK_VIEW
 2   (VIEW_NAME IN VARCHAR2) RETURN BOOLEAN IS
 3 TMP VARCHAR2(60);
 4   CURSOR_HANDLE INTEGER;
 5   CNT INTEGER;
 6 BEGIN
 7   TMP := 'INSERT INTO '||VIEW_NAME;
 8   TMP := TMP||' SELECT * FROM '||VIEW_NAME;
 9   TMP := TMP||' WHERE 1 = 0';
10 CURSOR_HANDLE := DBMS_SQL.OPEN_CURSOR;
11 DBMS_SQL.PARSE(CURSOR_HANDLE, TMP, DBMS_SQL.V7);
12 CNT := DBMS_SQL.EXECUTE(CURSOR_HANDLE);
13 RETURN TRUE;
14 EXCEPTION
15   WHEN OTHERS
16   THEN
17   RETURN FALSE;
18* END;
```

Lines 1 and 2 declare a stored function which is passed a view name and returns a Boolean value. Lines 3 through 5 create the temporary variables used by the function. Lines 7 through 10 put the type of INSERT statement shown in the prior steps into the TMP variable. Line 10 uses the OPEN_CURSOR function from the DBMS_SQL stored package to open a cursor that will execute the INSERT statement. The DBMS_SQL package allows dynamic SQL to be created and executed against the database. Since the view name is passed as a parameter, a fixed SQL statement cannot be created in the PL/SQL function. Line 11 parses the INSERT statement contained in the TMP variable by executing the PARSE procedure in the DBMS_SQL package. Line 12 executes the INSERT statement, using the EXECUTE function from the same package. Line 13 returns TRUE if an error does not occur. Lines 14 through 17 handle an error created if the INSERT statement fails, by returning FALSE.

6. Execute the statement to create the stored function.

```
SQL>  /
```

```
Function created.
```

7. Load CHP5.7.sql into the SQL buffer. The file contains a PL/SQL statement to test the operation of the stored function created in the previous step.

```
SQL>  GET CHP5.7
 1 DECLARE
 2   X BOOLEAN;
 3 BEGIN
 4   X := CHECK_VIEW('VIEW5_4A');
 5 IF X THEN
 6   DBMS_OUTPUT.PUT_LINE('Can update VIEW5_4A');
 7 ELSE
 8   DBMS_OUTPUT.PUT_LINE('Cannot update VIEW5_4A');
 9 END IF;
```

```
10  X := CHECK_VIEW('VIEW5_4B');
11 IF X THEN
12     DBMS_OUTPUT.PUT_LINE('Can update VIEW5_4B');
13   ELSE
14    DBMS_OUTPUT.PUT_LINE('Cannot update VIEW5_4B');
15   END IF;
16*  END;
```

Line 4 executes the TEST_CHECK function for TEST_VIEW1. Lines 5 through 9 display the results of the function call. Line 10 executes the TEST_CHECK function for TEST_VIEW2. Lines 11 through 15 display the results of the function call.

8. Set the SERVEROUTPUT system variable to ON with the SET command and execute the statement to test the function. TEST_VIEW1 is updatable, and TEST_VIEW2 is not.

```
SQL> SET SERVEROUTPUT ON
SQL> /

Can update VIEW5_4A
Cannot update VIEW5_4B

PL/SQL procedure successfully completed.
```

How It Works

Steps 1 and 2 create the two sample tables and two views used in the example. Steps 3 and 4 present a method for testing a view by inserting records into it with a SELECT statement. The INSERT statement will not create any rows in the table if successful, and will fail if the operation is not allowed. Step 4 attempts to execute the INSERT statement and fails since VIEW5_4B cannot be updated. Steps 5 and 6 create a stored function which is passed a view name, returning TRUE if the view data can be modified, FALSE if it cannot. The function uses the DBMS_SQL package to execute a dynamic SQL statement that tests the INSERT statement on the view. Steps 7 and 8 test the operation of the stored function created in steps 5 and 6.

Comments

The steps shown in this How-To test a view to determine if data management operations can be performed on the view. When the data in the view can be modified, views can provide benefits over using base tables in your applications.

5.4 How do I...
Simulate a cross-tab query using a view?

Problem

In Microsoft Access, I use a cross-tab query to view records horizontally. In my table, I have one record for each month. In my reports and inquiry screens, I want to display the data for a year horizontally, even though a record exists for each month. How do I simulate a cross-tab query using a view to present the combination of multiple records as a single row?

Technique

The DECODE function is a very owerful tool for creating advanced queries. DECODE works like an in-line IF..THEN..ELSE statement. It can be used to view data horizontally by returning a value if the row is in the correct column.

Steps

1. Run SQL*Plus and connect as the WAITE user account. The CHP5.8.sql file, shown in Figure 5-6, builds a table that will be the basis for the cross-tab view and inserts sample data.

```
CHP5-8.sql - Notepad
File  Edit  Search  Help
CREATE TABLE CROSS_TAB (
    YEAR        NUMBER(4),
    MONTH       NUMBER(2),
    VALUE       NUMBER(12,2));

INSERT INTO CROSS_TAB VALUES (1994, 1, 235);
INSERT INTO CROSS_TAB VALUES (1994, 2, 180);
INSERT INTO CROSS_TAB VALUES (1994, 3, 185);
INSERT INTO CROSS_TAB VALUES (1995, 1, 245);
INSERT INTO CROSS_TAB VALUES (1995, 2, 200);
INSERT INTO CROSS_TAB VALUES (1995, 3, 188);
COMMIT;
```

Figure 5-6 CHP5.8.sql creates the sample objects used in How-To 5.4

Setting the TERMOUT system variable OFF in line 1 hides the output of the script file when the table and its records are created. The CROSS_TAB table contains one row for each year, month combination. The VALUE column represents the value for the given month.

2. Run the command to create the table and build sample data.

```
SQL>   START CHP5.8

Table created.

1 row created.

1 row created.

1 row created.

1 row created.

1 row created.

1 row created.

Commit complete.
```

3. Load CHP5.9.sql into the SQL buffer. The file contains an SQL script to query the table created in the previous steps, displaying the data horizontally.

```
SQL>   GET CHP5.9
 1 SELECT YEAR,
 2   SUM(DECODE(month,1,VALUE,0)) January,
 3   SUM(DECODE(month,2,VALUE,0)) February,
 4   SUM(DECODE(month,3,VALUE,0)) March
 5 FROM
 6   CROSS_TAB
 7   GROUP BY YEAR
 8* ORDER BY YEAR
```

Line 1 begins the query statement and selects the YEAR column. The YEAR column is the only column not modified by a GROUP BY operator. Lines 2 through 4 return the values for the first three months. The DECODE function returns the VALUE if the MONTH column is correct for the column, otherwise it returns 0. The SUM operator displays one row for each year. Since 0 will be returned for each column whose month is not correct, the SUM operator doesn't effect the data besides grouping it as a single row. Line 7 groups the data by the YEAR column. Since the YEAR column retrieved in line 1 is not a GROUP BY expression, the GROUP BY clause in line 7 is required.

4. Run the query. Since sample data was created for two years, two rows will be returned by the query.

YEAR	JANUARY	FEBRUARY	MARCH
1994	235	180	185
1995	245	200	188

5. Load CHP5.10.sql into the SQL buffer. The file contains a CREATE VIEW statement to create a view based on the query shown in step 3.

```
SQL>  GET CHP5.10
  1   CREATE VIEW YEAR_VIEW
  2   AS
  3   SELECT YEAR,
  4      SUM(DECODE(MONTH,1,VALUE,0))  January,
  5      SUM(DECODE(MONTH,2,VALUE,0))  February,
  6      SUM(DECODE(MONTH,3,VALUE,0))  March,
  7      SUM(DECODE(MONTH,4,VALUE,0))  April,
  8      SUM(DECODE(MONTH,5,VALUE,0))  May,
  9      SUM(DECODE(MONTH,6,VALUE,0))  June,
 10      SUM(DECODE(MONTH,7,VALUE,0))  July,
 11      SUM(DECODE(MONTH,8,VALUE,0))  August,
 12      SUM(DECODE(MONTH,9,VALUE,0))  September,
 13      SUM(DECODE(MONTH,10,VALUE,0)) October,
 14      SUM(DECODE(MONTH,11,VALUE,0)) November,
 15      SUM(DECODE(MONTH,12,VALUE,0)) December,
 16      SUM(VALUE) Total
 17   FROM
 18      CROSS_TAB
 19*  GROUP BY YEAR
```

Lines 2 through 15 create a column for each month of the year. Line 16 creates a total for each year.

6. Run the statement to create the view.

```
SQL>  /

View created.
```

7. Look at the description of the view created with the DESCRIBE statement. Figure 5-7 shows the results of the operation within SQL*Plus.

How It Works

The DECODE function works like an in-line IF statement and can be used within a query to present records horizontally. Steps 1 and 2 create the tables used in this How-To. Step 3 uses the DECODE function to transform data from a vertical view to a horizontal view. For each column, the VALUE field is only added to the column if the MONTH belongs in it. Steps 5 and 6 build a view that hides the complexity of the query from the user. Step 7 shows that the view represents the data as 12 columns instead of 12 separate rows.

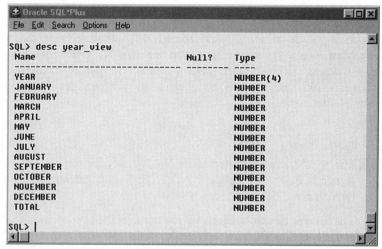

Figure 5-7 The description of the YEAR_VIEW
view in SQL*Plus

Comments

Data normalization creates this type of requirement. This DECODE function technique uses a very powerful feature of Oracle. Each time the view is queried, many more rows from the base tables are queried than are actually shown by the view. This may cause inadequate performance. Consider creating summary tables to represent data of this type if the performance of your views is unacceptable.

COMPLEXITY
INTERMEDIATE

5.5   How do I...
Restrict access to data using views?

Problem

We have certain tables which are used throughout the organization. We want all users to be able to work with the same table, but only see the data for their job function. I know that I can use views to query selective data, but how do I restrict access to data using views?

Technique

The USER pseudo-column contains the account of the user connected to the database. Most pseudo-columns can be used in views. The USER pseudo-column can restrict access to certain users, and the SYSDATE pseudo-column can restrict access from old data. Sub-queries can be used to produce lists of valid values within in an IN operator.

Steps

1. Run SQL*Plus and connect as the WAITE user account. CHP5.11.sql, shown in Figure 5-8, contains a CREATE TABLE statement for building a table that will be restricted by a view.

The SALES_ID column contains the name of the user account that creates the record. The ORDER_DATE column contains the date the order is placed, and the ORDER_DESC column describes the order.

2. Run the statement to create the table.

```
SQL> START CHP5.11

Table created.
```

3. Load CHP5.12.sql into the SQL buffer. The file contains a statement to restrict data based on the ORDER_DATE column. In this example, the customer service department can only work with orders that have an order date of today or later.

```
SQL>   GET CHP5.12
  1    CREATE OR REPLACE VIEW VIEW5_12 AS
  2    SELECT SALES_ID,
  3         ORDER_DATE,
  4         ORDER_DESC
  5    FROM
  6         SALES5_11
  7    WHERE
  8*       ORDER_DATE < SYSDATE
```

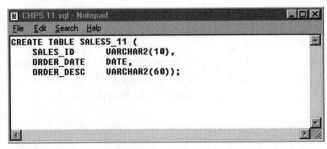

Figure 5-8 CHP5.11.sql creates the sample table used in How-To 5.5

Line 1 contains the CREATE OR REPLACE VIEW keywords to build the view and provides the name of the view. Lines 2 through 8 contain the query which generates the view's records. The WHERE clause in lines 7 and 8 specifies that the view will only return records where the ORDER_DATE column is less than the SYSDATE.

4. Run the statement to create the view.

```
SQL> /

View created.
```

5. Load CHP5.13.sql into the SQL buffer. The file contains a statement to insert a sample record into the table.

```
SQL>   GET CHP5.13
  1    INSERT INTO SALES5_11 (
  2      SALES_ID, ORDER_DATE, ORDER_DESC)
  3    VALUES
  4*     (USER, SYSDATE+5, 'FIVE DAYS LATER');
```

6. This statement inserts a record with an order date after today into the table. Even though the record will exist in the table, it will not appear in the view created in the previous steps. Run the statement to insert the record into the table and commit the transaction.

```
SQL> /

1 row created.

SQL> COMMIT;

Commit complete
```

7. Query the record from the SALES5_11 table. Since the table is not restricted, the row will be displayed.

```
SQL> SELECT * FROM SALES5_11;

SALES_ID   ORDER_DATE   ORDER_DESC
---------  -----------  --------------------------------
WAITE      06-APR-96    FIVE DAYS LATER
```

8. Query the record from the view. Since the view will not contain any rows with the ORDER_DATE column after the system date, no records will be retrieved.

```
SQL> SELECT * FROM VIEW5_12;

no rows selected.
```

9. Load CHP5.14.sql into the SQL buffer. The file contains a view that only returns rows with the SALES_ID column equal to the USER pseudo-column. Using the USER pseudo-column in the WHERE clause causes the view to return different results for each user account.

```
SQL>   GET CHP5.14
  1    CREATE OR REPLACE VIEW VIEW5_14 AS
  2    SELECT SALES_ID,
  3         ORDER_DATE,
  4         ORDER_DESC
  5    FROM
  6         CUST_SALES
  7    WHERE
  8*        SALES_ID = USER
```

Line 1 contains the keywords required to create the view and specifies the name of the view. Lines 2 through 8 contain the query used to generate records for the view. The WHERE clause in lines 7 and 8 returns rows only where the SALES_ID field is equal to the user account.

10. Create the view which restricts records based on the user account.

```
SQL> /

View created.
```

11. Query the view to determine if the record created in steps 5 and 6 exists in the view.

```
SQL> SELECT * FROM VIEW5_14;

SALES_ID ORDER_DATE  ORDER_DESC
-------- ----------- ------------------------------
WAITE    06-APR-96   FIVE DAYS LATER
```

How It Works

Steps 1 and 2 build a table that is the basis for the restricted view. Steps 3 and 4 create a view that only returns data if the ORDER_DATE column is less than SYSDATE. Steps 5 and 6 insert a record into the base table, which violates the WHERE clause of the view. Step 7 queries the table directly to display the data stored in it. Step 8 queries the view to show that the row is not returned by it. Steps 9 and 10 create a view that only lets a user whose account name is the same as the SALES_ID field display data. Step 11 queries the view to show that the user's data is returned by a query of the view.

Comments

Restricted views should be utilized to limit users to viewing data for their job function only. Restricting views can have a cascading effect. Restricting one table will have the effect of limiting the rows returned by other queries using the table.

COMPLEXITY
INTERMEDIATE

5.6 How do I...
Restrict insert of data into a view?

Problem

I use updatable views in my application to present a subset of the underlying table to the users. The users only see the data related to their job function, even though the table contains data for other areas. Although the users can only see their own data, I need to ensure that they cannot insert data for other areas. How do I restrict the insertion of data into a view?

Technique

The WITH CHECK OPTION clause of the CREATE VIEW statement restricts users from inserting data violating the WHERE clause of the view's query. If the user couldn't query a record from the view, he or she wouldn't be able to insert the record. The WITH CHECK OPTION clause is specified at the end of the CREATE VIEW statement.

Steps

1. Run SQL*Plus and connect as the WAITE user account. CHP5.15.sql, shown in Figure 5-9, creates the sample table that is the base table for the view created in the example.

The CREATE TABLE statement builds the DEPT5_15 table that will be the base table of the view created in the following steps. Run the statement to create the table.

2. Load CHP5.16.sql into the SQL buffer. The file contains a CREATE VIEW statement with the check option.

```
SQL> GET CHP5.16
  1   CREATE OR REPLACE VIEW VIEW5_16 AS
  2   SELECT DEPT_NO,
  3      DNAME
  4   FROM
  5     DEPT5_15
  6   WHERE
  7      DEPT_NO IN (4,5,6)
  8*  WITH CHECK OPTION
```

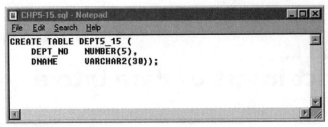

Figure 5-9 CHP5.15.sql creates the sample
objects used in How-To 5.6

Line 1 instructs Oracle to create the view or replace an existing one. Lines 2
and 3 show the two columns contained in the view. Lines 4 and 5 specify
the DEPT5_15 table as the base table of the view. Lines 6 and 7 specify the
departments to which the user account has access. Line 8 specifies the
WITH CHECK CONSTRAINT option.

3. Execute the statement to create the view.

```
SQL>  /
```

```
View created.
```

4. Load CHP5.17.sql into the SQL buffer. The file contains an INSERT statement to attempt to create an invalid record.

```
SQL>  GET CHP5.17
  1    INSERT INTO
  2      VIEW5_16(DEPT_NO, DNAME)
  3*   VALUES (1, 'TEST DEPARTMENT')
```

5. Execute the statement to insert the record.

```
SQL>  /
insert into view5_16(dept_no, dname) values
*
ERROR at line 1:
ORA-01402: view WITH CHECK OPTION where-clause violation
```

How It Works

Step 1 creates the sample table used as the base table in the following steps. Steps
2 and 3 create a view restricting the data which can be queried from the view or inserted into it. The WITH CHECK OPTION clause on the CREATE TABLE statement prevents
data that would not satisfy the query's WHERE clause from being inserted. Steps 4
and 5 attempt to insert invalid data into the table. Step 5 fails since the invalid record
cannot be inserted into the view.

Comments

If a user account is restricted from accessing data through a view, you will want to restrict the user from inserting data he or she couldn't normally query. If views are being used to restrict data, the WITH CHECK OPTION clause is a good way to stop users from inserting unwanted data.

COMPLEXITY
ADVANCED

5.7 How do I...
Create a view with errors?

Problem

I need to be able to force the creation of views, even if the SELECT statement of the view is invalid. The query used in the view does not contain syntax errors, but the tables used in the query may not exist when the view is created. As part of our batch operations, the tables will be created later in the process. How do I create a view containing errors?

Technique

The FORCE option in the CREATE VIEW statement forces the view to be created even if the query cannot be run. The statement will show compilation errors when run, but the view will still be created in the data dictionary. The view will be marked as INVALID in the data dictionary and must be recompiled in order to execute. The view will be recompiled automatically the first time it is used, or it can be compiled manually with an ALTER VIEW statement containing a COMPILE clause.

Steps

1. Run SQL*Plus and connect as the WAITE user account. Load CHP5.18.sql into the SQL buffer. The file contains a CREATE VIEW statement with the FORCE option to create a view on a non-existent base table.

```
SQL>   GET CHP5.18
  1    CREATE FORCE VIEW
  2         VIEW5_18
  3    AS SELECT
  4         DEPT_NO,
  5         DNAME,
  6         MGR_ID
  7*   FROM TAB5_19
```

Line 1 contains a FORCE clause which will create the view in the data dictionary even if the query is invalid. Line 7 specifies a table in the FROM clause, which does not exist.

2. Execute the statement to create the view.

```
SQL>  /
```

Warning: View created with compilation errors.

3. Attempt to query the view.

```
SQL>  SELECT *
  2>      FROM VIEW5_18;
```

```
select * from view5_18
         *
ERROR at line 1:
ORA-04063: view "WAITE.VIEW5_18" has errors
```

The Oracle ORA-04063 error is returned since the view is invalid. Oracle attempts to recompile an invalid view when it is referenced by a query. Since the table does not exist, the recompile fails.

4. Load CHP5.19.sql into the SQL buffer. The file contains a CREATE TABLE statement to build the table referenced in the view.

```
SQL>  GET CHP5.19
  1   CREATE TABLE TAB5_19 (
  2       DEPT_NO   NUMBER(10),
  3       DNAME     VARCHAR2(10),
  4*      MGR_ID    NUMBER(10))
```

The TAB5_19 table contains all of the columns referenced by the view. If it did not, the view would remain invalid after the next compile attempt.

5. Execute the statement to create the table.

```
SQL>  /
```

Table created.

The view is still invalid until the next attempt to reference it.

6. Load CHP5.20.sql into the SQL buffer. The file contains an ALTER VIEW statement with a COMPILE clause that forces the compilation of the view.

```
SQL>  GET CHP5.20
  1*  ALTER VIEW VIEW5_18 COMPILE
```

7. Execute the statement to compile the view.

```
SQL>  /
```

View altered.

The statement compiles the view and makes it valid. Any references to the view will not return errors.

How It Works

Steps 1 and 2 create a view using a CREATE VIEW statement with a FORCE clause. The query used in the view is invalid since the table referenced does not exist. The view is created with a warning explaining that the view has errors. Step 3 attempts to query the invalid view and returns an error. Steps 4 and 5 create the table referenced by the view. Creating the table does not automatically recompile the view. Steps 6 and 7 manually compile the view by using an ALTER VIEW statement with the COMPILE clause. If Steps 6 and 7 were not performed, the view would be recompiled automatically the next time it is referenced.

Comments

It is possible to create a view which contains an invalid query. The query cannot contain syntax errors, but tables or columns referenced in the query do not have to exist. The FORCE option in the CREATE VIEW statement allows invalid views to be created. When performing system maintenance or rebuilding a database, the FORCE option is useful.

COMPLEXITY
INTERMEDIATE

5.8 How do I...
Simplify privilege maintenance using views?

Problem

Whenever a table is dropped and re-created, the privileges granted to user accounts and roles are lost and must be regranted. Tables are re-created in our system regularly as part of some data transfer processes. How can I simplify privilege maintenance using views?

Technique

Views can be granted many of the same privileges as tables. If data management operations can be performed on the view, granting privileges to the view has the same effect as granting privileges to the base table. Unlike tables, views can be replaced using the CREATE OR REPLACE keywords. When a view is replaced, privileges granted to the view are not lost. If the base table of a view is removed, the view becomes invalid but the privileges remain intact. If the base tables are re-created before an operation is performed on the view, no errors will occur.

Steps

1. Run SQL*Plus and connect as the WAITE user account. CHP5.21.sql, shown in Figure 5-10, creates a base table, view, and user account and grants privileges on the view to the new user account.

The table TAB5_21 is created by the CREATE TABLE statement. The view VIEW5_21 queries all of the records from the table. The first GRANT statement creates the HENRY user account and grants the CONNECT default role to it. The last statement grants all privileges on the view to the new user account. Run the file to create the base table, view, and user account.

```
Table created.

View created.

Grant succeeded.

Grant succeeded.
```

Once the sample objects are created, the HENRY user account can perform data manipulation operations which affect the base table by using the view. The user account cannot perform these operations directly on the table since it has only been granted privileges on the view.

2. Connect to the HENRY user account created in the last step and load CHP5.22.sql into the SQL buffer. The file contains an INSERT statement to insert data into the view. Since the HENRY user account was granted privileges on the view, the command will succeed.

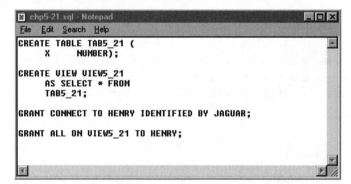

Figure 5-10 CHP5.21.sql creates the sample table and view used in How-To 5.8

```
SQL> CONNECT HENRY/JAGUAR

Connected.

SQL> GET CHP5.22
  1   INSERT INTO
  2       WAITE.VIEW5_21 (X)
  3   VALUES
  4*      (20)
```

The INSERT statement will create a single record in the base table by inserting the record into the view.

3. Run the statement to insert the record into the view.

```
SQL>  /

1 row created.
```

4. Load CHP5.23.sql into the SQL buffer. The file contains an INSERT table to insert a record into the base table referenced by the view.

```
SQL> GET CHP5.23
  1   INSERT INTO
  2     WAITE.TAB5_21 (DEPT_NO)
  3   VALUES
  4*      (21)
```

The INSERT statement attempts to insert a single record into the base table directly. Since the user account does not have privileges directly on the view, the operation will fail.

5. Run the statement to insert the record. Since the GREG user account was not granted privileges on the base table of the view, the statement will fail.

```
SQL>  /

insert into waite.tab5_21
*
ERROR at line 1:
ORA-00942: table or view does not exist
```

6. Connect as the WAITE user account and run CHP5.24.sql. The file shown in Figure 5-11 drops and re-creates the base table, but does not grant new privileges.

The DROP TABLE statement drops the base table of the view. The second statement rebuilds the table exactly like the original table created in Step 1.

```
SQL> CONNECT WAITE/PRESS

Connected.

SQL> START CHP5.24

Table dropped.

Table created.
```

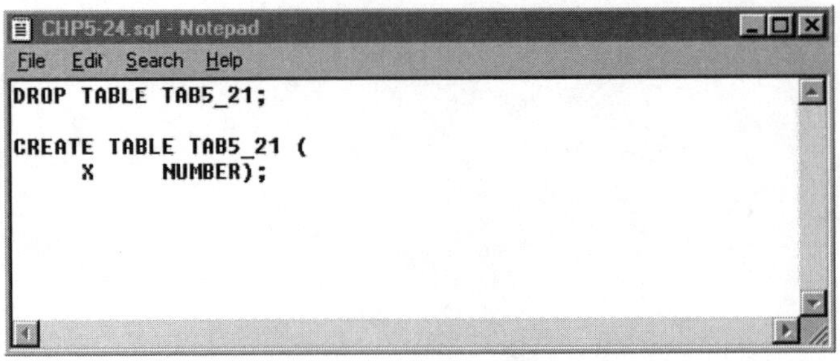

Figure 5-11 CHP5.24.sql drops and re-creates the base table of the view

Even though the table has been dropped and re-created, the GREG user account still has privileges on the view referencing the table. Data manipulation can still be performed through the view.

7. Connect as the HENRY user account and load CHP5.25.sql into the SQL buffer. Since the GREG user account was granted privileges on the view, the INSERT statement contained in the file will succeed.

```
SQL> CONNECT HENRY/JAGUAR

Connected.

SQL> GET CHP5.25
  1   INSERT INTO
  2       WAITE.VIEW5_21 (DEPT_NO)
  3   VALUES
  4*      (20)
```

8. Run the statement to insert the record. Even though the table was dropped and re-created, the privileges on the view remain intact.

```
SQL> /

1 row created.
```

How It Works

Step 1 creates a table and view and a user account to receive the privileges. It grants all privileges on the view to the new user account. Steps 2 and 3 connect to the new user account and insert a record into the base table through the view. Steps 4 and 5 attempt to insert a record directly into the base table. Since the privileges on the base table have not been granted to the new user account, the statement fails. Step 6 connects to the WAITE user account and drops and re-creates the base table of the view. Steps 7 and 8 show that the privileges on the view remain intact by inserting records into the view as the new user account.

Comments

The method presented in this How-To simplifies the maintenance of privileges in environments where tables are dropped and recreated regularly. In many environments where data is transferred from a mainframe database into Oracle, tables might be dropped as part of the process. The ability to grant privileges to views makes it easier to maintain privileges within the Oracle environment.

CHAPTER 6
SEQUENCES

6

SEQUENCES

How do I...

6.1 **Create a sequence to generate a unique number?**

6.2 **List the available sequences?**

6.3 **Change the minimum or maximum value of a sequence?**

6.4 **Change the current value of a sequence?**

6.5 **Retrieve the value of a sequence without incrementing it?**

A *sequence* generates a sequential number in Oracle. Prior to the availability of sequences in version 6.0, sequential values had to be generated programmatically. In order to generate a primary key, the application had to either maintain a table containing the next sequential value or query the largest key value from the table and increment it. Neither method worked very well, since only one user could create a new record at a time and locking problems would occur. Sequential numbers can be generated with sequences forward or backward, and a sequence can start at any number. Generating a number with a sequence is very fast, since sequence values are maintained in the System Global Area (SGA) while the database is running. This chapter explores the use of sequences within Oracle. The examples presented in this chapter can be found on the accompanying CD-ROM in the \SAMPLES\CHAP6 directory. You can copy them into your SQL*Plus working directory or specify the full pathname when using the START or GET command in SQL*Plus.

6.1 Create a sequence to generate a unique number

Sequences can be created with a variety of options. Where the sequences starts, how it is incremented, and the allowable range of values can all be specified when the sequence is created. This How-To covers the task of creating a new sequence and specifying its parameters.

6.2 List the available sequences

The sequences available to the user can be queried from data dictionary views. The ALL_SEQUENCES data dictionary view provides information about the sequences to which a user account has access. This How-To covers the topic of determining the sequences available to a user account.

6.3 Change the minimum or maximum value of a sequence

The minimum and maximum values of a sequence specify the sequence range. After a sequence is created, the values of these parameters can be changed using the ALTER SEQUENCE statement. This How-To covers the process of changing the parameter values of a sequence.

6.4 Change the current value of a sequence

It is sometimes necessary to change the value of a sequence. Oracle has no straightforward method for changing the current value of a sequence. This How-To presents the steps required to change the value of a sequence and the SQL scripts used to do so.

6.5 Retrieve the value of a sequence without incrementing it

It is sometimes necessary to retrieve the value of a sequence without incrementing it. Numerous times within a session a sequence can be referred to without incrementing it. This How-To covers the topic of retrieving a sequence value without incrementing the sequence.

COMPLEXITY
BEGINNING

6.1 How do I...
Create a sequence to generate a unique number?

Problem

I need to generate a sequential number for my application. The number will be used as the primary key of a table and must be unique. How do I create a sequence to generate a unique number?

```
                CREATE SEQUENCE Syntax

        CREATE SEQUENCE name
           { START WITH integer
           { INCREMENT BY integer }
           { MAXVALUE integer | NOMAXVALUE }
           { MINVALUE integer | NOMINVALUE }
           { CYCLE | NOCYCLE }
           { CACHE integer | NOCACHE }
           { ORDER | NOORDER }
```

Figure 6-1 CREATE SEQUENCE syntax

Technique

The CREATE SEQUENCE statement is used to create a new sequence. The syntax of the statement is shown in Figure 6-1.

The INCREMENT BY clause tells the sequence how to increment the counter. The value can be positive to increment forward, or negative to decrement backward. The START WITH clause defines the value the sequence will return the first time it is used. The MINVALUE and MAXVALUE clauses define the range of the sequence. If not specified, the sequence will have no minimum or maximum value. Information about sequences contained in the database can be queried from the USER_SEQUENCES and ALL_SEQUENCES data dictionary views. Figure 6-2 shows the description of the ALL_SEQUENCES view within SQL*Plus.

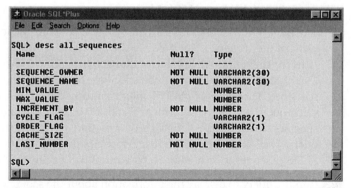

Figure 6-2 The ALL_SEQUENCES data dictionary view

Steps

1. Run SQL*Plus and connect as the WAITE user account. Load CHP6-1.sql into the SQL buffer. The file contains a CREATE SEQUENCE statement to create a new sequence.

```
SQL> GET CHP6-1
  1* CREATE SEQUENCE SEQ6_1
```

The CREATE SEQUENCE keywords are required to create a new sequence. Since no other options are specified, the sequence will contain default values for all the parameters and start with 1.

2. Execute the statement to create the sequence.

```
SQL> /
```

```
Sequence created.
```

Once the sequence is created, it can be used by the current user account or any user account granted SELECT privileges. The SEQ6_1.NEXTVAL pseudo-column can be queried within an application to increment the sequence and return the next value of the sequence.

3. Load CHP6-2.sql into the SQL buffer. The file contains a query of the USER_SEQUENCES data dictionary view to show information about the sequence created in the previous step.

```
SQL> GET CHP6-2
  1   SELECT
  2      MIN_VALUE,
  3      MAX_VALUE,
  4      INCREMENT_BY,
  5      LAST_NUMBER
  6   FROM USER_SEQUENCES
  7* WHERE SEQUENCE_NAME = 'SEQ6_1'
```

The MIN_VALUE column returned by line 2 contains the lowest possible value of the sequence. The MAX_VALUE column returned by line 3 contains the highest possible value of the sequence. Line 4 returns the INCREMENT_BY column, which specifies the value used to increment the sequence. The LAST_NUMBER column returned by line 4 contains the last value queried from the sequence. The FROM clause contained in line 6 specifies the USER_SEQUENCES data dictionary view as the source of the query. The WHERE clause in line 7 specifies that information about the SEQ6_1 sequence created in Steps 1 and 2 will be returned by the query.

4. Run the query to display the information about the sequence.

```
SQL> /
```

```
MIN_VALUE MAX_VALUE INCREMENT_BY LAST_NUMBER
--------- --------- ------------ -----------
        1 1.000E+27            1           1
```

The query returns a single record for the sequence. Since the sequence started with 1 by default and no maximum value was specified, 1 is returned as the minimum value and an extremely large number is returned as the maximum value.

5. Load CHP6-3.sql into the SQL buffer. The file contains a CREATE SEQUENCE statement which generates descending numbers.

```
SQL> GET CHP6-3
  1   CREATE SEQUENCE SEQ6_3
  2      START WITH 1000
  3      MAXVALUE 1000
  4*     INCREMENT BY -1
```

Line 1 contains the keywords required to create the sequence and give it a name. The START WITH clause contained in line 2 specifies that the sequence starts at 1,000. The MAXVALUE clause specified in line 2 provides the largest value the sequence can contain, and the negative number in the INCREMENT BY clause in line 4 creates a descending sequence.

6. Run the statement to create the sequence.

```
SQL> /
```

```
Sequence created.
```

The first value returned when the sequence is queried will be 1,000, since it was specified in the START WITH clause. The negative value in the INCREMENT BY clause decreases the sequence each time it is queried.

How It Works

Steps 1 and 2 create a sequence with default values for parameters. When a sequence is created with default values, it starts with 1 and has no upper limit. Steps 3 and 4 query the USER_SEQUENCES view to display information about the sequence created in the first two steps. Steps 5 and 6 create a sequence that starts with 1,000 and generates numbers in descending order. Sequential values are queried from a sequence using the NEXTVAL pseudo-column.

Comments

Sequences are the best way to generate sequential numbers in Oracle. After creating a sequence, privileges need to be granted to user accounts or roles just like tables. Synonyms can be created on sequences to provide ownership and location transparency. Chapter 7, Synonyms, covers tasks related to synonyms in detail.

6.2 How do I...
List the available sequences?

Problem

I need to determine the sequences I have available to use within my applications. It is possible to have many sequences available, and I need to know which ones I can use. How do I list the available sequences?

Technique

The USER_SEQUENCES and ALL_SEQUENCES views contain the sequences available to a user. The ALL_SEQUENCES view contains sequences owned by the user account and those granted to the user account. The columns contained in the ALL_SEQUENCES view is shown in Figure 6-2 in How-To 6.1.

Steps

1. Run SQL*Plus and connect as the WAITE user account. Load CHP6-4.sql into the SQL buffer. The file contains a query to display the sequences in the user account's schema and sequences on which the user account has privileges.

```
SQL> GET CHP6-4
  1  SELECT
  2     SEQUENCE_OWNER||'.'||SEQUENCE_NAME
  3* FROM ALL_SEQUENCES
```

Line 2 uses the concatenation operator (||) to concatenate the owner of the sequence and the name of the sequence. This produces a single column in the standard owner.object format. The FROM clause in line 3 specifies the ALL_SEQUENCES view as the source of the data.

2. Run the query to view the sequences. Since the WAITE user account has been granted the DBA role, the list of sequences is very long. The listing shown below has been abbreviated to conserve space.

```
SQL> /

SEQUENCE_OWNER||'.'||SEQUENCE_NAME
------------------------------------------------------------
SYS.AUDSES$
SYS.BROWSER_SEQ
SYS.DBMS_LOCK_ID
SYS.JOBSEQ
SYS.LABEL_TRANSLATION
SYS.OBJECT_GRANT
```

```
SYS.ORA_TQ_BASE$
SYS.PROFNUM$
SYS.RGROUPSEQ
SYS.SYSTEM_GRANT
```

Because the concatenation operator was used to combine the owner of the sequence with its name, the output is displayed in the format that would be used to reference the sequence.

How It Works

Steps 1 and 2 query the ALL_SEQUENCES data dictionary view to list the sequences available to the user. The SEQUENCE_OWNER column contains the owner of the column. The SEQUENCE_NAME column contains the name of the sequence. The concatenation operator (||) was used to generate the output in the same format used to reference the sequence.

Comments

The data dictionary is the source of information about objects in the database. The ALL_SEQUENCES and USER_SEQUENCES data dictionary views provides information about sequences in the database. If you need to list information about the sequences in your schema, use the USER_SEQUENCES view. If you need to know about sequences to which you have been granted privileges, use the ALL_SEQUENCES view.

COMPLEXITY
INTERMEDIATE

6.3 How do I...
Change the minimum or maximum value of a sequence?

Problem

When I created a sequence, I specified a minimum and maximum value. I need to change the values or remove them completely. How do I change the minimum or maximum value of a sequence?

Technique

The ALTER SEQUENCE statement shown in Figure 6-3 is used to change the values of certain sequence parameters. The MINVALUE and MAXVALUE parameters can be changed using this statement. The NOMINVALUE parameter removes the

```
              ALTER SEQUENCE Syntax


       ALTER SEQUENCE name
          { INCREMENT BY integer }
          { MAXVALUE integer | NOMAXVALUE }
          { MINVALUE integer | NOMINVALUE }
          { CYCLE | NOCYCLE }
          { CACHE integer | NOCACHE }
          { ORDER | NOORDER }
```

Figure 6-3 The syntax of the ALTER SEQUENCE statement

minimum value from the sequence. The NOMAXVALUE parameter removes the maximum value from the sequence.

Steps

1. Run SQL*Plus and connect as the WAITE user account. Load CHP6-5.sql into the SQL buffer. The file contains a CREATE SEQUENCE statement to build a sequence containing minimum and maximum value parameters.

```
SQL> GET CHP6-5
    1   CREATE SEQUENCE
    2       SEQ6_5
    3   START WITH 100
    4   INCREMENT BY 1
    5   MINVALUE 1
    6*  MAXVALUE 1000
```

Line 1 contains the required keywords to create a new sequence. Line 2 provides the name of the sequence. The START WITH clause contained in line 3 causes the sequence to start with 100. Line 4 contains the INCREMENT BY clause, which causes the sequence to increment forward one value each time it's used. The MINVALUE clause in line 5 specifies the lowest possible value for the sequence as 1, and the MAXVALUE clause specifies the highest possible value of the sequence as 1,000.

2. Run the statement to create the sequence.

```
SQL> /
```

```
Sequence created.
```

The sequence created in the first two steps will be altered in the following steps using the ALTER SEQUENCE statement.

3. Load CHP6-6.sql into the SQL buffer. The file contains an ALTER SEQUENCE statement to change the minimum and maximum value parameters of the sequence.

```
SQL> GET CHP6-6
  1  ALTER SEQUENCE
  2     SEQ6_5
  3  MINVALUE 50
  4* MAXVALUE 10000
```

Line 1 contains the ALTER SEQUENCE keywords to specify that a sequence will be modified by the statement. Line 2 contains the name of the sequence created in the previous steps. Line 3 contains the MINVALUE clause, setting the new minimum value for the sequence at 50. The MAXVALUE clause in line 4 sets the new maximum value of the sequence to 10,000.

4. Run the statement to modify the sequence.

```
SQL> /
```

```
Sequence altered.
```

Once the sequence is altered, the new parameters take effect immediately.

5. Load CHP6-7.sql into the SQL buffer. The file contains an ALTER SEQUENCE statement to remove the minimum and maximum values from the sequence.

```
SQL> GET CHP6-7
  1  ALTER SEQUENCE
  2     SEQ6_5
  3  NOMINVALUE
  4* NOMAXVALUE
```

Line 1 contains the keywords required to modify the parameters of a sequence. Line 3 removes the minimum value of the sequence by specifying the NOMINVALUE clause. Line 4 removes the maximum value of the sequence by specifying the NOMAXVALUE clause. The other parameter values are left unchanged by the statement.

6. Run the statement to modify the sequence.

```
SQL> /
```

```
Sequence altered.
```

How It Works

Steps 1 and 2 create the sample sequence modified in this How-To. A minimum value of 1 and a maximum value of 1,000 are specified in the CREATE SEQUENCE statement. Steps 3 and 4 use the ALTER SEQUENCE statement to change the minimum value to 50 and maximum value to 10,000. Steps 5 and 6 remove both the minimum and maximum values by using the NOMINVALUE and NOMAXVALUE parameters in the ALTER SEQUENCE statement.

Comments

The ALTER SEQUENCE statement can be used to change most of the parameters set for a sequence, but not the value of a sequence. How-To 6.4 covers the method used to change the value of a sequence.

COMPLEXITY
ADVANCED

6.4 How do I...
Change the current value of a sequence?

Problem

There are occasions when I want to change the value of a sequence. For example, at the beginning of every year we want our invoice numbers to start at 1 again. I noticed that the START WITH clause is not available in the ALTER SEQUENCE statement. How do I change the value of a sequence?

Technique

There is no direct way to change the value of a sequence. In order to change the value of a sequence, the sequence must be dropped and re-created with the new parameters. The USER_SEQUENCES data dictionary view contains the information needed to build a CREATE SEQUENCE statement from an existing sequence. This statement can be modified so the new sequence starts with a different number. When the original sequence is dropped, all of the privileges granted to it are lost. When the sequence is rebuilt, the privileges the original sequence had must be re-created.

Steps

1. Run SQL*Plus and connect as the WAITE user account. CHP6-8.sql, shown in Figure 6-4, contains a CREATE SEQUENCE statement to create the sequence used in this How-To.

The sequence created in the script starts with a value of 1 and grants all privileges to the PUBLIC user group. Granting all privileges to the PUBLIC

user group gives all users of the database access to the sequence. Run the
file to create the sample sequence.

```
SQL> START CHP6-8

Sequence created.

Grant complete.
```

2. Load CHP6-9.sql into the SQL buffer. The file contains a query to re-create
all grants on a sequence. Since the sequence value must be changed by
dropping and re-creating the sequence, we need to restore the privileges
granted to the sequence when re-creating it.

```
SQL> GET CHP6-9
  1  SELECT 'GRANT '||
  2     PRIVILEGE||
  3     ' ON '||
  4     TABLE_SCHEMA||'.'||TABLE_NAME||
  5     ' TO '||GRANTEE||';'
  6  FROM ALL_TAB_PRIVS
  7     WHERE
  8     TABLE_SCHEMA = USER AND
  9     TABLE_NAME = '&SEQUENCE'
 10  UNION
 11  SELECT 'GRANT '||
 12     PRIVILEGE||
 13     ' ON '||
 14     OWNER||'.'||TABLE_NAME||
 15     ' TO '||ROLE||';'
 16  FROM ROLE_TAB_PRIVS
 17     WHERE
 18     OWNER = USER AND
 19*    TABLE_NAME = '&SEQUENCE'
```

Privileges must be re-created for grants made directly to user accounts, as
well as privileges granted through roles. Lines 1 through 7 create GRANT
statements for all user accounts granted privileges on the sequence by
querying the ALL_TAB_PRIVS data dictionary view. Lines 9 through 17 create GRANT statements for all roles granted privileges on the sequence by
querying the ROLE_TAB_PRIVS data dictionary view. The UNION operator

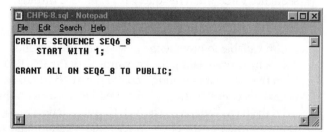

Figure 6-4 CHP6-8.sql creates the sequence used
in How-To 6.4

is used to connect the two queries. For more information about the UNION operator, see How-To 9.11.

3. Set the HEADING and FEEDBACK system variables OFF and spool the output of the statement to a file. Run the statement to build the GRANT statements, replacing the &SEQUENCE substitution variable with SEQ6_8.

```
SQL> SET HEADING OFF
SQL> SET FEEDBACK OFF
SQL> SET VERIFY OFF
SQL> SPOOL GRANTS.sql
SQL> /

Enter value for sequence: SEQ6_8
Enter value for sequence: SEQ6_8

GRANT ALTER ON WAITE.SEQ6_8 TO PUBLIC;
GRANT SELECT ON WAITE.SEQ6_8 TO PUBLIC;
```

The SELECT and ALTER privileges were granted to the sequence in Step 1 when ALL privileges were granted to the PUBLIC user account.

4. Execute the SPOOL OFF command to close the output file, and load CHP6-10.sql into the SQL buffer. The file contains a statement to build the CREATE SEQUENCE statement for re-creating a sequence. The START WITH clause is modified to start the sequence with the new sequence number.

```
SQL> SPOOL OFF
SQL> GET CHP6-10
  1  SELECT 'CREATE SEQUENCE '||SEQUENCE_NAME||
  2      ' START WITH '||'&STARTVALUE'||
  3      ' INCREMENT BY '||INCREMENT_BY||
  4      ' MINVALUE '||TO_CHAR(MIN_VALUE,'9.99EEEE')||
  5      ' MAXVALUE '||TO_CHAR(MAX_VALUE,'9.99EEEE')||
  6      DECODE(CYCLE_FLAG,'Y',' CYCLE',' NOCYCLE')||
  7      ' CACHE '||TO_CHAR(CACHE_SIZE)||';' A
  8  FROM USER_SEQUENCES
  9  WHERE
 10* SEQUENCE_NAME = '&SEQUENCE'
```

The substitution variable &STARTVALUE in line 2 is replaced by the new sequence value when the query runs. Lines 2 through 7 query the existing parameters of the sequence from the data dictionary to build the statement. Line 2 builds the START WITH clause and uses the &STARTVALUE substitution variable to provide the new value. Line 3 builds the INCREMENT BY clause by concatenating the keywords with the INCREMENT_BY column from the view. Lines 4 and 5 rebuild the MINVALUE and MAXVALUE clauses by concatenating the required keywords with the values returned from the data dictionary. The TO_CHAR function is used to convert the value returned by the query to scientific notation. Line 6 uses the DECODE function to build the CYCLE or NOCYCLE clauses, based on the value of the CYCLE_FLAG column in the view. Line 7 creates the CACHE SIZE clause using the CACHE_SIZE column from the view. The WHERE clause in lines 9 and 10 executes the query for the sequence represented by the &SEQUENCE substitution variable.

5. Set the HEADING system variable to OFF to remove the heading from the output of the query. Format the column with a COLUMN command to wrap the query output to multiple lines. Spool the output of the query to a file and execute the statement.

```
SQL> SET HEADING OFF
SQL> COLUMN A FORMAT A50
SQL> SET VERIFY OFF
SQL> SPOOL CREATES.sql
SQL> /

Enter value for startvalue: 100
Enter value for sequence: SEQ6_8

CREATE SEQUENCE SEQ6_8 START WITH 100 INCREMENT BY 1 MINVALUE
  1.00E+00 MAXVALUE  1.00E+27 NOCYCLE CACHE 20;
```

The SET HEADING OFF command removes the unwanted heading information. The SET VERIFY OFF command removes the extra lines generated when the substitution variables are set.

6. Stop spooling the file and drop the sequence.

```
SQL> SPOOL OFF
SQL> DROP SEQUENCE SEQ6_8;

Sequence dropped.
```

7. Set the values of the FEEDBACK and HEADING system variables to ON, and rebuild the sequence by running the file created in Step 5.

```
SQL> SET FEEDBACK ON
SQL> SET HEADING ON
SQL> START CREATES.sql
unknown command beginning "Enter valu..." - rest of line ignored.
unknown command beginning "Enter valu..." - rest of line ignored.

Sequence created.

unknown command beginning "SQL> spool..." - rest of line ignored.
```

The errors displayed are from the unnecessary text included in the output file from Step 5. The errors can be ignored or removed by editing the script file in a text editor before executing it.

8. Re-create the privileges granted on the sequence by running the script created in Step 3.

```
SQL> START GRANTS
unknown command beginning "Enter valu..." - rest of line ignored.
unknown command beginning "Enter valu..." - rest of line ignored.
```

continued on next page

continued from previous page
Grant succeeded.

Grant succeeded.

Once the grants are re-created on the sequence, you can can use it in applications.

How It Works

In order to change the value of a sequence, it must be re-created with a new starting value. Step 1 creates the sequence used throughout this How-To to demonstrate this technique. Once the sequence is dropped and re-created, the privileges granted on the sequence must be regranted. Steps 2 and 3 build a SQL script to re-create the privileges granted on the sequence. Steps 4 and 5 build a script file which re-creates the sequence with the new starting value. Step 6 drops the existing sequence. Step 7 re-creates the sequence using the script created in Steps 4 and 5. Step 8 grants privileges on the sequence using the script created in Steps 2 and 3.

Comments

Unfortunately, Oracle does not have an easy method for changing the value of a sequence. The NEW_SEQUENCE_VALUE procedure contained in the DBA_TOOLS package on the accompanying CD-ROM performs all of the tasks from this How-To in a single step for users of Oracle 7.1 or higher.

COMPLEXITY
BEGINNING

6.5   How do I...
Retrieve the value of a sequence without incrementing it?

Problem

After I retrieve a value from a sequence, I want to use that same value in other places in the application without incrementing the sequence. How do I retrieve a value from a sequence without incrementing it?

Technique

The CURRVAL pseudo-column within a sequence allows a sequence value to be queried without incrementing it. The CURRVAL pseudo-column cannot be queried until a NEXTVAL pseudo-column is queried for the sequence during the session. This keeps an application from using a sequence value created by another user or application.

Steps

1. Run SQL*Plus and connect as the WAITE user account. CHP6-11.sql, shown in Figure 6-5, contains a CREATE SEQUENCE statement that develops the sequence used throughout this How-To.

Run the file to create the sequence.

```
SQL> START CHP6-11

Sequence created.
```

2. Load CHP6-12.sql into the SQL buffer. The file contains a query of the NEXTVAL pseudo-column from the SEQ6_11 sequence. The NEXTVAL pseudo-column increments the sequence and retrieves the next value.

```
SQL> GET CHP6-12
  1   SELECT
  2       SEQ6_11.NEXTVAL
  3*  FROM DUAL
```

Line 2 provides the syntax used to retrieve the next value from a sequence. The DUAL system table is used as the source of the query and always returns a single value.

3. Execute the statement to query the sequence.

```
NEXTVAL
---------
        1
```

Once the NEXTVAL pseudo-column is retrieved from the sequence in the current session, the CURRVAL pseudo-column can be used to retrieve the same number repeatedly.

4. Load CHP6-13 into the SQL buffer. The file contains a query that uses the CURRVAL pseudo-column to retrieve a value from the sequence without incrementing it.

```
SQL> GET CHP6-13
  1   SELECT
  2       SEQ6_11.CURRVAL
  3*  FROM DUAL
```

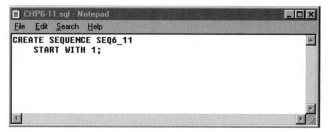

Figure 6-5 CHP6-11.sql creates the sequence used in How-To 6.5

Line 2 presents the CURRVAL pseudo-column used to return the current value from a sequence. The value returned will always be the last value returned by the NEXTVAL pseudo-column in the same session.

5. Execute the query to retrieve the current value of the sequence.

```
SQL> /

CURRVAL
---------
        1
```

The value returned by the query is the same as the value returned by the NEXTVAL pseudo-column in Step 3.

How It Works

The same value can be repeatedly retrieved from a sequence by first querying the NEXTVAL pseudo-column, then the CURRVAL pseudo-column for all subsequent queries. Step 1 creates the sample sequence used throughout this How-To and specifies a starting value of 1. Steps 2 and 3 retrieve a value from the sequence by querying the NEXTVAL pseudo-column from it. Once the value has been queried, the CURRVAL pseudo-column can be used in the session. Steps 4 and 5 query the same value by specifying the CURRVAL pseudo-column sequence.

Comments

The NEXTVAL pseudo-column must be queried before the CURRVAL pseudo-column can be queried within the session. An alternate method is to query NEXTVAL into a global variable to use throughout your application.

CHAPTER 7
SYNONYMS

SYNONYMS

How do I...

A *synonym* is an alias for a database object. A synonym provides a name for the object hiding the actual owner, location, or name of the object. Synonyms are created so the application only needs to know the name of the synonym, instead of the schema, name, and location of the object. By using synonyms, the application developer does not need to know which user account will eventually own the database object or where the object will reside on the network. A developer uses a synonym within an application just like a table or view contained in the user account's schema. The synonym is used without referencing a schema name. The examples presented in this chapter are located on the accompanying CD in the \SAMPLES\CHAP7 directory. Copy the .SQL files into your SQL*Plus working directory, or specify the full pathname when executing GET or START commands in SQL*Plus.

7.1 Determine the object a synonym references

Each synonym references an object within Oracle. If an incorrect object is referenced by a synonym, applications may not perform correctly. This How-To explains how to determine the object that a synonym references.

7.2   Create synonyms for all objects in a schema

If an application is not using public synonyms, a user account may create private synonyms referencing the application's objects in the object owner's schema. If synonyms do not exist, objects owned by other user accounts must be referenced using the schema.objectname format. This How-To presents a method for creating private synonyms for all objects in another user account's schema.

7.3   List synonyms referencing an object

An object can be referenced by many synonyms, including one or more public synonyms and many user account's private synonyms. Deleting or changing the name of an object will invalidate all the synonyms referencing the object. This How-To presents a method to list all synonyms pointing to an object.

7.4   Drop all invalid synonyms in a schema

When the object referenced by a synonym no longer exists, the synonym becomes invalid. It is an important system maintenance task to remove invalid synonyms. This How-To presents a method for deleting invalid synonyms from a user account's schema.

COMPLEXITY
BEGINNING

7.1   How do I...
Determine the object a synonym references?

Problem

I have many private synonyms in my schema, and there are many public synonyms in the database. Sometimes an application does not perform as expected when a synonym references a different object than I had anticipated. How do I determine the object to which a synonym points?

Technique

The USER_SYNONYMS and ALL_SYNONYMS data dictionary views provide information about the synonyms to which a user has access. The USER_SYNONYMS view contains only private synonyms existing in the user account's schema. The ALL_SYNONYMS view, shown in Figure 7-1, contains information about both public and private synonyms.

Steps

1. Run SQL*Plus and connect as the WAITE user account. CHP7-1.sql, shown in Figure 7-2, creates the synonym used throughout this How-To.

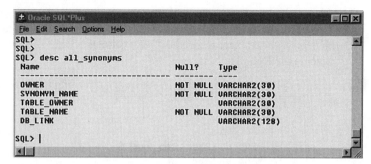

Figure 7-1 The ALL_SYNONYMS data dictionary view

The DUAL7_1 synonym is created by the CREATE SYNONYM statement and references the SYS.DUAL table. Run the file to create the sample synonym.

```
SQL> START CHP7-1

Synonym created.
```

Once the synonym is created, information about it can be queried from the ALL_SYNONYMS data dictionary view.

2. Load CHP7-2.sql into the SQL buffer. The file contains a query to determine the object a synonym references.

```
SQL>   GET CHP7-2
  1   SELECT
  2     OWNER,
  3     TABLE_OWNER,
  4     TABLE_NAME,
  5     DB_LINK
  6   FROM
  7     ALL_SYNONYMS
  8   WHERE
  9     SYNONYM_NAME = '&SYNONYM_NAME'
 10   AND OWNER IN (USER, 'PUBLIC')
```

The OWNER column in line 2 returns the owner of the synonym. If the value is PUBLIC, the synonym is public and available to all users of the database. The TABLE_OWNER and TABLE_NAME columns in lines 3 and

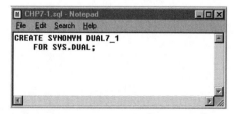

Figure 7-2 CHP7-1.sql creates the synonym used throughout How-To 7.1

4 return the owner and name of the object referenced by the synonym. The DB_LINK column in line 5 returns the database link identifying where on the network the object is located. If the value is NULL, the location of the object is the local database.

3. Execute the statement to perform the query replacing the substitution variable with DUAL7_1.

```
SQL> /

old  9:     SYNONYM_NAME = '&SYNONYM_NAME'
new  9:     SYNONYM_NAME = 'DUAL7_1'

OWNER            TABLE_OWNER       TABLE_NAME        DB_LINK
---------------- ----------------- ----------------- --------------------
WAITE            SYS               DUAL
```

The synonym created in Step 1 is the only synonym contained in the ALL_SYNONYMS view, unless other synonyms were created in the current user account's schema or public synonyms were created.

How It Works

Step 1 creates the sample synonym used throughout this How-To. Steps 2 and 3 provide a query to retrieve synonym information from the ALL_SYNONYMS data dictionary view. The OWNER column represents the user account that owns the synonym. A value of PUBLIC represents a public synonym. The TABLE_OWNER and TABLE_NAME fields represent the object the synonym references. The DB_LINK column represents the remote database if the object is not stored on the local database.

Comments

A synonym can reference any table, view, snapshot, sequence, procedure, function, or package. A synonym can even reference another synonym. If a synonym does not reference the object you expect, unpredictable results can occur. The management of synonyms can become a difficult task if your database contains many private synonyms. Public synonyms help reduce the maintenance of synonyms.

COMPLEXITY
INTERMEDIATE

7.2 How do I...
Create synonyms for all objects in a schema?

Problem

In our development environment, we create private synonyms for all developers to reference a common set of objects. I need a method to create private synonyms for all objects in another schema. How do I create synonyms for all objects in a schema?

Technique

The CREATE SYNONYM statement is used to develop a synonym for an object. As we have done throughout this book, we will use SQL*Plus and the data dictionary to build SQL statements to perform the task. Since synonyms can be created for many types of objects, the method uses many data dictionary views. As we've already seen, a synonym can reference tables, views, snapshots, sequences, procedures, functions, and packages. Table 7-1 shows the data dictionary view used for each type of object.

OBJECT TYPE	DATA DICTIONARY VIEW
Table	ALL_TABLES
View	ALL_VIEWS
Snapshot	ALL_SNAPSHOTS
Sequence	ALL_SEQUENCES
Procedure	ALL_SOURCE
Packages	ALL_SOURCE

Table 7-1 Data dictionary views used to create all objects in a schema

Steps

1. Run SQL*Plus and connect as the WAITE user account. Load CHP7-3.sql into the SQL buffer. The file contains a query to build CREATE SYNONYM statements for tables, views, synonyms, stored procedures, and packages in a user account's schema.

```
SQL> GET CHP7-3
  1  SELECT
  2    'CREATE SYNONYM '||TABLE_NAME||
  3      ' FOR '||OWNER||'.'||TABLE_NAME||';'
  4  FROM ALL_TABLES
  5    WHERE OWNER = '&&SCHEMA_OWNER'
  6  UNION
  7  SELECT
  8    'CREATE SYNONYM '||VIEW_NAME||
  9      ' FOR '||OWNER||'.'||VIEW_NAME||';'
 10  FROM ALL_VIEWS
 11    WHERE OWNER = '&&SCHEMA_OWNER'
 12  UNION
 13  SELECT
 14    'CREATE SYNONYM '||SEQUENCE_NAME||
 15      ' FOR '||OWNER||'.'||SEQUENCE_NAME||';'
 16  FROM ALL_SEQUENCES
 17    WHERE OWNER = '&&SCHEMA_OWNER'
 18  SELECT DISTINCT
 19    'CREATE SYNONYM '||NAME||
 20      ' FOR '||OWNER||'.'NAME
 21  FROM ALL_SOURCE
 22    WHERE OWNER = '&&SCHEMA_OWNER'
 23  ORDER BY 1
```

Lines 1 through 5 query ALL_TABLES to build CREATE SYNONYM statements referencing tables. The CREATE SYNONYM keywords are
concatenated with the owner and name of the object. Lines 7 through 11
query ALL_VIEWS to build CREATE SYNONYM statements to reference
views in the schema. Lines 13 through 17 query ALL_SEQUENCES to
build statements referencing sequences. Lines 18 through 22 query
ALL_SOURCE to build statements referencing stored procedures and packages. Since the ALL_SOURCE view contains one record for each line of
source code, the DISTINCT operator is used in line 18 to return a single
record for each object.

2. Set the HEADING, FEEDBACK, and VERIFY system variables to OFF to
suppress unwanted text. Spool an output file to contain the SQL script. Run
the query to build the statements for the SYS user account.

```
SQL> SET HEADING OFF
SQL> SET FEEDBACK OFF
SQL> SET VERIFY OFF
SQL> SPOOL CREATES.sql
SQL> /

Enter value for schema_owner: SYS

CREATE SYNONYM V_$BACKUP FOR SYS.V_$BACKUP;
CREATE SYNONYM V_$BGPROCESS FOR SYS.V_$BGPROCESS;
CREATE SYNONYM V_$CIRCUIT FOR SYS.V_$CIRCUIT;
CREATE SYNONYM V_$COMPATIBILITY FOR SYS.V_$COMPATIBILITY;
CREATE SYNONYM V_$COMPATSEG FOR SYS.V_$COMPATSEG;
```

Because the SYS user account contains a large number of objects, the output is abbreviated to conserve space.

3. Stop spooling the output file and run the script to create the synonyms.

```
SQL> SPOOL OFF
SQL> START CREATES

Synonym created.

Synonym created.

Synonym created.

Synonym created.

Synonym created.
```

How It Works

Step 1 builds CREATE SYNONYM statements for all objects in a schema, by concatenating the statement keywords with the query results of the ALL_TABLES, ALL_VIEWS, ALL_SEQUENCES, and ALL_SOURCE views. Since synonyms can be created on many types of objects, all the related data dictionary views must be queried. The double ampersand (&&) is used in the substitution variables, so the user does not have to enter the same information repeatedly.

Comments

Creating SQL scripts to perform many of the mundane tasks of managing a database can save you time and aggravation. A simple modification of the query presented in this How-To can be used to create public synonyms for all objects in a schema.

COMPLEXITY
BEGINNING

7.3 How do I...
List synonyms referencing an object?

Problem

I need to determine what synonyms are referencing an object in my schema. If I drop an object, all of the synonyms pointing to the object become invalid. It is possible that many synonyms reference an object. How do I list synonyms referencing an object?

Technique

The ALL_SYNONYMS data dictionary view can be used to determine the synonyms referencing an object. The TABLE_OWNER column contains the user account that owns the object. The TABLE_NAME column contains the name of the object the synonym references.

Steps

1. Run SQL*Plus and connect as the WAITE user account. CHP7-4.sql, shown in Figure 7-3, contains the CREATE TABLE and multiple CREATE SYNONYM statements, which are used throughout this How-To.

TAB7_4, the sample table created in the script, is referenced by two separate synonyms: SYN7_4A and SYN7_4B. In later steps, the two synonyms are queried based on the object they reference. Run CHP7-4.sql to create the sample table and synonyms.

```
SQL> START CHP7-4

Table created.

Synonym created.

Synonym created.
```

2. Load CHP7-5.sql into the SQL buffer. The file contains a query to view all synonyms referencing an object by querying the ALL_SYNONYMS data dictionary view.

```
SQL> GET CHP7-5
  1   SELECT
  2     OWNER,
  3     SYNONYM_NAME
  4   FROM
  5     ALL_SYNONYMS
```

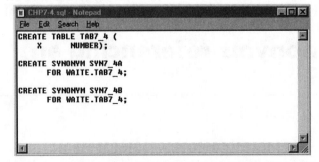

Figure 7-3 CHP7-4.sql creates the sample objects used in How-To 7.3

```
6   WHERE
7       TABLE_OWNER = '&TABLE_OWNER'
8       AND TABLE_NAME = '&TABLE_NAME'
```

Lines 2 and 3 specify that the OWNER and SYNONYM_NAME columns are returned by the query. Lines 4 and 5 specify the ALL_SYNONYMS data dictionary view as the source of the query. Lines 7 and 8 use the &TABLE_OWNER and &TABLE_NAME substitution variables to return the owner and name of the object referenced by the synonym.

3. Execute the statement, replacing the &TABLE_OWNER substitution variable with WAITE and the &TABLE_NAME substitution variable with TAB7_4.

```
SQL> /
Enter value from table_owner:  WAITE
Enter value for table_name: TAB7_4

OWNER                              SYNONYM_NAME
--------------------------------   --------------------------
PUBLIC                             SYN7_4A
PUBLIC                             SYN7_4B
```

The two records returned are the two synonyms created in Step 1 of this How-To. Since both synonyms reference the TAB7_4 table, both are returned by the query.

How It Works

Step 1 creates the sample table and synonyms used in this How-To. Steps 2 and 3 present a query of the ALL_SYNONYMS data dictionary view. This displays the OWNER and SYNONYM_NAME of all synonyms referencing the object specified in the query. If the OWNER column is PUBLIC, the synonym is a public synonym available to all user accounts.

Comments

An object can be referenced by more than one synonym, including one or more public synonyms and many private synonyms. When an object referenced by a synonym is removed, all synonyms referencing the object become invalid. Whenever you remove an object, you should remove the synonyms referencing it immediately since it will be difficult to identify the synonyms later.

COMPLEXITY
ADVANCED

7.4 How do I...
Drop all invalid synonyms in a schema?

Problem

I need an easy method to drop all invalid synonyms in a user account's schema. As our database changes, synonyms become invalid and very difficult to identify. How do I identify and drop all invalid synonyms in a schema?

Technique

The USER_SYNONYMS view contains all private synonyms for the connected user account. When an invalid synonym is queried, an ORA-00980 error occurs. A query to a synonym referencing a stored procedure or package also generates an error, but not the same error. The DBMS_SQL package creates SQL statements dynamically and executes them within a PL/SQL block. See How-To 14.2 for more information about using dynamic SQL. A script is created to test each synonym and drop all synonyms returning the ORA-00980 error.

Steps

1. Run SQL*Plus and connect as the WAITE user account. CHP7-6.sql, shown in Figure 7-4, creates two invalid synonyms and one valid synonym.

```
CHP7-6.sql - Notepad
File  Edit  Search  Help

CREATE SYNONYM DUAL7_6
        FOR SYS.DUAL;

CREATE SYNONYM BAD7_6A
        FOR WAITE.NO_TABLE1;

CREATE SYNONYM BAD7_6B
        FOR WAITE.NO_TABLE2;
```

Figure 7-4 CHP7-6.sql creates the sample synonyms used in How-To 7.4

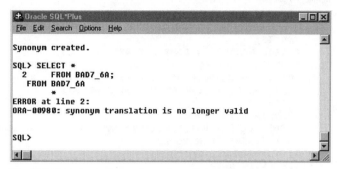

Figure 7-5 A query of an invalid synonym

The DUAL7_6 synonym references the SYS.DUAL table, which is a valid object. The BAD7_6A and BAD7_6B synonyms reference tables that do not exist in the WAITE schema. Run the file to create the sample synonyms.

```
SQL>  START CHP7-6

Synonym created.

Synonym created.

Synonym created.
```

2. Query the synonym BAD7_6A. Since the synonym references a table that does not exist, an error will be returned. Figure 7-5 shows the results of the operation in SQL*Plus.

The ORA-00980 error is returned when an invalid synonym is queried.

3. Load CHP7-7.sql into the SQL buffer. The file contains a PL/SQL statement to list all invalid synonyms within a user account's schema.

```
SQL> GET CHP7-7
  1   DECLARE
  2    T VARCHAR2(60);
  3    TMP VARCHAR2(60);
  4    CURSOR_HANDLE INTEGER;
  5    CNT INTEGER;
  6    CURSOR C1 IS
  7       SELECT SYNONYM_NAME
  8          FROM USER_SYNONYMS;
  9    INVALID_SYNONYM EXCEPTION;
 10    PRAGMA EXCEPTION_INIT (INVALID_SYNONYM, -00980);
 11   BEGIN
 12      OPEN C1;
 13      FETCH C1 INTO T;
 14      WHILE C1%FOUND LOOP
 15      BEGIN
 16       TMP := 'SELECT 0 FROM '||T;
 17       TMP := TMP||' WHERE ROWNUM = 1';
```

continued on next page

continued from previous page

```
18       IF DBMS_SQL.IS_OPEN(CURSOR_HANDLE) THEN
19           DBMS_SQL.CLOSE_CURSOR(CURSOR_HANDLE);
20       END IF;
21       CURSOR_HANDLE := DBMS_SQL.OPEN_CURSOR;
22       DBMS_SQL.PARSE(CURSOR_HANDLE, TMP, DBMS_SQL.V7);
23       CNT := DBMS_SQL.EXECUTE(CURSOR_HANDLE);
24       DBMS_SQL.CLOSE_CURSOR(CURSOR_HANDLE);
25       EXCEPTION
26       WHEN INVALID_SYNONYM THEN
27         DBMS_OUTPUT.PUT_LINE('Synonym '||T||' Invalid');
28       WHEN OTHERS THEN NULL;
29     END;
30     FETCH C1 INTO T;
31     END LOOP;
32*  END;
```

Lines 1 through 10 contain the declarative section of the PL/SQL block. The variable defined in line 2 is used to hold the name of the synonym currently processed by the module. The variable CURSOR_HANDLE defined in line 4 references the cursor used in dynamic SQL to test each synonym. The cursor defined in lines 6 through 8 returns all the synonyms in the current user account's schema by querying the USER_SYNONYMS data dictionary view. Lines 9 and 10 create an exception handler and define error code -00980 as INVALID_SYNONYM. Line 12 opens the cursor and executes the query of the ALL_SYNONYMS data dictionary view. Line 13 retrieves the value in the first record and puts it into the variable defined in line 2. Lines 14 through 31 contain a WHILE loop that continues to process synonyms until the cursor cannot fetch any more synonyms. The loop goes through all rows in the cursor to determine if they are valid synonyms. Lines 16 and 17 prepare a SQL statement that reads a single row from a synonym. If the statement fails, it is handled by the exception handler beginning on line 25. If the error code is -00980, line 27 displays a message that the synonym is invalid. If it displays a different error code, the synonym is valid. If the statement querying the synonym is successful, the synonym is also valid. If the cursor is open, lines 18 through 20 close it before trying to reopen it with another query. Lines 21 through 24 use the DBMS_SQL package to execute the SQL contained in the TMP variable declared in line 3.

4. Set the SERVEROUTPUT system variable to ON to display output from he DBMS_OUTPUT package. Run the PL/SQL block to view the invalid synonyms.

```
SQL>  SET SERVEROUTPUT ON
SQL>  /

BAD7_6A - BAD SYNONYM
BAD7_6B - BAD SYNONYM
```

Because the BAD7_6A and BAD7_6B synonyms reference invalid database objects, the BAD SYNONYM message is displayed. The DUAL7_6 synonym does not generate the ORA-00980 error when it is queried, so no record is returned.

5. Load CHP7-8.sql into the SQL buffer. The file contains modifications to the previous script which drops all invalid synonyms. The method presented in Steps 3 and 4 is used to identify the invalid synonyms.

```
SQL> GET CHP7-8
  1  DECLARE
  2    T VARCHAR2(60);
  3    TMP VARCHAR2(60);
  4    CURSOR_HANDLE INTEGER;
  5    CNT INTEGER;
  6    DROPPED INTEGER := 0;
  7    CURSOR C1 IS
  8      SELECT SYNONYM_NAME
  9         FROM USER_SYNONYMS;
 10    INVALID_SYNONYM EXCEPTION;
 11    PRAGMA EXCEPTION_INIT (INVALID_SYNONYM, -00980);
 12  BEGIN
 13    OPEN C1;
 14    FETCH C1 INTO T;
 15    WHILE C1%FOUND LOOP
 16    BEGIN
 17        TMP := 'SELECT 0 FROM '||T;
 18        TMP := TMP||' WHERE ROWNUM = 1';
 19        IF DBMS_SQL.IS_OPEN(CURSOR_HANDLE) THEN
 20              DBMS_SQL.CLOSE_CURSOR(CURSOR_HANDLE);
 21        END IF;
 22        CURSOR_HANDLE := DBMS_SQL.OPEN_CURSOR;
 23        DBMS_SQL.PARSE(CURSOR_HANDLE, TMP, DBMS_SQL.V7);
 24        CNT := DBMS_SQL.EXECUTE(CURSOR_HANDLE);
 25        DBMS_SQL.CLOSE_CURSOR(CURSOR_HANDLE);
 26    EXCEPTION
 27        WHEN INVALID_SYNONYM THEN
 28        BEGIN
 29            TMP := 'DROP SYNONYM '||T;
 30            IF DBMS_SQL.IS_OPEN(CURSOR_HANDLE) THEN
 31                DBMS_SQL.CLOSE_CURSOR(CURSOR_HANDLE);
 32            END IF;
 33            CURSOR_HANDLE := DBMS_SQL.OPEN_CURSOR;
 34            DBMS_SQL.PARSE(CURSOR_HANDLE, TMP, DBMS_SQL.V7);
 35            CNT := DBMS_SQL.EXECUTE(CURSOR_HANDLE);
 36            DBMS_OUTPUT.PUT_LINE('Synonym '||T||' Removed');
 37            DBMS_SQL.CLOSE_CURSOR(CURSOR_HANDLE);
 38        EXCEPTION
 39            WHEN OTHERS THEN
 40                  DBMS_SQL.CLOSE_CURSOR(CURSOR_HANDLE);
 41        END;
 42    WHEN OTHERS THEN
 43        IF DBMS_SQL.IS_OPEN(CURSOR_HANDLE) THEN
 44              DBMS_SQL.CLOSE_CURSOR(CURSOR_HANDLE);
```

continued on next page

continued from previous page

```
45              END IF;
46        END;
47        FETCH C1 INTO T;
48        END LOOP;
49* END;
```

This code works the same as the PL/SQL code shown in Step 4, except that it drops invalid synonyms when it finds them. Lines 27 through 41 build a DROP SYNONYM statement for each synonym found to be invalid. Lines 30 through 32 close the cursor currently open. Lines 33 through 35 open, parse, and execute the cursor to perform the DROP SYNONYM statement and remove the invalid synonym.

How It Works

Step 1 creates invalid synonyms which are used throughout this How-To. Step 2 queries an invalid synonym to show the error that occurs. Steps 3 and 4 present a PL/SQL statement to analyze each synonym in a schema and display whether or not the synonym is valid. Steps 5 and 6 present a modified script to drop all invalid synonyms in a user schema.

Comments

The number of invalid synonyms can get very large in development environments. Tables are created and dropped for development projects, but synonyms tend to never get removed. Private synonyms for user accounts referencing invalid database objects should be dropped regularly. DROPSN2.sql on the accompanying disc contains a stored procedure which performs the task of dropping invalid synonyms.

MANIPULATING DATA

MANIPULATING DATA

How do I...

Working with Oracle data does not always consist of inserting records and querying them later. Data can be inserted, updated, and deleted through complex SQL statements that depend on the results of sub-queries. Dates and times are stored in columns of the DATE datatype and can be manipulated through date functions. The How-Tos presented in this chapter are designed to save you hours of aggravation while manipulating data within your database. The data manipulation techniques presented in this chapter can be used in SQL*Plus for data maintenance or within your applications to enforce complex business rules.

8.1   Insert the result set of a query

Records can be inserted into a table from a query of one or more other tables or views. A single INSERT statement can use a query to populate a table with multiple rows. This How-To demonstrates using a query to insert records into an existing table. This technique can be used to manually replicate data between servers, create summary data, and perform a variety of system maintenance tasks.

8.2   Insert dates and times

Dates and times are stored in the database in columns of the DATE datatype. The DATE datatype contains both the date and time. Each date column contains the century, year, month, day, hour, minute, and second. This How-To presents methods for inserting dates and times into a table.

8.3   Update a record with results from a query

Columns within a table can be set to the results of a query. A sub-query can be used within an UPDATE statement to set the value of a column. This How-To presents the method for updating one or more records with the results of a query. The technique shown in this How-To is useful for both application development and database maintenance.

8.4   Update the value of a column to NULL

It is sometimes necessary to change the value of a column to NULL. A NULL value is an empty value; it is not the same as zero for numeric datatypes or an empty string for character datatypes. NULL values are handled differently than other values in Oracle. This How-To presents the method for updating the value of a column to NULL.

8.5   Delete all rows from a table quickly

The DELETE statement is used to delete rows from a table. When all records are deleted from a table using DELETE, the statement may execute very slowly. This How-To presents a method that deletes all records from a table quickly.

8.6   Delete duplicate rows from a table

Duplicate rows prevent primary keys and unique indexes from being created on a table. Applications can create duplicate rows if they are not programmed correctly. If a unique index does not exist when the duplicate records are created, Oracle inserts the records. This How-To presents the method used to delete duplicate rows from a table, while preserving one of the unique rows.

8.7   Delete data that exists in another table

Sub-queries can be used in the WHERE clause of a DELETE statement to delete rows where the key value exists in another table. This How-To presents the use of the IN and EXISTS clauses to delete data existing in a sub-query.

8.8   Delete data in sections to avoid errors

The deletion of a large number of records from a table with the DELETE statement can cause rollback segment errors. In order to avoid these errors, a COMMIT statement needs to be performed before the rollback segment fills. This How-To presents a method for deleting large amounts of data in sections to avoid errors.

8.9   Insert date columns compliant with the year 2000 issue

Most users like to enter dates using a two-digit year format. As the year 2000 approaches, it is important that dates get stored internally with the correct century. This How-To presents the method used to ensure that dates with two-digit years are stored with the correct century.

8.10   Update date columns for the year 2000 issue

Until recently, nobody cared about date issues surrounding the turn of the century. Most older applications inserted dates using a two-digit year format. Unfortunately, a date inserted as 01-JAN-02 was stored as the year 1902, not 2002. This How-To presents a method for correcting the century representation of date columns originally created with a two-digit year.

COMPLEXITY

INTERMEDIATE

8.1   How do I...
Insert the result set of a query?

Problem

I need to insert the results of a query into an existing table. The query can return multiple rows from one or more source tables. In many cases, I need to insert the results of a complex query into a table. How do I insert the result set of a query into a table?

Technique

The INSERT statement inserts the results of a query into an existing table. The datatypes of the source columns from the query must match the datatypes of the columns specified in the INSERT statement. A SELECT clause in an INSERT statement ensures that the rows will be created as the results of a query. The creation of multiple rows is performed as a single transaction. If an error is caused by any record, the entire transaction will fail.

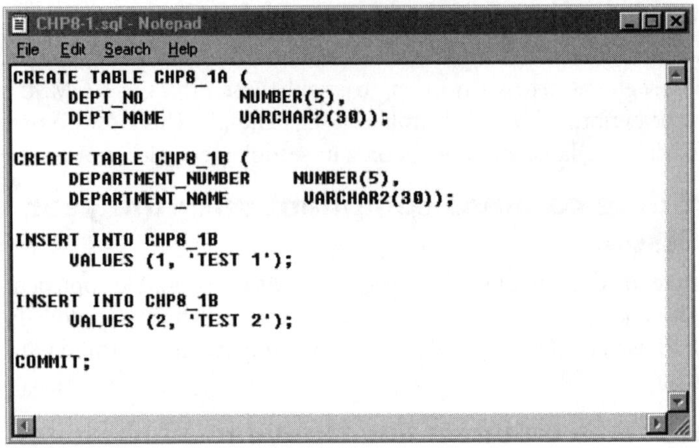

Figure 8-1 CHP8-1.sql creates the sample tables
used in How-To 8.1

Steps

1. Run SQL*Plus and connect as the WAITE user account. CHP8-1.sql,
shown in Figure 8-1, builds the sample tables used in this How-To.

The two tables created by the script contain columns of the same datatypes.
The CHP8_1A table will have records inserted with a query of the
CHP8_1B table. Run the file to create the sample tables.

```
SQL> START CHP8-1

Table created.

Table created.

1 row inserted.

1 row inserted.

Commit complete.
```

2. Load CHP8-2.sql into the SQL buffer. The file contains an INSERT statement to create new rows in the CHP8_1A table.

```
SQL> GET CHP8-2
  1  INSERT INTO
  2   CHP8_1A (DEPT_NO, DEPT_NAME)
  3  SELECT
  4   DEPARTMENT_NUMBER,
  5   DEPARTMENT_NAME
  6  FROM
  7   CHP8_1B
```

The DEPARTMENT_NUMBER and DEPARTMENT_NAME columns from the CHP8_1B table are inserted into the DEPT_NO and DEPT_NAME columns in the CHP8_1A table. The datatypes in the source and destination columns must match, and data from the source column must fit in the destination column. If an error occurs on any record, the entire transaction will fail.

3. Run the statement to insert rows into the table.

```
SQL>   /

2 rows created.
```

How It Works

Step 1 builds the sample tables used throughout this How-To. Step 2 inserts records into the CHP8_1A table as a query from the CHP8_1B table. The column names receiving the data are specified before the SELECT clause of the statement. If the columns are not specified in the statement, Oracle expects every column from the table to be provided in the order the columns are listed in the table. The datatypes of the source and destination columns must be the same.

Comments

Creating records as the result of a query can be used for many data management tasks. Data can be replicated between tables or servers using this technique. Summary data can be created using this technique for reporting or analysis purposes. If you get in the habit of using this technique, you will find many places in which creating records from a query can solve problems.

COMPLEXITY

INTERMEDIATE

8.2   How do I...
Insert dates and times?

Problem

I am having trouble inserting dates and times into a table. In some of my date columns no time portion exists, while other fields contain both dates and times. How do I insert dates and times into a table?

Technique

The TO_DATE function is used to convert a value to Oracle's internal date format. The TO_CHAR function is used to convert a text value into one of many different character formats. Any time you insert dates in a format other than the standard Oracle format, a TO_DATE function must be used. The TO_DATE function can also be used to format a time into a date column.

Steps

1. Run SQL*Plus and connect as the WAITE user account. CHP8-3.sql, shown in Figure 8-2, is used to create the sample table used in this How-To.

The CHP8_3 table contains a single date column used to hold date and time values. Run the file to create the sample table.

```
SQL> START CHP8-3
```

Table created.

2. Load CHP8-4.sql into the SQL buffer. The file contains an INSERT statement to insert a time into the sample table. The date portion of the column is omitted.

```
SQL> GET CHP8-4
  1   INSERT INTO
  2   CHP8_3 (TIMEFLD)
  3*  VALUES (TO_DATE('13:20','HH24:MI'))
```

Line 1 specifies the INSERT keyword used to create new records in a table. Line 2 specifies the table that will receive the new records. The TO_DATE function is used in line 3 to specify the format of the date value. In this example, only the time portion of the date is specified.

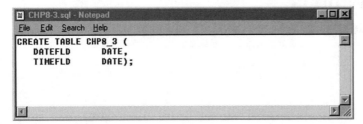

Figure 8-2 CHP8-3.sql creates the sample table used in How-To 8.2

3. Run the statement to insert the time value into the date column.

```
SQL>  /

1 row created.
```

4. Load CHP8-5.sql into the SQL buffer. The file contains a query to view the some of the different formats in which the column can be displayed.

```
SQL> GET CHP8-5
  1   SELECT
  2     TIMEFLD A,
  3     TO_CHAR(TIMEFLD,'HH24:MI') B,
  4     TO_CHAR(TIMEFLD,'HH24:MI:SS') C
  5   FROM
  6*    CHP8_3
```

Lines 2 through 3 specify the columns returned by the query. Line 2 returns the column in its default format. Line 3 returns the column in the format in which it was inserted in Step 3, and line 4 includes the seconds from the time. Line 6 specifies the CHP8_3 table as the source of the query.

5. Execute COLUMN statements to format the output of the three columns and execute the query formats. Execute the ROLLBACK statement to remove the row created in Step 3.

```
SQL> COLUMN A FORMAT A12
SQL> COLUMN B FORMAT A12
SQL> COLUMN C FORMAT A12
SQL> /

A             B             C
------------- ------------- -------------
01-APR-96     13:28         13:28:00

SQL>  ROLLBACK;

Rollback complete.
```

Querying the column in its default format provides ambiguous data. No date portion was inserted into the column, so querying the date part of the column provides useless information. Column B shows the column in the format in which it was created. Column C includes the seconds from the time. Since the data was not created with this level of precision, the seconds default to 00.

6. Load CHP8-6.sql into the SQL buffer. The file contains an INSERT statement to insert a date into the sample table.

```
SQL> GET CHP8-6
  1   INSERT INTO
  2     CHP8_3 (DATEFLD)
  3*  VALUES (TO_DATE('10/01/96','MM/DD/YY'))
```

The TO_DATE function is used in the VALUES clause in line 3, specifying the format in which the date is specified. In this case, no time is specified with the date.

7. Run the statement to insert the date value into the DATE column.

```
SQL>  /

1 row created.
```

8. Load CHP8-7.sql into the SQL buffer. The file contains a query to view some of the different formats in which the column can be displayed.

```
SQL> GET CHP8-7
  1  SELECT
  2     DATEFLD A,
  3     TO_CHAR(DATEFLD,'MM/DD/YY') B,
  4     TO_CHAR(DATEFLD,'HH24:MI:SS') C
  5  FROM
  6*    CHP8_3
```

Lines 2 through 4 specify the columns returned by the query. Line 2 returns the date value in its default format. Line 2 returns the month, day, and year separated by the foreward slash symbol, /. Line 3 returns the time portion of the date. Line 6 specifies the CHP8_3 table as the source of the query.

9. Execute the query to display the date value formatted with the TO_CHAR function.

```
SQL> /

A          B             C
---------- ------------- -------------
01-OCT-96  10/01/96      00:00:00
```

Column A displays the date in the default format for a date field. Although it is not the format in which the date was created, the date value is correct. Column B contains the date column formatted in the same format in which it was inserted. Column C displays the time portion of the date. Since no time was specified, the time defaults to 00:00:00.

How It Works

Step 1 creates the sample tables used throughout this How-To. Steps 2 and 3 insert a time value into a column of the DATE datatype by using the TO_DATE function. When the value is formatted with the TO_DATE function, the month, day, year, hour, minute, and second values can all be specified. Steps 4 and 5 query the data from the table, displaying it in different formats. Steps 6 and 7 insert a date value into a table without a time value, without specifying the time portion of the date. Steps 8 and 9 query the data, displaying the different parts of the date value when the time portion is missing.

Comments

The TO_DATE and TO_CHAR functions are important when manipulating dates and times. Dates and times are stored together in columns of the DATE datatype. When working with the DATE datatype, you must keep track of the format of the information in the column. Problems can occur if you store dates in one format and use them in another.

COMPLEXITY
INTERMEDIATE

8.3 How do I...
Update a record with results from a query?

Problem

I need to update one or more columns in a table. The value to which I am setting the columns is the result of a complex query dependent on the record I am updating. How do I update a record with the results of a query?

Technique

A sub-query can be used as the source of the information in an UPDATE statement. When updating a column, the value can be provided by a sub-query contained in parentheses. If a sub-query is used to generate a value for a column, the sub-query must only return one row. An error will occur if an attempt is made to update a single record with multiple values, or if the sub-query returns no rows.

Steps

1. Run SQL*Plus and connect as the WAITE user account. The file CHP8-8.sql, shown in Figure 8-3, builds the tables used in this How-To.

The CHP8_8A and CHP8_8B tables are created to demonstrate how records can be updated with the results of a query. Two records are inserted into each of the tables. In the following steps, the records in the CHP8_8A table will be updated with values queried from the CHP8_8B table. Execute the statement to build the sample tables.

```
SQL> START CHP8-8

Table created.

Table created.
```

continued on next page

continued from previous page

```
1 row created.

1 row created.

1 row created.

1 row created.

Commit complete.
```

2. Load CHP8-9.sql into the SQL buffer. The file contains an UPDATE statement that sets all of the DEPT_NO columns in the CHP8_8A table to the values of the DEPARTMENT_NO column in the CHP8_8B table.

```
SQL> GET CHP8-9
  1  UPDATE CHP8_8A
  2     SET DEPT_NAME = (SELECT
  3            DEPARTMENT_NAME
  4        FROM
  5            CHP8_8B
  6        WHERE
  7*           CHP8_8B.DEPARTMENT_NUMBER = CHP8_8A.DEPT_NO)
```

Line 1 specifies the UPDATE keyword used to modify data in a table. Line 2 sets the DEPT_NAME column to the result of the query contained in parentheses. Lines 2 through 7 contain the sub-query used to modify records in the CHP8_8A table. The sub-query selects the DEPARTMENT_NAME column from the CHP8_8B table. Line 7 joins the

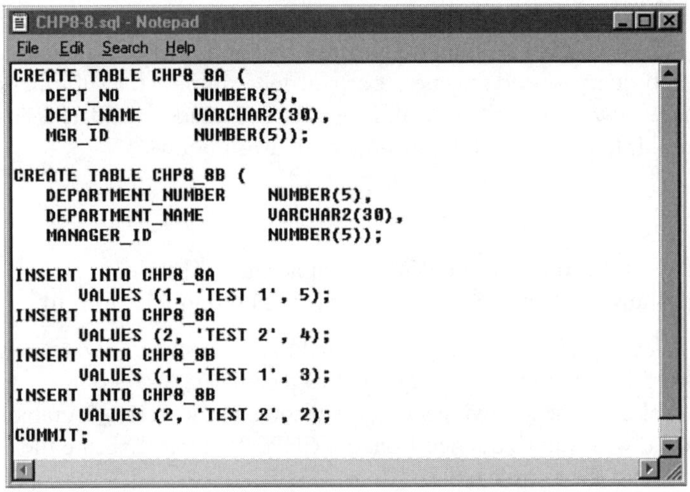


```
CREATE TABLE CHP8_8A (
   DEPT_NO        NUMBER(5),
   DEPT_NAME      VARCHAR2(30),
   MGR_ID         NUMBER(5));

CREATE TABLE CHP8_8B (
   DEPARTMENT_NUMBER    NUMBER(5),
   DEPARTMENT_NAME      VARCHAR2(30),
   MANAGER_ID           NUMBER(5));

INSERT INTO CHP8_8A
     VALUES (1, 'TEST 1', 5);
INSERT INTO CHP8_8A
     VALUES (2, 'TEST 2', 4);
INSERT INTO CHP8_8B
     VALUES (1, 'TEST 1', 3);
INSERT INTO CHP8_8B
     VALUES (2, 'TEST 2', 2);
COMMIT;
```

Figure 8-3 CHP8-8.sql creates the sample tables used in How-To 8.3

DEPARTMENT_NO column from the CHP8_8B query with the DEPT_NO column from the updated table.

3. Execute the query to update the records.

```
SQL> /
```

2 rows updated.

4. Load CHP8-10.sql into the SQL buffer. The file contains an UPDATE statement which updates multiple columns with a single sub-query.

```
SQL> GET CHP8-10
  1  UPDATE CHP8_8A
  2    SET (DEPT_NAME, MGR_ID) = (SELECT
  3          DEPARTMENT_NAME, MANAGER_ID
  4      FROM
  5          CHP8_8B
  6      WHERE
  7*         CHP8_8B.DEPARTMENT_NUMBER = CHP8_8A.DEPT_NO)
```

Line 1 presents the UPDATE keyword which modifies records by the statement. Line 2 specifies the list of columns being updated as the result of the statement. The columns updated are listed in parentheses before the equal sign. The sub-query contained in lines 2 through 7 must return one column for each column listed in line 2.

5. Execute the query to update the records.

```
SQL> /
```

2 rows updated.

6. Load CHP8-11.sql into the SQL buffer. The file contains an UPDATE statement ensuring that the data returned by the sub-query exists and only one row is returned. The UPDATE statements in the previous two examples will fail if the sub-query does not return exactly one record.

```
SQL> GETP CHP8-11
  1  UPDATE CHP8_8A
  2    SET (DEPT_NAME, MGR_ID) = (SELECT
  3        DEPARTMENT_NAME, MANAGER_ID
  4      FROM
  5          CHP8_8B
  6      WHERE
  7          CHP8_8B.DEPARTMENT_NUMBER = CHP8_8A.DEPT_NO
  8      AND ROWNUM = 1)
  9    WHERE
 10      EXISTS (SELECT 'x'
 11           FROM
 12               CHP8_8B
 13           WHERE
 14*              CHP8_8B.DEPARTMENT_NUMBER = CHP8_8A.DEPT_NO)
```

Lines 2 through 8 specify the columns modified by the statement and query providing the new column values. Line 8 ensures that only one row is returned by the sub-query by using the ROWNUM pseudo-column. If more than one record is returned by a sub-query in an UPDATE statement, an error will occur. Lines 10 through 14 only attempt updates where the inner query returns at least one row. The EXISTS clause in line 10 evaluates to TRUE if at least one record is returned by the sub-query in lines 10 through 14. The WHERE clause in lines 13 and 14 is the same as the WHERE clause in lines 6 and 7. This ensures that records will only be updated where the sub-query returns at least one row.

7. Run the statement to update the records.

```
SQL> /

2 rows updated.
```

How It Works

Step 1 builds the sample tables used in this How-To. The CHP8_8A table contains records updated with a query of the records in the CHP8_8B table. A sub-query can be used in an UPDATE statement to set one or more column values, as long as the sub-query returns exactly one row. Steps 2 and 3 update all records in the CHP8_8A table. The DEPT_NO column is set to the results of a query of the CHP8_8B table. The statement will fail if there is not exactly one row per record in CHP8_8B table. Steps 4 and 5 update multiple columns with a sub-query. More than one column can be updated with a single sub-query, by specifying the column names in parentheses before the equal sign. Steps 6 and 7 guarantee that no errors occur, by restricting the inner query to return one row and creating a WHERE clause to only update records contained in the sub-query.

Comments

Updating records with the results of a query is a very useful data management technique. In many cases, the correct value of a column can be derived from a query of other tables. Steps 6 and 7 show important techniques to ensure that errors do not occur in the statement.

8.4 How do I...
Update the value of a column to NULL?

Problem

I need to change the value of a column to NULL. The column contains data, and I want to remove it. I know that an empty string is not the same as NULL, so I cannot set my character column to an empty string. How do I set the value of a column to NULL?

Technique

The NULL keyword represents a NULL value. In an UPDATE statement, a value can be set to NULL by specifying the NULL keyword after the assignment operator, =. The only place you will see the construct = NULL is in an UPDATE statement in which you are setting a value to NULL. When NULL is used in the WHERE clause of a query, the IS NULL or IS NOT NULL constructs are used.

Steps

1. Run SQL*Plus and connect as the WAITE user account. CH8-12.sql, shown in Figure 8-4, contains a SQL script to create the sample table and data used throughout this How-To.

```
CREATE TABLE DEPT8_12 (
    DEPT_NO         NUMBER(5),
    DEPT_NAME       VARCHAR2(30),
    MGR_ID          NUMBER(5));

INSERT INTO DEPT8_12
    VALUES (1, 'TEST 1', 5);

COMMIT;
```

Figure 8-4 CH8-12.sql creates the sample table used in How-To 8.4

The SQL script creates the DEPT8_12 table and a single record. Each of the columns in the new record contain values. In the steps that follow, the value of a column is set to NULL. Run the file to create the sample table and data.

```
SQL>   START CH8-12

Table created.

1 row inserted.
```

2. Load CH8-13.sql into the SQL buffer. The file contains an UPDATE statement to change the value of the DEPT_NO column to NULL.

```
SQL> GET CH8-13
  1   UPDATE DEPT8_12
  2   SET
  3      DEPT_NO = NULL
  4   WHERE
  5*     DEPT_NO IS NOT NULL
```

Line 1 specifies the UPDATE keyword used to modify data in a table. It also specifies the table to be modified. Line 3 shows the proper syntax used to set the value of a column to NULL. The assignment operator, =, is used to assign a NULL value in an UPDATE statement. Line 5 shows how NULL is referenced in the WHERE clause of a statement. The IS NULL or IS NOT NULL clause is used to specify NULL values in the WHERE clause.

3. Run the statement to update the record.

```
SQL>   /

1 row updated.
```

How It Works

Step 1 creates the sample table and data used in this How-To. The DEPT8_12 table is created with a single record containing values for all the columns. Steps 2 and 3 set the value of the DEPT_NO column to NULL and show the proper syntax used. The assignment operator, =, assigns NULL to a column value. The expression IS NULL or IS NOT NULL evaluates NULL values in the WHERE clause of a SQL statement.

Comments

Updating a column to NULL is a common operation that confuses many people. Within an UPDATE statement, NULL is treated like any other value that can be set with the assignment operator, =.

COMPLEXITY
BEGINNING

8.5 How do I...
Delete all rows from a table quickly?

Problem

In our development environment, I create test data in many tables. In order to test the application, I need to delete all the data from the tables repeatedly. Deleting all rows from a table can be very slow when I use the DELETE statement. How do I delete all rows from a table quickly?

Technique

The TRUNCATE TABLE statement can be used to delete all records from a table. Figure 8-5 shows the syntax of the TRUNCATE TABLE statement.

Steps

1. Run SQL*Plus and connect as the WAITE user account. CHP8-14.sql, shown in Figure 8-6, creates the table used throughout this How-To.

The SAMPLE8_14 table is created with the CREATE TABLE statement and populated with the INSERT statement. Two hundred rows of data are inserted by querying the SYS.DBA_OBJECTS data dictionary view. Because it would take a while to delete these rows with a DELETE statement we use the TRUNCATE TABLE statement, as demonstrated in the following steps. Run the file to create the sample tables.

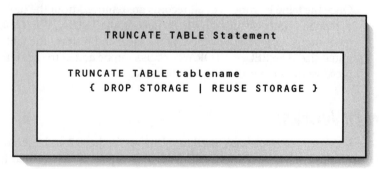

Figure 8-5 The TRUNCATE TABLE statement

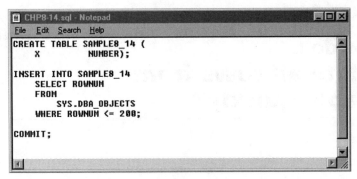

Figure 8-6 CHP8-14.sql creates the sample table
used in How-To 8.5

```
SQL> START CHP8-14

Table created.

200 rows inserted.

Commit complete.
```

2. Load CHP8-15.sql into the SQL buffer. The file contains a TRUNCATE
TABLE statement to remove all rows from the sample table.

```
SQL> GET CHP8-15
  1   TRUNCATE TABLE SAMPLE8_14
```

The SAMPLE8_14 table created in Step 1 will have all data removed by the
statement.

3. Run the statement to remove the data.

```
SQL> /

Table truncated.
```

Once the table is truncated, all records are removed from the table and the
operation cannot be rolled back. By default, the TRUNCATE TABLE statement drops the storage allocated to the table and restores the table to its
initial size. The REUSE STORAGE clause can be added to the statement to
preserve the storage allocated to the table.

How It Works

Step 1 creates the sample table used in this How-To. Steps 2 and 3 remove all rows
from the table using the TRUNCATE TABLE statement. If the table has indexes, all

data is deleted from them when the table is truncated. The table must be in the schema of the connected user account, or the account must have the DELETE ANY TABLE system privilege.

Comments

If you are deleting all rows from a table, the TRUNCATE TABLE statement is useful. The operation of truncating a table cannot be rolled back. As soon as the statement is executed, all data is permanently removed. Views cannot be truncated even if data management operations are allowed on the view. In order to quickly remove all data from a view, the TRUNCATE TABLE statement must be executed on the view's base table.

COMPLEXITY
ADVANCED

8.6   How do I...
Delete duplicate rows from a table?

Problem

I want to create a unique index on a table but cannot because it contains duplicate rows. I want to identify the rows that are duplicates and delete all but one of them. How do I identify and delete duplicate rows from a table?

Technique

In Oracle, every row is unique because of the ROWID column. Even duplicate records are unique in Oracle because of ROWID. The ROWID column exists in every row in the database, and no two ROWIDs are the same. ROWID identifies the data file, block, and physical row within the block of the record. Duplicate rows can be deleted from the table using a single statement. This technique requires three features which distinguish Oracle as a powerful tool: ROWID, sub-queries, and aliases. Since the ROWID is unique for each record in the table, records with duplicate data still maintain unique ROWIDs. A sub-query can be used to select the maximum or minimum ROWID from the same table where the key fields are duplicate. Since only one record can have the maximum ROWID, the others can be identified and deleted. In order to join a table to itself in the sub-query, an alias must be used. *Aliases* allow different names to be defined for a table in a SQL statement. This allows the same table to be used in a statement more than once and treated as two separate tables.

Steps

1. Run SQL*Plus and connect as the WAITE user account. CHP8-16.sql, shown in Figure 8-7, creates a sample table with duplicate rows.

The DEPT8_16 table created with the CREATE TABLE statement contains two columns. The seven records inserted into the column contain duplicate values for DEPT_NO = 1 and DEPT_NO = 2. In the following steps, the duplicate records will be identified and deleted. Run CHP8-16.sql to create the sample table with its data.

```
SQL> /

Table created.

1 row created.

1 row created.

1 row created.

1 row created.

1 row created.

1 row created.

1 row created.

Commit complete.
```

2. Load CHP8-17.sql into the SQL buffer. The file contains a query to determine duplicate rows using ROWID.

```
CREATE TABLE DEPT8_16 (
    DEPT_NO      NUMBER,
    DNAME        VARCHAR2(30));

INSERT INTO DEPT8_16 VALUES (1, 'DEPT 1');
INSERT INTO DEPT8_16 VALUES (1, 'DEPT 1');
INSERT INTO DEPT8_16 VALUES (1, 'DEPT 1');
INSERT INTO DEPT8_16 VALUES (2, 'DEPT 2');
INSERT INTO DEPT8_16 VALUES (2, 'DEPT 2');
INSERT INTO DEPT8_16 VALUES (3, 'DEPT 3');
INSERT INTO DEPT8_16 VALUES (4, 'DEPT 4');
COMMIT;
```

Figure 8-7 CHP8-16.sql creates the sample table used in How-To 8.6

```
SQL> GET CHP8-17
  1  SELECT
  2       DISTINCT DEPT_NO
  3  FROM DEPT8_16
  4  WHERE
  5    ROWID != (SELECT MAX(ROWID) FROM
  6              DEPT8_16 D
  7         WHERE
  8*            DEPT8_16.DEPT_NO = D.DEPT_NO)
```

Line 2 specifies the distinct DEPT_NO columns that will be returned by the query. The DISTINCT keyword causes only unique values to be returned by the query. Line 3 specifies the sample table created in Step 1 as the source of the query. The WHERE clause starting on line 4 uses a sub-query to return the largest ROWID for the given record. The sub-query contained in lines 5 through 8 returns the maximum ROWID for the record the WHERE clause is processing. The FROM clause for the sub-query shown in line 6 aliases the DEPT8_16 table with the name D. This allows the WHERE clause in lines 7 and 8 to compare the value of the DEPT_NO column in the sub-query with the value of the DEPT_NO column in the outer query. If the record processed by the WHERE clause in the outer query is unique, it will always have the largest ROWID and not be returned. If the record does not have the largest ROWID, it will be returned by the query.

3. Execute the query to display the duplicate department numbers.

```
SQL> /

DEPT_NO
---------
  1
  2
```

Two records are returned by the query identifying the duplicate records. The DISTINCT operator in the query causes the first record to be returned only once, even though there are more than two occurrences of DEPT_NO = 1.

4. Load CHP8-18.sql into the SQL buffer. The statement contained in the file replaces the SELECT statement and column list in the previous query with the DELETE keyword. The DELETE statement removes all records from the table that do not have the largest ROWID for its unique attributes.

```
SQL> GET CHP8-18
  1  DELETE
  2     FROM DEPT8_16
  3  WHERE
  4    ROWID != (SELECT MAX(ROWID) FROM
  5              DEPT8_16 D
  6         WHERE
  7*            DEPT8_16.DEPT_NO = D.DEPT_NO)
```

Line 1 contains the DELETE keyword, which causes the statement to delete all records satisfying the conditions of the WHERE clause. Lines 3 through 7 contain the WHERE clause, which removes records from the table specified in line 2. The logic used in the WHERE clause is the same as that presented in Step 2.

5. Run the statement to delete the duplicate rows.

```
SQL> /

3 rows deleted.
```

How It Works

ROWID is unique for every row in the database. Even if two records are identical in every other attribute, only one of them can have the largest ROWID. Step 1 creates the sample data used in this How-To and populates it with records containing duplicate values. Steps 2 and 3 show a query that returns all duplicate records. Steps 4 and 5 present a DELETE statement that deletes all but one instance of the duplicate records.

Comments

The easiest way to deal with duplicate records in a table is to not allow them. You can eliminate the possibility of duplicate records by placing a primary key or unique index on the table before inserting data. Since the sub-query used in the WHERE clause is executed once for every row in the table, it is important that the table be properly indexed. If the table is large, you could invoke a full table scan of a million-row table a million times.

COMPLEXITY

INTERMEDIATE

8.7 How do I...
Delete data that exists in another table?

Problem

I want to delete rows from a table if a record with the same keys exists in another table. In some of my applications, I move data out of its primary table into a historical table. Once this is done, I want to delete the records from the primary table. How do I delete data that exists in another table?

```
CHP8-19.sql - Notepad                                    _ □ ×
File  Edit  Search  Help
CREATE TABLE DEPT8_19A (
    DEPT_NO        NUMBER(5));

CREATE TABLE DEPT8_19B (
    DEPT_NO        NUMBER(5));

INSERT INTO DEPT8_19A VALUES (1);
INSERT INTO DEPT8_19A VALUES (2);
INSERT INTO DEPT8_19B VALUES (1);

COMMIT;
```

Figure 8-8 CHP8-19.sql creates the sample tables
used in How-To 8.7

Technique

Sub-queries used in the HERE clause of INSERT, UPDATE, or DELETE statements
can query other tables to determine whether to process a record. The EXISTS and
IN clauses can both be used within the WHERE clause to help determine which rows
to delete from a table. The IN clause can use a sub-query to create a list of values
evaluated in the WHERE clause. If the value specified prior to the IN clause is contained in the list, the expression evaluates to TRUE. The EXISTS clause executes a
sub-query once for each row evaluated, to determine if the record causes the sub-
query to return rows. If the sub-query returns one or more rows, the expression evaluates
to TRUE.

Steps

1. Run SQL*Plus and connect as the WAITE user account. The CHP8-19.sql
file, shown in Figure 8-8, creates the sample tables used in this How-To.

The SQL script creates two tables, DEPT8_19A and DEPT8_19B. Two
records are created in the DEPT8_19A table, and one record is created in
the DEPT8_19B table. In the following steps, the record in the DEPT8_19A
table that also exists in the DEPT8_19B table will be deleted. Run the file to
create the sample tables.

```
SQL>   START CHP8-19

Table created.

Table created.

1 row created.
```

continued on next page

continued from previous page

1 row created.

1 row created.

Commit complete.

> **2.** Load CHP8-20.sql into the SQL buffer. The file contains a DELETE statement using an EXISTS clause to delete all records in the DEPT8_19A table that already exist in the DEPT8_19B table.

```
SQL> GET CHP8-20
  1   DELETE FROM
  2      DEPT8_19A
  3   WHERE
  4    EXISTS
  5    (SELECT 'X' FROM
  6       DEPT8_19B WHERE
  7*      DEPT8_19B.DEPT_NO = DEPT8_19A.DEPT_NO)
```

> Line 1 specifies the DELETE keyword used to remove records from a table. Lines 4 through 7 specify an EXISTS clause which deletes any records meeting the criteria of the sub-query. The sub-query will determine whether each record evaluated by the statement's WHERE clause exists in the DEPT8_19B table. Line 7 specifies that the DEPT_NO field from the sub-query must equal the DEPT_NO field from the table in the DELETE statement.

> **3.** Run the statement to delete the records, and rollback the transaction with the ROLLBACK statement.

```
SQL> /
```

1 row deleted.

```
SQL> Rollback;
```

Rollback complete.

> **4.** Load CHP8-21.sql into the SQL buffer. This file contains a DELETE statement with an IN clause, which deletes all records in the DELTEST table that already exist in the DELSOURCE table.

```
SQL> GET CHP8-21
  1   DELETE FROM
  2      DEPT8_19A
  3   WHERE
  4      DEPT_NO IN
  5    (SELECT DEPT_NO FROM
  6*      DEPT8_19B)
```

This statement performs the same task as the statement listed in Step 2, but Oracle parses its execution differently. Lines 5 and 6 specify a query listing all the DEPT_NO values in the DEPT8_19B table. The resulting list is used by the IN clause to determine which records to delete. If you know that the number of rows returned by the sub-query is small, use this approach; otherwise, use the EXISTS clause.

5. Execute the statement to delete the rows.

```
SQL>  /

1 row deleted.
```

How It Works

Step 1 builds the sample tables used in this How-To. The DEPT8_19A table is created and populated with two records. The DEPT8_19B table is created and populated with a single record. The record created in the DEPT8_19B table exists in DEPT8_19A. Steps 2 and 3 use the EXISTS clause in a DELETE statement to delete the record from DEPT8_19A which exists in DEPT8_19B. Steps 4 and 5 use the IN operator in the WHERE clause of a DELETE statement to perform the same task. The better method to use depends on the characteristics of the data in the tables. The EXISTS clause uses the table being deleted as the driving table. The sub-query is executed once for each row in the table. The IN clause executes the sub-query once and uses the results when evaluating the table being deleted. The sub-query is performed to create a list of values to check with the DELETE statement. If the table used in the sub-query is small, using the IN clause is usually the better method. If the table used in the sub-query is large, make sure that an index exists on the columns used to join it to the deleted table.

Comments

The NOT EXISTS and NOT IN clauses can be used to delete data from a table when it does not exist in the other table. The method for creating the sub-queries is exactly the same as the method used with the EXISTS and IN clauses. It is possible for the DELETE statements to take a very long time if the tables are large and the correct indexes do not exist.

COMPLEXITY
ADVANCED

8.8 How do I...
Delete data in sections to avoid errors?

Problem

When I delete large amounts of data, I get rollback segment errors because the DELETE statement uses rollback segments when executed. How can I delete data in sections in order to avoid rollback segment errors?

Technique

The ROWNUM pseudo-column can be used in a DELETE statement to delete a limited number of rows. The DELETE statement can be put in a loop within PL/SQL to execute repeatedly. After each group of data is deleted, a COMMIT statement is executed. When no more data to be deleted exists, the PL/SQL loop is exited.

Steps

1. Run SQL*Plus and connect as the WAITE user account. CHP8-22.sql, shown in Figure 8-9, is used to create the tables used in this How-To.

```
CREATE TABLE SAMPLE8_22 (
     X        NUMBER);

INSERT INTO SAMPLE8_22
   SELECT ROWNUM
   FROM
       SYS.DBA_OBJECTS
   WHERE
       ROWNUM <= 200;

COMMIT;
```

Figure 8-9 CHP8-22.sql creates the sample table used in How-To 8.8

The SQL script creates the SAMPLE8_22 table and populates it with 200 records generated by a query. In the steps that follow, the data will be deleted in sections. Run CHP8-22.sql to create the sample table.

```
SQL> START CHP8-22

Table created.

200 rows created.

Commit complete.
```

2. Load CHP8-23.sql into the SQL buffer. The file contains a PL/SQL statement to delete all the rows from a table, committing the transaction every 20 rows. In a real situation, you would commit the transaction every few hundred rows.

```
SQL> GET CHP8-23
  1   DECLARE
  2      TMP VARCHAR2(1);
  3   BEGIN
  4      LOOP
  5        BEGIN
  6          SELECT 'X'
  7             INTO TMP
  8           FROM
  9             SAMPLE8_22
 10          WHERE ROWNUM = 1;
 11          DELETE FROM SAMPLE8_22
 12            WHERE ROWNUM < 20;
 13          COMMIT;
 14        EXCEPTION
 15            WHEN NO_DATA_FOUND THEN
 16              EXIT;
 17        END;
 18      END LOOP;
 19*  END;
```

Lines 1 and 2 contain the declarative section of the PL/SQL block and create a temporary variable used in line 7 of the code. Lines 4 and 18 define a simple loop, which will continue to execute until the EXIT statement runs. Lines 5 and 17 define the block of PL/SQL code executed within the loop. Lines 6 through 10 query the SAMPLE8_22 table to determine if any more rows fitting the deletion criteria exist. In this case, all rows fit the criteria. If there are no rows left in the table, the exception handler in lines 15 and 16 exits the PL/SQL statement. If there are rows left, line 12 deletes a chuck of records limited by the ROWNUM pseudo-column. Line 13 commits the transaction.

3. Run the statement to delete the records from the sample table.

```
SQL> /

PL/SQL procedure successfully completed.
```

How It Works

Step 1 creates the sample table used in this How-To and populates it with 200 rows of sample data. Steps 2 and 3 delete records from the table, 20 at a time, committing after every 20 records. The ROWNUM pseudo-column is used in the DELETE statement to remove only 20 records when the statement is executed. A loop within PL/SQL continues to process records until the NO_DATA_FOUND exception occurs in the PL/SQL block. The exception occurs when a query of the table returns no rows.

Comments

The TRUNCATE statement can be used to delete all rows from a table quickly. Unfortunately, this statement cannot delete a subset of rows. The method shown in this How-To can be used when you are deleting a large number of rows in the table, but not all of them.

COMPLEXITY
INTERMEDIATE

8.9   How do I...
Insert date columns compliant with the year 2000 issue?

Problem

Our users like to enter dates using a two-digit year format. We need to ensure that dates inserted into the database represent the correct century. Currently when a user enters the date 01/01/00, it is stored in the table as the year 1900. How do I insert date columns compliant with the year 2000 issue?

Technique

Oracle has included the RR date format mask to solve problems caused by the turn of the century. Replacing the YY format mask in applications with the RR format mask creates all years between 00 and 49 in the next century. In other words, the century portion of the year would be 20. Years between 50 and 99, however, are created in the current century and begin with 19.

Steps

1. Run SQL*Plus and connect as the WAITE user account. CHP8-24.sql, shown in Figure 8-10, creates the sample table used in this How-To.

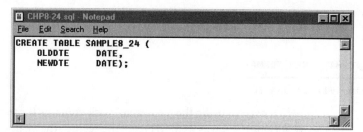

Figure 8-10 CHP8-24.sql creates the sample table used in How-To 8.9

The SAMPLE8_24 table is created by the script and contains two date columns which will be used to demonstrate the RR format mask. Run the file to create the sample table.

```
SQL>   /

Table created.
```

2. Load CHP8-25.sql into the SQL buffer. The file contains an INSERT statement to create a record containing two columns. One of the columns uses the RR format mask, and the other uses the YY format mask.

```
SQL> GET CHP8-25
  1   INSERT INTO SAMPLE8_24
  2        (OLDDTE, NEWDTE)
  3   VALUES
  4        (TO_DATE('01/01/11','MM/DD/YY'),
  5*        TO_DATE('01/11/11','MM/DD/RR'));
```

Line 4 formats the date using the YY format mask. The year will be stored as 1911. Line 5 uses the RR format mask to create the date stored in the next century. In this case, the date will be stored as 2011.

3. Run the statement to insert the records into the table.

```
SQL>   /

1 row created.
```

4. Load CHP8-26.sql into the SQL buffer. The file contains a statement to query the records created in the previous step.

```
SQL> GET CHP8-26
  1   SELECT
  2        TO_CHAR(OLDDTE,'DD-MON-YYYY') OLD_FORMAT,
  3        TO_CHAR(NEWDTE,'DD-MON-YYYY') NEW_FORMAT
  4   FROM
  5*        SAMPLE8_24
```

5. Format the columns using the COLUMN command and run the statement to query the records.

```
SQL> COLUMN OLD_FORMAT FORMAT A11
SQL> COLUMN NEW_FORMAT FORMAT A11
SQL> /

OLD_FORMAT   NEW_FORMAT
-----------  -----------
01-JAN-1911  01-JAN-2011
```

The record created using the YY format mask contains the year 1911. When the RR format mask was used to create the record, the year was stored as 2011.

How It Works

Step 1 creates the sample table used throughout this How-To. The SAMPLE8_24 table contains two date columns. Steps 2 and 3 create a record using an INSERT statement with the TO_DATE function. One column is inserted using the YY format mask and another using the RR format mask. Steps 4 and 5 query the record inserted in the previous steps, formatting the date with a four-digit year. When the YY format mask is used, the date is always created in the current century. When the RR format mask is used, the date is created in the current century if the two-digit year is between 50 and 99, and the next century if it is between 0 and 49.

Comments

The RR format mask should be used where needed to help resolve the year 2000 issue. However, be careful using this mask since there are many cases where YY should still be used. Since nobody has yet been born in the 21st century and many people were born before 1950, birthdays are one place to avoid using the RR format mask.

COMPLEXITY
INTERMEDIATE

8.10 How do I...
Update date columns for the year 2000 issue?

Problem

Many of our older applications insert and update records using the two-digit year format. As we approach the turn of the century, we are inserting dates past the year 2000. Oracle is storing the dates in the wrong century. As part of the process to upgrade our system to handle the year 2000, I need to update existing date columns to the correct internal representation. How do I update date columns to handle the year 2000 issue?

Technique

To help resolve year 2000 issues, Oracle7 included the RR date format mask. When the RR format mask is used, the year is stored with the next century if the last two digits of the year are between 0 and 49. The year is stored in the current century if the two-digit year is between 50 and 99. We will use the TO_DATE function in an UPDATE statement to correct existing data.

Steps

1. Run SQL*Plus and connect as the WAITE user account. CHP8-27.sql, shown in Figure 8-11, creates the sample table and data used in this example.

The SQL script creates the table SAMPLE8_27 and populates it with two records. The first record contains a date with a two-digit year of 11. When the record is created, it is stored as 1911. The second record is created with a two-digit year of 90, which is stored as 1990. The steps that follow update the first record to 2011, while leaving the second record as 1990. Run the file to create the sample table and two sample records.

```
SQL>  /

Table created.

1 row inserted.

1 row inserted.

Commit complete.
```

2. Load CHP8-28.sql into the SQL buffer. The file contains an UPDATE statement to modify records to the correct century using the RR format mask.

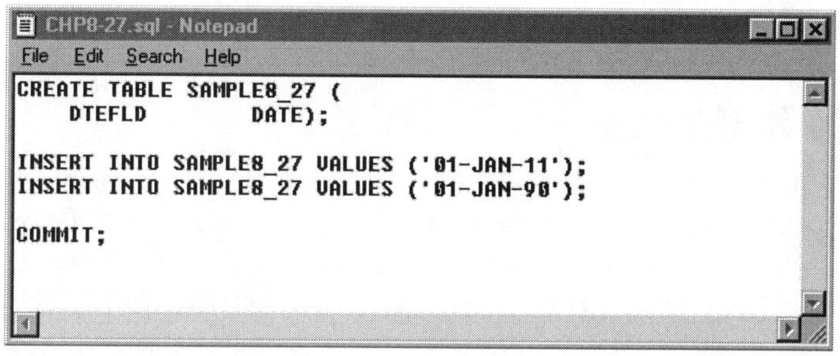

Figure 8-11 CHP8-27.sql creates the sample table used in How-To 8.10

```
SQL> GET CHP8-28
  1   UPDATE SAMPLE8_27
  2   SET
  3       DATEFLD = TO_DATE(TO_CHAR(DATEFLD,'DD-MON-YY HH24:MI:SS'),
  4*                        'DD-MON-RR HH24:MI:SS')
```

Lines 3 and 4 use the TO_CHAR function to convert the date in the column to a format including a two-digit year, hours, minutes, and seconds. If the time portion of the format mask is not included, the time gets lost in the conversion. The TO_DATE function uses the RR format mask to convert the two-digit year to the correct century. With the exception of the RR portion of the format mask, the format masks used by the TO_CHAR and TO_DATE functions must match exactly.

3. Run the statement to update the records in the table.

```
SQL>  /
```

2 rows updated.

4. Load CHP8-29.sql into the SQL buffer. The file was used in Steps 2 and 3 to query the original data. Because the RR format mask was used, one of the two rows should be modified to the new century.

```
SQL>  GET CHP8-29
  1   SELECT
  2       TO_CHAR(DATEFLD,'DD-MON-YYYY') DATEFLD
  3   FROM
  4       SAMPLE8_27
```

5. Run the statement to query the new data.

```
SQL>  /

DATEFLD
-----------------------------------------------------------------
01-JAN-2011
01-JAN-1990
```

How It Works

Step 1 creates the sample table and data used throughout this How-To. The sample table contains a date field, and two rows are inserted with the year formatted using the YY format mask. The first record is created with 11 as the two-digit year and stored as 1911 in the database. The second record is created with 90 as the two-digit year and stored as 1990 in the database. Steps 2 and 3 update the value of the column using the RR format mask. Both the date and time are included in the format mask to ensure that the time values are not lost in the conversion. Steps 4 and 5 show the records after conversion. The 1911 record is converted to 2011, and the 1990 record remains unchanged.

Comments

Not all date columns should be converted using this method. If a date prior to 1950 is valid for the column, do not use this method. Updating very large tables can cause problems, because the UPDATE statement will be processed as a single transaction. If the size of the table is very large, a PL/SQL script should be used to commit the transaction every few hundred rows.

QUERYING DATA

9

QUERYING DATA

How do I...

9.15   Perform greater than and less than logic with the DECODE function?

9.16   Query a record by ROWID?

9.17   Lock rows when I query them?

9.18   Traverse a tree structure?

9.19   Return records based on a group function?

One of the most powerful features of Oracle is the sophisticated way it retrieves data from the database. Querying data can be as simple as retrieving all records from a single table, or as complex as querying the hierarchy of tree-structured data. Many of the topics covered in this chapter are common to all relational databases supporting SQL. Others are specific to Oracle. Oracle has created powerful functions to enhance SQL. Using the power of Oracle to create sophisticated queries within your application means records do not need to be manipulated within your application. This chapter explores methods of querying data from the database. Chapter 10 explores methods used to format data when it is queried. The examples presented in this chapter are found on the accompanying CD in the \SAMPLES\CHAP10 directory.

9.1   Join two related tables

Joining tables within a query is a fundamental operation in a relational database. Two or more tables can be combined in a single query to return results as if all the data came from a single source. The join condition specified in the query defines the relationships between the tables used in the query. The join condition is specified in the WHERE clause of a query by matching like columns between tables. This How-To provides an explanation and example of joining tables within a query.

9.2   Group data in logical groups

Group operations, such as calculating the sum or average of columns in a table, return a calculation of multiple rows as a single value. Data can be grouped to return multiple groups of data in a single query. Group functions and the GROUP BY clause are used in a query to group like data. This How-To presents techniques for using group operations within a query.

9.3   Limit the number of rows returned by a query

In many situations, you will not want to retrieve all the rows normally returned by a query. If you are populating static text on a form or a listbox, you may need to limit the number of rows returned by a query. The number of rows returned by a query can by limited by using the ROWNUM pseudo-column in the WHERE clause of the query. This How-To presents the method used to limit the number of rows returned by a query.

9.4   Prevent the selection of duplicate rows

Sometimes a query will return duplicate records based on its selection criteria. If you are looking for all the unique values contained in a column, you can remove duplicate values by using the DISTINCT operator in a query. This How-To covers the technique used to prevent duplicate results in a query.

9.5   Join a table to itself

There are many cases when it is desirable to join a table to itself in a query. It can be necessary when creating complicated queries with the DECODE function or when using group functions. A table can be joined to itself by using aliases on the table-name in the FROM clause of the query. Aliases allow the same table to be used more than once in a query. This How-To presents methods for joining a table to itself within in a query.

9.6   Use wildcards in a query

You will not always know the exact spelling of values in a character field. Wildcards allow the user to query information without knowing the exact value of a field. The LIKE operator in Oracle is a powerful tool for pattern matching. In Oracle, the percent sign (%) is the wildcard and can represent any number of characters. The underscore (_) character is a position marker. It can represent any single character in its position. This How-To covers to the process of using wildcards in a query.

9.7   Count the number of records in a table

Within Oracle, it is possible to count the number of rows in a table or the number of rows that satisfy certain conditions. The COUNT function is a group function used on an entire table or a table's subset. This How-To presents methods for counting records within a table.

9.8   Order rows in descending order

An ORDER BY clause is used to specify the order in which rows are retrieved. By default, records are returned by the ORDER BY clause in ascending order. The DESC modifier is used to reverse the order of the query. The ASC modifier returns the records in ascending order. A combination of DESC and ASC modifiers can be used in a single query. This How-To presents techniques for ordering data in a query.

9.9   Order rows in a non-standard order

An ORDER BY clause retrieves records in ascending or descending order. However, it is sometimes necessary to return rows in a non-standard order. If you want to put the most common values at the beginning of a list, a different technique must be used. The DECODE function can be used in the ORDER BY clause to force records to be returned in a non-standard order. This How-To presents a technique to perform non-standard ordering.

9.10 Create a query that depends on the results of another query

The results of a query can be dependent on the results of a sub-query. The IN and EXISTS operators return records using a sub-query as part of the WHERE clause. This How-To presents methods for using sub-queries within a query.

9.11 Combine two queries

In many situations, all of the data you want returned by a query cannot be presented in a single SELECT statement. *Unions* allow multiple queries to be executed and returned by Oracle as a single result set. This How-To presents the method for using the UNION operator in a query.

9.12 Return the intersection of two queries

Sometimes you need to return records existing in two related queries. If a record only exists in one of the two queries, you do not want to return the record. The INTERSECT operator allows you to perform two related queries and return only records identical in both queries. This How-To presents the process of using the INTERSECT operator in a query.

9.13 Subtract the results of a query from another

The results of a query can be subtracted from another query to return a calculated result set. If an identical record exists in the subtracted query, it is not returned by the query. The MINUS operator is used to subtract queries. This How-To presents the method used to subtract one query from another and return a calculated result set.

9.14 Return rows even when a join condition fails

When two tables are joined, only rows that meet the join condition are returned by the query. In many cases, you want to return all rows from one side of the join condition, even if the join condition fails. The *outer join operator*, (+), is used to force a join condition to succeed even if one side of the join condition fails. This How-To explores the use of the outer join operator in Oracle.

9.15 Perform greater than and less than logic with the DECODE function

The DECODE function is a very powerful function used to perform equality tests in a query. You many want to perform greater than or less than logic within a DECODE function. On the surface, the DECODE function does not look like it can perform these types of tests. This How-To presents a method for expanding the use of the DECODE function to perform greater than and less than logic in a query.

9.16 Query a record by ROWID

The ROWID column is unique within the database. Querying a record by ROWID is the fastest way to retrieve a row. The ROWID can be used in a query or to modify a record. This How-To covers the process used to query a record using the ROWID.

9.17   Lock rows when I query them

If you are planning to update a row after it has been queried, it is important to lock the row to prevent other users from unexpectedly updating it. The FOR UPDATE clause in a query locks the record it returns, until a COMMIT statement is executed or the session is terminated. This How-To presents the method for locking records with a query.

9.18   Traverse a tree structure

Data can be stored in a hierarchical structure within a table. An example of this is the reporting structure within an organization. Oracle provides support for a hierarchical structure through the CONNECT BY clause. This How-To presents the method for navigating a tree structure in Oracle.

9.19   Return records based on a group function

Group functions such as SUM, COUNT, MAX, and MIN cannot be used in the WHERE clause of a query. It is sometimes necessary to base the results of a query on a group function. The HAVING clause allows records to be returned based on the results of a group function. This How-To explores the use of the HAVING clause within queries.

COMPLEXITY
BEGINNING

9.1   How do I...
Join two related tables?

Problem

I want to create a query which joins two or more tables. The structure of the data model makes it impossible to get all the information I need from a single table. Within my application, it is important to be able to create queries containing data from more than one table or view. The tables I want to join are related through common columns. How do I join two related tables?

Technique

Data in two or more related tables or views can be joined in a query. Within the FROM clause of the query, all tables that are part of the query must be listed. The WHERE clause must specify the relationship between the tables by making like columns equal. Figure 9-1 shows the relationship between the two tables used in this How-To.

Both tables contain the DEPT_NO column. The WHERE clause of a query of these two tables must specify DEPT92.DEPT_NO = EMP92.DEPT_NO. In order for a row to be retrieved by the query, matching data must exist in both tables. If a value exists in one of the tables but not the other, the record will not be returned.

```
CHP9-1.sql - Notepad                                    _ □ ×
File  Edit  Search  Help
CREATE TABLE DEPT9_2 (
    DEPT_NO     NUMBER(10),
    DEPT_NAME   VARCHAR2(20),
    MGR_ID      NUMBER(10));

CREATE TABLE EMP9_2 (
    EMP_NO      NUMBER(10),
    EMP_NAME    VARCHAR2(20),
    DEPT_NO     NUMBER(10),
    MGR_ID      NUMBER(10));

INSERT INTO DEPT9_2
    VALUES (1,'MARKETING',1);
INSERT INTO EMP9_2
    VALUES (1, 'JOHN SMITH', 1, 2);
INSERT INTO EMP9_2
    VALUES (2, 'MARY HENRY',1, 1);
INSERT INTO EMP9_2
    VALUES (3, 'BILL JONES',2, 2);
COMMIT;
```

Figure 9-1 The relationship between related tables

Steps

1. Run SQL*Plus and connect as the WAITE user account. CHP9-1.sql, shown in Figure 9-2, creates the sample tables and data used in this How-To.

The DEPT_92 table contains the departments within an organization. The EMP_92 table contains the employees that work in the organization. The DEPT_NO column contained in both tables will join the tables. Four records demonstrating how tables are joined in a query are created. One record is created in the DEPT_92 table, joined to two of the records in the EMP_92 table by the common DEPT_NO column. Run the file to create the sample tables and data.

```
SQL>  START CHP9-1

Table created.

Table created.

1 row created.

1 row created.

1 row created.

1 row created.

Commit complete.
```

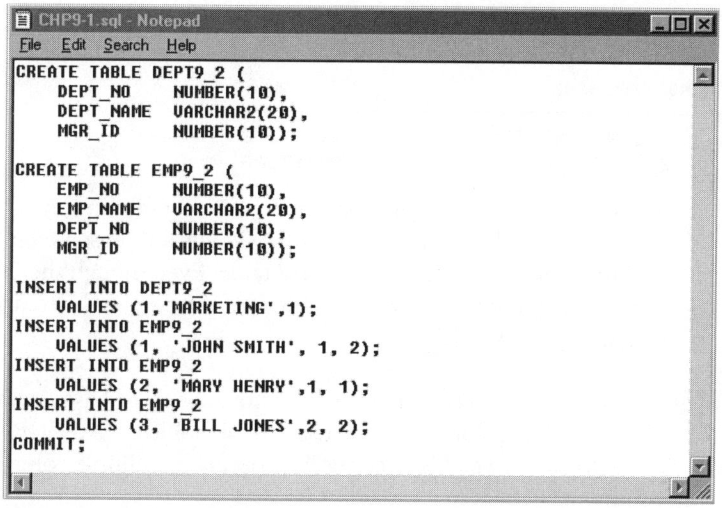

Figure 9-2 CHP9-1.sql creates the sample tables
used in How-To 9.1

2. Load CHP9-2.sql into the SQL buffer. The file contains a query joining the two sample tables created in the last step.

```
SQL> GET CHP9-2
  1  SELECT
  2      EMP9_2.EMP_NO,
  3      EMP9_2.EMP_NAME,
  4      DEPT9_2.DEPT_NAME
  5  FROM
  6      EMP9_2,
  7      DEPT9_2
  8  WHERE
  9*      EMP9_2.DEPT_NO = DEPT9_2.DEPT_NO
```

Lines 2 through 4 specify the columns to be returned by the query. The tablename is specified along with the column name. The table name does not need to be specified if the column name is unique within the tables used in the query. Lines 6 and 7 specify the tables used in the query. If a table is used in the select list or the WHERE clause without being specified in the FROM clause, an error will occur. Line 9 specifies the join condition. Each table contains a DEPT_NO column which relates the two tables. If the join condition is not specified, many invalid rows will be returned by the query.

3. Run the statement to show the results of the query.

```
SQL> /

EMP_NO EMP_NAME              DEPT_NAME
-------- --------------------- ----------------------
     1 JOHN SMITH            MARKETING
     2 MARY HENRY            MARKETING
```

The DEPT_NAME column from the DEPT_92 table and the EMP_NO and EMP_NAME columns from the EMP_92 table are presented in the result set as if they came from the same source table. Even though the DEPT_NO column is used to join the two tables, it does not need to be returned by the query.

4. A join condition between tables does not have to be based on a single column. Multiple columns can be used to join tables. Load CHP9-3.sql into the SQL buffer. The file contains a query using multiple columns in the join condition.

```
SQL> GET CHP9-3
  1  SELECT
  2      EMP9_2.EMP_NO,
  3      EMP9_2.EMP_NAME,
  4      DEPT9_2.DEPT_NAME,
  5      EMP9_2.MGR_ID
  6  FROM
  7      EMP9_2,
  8      DEPT9_2
  9  WHERE
 10      EMP9_2.DEPT_NO = DEPT9_2.DEPT_NO AND
 11*     EMP9_2.MGR_ID = DEPT9_2.MGR_ID
```

Lines 2 through 5 specify the columns returned by the query. Lines 7 and 8 specify the tables used in the query. The EMP9_2 table is the source of three columns in the select list, and the DEPT9_2 table is the source of one column. Lines 10 and 11 join the EMP9_2 and DEPT9_2 tables using two columns. Both of the columns must be equal in order for a record to be returned.

5. Run the query to display the results.

```
SQL> /

EMP_NO EMP_NAME              DEPT_NAME                MGR_ID
-------- --------------------- ----------------------  ----------
     2 MARY HENRY            MARKETING                     1
```

Unlike Step 3 where two records were returned by the query, only one record is returned by this query. Although both employees have the same DEPT_NO column, only one employee has both the same DEPT_NO and MGR_ID columns. When the primary key of a table contains multiple columns, it is important to include all of the columns when specifying the join condition.

How It Works

Step 1 creates the sample tables used throughout this How-To. Steps 2 and 3 present a query that joins two tables, returning information from both in a single query. The columns joining the two tables must be specified in the WHERE clause of the query. Each table used within the query must be specified in the FROM clause. If a column name exists in more than one table in the query, the table name must be specified to identify which table is the data source. Steps 4 and 5 join the same tables by two columns. In order for a row to be returned by the query, both columns in the join condition must be identical.

Comments

Joining tables is an important operation when using a relational database. The more proficient you become at using multiple tables within a query, the more flexible the Oracle database will become for you. With a normalized data model, it is almost impossible to avoid joining tables. Do not denormalize your database in order to avoid joins!

COMPLEXITY
INTERMEDIATE

9.2 How do I...
Group data in logical groups?

Problem

I want to use group functions such as SUM, MIN, MAX, and AVG within my queries. I do not always want to perform these functions on the entire table. I need to group information based on the values in one or more of the columns. How do I group data in logical groups within a query?

Technique

Group functions allow calculations to be performed on the entire table or groups of related records. Figure 9-3 shows how data can be grouped within a table.

Within the table shown in Figure 9-3, employee records are grouped by their department number. In addition to querying the sum of all the employees' salaries listed in the table, we can query the sum of each department number by specifying a GROUP BY clause in the query. The GROUP BY clause specifies how data should be grouped when performing group operations. If group functions are used in a query, any column which is not a group function must be specified in the GROUP BY clause.

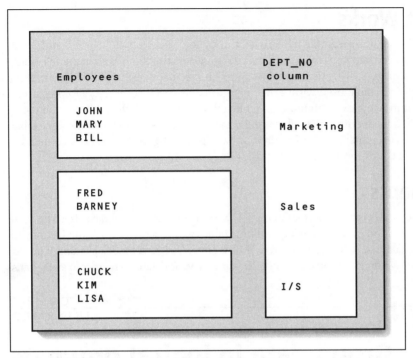

Figure 9-3 The grouping of logical data

Steps

1. Run SQL*Plus and connect as the WAITE user account. CHP9-4.sql, shown in Figure 9-4, creates the sample table and data used throughout this How-To.

The sample table contains employees who work in an organization. Although each record contains information about specific employees, the queries run in this How-To will calculate information about their department. The DEPT_NO column identifies the department for which the employee works. Group functions will be used and employee records grouped by the DEPT_NO column. Run the statement to create the sample table and data.

```
SQL> START CHP9-4

Table created.

1 record created.

1 record created.

1 record created.
```

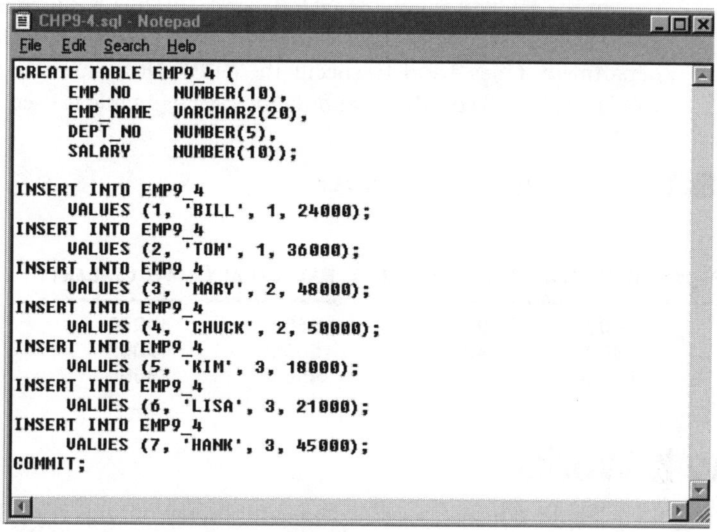

Figure 9-4 CHP9-4.sql creates the sample tables used in
How-To 9.2

```
1 record created.

1 record created.

1 record created.

1 record created.

Commit complete.
```

2. Load CHP9-5.sql into the SQL buffer. The file contains a query that groups
data and performs group functions on the data.

```
SQL> GET CHP9-5
  1  SELECT
  2    DEPT_NO,
  3    SUM(SALARY),
  4    MIN(SALARY),
  5    MAX(SALARY),
  6    AVG(SALARY)
  7  FROM
  8    EMP9_4
  9  GROUP BY
 10*   DEPT_NO
```

Lines 3 through 6 specify the columns returned by the query. The
DEPT_NO column specified in line 2 is the only column that isn't a group
function. Since it is not a group function, it must be specified in the
GROUP BY clause. Line 3 calculates the sum of the grouped data. Line 4

returns the smallest salary for each department, line 5 returns the largest salary for each department, and line 6 returns the average salary for each department. Lines 9 and 10 specify the DEPT_NO column in the GROUP BY clause. Line 8 specifies that only the EMP9_3 table is used in the query.

3. Run the query to display the results.

```
SQL>  /

    DEPT_NO  SUM(SALARY)  MIN(SALARY)  MAX(SALARY)  AVG(SALARY)
    -------  -----------  -----------  -----------  -----------
       1        60000        24000        36000        30000
       2        98000        48000        50000        49000
       3        84000        18000        45000        28000
```

How It Works

Step 1 creates the sample table and data used throughout this How-To. Steps 2 and 3 present a query that groups data logically by the DEPT_NO column. Any time a group function is used in a query with non-group functions, a GROUP BY clause must be specified. Each column that is not a group function must be listed in the GROUP BY clause. Table 9-1 shows the group functions contained in Oracle. The GROUP BY clause makes the query return one record for each distinct combination of values listed. A group function cannot be used in the WHERE clause of a query. How-To 9.19 presents the HAVING clause and the technique used to return records based on the results of a group function.

FUNCTION	DESCRIPTION
AVG	Calculates the average values of the group.
COUNT	Counts the number of records in the group.
MAX	Returns the maximum value in the group.
MIN	Returns the minimum value in the group.
STDDEV	Returns the standard deviation of the group.
VARIANCE	Returns the variance of the group.

Table 9-1 Group functions

Comments

Group functions let a query perform many of the operations you would normally have to execute in your applications. It is much easier to use a group function like SUM than query all the records and calculate the total in your application. The GROUP BY clause can be confusing at times. When using group functions, just remember if a column is not a group function, it must be listed in the GROUP BY clause.

COMPLEXITY
BEGINNING

9.3 How do I...
Limit the number of rows returned by a query?

Problem

I need to limit the number of rows my query returns. In some cases I need to be sure the query only returns one row. In other queries, I need to populate fields on a screen and do not want to return more rows than I have room for. The information in my WHERE clause is not complete enough to limit the number of rows the query returns. How can I limit the number of rows returned by a query?

Technique

The ROWNUM pseudo-column returns a unique number for each record, starting with 1. The first value for ROWNUM in a query is always 1, the second is 2, and so on. In many cases, ROWNUM can be used in a WHERE clause to limit the number of rows returned. ROWNUM counts the rows returned by the query, not by each table in the query. The ROWNUM pseudo-column cannot be prefixed by a table name.

Steps

1. Run SQL*Plus and connect as the WAITE user account. CHP9-6.sql, shown in Figure 9-5, creates the sample table and data used throughout this How-To.

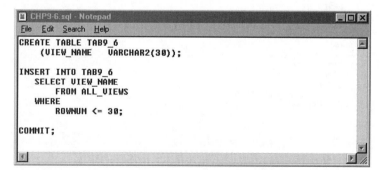

Figure 9-5 CHP9-6.sql creates the sample objects used in How-To 9.3

The sample table is populated with the data from the ALL_VIEWS data dictionary view. The ROWNUM pseudo-column is used in the creation of the sample table to create only 30 records. Run the file to create the sample table and data.

```
SQL>   START CHP9-6
```

Table created.

30 rows created.

Commit complete.

2. Load CHP9-7 into the SQL buffer. The file contains a query limiting the number of rows returned by using the ROWNUM pseudo-column.

```
SQL> GET CHP9-7
  1   SELECT VIEW_NAME
  2        FROM TAB9_6
  3   WHERE
  4        ROWNUM <= 5
  5   ORDER BY
  6*       VIEW_NAME
```

Line 1 specifies the column to be returned by the query. Line 2 specifies the table which is the source of the data. Line 4 uses the ROWNUM pseudo-column to ensure that no more than five records are returned by the query.

3. Run the statement to return the results of the query. Figure 9-6 shows the results of the query in SQL*Plus.

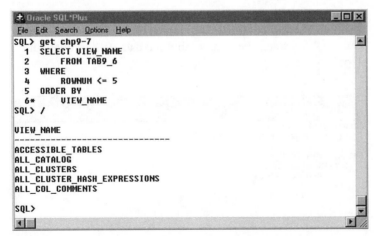

Figure 9-6 The results of CHP9-7.sql in SQL*Plus

4. Since the ROWNUM pseudo-column counts rows returned by the query, you cannot query records where ROWNUM is greater than a positive number. Load CHP9-8.sql into the SQL buffer. This attempts to return records where ROWNUM is greater than 5.

```
SQL> GET CHP9-8
  1  SELECT VIEW_NAME
  2      FROM TAB9_6
  3  WHERE
  4      ROWNUM > 5
  5  ORDER BY
  6*     VIEW_NAME
```

Line 4 specifies that records are only returned when the ROWNUM is greater than 5.

5. Run the query to display the results returned.

```
SQL>  /

No rows selected.
```

Even though there are more than five records in the table, no rows are returned by the query. Since ROWNUM is a pseudo-column which always begins with 1, there is never a value greater than 5.

How It Works

Step 1 creates the sample table and data used in this How-To. Steps 2 and 3 present a query limiting the number of records returned by specifying ROWNUM in the WHERE clause. Steps 4 and 5 attempt to perform an invalid query using ROWNUM. Since ROWNUM is created as the rows are returned and always begins with 1, the WHERE clause must not eliminate records where the ROWNUM is 1.

Comments

ROWNUM is very useful for limiting the number of rows in a query or putting a line counter in a report. Do not use ROWNUM as a join condition in queries or to update a specific row in the database. ROWNUM is a pseudo-column based on the query, not the tables within the query. You cannot predict the value of ROWNUM when you use it as part of a join condition in a complex query.

9.4 How do I...
Prevent the selection of duplicate rows?

Problem

In some of my queries, duplicate rows are returned. Even though the records are valid for the query, I do not want to return duplicate rows from the query. In many cases I want to view the unique values within a column. How do I prevent the selection of duplicate rows and present unique results?

Technique

The DISTINCT operator causes only unique rows to be returned by a query. If any column in the query makes the row unique, the row is returned. The keyword is placed at the beginning of the select list and only needs to be specified once in the query.

Steps

1. Run SQL*Plus and connect as the WAITE user account. CHP9-9.sql, shown in Figure 9-7, creates the sample tables and records used in this How-To.

```
CHP9-9.sql - Notepad

File  Edit  Search  Help

CREATE TABLE EMP9_9 (
     EMP_NO    NUMBER(10),
     EMP_NAME  VARCHAR2(20),
     DEPT_NO   NUMBER(5));

INSERT INTO EMP9_9
     VALUES (1, 'BILL', 1);
INSERT INTO EMP9_9
     VALUES (2, 'TED', 1);
INSERT INTO EMP9_9
     VALUES (3, 'MARY', 2);
INSERT INTO EMP9_9
     VALUES (4, 'JOHN', 2);
COMMIT;
```

Figure 9-7 CHP9-9.sql creates the sample objects used in How-To 9.4

The data created in the sample table contains duplicate values for some of the columns. When the data is queried using the DISTINCT operator, the duplicate column values will be eliminated. Run the statement to create the table and data.

```
SQL> START CHP9-9

Table created.

1 row created.

1 row created.

1 row created.

1 row created.

Commit complete.
```

2. Load CHP9-10.sql into the SQL buffer. The file contains a query of the sample table that does not use the DISTINCT keyword to eliminate duplicate rows.

```
SQL> GET CHP9-10
  1   SELECT
  2       DEPT_NO
  3   FROM
  4       EMP9_9
  5*  ORDER BY DEPT_NO
```

Line 2 specifies the column returned by the query. Line 4 presents the sample table as the source of the data, and line 5 specifies the order of the resulting data.

3. Run the statement to show the results.

```
SQL>  /

  DEPT_NO
----------
        1
        1
        2
        2
```

If the purpose of the query was to display the unique department numbers, the duplicate data makes the query results hard to read. Even though each record contains a unique employee, the DEPT_NO column is duplicated among records. If the source table contained hundreds of records, the results of this query would be unreadable.

4. Load CHP9-11.sql into the SQL buffer. The file contains a query that returns unique department numbers by specifying the DISTINCT keyword before the select list.

```
SQL>   GET CHP9-11
  1    SELECT
  2        DISTINCT DEPT_NO
  3    FROM
  4        EMP9_9
  5*   ORDER BY DEPT_NO
```

Line 2 uses the DISTINCT keyword to prevent the query from returning duplicate department numbers. The remaining lines of the query are identical to the query presented in Step 2.

5. Run the statement to display the results.

```
SQL> /

    DEPT_NO
----------
          1
          2
```

Regardless of the number of rows in the table, only distinct departments are returned by the query. The DISTINCT keyword applies to all columns following it in the select list.

6. Load CHP9-12.sql into the SQL buffer. The query returns two columns after the DISTINCT operator.

```
SQL> GET CHP9-12
  1    SELECT
  2        DISTINCT DEPT_NO, EMP_NO
  3    FROM
  4        EMP9_9
  5* ORDER BY DEPT_NO
```

Line 2 specifies two columns to be returned by the query. The DISTINCT keyword will cause distinct DEPT_NO, EMP_NO combinations to be returned by the query.

7. Run the query to display the results.

```
   DEPT_NO       EMP_NO
---------- ----------
         1            1
         1            2
         2            3
         2            4
```

Even though there are duplicate DEPT_NO columns returned by the query, all of the rows returned are distinct.

How It Works

The DISTINCT keyword is used to prevent queries from returning duplicate rows. Step 1 creates the sample tables and records used throughout this How-To. Steps 2 and 3 query the records in the table without using the DISTINCT keyword. Steps 4 and 5 use the DISTINCT keyword to return distinct DEPT_NO columns from the sample table. Steps 6 and 7 show the results of a query with two columns specified in a select list using the DISTINCT keyword.

Comments

The DISTINCT operator is very useful in analyzing data in a table. When you use the DISTINCT keyword, keep in mind that it affects the entire select list. You do not need to specify the keyword for each column in the list. The keyword is useful within sub-queries to limit the number of rows to be processed by the query.

COMPLEXITY
INTERMEDIATE

9.5 How do I...
Join a table to itself?

Problem

In one of my tables, I have a foreign key which references a primary key in the same table. When I create a query based on this table, I need to join the table to itself. An error occurs if the same table is used twice in the FROM clause of a query. How do I join a table to itself in a query?

Technique

Figure 9-8 shows a situation where it is necessary to join a table to itself. The sample table, EMP_13, contains a manager ID, which is also another employee's ID. In order to query an employee and his or her manager at the same time, the table must be joined to itself.

In order to use the same table twice in a query, an alias must be employed. An alias is specified by being included after the table name in the FROM clause of the query. When an alias is specified, using the actual table name in the query will cause an error. Aliases are also useful when the name of a table is long and you do not wish to type it repeatedly in a query.

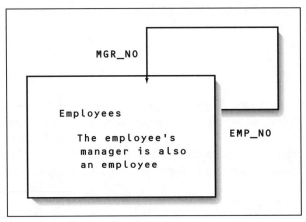

Figure 9-8 A self join

Steps

1. Run SQL*Plus and connect as the WAITE user account. CHP9-13.sql, shown in Figure 9-9, creates the sample table and records used in this How-To.

The EMP_NO and MGR_NO columns create a join condition between records in the same table. The MGR_NO represents the employee number of the manager. Run the file to create the table and sample records.

```
SQL> START CHP9-13

Table created.

1 row inserted.
```

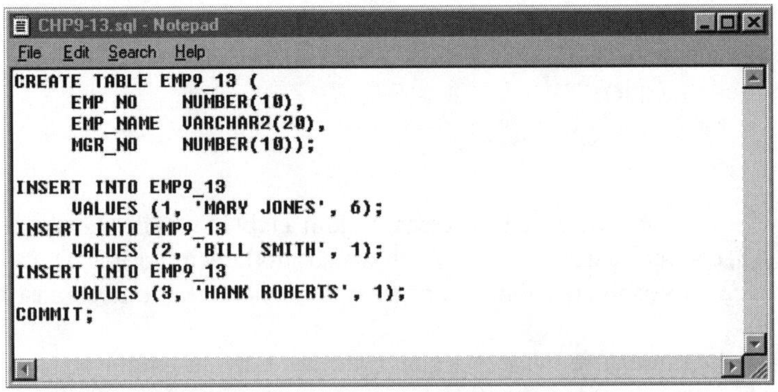

```
CHP9-13.sql - Notepad
File  Edit  Search  Help
CREATE TABLE EMP9_13 (
    EMP_NO     NUMBER(10),
    EMP_NAME   VARCHAR2(20),
    MGR_NO     NUMBER(10));

INSERT INTO EMP9_13
    VALUES (1, 'MARY JONES', 6);
INSERT INTO EMP9_13
    VALUES (2, 'BILL SMITH', 1);
INSERT INTO EMP9_13
    VALUES (3, 'HANK ROBERTS', 1);
COMMIT;
```

Figure 9-9 CHP9-13.sql creates the sample objects used in How-To 9.5

1 row inserted.

1 row inserted.

Commit complete.

> **2.** Load CHP9-14.sql into the SQL buffer. The file contains a query where a table is used twice and joined to itself.

```
SQL> GET CHP9-14
  1  SELECT
  2      E.EMP_NO,
  3      E.EMP_NAME EMP_NAME,
  4      M.EMP_NAME MGR_NAME
  5  FROM
  6      EMP9_13 E,
  7      EMP9_13 M
  8  WHERE
  9*     E.MGR_NO = M.EMP_NO
```

> Lines 2 through 4 specify the columns to be returned by the query. Each of the columns uses the aliases declared in the FROM clause. A column alias is also specified to give each column a unique name in the query. The table alias is required with the column name in the select list, because the column name cannot be unique among tables in the query. Lines 6 and 7 specify that the EMP9_13 table be used in the query twice, once with the alias M and once with the alias E. Line 9 joins the foreign key from the E instance of the table with the primary key from the M instance of the table.

> **3.** Run the statement to perform the query. Figure 9-10 shows the results of the query in SQL*Plus.

> Because the MARY JONES record does not contain a MGR_NO value that exists in the query, the record is not returned by the query. Only records containing a valid MGR_NO column are returned by the query.

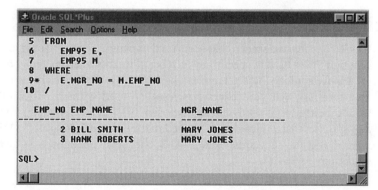

Figure 9-10 The results of CHP9-14.sql in SQL*Plus

How It Works

Step 1 creates the sample table and data used in this How-To. The foreign key of the EMP9_13 table joins to the primary key of the same table. When the same table is used twice within a query, aliases must be used to identify the table throughout the query. Since the same table is used twice in the query, the column names in the select list must contain the table alias. Steps 2 and 3 provide a query which performs a *self join*.

Comments

There are times when it is necessary to join a table to itself. If the same table is specified twice in a FROM clause without specifying an alias, an error will occur. When aliases are used within a query, the Oracle parser does not care that the same table is used more than once. This technique is useful when you want to return group functions and column values from the same table in a query.

COMPLEXITY
INTERMEDIATE

9.6 How do I...
Use wildcards in a query?

Problem

I want to use wildcard characters in some of my queries. For example, I want to return all records where the first three letters of the person's last name is JON. The user of the system does not always know the exact spelling of the data in a character field, and pattern matching is necessary. How do I use wildcards in a query?

Technique

Oracle contains two special characters used in pattern matching operations. The percent sign (%) is used to specify any number of unknown characters. The underscore (_) is a placeholder character and can be replaced by only one character in the specified location. Wildcard characters must be used with the LIKE operator. If a wildcard character is used with an equal sign (=), it is taken literally. The LIKE operator specifies that wildcards can be used in the specified string. If the LIKE operator is used and no wildcards are specified, the LIKE operator is equivalent to the equal sign.

Steps

1. Run SQL*Plus and connect as the WAITE user account. CHP9-15.sql, shown in Figure 9-11, creates the sample tables and data used in this How-To.

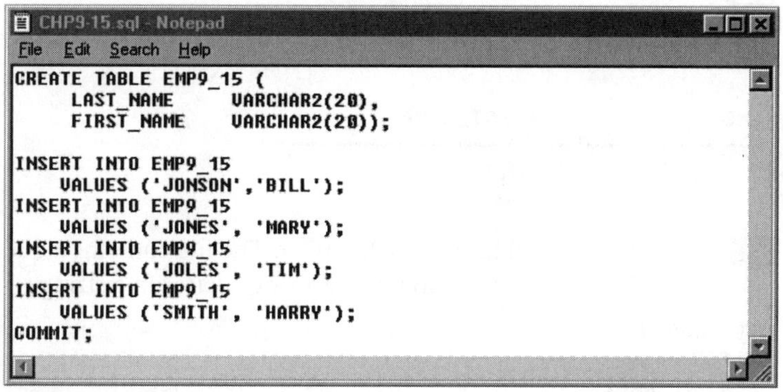


```
CREATE TABLE EMP9_15 (
     LAST_NAME      VARCHAR2(20),
     FIRST_NAME     VARCHAR2(20));

INSERT INTO EMP9_15
    VALUES ('JONSON','BILL');
INSERT INTO EMP9_15
    VALUES ('JONES', 'MARY');
INSERT INTO EMP9_15
    VALUES ('JOLES', 'TIM');
INSERT INTO EMP9_15
    VALUES ('SMITH', 'HARRY');
COMMIT;
```

Figure 9-11 CHP9-15.sql creates the sample objects used in How-To 9.6

The sample table is populated with data to demonstrate the use of wildcard characters. Run the file to create the sample table and data.

```
SQL>  START CHP9-15

Table created.

1 row created.

1 row created.

1 row created.

1 row created.

Commit complete.
```

2. Load CHP9-16.sql into the SQL buffer. The file contains a query that uses a wildcard character to return all rows in which the first three letters of the LAST_NAME column are JON.

```
SQL> GET CHP9-16
  1  SELECT
  2     LAST_NAME,
  3     FIRST_NAME
  4  FROM
  5     EMP9_15
  6  WHERE
  7*    LAST_NAME LIKE 'JON%'
```

Lines 2 and 3 specify the columns returned by the query. Line 5 specifies the source table for the data. Line 7 uses the LIKE operator and the % wildcard character in the WHERE clause of the query. The query will return all records in which the LAST_NAME column begins with the letters JON.

3. Run the statement to view the results.

```
SQL>  /

LAST_NAME                 FIRST_NAME
-------------------       --------------------
JONSON                    BILL
JONES                     MARY
```

4. Load CHP9-17.sql into the SQL buffer. The file contains a query which uses the _ wildcard character to replace a single letter in a string.

```
SQL>  GET CHP9-17
   1    SELECT
   2        LAST_NAME
   3    FROM
   4        EMP9_15
   5    WHERE
   6*      LAST_NAME LIKE 'JO_ES'
```

The _ wildcard character in line 6 specifies that only the third letter in the name can be replaced in the query. The first two letters in the LAST_NAME column must be JO, and the final two letters must be ES. The column must be five characters long.

5. Run the statement to display the results.

```
SQL>  /

LAST_NAME
--------------------------
JONES
JOLES
```

How It Works

Step 1 creates the sample table and records used in this How-To. Steps 2 and 3 use the % wildcard character to replace any number of characters. The query returns all records in which a column begins with a specific string. Steps 4 and 5 use the _ wildcard character to specify that only a single character can be replaced in the query. When the underscore wildcard is used, only a single character can be replaced in the query.

Comments

Wildcard characters make it easier to find data in a table. The % character is equivalent to the * character in UNIX or DOS. Remember to use the LIKE operator when working with wildcard characters, or they will treated as literal values.

COMPLEXITY
BEGINNING

9.7 How do I...
Count the number of records in a table?

Problem

I want to count the number of records in a table. I also want to count the rows that satisfy the criteria specified in the WHERE clause. I know the COUNT function is a group function and can be used with a GROUP BY clause. How do I count the number of records in a table?

Technique

The COUNT function is a group function used to return the number of rows in a set. The set of records can be the entire table, the number of rows returned by a WHERE clause, or the number or rows in a group defined in a GROUP BY clause. If the COUNT function is used alone in the select list without a GROUP BY or WHERE clause, the entire table is counted. If it is used alone with a WHERE clause, a single record is still returned but the number of records counted decreases. If the COUNT function is used with non-grouped columns, a GROUP BY clause must be included and all non-grouped columns must be listed in the clause.

Steps

1. Run SQL*Plus and connect as the WAITE user account. CHP9-18.sql, shown in Figure 9-12, creates the sample tables used in this How-To and populates it with data.

The sample table is created with the CREATE TABLE statement. Five records are created by the script, which will be counted in the examples. Run the statement to create the sample table and its data.

```
SQL>  START CHP9-18

Table created.

1 row created.

1 row created.

1 row created.
```

continued on next page

continued from previous page

```
1 row created.

1 row created.

Commit complete.
```

2. Load CHP9-19 into the SQL buffer. The file contains a query to count the number of records in the table.

```
SQL> GET CHP9-19
  1  SELECT
  2         COUNT(*)
  3  FROM
  4*        DEPT9_18
```

Line 2 specifies the COUNT function in order to count the number of records returned by the query. The COUNT function is a group function and can be used to count groups of records. Line 4 specifies the table to be counted. Since there is no WHERE clause in the query, all rows in the table are processed by the query.

3. Run the statement to count the number of records in the table.

```
SQL>  /

COUNT(*)
----------
         5
```

A single row is returned by the query because the COUNT function is a group function, and there is no GROUP BY clause in the query. The GROUP BY clause returns multiple rows in group expressions.

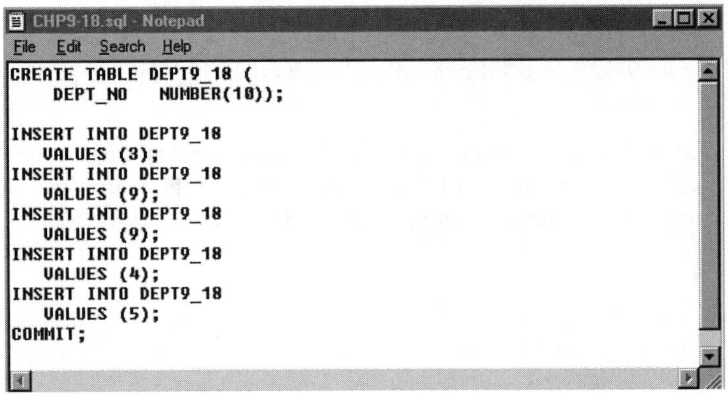


```
CREATE TABLE DEPT9_18 (
    DEPT_NO   NUMBER(10));

INSERT INTO DEPT9_18
   VALUES (3);
INSERT INTO DEPT9_18
   VALUES (9);
INSERT INTO DEPT9_18
   VALUES (9);
INSERT INTO DEPT9_18
   VALUES (4);
INSERT INTO DEPT9_18
   VALUES (5);
COMMIT;
```

Figure 9-12 CHP9-18.sql creates the sample objects used in How-To 9.7

4. Load CHP9-20.sql into the SQL buffer. The file contains a query to count the number of records in which the DEPT_NO field is 9.

```
SQL> GET CHP9-20
  1  SELECT
  2      COUNT(*)
  3  FROM
  4      DEPT9_18
  5  WHERE
  6*     DEPT_NO = 9
```

In the previous steps, all records in the table were counted. The WHERE clause in lines 5 and 6 causes a subset of the table to be processed by the query.

5. Run the statement to count the records.

```
SQL>  /

COUNT(*)
-----------
          2
```

Since there is no GROUP BY clause in the query, one row is returned. The WHERE clause limits the number of records the query processes, but does not change the number of records returned.

6. Load CHP9-21.sql into the SQL buffer. The file contains a query with a GROUP BY expression and counts the records for each department number.

```
SQL> GET CHP9-21
  1  SELECT
  2      DEPT_NO,
  3      COUNT(*)
  4  FROM
  5      DEPT9_18
  6  GROUP BY
  7*     DEPT_NO
```

Line 2 specifies that the DEPT_NO column is included in the query. Line 3 returns the COUNT function, which is a group function. Since the DEPT_NO column is not a group function and line 3 contains a group function, a GROUP BY clause must be included. Lines 6 and 7 specify the GROUP BY clause of the query.

7. Run the statement to view the results.

```
SQL>   /

DEPT_NO   COUNT(*)
--------- ---------
        3         1
        4         1
        5         1
        9         2
```

The GROUP BY clause returns one row for each distinct DEPT_NO value. The COUNT function is processed for each department number instead of the entire result set.

How It Works

Step 1 creates the sample table and data used throughout this How-To. Steps 2 and 3 present a query using the COUNT function to count the number of records in the table. Since no WHERE clause or GROUP BY clause was specified, a single row is retrieved and the entire table is processed. Steps 3 and 4 present a query that counts the number of records satisfying a certain condition. Including a WHERE clause in the query limits the number of records processed but does not change the number of rows returned. Steps 5 and 6 use the GROUP BY operator to return multiple rows with the COUNT group function.

Comments

The COUNT function is very useful in performing system management tasks. If the table is very large, a query of every record in the table can take an extremely long time. The COUNT function can be used in any query, as long as a GROUP BY clause is included to group logical data. How-To 9.2 presents the topic of grouping data with the GROUP BY clause.

COMPLEXITY
INTERMEDIATE

9.8   How do I...
Order rows in descending order?

Problem

In my queries, I use the ORDER BY clause to specify the order of the returned rows. The ORDER BY clause returns rows in ascending order. This is not always the way I want the records returned. In some cases, I want the records returned in descending order. I also want to be able to use multiple columns in an ORDER BY clause, with some in ascending order and others in descending order. How do I specify the ordering direction in an ORDER BY clause?

Technique

The ASC and DESC modifiers are used in the ORDER BY clause to specify the direction of the ordering. The default is ascending. If necessary, modifiers can be specified on multiple columns within the ORDER BY clause.

Steps

1. CHP9-22.sql, shown in Figure 9-13, creates the sample table and data used throughout this How-To.

CHP9-22 creates a single table with two VARCHAR2 columns to demonstrate ordering data by one or more columns. The table is populated with sample data to demonstrate the technique. Run the file to create the sample table and its data.

```
SQL>  START CHP9-22

Table created.

1 row created.

1 row created.

1 row created.

1 row created.

Commit complete.
```

2. Load CHP9-23.sql into the SQL buffer. The file contains a query including an ORDER BY clause with the DESC operator, which returns rows in descending order.

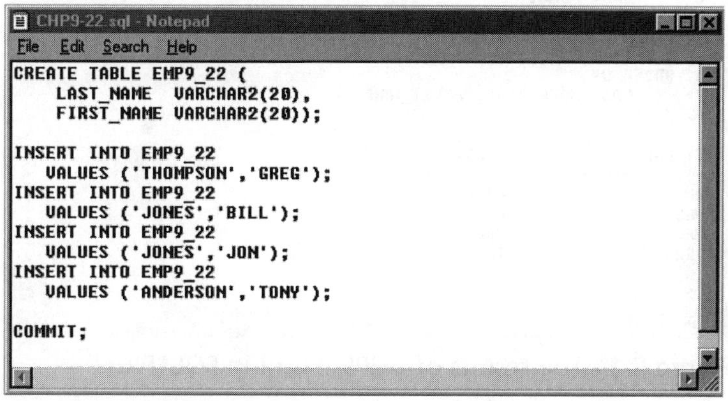


```
CREATE TABLE EMP9_22 (
     LAST_NAME  VARCHAR2(20),
     FIRST_NAME VARCHAR2(20));

INSERT INTO EMP9_22
   VALUES ('THOMPSON','GREG');
INSERT INTO EMP9_22
   VALUES ('JONES','BILL');
INSERT INTO EMP9_22
   VALUES ('JONES','JON');
INSERT INTO EMP9_22
   VALUES ('ANDERSON','TONY');

COMMIT;
```

Figure 9-13 CHP9-22.sql creates the sample objects used in How-To 9.8

```
SQL> CHP9-23
  1  SELECT
  2       LAST_NAME,
  3       FIRST_NAME
  4  FROM
  5       EMP9_22
  6  ORDER BY
  7*      LAST_NAME DESC, FIRST_NAME
```

Lines 2 and 3 specify the columns returned by the query. Line 5 identifies the table that is the data source. Line 7 identifies the ordering of the records. The DESC modifier is specified after the LAST_NAME column. This will organize the column in descending order. Since no modifier is specified in the FIRST_NAME column, it is returned in ascending order. The ASC modifier could be specified after the FIRST_NAME column to yield the same results.

3. Run the statement to display the results of the query. Figure 9-14 shows the results of the query within SQL*Plus.

The records are organized in descending order by the LAST_NAME column. The second and third records are the only records in which the second column in the ORDER BY clause matters. Since the DESC keyword was not specified for the column, the records are organized in ascending order.

4. Load CHP9-24.sql into the SQL buffer. The file contains the same query as the previous example, but organizes both columns in descending order by specifying the DESC modifier after each.

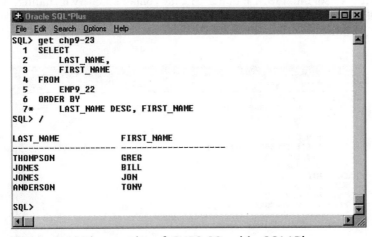

Figure 9-14 The results of CHP9-23.sql in SQL*Plus

```
SQL> CHP9-24
  1  SELECT
  2      LAST_NAME,
  3      FIRST_NAME
  4  FROM
  5      EMP9_22
  6  ORDER BY
  7*      LAST_NAME DESC, FIRST_NAME DESC
```

Line 7 specifies that both the LAST_NAME and FIRST_NAME columns are returned in descending order. The DESC modifier is specified after each column in the ORDER BY clause.

5. Run the query to display the results. Since both columns are organized in descending order, the second and third records are reversed. Figure 9-15 displays the results of CHP9-24.sql in SQL*Plus.

In this case, the order of the second and third records has reversed. The FIRST_NAME column is also organized in descending order.

How It Works

Step 1 creates the sample table and data used throughout this How-To. Steps 2 and 3 use the DESC modifier on a single column to reverse the order in which the query returns the records. Since the ORDER BY clause contained two columns and only one was specified as descending, the secondary column returned records in ascending order. Steps 4 and 5 specify both columns in the ORDER BY clause as descending.

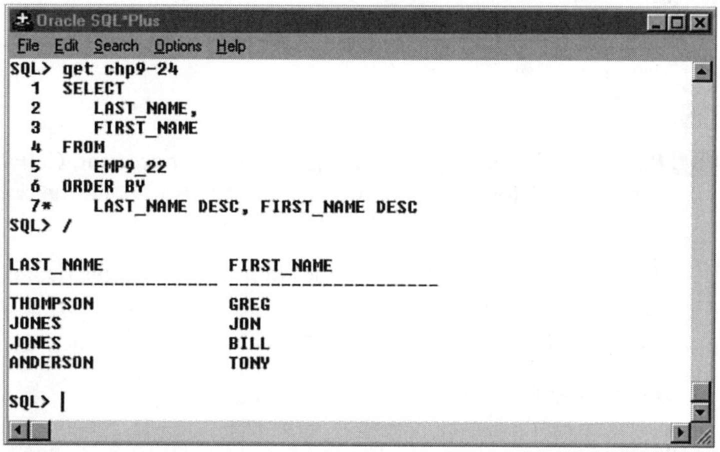

Figure 9-15 The results of CHP9-24.sql in SQL*Plus

Comments

The ASC and DESC keywords can be used to specify the direction in which the ORDER BY clause returns rows. The default direction is ascending. The ASC keyword makes complex ORDER BY clauses easier to read, but is not necessary.

COMPLEXITY
ADVANCED

9.9 How do I...
Order rows in a non-standard order?

Problem

In my applications, I do not always want to order records in a way that can be represented by a standard ORDER BY clause. When I populate a list box, I want to move the most common values to the top of it. The data in the table is not in this order. How do I organize records in a non-standard order in a query?

Technique

The DECODE function can replace the actual value of a column with an index value used within an ORDER BY clause. The DECODE function acts like an in-line IF statement. The technique forces columns to be ordered in a way not directly represented by the data. This allows you to move the most commonly used, or most important, records to the top of the query.

Steps

1. Run SQL*Plus and connect as the WAITE user account. CHP9-25.sql, shown in Figure 9-16, contains the statements to build the sample table used throughout this How-To.

The sample table contains a single column. The sample data contains three records which will be used to display non-standard ordering techniques. Run the file to create the sample tables.

```
SQL>   START CHP9-25

Table created.

1 row created.

1 row created.
```

1 row created.

Commit complete.

> **2.** Load CHP9-26.sql into the SQL buffer. The file contains a query to retrieve
> records from the table ordered by the DEPT_NO column.

```
SQL> GET CHP9-26
  1   SELECT
  2        DEPT_NO
  3   FROM
  4        DEPT9_25
  5   ORDER BY
  6*       DEPT_NO
```

> Line 2 specifies the column returned by the query. Line 4 identifies the
> table which is the data source. Line 6 identifies the ordering of records
> returned by the query. Since the DEPT_NO column is specified in the
> ORDER BY clause without any modification, records will be returned in
> ascending order.

> **3.** Run the statement to view the data.

```
SQL> /

DEPT_NO
---------
        1
        2
        3
```

> **4.** Load CHP9-27.sql into the SQL buffer. The file contains a WHERE clause
> using the DECODE function to order the data.

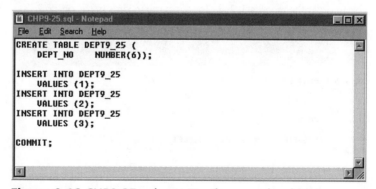

Figure 9-16 CHP9-25.sql creates the sample objects
used in How-To 9.9

```
SQL> GET CHP9-27
  1  SELECT
  2      DEPT_NO
  3  FROM
  4      DEPT9_25
  5  ORDER BY
  6*     DECODE(DEPT_NO,2,-3,3,-2,DEPT_NO)
```

Lines 1 through 4 contain a standard query of the sample table created in Step 1. The ORDER BY clause contained in lines 5 and 6 uses the DECODE function to specify the order of the resulting query. A DEPT_NO value of 2 is treated by the ORDER BY clause as a -3. A value of 3 is treated as -2. The actual value of the DEPT_NO column is used by the ORDER BY clause if it is not 2 or 3. This forces the records with a DEPT_NO column equal to 2 or 3 to the top of the query.

5. Run the statement to view the results of the query. Figure 9-17 shows the results of the query in SQL*Plus.

Since the minimum value of the DEPT_NO column is 1, using the DECODE function to translate a value to a column less than 1 forces the record to the beginning of the list. A single DECODE function can move multiple records to the beginning of the list.

How It Works

Step 1 creates the sample table and data used throughout this How-To. The DEPT_NO column contains the values 1, 2, and 3 in the three records. Steps 2 and 3 query the data using a standard ORDER BY clause, which causes the records to be displayed in the order 1, 2, 3. If the DESC modifier were added, it would be possible to order the records 3, 2, 1. To return the records in the order, 2, 3, 1, the DECODE

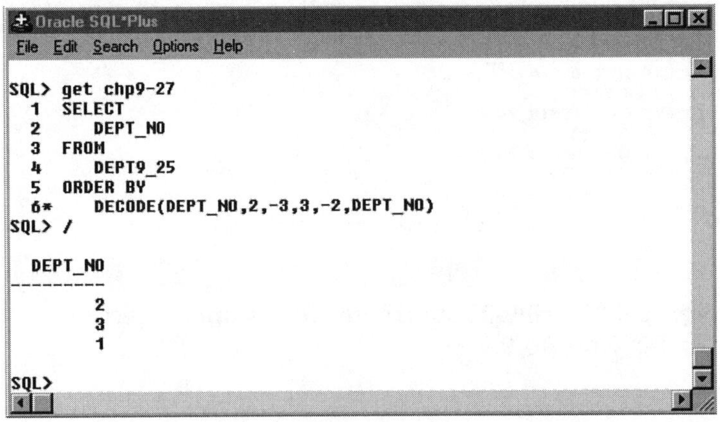

Figure 9-17 The results of CHP9-27.sql in SQL*Plus

function can be used in the ORDER BY clause to replace the values you want sorted to the top with lower values. Steps 4 and 5 use the DECODE function in the ORDER BY clause to force the values 2 and 3 to the top of the list. The DECODE function causes the value 2 to be treated as -3, and 3 to be treated as -2.

Comments

This technique is very useful in populating a list box with a query when you need to move the most used or most logical selections to the top of the list. When you use the DECODE function in an ORDER BY clause, make sure the values returned by the DECODE function are unique and that they fall in the proper list location.

COMPLEXITY
INTERMEDIATE

9.10 How do I...
Create a query that depends on the results of another query?

Problem

I only want records to be returned by a query where the key values exist in a sub-query. For example, I only want to display employees in departments on the west coast. I can get the list of departments on the west coast using a sub-query and want to use the results to determine which employees to display. How do I create a query that depends on the results of another query?

Technique

The IN and EXISTS operators, as well as the NOT IN and NOT EXISTS operators, can be used in a WHERE clause with sub-queries. The IN and NOT IN clauses use a sub-query to generate a list of key values that are compared to a column in the primary table. The EXISTS and NOT EXISTS operators use a sub-query dependent on one or more columns from the primary table. If the sub-query returns one or more rows, the condition is met. If no records are returned, the condition is not met. The values returned by the sub-query do not matter, only the existence of valid records.

Steps

1. Run SQL*Plus and connect as the WAITE user account. CHP9-28.sql, shown in Figure 9-18, creates the sample tables and records used in this How-To.

```
CHP9-28.sql - Notepad                                    _ □ X
File  Edit  Search  Help
CREATE TABLE REGION9_28 (
     REGION_NO     NUMBER(5),
     LOCATION      VARCHAR2(15));

CREATE TABLE DEPT9_28 (
     DEPT_NO       NUMBER(5),
     DEPT_NAME     VARCHAR2(15),
     REGION_NO     NUMBER(5));

INSERT INTO REGION9_28
     VALUES (1,'WEST COAST');
INSERT INTO REGION9_28
     VALUES (2,'EAST COAST');
INSERT INTO DEPT9_28
     VALUES (1,'SALES', 1);
INSERT INTO DEPT9_28
     VALUES (2,'MARKETING', 1);
INSERT INTO DEPT9_28
     VALUES (3,'I/S', 2);
COMMIT;
```

Figure 9-18 CHP9-28.sql creates the sample objects
used in How-To 9.10

Two sample tables are created by the script. The REGION9_28 table will be
used in the sub-queries in this How-To. Run the file to create the sample
data.

SQL> START CHP9-28

Table created.

Table created.

1 row created.

1 row created.

1 row created.

1 row created.

1 row created.

Commit complete.

2. Load CHP9-29.sql into the SQL buffer. The file contains a query which uses
the EXISTS clause to return records based on the results of a query.

SQL> GET CHP9-29
```
  1   SELECT
  2       DEPT_NAME
  3   FROM
  4       DEPT9_28
```

```
 5   WHERE
 6      DEPT_NO BETWEEN 1 AND 10 AND
 7      EXISTS (SELECT 'X' FROM
 8         REGION9_28 WHERE
 9            DEPT9_28.REGION_NO = REGION9_28.REGION_NO AND
10*           REGION9_28.LOCATION = 'WEST COAST')
```

Line 2 specifies the DEPT_NAME column to be returned by the query.
Lines 6 through 9 specify the WHERE clause of the query. Line 6 specifies
that the DEPT_NO column must be between 1 and 10. Lines 7 through 9
use the EXISTS operator with a sub-query to eliminate rows from the query.
Line 7 specifies that the constant X is returned by the sub-query. Since the
EXISTS clause only checks for the existence of records, the resulting value
of the sub-query does not matter. Line 9 joins the REGION_NO column
from the sub-query with a column from the outer query. The WHERE
clause in the sub-query must use values from the outer query to tie the two
queries together.

3. Run the statement to display the results. The results of the query are shown
in Figure 9-19.

4. Load CHP9-30.sql into the SQL buffer.

```
SQL> GET CHP9-30
 1   SELECT
 2      DEPT_NAME
 3   FROM
 4      DEPT9_28
 5   WHERE
 6      DEPT_NO BETWEEN 1 AND 10 AND
 7      REGION_NO IN (SELECT REGION_NO FROM
 8*        REGION9_28 WHERE LOCATION = 'WEST COAST')
```

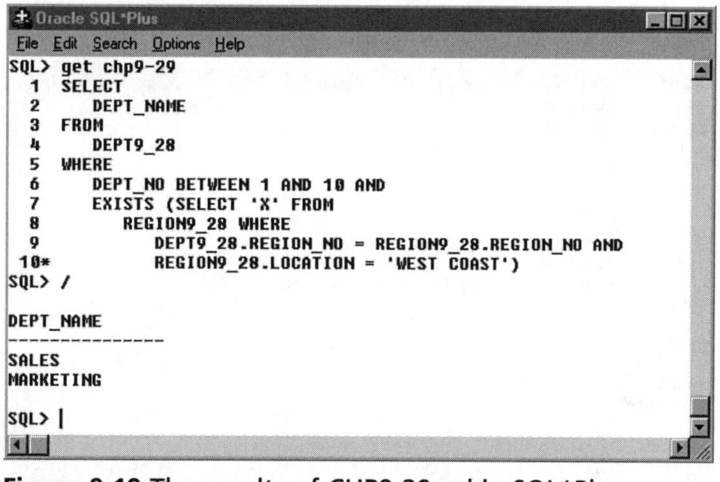

Figure 9-19 The results of CHP9-29.sql in SQL*Plus

Line 2 specifies the column to be returned by the query. Line 6 causes only departments to be returned if the DEPT_NO column is between 1 and 10. Lines 7 and 8 specify that only rows will be returned if the region number is in the list of regions generated by the sub-query.

5. Run the query to return the results. Figure 9-20 shows the results of the query in SQL*Plus.

The results of the query using the IN clause are the same as the similar query using the EXISTS clause. The difference between the queries is how the statement is executed.

How It Works

Step 1 creates the sample tables and data used in this How-To. Steps 2 and 3 use the EXISTS operator to return rows in which a value exists in a sub-query. The results of the sub-query are dependent on one or more values in the outer query. The value of the data returned by the sub-query is not important, only the existence or non-existence of the results. Steps 4 and 5 use the IN operator to create a list of valid key values in a sub-query and check to ensure that the key value in the outer query is part of the list.

Comments

Whether you use the IN or EXISTS operator depends on the data you are querying. If the table referenced in the sub-query is small, the IN operator performs the sub-query first and uses the results to perform the outer query. The EXISTS operator executes the sub-query once for every record analyzed in the outer query. This can cause the sub-query to execute thousands, or perhaps millions, of times if the outer query is very large.

```
Oracle SQL*Plus
File  Edit  Search  Options  Help
SQL> get chp9-30
  1   SELECT
  2      DEPT_NAME
  3   FROM
  4      DEPT9_28
  5   WHERE
  6      DEPT_NO BETWEEN 1 AND 10 AND
  7      REGION_NO IN (SELECT REGION_NO FROM
  8*        REGION9_28 WHERE LOCATION = 'WEST COAST')
SQL> /

DEPT_NAME
----------------
SALES
MARKETING

SQL>
```

Figure 9-20 The results of CHP9-30.sql in SQL*Plus

COMPLEXITY
INTERMEDIATE

9.11 How do I...
Combine two queries?

Problem

I cannot always create a single query that returns all the records I need. I need to combine two queries into one so I can organize the records in the proper order. Both my queries return the same number of columns and are the same datatype. How do I combine the two of them into a single query?

Technique

The UNION operator can be used to combine multiple queries into a single one. Queries can be combined with the UNION operator if they return the same number of columns and the same datatypes. A query with a UNION operator can only have one ORDER BY clause, which gets placed at the end of the query. The column position is used in the ORDER BY clause to represent the ordering of the data.

Steps

1. Run SQL*Plus and connect as the WAITE user account. CHP9-31.sql, shown in Figure 9-21, creates the sample tables used in this How-To.

```
CHP9-31.sql - Notepad
File  Edit  Search  Help
CREATE TABLE DEPT9_31 (
    DEPT_NO    NUMBER(5),
    DEPT_NAME  VARCHAR2(15));

CREATE TABLE DEPT9_31B (
    DEPARTMENT_NO    NUMBER(5),
    DEPARTMENT_NAME  VARCHAR2(15));

INSERT INTO DEPT9_31
    VALUES (1, 'SALES');
INSERT INTO DEPT9_31B
    VALUES (2, 'MARKETING');
INSERT INTO DEPT9_31B
    VALUES (3, 'I/S');

COMMIT;
```

Figure 9-21 CHP9-31.sql creates the sample objects used in How-To 9.11

Two tables are created with columns of the same datatype, but different column names. The sample data will demonstrate the UNION operator. Run the statement to create the sample tables and records.

```
SQL>  START CHP9-31

Table created.

Table created.

1 row created.

1 row created.

1 row created.

Commit complete.
```

2. Load CHP9-32.sql into the SQL buffer. The file contains a query that combines two queries using the UNION operator.

```
SQL> GET CHP9-32
  1    SELECT
  2         DEPT_NO,
  3         DEPT_NAME
  4    FROM
  5         DEPT9_31
  6    UNION
  7    SELECT
  8          DEPARTMENT_NO,
  9          DEPARTMENT_NAME
 10    FROM
 11         DEPT9_31B
 12*   ORDER BY 1
```

Lines 1 through 5 query the DEPT_NO and DEPT_NAME columns from the DEPT9_31 table. Lines 7 through 11 query the DEPARTMENT_NO and DEPARTMENT_NAME columns from the DEPT9_31B table. The UNION operator in line 6 combines the two queries. The ORDER BY clause in line 12 specifies that the output will be ordered by the first column in the select list.

3. Execute the query to view the results. Figure 9-22 shows the results of the query in SQL*Plus.

The columns take their names from the first query. Any records that are identical in both queries will only be returned once by the query.

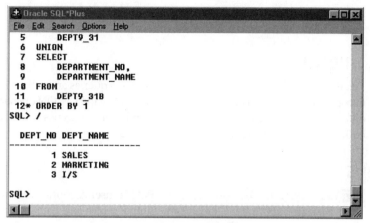

Figure 9-22 The results of CHP9-32.sql in SQL*Plus

How It Works

Step 1 creates the sample tables and records used throughout this How-To. Steps 2 and 3 present a query that combines two queries using the UNION operator. Only a single instance of duplicate records is returned by the query. If a record exists in both queries, it is only displayed once. The ORDER BY clause specifies the order of the results. The results are ordered after the union is performed, generating an ordered list.

Comments

The UNION operator is very useful when the data you need for your query is distributed over multiple objects. The UNION operator is often used in the data dictionary views. Related information is stored in different data dictionary tables and presented using complex queries containing the UNION operator.

COMPLEXITY
INTERMEDIATE

9.12 How do I...
Return the intersection of two queries?

Problem

I want to create a query that returns only records contained in two separate queries. I can use the UNION operator to combine two queries, but in this case I want to exclude records that are not in both queries. How do I create a query that returns the intersection of two queries?

Technique

The INTERSECT operator is used to combine two queries and return rows that exist in both queries. The INTERSECT operator is used like the UNION operator but returns different results. The number of columns and their datatypes must be identical in both queries. If they are not, an error will occur.

Steps

1. Run SQL*Plus and connect as the WAITE user account. CHP9-33.sql, shown in Figure 9-23, creates the sample tables and data used in this How-To.

Two tables that are the source of the data in the examples are created. The sample data created overlaps so an intersection of it can be returned by the query. Run the statement to create the sample tables and data.

```
SQL> START CHP9-33

Table created.

Table created.

1 row created.

1 row created.

1 row created.

Commit complete.
```

2. Load CHP9-34.sql into the SQL buffer. The file contains a query using the INTERSECT operator to return the intersection of two queries.

```
SQL> GET CHP9-34
  1   SELECT
  2       DEPT_NO
  3   FROM
  4       DEPT9_33
  5   INTERSECT
  6   SELECT
  7       DISTINCT DEPT_NO
  8   FROM
  9*      EMP9_33
```

The INTERSECT operator in line 5 returns the intersection of the two queries as the query results. Lines 2 and 7 specify the columns returned by the query. The column listed in line 7 includes a DISTINCT operator,

```
CHP9-33.sql - Notepad
File  Edit  Search  Help
CREATE TABLE DEPT9_33 (
    DEPT_NO   NUMBER(5),
    DEPT_NAME VARCHAR2(15));

CREATE TABLE EMP9_33 (
    EMP_NO    NUMBER(5),
    DEPT_NO   NUMBER(5));

INSERT INTO DEPT9_33
    VALUES (1, 'MARKETING');
INSERT INTO DEPT9_33
    VALUES (2, 'SALES');
INSERT INTO EMP9_33
    VALUES (1,  1);

COMMIT;
```

Figure 9-23 CHP9-33.sql creates the sample tables and data used in How-To 9.12

which makes the EMP9_33 table return distinct DEPT_NO columns. The datatypes of the columns are identical, and the same number of columns are returned by each query.

3. Run the query to return the results. Figure 9-24 contains the results of the query in SQL*Plus.

Because only one record exists in both queries, only one record is returned by the query containing the INTERSECT operator.

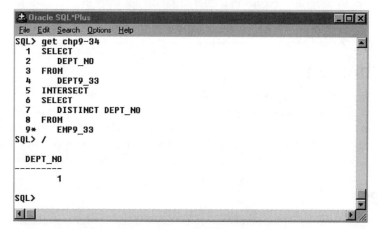

```
Oracle SQL*Plus
File  Edit  Search  Options  Help
SQL> get chp9-34
  1  SELECT
  2      DEPT_NO
  3  FROM
  4      DEPT9_33
  5  INTERSECT
  6  SELECT
  7      DISTINCT DEPT_NO
  8  FROM
  9*     EMP9_33
SQL> /

  DEPT_NO
---------
        1

SQL>
```

Figure 9-24 The results of CHP9-34.sql in SQL*Plus

How It Works

Step 1 creates the sample tables and records used throughout this How-To. Steps 2 and 3 present a query using the INTERSECT operator to return the intersection of two queries. The same number of columns must be returned by each query, and the datatypes of the columns in each query must be the same.

Comments

The INTERSECT operator is very useful for comparing the contents of tables. If you need to identify duplicate records in two distributed tables, the INTERSECT operator can be used to display all records in both tables. The INTERSECT operator, along with the UNION and MINUS operators, enhance your ability to create complex queries that may not be possible using a single SELECT statement.

COMPLEXITY
INTERMEDIATE

9.13 How do I...
Subtract the results of a query from another?

Problem

I need to return records in a query that do not exist in a second query. In effect, I want to subtract the results of one query from another. How do I subtract the results of a query from another?

Technique

The MINUS operator is used within a statement to subtract the results of one query from another. When using the MINUS operator, the same number of columns must exist in each of the queries, and the columns must be of the same datatype. If an exact match is found in the subtracted query, the record is not returned by the source query. If any of the columns in the subtracted query are different, the source record is returned.

Steps

1. Run SQL*Plus and connect as the WAITE user account. CHP9-35.sql, shown in Figure 9-25, creates the sample tables and records used throughout this How-To.

Two sample tables are created with data in order to demonstrate the MINUS operator. Run the statement to create the sample tables and records.

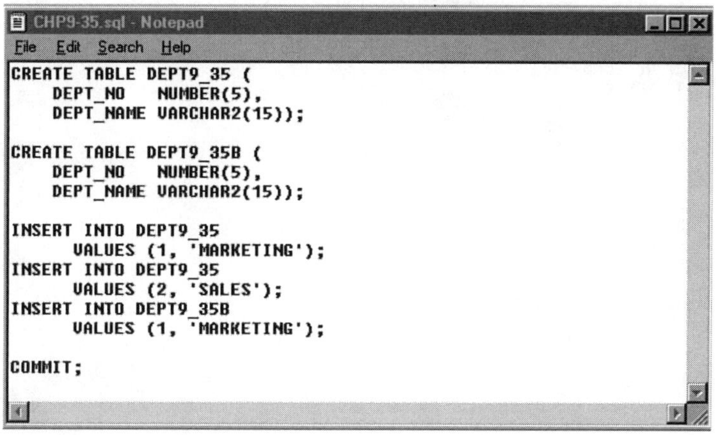

```
CREATE TABLE DEPT9_35 (
    DEPT_NO   NUMBER(5),
    DEPT_NAME VARCHAR2(15));

CREATE TABLE DEPT9_35B (
    DEPT_NO   NUMBER(5),
    DEPT_NAME VARCHAR2(15));

INSERT INTO DEPT9_35
      VALUES (1, 'MARKETING');
INSERT INTO DEPT9_35
      VALUES (2, 'SALES');
INSERT INTO DEPT9_35B
      VALUES (1, 'MARKETING');

COMMIT;
```

Figure 9-25 CHP9-35.sql creates the sample tables and records used in How-To 9.13

```
SQL>  START CHP9-35

Table created.

Table created.

1 row inserted.

1 row inserted.

1 row inserted.

Commit complete.
```

2. Load CHP9-36.sql into the SQL buffer. The file contains a query that causes the MINUS operator to subtract the results of a query from another.

```
SQL> GET CHP9-36
  1  SELECT
  2      DEPT_NO,
  3      DEPT_NAME
  4  FROM DEPT9_35
  5  MINUS
  6  SELECT
  7      DEPT_NO,
  8      DEPT_NAME
  9* FROM DEPT9_35B
```

Lines 1 through 5 specify the query that will return the rows. Lines 6 through 9 specify a query to be subtracted from the first query. Any records returned by the query in lines 1 through 5 will not be displayed if they exist in the query in lines 6 through 9.

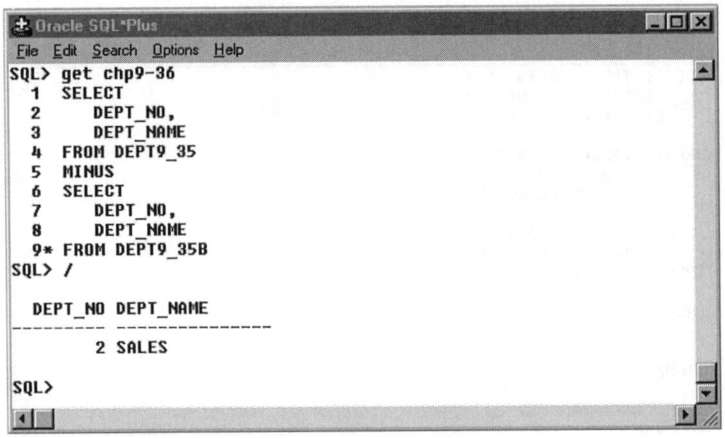

Figure 9-26 The results of a query using
the MINUS operator

3. Run the statement to display the results of the query. Figure 9-26 shows the
results of the query in SQL*Plus.

Because a record for the Marketing department existed in both queries, the
record is not displayed in the results.

How It Works

Step 1 creates the table and sample records used in this How-To. The sample data
contains records used to demonstrate the MINUS operator. Steps 2 and 3 present
a query which uses the MINUS operator to subtract the results of one query from
another. The row subtracted by the second query in the statement must be identical to the row in the first query, in order to prevent the row from being displayed.
No records returned by the subtracted query are displayed in the result set.

Comments

The MINUS operator is useful when searching for rows that do not exist in a table.
If you want to ensure that all records in a table exist in another table, you can use
the MINUS operator to subtract one query from another. If any rows are returned
by the query, they are missing in the first query.

COMPLEXITY
ADVANCED

9.14 How do I...
Return rows even when a join condition fails?

Problem

I need to join two tables, but one of the tables does not always contain the records needed to satisfy the join condition. I want the records to be returned by the query even if the join condition fails because of this table. How do I return rows from a query even if the join condition fails?

Technique

An outer join operator (+) retrieves records even if one side of the join condition fails. The outer join operator is placed on the side of the expression which may not exist. This causes the expression to return all records from the opposite table as if the related records in the joined table were present. The location of the operator is important to its success. Any columns in the table's select list that fail the join condition will return NULL.

Steps

1. Run SQL*Plus and connect as the WAITE user account. CHP9-37.sql, shown in Figure 9-27, creates the sample tables and records used throughout this How-To.

```
CREATE TABLE DEPT9_37 (
    DEPT_NO    NUMBER(5),
    DEPT_NAME VARCHAR2(15));
CREATE TABLE EMP9_37 (
    EMP_NO    NUMBER(5),
    EMP_NAME  VARCHAR2(15),
    DEPT_NO   NUMBER(5));

INSERT INTO DEPT9_37
    VALUES (1, 'MARKETING');
INSERT INTO EMP9_37
    VALUES (1, 'JOHN SMITH', 1);
INSERT INTO EMP9_37
    VALUES (2, 'BILL JONES', 2);
INSERT INTO EMP9_37
    VALUES (3, 'MARY BROWN', 2);
COMMIT;
```

Figure 9-27 CHP9-37.sql creates the sample tables and records used in How-To 9.14

The DEPT9_37 table contains the departments in an organization. The EMP9_37 table contains employees in the same organization. In the sample query we want to return all employees, even if the department number is invalid for their record. Run the file to create the sample tables and records.

```
SQL> START CHP9-37

Table created.

Table created.

1 row created.

1 row created.

1 row created.

1 row created.

Commit complete.
```

2. Load CHP9-38.sql into the SQL buffer. The file contains a query joining the two sample tables without using an outer join. The query will only return records in which both sides of the join condition exists.

```
SQL> GET CHP9-38
  1   SELECT
  2       EMP.EMP_NO EMP_NO,
  3       EMP.EMP_NAME ENAME,
  4       EMP.DEPT_NO DEPT_NO,
  5       DEPT.DEPT_NAME DEPT_NAME
  6   FROM
  7       EMP9_37 EMP,
  8       DEPT9_37 DEPT
  9   WHERE
 10*      EMP.DEPT_NO = DEPT.DEPT_NO
```

Lines 2 through 4 specify three columns from the EMP9_37 tables to be returned by the query. Line 5 specifies a column from the DEPT9_37 table to be returned. Lines 7 and 8 specify the source tables for the data. The WHERE clause in line 10 joins the two tables on the DEPT_NO column. Without an outer join, records will be returned only when they meet the join condition.

3. Run the statement to execute the query.

```
SQL> /

EMP_NO ENAME            DEPT_NO  DEPT_NAME
------ ---------------- -------- ----------------
     1 JOHN SMITH              1 MARKETING
```

Although there are three records in the EMP9_37 table, there is only one which satisfies the join condition. This is not the desired result of the query since the other two employees are still valid.

4. Load CHP9-39.sql into the SQL buffer. The file contains the same query but includes an outer join operator on the DEPT9_37 table. Since employees without a valid department number are still considered valid employees, they will be included in the results of the query.

```
SQL> GET CHP9-39
  1  SELECT
  2      EMP.EMP_NO EMP_NO,
  3      EMP.EMP_NAME ENAME,
  4      EMP.DEPT_NO DEPT_NO,
  5      DEPT.DEPT_NAME DEPT_NAME
  6  FROM
  7      EMP9_37 EMP,
  8      DEPT9_37 DEPT
  9  WHERE
 10*     EMP.DEPT_NO = DEPT.DEPT_NO (+)
```

Records in the EMP9_37 table will be returned even if they do not match the join condition, because of the outer join operator (+) in line 10. The outer join operator is on the side of the expression that may not exist. The placement of the operator is important to the results of the query.

5. Run the query to display the results. Figure 9-28 shows the results of the query in SQL*Plus.

All three records in the EMP9_37 table are represented in the results of the query. For the two EMP9_37 records which do not contain a valid value in the DEPT_NO column, the DEPT_NAME column returns NULL.

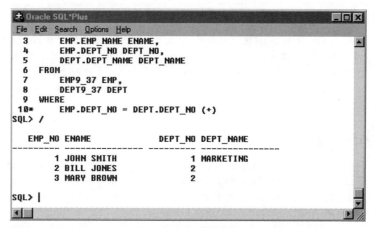

Figure 9-28 The results of CHP9-39.sql in SQL*Plus

How It Works

The outer join operator (+) lets a join condition succeed even if one side of the join condition fails. Step 1 creates the sample tables and records used throughout this How-To. Three employee records are created, and two have an invalid DEPT_NO column. Step 2 queries the tables without an outer join operator. The join condition causes one row to be returned, because only one row satisfies both sides of the join condition. Steps 4 and 5 include an outer join operator to force the query to return all rows from the EMP9_37 table.

Comments

The outer join is an important technique used in complex reporting. It is possible that the join operation does not always contain records in both tables. It is possible that a valid record exists in a table with no corresponding foreign key. This is common when the table that's usually the foreign key table is used as the driving table of the query.

COMPLEXITY
ADVANCED

9.15 How do I...
Perform greater than and less than logic with the DECODE function?

Problem

In my query, I want to return one value if the resulting value is larger than a certain number and a different value if it's not. I use the DECODE function to perform IF..THEN..ELSE logic in other places, but DECODE tests equality. I want to test if a value is greater than another. How do I use DECODE to test greater than or less than logic?

Technique

The DECODE function performs IF..THEN..ELSE logic based on equality tests. The SIGN function can be used within the DECODE function to test if a value is greater than, less than, or equal to another value. There are three possible values which the SIGN function can return. If the number passed to the function is positive, SIGN returns 1. If the value is negative, SIGN returns -1. If the value is 0, SIGN returns 0. If a number is greater than another number then SIGN (number - other number) = 1, since the number minus the other number is positive. This same method can be used to test less than or equal to logic.

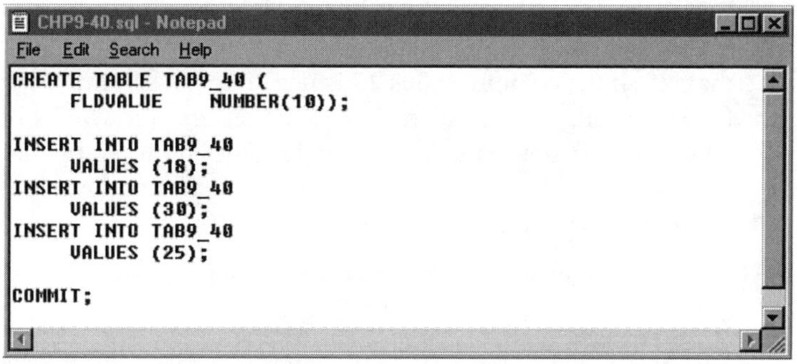

Figure 9-29 CHP9-40.sql creates the sample objects used in How-To 9.15

Steps

1. Run SQL*Plus and connect as the WAITE user account. CHP9-40.sql, shown in Figure 9-29, creates the sample tables used throughout this How-To.

A sample table is created with a single column. Three records are inserted into the table used to demonstrate the technique. One record is inserted with a column value greater than 25, another with a value less than 25, and a third equal to 25. Run the statement to create the sample table and its data.

```
SQL> START CHP9-40

Table created.

1 row created.

1 row created.

1 row created.

Commit complete.
```

2. Load CHP9-41.sql into the SQL buffer. The file contains a SQL statement using a DECODE function to return values based on greater than and less than operations. If the value in the column is 25, the string EXACTLY 25 is returned by the query. If the value is less than 25, the string LESS THAN 25 is returned by the query. If the value is greater than 25, the string GREATER THAN 25 is returned by the query.

```
SQL> GET CHP9-41
  1   SELECT
  2       FLDVALUE,
  3       DECODE(SIGN(FLDVALUE - 25),0,'EXACTLY 25',
  4                              -1,'LESS THAN 25',
  5                               1,'GREATER THAN 25') A
  6* FROM TAB9_40
```

Line 3 subtracts 25 from the column value and passes the result into the SIGN function. If the column minus 25 is positive, the column is greater than 25. If the column minus 25 is negative, the column is less than 25. Lines 3 through 5 use the three possible results of the SIGN function in a DECODE function. The three possible values returned by the SIGN function are handled in the DECODE function to return the value of the column in relation to the number 25.

3. Run the statement to view the results of the function. Figure 9-30 shows the results of the query in SQL*Plus.

One of the records returned by the query is exactly 25, another is less than 25, and another is greater than 25. The query used the SIGN function and DECODE function together to generate these records.

How It Works

The SIGN function is used in the DECODE function to create greater than and less than logic. The SIGN function returns 0, 1, or -1 depending on whether a value is 0, positive, or negative. A value minus the tested constant in a SIGN function will return 1 if the value is greater than the tested number. It will return -1 if it is less than the tested number. This limits the number of values for which the DECODE function must test. Step 1 creates the sample table and data used throughout this How-To. Steps 2 and 3 show the use of the SIGN function within the DECODE function. If the value of a record is greater than, less than, or equal to 25, a different response is generated.

```
Oracle SQL*Plus
File  Edit  Search  Options  Help
SQL> get chp9-41
  1  SELECT
  2     FLDVALUE,
  3     DECODE(SIGN(FLDVALUE - 25),0,'EXACTLY 25',
  4                               -1,'LESS THAN 25',
  5                                1,'GREATER THAN 25') A
  6* FROM TAB9_40
SQL> /

 FLDVALUE A
--------- ----------------
       18 LESS THAN 25
       30 GREATER THAN 25
       25 EXACTLY 25

SQL>
```

Figure 9-30 The results of CHP9-41.sql in SQL*Plus

Comments

The SIGN function allows you to work around one of the limitations of the DECODE function, making the DECODE function even more powerful. It expands the DECODE function from a function that only performs equality tests, to a function that can perform greater than and less than logic. When working with Oracle, keep in mind that almost anything is possible within SQL.

COMPLEXITY
INTERMEDIATE

9.16 How do I...
Query a record by ROWID?

Problem

I want to retrieve a record in the fastest way possible. I know that querying a record by ROWID is the fastest method. Within SQL*Plus, automatic type conversion allows me to specify a ROWID as a character string. How do I query a record by ROWID in other tools which do not support automatic type conversion?

Technique

The CHARTOROWID function converts a character string to the ROWID datatype. The ROWID column can be queried from a table or used in the WHERE clause to query a record. To query a record by ROWID, convert the character representation of the ROWID with the CHARTOROWID function. The ROWID column is unique in the database and the fastest way to query or update a single record.

Steps

1. Run SQL*Plus and connect as the WAITE user account. CHP9-42.sql, shown in Figure 9-31, creates the sample table used in this How-To.

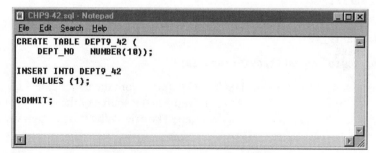

Figure 9-31 CHP9-42.sql creates the sample table used in How-To 9.16

A single table is created and populated with a single record to demonstrate a query by ROWID. The upcoming steps will query this record's ROWID and use the value to query the record. Run the statement to create the sample table and its record.

```
SQL>   START CHP9-42

Table created.

1 row inserted.

Commit complete.
```

2. Load CHP9-43.sql into the SQL buffer. The file contains a query of the DEPT9_42 table to display the ROWID of the record in the table.

```
SQL> GET CHP9-43
  1   SELECT
  2       DEPT_NO,
  3       ROWID
  4   FROM
  5*      DEPT9_42
```

Line 2 returns the DEPT_NO column from the table. Line 3 returns the ROWID pseudo-column. ROWID can be included in any query. Line 5 specifies the source of the data as the sample table created in Step 1.

3. Run the statement to perform the query.

```
SQL> /

  DEPT_NO ROWID
---------- --------------------
        1 00000EFC.0000.0001
```

The value for your ROWID when executing the query will be different, because the ROWID is generated by the system according to the location of the row within the database.

4. Load CHP9-44.sql into the SQL buffer. The file contains a query of the sample table in which ROWID is used in the WHERE clause.

```
SQL> GET CHP9-44
  1   SELECT
  2       DEPT_NO
  3   FROM
  4     DEPT9_42
  5   WHERE
  6*   ROWID = CHARTOROWID('&ROWID')
```

Line 2 returns the DEPT_NO column from the table. Line 4 specifies that the sample table created in Step 1 is the source of the data. Line 6 specifies the WHERE clause of the query. The &ROWID substitution variable is used in line 6, since you will need to enter the ROWID your database made when you created the record. The CHARTOROWID function converts the character representation of the ROWID to its internal representation. In SQL*Plus this conversion is automatic, but you would need to use the function in other development tools.

5. Run the query, replacing the &ROWID substitution variable with the ROWID your query returned in Step 3. Figure 9-32 displays the results of the operation in SQL*Plus.

The DEPT_NO column of the sample record is returned, and the ROWID is used to query the record. Using ROWID in the WHERE clause of a query is a very fast way to return a record.

How It Works

Step 1 creates the sample table used throughout the How-To and inserts a sample record. Inserting the sample record generates a ROWID that is unique throughout the system. Steps 2 and 3 query the ROWID from the column by specifying the ROWID column in the query. Steps 4 and 5 query the sample records, by using ROWID in the WHERE clause of the query and using the CHARTOROWID function to convert the character representation of ROWID to its internal datatype.

Comments

Using the ROWID column is the fastest way to query or update a record in a table. In your applications, you can query the ROWID for any record you need to update later in your application. The ROWIDTOCHAR function can be used to query ROWID into a VARCHAR2 (or string) variable.

```
Oracle SQL*Plus
File  Edit  Search  Options  Help
   1   SELECT
   2        DEPT_NO
   3   FROM
   4        DEPT9_42
   5   WHERE
   6*       ROWID = CHARTOROWID('&ROWID')
SQL> /
Enter value for rowid: 00000EFC.0000.0001
old   6:      ROWID = CHARTOROWID('&ROWID')
new   6:      ROWID = CHARTOROWID('00000EFC.0000.0001')

   DEPT_NO
---------
         1

SQL>
```

Figure 9-32 The results of CHP9-44.sql in SQL*Plus

COMPLEXITY
INTERMEDIATE

9.17 How do I...
Lock rows when I query them?

Problem

In our programs, we have procedures that perform queries and later update the results. I need to ensure that other users cannot update the records while the procedures are processing data. How do I lock rows when I query them?

Technique

The FOR UPDATE clause of a SELECT statement locks the rows returned by the query until a COMMIT statement is executed. When the FOR UPDATE clause is used in a query, another user cannot update, delete, or lock the rows until the lock is released. If the rows you are attempting to query for update are locked, the query will wait until the lock is released unless the NO WAIT clause is specified.

Steps

1. Run SQL*Plus and connect as the WAITE user account. CHP9-45.sql, shown in Figure 9-33, creates the sample tables used in this How-To.

```
CREATE TABLE DEPT9_45 (
    DEPT_NO     NUMBER(5),
    DEPT_NAME   VARCHAR2(20));

CREATE TABLE EMP9_45 (
    EMP_NO      NUMBER(5),
    EMP_NAME    VARCHAR2(20),
    DEPT_NO     NUMBER(5));

INSERT INTO DEPT9_45
    VALUES (25, 'MARKETING');
INSERT INTO DEPT9_45
    VALUES (26, 'SALES');
INSERT INTO EMP9_45
    VALUES (1, 'BILL SMITH', 25);
INSERT INTO EMP9_45
    VALUES (2, 'MARY ROBERTS', 26);

COMMIT;
```

Figure 9-33 CHP9-45.sql creates the sample tables used in How-To 9.17

The sample table is a simple table containing the departments in an organization. Data used to demonstrate the locking capabilities of the FOR UPDATE clause is created. Run the file to create the sample table and data.

```
SQL>   START CHP9-45

Table created.

1 row inserted.

1 row inserted.

1 row inserted.

Commit complete.
```

2. Load CHP9-46.sql into the SQL buffer. The file contains a query which locks the rows as they are queried.

```
SQL> GET CHP9-46
  1   SELECT DEPT_NO
  2   FROM
  3       DEPT9_45
  4   WHERE
  5       DEPT_NO = 25
  6*  FOR UPDATE
```

Lines 4 and 5 specify the WHERE clause identifying which rows the query will retrieve. Line 6 tells Oracle to lock the rows retrieved by the query.

3. Run the query to return the results and lock the rows.

```
SQL>  /

DEPT_NO
-------
     25
```

4. Load CHP9-47.sql into the SQL buffer. The file contains a query of multiple tables, but only locks one of them.

```
SQL>   GET CHP9-47
  1    SELECT DEPT9_45.DEPT_NO, EMP_NO
  2       FROM DEPT9_45, EMP9_45
  3    WHERE
  4       DEPT9_45.DEPT_NO = EMP9_45.DEPT_NO
  5*   FOR UPDATE OF DEPT9_45.DEPT_NO
```

The FROM clause in line 2 specifies the two tables used in the query. Line 4 contains the join condition between the two tables. Line 5 specifies that only DEPT9_45 will have rows returned by the query locked. Rows from EMP9_45 will not be locked and can be updated by another process.

5. Run the query to lock the rows.

```
SQL>   /

DEPT_NO     EMP_NO
```

continued on next page

continued from previous page

```
--------- ----------
     25          1
     26          2
```

The query locks the DEPT_45 records returning the two rows.

6. Execute a COMMIT statement to unlock the rows. When rows are locked using the SELECT statement with a FOR UPDATE clause, they remain locked until a COMMIT or ROLLBACK statement is executed or until the session is terminated.

```
COMMIT;
```

How It Works

Step 1 creates two sample tables and records used throughout this How-To. Steps 2 and 3 use the FOR UPDATE clause in a SELECT statement to lock all rows returned by the query. The query only has a single source table, so the FOR UPDATE clause knows which table to lock. Steps 4 and 5 demonstrate a query from multiple tables, only one of which is locked. The table name is specified in the FOR UPDATE clause, telling Oracle to only lock that one table. If the table name was not specified in the clause, records from both tables would be locked. Step 6 unlocks any locked records by executing a COMMIT statement.

Comments

If you are planning to update a record that will be first returned by a query, it is a good idea to lock the record to prevent other users from updating it. Remember to unlock the record if you decide not to commit the changes you make.

COMPLEXITY
ADVANCED

9.18 How do I...
Traverse a tree structure?

Problem

In my application, I have a table containing data in a hierarchical structure. I need to create a query that navigates the tree structure to create a report. I have not been able to generate a simple query to traverse a tree structure. How do I traverse a tree structure in a query?

Technique

The CONNECT BY clause in a query provides support for hierarchical data structures. Unfortunately, using the CONNECT BY clause can be confusing. Navigating a tree structure requires two clauses. The START WITH clause identifies where the query begins in the tree structure. The CONNECT BY PRIOR clause identifies the parent/child relationship between key fields. The format of the query is shown below:

```
SELECT fields
FROM table
START WITH column = value
CONNECT BY PRIOR parent primary key = child foreign key;
```

An additional WHERE clause or an ORDER BY clause is not allowed by Oracle in a query using the CONNECT BY structure.

Steps

1. Run SQL*Plus and connect as the WAITE user account. CHP9-48.sql, shown in Figure 9-34, creates the sample table and data used in this How-To.

The sample table contains employees for an organization. Each record contains an EMP_NO column to uniquely identify the employee and a MGR_NO column to identify his or her manager. If the MGR_NO column is NULL, the employee is at the top of the corporate structure. Run the file to create the sample table and data.

```
CHP9-48.sql - Notepad
File  Edit  Search  Help
CREATE TABLE EMP9_48 (
    EMP_NO      NUMBER(5),
    EMP_NAME    VARCHAR2(15),
    MGR_NO      NUMBER(5));

SET TERMOUT OFF
INSERT INTO EMP9_48 VALUES (1, 'JONES, TOM', NULL);
INSERT INTO EMP9_48 VALUES (2, 'SMITH, JIM', 1);
INSERT INTO EMP9_48 VALUES (3, 'GREEN, JACK', 2);
INSERT INTO EMP9_48 VALUES (4, 'WHITE, MARY', 2);
INSERT INTO EMP9_48 VALUES (5, 'PINK, LISA', 2);
INSERT INTO EMP9_48 VALUES (6, 'BLACK, GREG', 3);
INSERT INTO EMP9_48 VALUES (7, 'YELLOW, STEVE', 3);
INSERT INTO EMP9_48 VALUES (8, 'RED, BILL', 4);
INSERT INTO EMP9_48 VALUES (9, 'GATES, TOM', 5);
INSERT INTO EMP9_48 VALUES (10, 'RED, MIKE', 9);

COMMIT;
SET TERMOUT ON
```

Figure 9-34 CHP9-48.sql creates the sample table and data used in How-To 9.18

```
SQL> START CHP9-48
```

Table created.

> **2.** Load CHP9-49.sql into the SQL buffer. The file contains a query of the sample table for the hierarchical structure of the data.

```
SQL> GET CHP9-49
  1  SELECT
  2    LPAD(' ',4*(LEVEL-1))||EMP_NAME EMP_NAME
  3  FROM
  4    EMP9_48
  5  START WITH MGR_NO IS NULL
  6* CONNECT BY PRIOR EMP_NO = MGR_NO
```

> Line 2 uses the LEVEL pseudo-column to left pad the EMP_NAME column with four spaces for each level of the hierarchy. The START WITH clause in line 5 begins the tree navigation for records in which the MGR_NO column is NULL. Since a NULL MGR_NO column represents an employee at the top of the corporate structure, we want the tree navigation to start there. The CONNECT BY PRIOR clause identifies that the EMP_NO column of the previous level joins to the MGR_NO column from the next level down.

> **3.** Run the statement to display the results of the query. The results of the query are shown in Figure 9-35.

> The query used the LEVEL pseudo-column to indent the results of the query and display the records in the tree structure. Since the JONES, TOM record contained no MGR_NO column, the query results begin with that column. The CONNECT BY PRIOR clause caused the tree to be navigated beginning at the record.

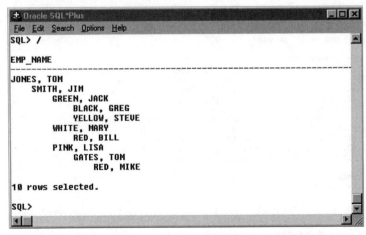

Figure 9-35 The results of CHP9-49.sql in SQL*Plus

How It Works

Step 1 creates the sample table and records used in this How-To. Steps 2 and 3 present a query using the START WITH and CONNECT BY PRIOR clauses to navigate the data's hierarchical structure. The START WITH clause identifies the root of the tree structure and the CONNECT BY PRIOR clause identifies the columns linking the hierarchy. The LEVEL pseudo-column is used in the select list to indent the results based on the level of the tree structure.

Comments

A hierarchical structure of data is definitely not easy to work with. The CONNECT BY PRIOR clause in a query allows Oracle to perform this task. Remember to include the START WITH clause. Also keep in mind that the ordering of the columns in the CONNECT BY prior clause is important.

COMPLEXITY
INTERMEDIATE

9.19 How do I...
Return records based on a group function?

Problem

I want to return rows in a query based on the results of a group function. For example, I want to return all records where the MIN value is greater than a constant. Since MIN is a group function, it cannot be used in a WHERE clause. How do I return records based on the value of a group function?

Technique

Group functions such as MAX, MIN, COUNT, and AVG cannot be used in a WHERE clause. The HAVING clause can be used to achieve the desired effect. The HAVING clause is used after the GROUP BY clause in a query. A HAVING clause can include one or more group functions.

Steps

1. Run SQL*Plus and connect as the WAITE user account. CHP9-50.sql, shown in Figure 9-36, creates the sample tables and data used in this How-To.

The sample table contains employees that work for the organization. The table is populated with employees working for different departments,

```
CHP9-50.sql - Notepad

File  Edit  Search  Help

CREATE TABLE EMP9_50 (
     EMP_NO      NUMBER(10),
     EMP_NAME    VARCHAR2(20),
     DEPT_NO     NUMBER(5),
     SALARY      NUMBER(10));

INSERT INTO EMP9_50
     VALUES (1, 'BILL', 1, 24000);
INSERT INTO EMP9_50
     VALUES (2, 'TOM', 1, 36000);
INSERT INTO EMP9_50
     VALUES (3, 'MARY', 2, 48000);
INSERT INTO EMP9_50
     VALUES (4, 'CHUCK', 2, 50000);
INSERT INTO EMP9_50
     VALUES (5, 'KIM', 3, 18000);
INSERT INTO EMP9_50
     VALUES (6, 'LISA', 3, 21000);
INSERT INTO EMP9_50
     VALUES (7, 'HANK', 3, 45000);
COMMIT;
```

Figure 9-36 CHP9-50.sql creates the sample tables and data used in How-To 9.19

which will allow group functions to be performed by department numbers. Run the file to create the sample tables and their data.

```
SQL> START CHP9-50

Table created.

1 row created.

1 row created.

1 row created.

1 row created.

1 row created.

1 row created.

1 row created.

Commit complete.
```

2. Load CHP9-51.sql into the SQL buffer. The file contains a query using group functions within a query. There is no WHERE clause in the query to limit data.

```
SQL> GET CHP9-51
  1  SELECT
```

```
2       DEPT_NO,
3       SUM(SALARY),
3       MIN(SALARY),
4       MAX(SALARY),
5       AVG(SALARY)
6    FROM
7       EMP9_50
8    GROUP BY
9*      DEPT_NO
```

Lines 2 through 5 specify the columns returned by the query. Since the DEPT_NO column is not a group function and the rest of the columns contain group columns, the DEPT_NO column is specified in the GROUP BY clause in lines 8 and 9. Since group functions cannot be used in the WHERE clause of a query, this query cannot limit the result set based on the results of one of the group functions.

3. Run the query to display its results.

```
SQL>  /
```

DEPT_NO	SUM(SALARY)	MIN(SALARY)	MAX(SALARY)	AVG(SALARY)
1	60000	24000	36000	30000
2	98000	48000	50000	49000
3	84000	18000	45000	28000

4. Load CHP9-52.sql into the SQL buffer. The file contains the query from the previous step with a HAVING clause that will only return rows where MIN(SALARY) is greater than 25,000.

```
SQL>  GET CHP9-52
 1    SELECT
 2       DEPT_NO,
 3       MIN(SALARY),
 4       MAX(SALARY),
 5       AVG(SALARY)
 6    FROM
 7       EMP9_50
 8    GROUP BY
 9       DEPT_NO
10    HAVING
11*      MIN(SALARY) > 25000
```

The HAVING clause in lines 9 and 10 operates like a group function in a WHERE clause. The query will only return records in which MIN(SALARY) is greater than 25,000. The HAVING clause is positioned after the WHERE clause in a query.

5. Run the statement to display the results of the query. The results of the query are shown in Figure 9-37.

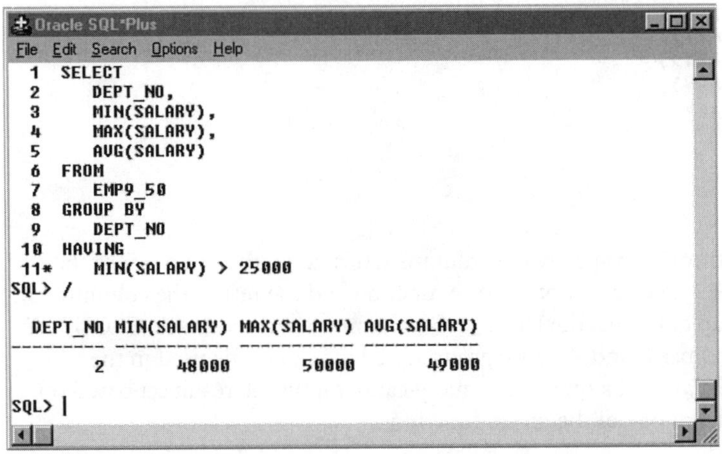

Figure 9-37 The results of CHP9-52.sql in SQL*Plus

The number of records returned by the query is limited to those in which the minimum salary for the department is greater than 25,000. The HAVING clause effectively created a WHERE clause using group functions.

How It Works

Step 1 creates the sample table and records used in this How-To. Steps 2 and 3 present a query that uses group functions and a GROUP BY clause. Since no WHERE or HAVING clause exists in the query, all records in the table are processed by the query. Steps 4 and 5 add a HAVING clause to the query to return only records with MIN(SALARY) greater than 25,000. The HAVING clause has the same effect as the WHERE clause, only it works with group functions.

Comments

Since group functions cannot be used in the WHERE clause of a query, the HAVING clause is used to perform this operation. You can use the HAVING clause any time a GROUP BY clause exists in a statement.

CHAPTER 10
DATES, TEXT, AND NUMBERS

10

DATES, TEXT, AND NUMBERS

How do I...

Oracle provides functions that enable you to manipulate records as they are queried from the database and manipulate information used in SQL statements. When most people think of performing queries, they think of displaying database columns or retrieving them and putting them directly into their applications. Using functions to manipulate values in SQL statements reduces development time by yielding usable

321

results directly from the query. In other words, you don't have to perform manipulation at a later point in time. This chapter deals with the manipulation of database values using Oracle's built-in functions. Single value functions return a value from a calculation performed on a single record. Dates, text, and numeric values can all be modified using single value functions. Group functions calculate a result from multiple records, usually on a single column or a series of columns. In most cases, group functions return a numeric result.

10.1   Format date and time values

Date values are stored in the database with the month, day, year, hour, minute, and second. The value of a date column can be presented in a variety of formats using date functions. If you query a date value without using a date function, the time portion of the date will not be displayed and the format will be the default date format. This How-To presents the suite of date and time formatting functions.

10.2   Trim trailing spaces from day and month names

When the day of the week or name of a month is written using Oracle's date manipulation functions, the values are padded with spaces. This How-To presents the specific date format masks for trimming trailing spaces from these values, without using string manipulation functions.

10.3   Perform date and time math

Oracle provides functions for calculating the number of months, days, or weeks between dates. Using date functions, it is possible to add months to a date, determine the last date in a month, find the next occurrence of a specific weekday, and convert time zones. This How-To covers the suite of date and time manipulation functions for performing date and time math.

10.4   Replace a NULL value with a string or number

In Oracle, a NULL value is not the same as zero and is not an empty string. A NULL value is an unknown value and cannot be used in calculations. If a calculation includes a NULL value, a NULL result will be returned. This How-To presents the function used to substitute a NULL value with a valid value.

10.5   Convert a number to a string

In order to use string functions such as INSTR or SUBSTR, it is necessary to convert a numeric value to a string. In addition to simple type casting, it is possible to format a numeric value in a variety of string formats. This How-To covers the method used to convert a number to a string.

10.6   Concatenate strings

You will often need to concatenate the values of two strings or attach static text to a column's value. Throughout this book, you will find many situations where string concatenation is required to perform a task. There are two methods used to concatenate strings to create a single string value. One method uses a string function, and the other uses the concatenation operator. This How-To presents the methods for concatenating strings.

10.7 Capitalize the first letter of each word in a string

A common text conversion requirement is to capitalize the first letter of each word in a string. The method presented in this How-To lets you improve the presentation of text data in reports and within applications.

10.8 Write a number as words

It is possible to write a number in words using a query. The printing of checks in a financial system is a common example of an instance when you would want to write a number in words. This How-To presents a method used to perform the task.

10.9 Return a section of a string

In many cases, only a section of a column value is required by your application. For example, you may want to use the first three letters, a few letters from the middle, or the last few letters from a text column to provide an abbreviation. This How-To presents the method used to return a section of a string.

10.10 Find and replace patterns within a string

A common text manipulation requirement is to find a pattern within a string and replace it with another value. This How-To presents techniques that let you perform search and replace operations within Oracle data.

10.11 Change the case of a string

Text is often stored in the database with all characters capitalized or forced lower case. Within your reports and applications, it is often necessary to change the case of text stored in the database. This How-To covers the process used to change the case of a string.

COMPLEXITY
BEGINNING

10.1 How do I...
Format date and time values?

Problem

I need to be able to format date and time values. The default representation of the date columns' type is not acceptable for my applications and reports. My applications need date and time values formatted in a variety of ways. How do I format date and time values in Oracle?

Technique

The TO_CHAR function is used to convert a date value to character representations. It can be used within SQL statements or PL/SQL modules to present date values in more useful formats. The TO_CHAR function is overloaded in Oracle and has different uses depending on the parameter list passed to the function. The syntax of the TO_CHAR function used to format date values is shown here:

```
TO_CHAR(date_value, 'format mask')
```

The format mask specifies the format of the date when it is returned by the function. You can specify the output format any way you want by using valid date format models. Table 10-1 shows the valid date format models.

FORMAT	DESCRIPTION
MM	The number of the month (1-12).
RM	The month specified as a roman numeral.
MON	A three-letter abbreviation of the month.
MONTH	The month fully spelled out.
D	The number of the day in the week.
DD	The number of the day in the month.
DDD	The number of the day in the year.
DY	The three letter abbreviation of the day.
DAY	The day fully spelled out.
Y	The last digit of the year.
YY	The last two digits of the year.
YYY	The last three digits of the year.
YYYY	Full four-digit year.
SYYYY	The year in a signed format. BC values represented negative.
RR	The last two digits of the year used for year 2000 issues.
YEAR	The year spelled out.
Q	The number of the quarter.
WW	The number of the week in the year.
W	The number of the week in the month.
J	The number of days since December 31, 4713 B.C.
HH	The hour of the day (1-12).
HH24	The hour of the day (1-24).
MI	The minutes of the hour.
SS	The seconds of the minute.
SSSSS	The seconds since midnight.
A.M.	Displays A.M. or P.M. depending on time of day.

FORMAT	DESCRIPTION
P.M.	Displays A.M. or P.M. depending on time of day.
AM	Displays AM or PM depending on time of day.
PM	Displays AM or PM depending on time of day.
A.D.	Displays B.C. or A.D. depending on date.
B.C.	Same as A.D.
AD	Displays BC or AD depending on date.
BC	Same as AD.
fm	Prefix to MONTH or DAY to suppress padded spaces.
th	Suffix to number format to cause th, st, or rd to be added to the end of the number.
sp	Suffix to number to force the number to be spelled out.
spth	Suffix to number to force it to be spelled out and given an ordinal suffix.
thsp	Same as spth.

Table 10-1 Date format models

Combinations of the format models can be used with punctuation symbols in order to create an enormous number of possibilities.

Steps

1. Run SQL*Plus and connect as the WAITE user account. CHP10-1.sql, shown in Figure 10-1, creates the sample table used in this How-To.

```
CREATE TABLE SAMPLE102 (
    DATEFLD     DATE);

INSERT INTO SAMPLE102 VALUES
    (TO_DATE('25-FEB-95 11:23:03','DD-MON-YY HH:MI:SS'));

COMMIT;

COLUMN MMDDYY FORMAT A8
COLUMN MMDDYYYY FORMAT A10
COLUMN DAY FORMAT A15
COLUMN MONTH FORMAT A15
COLUMN DY FORMAT A10
COLUMN DDD FORMAT A10
COLUMN WW FORMAT A5
COLUMN MON FORMAT A5
COLUMN YEAR FORMAT A20
COLUMN RM FORMAT A5
COLUMN CC FORMAT A5
COLUMN HH FORMAT A5
COLUMN HHPM FORMAT A10
COLUMN HH24 FORMAT A5
COLUMN MI FORMAT A5
COLUMN SS FORMAT A5
COLUMN SSSSS FORMAT A5
```

Figure 10-1 CHP10-1.sql creates the sample table used in How-To 10.1

The SAMPLE102 table is created and populated with a single date value, which is queried in the examples using date formatting functions. The COLUMN commands contained in the script format the columns in the examples to make the output more readable. Run the file to create the sample table and sample record.

```
SQL> START CHP10-1

Table created.

1 row created.

Commit complete.
```

2. Load CHP10-2.sql into the SQL buffer. The file contains a query of the sample table that returns a date column in a variety of formats.

```
SQL> GET CHP10-2
  1  SELECT
  2      DATEFLD,
  3      TO_CHAR(DATEFLD,'MM/DD/YY') MMDDYY,'
  4      TO_CHAR(DATEFLD,'MM/DD/YYYY') MMDDYYYY,
  5      TO_CHAR(DATEFLD,'DAY') DAY,
  6      TO_CHAR(DATEFLD,'MONTH') MONTH
  7  FROM
  8*     SAMPLE102
```

Line 2 returns the date column in the default Oracle format. Lines 3 through 6 format the date in a variety of ways. Line 3 demonstrates the two-digit year format. Line 4 shows the day and month with the year in a four-digit format. Line 5 uses the DAY format mask to spell out the day of the week. Line 6 uses the MONTH format mask to spell out the month. Line 8 specifies that the sample table created in Step 1 is the source of the data.

3. Run the query to display the output. Figure 10-2 shows the output of the query within SQL*Plus.

The first three columns of the query display the date in the most commonly used formats. The DAY and MONTH columns show how the date can be converted and displayed in different formats. Both columns are shown in all capital letters. If the format mask was specified in all lower case, or with only the first letter capitalized, the case of the output would change.

4. Load CHP10-3.sql into the SQL buffer. The query contained in the file presents more formats in which date values can be presented.

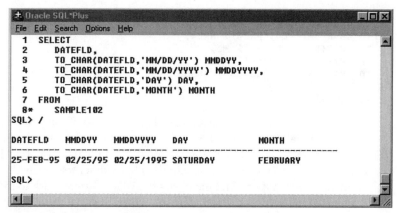

Figure 10-2 The output of the date formatting functions in SQL*Plus

```
SQL> GET CHP10-3
  1   SELECT
  2       TO_CHAR(DATEFLD,'DY') DY,
  3       TO_CHAR(DATEFLD,'DDD') DDD,
  4       TO_CHAR(DATEFLD,'WW') WW,
  5       TO_CHAR(DATEFLD,'MON') MON,
  6       TO_CHAR(DATEFLD,'YEAR') YEAR
  7   FROM
  8*      SAMPLE102
```

Line 2 displays the day of the week abbreviated in the three-digit format. Line 3 uses the DDD format mask to display the number of days from the beginning of the year. Line 4 uses the WW format mask to display the week of the year from 1 to 53. Line 5 uses the MON format mask to display the month in its three-digit abbreviation. Line 6 uses the YEAR format mask to display the year spelled out.

5. Run the statement to display the formatted results. Figure 10-3 shows the results of the query.

The formats displayed by the query can be used for specific requirements within applications. Information such as the day of year or week of year can be useful in batch operations.

6. Load CHP10-4.sql into the SQL buffer. The query contained in the file displays format masks based on the year and the time portion of the date variable.

```
SQL> GET CHP10-4
  1   SELECT
  2       TO_CHAR(DATEFLD,'RM') RM,
  3       TO_CHAR(DATEFLD,'CC') CC,
  4       TO_CHAR(DATEFLD,'HH') HH,
```

continued on next page

continued from previous page

```
  5        TO_CHAR(DATEFLD,'HH PM') HHPM,
  6        TO_CHAR(DATEFLD,'HH24') HH24,
  7        TO_CHAR(DATEFLD,'MI') MI,
  8        TO_CHAR(DATEFLD,'SS') SS,
  9        TO_CHAR(DATEFLD,'SSSSS') SSSSS
 10   FROM
 11*      SAMPLE102
```

Line 2 uses the RM format mask to display the month of the year as a roman numeral. Line 3 uses the CC format mask to format the century. Line 4 uses the HH format mask to display the hour of the day from 0 to 12. Line 5 uses the HH format mask with the PM modifier to display the hour of the time with AM or PM. Line 6 uses the HH24 format mask to display the hour in military time. Line 7 formats the minutes with the MI format mask. Line 8 uses the SS format mask to display the seconds. Line 9 uses the SSSSS format mask to display the number of seconds past midnight.

7. Run the statement to display the results.

The results of the query show how year values can be presented as roman numerals and the century can be calculated. The time formats contained in the query show that the time portion of the date column can be displayed in a variety of ways. (See Figure 10-4).

How It Works

The TO_CHAR function is used to display a date value in a variety of formats. The format models shown in Table 10-1 can be used to create date output in almost any conceivable format. The opposite of the TO_CHAR function is the TO_DATE function. The TO_DATE function is used to convert a character string to the internal Oracle date format. Step 1 creates the sample table and data used throughout this How-To. The sample table contains a date column and a single record, which

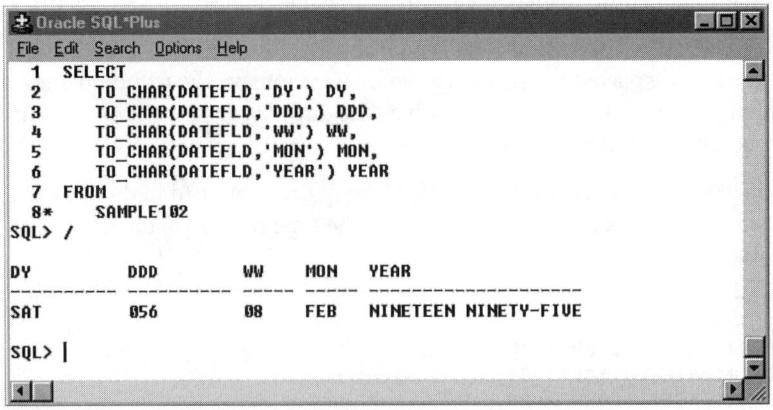

Figure 10-3 The result of date formatting functions

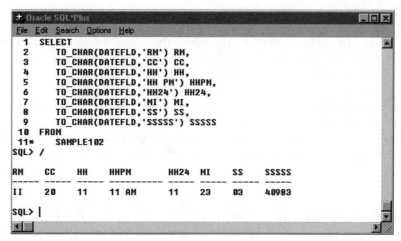

Figure 10-4 The time portion of the date column displayed in a variety of ways

are queried in the later steps. Steps 2 through 7 present queries which format the date column to present formatted output.

Comments

Date and time values can be formatted easily using the TO_CHAR function. The power of the function can be used to solve a variety of problems. How-To 10.9 uses the date formatting functions to write a number as text.

COMPLEXITY
BEGINNING

10.2 How do I...
Trim trailing spaces from day and month names?

Problem

When I use the DAY and MONTH format masks with the TO_CHAR function, Oracle pads the right side of the output with spaces. This makes the format mask difficult to use in my applications. I do not want to TRIM the output of the TO_CHAR function every time I use these format masks. How do I trim trailing spaces from the day and month names?

Technique

The TO_CHAR function is used to display the values of dates and times in a variety of formats. How-To 10-1 presents the TO_CHAR function to display date values. The FM modifier to the DAY and MONTH format masks trims the trailing spaces from the output generated by the TO_CHAR function. The format masks fmDAY and fmMONTH output the results with the trailing spaces removed. The FM modifier should only be specified once in the format mask. The first instance of the modifier trims trailing spaces for the remainder of the format mask or until another FM modifier is found. A second modifier terminates the action of this modifier.

Steps

1. Run SQL*Plus and connect as the WAITE user account. CHP10-5.sql, shown in Figure 10-5, creates the sample tables used in this How-To.

Run the file to create the sample table and a sample record. The SAMPLE105 table used in the example contains a single date column and is populated with one record. The COLUMN commands format the output of the queries in SQL*Plus to make them more readable.

```
SQL>   START CHP10-5

Table created.

1 row created.

Commit complete.
```

2. Load CHP10-6.sql into the SQL buffer. The file contains a query of the sample table using format masks with and without the FM modifier.

```
SQL> GET CHP10-6
  1   SELECT
  2       TO_CHAR(DATEFLD,'Day, Month DD') A,
  3       TO_CHAR(DATEFLD,'fmDay, Month DD') B
  4   FROM
  5*      SAMPLE105
```

Line 2 returns the date column using the DAY and MONTH format models. Without the FM modifier, both values will be padded with spaces. In line 3, the FM modifier is used only once for the entire format mask to trim trailing spaces off both values. Including a second modifier terminates the function of the modifier.

3. Run the statement to display the results. Figure 10-6 shows the results of the query in SQL*Plus.

The first column, which does not contain the FM modifier, has unwanted spaces after the day and month values. The second column, which contains the FM modifier, has a much more useable format.

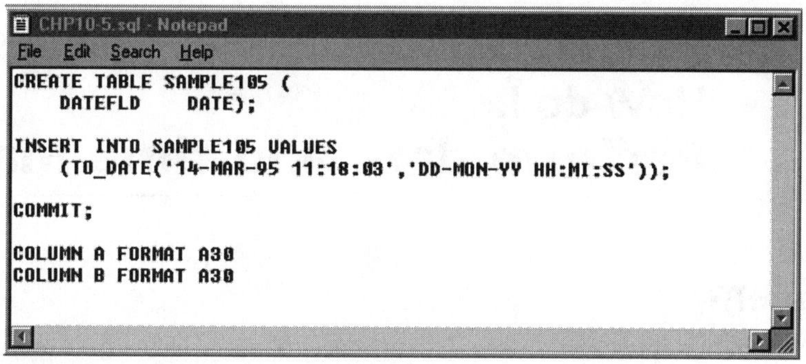

Figure 10-5 CHP10-5.sql creates the sample tables used in How-To 10.2

How It Works

The FM format mask modifier is used within the TO_CHAR function to trim unwanted spaces from the DAY and MONTH format models. Step 1 creates the sample table and record used throughout the How-To. Steps 2 and 3 display the use of the FM format mask by displaying the output using the same format mask with and without the modifier. The modifier only needs to be specified once for the entire format mask. Specifying a second modifier stops the format modification.

Comments

The trailing spaces returned by the DAY and MONTH format masks can be annoying. The FM modifier is an easy way to remove the trailing spaces without resorting to string modification functions. The FM modifier should only be specified once in the format mask.

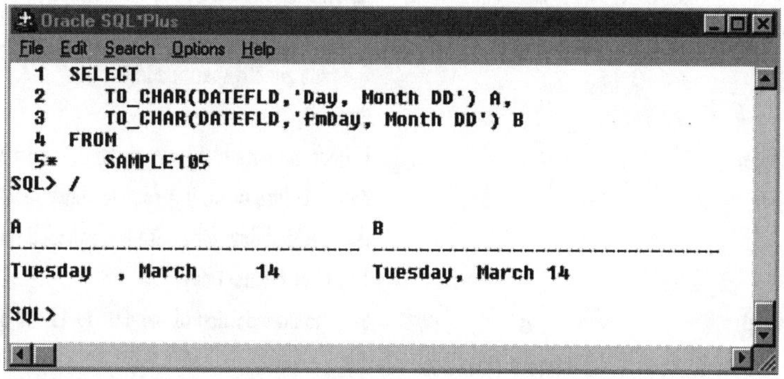

Figure 10-6 The output of a query using the FM modifier in a format mask

10.3   How do I...
Perform date and time math?

Problem

Within our applications, we use many date columns. In many of our reports and PL/SQL processes, we need to perform date math. This includes adding and subtracting days, months, and years and calculating the number of weeks or months between dates. How do I perform date math within Oracle?

Technique

Oracle provides a complete set of functions for performing date math. Table 10-2 shows the date modification functions available.

FUNCTION/PARAMETERS	DESCRIPTION
ADD_MONTHS(date, value)	Adds *value* months to the date.
GREATEST(date1, date2, ...)	Returns the latest date from a list of dates.
LEAST(date1, date2, ...)	Returns the earliest date from a list of dates.
LAST_DAY(date)	Returns the last day of the month the date is in.
MONTHS_BETWEEN(date2, date1)	Calculates *date2 - date1* in months.
NEXT_DAY(date, 'day')	Returns the date of the next 'day' that is after *date*.
	Day is specified as 'Monday', 'Tuesday', etc.
NEW_TIME(date, 'this_zone,' 'new_zone')	Returns the time of day in the new time
	zone, 'new_zone,' when it is stored in 'this_zone.'
	The time zone is specified in its
	three-digit abbreviation.
ROUND(date)	Rounds the date to 12 AM. If the time portion of the
	date is before noon, it is rounded back to 12 AM of
	the specified day; otherwise it is rounded forward to
	12 AM of the next day.
TRUNC(date)	Sets the time portion of the date to 12 AM of the specified day.

Table 10-2 Date and time functions

In addition to the date functions provided by Oracle, the addition operator (+) and subtraction operator (–) can be used to add and subtract dates.

Steps

1. Run SQL*Plus and connect as the WAITE user account. CHP10-7.sql, shown in Figure 10-7, creates the sample table used in this How-To.

The sample table contains a single date column populated with a record containing both the date and time portions of the value. The COLUMN commands in the script format the output of the columns in this How-To. Run the file to create the sample table and record.

```
SQL>  /

Table created.

1 row created.

Commit complete.
```

2. Load CHP10-8.sql into the SQL buffer. The file contains a query to demonstrate date modification functions.

```
SQL>  GET CHP10-8
   1   SELECT
   2      DATEFLD+1 DATEFLD,
   3      ADD_MONTHS(DATEFLD,1) ADDMONTHS,
   4      MONTHS_BETWEEN('_01-JAN-98',DATEFLD) MONTHSBETWEEN,
   5      LAST_DAY(DATEFLD) LASTDAY,
   6      NEXT_DAY(DATEFLD,'FRIDAY') NEXTDAY
   7   FROM
   8*     SAMPLE107
```

Line 2 adds one day to the date field using the standard addition operator. Line 3 uses the ADD_MONTHS function to add one month to the date field. Line 4 uses the MONTHS_BETWEEN function to return the number

```
█ CHP10-7.sql - Notepad                                           _ □ ×
 File  Edit  Search  Help
CREATE TABLE SAMPLE107 (
    DATEFLD      DATE);

INSERT INTO SAMPLE107 VALUES
    (TO_DATE('01-MAR-96 10:22:09','DD-MON-YY HH:MI:SS'));

COMMIT;

COLUMN DATEFLD FORMAT A10
COLUMN ADDMONTHS FORMAT A10
COLUMN MONTHSBETWEEN FORMAT 9999.99
COLUMN LASTDAY FORMAT A10
COLUMN NEXTDAY FORMAT A10
```

Figure 10-7 CHP10-7.sql creates the sample table used in How-To 10.3

of months between the date field and 01-JAN-98. Line 5 uses the LAST_DAY function to return the last date of the month that the date in the date fields is in. Line 6 uses the NEXT_DAY function to return the date of the Friday following the value in the date field.

3. Run the query to display the results. Figure 10-8 shows the results of the query in SQL*Plus.

The value returned in the first column is one day after the date in the table. The value returned in the second column is one month after the date in the column, as calculated by the ADD_MONTHS function. The third column shows that there are exactly 22 months between the date in the table and January 1, 1998. The value returned by the fourth column shows the last day of the month in the column, and the fifth column shows the date of the following Friday.

How It Works

Oracle provides a powerful set of date functions for performing date and time math. In addition, values can be added and subtracted to a date value with the addition and subtraction operators. Step 1 creates a sample table containing a date file used to demonstrate the capabilities of some of the Oracle date functions. Steps 2 and 3 present a query displaying the use of the addition operator and the some of the date functions. The ADD_MONTHS function is used to add a number of months to date values. The MONTHS_BETWEEN function is used to calculate the number of months between two dates. The LAST_DAY function is used to determine the last date of the month, and the NEXT_DAY function is used to determine the next date that falls on a certain day of the week.

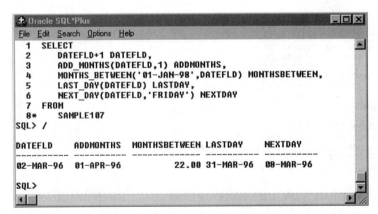

Figure 10-8 The results of the query in SQL*Plus

Comments

Performing date math in Oracle can be confusing, which is why the Oracle built-in date functions should be used whenever you need to work with dates. Oracle provides functions for almost any type of date calculation you will need to perform.

COMPLEXITY
BEGINNING

10.4 How do I...
Replace a NULL value with a string or number?

Problem

When my query returns NULL values, I need the value to be a specific string or number. Since a NULL value represents nothing and not zero or a zero-length string, using NULL values in my operations presents a problem. Whenever a NULL value is used in one of my calculations, the result is always NULL. How do I replace a NULL value with a string or number?

Technique

The NVL function replaces a NULL value with a substitute value that can be used in an expression. The syntax of the NVL function is shown here:

```
NVL(value, substitute)
```

If the value passed to the function is NULL, the substitute is returned as the result; otherwise the value is returned. The NVL function can be used with many datatypes; however, the value and its substitute must be of the same datatype.

Steps

1. Run SQL*Plus and connect as the WAITE user account. CHP10-9.sql, shown in Figure 10-9, creates the sample table and data used throughout this How-To.

The sample table contains one numeric column and is populated with two records. One of the records contains a value for the column, and the other contains a NULL value. Run the statement to create the sample table and its data.

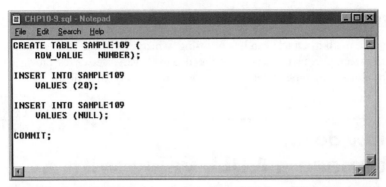

Figure 10-9 CHP10-9.sql creates the sample table and data
used throughout How-To 10.4

```
SQL>    START CHP10-9

Table created.

1 row created.

1 row created.

Commit complete.
```

2. Load CHP10-10.sql into the SQL buffer. The file contains a query of the sample table.

```
SQL> GET CHP10-10
  1   SELECT
  2      ROWNUM,
  3       ROW_VALUE,
  4       ROW_VALUE * 6
  5   FROM
  6*      SAMPLE109
```

The ROWNUM pseudo column is returned by line 2 to help identify the records returned. The value of the column in the sample table is returned by line 3 and is used in an expression in line 4. The FROM clause contained in lines 5 and 6 specifies the sample table created in step 1 as the source of the data.

3. Run the statement to view the data contained in the table. Figure 10-10 shows the results of the query.

The second record identified by the ROWNUM value of 2 contains NULL data for both the value and the expression containing it. This could cause a problem in applications expecting a valid value for the result of an expression. The query presented in the next step uses the NVL function to solve the problem.

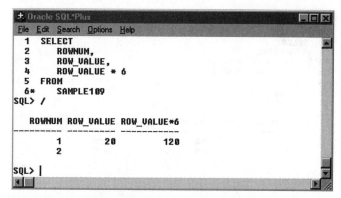

Figure 10-10 The results of the query
containing NULL data

4. Load CHP10-11.sql into the SQL buffer. The query contained in the file
uses the NVL function to return a value for columns and expressions containing NULL.

```
SQL> GET CHP10-11
  1   SELECT
  2       ROWNUM,
  3       NVL(ROW_VALUE,0),
  4       NVL(ROW_VALUE,0) * 6
  5   FROM
  6*      SAMPLE109
```

The ROW_VALUE column used in lines 3 and 4 is replaced by 0 any time it
contains a NULL value. This will return a value in the expression as NOT
NULL, even if the column contains a NULL value.

5. Run the query to display the records containing NULL values. Figure 10-11
shows the results of the query in SQL*Plus.

The value of 0 is returned by the second record because the NVL function
converted the value of the NULL column to 0. The NVL function solves the
problem of the application which uses the query expecting a non-NULL
value in the expression.

How It Works

The NVL function is used to replace a NULL value with a substitute value. The value
used in the function and the substitute value must be of the same datatype. Step 1
creates a sample table populated with two records. One of the records contains a value
in the column, and the other contains NULL. Steps 2 and 3 present a query which
displays the column value and uses it in an expression. Both the column value and

```
Oracle SQL*Plus                                            _ □ X
File  Edit  Search  Options  Help
  1   SELECT
  2      ROWNUM,
  3      NVL(ROW_VALUE,0),
  4      NVL(ROW_VALUE,0) * 6
  5   FROM
  6*     SAMPLE109
SQL> /

   ROWNUM NVL(ROW_VALUE,0) NVL(ROW_VALUE,0)*6
--------- ---------------- ------------------
        1               20                120
        2                0                  0

SQL>
```

Figure 10-11 The results of the query when
the NVL function is used

the expression return NULL, because any NULL values in an expression return it
as NULL. Steps 4 and 5 use the NVL function in the same query to replace the NULL
value with 0. By using 0 instead of NULL in the expression, a valid result is
returned.

Comments

It is a common error to think of NULL as zero or a zero-length string. This can cause
problems in queries and applications that expect a valid value to be returned. The
NVL function is a very easy way to ensure that NULL values do not appear in expressions where unexpected. You can use the NVL function any time you are not sure
of the data contained in a column.

COMPLEXITY
INTERMEDIATE

10.5   How do I...
Convert a number to a string?

Problem

I need to convert a numeric value to a string in order to perform operations like concatenating strings and string functions, such as INSTR and SUBSTR. I also want to
display numeric values in a variety of formats, such as scientific notation. How do
I convert a number to a string to display it in different formats?

Technique

The TO_CHAR function can be used to convert a numeric value to a string datatype. The output of the function can be specified in many different formats. TO_CHAR is an overloaded function that works differently depending on the parameters passed to it. When TO_CHAR is used to convert a number to a string, a format mask may be specified to provide the conversion format. Table 10-3 shows the numeric format masks that can be used with the TO_CHAR function.

FORMAT	DEFINITION
999990	The number of nines or zeros determines how many digits can be displayed.
999,999.00	Commas and decimals will be displayed. Leading zeros shown as blank.
099999	Displays number with leading zeros.
$99999	Dollar sign placed in from of number.
99999S	If number is negative, the minus sign is displayed to the left.
S99999	Displays a plus or minus sign at the beginning of the number.
L99999	Displays the local currency character in the location of the L.
RN	Displays the number as a Roman numeral.
99999PR	Negative numbers are surrounded by <>.
9.999EEEE	Displays the number in scientific notation. (Must be exactly four Es.)
999V99	Multiplies the number by 10n, where n is the number of digits to the right of V.

Table 10-3 Numeric format models

Steps

1. Run SQL*Plus and connect as the WAITE user account. CHP10-12.sql, shown in Figure 10-12, creates the sample table used throughout this How-To.

The sample table created by the script contains a single numeric column which will be formatted in the following steps. A single record which will be queried in a variety of formats is created. Run the file to create the table and data.

```
SQL>   START CHP10-12

Table created.

1 row created.

Commit complete.
```

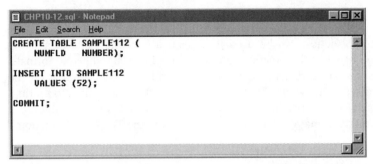

Figure 10-12 CHP10-12.sql creates the sample table
used in How-To 10.5

2. Load CHP10-13.sql into the SQL buffer. The file contains a query which
presents number conversion formats.

```
SQL> GET CHP10-13
  1   SELECT
  2      TO_CHAR(NUMFLD,'099999') F099999,
  3      TO_CHAR(NUMFLD,'$999,999.99') MONEY,
  4      TO_CHAR(NUMFLD,'99999.99S') F9999S,
  5      TO_CHAR(NUMFLD,'RN') RN,
  6      TO_CHAR(NUMFLD,'9.999EEEE') EE
  7   FROM
  8*     SAMPLE112
```

Line 2 returns the value from the table padded with zeros. The format mask
specified in line 3 returns the value of the column formatted as a monetary
amount, including the dollar sign and appropriate commas. The format
mask specified in line 4 formats the column to include two digits after the
decimal point and a sign at the end of the value. Line 6 formats the value of
the column in scientific notation. The format mask used in line 6 cannot be
varied. The FROM clause in lines 7 and 8 specifies the sample table created
in step 1 as the source of the query.

3. Run the statement to display the results. Figure 10-13 shows the results of
the query in SQL*Plus.

The first column displays the value padded with zeros. The second column
shows the same value as a monetary amount. The third column displays a
sign at the end of the value. The Roman numeral shown in the fourth column will only be valid if the number does not contain a decimal point and
is positive and relatively small. The format mask used in the fifth column to
generate the value in scientific notation must be specified exactly as shown
in the query to generate this result.

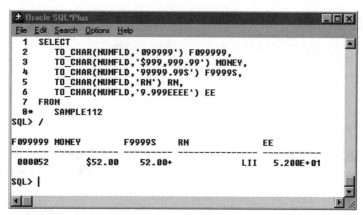

Figure 10-13 The results of the number formatting query

How It Works

The TO_CHAR function can be used to convert numeric values to a character representation. A format mask can be provided containing the models shown in Table 10-3, which convert the number to a variety of formats. Step 1 creates a sample table populated with a single record. The table contains a numeric column, which is formatted in steps 2 and 3. Steps 2 and 3 use the TO_CHAR function to convert the numeric value in the sample table to various string formats.

Comments

Numeric values can be formatted almost any way you like using the TO_CHAR function. If you only need to typecast the number so it can be used with string functions, do not include a format mask with the TO_CHAR function.

COMPLEXITY
BEGINNING

10.6 How do I...
Concatenate strings?

Problem

I often need to concatenate two or more strings into a longer one. Many of the queries I use in the data dictionary need to concatenate a static text string with the value returned from a column. How do I concatenate strings in Oracle?

Technique

The string concatenation operator (||) can be used to combine two strings into one. The CONCAT function can also be used in SQL and PL/SQL to concatenate strings. When you use either of these methods, you need to ensure that both values to be concatenated are strings.

Steps

1. Run SQL*Plus and connect as the WAITE user account. CHP10-14.sql, shown in Figure 10-14, creates the sample table and data used in the examples.

The sample table contains two text columns which will be concatenated using different methods in the rest of this How-To. Run the file to create the sample table and data.

```
SQL> START CHP10-14

Table created.

1 row created.

Commit complete.
```

2. Load CHP10-15.sql into the SQL buffer.

```
SQL> GET CHP10-15
  1   SELECT
  2       FLD1||FLD2 COLUMN1,
  3       CONCAT(FLD1,FLD2) COLUMN2
  4   FROM
  5*      SAMPLE114
```

```
CHP10-14.sql - Notepad
File  Edit  Search  Help

CREATE TABLE SAMPLE114 (
    FLD1   VARCHAR2(20),
    FLD2   VARCHAR2(20));

INSERT INTO SAMPLE114
    VALUES ('HELLO','WORLD');

COMMIT;
```

Figure 10-14 CHP10-14.sql creates the sample table and data used throughout How-To 10.6

Line 2 uses the concatenation operator (||) to concatenate the two columns from the table. The column is aliased as COLUMN1. Line 3 uses the CONCAT function to concatenate the same two columns. The column is aliased as COLUMN2. Both methods will return the same result. The FROM clause in lines 4 and 5 specifies the sample table created in step 1 as the source of the data.

3. Run the statement to display the results. Figure 10-15 shows the results of the query in SQL*Plus.

Both the concatenation operator and the CONCAT function return identical results. The method you use in a query depends on your personal preference. The next step uses both methods to concatenate strings in PL/SQL.

4. Load CHP10-16.sql into the SQL buffer. The PL/SQL module contained in the file concatenates strings using both the concatenation operator and the CONCAT function.

```
SQL> GET CHP10-16
  1   DECLARE
  2      X     VARCHAR2(30);
  3      Y     VARCHAR2(30);
  4      Z     VARCHAR2(60);
  5   BEGIN
  6      X := '_HELLO';
  7      Y := '_WORLD';
  8      Z := X||Y;
  9      DBMS_OUTPUT.PUT_LINE(Z);
 10      Z := NULL;
 11      Z := CONCAT(X,Y);
 12      DBMS_OUTPUT.PUT_LINE(Z);
 13*  END;
```

Lines 2 through 4 declare three string variables used in the PL/SQL block. Line 6 sets the value of variable X to HELLO. Line 7 sets the value of variable Y to WORLD. Line 8 uses the concatenate operator to concatenate the

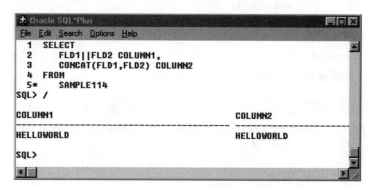

Figure 10-15 The results of the query in SQL*Plus

two strings and put the results in Z. The DBMS_OUTPUT.PUT_LINE procedure is used in line 9 to display the results of the operation. The value of variable Z is set back to NULL in line 10. Line 11 uses the CONCAT function to concatenate the variables X and Y and put the results in Z. Line 12 displays the value of Z.

5. Set the SERVEROUTPUT system variable to ON to display the output and run the module to show the results. Figure 10-16 shows the results of the operation in SQL*Plus.

Once again, both the concatenation operator and the CONCAT function return identical results.

How It Works

Strings can be concatenated in Oracle using the concatenation operator (||) or the CONCAT function. Both methods return identical results. Step 1 creates a sample table and populates it with a single record. The table contains two columns, both of which are string variables. Steps 2 and 3 present a query which uses the concatenate operator (||) and the CONCAT function to concatenate two strings. Steps 4 and 5 present a PL/SQL module using the same two methods to concatenate string values.

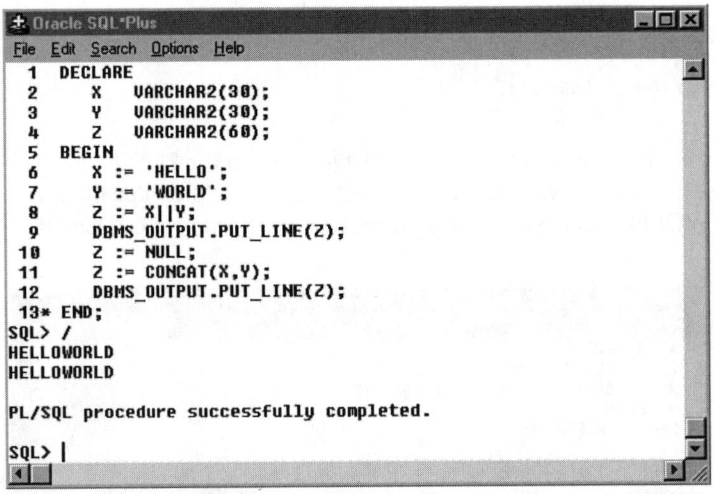

Figure 10-16 The results of the concatenation operation performed in PL/SQL

Comments

String concatenation will be necessary in almost every application you develop. The concatenation operator and the CONCAT function return identical results. Which method you use depends on your personal preference.

COMPLEXITY
BEGINNING

10.7 How do I...
Capitalize the first letter of each word in a string?

Problem

In our database, names are stored in all capital letters. When I retrieve a name from a table, I want to capitalize the first letter of each word in the name. I know there are functions to convert strings to all uppercase or all lowercase, but how do I capitalize the first letter of each word in a string?

Technique

The INITCAP function capitalizes the first letter of every word in a string. The function is very useful when strings are stored in the database in all upper- or lowercase. The function is passed a string as a parameter and returns a string value containing the case modification.

Steps

1. Run SQL*Plus and connect as the WAITE user account. Load CHP10-17.sql into the SQL buffer. The file demonstrates the INITCAP function by selecting a value from DUAL.

```
SQL> GET CHP10-17
  1  SELECT
  2      INITCAP('_THIS STRING IS ALL CAPS') A
  3* FROM DUAL
```

The INITCAP function is used in line 1 to capitalize the first letter of each word in the string. The FROM clause in line 3 specifies the DUAL system table as the source of the data.

2. Run the statement to display the output of the query.

```
SQL>  /

A
------------------------------------
This String Is All Caps
```

The INITCAP function capitalizes the first letter of each word in the string. This can be very useful when working with strings containing names.

3. Load CHP10-18.sql into the SQL buffer. The file contains a PL/SQL module presenting the use of the INITCAP function within PL/SQL. The INITCAP function can be used within PL/SQL like any other function.

```
SQL>  GET CHP10-18
  1   DECLARE
  2       X VARCHAR2(50);
  3   BEGIN
  4       X := INITCAP('_THIS STRING IS ALL CAPS');
  5       DBMS_OUTPUT.PUT_LINE(X);
  6*  END;
```

Line 2 declares a variable to be set to the value of the INITCAP function in line 4. Line 5 uses the DBMS_OUTPUT.PUT_LINE procedure to display the value of the variable.

4. Set the SERVEROUTPUT system variable to ON to make SQL*Plus display output from the DBMS_OUTPUT package and run the statement. Figure 10-17 shows the results of the operation.

The results of the INITCAP function in PL/SQL are identical to its results when used in a query. The first letter of each word in the string is capitalized by the function.

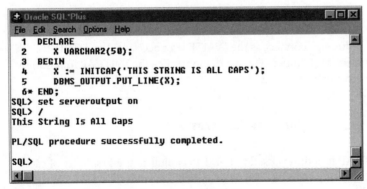

Figure 10-17 The results of the PL/SQL
statement in SQL*Plus

How It Works

The INITCAP function capitalizes the first letter of each word in a string and converts all of the other letters to lowercase. The function can be used in SQL statements and in PL/SQL modules. Steps 1 and 2 use the INITCAP function in a query. The INITCAP function formats character columns as they are queried. Steps 3 and 4 show the use of the INITCAP function within a PL/SQL module. The function can be used like any other built-in function in PL/SQL.

Comments

The INITCAP function is very useful for formatting strings in SQL and PL/SQL. You will find it most useful for formatting names stored in the database in all uppercase letters or all lowercase letters. How-To 10.11 presents the other functions used to change the case of strings in Oracle.

COMPLEXITY
ADVANCED

10.8   How do I...
Write a number as words?

Problem

In the payroll system we are developing, we need to print checks. One of the requirements is that the dollar amount of the check be written as words on the check. I need a method to write a number in words using both SQL and PL/SQL. How do I spell out a number in words?

Technique

One of the format mask modifiers in the TO_CHAR date formatting function writes the number portions of a date as words. The number can be changed to written text by converting it to the internal date format using the TO_DATE function, then converting it to text with the TO_CHAR function and the SP format mask modifier. The SP modifier converts a number to written text when used in a format mask. The J format mask converts a date to the number of days since December 31, 4713 B.C. Converting a number to a date using the J format mask in the TO_DATE function, then converting it back with the TO_CHAR function using the same format mask, always generates the same number. Adding the SP modifier in the conversion back transforms the number to written text.

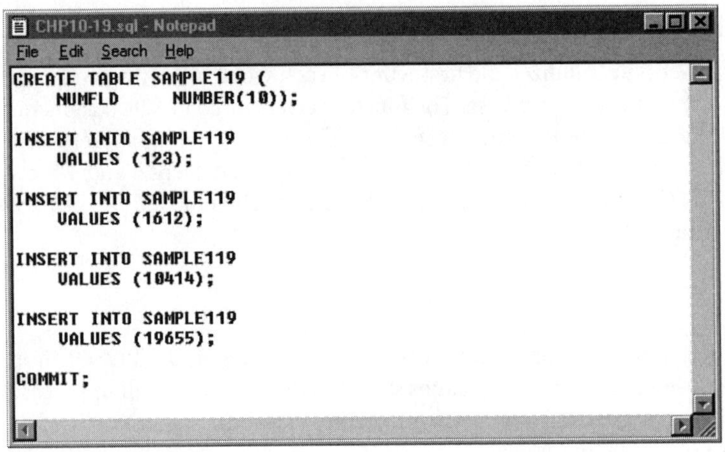

```
CREATE TABLE SAMPLE119 (
    NUMFLD     NUMBER(10));

INSERT INTO SAMPLE119
    VALUES (123);

INSERT INTO SAMPLE119
    VALUES (1612);

INSERT INTO SAMPLE119
    VALUES (10414);

INSERT INTO SAMPLE119
    VALUES (19655);

COMMIT;
```

Figure 10-18 CHP10-19.sql creates the sample table used in How-To 10.8

Steps

1. Run SQL*Plus and connect as the WAITE user account. CHP10-19.sql, shown in Figure 10-18, creates the sample table used throughout this How-To.

The sample table contains a numeric column and is populated with four records which will display the use of the technique. Run the script to create the table and sample records.

```
SQL>  START CHP10-19

Table created.

1 row created.

1 row created.

1 row created.

1 row created.

Commit complete.
```

2. Load CHP10-20.sql into the SQL buffer. The file contains a query which converts the numbers in the table to their written text representation by using the TO_CHAR and TO_DATE functions.

```
SQL> GET CHP10-20
  1  SELECT
  2      TO_CHAR(TO_DATE(NUMFLD,'J'),'JSP')
```

```
3   FROM
4*     SAMPLE119
```

Line 2 uses the TO_DATE function to convert the number field to the Oracle date format by using the J format mask. The date returned by the function does not matter because it is immediately converted back using the TO_CHAR function. In the JSP format mask, the J portion converts the date back to a number and the SP modifier writes the number out in words.

3. Run the query in SQL*Plus to display the values from the table written out as text. Figure 10-19 shows the results of the query.

Each of the numeric values returned by the query is converted to written text using the TO_CHAR and TO_DATE functions. Since the TO_CHAR and TO_DATE functions can both be used in PL/SQL modules, the same technique can be used in PL/SQL.

How It Works

The TO_DATE and TO_CHAR functions can format a numeric value as written text because of the format masks they contain. The TO_DATE function can convert a number to the Oracle date format using the J format mask. Once the number is in date format, the TO_CHAR function can be used with the JSP format mask to write the number as text. Step 1 creates a sample table with a numeric column and populates it with four records. The sample table displays the output generated by the technique. Steps 2 and 3 present the method used to convert the numeric values to written text. Using the technique previously described, the sample table is queried to display each of the numeric values as a text string.

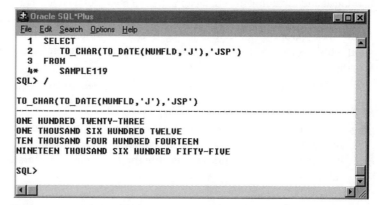

Figure 10-19 The data from the sample table written as text

Comments

Formatting a number as written words is a common task in financial functions. The stored procedure presented in this How-To can be used to simplify the task of converting numbers. The method presented in this How-To can by used in PL/SQL or as part of a query of a field.

COMPLEXITY
BEGINNING

10.9 How do I...
Return a section of a string?

Problem

In my applications, I need characters of the value. In other cases, I need to return a specified number of characters from the middle of the string value. How do I return a section of a string?

Technique

The SUBSTR function is used to return a string section of a specified length, starting at a specific location within the string. The syntax of the SUBSTR function is shown here:

```
SUBSTR(value, starting_position, chars_returned)
```

The function returns the number of characters represented by CHARS_RETURNED, starting at and including the character at STARTING_POSITION. The SUBSTR function can be used within SQL statements and in PL/SQL modules. If the STARTING_POSITION specified is negative, it is counted from the end of the column. This lets you return sections from the end of the column without knowing its length.

Steps

1. Run SQL*Plus and connect as the WAITE user account. Load CHP10-21.sql into the SQL buffer. The file contains a query of the ALL_VIEWS data dictionary view and returns only the first four characters of the column value.

```
SQL> GET CHP10-21
  1  SELECT
  2      SUBSTR(VIEW_NAME, 1,4) VN
  3  FROM
```

```
4     ALL_VIEWS
5  WHERE
6*    ROWNUM  <=  10
```

Line 2 uses the SUBSTR function to return the first four characters of the VIEW_NAME column from the ALL_VIEWS data dictionary view. The first parameter specifies the starting location for cutting characters. The second parameter specifies the number of characters to return. The WHERE clause contained in lines 5 and 6 only causes the query to return the first ten rows.

2. Run the statement to execute the query. The results of the operation are shown in Figure 10-20.

The query displays the first four characters of each row. The SUBSTR function lets you specify the number of characters to return and the starting location in the string.

3. It is often necessary to return the last few characters from a text string. Load CHP10-22.sql into the SQL buffer. The file contains a query using the SUBSTR function with a negative starting location to return the last four characters from the VIEW_NAME column.

```
SQL> GET CHP10-22
  1  SELECT
  2    SUBSTR(VIEW_NAME,-4,4),
  3    VIEW_NAME
  4  FROM
  5    ALL_VIEWS
  6  WHERE
  7*   ROWNUM  <=  10
```

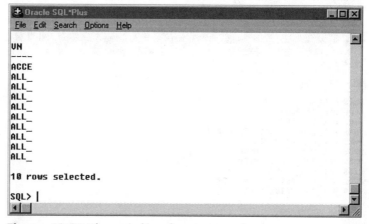

Figure 10-20 The results of a query using the SUBSTR function

Line 2 uses the SUBSTR function and specifies a negative number for the starting position, thus causing the location to be calculated from the end of the column. The VIEW_NAME column is returned in line 3 in order to show the unaltered value. Lines 4 and 5 specify the ALL_VIEWS data dictionary view as the data source.

4. Run the statement to view the results of the operation. Figure 10-21 displays these results.

As long as there are at least four characters in the VIEW_NAME column, the function will return exactly four characters. If there are less than four characters, the function will return them all.

How It Works

The SUBSTR function is used to return a section of a string starting at a specified position within the string. The starting position and the number of characters to return are provided to the SUBSTR function as parameters. Steps 1 and 2 present the SUBSTR function in a query to return the first four characters of a column in a data dictionary view. Steps 2 and 3 use the SUBSTR function with a negative starting position to return characters from the end of the string.

Comments

The SUBSTR function gives you the flexibility needed to manipulate strings in Oracle. The function can be used in both SQL statements and PL/SQL modules. If you specify a negative starting location, the value will be calculated from the end of the

```
Oracle SQL*Plus
File  Edit  Search  Options  Help
SQL> /

VN    VIEW_NAME
----  -------------------------------
BLES  ACCESSIBLE_TABLES
ALOG  ALL_CATALOG
TERS  ALL_CLUSTERS
IONS  ALL_CLUSTER_HASH_EXPRESSIONS
ENTS  ALL_COL_COMMENTS
MADE  ALL_COL_GRANTS_MADE
RECD  ALL_COL_GRANTS_RECD
RIVS  ALL_COL_PRIVS
MADE  ALL_COL_PRIVS_MADE
RECD  ALL_COL_PRIVS_RECD

10 rows selected.

SQL> |
```

Figure 10-21 The results of the query using the SUBSTR function with a negative starting location

column. This can only be performed on VARCHAR2 columns, since CHAR columns are right-padded with spaces.

10.10 How do I...
Find and replace patterns within a string?

Problem

I need to search a string and return the first occurrence of another string within it. I also want to replace a string contained in the other string. I want to use this process in both queries and PL/SQL code.

Technique

The INSTR function is used to find the occurrences of a string in another string. The syntax of the INSTR function is shown here:

```
INSTR(string, set [,start [,occurrence]])
```

The function searches the string for the set of characters. If no occurrences of the set of characters are found, the function returns 0; otherwise it returns the starting location of the string. The START parameter lets you specify a starting location for the search. The OCCURRENCE parameter allows you to skip a number of occurrences of the set. If you wish to find the second occurrence of the set, you would specify 2 for the OCCURRENCE parameter. The REPLACE function returns a string in which all occurrences of a specified string are replaced with another one. If you do not specify a replacement string, all occurrences of the search string are removed. The syntax of the REPLACE function is shown here:

```
REPLACE(string, if, then)
```

Each occurrence of the string represented by the IF parameter is replaced by the string represented by the THEN parameter.

Steps

1. Run SQL*Plus and connect as the WAITE user account. Load CHP10-23.sql into the SQL buffer. The query contained in the file demonstrates the use of the INSTR function.

```
SQL> GET CHP10-23
  1  SELECT
```

continued on next page

continued from previous page

```
 2     INSTR('HELLO WORLD','WORLD') D,
 3     INSTR('HELLO WORLD','O',1,2) E
4* FROM DUAL
```

Line 2 returns the position of the WORLD string in the HELLO WORLD string. If the search string is not found, 0 is returned; otherwise the starting position is returned. Line 3 returns the second occurrence of the letter O in the same string. The parameter 1 specifies to begin the search at the first character, and the parameter 2 specifies to search for the second occurrence of the string. The FROM clause contained in line 4 specifies the DUAL table as the source of the query.

2. Run the statement to display the results. Figure 10-22 shows the results of the query in SQL*Plus.

The string WORLD was found at the seventh character, as shown by the first column. The second occurrence of the letter was found at the eighth character.

3. Run SQL*Plus and connect to the WAITE user account. Load CHP10-24.sql into the SQL buffer. The file contains a query from DUAL replacing the value of a string with another string.

```
SQL> GET CHP10-24
  1   SELECT
  2      REPLACE('IT IS HOT OUTSIDE','HOT', 'COLD') TEMP
  3   FROM
 4*      DUAL
```

Line 2 contains the REPLACE function to replace the word HOT in the source string with the word COLD. The FROM clause in lines 3 and 4 specifies the DUAL table as the source of the query.

4. Run the query to display the results.

Figure 10-22 The results of a query containing the INSTR function

```
SQL> /

TEMP
--------------------------
IT IS COLD OUTSIDE
```

The word HOT was replaced with the word COLD in the query, making the length of the string one character longer.

5. Load CHP10-25.sql into the SQL buffer. The file contains a PL/SQL statement using the REPLACE function.

```
SQL> GET CHP10-25
  1   DECLARE
  2      X VARCHAR2(30);
  3   BEGIN
  4      X := REPLACE('_IT IS HOT OUTSIDE','HOT','COLD');
  5      DBMS_OUTPUT.PUT_LINE(X);
  6*  END;
```

Line 2 creates a variable which receives the results of the REPLACE function in line 4. Line 4 uses the REPLACE function in PL/SQL to replace the word HOT with the word COLD. Line 5 uses the PUT_LINE function from the DBMS_OUTPUT built-in package to display the value of the variable set by the REPLACE function.

6. Set the SERVEROUTPUT system variable to ON to display the results from the DBMS_OUTPUT package in SQL*Plus. Run the statement to show the results. Figure 10-23 shows the results of the operation in SQL*Plus.

The PL/SQL module replaced the word HOT with the word COLD and displayed the output using the DBMS_OUTPUT.PUT_LINE function. The REPLACE function replaces all occurrences of the word HOT in the string.

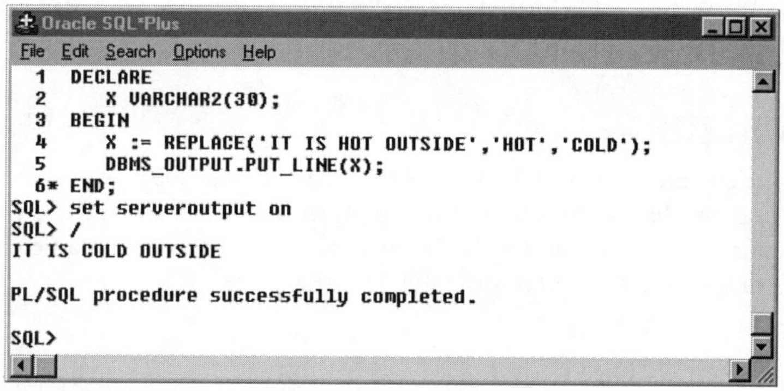

Figure 10-23 The results of the PL/SQL operation in SQL*Plus

How It Works

The INSTR function is used to find the location of a set of characters within a string. The REPLACE function is used to replace a set of characters in a string with a different set of characters. Steps 1 and 2 present a query of the DUAL table, which uses the INSTR function to return the location of a word within a text string and the second occurrence of a letter in the string. Steps 3 and 4 present a query of the DUAL table, which uses the REPLACE function to replace all occurrences of a word in a string with another word. Steps 5 and 6 perform the same operation in a PL/SQL module to display the use of the REPLACE function.

Comments

The find and replace operations in text strings are basic tasks in many applications. The INSTR and REPLACE functions in PL/SQL make these operations easy. The INSTR function can be used to determine if a string exists in another string. In this way, it can be used as the LIKE operator in a SQL statement.

COMPLEXITY
BEGINNING

10.11 How do I...
Change the case of a string?

Problem

I need to use string manipulation functions to change the case of a string. In some cases, I want to make a string uppercase. In other cases, I want to force the string to be lowercase. In many of our applications, the strings are stored in all uppercase, but I need to print reports using lowercase. How do I change the case of a string?

Technique

The UPPER and LOWER functions are used to change the case of a string. The UPPER function changes the entire string to uppercase. The LOWER function changes the entire string to lowercase. Both functions require a single parameter, which is the string to convert, and return a VARCHAR2 value.

Steps

1. Run SQL*Plus and connect as the WAITE user account. CHP10-26.sql, shown in Figure 10-24, creates the sample table and data used throughout this How-To. The sample table includes one column containing the text to be manipulated by the UPPER and LOWER functions.

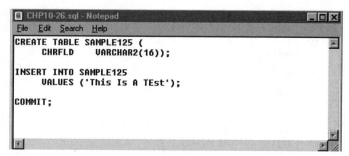

Figure 10-24 CHP10-26.sql creates the sample table and data used in How-To 10.11

The sample table, SAMPLE125, contains a text field and is populated with a record of mixed text. Run the file to create the table and sample data.

```
SQL>   START CHP10-26

Table created.

1 row created.

Commit complete.
```

2. Load CHP10-27.sql into the SQL buffer. The file contains a query of the SAMPLE125 table created in the previous step. The query uses the UPPER function to convert the value of a column to uppercase and the LOWER function to convert it to lowercase.

```
SQL> GET CHP10-27
  1   SELECT
  2       CHRFLD,
  3       UPPER(CHRFLD),
  4       LOWER(CHRFLD)
  5   FROM
  6*       SAMPLE125
```

Line 2 returns the column from the sample table without modification. Line 3 uses the UPPER function to convert the value in the field to uppercase, and line 4 uses the LOWER function to covert the column to lowercase. Lines 5 and 6 contain the FROM clause, which specifies the sample table created in step 1 as the source of the data.

3. Run the statement to query the data. Figure 10-25 shows the results of the query in SQL*Plus.

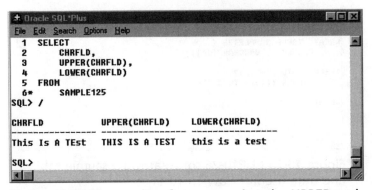

Figure 10-25 The results of a query using the UPPER and
LOWER functions

The first column shows the data without any modification. The output generated by the UPPER function in the second column returns the value in uppercase. The LOWER function used in the third column returns the value in lowercase.

How It Works

The UPPER and LOWER functions are used to convert the case of a text string to uppercase or lowercase. Step 1 creates the sample table which has a text column and is populated with a record containing mixed case. Steps 2 and 3 query the sample table using the UPPER and LOWER functions to change the case of the column's value.

Comments

The string conversion functions allow you to work with a text string and not worry about its case. The UPPER and LOWER functions can be used in the WHERE clause of queries to guarantee that the equality operations are performed correctly. The functions can also be used in PL/SQL code to ensure that values are generated in the proper case.

DISTRIBUTED DATABASES

11

DISTRIBUTED DATABASES

How do I...

Oracle's distributed database capabilities allow you to develop applications which treat multiple databases as a single integrated database. SQL*Net allows two or more computers running Oracle products to communicate. The Distributed Option in Oracle7 allows data to be manipulated on a remote database transparently to the user. Databases can be implemented to handle workgroups, departments, or geographical regions and linked together to appear as one large database to the application. This chapter covers topics related to the creation and management of distributed databases and applications. Since it cannot be assumed that you have multiple databases to run the examples presented in this chapter, the local database is referenced as a remote database through database links. The scripts presented in this chapter can be tested on a single database and will work for remote databases. The examples presented in this chapter are located on the accompanying CD in the \SAMPLES\CHAP11 directory. Copy the .SQL files into your SQL*Plus working directory, or specify the full pathname of the directory when executing the GET command.

11.1   Create a link to another database

Database links allow access to data on remote databases. A database link is used to establish a connection to the remote database. It specifies the database, user account, and password for the remote database. A database link can be public, meaning it is available to all users of the database, or private, making it only available to the user account that created it. This How-To covers the process of creating public and private database links.

11.2   Determine the database links available

Within a database, it is possible to have many database links referencing remote databases. A database link identifies a user account on the remote database with which to connect. Therefore, several database links referencing different user accounts on the same database can be created. This How-To provides the data dictionary views and queries for determining the database links available.

11.3   Retrieve data from another database

Users access data from remote databases through database links. The database link can be included in a query to retrieve data from the remote database. This How-To presents the technique for querying data from a remote database using a database link.

11.4   Create a synonym referencing another database

Synonyms hide the actual schema, name, and location of a database object. A synonym can be used to provide an alias for an object on a remote database. An application can use a synonym to reference an object without knowing the actual location of the object. This How-To presents the technique for creating synonyms that reference remote objects.

11.5   Insert or update data on a remote database

If a remote database is running Oracle7 with the distributed option, data can be inserted, updated, or deleted on it. A database link can be included as part of the data manipulation statements only if the distributed option is installed on the remote computer. This How-To presents the technique used to perform data manipulation operations on a remote database.

11.6   Create a snapshot

Performance of applications using data from remote databases can be improved by using snapshots. A snapshot provides a local copy of a remote table. It can contain all or part of the remote table and be refreshed automatically. This How-To presents the commands for creating a snapshot and managing an existing snapshot. Creating snapshots requires Oracle7 with the distributed option.

11.7   Refresh a snapshot manually

It is sometimes necessary to perform a manual refresh of the data within a snapshot. It is important that the data within a snapshot accurately represent the data in the remote table. Oracle provides the DBMS_SNAPSHOT package to manage snapshots. This How-To presents the method used to refresh a snapshot manually.

11.8   View information about existing snapshots

Information about snapshots such as the name of the base table, the owner of the snapshot, and the date and time of the last refresh can be queried from the data dictionary. The USER_SNAPSHOTS and ALL_SNAPSHOTS data dictionary views provide important information about the management of snapshots. This How-To presents the queries used to view information about existing snapshots.

11.9   Execute a remote stored procedure

It is possible to execute stored procedures and functions that exist on remote databases. If an application needs to process a large amount of data on a remote database, a stored object located there can improve performance. The stored procedure or function will be executed on the remote database, and only the results will be returned to the local application. This How-To presents the method used to execute stored procedures and functions on a remote database.

COMPLEXITY

INTERMEDIATE

11.1   How do I...
Create a link to another database?

Problem

I need to access data from a remote database in my applications. I want to create a link to the database to make it possible to access data. I know that without a database link I cannot access or manipulate remote data. How do I create a database link?

Technique

A database link is used to establish a connection to the remote database. It specifies the database, user account, and password for a connection to the remote database. The database link resides in the data dictionary of the "local" computer. When the database link is used, it connects to the specified database as the user account of the remote database. When the operation is complete, the database link logs out of the remote database. A database link can be used for remote updates if the remote database is running the distributed option. If the remote database is not running the distributed option, only queries to the database are allowed. A database link is created with the CREATE DATABASE LINK statement. The syntax of the statement is shown in Figure 11-1.

The PUBLIC keyword lets any user account work with the database link. If the PUBLIC keyword is not specified, the database link can only be accessed by the user account that created it. The exact syntax of the statement depends on the version of SQL*Net running and the use of default or explicit logins on the remote database. The DROP DATABASE LINK statement removes a database link from the system.

Steps

1. Run SQL*Plus and connect as the WAITE user account. Since your environment may not have any remote databases, this How-To will create a database link that references the local database. Actions performed on the database link will work as if a database on another computer in the network were referenced by the link. Load CHP11-1.sql into the SQL buffer. The file contains a CREATE DATABASE LINK statement to create a private database link.

```
SQL>  GET CHP11-1
  1    CREATE DATABASE LINK
  2        DBLINK11_1
  3    CONNECT TO WAITE IDENTIFIED BY PRESS
  4    USING '2:'
```

Line 1 provides the CREATE DATABASE LINK keywords required by the operation. Line 2 specifies the name of the database link to be created. Line 3 identifies the user account and password that will connect to the remote database. If this clause is omitted, the database link employs the user account and password of the person using the database link. Line 4 specifies the connect string of the remote database. The format of the connect

```
CREATE [PUBLIC]DATABASE LINK linkname
    [CONNECT TO username IDENTIFIED BY password]
    [USING 'connect_string']
```

Figure 11-1 The syntax of the CREATE DATABASE LINK statement

string depends on the version of SQL*Net running on your system. Connect strings used in SQL*Net 1.X contain three sections separated by colons. The first section represents the network interface driver. The second section specifies the name of the server, and the third section represents the database instance. SQL*Net 2.X uses a single word alias to represent the database. The TNSNAMES.ORA file contains information about the network interface driver, server name, and database instance referenced by SQL*Net 2.X aliases.

NOTE

The examples in this chapter specify the connect string as '2:'. This is the connect string of the local database and ensures that there is a "remote" database to connect to.

2. Run the statement to create the database link. Creating the database link stores it in the data dictionary, but does not validate the user account, password, or connect string supplied in the statement.

```
SQL>  /

Database link created.
```

The database link created is a private database link available only to the current user account.

3. Load CHP11-2.sql into the SQL buffer. The file contains a statement to create a new PUBLIC database link. The user account creating a public database link must have the CREATE PUBLIC DATABASE LINK system privilege. User accounts with the DBA role have this privilege.

```
SQL>  GET CHP11-2
  1    CREATE PUBLIC DATABASE LINK
  2         DBLINK11_2
  3    CONNECT TO WAITE IDENTIFIED BY PRESS
  4    USING '2:'
```

Line 1 includes the PUBLIC keyword to identify the database link as public. Line 2 specifies the name of the database link. Public database link names must be unique. You cannot create a public database link with the same name as one created by another user. Line 3 contains the CONNECT and IDENTIFIED BY clause which identifies the user account and password for connecting to the remote database. The clause may be omitted, activating the account and password of the user employing the link to be used on the remote database. If the user account and password do not exist on the remote database, an error will occur. Line 4 contains the USING clause, which specifies the string connecting to the remote computer. The '2:' shown in the statement represents the local database.

4. Run the statement to create the database link.

```
SQL> /
```

Database link created.

The database link created by this statement is a public database link and available to all user accounts in the database.

5. Load CHP11-3.sql into the SQL buffer. The file contains a DROP DATA-BASE LINK statement to remove the database link created in Step 1.

```
SQL> GET CHP11-3
  1  DROP DATABASE LINK
  2       DBLINK11_1
```

Line 1 specifies the required DROP DATABASE LINK keywords. Line 2 specifies the name of the database link to be removed. If the database link is PUBLIC, the PUBLIC keyword must be specified in the statement. Line 1 would be replaced with DROP PUBLIC DATABASE LINK.

6. Run the statement to remove the database link.

```
SQL> /
```

Database link dropped.

When a database link is dropped, any references to it will return an error. Be careful when you drop database links, and make sure they are not referenced in SQL statements and synonyms used throughout the system.

How It Works

Steps 1 and 2 create a new private database link using the CREATE DATABASE LINK statement. The database name referenced in the USING clause is the local database. Steps 3 and 4 create a public synonym named PUBLICDB, by using the CREATE DATABASE LINK statement and specifying the PUBLIC keyword. In order to create a public database link, the user account must have the CREATE PUBLIC DATABASE LINK system privilege. Steps 5 and 6 use the DROP DATABASE LINK statement to remove the database link created in Step 1.

Comments

Database links are the fundamental objects used in creating distributed applications. How-Tos 11.3 through 11.5 present the use of database links within queries and data management statements. How-To 11.4 presents the use of synonyms to hide the location of objects referenced through database links.

COMPLEXITY
BEGINNING

11.2 How do I...
Determine the database links available?

Problem

Within our database, we have several links referencing different databases. I need a method to identify which database links are available and which databases and user accounts they reference. How do I determine the database links available?

Technique

The ALL_DB_LINKS data dictionary view contains information about the database links to which a user account has access. The view will contain public and private database links created by the connected user. The description of the view is shown in Figure 11-2.

The OWNER column specifies the owner of the database link. A value of PUBLIC represents a public database link. The DB_LINK column contains the name of the database link. The HOST column represents the database the link references. The USERNAME column contains the user account name the database link will connect with. The password for the user account is not contained in the view. The USER_DB_LINKS data dictionary view shown in Figure 11-3 contains all the private database links for a user account.

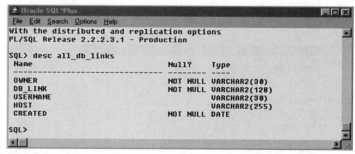

Figure 11-2 The ALL_DB_LINKS data dictionary view

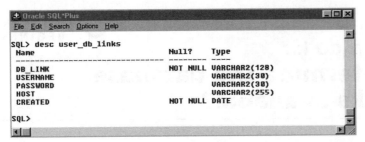

Figure 11-3 The USER_DB_LINKS data dictionary view

The PASSWORD column contains the password of the user account used for the remote connection. This column is not available in the ALL_DB_LINKS view; it is only available in the USER_DB_LINKS view.

Steps

1. Run SQL*Plus and connect as the WAITE user account. CHP11-4.sql, shown in Figure 11-4, creates the sample database links queried in this How-To.

The column commands at the end of the script format the output of the query in Step 2 to make it more readable. Run the file to create the sample database links.

```
SQL>   START CHP11-4

Database link created.

Database link created.

Database link created.
```

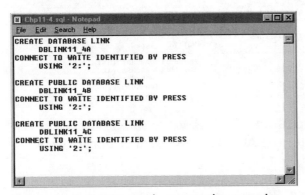

Figure 11-4 CHP11-4.sql creates the sample database links used in How-To 11.2

Two public and one private database links to be queried in the following steps are created.

2. Load CHP11-5.sql into the SQL buffer. The file contains a query of the ALL_DB_LINKS data dictionary view.

```
SQL> GET CHP11-5
  1    SELECT
  2        DB_LINK,
  3        OWNER,
  4        USERNAME,
  5        HOST
  6    FROM
  7        ALL_DB_LINKS
  8*   ORDER BY DB_LINK
```

Lines 2 through 5 specify the columns returned by the query. Line 2 returns the name of the database link. Line 3 returns the owner of the database link. Line 4 returns the user account name the database link uses to connect. Line 5 returns the connect string of the database referenced by the link. The SUBSTR function on every column truncates the data returned on each, making the data from a record fit on a single line. Line 7 specifies the ALL_DB_LINKS data dictionary view as the source of the data.

3. Run the query to view the results. The query displays the sample database links created in Step 1 and any other database links to which the user account has access.

```
SQL> /
```

DB_LINK	OWNER	USERNAME	HOST
DBLINK11_4A.WORLD	WAITE	WAITE	2:
DBLINK11_4B.WORLD	PUBLIC	WAITE	2:
DBLINK11_4C.WORLD	PUBLIC	WAITE	2:

When reading the results of the query, ignore the .WORLD suffix in the DB_LINK column. It should not be specified when the database link is used. If the USER_DB_LINKS view were used instead of the ALL_DB_LINKS view, only the first record would be returned. The OWNER column returns the value of PUBLIC for public database links.

How It Works

Step 1 creates the sample database links queried in the How-To. Steps 2 and 3 present a query of the ALL_DB_LINKS data dictionary view, displaying database links available to the connected user account. The DB_LINK column returns the name of the database link. The OWNER column contains the value PUBLIC if the database link is public and available to all users; otherwise, it's owned by the connected user account. The USER_NAME column returns the name of the user account connecting to the remote database. The HOST column contains the connect string or alias of the remote database.

Comments

Before using a database link, make sure the user account it connects with on the remote database has the privileges you need. The database link only provides you with objects visible to the user account the link specifies. Since the database link connects to the remote database as the user account the link specifies, links referencing the same database may provide different objects.

COMPLEXITY
INTERMEDIATE

11.3 How do I...
Retrieve data from another database?

Problem

I need to query data from a remote database. I have created a database link as shown in How-To 11.1, but I need to use it in a query. How do I query data from a remote database using a link?

Technique

The ampersand (&) is used to specify a database link in a query. Placing an ampersand after a table name specifies the following name as a database link. The syntax of a statement using a database link is

```
SELECT col1, col2,....
    FROM tablename@db_link;
```

When the statement is executed, the referenced database link will specify the location of the object. An error will be returned if the database link does not reference a correct user name, password, or database.

Steps

1. Run SQL*Plus and connect as the WAITE user account. CHP11-6.sql, shown in Figure 11-5, creates the sample database link and table used throughout this How-To.

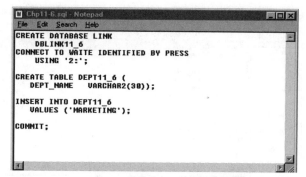

Figure 11-5 CHP11-6.sql creates the sample database link and table used in How-To 11.3

The sample database link DBLINK11_6 connects to the WAITE user account on the local database. In effect, this database link loops back to the local database to retrieve the data. Replacing the '2:' specified in the USING clause with another database makes the database link reference a different database. The sample table DEPT11_6 is populated with data and will be queried using the database link. Run the file to create the database link and sample table.

```
SQL>   START CHP11-6

Database link created.

Table created.

1 row created.

Commit complete.
```

2. Load CHP11-7.sql into the SQL buffer. The file contains a query of the sample table created in Step 1 using a database link.

```
SQL>   GET CHP11-7
  1    SELECT DEPT_NAME
  2       FROM
  3    DEPT11_6@DBLINK11_6
```

Line 1 specifies the column returned by the query. Line 3 specifies the table name that is the source of the data and the database link identifying the table location. The ampersand is used to identify DBLINK11_6 as a database link.

3. Run the statement to execute the query. Figure 11-6 shows the operation and its results.

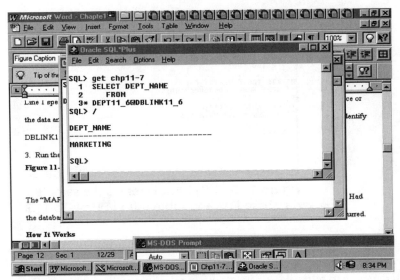

Figure 11-6 The results of CHP11-7.sql in SQL*Plus

The MARKETING record is queried through the database link as if it were on the local database. Had the database link not specified a valid database, user account, or password, an error would have occurred.

How It Works

Step 1 creates the sample database link and table used throughout the How-To. Steps 2 and 3 present a query which uses a database link to specify the location of a table. The at symbol is used to identify that the table is located on a remote database. The database link created in Step 1 is a valid database link, even though it references data on the local database. The user account the link on the database employs must have privileges on the object specified in the query.

Comments

Database links make it easy to query data from remote databases. Querying data from a remote database can be very slow, depending on the type of connection you have to the database. If the performance of your queries is very slow, consider replication or snapshots to increase performance. How-Tos 11.6 through 11.8 present information on snapshots.

COMPLEXITY
INTERMEDIATE

11.4 How do I...

Create a synonym referencing another database?

Problem

Within my application, I access data from a remote database. Although I can specify the database link with the table name in the application, I do not want to change the application if the location of the table changes. I want to use a synonym to provide location transparency to my application. How do I create a synonym referencing another database?

Technique

A database link can be specified within a CREATE SYNONYM statement. You can specify the database link with the table using the same syntax as you would when you query a remote object. The synonym will hide the actual location of the object from the application. Chapter 7, Synonyms, presents many tasks related to synonyms.

Steps

1. Run SQL*Plus and connect as the WAITE user account. CHP11-8.sql, shown in Figure 11-7, creates a database link and table which will be referenced by a synonym.

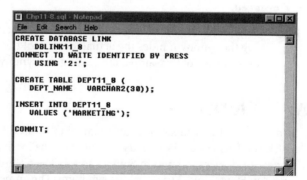

Figure 11-7 CHP11-8.sql creates the sample database link and table used in How-To 11.4

The database link DBLINK11_8 references the WAITE user account on the local database. The sample table DEPT11_8 is populated with data so that the synonym can be tested in later steps. Run the file to create the sample objects.

```
SQL>   START CHP11-8

Database link created.

Table created.

1 row created.

Commit complete.
```

2. Load CHP11-9.sql into the SQL buffer. The file contains a CREATE SYNONYM statement, which references the database link created in Step 1. Since a synonym is processed when a reference is made to it, the CREATE SYNONYM statement does not analyze the object it references. If the database link does not exist when the synonym is created, an error will not occur until the synonym is used.

```
SQL>  GET CHP11-9
  1    CREATE SYNONYM
  2         DEPT11_9
  3    FOR
  4       DEPT11_8@DBLINK11_8
```

Line 1 provides the required CREATE SYNONYM keywords. Line 2 specifies the name of the synonym created. Line 4 specifies the object the synonym references: the DEPT11_8 table on the DBLINK11_8 database.

3. Run the statement to create the synonym.

```
SQL>  /

Synonym created.
```

4. The synonym can be used in a query without specifying the database link. Using the synonym hides the actual location of the object. Figure 11-8 shows a query of the sample table using the synonym.

How It Works

Step 1 creates the database link and sample table used in this How-To. The database link references the WAITE user account on the local database. The sample table is referenced by a synonym in Steps 2 and 3. The CREATE SYNONYM statement is used in Steps 2 and 3 to create the synonym. The ampersand symbol (&) is used with the table name to identify a database link. Step 4 presents a query to the

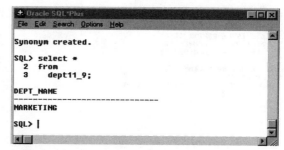

Figure 11-8 A query of a synonym referencing a remote table

synonym and the results returned. Since a synonym is used in the query, the location of the table is transparent.

Comments

If you are developing applications that access tables on remote databases, create synonyms to hide the table location from the application. If you decide to move your table, it is much easier to change a single synonym than all the object references in your applications.

COMPLEXITY
INTERMEDIATE

11.5 How do I...

Insert or update data on a remote database?

REQUIRES DISTRIBUTED OPTION

Problem

I use links to access data on other databases and want to modify data in the remote tables. The remote databases have the *d*, which allows remote updates. How do I insert or update data on a remote database?

Technique

If the remote database is running the distributed option, data can be manipulated through a database link. The table in the data manipulation statement is referenced with the ampersand to specify the database link used. INSERT, UPDATE, and DELETE statements all support the use of database links in the table specification.

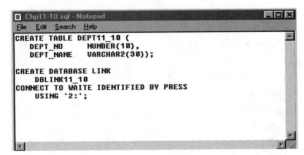

Figure 11-9 CHP11-10.sql creates the sample database link used in How-To 11.5

Steps

1. Run SQL*Plus and connect as the WAITE user account. CHP11-10.sql, shown in Figure 11-9, creates the sample database link used throughout this How-To.

The database link DBLINK11_10 connects to the WAITE user account on the local database. The table DEPT11_10 has data manipulation statements running against it in the following steps. Run the file to create the sample objects.

```
SQL> START CHP11-10
```

```
Table created.
```

```
Database link created.
```

2. Load CHP11-11.sql into the SQL buffer. The file contains an INSERT statement to create data in the table on the remote database.

```
SQL> GET CHP11-11
  1   INSERT INTO
  2       DEPT11_10@DBLINK11_10
  3   VALUES (1,'MARKETING')
```

Line 1 specifies the required keywords of the statement. Line 2 specifies the table name and database link name. The ampersand is used to identify the database link in the statement. Line 3 supplies the data to be created with the VALUES clause.

3. Run the statement to create the new record. The INSERT statement uses the database link specified with the table to determine the location of the object. If the database link is invalid, the statement will fail.

```
SQL> /
```

```
1 row inserted.
```

4. Load CHP11-12.sql into the SQL buffer. The file contains an UPDATE statement to modify data in the remote table.

```
SQL>  GET CHP11-12
  1   UPDATE
  2       DEPT11_10@DBLINK11_10
  3   SET DEPT_NAME = 'NEW NAME'
```

Line 1 presents the statement's required keyword. Line 2 specifies the table name and location. The location is specified by the database link. Line 3 uses the SET clause to give the DEPT_NAME column a new value.

5. Run the statement to update the existing data. The REMOTE119 database link is used to determine the location of the remote table.

```
SQL>  /
```

```
1 row updated.
```

6. Load CHP11-13.sql into the SQL buffer. The file contains a DELETE statement to remove records from the remote table.

```
SQL>  GET CHP11-13
  1   DELETE FROM
  2       DEPT11_10@DBLINK11_10
```

Line 1 presents the DELETE keyword required to delete one or more records. Line 2 specifies the table name and location. The database link is included with the table name to specify the remote database where the object is.

7. Run the statement to delete the record.

```
SQL>  /
```

```
1 row deleted.
```

How It Works

Step 1 creates the database link and table used throughout this How-To. Steps 2 and 3 insert data into the remote table using an INSERT statement and specifying the database link with the table. Steps 4 and 5 update existing records in a remote table by specifying a database link within an UPDATE statement. Steps 6 and 7 delete records from a remote table by specifying a database link in a DELETE statement.

Comments

When the distributed option is installed on the remote computer, data manipulation statements can be executed through a database link. You can create synonyms which use database links to hide the location of the remote object. If you plan to use database links in your applications, refer to How-To 11.4 for the process of creating synonyms.

COMPLEXITY
INTERMEDIATE

11.6 How do I...
Create a snapshot?

REQUIRES DISTRIBUTED OPTION

Problem

There are some common tables used throughout our distributed environment. The distributed option of Oracle 7 is required to create a snapshot. These tables are read only and reside in a central location. I have created database links to the remote database, but find performance to be very slow referencing the remote object. Our network communications between locations is very slow. I want to use a snapshot to improve performance. How do I create a snapshot?

Technique

Snapshots let you keep local copies of tables residing in a remote database. All or part of the table can be stored in the snapshot. Snapshots do not have to represent a single remote object. A snapshot can be based on a query of multiple tables. A snapshot can be refreshed automatically at preset intervals, and depending on the version of Oracle 7 you are running, may be updatable. The CREATE SNAPSHOT statement is used to create a snapshot. The syntax of the CREATE SNAPSHOT statement is shown in Figure 11-10.

```
CREATE SNAPSHOT snapshot_name
    [STORAGE(storage parameters)]
    [TABLESPACE tablespace_name ]
    [REFRESH[FAST\COMPLETE\FORCE][START WITH start date
    NEXT next date]
    AS query
```

Figure 11-10 The syntax of the CREATE SNAPSHOT statement

The first section of the CREATE SNAPSHOT statement lets you specify many of the same storage parameters as you can when creating a table. The REFRESH clause specifies when the snapshot will be refreshed. In order to create a snapshot, the user account must have CREATE SNAPSHOT, CREATE TABLE, CREATE VIEW, and CREATE INDEX system privileges. If the user wants to create snapshots in the schema of another user account, the CREATE ANY SNAPSHOT system privilege is required.

Steps

1. Run SQL*Plus and connect as the WAITE user account. CHP11-14.sql, shown in Figure 11-11, creates the sample database links and tables used in this How-To.

Run the file to create the objects required by the example.

```
SQL>   START CHP11-14

Database link created.

Table created.

Table created.

1 row created.

1 row created.

1 row created.

Commit complete.
```

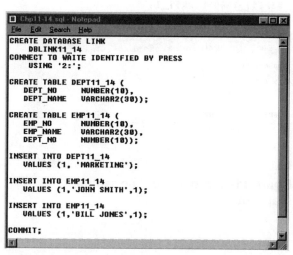

Figure 11-11 CHP11-14.sql creates the sample database links and tables used in How-To 11.6

2. Load CHP11-15.sql into the SQL buffer. The file contains a CREATE SNAPSHOT table to create a snapshot of a remote table.

```
SQL>   GET CHP11-15
  1    CREATE SNAPSHOT
  2        SNAP11_14
  3    AS SELECT *
  4    FROM
  5    DEPT11_14@DBLINK11_14
```

Line 1 contains the required keywords to create a snapshot. Line 2 contains the name of the snapshot created by the statement. Lines 3 through 5 contain the query used to create the snapshot, specifying the database link name in line 5.

3. Run the statement to create the snapshot.

```
SQL>   /
```

```
Snapshot created.
```

4. Run a query of the snapshot. A snapshot can be queried just like a table or view. Figure 11-12 shows a simple query and its results.

5. Load CHP11-16.sql into the SQL buffer. The file contains a statement to create a snapshot specifying refresh parameters.

```
SQL>   GET CHP11-16
  1    CREATE SNAPSHOT
  2        SNAP11_16
  3    REFRESH COMPLETE
  4    START WITH sysdate NEXT sysdate+1
  5    AS SELECT *
  6    FROM
  7    DEPT11_14@DBLINK11_14
```

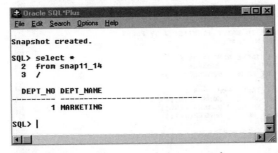

Figure 11-12 A query of the sample snapshot

Line 3 specifies the refresh type of the snapshot. The COMPLETE option tells Oracle to completely refresh the snapshot. Line 4 specifies the starting date and interval of the automatic refreshes. The starting date is a date value which can include a time portion. The next date is also a date value with a time portion. A snapshot can be refreshed more than once per day, by specifying the next date value to be the same date as the start date and including a time portion with the date value.

6. Run the statement to create the snapshot.

```
SQL> /
```

Snapshot created.

7. Load CHP11-17.sql into the SQL buffer. The file contains a statement which creates a complex snapshot by joining two remote tables and specifying storage parameters.

```
SQL>   GET CHP11-17
   1    CREATE SNAPSHOT
   2       SNAP1117
   3    STORAGE (INITIAL 50K NEXT 50K)
   4    TABLESPACE SYSTEM
   5    REFRESH COMPLETE
   6    START WITH SYSDATE NEXT SYSDATE + 1
   7    AS SELECT
   8        E.EMP_NO,
   9        E.DEPT_NO,
  10        D.DEPT_NAME
  11    FROM
  12        EMP11_14@DBLINK11_14 E, DEPT11_14@DBLINK11_14 D
  13    WHERE
  14        E.DEPT_NO = D.DEPT_NO
```

Line 3 specifies the storage parameters for the snapshot. Line 4 specifies the tablespace where the snapshot is to be located. Lines 5 and 6 specify a complete refresh every day, starting immediately. A fast refresh is not possible for this snapshot because of the complexity of the query. Fast refreshes are only possible for simple queries. Lines 7 through 14 create the query as a join of two remote tables.

8. Run the statement to create the snapshot.

```
SQL> /
```

Snapshot created.

9. Execute a query of the snapshot created in the previous step by using its name as the query source. Figure 11-13 shows a simple query using the snapshot name in the FROM clause.

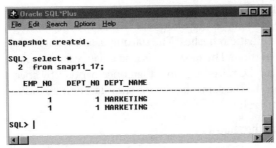

Figure 11-13 A query of the complex
snapshot

The simple query returns all columns and rows from the snapshot created
in the previous steps. The snapshot name can be used in a query just like a
table.

How It Works

Step 1 creates the objects used throughout this How-To. Steps 2 and 3 create a simple database link. Storage and refresh options are not specified in the CREATE SNAPSHOT
statement. The snapshot is created in the default tablespace for the user account and
uses the default storage parameters for the tablespace. Step 4 presents a simple query
of the snapshot, showing how a snapshot can be queried like a table. Steps 5 and
6 create a snapshot which uses one remote table as its source and includes tablespace, storage, and refresh parameters. Steps 7 and 8 create a snapshot which joins
multiple remote tables to create a snapshot providing data in a format different than
stored on the remote database.

Comments

It is very important to choose the correct method for table replication. Database performance can be unnecessarily degraded by making too many calls to remote
objects. Snapshots increase performance by creating a local copy of data.

COMPLEXITY
INTERMEDIATE

11.7   How do I...
Refresh a snapshot manually?

REQUIRES DISTRIBUTED OPTION

Problem

Prior to large operations, I want to be sure that the data in the snapshot references
in the SQL*Plus scripts are refreshed. If the data in the snapshot is old, my

operations may get incorrect results. I want to manually refresh a snapshot before using it in my operations. How do I refresh a snapshot manually?

Technique

The DBMS_SNAPSHOT package provided by Oracle lets you manually refresh a snapshot. The REFRESH procedure performs a refresh on a single snapshot. The REFRESH_ALL procedure refreshes all snapshots with automatic refresh parameters. Each snapshot is refreshed sequentially. The procedure call for the REFRESH procedure of the DBMS_SNAPSHOT package is shown here:

```
DBMS_SNAPSHOT.REFRESH(snapshot_name,refresh_type);
```

The refresh types are F for a fast refresh, C for a complete refresh, and ? to execute the default refresh type. A *fast refresh* will refresh the snapshot with changed records from the snapshot log. A *complete refresh* will completely refresh the snapshot.

Steps

1. Run SQL*Plus and connect as the WAITE user account. CHP11-18.sql, shown in Figure 11-14, creates the sample objects used in this How-To.

Run the file to create the sample objects.

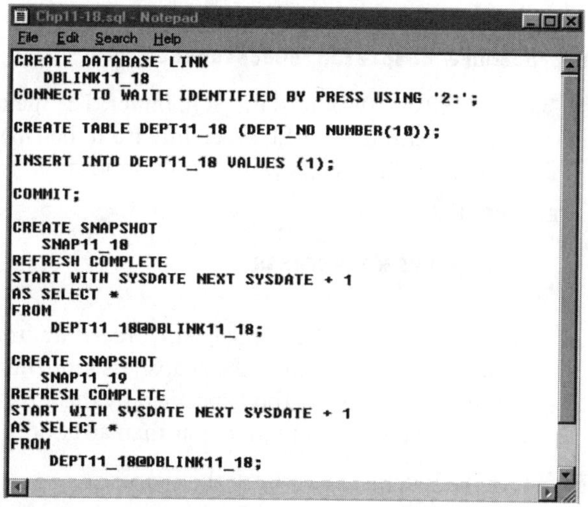

Figure 11-14 CHP11-18.sql creates the sample objects used in How-To 11.7

```
SQL>   START CHP11-18

Database link created.

Table created.

1 row created.

Commit complete.

Snapshot created.

Snapshot created.
```

2. Load CHP11-19.sql into the SQL buffer. The file contains a PL/SQL block to refresh a single snapshot.

```
SQL> GET CHP11-19
  1   BEGIN
  2       DBMS_SNAPSHOT.REFRESH('SNAP11_19','C');
  3   END;
```

Line 2 runs the REFRESH procedure from the DBMS_SNAPSHOT package to perform a complete refresh on SNAP11_19. The second parameter passed to the procedure identifies the type of refresh performed on the snapshot.

3. Run the statement to refresh the snapshot.

```
SQL>  /

PL/SQL procedure completed successfully.
```

4. Load CHP11-20.sql into the SQL buffer. The file contains a PL/SQL block using the REFRESH_ALL procedure from the DBMS_SNAPSHOT package to refresh all snapshots with refresh options.

```
SQL>   GET CHP11-20
  1   BEGIN
  2       DBMS_SNAPSHOT.REFRESH_ALL;
  3   END;
```

Line 2 executes the REFRESH_ALL procedure from the DBMS_SNAPSHOT package to refresh each of the snapshots sequentially. Each snapshot is refreshed using the method specified by the refresh options. The snapshots are refreshed one at a time, rather than all at once.

5. Run the statement to refresh the snapshots.

```
SQL>  /

PL/SQL procedure completed successfully.
```

How It Works

The DBMS_SHAPSHOT package allows manual refreshes of snapshots. The REFRESH procedure in used to refresh a single snapshot. The REFRESH_ALL procedure refreshes each snapshot with refresh options. The type of refresh performed depends on the type specified in the refresh options of the snapshot. Step 1 creates sample tables and snapshots refreshed in the other steps. Steps 2 and 3 use the REFRESH procedure to refresh a single snapshot. Steps 4 and 5 use the REFRESH_ALL procedure to refresh all the snapshots.

Comments

It is important to make sure the snapshots are current if you are performing a large amount of processing with the snapshot. It is much faster to refresh the snapshot once at the beginning of your procedure than to repeatedly return to the source database. The DBMS_SNAPSHOT package makes it easy to manually refresh snapshots. If you find yourself manually refreshing snapshots often, you should consider changing the refresh options of the snapshots.

COMPLEXITY
BEGINNING

11.8   How do I...
View information about existing snapshots?

REQUIRES DISTRIBUTED OPTION

Problem

I need to get information about the snapshots that exist in the database. Snapshots have been created by various users and database administrators to bring remote data to the local database, to improve performance. If a snapshot containing the data I need exists, I do not want to create another snapshot or access the data over the network. In addition to the snapshot name and the query that created it, I need to know the date and time the snapshot was last refreshed. How can I do this?

Technique

The ALL_SNAPSHOTS view contains information about the snapshots in the database. Privileges are granted on snapshots just like tables and views. If you have not been granted access to the snapshot, it will not be contained in the ALL_SNAPSHOTS view. If your user account has been granted the DBA role, you will see all snapshots in the database. Figure 11-15 shows the description of the view.

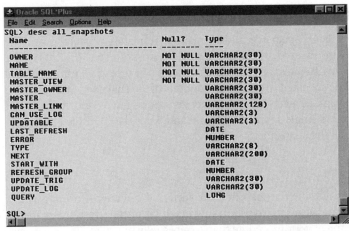

Figure 11-15 ALL_SNAPSHOTS data dictionary view

The NAME column returns the name of the snapshot. If you use the snapshot in your applications, it is referenced by the value in this column. The QUERY column contains the query used to build and refresh the snapshot. You can use this column to determine whether the snapshot contains the right data for your application. The LAST_REFRESH column is a DATE column containing the date and time of the last refresh. The NEXT column contains the formula used to calculate the date and time of the next refresh. You can use the LAST_REFRESH and NEXT columns to determine whether the refresh rate of the snapshot is acceptable for your application.

Steps

1. Run SQL*Plus and connect as the WAITE user account. CHP11-21.sql, shown in Figure 11-16, builds the sample objects used throughout this How-To.

Run the file to create the sample snapshots.

```
SQL> START CHP11-21

Table created.

1 row created.

Commit complete.

Snapshot created.

Snapshot created.
```

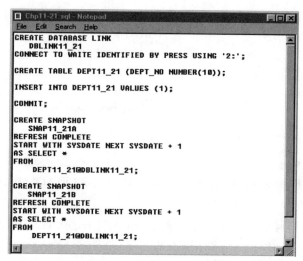

Figure 11-16 CHP11-21.sql creates the sample objects used in How-To 11.8

2. Load CHP11-22.sql into the SQL buffer. The file contains a query of the ALL_SNAPSHOTS data dictionary view to display the snapshot name and the query refreshing it.

```
SQL> GET CHP11-22
  1  SELECT
  2     NAME,
  3     QUERY
  4  FROM ALL_SNAPSHOTS
```

The NAME column returns the name of the snapshot. The QUERY column contains the query used to populate and refresh the snapshot. The QUERY column is of the LONG datatype, so it must be formatted before executing the query.

3. Execute a COLUMN command for the QUERY column to fit the data on the screen. Set the LONG environment variable to ensure that the values in the QUERY column are not truncated.

```
SQL> COLUMN QUERY FORMAT A30
SQL> SET LONG 1000
SQL>
```

4. Run the statement to display the results. The snapshots created in Step 1 and any other snapshots existing on the system are displayed in the results. The results of the operation are shown in Figure 11-17.

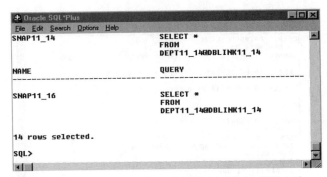

Figure 11-17 The results of CHP11-22 in SQL*Plus

5. Load CHP11-23.sql into the SQL buffer. The file contains a query to display refresh information about a snapshot.

```
SQL>   GET CHP11-23
  1    SELECT
  2       NAME,
  3       OWNER,
  4       LAST_REFRESH,
  5       SUBSTR(NEXT,1,20) NEXT
  6    FROM
  7       ALL_SNAPSHOTS
```

The OWNER column returned by line 2 contains the owner of the snapshot. The LAST_REFRESH column returned by line 4 contains the date of the snapshot's last refresh. The NEXT column returned by line 5 contains the data function used to calculate the next refresh date. The SUBSTR function is used in line 5 to only display the first 20 characters of the column, making the output more readable. Line 7 specifies the ALL_SNAPSHOTS data dictionary view as the data source.

6. Run the COLUMN command to format the NAME and OWNER columns. Format each of the columns to a 15-character text column.

```
SQL>   COLUMN NAME FORMAT A15
SQL>   COLUMN OWNER FORMAT A15
SQL>
```

7. Run the query to view the snapshot information. The results of the query are shown in Figure 11-18.

How It Works

Step 1 creates two sample snapshots, displayed in the results of the later steps. Steps 2 and 3 query information about queries used to create the snapshots. The QUERY

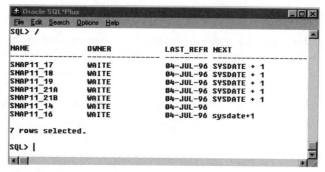

Figure 11-18 The results of CHP11-23.sql
in SQL*Plus

column is of the LONG datatype. The LONG system variable ensures the results of
the query are not truncated. Steps 6 and 7 query refresh information about the
snapshots.

Comments

Snapshots can dramatically improve the performance of applications using data from
remote databases. It is important to know what snapshots are available and how they
are structured. If a snapshot containing the remote data you need is available and
the refresh options meet your needs, you should use the snapshot instead of the database link.

COMPLEXITY
ADVANCED

11.9   How do I...
Execute a remote stored procedure?

Problem

Within my application, I want to execute stored procedures and functions existing
on a remote database. The stored procedures perform complex logic and queries,
meaning performance would be very poor if I created these program units locally
and referenced remote tables. How do I execute a remote stored procedure or
function?

Technique

A stored procedure can be executed on a remote database by specifying a link with the call to the procedure or function. The account the link uses for connecting to the remote database must have EXECUTE privileges on the procedure or function you are executing. Parameters can be passed to the modules by specifying the parameter list after the database link. The exact syntax of the procedure and function calls are shown in this How-To.

Steps

1. Run SQL*Plus and connect as the WAITE user account. CHP11-24.sql, shown in Figure 11-19, creates the sample database objects required by this How-To.

A sample stored procedure, stored function, and database link are created. The stored procedure and function will be executed through the database links in the following steps. The stored procedure performs no action other than execution. The stored function returns a text string containing the parameter passed to the function. For more information about creating stored procedures and functions, see Chapter 13, Procedures, Functions, and Packages. Run the file to create the required objects.

```
SQL> START CHP11-24

Procedure created.

Function created.

Database link created.
```

```
Chp11-24.sql - Notepad
File  Edit  Search  Help
CREATE OR REPLACE PROCEDURE PROC11_24 (X IN NUMBER) AS
BEGIN
     NULL;
END;
/

CREATE OR REPLACE FUNCTION FUNC11_24 (X IN NUMBER) RETURN VARCHAR2 AS
BEGIN
     RETURN 'THE PARAMETER IS '||TO_CHAR(X);
END;
/

CREATE DATABASE LINK
     DBLINK11_24
CONNECT TO WAITE IDENTIFIED BY PRESS USING '2:';
```

Figure 11-19 CHP11-24.sql creates the sample database objects used in How-To 11.9

2. Load CHP11-25.sql into the SQL buffer. The file contains a call to the stored procedure created in the previous step.

```
SQL>  GET CHP11-25
   1  BEGIN
   2    PROC11_24@DBLINK11_24(300);
   3  END;
```

Line 2 executes the PROC1124 procedure from the remote database. The database link is specified after the procedure name, but before the parameter list. The procedure is passed the parameter 300.

3. Run the statement to execute the procedure. The stored procedure contains no executable code, but will fail if the procedure or database link does not exist.

```
SQL>  /
```

```
PL/SQL procedure completed successfully.
```

4. Load CHP11-26.sql into the SQL buffer. The file contains a call to a stored function on a remote database and returns a value to the local PL/SQL code.

```
SQL> GET CHP11-26
   1  DECLARE
   2    X VARCHAR2(40);
   3  BEGIN
   4    X := FUNC11_24@DBLINK11_24(300);
   5    DBMS_OUTPUT.PUT_LINE(X);
   6  END;
```

Line 2 declares a variable that will receive the results of the function. Line 4 calls the remote function by specifying the database link with the function call. The database link is specified to identify the remote database. Line 5 displays the results from the function by using the PUT_LINE procedure from the DBMS_OUTPUT package.

5. Set the SERVEROUTPUT variable to ON to cause SQL*Plus to display the results of the DBMS_OUTPUT package. Run the statement to execute the PL/SQL module.

```
SQL> /
```

```
THE PARAMETER IS 300
```

```
PL/SQL procedure successfully completed.
```

How It Works

Stored procedures and functions can be executed through database links, by specifying the database link with the call to the module. Step 1 creates a stored procedure, stored function, and database link to demonstrate the process. Steps 2 and 3 execute a remote stored procedure through a database link. Steps 4 and 5 execute a remote stored function and return a value to the local PL/SQL code.

Comments

Stored procedures and functions executed on a remote database can dramatically improve the performance of operations with remote data. Executing the procedure on the database containing the data reduces network traffic. A local module using remote data can be much slower than the same module executed on the remote database.

PL/SQL

PL/SQL

How do I...

PL/SQL is the procedural language of Oracle. It is a sophisticated programming language that provides the flexibility of third-generation languages not available in SQL. PL/SQL includes a full range of datatypes, conditional structures, loop structures, and exception handling structures. Procedures and functions can be created in PL/SQL, promoting the development of modular code. PL/SQL is tightly integrated with SQL, allowing SQL statements to be executed within PL/SQL programs and PL/SQL functions to be used within SQL statements. This chapter presents techniques to help you use PL/SQL effectively. The How-Tos presented in this chapter provide a foundation that will help you develop better applications. The examples presented in this chapter are found in the \SAMPLES\CHAP12 directory on the accompanying CD.

12.1 Create a PL/SQL block to perform an action

A block is the basic unit of PL/SQL code. All PL/SQL programs are made up of one or more blocks. A PL/SQL block can contain the constructs of PL/SQL and SQL statements. Each block performs a unit of work within the application, and blocks can be nested to create modular code. This How-To presents PL/SQL blocks and examples that create them.

12.2 Display debug statements from PL/SQL

When PL/SQL code is executed within SQL*Plus, nothing but a completion message is displayed. Without the ability to display statements from PL/SQL, it would be very difficult to debug PL/SQL modules within SQL*Plus. The DBMS_OUTPUT package allows you to print text from PL/SQL through SQL*Plus. This How-To presents the method for displaying text from a PL/SQL statement when using SQL*Plus.

12.3 Handle exceptions in PL/SQL

Exception handlers are used to handle unexpected occurrences in normal processing. The exception section of a block handles predefined and user-defined errors. Unhandled exceptions cause the abnormal termination of a PL/SQL block. This How-To covers the process of handling exceptions in PL/SQL.

12.4 Perform conditional statements

Like other procedural languages, PL/SQL contains conditional control structures which provide flexibility to the language. The IF..THEN..ELSE statement is used to control the execution of statements based on boolean conditions. This How-To presents the IF..THEN..ELSE statement and code demonstrating it.

12.5 Perform looping operations

PL/SQL contains three basic types of looping constructs. The SIMPLE loop performs a sequence of statements repeatedly until an EXIT statement terminates it. A numeric FOR loop performs a series of statements repeatedly for a specified number of iterations. The WHILE loop tests a boolean expression and executes the statements as long as the expression evaluates to TRUE. This How-To demonstrates using the looping constructs in PL/SQL.

12.6 Create user-defined exceptions

An exception does not have to be a system error returned by Oracle. It is possible to create a user-defined exception which can be raised and handled within your code.

User-defined exceptions let you treat a violation of business rules as an exception. This How-To presents the method used to create, raise, and handle user-defined exceptions.

12.7 Handle user-defined errors from a stored procedure

When an error occurs in a stored procedure, the RAISE_APPLICATION_ERROR procedure can be called to return a user-defined error number and error text to the calling module. When a user-defined error occurs in a stored procedure, the calling PL/SQL code must trap and handle the exception, or an error will occur. This How-To presents the technique for handling user-defined errors from stored procedures.

12.8 Perform single record queries in PL/SQL

Within PL/SQL, it is possible to query a single record into variables without declaring an explicit cursor. The SELECT...INTO statement allows you to query one record directly into PL/SQL variables. If more than one record is returned, an exception occurs, and the technique presented in How-To 12.9 should be used to handle the query. This How-To presents the method used to query a single record in PL/SQL using the SELECT...INTO statement.

12.9 Perform multiple record queries using cursors

Whenever you want to perform a query in PL/SQL that returns more than one row, an explicit cursor must be declared to handle the result set. A *cursor* performs a query on the server and provides you with the methods for retrieving the records to your PL/SQL block. This How-To presents the techniques used to open, navigate, and close a cursor within PL/SQL.

12.10 Create variables to represent database records and columns

The %TYPE and %ROWTYPE attributes define the datatype of a variable in the declarative section of a block. The %TYPE attribute declares a variable to represent a column within a table, ensuring that the variable datatype can handle the values in the column. The %ROWTYPE attribute creates a record variable representing all the columns in a record. This How-To uses these attributes to declare variables representing database columns and rows.

12.11 Achieve array functionality with PL/SQL tables

PL/SQL tables are similar to one-dimensional arrays in other procedural languages like C. The implementation of a PL/SQL table requires the creation of a datatype and a separate variable declaration. This How-To presents the method for creating a PL/SQL table and using it like an array.

12.1 How do I...
Create a PL/SQL block to perform an action?

Problem

I want to perform tasks not well-suited for SQL on the database. I need to perform conditional logic and work with the procedural components available in PL/SQL. Since the PL/SQL block is the smallest logical unit of PL/SQL code, I want to start by creating a PL/SQL block to perform a simple action. How do I create a PL/SQL block in Oracle?

Technique

A block is the smallest piece of PL/SQL code, and every PL/SQL program must contain at least one block. A block is made up of as many as three sections, as shown here:

```
DECLARE
    The declarative section is an optional section which declares
    variables, type declarations, cursors, and PL/SQL procedures
    and functions that are local to the module.
BEGIN
    The executable section contains the code which is executed
    when the block is run. This section is required.
EXCEPTION
    The exception section is an options section that handles
    errors and user-defined exceptions.
END;
```

The *declarative section*, started with the DECLARE statement, is where variables are declared. Variables defined in the declarative section are local to the block. They cannot be seen outside the block where they are declared. Programmer defined datatypes, cursors, and names of PL/SQL modules local to the block are also defined in the declarative section. The *executable section*, started with the BEGIN statement, contains the code that is executed when the block is run. The *exception section*, started with the EXCEPTION statement, handles exceptions that occur during processing. The code contained in the exception section is only executed when an error occurs. A PL/SQL block is terminated with the END statement and a semicolon.

Steps

1. Run PL/SQL and connect to the database as the WAITE user account. Load CHP12-1 into the SQL buffer. The PL/SQL block contained in the file declares and uses a numeric variable.

```
SQL>  GET CHP12-1
  1   DECLARE
  2     X NUMBER(3);
  3   BEGIN
  4     X := 3;
  5   EXCEPTION
  6     WHEN OTHERS THEN NULL;
  7*  END;
```

Lines 1 and 2 contain the declarative section of the block. The section is started with the DECLARE keyword and continues until the BEGIN keyword. When declaring variables in PL/SQL, the datatype is specified after the variable name. Lines 3 and 4 contain the code segment executed when the block is run. The statement on line 4 sets the value of the variable X to the number 3. The colon-equals (:=) operator is used to set a variable to a value in PL/SQL. Table 12-1 contains the operators used in PL/SQL. If an exception occurs, it is handled in the exception section starting on line 5. The WHEN OTHERS exception handles any exceptions not dealt with by other exception handlers and must be the last exception handler. How-To 12.3 covers the process of handling exceptions in detail. Both the declaration section and the exception section are optional. If you do not need any local variables for your module or you do not want to handle exceptions which occur, these sections can be removed.

OPERATOR	DESCRIPTION
+	Addition
-	Subtraction
*	Multiplication
/	Division
=	Equality
<	Less than
>	Greater than
!=	Not equals
<>	Not equals
~	Not equals
^=	Not equals
<=	Less than or equal

continued on next page

continued from previous page

OPERATOR	DESCRIPTION
>=	Greater than or equal
:=	Assignment
=>	Association
..	Range operator
||	String concatenation

Table 12-1 PL/SQL operators

2. Run the statement to execute the PL/SQL code.

```
SQL>  /

PL/SQL procedure successfully completed.
```

When a PL/SQL block is executed in SQL*Plus, a successful completion message is the only message displayed. How-To 12.2 presents the method used to display text and debugging statements within PL/SQL.

3. Load CHP12-2.sql into the SQL buffer. The PL/SQL code contained in the file nests PL/SQL blocks by declaring a PL/SQL block inside another block. The block also presents the methods for creating comments within PL/SQL code.

```
SQL> GET CHP12-2
  1    DECLARE
  2     X NUMBER; -- A variable used in the block.
  3    BEGIN
  4     /* This is the beginning execution section of the outer block.
  5        Only the variables declared in its declarative
  6        section are visible. */
  7     X := 6;
  8     DECLARE
  9      Y VARCHAR2(30);
 10      BEGIN
 11       X := 3;
 12       Y := _WORLD ;
 13      EXCEPTION
 14       WHEN OTHERS THEN NULL;
 15      END;
 16*   END;
```

Lines 1 and 2 present the declarative section of the outermost block. The variable defined in line 2 declares a variable visible throughout the entire PL/SQL code. Line 2 also presents the syntax of a single line comment, specified with two dashes (--). Lines 4 through 6 present the syntax for a multiline comment. *Multiline comments* use the same style as the C language and start with /* and end with */. The nested PL/SQL block begins on line 8 and ends on line 16. The declarative section for the innermost block begins on line 8 and ends on line 9. The variable declared on line 6 is visible within the nested block, but not in the outside block. The execution section of the innermost block can access variables created in both the innermost and outermost blocks. The exception section defined in lines 10 through 12 only handles exceptions for the innermost block. There is no exception section defined for the outermost block.

4. Run the statement to execute the PL/SQL code.

```
SQL> /
```

```
PL/SQL procedure successfully completed.
```

5. Load CHP12-3.sql into the SQL buffer. The PL/SQL block contained in the file declares variables with a variety of datatypes. It also declares constants and variables with default values.

```
SQL> GET CHP12-3
  1    DECLARE
  2      ORDER_NO      NUMBER(3); - Numeric variable with precision of 3.
  3      CUST_NAME     VARCHAR2(20); --Character variable with width of 20.
  4      ORDER_DATE    DATE;
  5      EMP_NO        INTEGER := 25; --Default value of 25
  6      PI            CONSTANT NUMBER := 3.1416;
  7    BEGIN
  8      NULL;
  9*   END;
```

Lines 1 through 6 contain the declarative section of the block. Lines 1 through 3 declare variables of the most common datatypes used in Oracle: NUMBER, VARCHAR2, and DATE. Line 5 declares an INTEGER variable and sets its default value to 25. The INTEGER datatype is a subtype constraining the legal values of another datatype. Line 6 declares a constant numeric value. Table 12-2 contains the PL/SQL datatypes and the subtypes available to all PL/SQL modules.

NAME	TYPE	DESCRIPTION
NUMBER	numeric	Can hold integer and real values and may be defined with a precision and scale.
BINARY_INTEGER	numeric	Can store signed integers. Optimized to performance in integer calculations.
DEC	numeric	Subtype of number. Decimal.
DOUBLE PRECISION	numeric	Subtype of number. Real numbers with high precision.
INTEGER	numeric	Subtype of number. Integer values only.

continued on next page

continued from previous page

NAME	TYPE	DESCRIPTION
INT	numeric	Subtype of number. Integer values only.
NUMERIC	number	Subtype of number. Equivalent to number.
REAL	number	Subtype of number. Equivalent to number.
SMALLINT	number	Subtype of number. Small range of integer.
VARCHAR2	character	Holds variable length strings with a maximum length.
CHAR	character	Fixed length strings.
LONG	character	Variable length string up to 32,767 bytes.
DATE	date	Holds date values in same format as the database.
BOOLEAN	Boolean	Contains TRUE or FALSE.
ROWID	ROWID	Holds database rowids.

Table 12-2 PL/SQL datatypes

The executable section is contained in lines 7 through 9. Since the executable section is required, it must contain at least one statement. The NULL statement in line 8 performs no action, but can serve as the required statement.

6. Run the statement to execute the PL/SQL code.

```
SQL>  /

PL/SQL procedure successfully completed.
```

How It Works

Step 1 presents a simple PL/SQL block showing the basic structure of a block. A block can contain a declarative section, an executable section, and an exception section. Both the declarative and exception sections are optional. When the block is executed in Step 2, the occurring SQL*Plus message is presented. Step 3 presents the way a block can be nested in PL/SQL. Nesting is very important when you need exceptions handled separately within a block. Both the outermost and innermost blocks can contain all three block sections. Step 5 presents a PL/SQL block declaring variables of a variety of datatypes, but performs no actions.

Comments

The PL/SQL block is the fundamental structure in PL/SQL. Do not hesitate to use PL/SQL code within SQL*Plus or other environments when it is not possible to perform an action using standard SQL statements.

COMPLEXITY
BEGINNING

12.2 How do I...
Display debug statements from PL/SQL?

Problem

When I run PL/SQL code in SQL*Plus, it does not display any results from the operation. It displays errors or a successful completion message, but not anything happening while the code is running. In order to determine if my code is operating correctly, I want to put debug statements in it to view its progress. How do I display debug statements from PL/SQL?

Technique

The PUT_LINE procedure from the DBMS_OUTPUT stored package lets you display information within PL/SQL. In order for the output of the DBMS_OUTPUT package to be displayed in SQL*Plus, the SERVEROUTPUT system variable must be set to ON. A *stored package* is a group of related procedures and functions executed on the server. The DBMS_OUTPUT package is a built-in package supplied by Oracle. For more information about packages, see Chapter 13, Procedures, Functions, and Packages, and Chapter 14, Built-In Packages.

Steps

1. Run SQL*Plus and connect as the WAITE user account. Load CHP12-4.sql into the SQL buffer. The PL/SQL block contained in the file uses the DBMS_OUTPUT.PUT_LINE to display a message in SQL*Plus.

```
SQL> GET CHP12-4
  1  BEGIN
  2    DBMS_OUTPUT.PUT_LINE('Output from the PUT_LINE function.');
  3* END;
```

The PUT_LINE procedure is passed a single text parameter displayed within SQL*Plus. In order to display data of other datatypes, a conversion function such as TO_CHAR must be used.

2. Set the SERVEROUTPUT system variable to ON using the SET command. The SERVEROUTPUT system variable controls the output of statements from the DBMS_OUTPUT package within SQL*Plus.

```
SQL> SET SERVEROUTPUT ON
SQL>
```

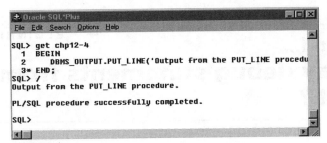

Figure 12-1 The output displayed by the
DBMS_OUTPUT.PUT_LINE procedure

Once the SERVEROUTPUT system variable is set to ON, output generated
by the DBMS_OUTPUT.PUT_LINE procedure is displayed in SQL*Plus. If
the value of the system variable is OFF, no output will be displayed even
though no error will occur.

3. Run the statement to display the results. Figure 12-1 shows the output of
the PL/SQL code in SQL*Plus.

How It Works

Step 1 presents a PL/SQL block containing the DBMS_OUTPUT.PUT_LINE procedure
to display output within SQL*Plus. Step 2 executes the SET SERVEROUTPUT ON
statement causing SQL*Plus to display the output of the PUT_LINE function.

Comments

The DBMS_OUTPUT.PUT_LINE procedure makes it possible to determine what is
happening within your PL/SQL blocks. Whenever you have PL/SQL code that is not
behaving the way you expected it to, you can put debugging statements in it to see
what is happening.

COMPLEXITY
BEGINNING

12.3 How do I...
Handle exceptions in PL/SQL?

Problem

Any time an exception occurs in my PL/SQL block, it terminates the block. I need
to handle exceptions in all my PL/SQL code to ensure that unexpected errors do not
terminate my PL/SQL module. When exceptions occur, I want to be sure errors are
handled gracefully. How do I handle exceptions in PL/SQL?

Technique

The *exception section* of each PL/SQL block can handle one or more exceptions. The EXCEPTION keyword identifies the beginning of the exception section. If an exception occurs and an exception handler does not exist in the exception section to handle it, an unhandled exception error occurs and execution of the module is terminated. Handlers are listed in the exception section following the WHEN clause, as shown here:

```
EXCEPTION
    WHEN first_exception THEN
        <code to handle first exception>
    WHEN second_exception THEN
        <code to handle second exception>
END;
```

Exceptions can be listed in any order, with one exception. The OTHERS exception handler, which handles all exceptions not explicitly listed, must be specified last. Predefined exceptions are supplied by Oracle and correspond to the most common Oracle errors. Table 12-3 contains the predefined exceptions.

EXCEPTION NAME	ORACLE ERROR	DESCRIPTION
CURSOR_ALREADY_OPEN	ORA-6511	Attempt to open a cursor that is already open.
DUP_VAL_ON_INDEX	ORA-0001	Attempt to violate a unique constraint.
INVALID_CURSOR	ORA-1001	Attempt to use an invalid cursor.
INVALID_NUMBER	ORA-1722	Attempt to perform a numeric operation on a non-number.
LOGIN_DENIED	ORA-1017	Invalid username or password.
NO_DATA_FOUND	ORA-1403	No data found in a query.
NOT_LOGGED_ON	ORA-1012	Attempt to perform a database operation when not connected.
PROGRAM_ERROR	ORA-6501	Internal error.
ROWTYPE_MISMATCH	ORA-6504	Host variable and cursor have incompatible types.
STORAGE_ERROR	ORA-6500	Internal error.
TIMEOUT_ON_RESOURCE	ORA-0051	Timeout occurred.
TOO_MANY_ROWS	ORA-1422	More than one row returned by SELECT INTO statement.
TRANSACTION_BACKED_OUT	ORA-006	Transaction rolled back due to deadlock.
VALUE_ERROR	ORA-6502	Conversion or truncation error.
ZERO_DIVIDE	ORA-1476	Attempt to divide by zero.

Table 12-3 Predefined exceptions

If an Oracle error that is not a predefined exception needs to be handled, an exception variable can be defined and linked to the error using the PRAGMA EXCEPTION_INIT statement in a block's declarative section. The syntax of the statement is shown here:

```
PRAGMA EXCEPTION_INIT(exception_name,error_number);
```

> **NOTE**
>
> Errors specified in the EXCEPTION_INIT statement are negative. Remember to include the minus sign (-) when defining the error, since error numbers are considered negative numbers.

Steps

1. Run SQL*Plus and connect as the WAITE user account. Set the SERVER-OUTPUT system variable to ON to display outputed. Load CHP12-5.sql into the SQL buffer. The PL/SQL block in the file generates an exception by placing a character value in a numeric variable. Since the PL/SQL block does not contain an exception section, the block will terminate abnormally.

```
SQL> SET SERVEROUTPUT ON
SQL> GET CHP12-5
  1   DECLARE
  2     X NUMBER;
  3   BEGIN
  4     X := _YYYY ;
  5     DBMS_OUTPUT.PUT_LINE(_IT WORKED );
  6*  END;
```

Lines 1 and 2 contain the declarative section of the block. Line 4 attempts to set the numeric variable defined in line 2 to a character value, which is an illegal operation. Since no exception handler is defined to handle the error, the program will terminate abnormally.

2. Run the statement to display the results of the operation. Figure 12-2 displays the results of the operation in SQL*Plus.

The Oracle error and its description are displayed whenever an unhanded exception occurs.

3. Load CHP12-6.sql into the SQL buffer. This PL/SQL block contained in the file handles the exception presented in the previous steps by creating an exception section and an exception handler.

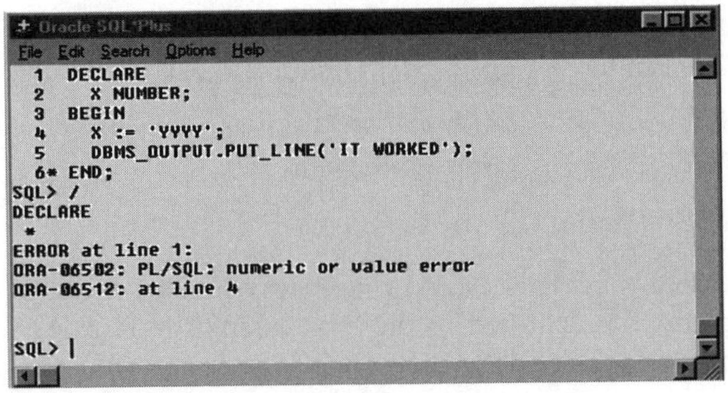

Figure 12-2 The error generated by an unhandled exception

```
SQL> GET CHP12-6
  1   DECLARE
  2       X NUMBER;
  3   BEGIN
  4       X := _YYYY ;
  5       DBMS_OUTPUT.PUT_LINE(_IT WORKS );
  6   EXCEPTION
  7       WHEN VALUE_ERROR THEN
  8           DBMS_OUTPUT.PUT_LINE(_EXCEPTION HANDLED );
  9*  END;
```

Lines 1 through 5 are the same as those presented in Step 1. The exception section starting on line 6 is added to the exception that occurs. The exception handler executes the code following the WHEN statement, until another exception handler is found or the END statement is found. The VALUE_ERROR exception is handled in lines 7 and 8. If a different exception occurs, it would not be handled and the execution of the process would still be terminated.

4. Run the statement to display the results of the operation.

```
SQL>  /

EXCEPTION HANDLED

PL/SQL procedure completed successfully.
```

The Oracle error generated by line 4 is handled by the exception handler in lines 7 and 8. The only way for this code to execute is for the exception to occur. The next step presents a sample PL/SQL block that includes the WHEN OTHERS exception handler, which handles all unhanded exceptions.

5. Load CHP12-7.sql into the SQL buffer. The PL/SQL block contained in the file uses the OTHERS exception to handle exceptions not specifically handled.

```
SQL> GET CHP12-7
  1   DECLARE
  2       X NUMBER;
  3   BEGIN
  4       X := 1 / 0;
  5       DBMS_OUTPUT.PUT_LINE(_IT WORKS );
  6   EXCEPTION
  7       WHEN VALUE_ERROR THEN
  8           DBMS_OUTPUT.PUT_LINE(_VALUE ERROR HANDLED );
  9       WHEN OTHERS THEN
 10           DBMS_OUTPUT.PUT_LINE(_OTHER ERROR HANDLED );
 11*  END;
```

Lines 1 and 2 contain the declarative section of the block. Line 4 attempts to divide by zero, which is not handled by a specific error handler. The exception section starting on line 6 only handles the VALUE_ERROR exception. The WHEN OTHERS exception handler starting on line 9 handles all other exceptions.

6. Run the statement to view its results. Figure 12-3 shows the results of the operation within SQL*Plus.

7. Load CHP12-8.sql into the SQL buffer. The PL/SQL block contained in the file creates an exception for an Oracle error not predefined.

```
SQL> GET CHP12-8
  1   DECLARE
  2     BAD_ROWID EXCEPTION;
  3     X ROWID;
  4     PRAGMA EXCEPTION_INIT(BAD_ROWID,-01445);
  5   BEGIN
  6     SELECT ROWID
  7       INTO X
  8       FROM ALL_VIEWS
  9      WHERE ROWNUM = 1;
 10   EXCEPTION
 11     WHEN BAD_ROWID THEN
 12       DBMS_OUTPUT.PUT_LINE('CANNOT QUERY ROWID FROM THIS VIEW');
 13* END;
```

Lines 1 through 3 contain the declarative section for the block. Line 2 declares an exception variable which will identify an Oracle error without a predefined exception. The statement contained in line 4 is executed at compile time to associate the newly defined exception with an Oracle error. When the Oracle error defined in the EXCEPTION_INIT procedure is encountered, the exception associated with it will be raised. Lines 6 through 9 attempt to query a ROWID from a view that joins tables. The error encounter is the one defined by the BAD_ROWID exception. Lines 11 and 12 handle the programmer-defined exception by displaying a message within SQL*Plus.

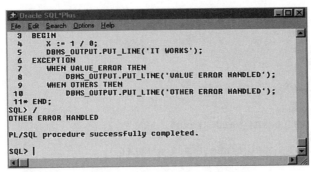

Figure 12-3 The output generated by the exception handler in CHP12-7.sql

8. Run the statement to display the results.

```
SQL> /

CANNOT QUERY ROWID FROM THIS VIEW

PL/SQL procedure successfully completed.
```

When the Oracle error ORA-1445 occurs in line 6 of the PL/SQL block, the programmer-defined exception handler processes the error and terminates the program normally.

How It Works

Errors are handled in PL/SQL blocks by exception handlers in the exception section. Steps 1 and 2 present a PL/SQL block which does not handle exceptions when they occur. When an exception occurs within the block, an error is generated and the program is terminated abnormally. Steps 3 and 4 present the same PL/SQL block with an exception handler for the VALUE_ERROR exception occurring. The exception handler causes the program to display a message and terminate normally when the error occurs. Steps 5 and 6 present the WHEN OTHERS exception handler for any exception not dealt with by a specific error handler. The WHEN OTHERS exception handler must be placed last in the exception section. Steps 7 and 8 present the technique for handling exceptions not predefined within PL/SQL. An exception variable is declared, and the PRAGMA EXCEPTION_INIT is used to associate an Oracle error with the exception defined.

Comments

It is very important to handle exceptions within your PL/SQL code. Exceptions can occur for a variety of reasons and can cause your code to terminate abnormally. You should attempt to handle exceptions specifically, not rely on the WHEN OTHERS exception to handle all your errors. How-To 12.7 presents the technique for handling programmer-defined errors occurring in stored procedures and functions.

COMPLEXITY
BEGINNING

12.4 How do I...
Perform conditional statements?

Problem

In the other procedural languages, I use conditional statements like IF . .THEN. . ELSE, which let me write flexible programs and control their behavior. In PL/SQL, I also need conditional statements since they do not exist in standard SQL. How do I perform conditional operations in PL/SQL?

Technique

The IF statement shown below allows you to incorporate conditional logic in your PL/SQL code.

```
IF <boolean expression> THEN
    PL/SQL and SQL statements
END IF;
```

The <boolean expression> is any expression that evaluates to a boolean value (TRUE or FALSE). The statement evaluates the boolean expression and executes the sequence of statements if the expression evaluates to TRUE. The IF. .THEN. .ELSE statement shown below provides an alternate sequence of statements to execute if the boolean expression evaluates to FALSE.

```
IF <boolean expression> THEN
    PL/SQL and SQL statements
ELSE
    Alternate statements
END IF;
```

If the boolean expression evaluates to TRUE, the first set of statements is executed; otherwise the alternate statements are executed. The ELSEIF construct evaluates additional boolean expressions when the first expression evaluates to FALSE. The syntax shown below presents the use of ELSEIF.

```
IF <boolean expression> THEN
    PL/SQL and SQL statements
ELSEIF <alternate boolean expression> THEN
    Alternate statements
END IF;
```

If the first boolean expression evaluates to FALSE, the boolean expression in the ELSEIF clause is evaluated. If the alternate boolean expression evaluates to TRUE, the alternate statements are executed. One or more ELSEIF clauses can be included with the IF statement to cause a chain of conditional statements.

Steps

1. Run SQL*Plus and connect as the WAITE user account. Load CHP12-9.sql into the SQL buffer. The PL/SQL block contained in the file demonstrates a simple IF statement with an ELSE clause.

```
SQL> GET CHP12-9
  1   DECLARE
  2     X NUMBER;
  3   BEGIN
  4     X := 3;
  5     IF X > 2 THEN
```

```
6         DBMS_OUTPUT.PUT_LINE('THE VALUE OF X IS GREATER THAN 2');
7     ELSE
8         DBMS_OUTPUT.PUT_LINE('THE VALUES OF X IS NOT GREATER THAN 2');
9     END IF;
10*  END;
```

Lines 1 and 2 containthe declarative section of the block. The variable declared in line 2 will be evaluated within the IF statement in the executable section. Lines 3 through 10 contain the executable section of the block. Line 4 assigns the number 3 to the variable X. The IF statement in line 5 evaluates the variable X within a boolean expression. If the value of X is greater than 2, the statement in line 6 is executed; otherwise the statement in line 8 is executed. The DBMS_OUTPUT stored package is used to display PL/SQL output in lines 6 and 8 in SQL*Plus. Refer to How-To 12.2 for more information about displaying debugging statements in PL/SQL.

2. Set the SERVEROUTPUT system variable to ON, and run the statement to display the results.

```
SQL>  /
```

```
THE VALUE OF X IS GREATER THAN 2.
```

```
PL/SQL procedure completed successfully
```

Since X was assigned to 3 in line 4, the boolean expression in line 5 evaluates to TRUE, displaying the first message.

3. Load CHP12-10.sql into the SQL buffer. The PL/SQL block contained in the file uses the IF..ELSEIF construct to perform conditional logic.

```
SQL> GET CHP12-10
 1 DECLARE
 2    X NUMBER;
 3 BEGIN
 4    X := 4;
 5    IF X > 5 THEN
 6        DBMS_OUTPUT.PUT_LINE('X IS GREATER THAN 5');
 7    ELSEIF X > 3 THEN
 8        DBMS_OUTPUT.PUT_LINE('X IS GREATER THAN 3 BUT NOT GREATER THAN 5');
 9    ELSE
10        DBMS_OUTPUT.PUT_LINE('X IS NOT GREATER THAN 3');
11    END IF;
12* END;
```

Lines 1 and 2 contain the declarative section on the PL/SQL block, and lines 3 though 12 contain the execution section. Lines 5 through 11 present the IF..ELSEIF construct. If the boolean expression contained in line 5 evaluates to TRUE, line 6 is executed. Otherwise, the boolean expression in line 7 is evaluated. If the expression evaluates to TRUE, line 8 is executed; otherwise line 10 is executed.

4. Run the statement to display the output.

SQL> /

X IS GREATER THAN 3 BUT NOT GREATER THAN 5

PL/SQL procedure completed successfully.

Line 4 assigns the value 4 to the variable X. This causes the expression on line 5 to be evaluated as FALSE, causing the expression on line 7 to be tested. Since X is greater than 3, the expression evaluates to TRUE, and the message in line 8 is displayed.

How It Works

The IF statement is used to perform conditional operations within PL/SQL by evaluating a boolean expression and performing statements based on the result. The operators that can be used in a boolean expression appear in Table 12-4.

OPERATOR	DESCRIPTION
=	Is equal to.
!=,<>,*=,^=	Is not equal to.
<	Is less than.
>	Is greater than.
>=	Is greater than or equal to.
<=	Is less than or equal to.
IS NULL	Is a null value.
BETWEEN	Is between two values.
IN	Is contained in a list of values.
AND	Logical conjunction.
OR	Logical inclusion.
NOT	Negation. Can be used as IS NOT NULL, NOT BETWEEN, NOT IN.

Table 12-4 PL/SQL logical operators

Steps 1 and 2 present the basic IF.THEN..ELSE construct within a PL/SQL block. Steps 3 and 4 present the ELSEIF clause, providing an easy way to make nested conditional statements.

Comments

Conditional statements give PL/SQL added flexibility not provided by SQL. As you develop applications using PL/SQL, you will find yourself using conditional statements often, since they are a fundamental part of the language.

COMPLEXITY
BEGINNING

12.5 How do I...
Perform looping operations?

Problem

I need to perform sequences of SQL and PL/SQL statements repeatedly within my PL/SQL modules. In third-generation languages like C, there are looping constructs that execute statements repeatedly. How do I perform looping operations in PL/SQL?

Technique

There are four types of looping constructs in PL/SQL: simple loops, FOR loops, WHILE loops, and cursor FOR loops. Simple loops execute a sequence of statements repeatedly with no apparent end. The syntax of a simple loop is shown here:

```
LOOP;
    Statements to be executed,
END LOOP;
```

The loop will continue to execute until it encounters an EXIT statement. The EXIT statement can be provided alone or with a WHEN clause, which includes a boolean expression to be evaluated. A FOR loop has a defined number of iterations performed and includes a loop counter which can be used within the loop. The syntax of a FOR loop is

```
FOR loop counter IN lower_bound .. upper_bound LOOP
    Statements to be executed,
END LOOP;
```

The loop is executed once for each value between the lower bound and upper bound. The WHILE loop evaluates a boolean expression before each iteration. If the expression evaluates to TRUE, the statements in the loop are executed. If the expression evaluates to FALSE, execution is passed to the statement following the loop. The syntax of the WHILE loop is shown here:

```
WHILE boolean expression LOOP
    Statements to be executed,
END LOOP;
```

If the boolean expression evaluates to FALSE the first time it's evaluated, the statements will never be executed. The cursor FOR loop is explored in How-To 12.9.

Steps

1. Load CHP12-11.sql into the SQL buffer. The PL/SQL block contained in the file executes a simple loop, using the EXIT WHEN statement to break out of the loop.

```
SQL> GET CHP12-11
  1  DECLARE
  2      X NUMBER;
  3  BEGIN
  4      X := 0;
  5      LOOP
  6          X := X + 1;
  7          DBMS_OUTPUT.PUT_LINE(TO_CHAR(X));
  8          EXIT WHEN X = 10;
  9      END LOOP;
 10* END;
```

Lines 1 and 2 contain the declarative section of the block, and lines 3 through 10 contain its execution section. Lines 5 though 9 present a simple loop which continues to perform iterations until the boolean expression contained in line 8 evaluates to TRUE. The PUT_LINE function contained in the loop displays a value within SQL*Plus for each iteration of the loop.

2. Set the SERVEROUTPUT system variable to ON, and run the statement to view the results of the operation. The output is shown in Figure 12-4.

The loop executes ten times before the expression in the EXIT WHEN statement evaluates to TRUE. Once the expression is TRUE, the loop is exited.

3. Load CHP12-12.sql into the SQL buffer. The PL/SQL block in the file contains a FOR loop which counts from 1 to 10 and displays the loop index.

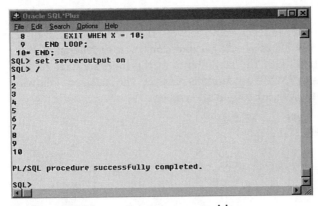

Figure 12-4 The output generated by a simple loop

```
SQL> GET CHP12-12
  1  BEGIN
  2    FOR I IN 1..10 LOOP
  3        DBMS_OUTPUT.PUT_LINE('THE VALUE OF I IS: '||TO_CHAR(I));
  4    END LOOP;
  5* END;
```

Lines 1 through 5 contain the execution section of the block. There is no declarative section, because the loop index can be declared implicitly by using it. The loop in lines 2 through 4 performs an iteration for each value between 1 and 10. The DBMS_OUTPUT.PUT_LINE statement in line 3 displays the value of the loop counter.

4. Run the statement. The results of the operation are shown in Figure 12-5.

The loop is performed ten times with the loop counter representing the number of the iteration performed.

5. Load CHP12-13.sql into the SQL buffer. The PL/SQL block in the file uses a WHILE loop to perform iterations.

```
SQL> GET CHP12-13
  1  DECLARE
  2    X NUMBER;
  3  BEGIN
  4    X := 1;
  5    WHILE X < 10 LOOP
  6        DBMS_OUTPUT.PUT_LINE(TO_CHAR(X)||' IS STILL LESS THAN 10');
  7        X := X + 1;
  8    END LOOP;
  9* END;
```

Lines 1 and 2 contain the declarative section of the block, and lines 3 through 9 contain the execution section. The variable defined in line 2 is used in the boolean expression in the WHILE loop. The WHILE loop in

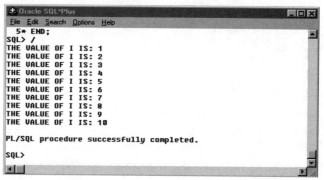

Figure 12-5 The output generated by a FOR loop

lines 5 through 8 performs iterations as long as the value of X is less than 10. Line 6 displays a message using the DBMS_OUTPUT.PUT_LINE procedure, and line 7 increments the value of X. If line 7 did not exist, the loop would be performed indefinitely.

6. Run the statement to display the results. The results of the operation are shown in Figure 12-6.

The loop is executed nine times, since the value of X is less than 10 for the first nine iterations.

How It Works

PL/SQL contains four types of looping constructs, three of which are presented in this How-To. The simple loop presented in steps 1 and 2 performs a loop indefinitely, until it encounters an EXIT statement. The FOR loop, presented in Steps 3 and 4, performs a defined number of iterations based on the value of a loop counter between a lower and upper bound. The WHILE loop, presented in Steps 5 and 6, evaluates a boolean expression before each iteration of the loop. As long as the boolean expression evaluates to TRUE, the loop is performed. If the expression never evaluates to TRUE, the statements contained in the loop are never performed.

Comments

Looping operations are a fundamental part of procedural languages. The type of loop you use in your programs depends on your personal preference. Each of the different loop structures have benefits for different types of operations.

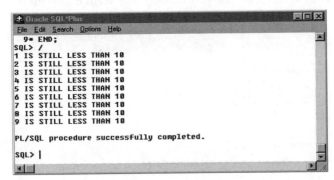

Figure 12-6 The output generated by a WHILE loop

12.6 How do I...
Create user-defined exceptions?

Problem

When certain business rules are violated within a PL/SQL block, I want to handle the error like an exception. I want to create and use my own exception within the code to treat certain situations like an error. How do I create and use a user-defined exception?

Technique

An exception can be declared in the declarative section of a PL/SQL block and raised using the RAISE statement. When an exception is raised, execution is passed to the exception section of the block. The exception handler created for the user-defined exception will be executed any time the exception is raised.

Steps

1. Run SQL*Plus and connect as the WAITE user account. Load CHP12-14.sql into the SQL buffer. The file contains a PL/SQL block that makes use of a user-defined exception.

```
SQL>   GET CHP12-14
  1    DECLARE
  2       SALARY_CODE VARCHAR2(1);
  3       INVALID_SALARY_CODE EXCEPTION;
  4    BEGIN
  5       SALARY_CODE := 'X';
  6       IF SALARY_CODE NOT IN ('A','B','C') THEN
  7          RAISE INVALID_SALARY_CODE;
  8       END IF;
  9       DBMS_OUTPUT.PUT_LINE('EVERYTHING IS OK');
 10    EXCEPTION
 11       WHEN INVALID_SALARY_CODE THEN
 12          DBMS_OUTPUT.PUT_LINE('INVALID SALARY CODE');
 13*   END;
```

Lines 1 though 3 contain the declarative section of the block. Line 3 declares an exception variable which can be raised in the executable section of the block and handled in the exception section. Lines 4 through 9 contain the executable section of the block. Line 5 sets the value of a variable to X. Lines 6 through 8 evaluate the value of the variable. If the value of the variable is not in a list of valid values, the RAISE statement will raise the exception in line 7. Lines 10 through 13 contain the exception section of the block. Lines 11 and 12 handle the user-defined exception by displaying a message with the DBMS_OUTPUT.PUT_LINE procedure.

2. Set the SERVEROUTPUT system variable to ON to display the output, and run the statement. The results of the operation are shown in Figure 12-7.

The user-defined exception is raised in the block and handled by the exception handler in lines 11 and 12. The message displayed in SQL*Plus is generated by the exception handler, rather than code in the executable section.

How It Works

A user-defined exception can be declared in the declarative section of a block and raised using the RAISE statement. When the exception is raised, the exception handler defined is executed. Steps 1 and 2 present a PL/SQL block employing a user-defined exception to exit the executable section of the code. If a user-defined exception is raised in the executable section, but not handled in the exception section, an error will occur and the block will terminate abnormally.

Comments

A user-defined exception allows you to perform a different type of logic in your PL/SQL code. If a business situation that makes you want to exit the PL/SQL block arises, an exception can be used to make a graceful exit. If you find yourself creating an IF statement containing most of the executable section, consider raising an exception when the boolean expression in the IF statement evaluates to FALSE.

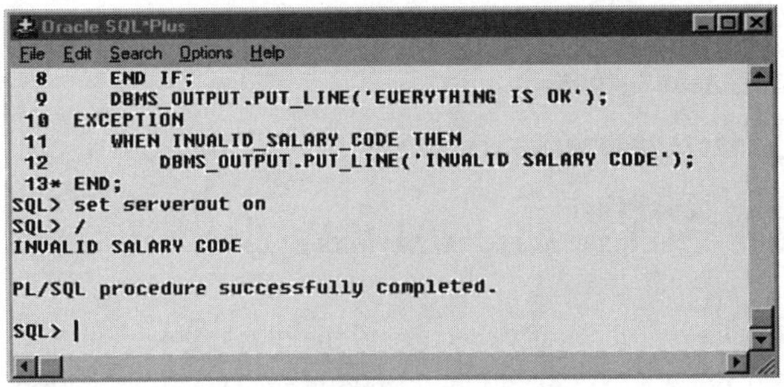

Figure 12-7 The output generated by a user-defined exception

COMPLEXITY
INTERMEDIATE

12.7 How do I...
Handle user-defined errors from a stored procedure?

Problem

Within my PL/SQL code, I use stored procedures. If a stored procedure returns an error with the RAISE_APPLICATION_ERROR procedure, I do not know how to handle the error. How do I handle a user-defined error caused by a stored procedure?

Technique

A EXCEPTION_INIT pragma is a special instruction to the compiler that associates an error code to an exception name. It can be used to define an exception name for each of the errors the stored procedure can return. An exception variable can be defined in the code's declarative section to be associated with the error and handled in the exception section.

Steps

1. Run SQL*Plus and connect as the WAITE user account. CHP12-15.sql, shown in Figure 12-8, creates a sample stored procedure used throughout this How-To.

The stored procedure contains the RAISE_APPLICATION_ERROR procedure, which terminates it and returns a user-defined error code to the calling module. The error code the stored procedure generates will be trapped in the following steps. Run the file to create the sample stored procedure.

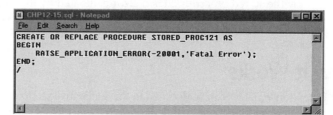

Figure 12-8 CHP12-15.sql generates a stored procedure that generates an error

```
SQL>   START CHP12-15
```

Procedure created.

> **2.** Load CHP12-16.sql into the SQL buffer. The PL/SQL block in the file calls
> the stored procedure created in the last step and handles the error returned.

```
SQL>  GET CHP12-16
  1   DECLARE
  2       INVALID_SP_CALL EXCEPTION;
  3       PRAGMA EXCEPTION_INIT(INVALID_SP_CALL,-20001);
  4   BEGIN
  5       STORED_PROC121;
  6       DBMS_OUTPUT.PUT_LINE(_NO ERROR OCCURRED );
  7   EXCEPTION
  8       WHEN INVALID_SP_CALL THEN
  9           DBMS_OUTPUT.PUT_LINE(_ERROR OCCURRED IN STORED PROCEDURE );
 10*  END;
```

> Lines 1 through 3 contain the declarative section of the block. Line 2
> declares an exception variable to handle the error returned by the stored
> procedure. Line 3 associates the error code returned by the stored proce-
> dure with the name of the exception, by defining a PRAGMA. Lines 4
> through 6 contain the executable section of the block. Line 5 executes the
> stored procedure. Any errors generated by the stored procedure must be
> handled, or the PL/SQL block will terminate abnormally. The exception
> handler in lines 8 and 9 handles the exception defined in the declarative
> section and returned by the stored procedure.

> **3.** Set the SERVEROUTPUT system variable to ON and run the statement to
> display the results of the operation.

```
SQL>   SET SERVEROUTPUT ON
SQL>   /
```

ERROR OCCURRED IN STORED PROCEDURE

PL/SQL procedure completed successfully.

> The exception created in the declarative section handles the error generated
> by the stored procedure. Each error generated by the stored procedure
> must be handled by the local PL/SQL block, or it will terminate abnormally.

How It Works

Exception variables can be declared in the declarative section of a PL/SQL block and
associated with the user-defined error by the PRAGMA EXCEPTION_INIT. A
pragma is executed when the PL/SQL module is compiled and the EXCEP-
TION_INIT procedure associates error numbers with exception variables. When an

error is generated from a stored procedure by the RAISE_APPLICATION_ERROR procedure, it can be handled by a user-defined exception. Step 1 creates a stored procedure that returns an error code when it is run. The PL/SQL code in Step 2 runs the stored procedure and handles the error generated.

Comments

If your stored procedures generate errors using the RAISE_APPLICATION_ERROR procedure, you must be sure to handle the errors in your PL/SQL code. If the errors are not handled, the PL/SQL module will terminate abnormally, even though the error generated is programmer defined.

COMPLEXITY
INTERMEDIATE

12.8   How do I...
Perform single record queries in PL/SQL?

Problem

Within PL/SQL, I need to query records from tables and views and use the results within my PL/SQL. In some cases, I need to return a single record and select it into a variable. I know that the query will return a single record and do not want to create an explicit cursor. How do I perform a single record query in PL/SQL?

Technique

The SELECT..INTO statement is used to query a single row into local PL/SQL variables. The variables receiving the columns must match the number and datatypes of the columns the query returns, and the query must return exactly one row. If it returns more than one row, the TOO_MANY_ROWS exception is raised. If the query returns no rows, the NO_DATA_FOUND exception is raised.

Steps

1. Run SQL*Plus and connect as the WAITE user account. CHP12-17.sql, shown in Figure 12-9, creates the sample table used in this How-To.

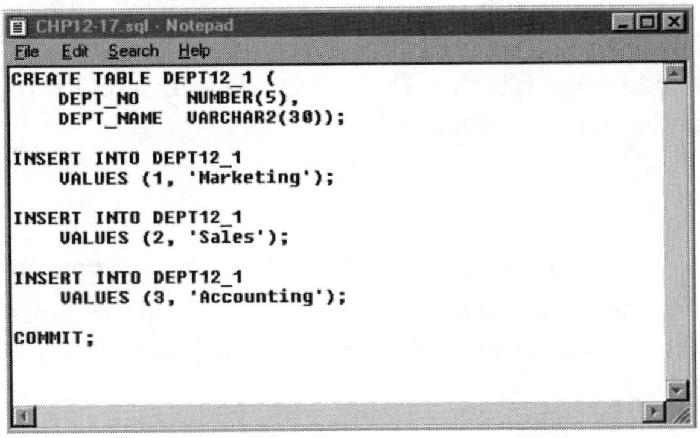

Figure 12-9 CHP12-17.sql creates a sample
table used in How-To 12.8

The sample table contains two columns, DEPT_NO and DNAME, and is
populated with three records that demonstrate a single record query. Run
the file to create the sample table with its data.

```
SQL> START CHP12-17

Table created.

1 row inserted.

1 row inserted.

1 row inserted.

Commit complete.
```

2. Load CHP12-18.sql into the SQL buffer. The PL/SQL block contained in
the file queries a record from the sample table into PL/SQL variables.

```
SQL> GET CHP12-18
  1  DECLARE
  2    DNO        NUMBER;
  3    DNAME      VARCHAR2(40);
  4  BEGIN
  5    SELECT DEPT_NO, DEPT_NAME
  6      INTO DNO, DNAME
  7    FROM
  8      DEPT12_1
  9    WHERE
 10      DEPT_NO = 1;
 11    DBMS_OUTPUT.PUT_LINE(_DEPT_NO =_||
 12                  TO_CHAR(DNO)||  DEPT_NAME =_||DNAME);
 13  EXCEPTION
 14    WHEN NO_DATA_FOUND THEN
 15          DBMS_OUTPUT.PUT_LINE(_NO_DATA_FOUND );
 16    WHEN TOO_MANY_ROWS THEN
 17          DBMS_OUTPUT.PUT_LINE(_TOO_MANY_ROWS );
 18* END;
```

Lines 1 through 3 contain the declarative section of the block. Lines 2 and 3 declare the variables to hold the results of the query. Lines 4 through 12 contain the execution section of the block. The SELECT..INTO statement in lines 5 through 10 queries the two table columns into the two variables lines 2 and 3 define. The INTO clause in line 6 is required of all queries in PL/SQL not using explicit cursors. The exception section is contained in lines 13 through 18 to handle the two most common errors with the SELECT..INTO statement. The NO_DATA_FOUND exception, handled in lines 14 and 15, is raised when a query returns no rows. The TOO_MANY_ROWS exception, handled in lines 16 and 17, is raised when the query returns more than one row.

3. Set the SERVEROUTPUT system variable to ON, and run the statement to display the results.

```
SQL>   SET SERVEROUTPUT ON
SQL>   /

DEPT_NO =1 DEPT_NAME =Marketing

PL/SQL procedure successfully completed.
```

Since one record matches the query criteria, the SELECT..INTO statement is successfully executed and the message displayed.

How It Works

The SELECT..INTO statement is used to query a single record into PL/SQL variables. The number of columns the query returns must match the number of PL/SQL variables supplied in the INTO clause. The datatypes of the columns and variables must match, or an error will occur. Step 1 creates a sample table used to demonstrate the SELECT..INTO statement in PL/SQL. Steps 2 and 3 use the SELECT..INTO statement to query a single record. If more than one record is returned by the statement, the TOO_MANY_ROWS exception is raised. If no records are returned, the NO_DATA_FOUND exception is raised.

Comments

When you use the SELECT..INTO statement, be sure to nest PL/SQL blocks in order to handle the exceptions correctly. Do not have more than one SELECT..INTO statement in a PL/SQL block. If more than one query is contained in a PL/SQL block, the same exception handler takes care of exceptions raised by any of the queries. When an exception is raised by a query, subsequent queries will not be executed. By nesting PL/SQL blocks, an exception section can exist for each query executed, ensuring all of the queries will execute.

COMPLEXITY
INTERMEDIATE

12.9 How do I...
Perform multiple record queries with cursors?

Problem

I need to perform multiple record queries in PL/SQL and use the results within the code. I do not know how many rows will be returned by the query. Once the results of the query have been moved into PL/SQL, I need to be able to navigate through the record set. How do I perform multiple record queries in PL/SQL?

Technique

In order to perform a multiple record query in PL/SQL, a cursor must be used. A *cursor* is a pointer to an area in the Process Global Area (PGA) on the server called the *context area*. When a query is executed on the server, the set of rows the query returns is contained in the context area and can be retrieved to the client application through operations on a cursor. All SQL statements use implicitly declared cursors if you do not explicitly define the cursor in your code. In order for a cursor to be controlled within a PL/SQL block, it must be given a name and declared explicitly. Processing an explicit cursor requires four steps. The first step is to declare the cursor in the declarative section of the PL/SQL block. The syntax is

```
CURSOR cursor_name IS query;
```

Parameters can be passed to the query by specifying them and their datatypes with the cursor name. The parameters can be used in the query to control the output generated. Once the cursor has been declared, it must be opened. Opening a cursor performs the query on the server. The OPEN statement is used to open the cursor. Its syntax is

```
OPEN cursor_name;
```

After the cursor has been opened, the records returned by the query must be fetched into the variables in the PL/SQL block using the FETCH statement. The syntax of the FETCH statement is

```
FETCH cursor_name INTO <column list seperated by commas>;
```

The columns in the column list must match the numbers and datatypes of the columns returned by the query. After the processing of the query is completed, the cursor must be closed with the CLOSE statement. The syntax of the CLOSE statement is

```
CLOSE cursor_name;
```

If you attempt to reopen a cursor without closing it first, an error will occur. The steps required to open and fetch the records can be consolidated by using a cursor FOR loop. The cursor FOR loop lets you loop through each record in a cursor. The syntax of the cursor FOR loop is

```
FOR loop_counter IN cursor_name LOOP
    <statements using records in the cursor>
END LOOP;
```

Columns in the cursor are referenced within the loop using the syntax LOOP_COUNTER.COLUMN_NAME.

Steps

1. Run SQL*Plus and connect as the WAITE user account. Load CHP12-19.sql into the SQL buffer. The PL/SQL block contained in the file defines a cursor to handle multiple rows returned by a query.

```
SQL> GET CHP12-19
  1   DECLARE
  2      CURSOR C1 IS
  3         SELECT VIEW_NAME
  4             FROM ALL_VIEWS
  5          WHERE ROWNUM <= 10
  6          ORDER BY VIEW_NAME;
  7      VNAME VARCHAR2(40);
  8   BEGIN
  9      OPEN C1;
 10      FETCH C1 INTO VNAME;
 11      WHILE C1%FOUND LOOP
 12         DBMS_OUTPUT.PUT_LINE(TO_CHAR(C1%ROWCOUNT)||  _||VNAME);
 13         FETCH C1 INTO VNAME;
 14      END LOOP;
 15* END;
```

Lines 1 through 7 contain the declarative section of the PL/SQL block. Lines 2 through 6 create a cursor that queries a data dictionary view to return multiple records. Lines 8 through 14 contain the executable section of the block. The OPEN statement in line 9 opens the cursor, performing the query on the server. The FETCH statement in line 10 retrieves the first record from the cursor into the variable defined in line 7. Lines 11 through 14 loop through the records of the cursor until the %FOUND attribute of the cursor returns FALSE. The cursor attributes used to control the processing cursors are shown in Table 12-5. Line 12 displays the value retrieved from the cursor, and line 13 fetches the next record.

ATTRIBUTE	MEANING
%FOUND	Boolean attribute which returns TRUE if the record returned by the last fetch attempt was successful.
%NOTFOUND	Boolean attribute which always returns the opposite of %FOUND.
%ISOPEN	Boolean attribute which returns TRUE if the cursor is open.
%ROWCOUNT	Numeric attribute which returns the number of records fetched from the cursor.

Table 12-5 Cursor attributes

2. Set the SERVEROUTPUT system variable to ON and run the statement to display its results. The results of the operation are shown in Figure 12-10.

The ten records returned by the query are displayed by the DBMS_OUTPUT.PUT_LINE procedure as the cursor is read by the FETCH statement. After the tenth record has been retrieved, the next FETCH statement fails, changing the value of the %FOUND attribute to FALSE and exiting the WHILE loop.

3. Load CHP12-20.sql into the SQL buffer. The PL/SQL module contained in the file creates a cursor and uses it in a cursor FOR loop.

```
SQL> GET CHP12-20
  1   DECLARE
  2      CURSOR C1 IS
  3         SELECT VIEW_NAME
  4            FROM ALL_VIEWS
  5         WHERE ROWNUM <= 10
  6         ORDER BY VIEW_NAME;
  7   BEGIN
  8      FOR III IN C1 LOOP
  9         DBMS_OUTPUT.PUT_LINE(III.VIEW_NAME);
 10      END LOOP;
 11* END;
```

Lines 1 through 7 contain the declarative section of the block. The cursor defined in lines 2 through 6 queries ten records from a data dictionary view. Lines 7 through 11 contain the executable section of the block. The cursor FOR loop contained in lines 8 through 10 loops through each record in the cursor and displays its column using the DBMS_OUTPUT.PUT_LINE procedure.

4. Run the statement to display the results. Figure 12-11 shows the results of the output.

The results of the output are the same as in the previous example, but there was less code required to perform the task.

5. Load CHP12-21.sql into the SQL buffer. The PL/SQL block contained in the file creates a cursor with parameters. Cursor parameters allow the same cursor to be used with variable information in the query.

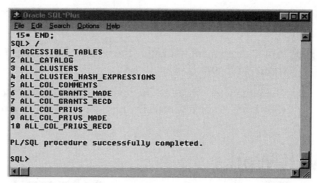

Figure 12-10 The output of records returned by a cursor in PL/SQL

```
SQL> GET CHP12-21
 1   DECLARE
 2      CURSOR C1 (VIEW_PATTERN VARCHAR2) IS
 3         SELECT VIEW_NAME
 4            FROM ALL_VIEWS
 5         WHERE VIEW_NAME LIKE VIEW_PATTERN||'%' AND
 6               ROWNUM <= 10
 7         ORDER BY VIEW_NAME;
 8   VNAME VARCHAR2(40);
 9   BEGIN
10      FOR III IN C1(_DBA_) LOOP
11         DBMS_OUTPUT.PUT_LINE(III.VIEW_NAME);
12      END LOOP;
13*  END;
```

Lines 1 through 7 contain the declarative section of the block. The cursor defined in lines 2 through 7 contains a parameter used in the WHERE clause in line 5. When the cursor is opened, the parameter must be supplied or an error will occur. Lines 9 through 13 contain the executable section of the block. The cursor FOR loop in lines 10 through 12 passes a

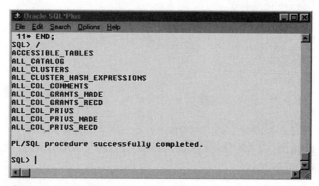

Figure 12-11 The output of records returned by a cursor using a cursor FOR loop

character parameter to the cursor, which is used when the query is executed.

6. Run the statement to display the results. The results of the operation are shown in Figure 12-12.

The parameter passed to the opened query only caused records beginning with DBA_ to be returned by the query and displayed in SQL*Plus.

How It Works

Cursors allow you to execute a query within a PL/SQL block and then retrieve the records. A cursor is declared in the declarative section of the block and provides the query to be executed. Within the executable section, the cursor must be opened, the records fetched, then the cursor closed. Steps 1 and 2 demonstrate the process of using a cursor in a PL/SQL block. The process of opening the cursor and fetching the records can be consolidated by using a cursor FOR loop to process a cursor. Steps 3 and 4 demonstrate the operation of a cursor FOR loop in PL/SQL. Steps 5 and 6 create a cursor which is passed parameters when opened. Cursors allow parameters to be created, providing greater flexibility and promoting their reuse in similar queries.

Comments

You will find it necessary to perform queries returning multiple rows in PL/SQL. Explicit cursors must be used when multiple rows are returned by a query. Whenever possible, use cursors containing parameters so you can reuse them in your code. This reduces the amount of overhead required.

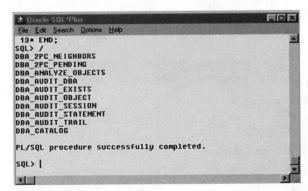

Figure 12-12 The output of a cursor containing a parameter

COMPLEXITY
INTERMEDIATE

12.10 How do I...
Create variables to represent database records and columns?

Problem

I need to declare variables in my PL/SQL code to represent columns retrieved from the database. Errors can occur if I do not create the variable with the correct datatype and column width. If the column changes in the table, my code needs to be modified. I want to create variables to represent columns. I also want to create structures to represent records in my PL/SQL code. How do I create variables to represent records and columns?

Technique

In PL/SQL, it is possible to declare the datatype of a variable as the datatype of a table column by using the %TYPE attribute. The %TYPE attribute ensures that the datatype of the variable is suitable for handling the column. The usage of the %TYPE attribute is shown here:

```
DECLARE
    variable_name table_name.column_name%TYPE
```

A variable must be declared for each of the columns retrieved from the database when using the %TYPE attribute. A single variable can be created to represent the entire row, by using the %ROWTYPE attribute. Variables declared with the %ROWTYPE attribute are structures containing all the columns in the table. The usage of the %ROWTYPE attribute is shown here:

```
DECLARE
    variable_name table_name%ROWTYPE
```

Once a variable is defined using the %ROWTYPE attribute, its components are referenced using the syntax VARIABLE_NAME.COLUMN_NAME.

Steps

1. Run SQL*Plus and connect as the WAITE user account. CHP12-22.sql, shown in Figure 12-13, creates the sample table used in this How-To.

Figure 12-13 CHP12-22.sql creates a sample
table used in How-To 12.10

The DEPT12_2 table created by the script contains two columns used to
define column and record type variables in the following steps. Run the file
to create the sample table and data.

```
SQL>   START CHP12-22

Table created.

1 row created.

Commit complete.
```

2. Load CHP12-23.sql into the SQL buffer. The PL/SQL block contained in
the file uses the %TYPE attribute when declaring variables to represent
database columns.

```
SQL> GET CHP12-23
  1   DECLARE
  2       D_NO    DEPT12_2.DEPT_NO%TYPE;
  3       D_NAME  DEPT12_2.DEPT_NAME%TYPE;
  4   BEGIN
  5       SELECT
  6           DEPT_NO, DEPT_NAME
  7       INTO
  8           D_NO, D_NAME
  9       FROM
 10           DEPT12_2;
 11       DBMS_OUTPUT.PUT_LINE(TO_CHAR(D_NO));
 12       DBMS_OUTPUT.PUT_LINE(D_NAME);
 13   EXCEPTION
 14       WHEN NO_DATA_FOUND THEN
 15           NULL;
 16*  END;
```

Lines 1 through 3 contain the declarative section of the block. Lines 2 and
3 declare variables using the %TYPE attribute. The D_NO and D_NAME
variables are declared with the datatype of the DEPT_NO and

DEPT_NAME columns in the sample table, even though the datatypes are not specified. Lines 4 through 12 contain the execution section of the block. The query contained in lines 5 through 10 selects a record from the sample table and puts the results in the variables declared with the %TYPE attribute. Even though the datatype is not known to the programmer when the module is created, it is assured of being correct by the %TYPE attribute. The DBMS_OUTPUT package is used in lines 11 and 12 to display the values returned by the query. The exception section contained in lines 13 through 15 handles the exception raised if no data is returned by the query.

3. Run the statement to view the results.

```
SQL>  /

1
Marketing

PL/SQL procedure completed successfully.
```

4. Load CHP12-24.sql into the SQL buffer. The PL/SQL block contained in the file declares a record variable using the %ROWTYPE attribute.

```
SQL> GET CHP12-24
  1   DECLARE
  2      D     DEPT12_2%ROWTYPE;
  3   BEGIN
  4      SELECT
  5         DEPT_NO, DEPT_NAME
  6      INTO
  7         D.DEPT_NO, D.DEPT_NAME
  8      FROM
  9         DEPT12_2;
 10      DBMS_OUTPUT.PUT_LINE(TO_CHAR(D.DEPT_NO));
 11      DBMS_OUTPUT.PUT_LINE(D.DEPT_NAME);
 12   EXCEPTION
 13      WHEN NO_DATA_FOUND THEN
 14         NULL;
 15* END;
```

Lines 1 through 3 contain the declarative section of the block. The variable defined in line 2 uses the %ROWTYPE attribute to declare a record variable representing all the columns in the DEPT122 table. Lines 3 through 11 contain the executable section of the block. The query defined in lines 4 through 9 retrieves a record from the sample table in Step 1 and places the columns in the components of the record variable. Line 7 shows how the columns of a record-type variable are referenced using dot notation. Lines 10 and 11 use the DBMS_OUTPUT package to display the values contained in the components of the record variable. The exception section contained in lines 12 through 14 handles the exception occuring if no data is returned by the query.

5. Run the statement to execute it.

```
SQL>  /

1
MARKETING

PL/SQL procedure completed.
```

How It Works

The %TYPE attribute can be used to declare variables of the datatype contained in the column of a table. This allows you to declare variables without knowing the datatype of the value it will receive. The %ROWTYPE attribute allows you to declare a composite datatype containing all the columns in a table. Step 1 creates a sample table used in the following steps. Steps 2 and 3 demonstrate the use of the %TYPE attribute by declaring variables to represent the columns in the sample table. The sample record is queried into the variables and displayed using the DBMS_OUTPUT.PUT_LINE procedure. Steps 4 and 5 use the %ROWTYPE attribute to declare a composite variable containing all the columns in the sample table. The sample record is queried into the variable, and the values are displayed.

Comments

It is good practice to use the %TYPE and %ROWTYPE attributes whenever you create a variable to represent a column in a table or create multiple variables to represent an entire record. Using the %TYPE and %ROWTYPE attributes ensures that your PL/SQL code will continue to work if the structure of the table or datatypes of a column change.

COMPLEXITY
INTERMEDIATE

12.11 How do I...
Achieve array functionality with PL/SQL tables?

Problem

I need to use arrays in my PL/SQL code, but PL/SQL does not contain array structures. I know the PL/SQL tables exist, and I want to use them the same way arrays are used. How do I achieve array functionality with PL/SQL tables?

Technique

One-dimensional arrays can be simulated in PL/SQL using PL/SQL tables. Since a PL/SQL table can have only one column, it is very similar to a one-dimensional array. A two-step process is required to create a PL/SQL table. A user-defined datatype containing a description of the table must be created before a table variable can be declared. The syntax used to create a datatype defining a table is shown here:

```
TYPE <type_name> IS
    TABLE OF <data_type>
    INDEX BY BINARY_INTEGER;
```

<type_name> is the name of the datatype representing the table. <data_type> represents the datatype of the elements contained in the table. The INDEX BY BINARY_INTEGER clause is required when creating the table, since BINARY_INTEGER is the only type of index currently supported. In PL/SQL versions 2.3 and higher you can use record variables as elements of a table. Once the datatype is defined to represent the table, variables can be defined as the new datatype.

Steps

1. Run SQL*Plus and connect as the WAITE user account. Load CHP12-25.sql into the SQL buffer. The PL/SQL code contained in the file uses a FOR loop to define a PL/SQL table and fill it with data. Once the table is filled, a second FOR loop moves through the table, displaying the values contained.

```
SQL> GET CHP12-25
  1   DECLARE
  2       TYPE ARRAY_TYPE IS
  3           TABLE OF NUMBER
  4               INDEX BY BINARY_INTEGER;
  5       MY_ARRAY ARRAY_TYPE;
  6   BEGIN
  7       FOR I IN 1..10 LOOP
  8           MY_ARRAY(I) := I * 2;
  9       END LOOP;
 10       FOR I IN 1..10 LOOP
 11           DBMS_OUTPUT.PUT_LINE(TO_CHAR(MY_ARRAY(I)));
 12       END LOOP;
 13* END;
```

Lines 1 through 5 contain the declarative section of the PL/SQL block. The TYPE statement started in line 2 creates a datatype called ARRAY_TYPE, which defines a table of numbers. Line 4 presents the required INDEX BY BINARY_INTEGER clause to create the index for the table. Currently, BINARY_INTEGER is the only datatype supported for the index. Line 5 declares a variable of the table type defined in the previous lines. Lines 5 through 13 contain the execution section of the block. The FOR loop contained in lines 7 through 9 populates the first ten values of the table with a calculated value. The FOR loop contained in lines 10 through 13 loops through the table, displaying the values contained in the records.

2. Set the SERVEROUTPUT system variable to ON to display the output of the DBMS_OUTPUT package and run the statement showing the results.

```
SQL>   /

2
4
6
8
10
12
14
16
18
20

PL/SQL procedure successfully completed.
```

When the statement is executed, the table is created and populated with elements. Once the table has been populated, the values of the table are displayed within SQL*Plus.

How It Works

PL/SQLtables are similar to one-dimensional arrays and are referenced like arrays. PL/SQL tables can be created containing any of the standard PL/SQL datatypes. In PL/SQL version 2.3 and higher, you can even use record variables in PL/SQL tables. To declare a PL/SQL table, a datatype defining the table characteristics must first be created. Once the datatype is created, variables of the new datatype can be declared. Steps 1 and 2 create a PL/SQL module which uses a PL/SQL table like an array. A datatype is created in the declarative section of the block with the TYPE statement. The statement TABLE OF NUMBER INDEX BY BINARY_INTEGER defines a table containing values of the NUMBER datatype. The INDEX BY BINARY_INTEGER clause is required of all table declarations, since BINARY_INTEGER is currently the only index type supported by PL/SQL. Once the table variable is created, it can be referenced like an array by specifying an index value in parentheses to represent an element in the table.

Comments

Array processing is a common need within procedural languages. PL/SQL tables can be used like one-dimensional arrays within your code. If your requirements include two-dimensional arrays, this requires considerably more effort. If you are running PL/SQL version 2.3, the additional support of record variables in PL/SQL tables lets you create array-type structures to represent records returned by a query.

CHAPTER 13

PROCEDURES, FUNCTIONS, AND PACKAGES

13

PROCEDURES, FUNCTIONS, AND PACKAGES

How do I...

Procedures, functions, and packages allow you to name your PL/SQL blocks to create modular code and promote the reuse of code. A procedure or function can be stored in the database and executed by any user granted EXECUTE privileges to the module. When a stored PL/SQL module is executed the processing is performed on the server, which can increase performance by reducing network traffic and optimizing your computer's power. Dividing the application into client- and server-side processing is called *application partitioning*. Procedures and functions can be created to run on the client or the server. Tools such as SQL*Plus and Developer 2000 let you create procedures and functions to run on the client. Such tools also allow you to execute modules stored in the database. A *package* groups related procedures and functions and lets them share a common set of variables, cursors, and user-defined datatypes. Procedures and functions can be overloaded in packages, greatly extending their flexibility. This chapter presents techniques related to the creation and management of procedures, functions, and packages. The examples presented in this chapter can be found in the accompanying CD in the \SAMPLES\CHAP13 directory.

13.1   Create a stored procedure

Stored procedures can be created within a user account's schema to execute PL/SQL modules on the database server. Parameters can be passed to and from stored procedures, creating modular units of reusable code. Using stored procedures within PL/SQL modules is as easy as writing a single PL/SQL statement. This How-To presents the technique used to create a stored procedure and call it from a PL/SQL module.

13.2   Create a stored function

A stored function executes on the server and returns a value to the calling PL/SQL module. Stored functions can accept parameters and return a value of standard datatypes, record variables, and since PL/SQL version 2.3, cursors. This How-To presents the technique used to create a stored function and call it from a local PL/SQL module.

13.3   Display compilation errors when creating a stored module

When you create a stored module, syntax errors can occur in the code. The only message displayed when you compile the module informs you that there are compilation errors. Errors in stored modules are contained in the USER_ERRORS data dictionary view and can be queried through SQL*Plus. This How-To presents the method used to display compilation errors generated when creating stored modules.

13.4   Create a procedure or function within a PL/SQL module

Procedures and functions can be created within a PL/SQL module to make the code more modular. A function within a PL/SQL module is created in the declarative section and has scope local to the module. This How-To presents the technique used to create a local procedure or function.

13.5   Create a stored package

A stored package groups related procedures and functions into a single package. Grouping related modules into packages allows you to take an object-oriented approach to stored procedure development. A package can contain its own local procedures, variables, and datatypes and expose only specified objects to the user. This How-To presents the technique for creating a stored package and using it within your local PL/SQL code.

13.6 View the source code of a stored module

The source code of stored modules can be queried from the ALL_SOURCE data dictionary view. A simple query of the data dictionary can be used to present the module's source code. This How-To presents the method used to view the source code of the stored module within the database.

13.7 Rebuild statements to create stored modules

As we have done throughout the book, you can use the data dictionary and SQL*Plus to rebuild DDL statements. Since the source code for stored modules is contained in the data dictionary, it is possible to rebuild the statements used to create the existing stored modules. This How-To presents the techniques for rebuilding the DDL statements that created stored modules.

13.8 Overload procedures and functions in packages

Procedure and function overloading is a very useful technique allowing a procedure or function to accept multiple parameter lists and perform differently for each. Overloading is used extensively in Oracle to make procedures and functions work with parameters of varying datatypes. This How-To presents the method used to overload procedures and functions within packages.

13.9 Use a stored function in a SQL statement

In PL/SQL version 2.1 and higher, stored functions can be used directly within SQL statements under certain conditions. When used in a select statement, the function is executed once for each record the query returns. This How-To presents the method used to call stored functions in SQL statements.

COMPLEXITY
INTERMEDIATE

13.1 How do I...
Create a stored procedure?

Problem

I want to create a stored procedure which performs an operation on the database. Since the procedure is used in many places throughout my application and does not require any interaction with the local environment when run, I want to create it on the database. This allows any of my PL/SQL modules to run it and makes the server perform the operation. How do I create a stored procedure?

Technique

A stored procedure is created with the CREATE PROCEDURE statement and consists of two parts. The procedure specification defines the name of the procedure and its parameters. The procedure body contains the PL/SQL module which is executed when the procedure is run. The procedure body has the same structure as the PL/SQL blocks presented in Chapter 12. It contains a declarative section, an executable section, and an exception section. The syntax used to create a stored procedure that does not contain parameters is shown here:

```
CREATE [OR REPLACE] PROCEDURE procedure_name AS
    Declarative section contains type, variable, and
    local subprogram declarations. (Note: There no
    DECLARE statement.)
BEGIN
    Executable section which is run when the procedure is
    executed.
EXCEPTION
    Optional exception section to handle errors that may
    occur.
END;
```

A stored procedure can contain parameters which may be passed into the procedure, back to the local module, or in both directions. When a parameter is defined in the procedure specification, a name, the parameter mode, and the datatype must be specified. The three possible parameter modes are IN (the default), which represents a parameter passed into the procedure; OUT, which represents a parameter passed back to the calling module; or IN OUT, which represents a parameter passed in both directions. A parameter can be defined with a default value used when the parameter is not specified. A sample procedure specification containing parameters is shown here:

```
CREATE OR REPLACE PROCEDURE Test_Proc
          (dept_no IN VARCHAR2,
           mgr_id OUT NUMBER,
           run_date IN DATE DEFAULT SYSDATE) AS
```

The third parameter shown in the example contains a default parameter. If a value for the run_date parameter is not specified, the current system date is used. When a procedure is called from a PL/SQL module, the parameters can be specified using two methods. *Positional notation* matches the parameter value with the order of the parameters in the procedure specification. A sample call using positional notation is shown here:

```
TEST_PROC(12, mgr_variable)
```

Named notation lets you specify a name for the parameter value, to ensure that the parameter is correct. When using named notation, the order of the parameters is not important. A sample call using named notation is shown here:

```
TEST_PROC(mgr_id => mgr_variable, dept_no => 12)
```

The assignment operator (=>) is used to relate the parameter name with its value. Named parameters ensure that the values are assigned correctly. They may be necessary when a procedure contains more than one default parameter.

Steps

1. Run SQL*Plus and connect as the WAITE user account. Load CHP13-1.sql into the SQL buffer. The CREATE PROCEDURE statement contained in the file creates a simple stored procedure that receives a parameter and displays it.

```
SQL> GET CHP13-1
  1   CREATE OR REPLACE PROCEDURE
  2           CHP13_1 (X IN NUMBER) AS
  3   BEGIN
  4           DBMS_OUTPUT.PUT_LINE('THE PARAMETER IS '||TO_CHAR(X));
  5*  END;
```

Lines 1 and 2 provide the procedure specification of the statement. The CREATE OR REPLACE clause instructs Oracle to create a new trigger if one does not exist, or replace the old one if it does. Line 2 specifies the name of the procedure and provides its parameter line. The parameter X is declared as an IN parameter of the NUMBER datatype. Lines 3 through 5 contain the procedure body. Line 4 displays the parameter passed to the procedure using the DBMS_OUTPUT.PUT_LINE procedure.

2. Run the statement to create the stored procedure.

```
SQL>  /
```

```
Procedure created.
```

Once the stored procedure is created, it can be executed by the procedure owner or any user account granted EXECUTE privileges for it.

3. Load CHP13-2.sql into the SQL buffer. The PL/SQL module contained in the file runs the stored procedure created in the previous step.

```
SQL> GET CHP13-2
  1   BEGIN
  2       CHP13_1(6);
  3*  END;
```

Line 2 calls the stored procedure created in the previous steps and passes it a parameter of 6. When the procedure is executed, the statements contained in the executable section of the procedure are run on the server.

4. Set the SERVEROUTPUT system variable to ON and run the PL/SQL module. Figure 13-1 shows the results of the module within SQL*Plus.

The message displayed by the DBMS_OUTPUT.PUT_LINE procedure contained in the stored procedure is displayed in SQL*Plus. The number displayed in the output line was passed to the stored procedure as a parameter.

5. Load CHP13-3.sql into the SQL buffer. The statement contained in the file creates a stored procedure demonstrating OUT parameters, default parameters, and the declaration of variables within a stored procedure.

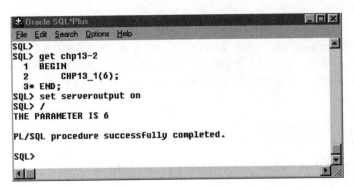

Figure 13-1 The results of a PL/SQL module calling a stored procedure

```
SQL> GET CHP13-3
  1  CREATE OR REPLACE PROCEDURE
  2      CHP13_3 (X IN VARCHAR2, Y OUT VARCHAR2, Z IN NUMBER := 7) AS
  3  LOCAL_VAR VARCHAR2(50);
  4  BEGIN
  5      LOCAL_VAR := X||' '||TO_CHAR(Z);
  6      Y := LOCAL_VAR;
  7* END;
```

Lines 1 and 2 present the procedure specification. Line 2 declares the name of the procedure and specifies its parameter list. Three parameters are passed to the procedure. The first parameter is an IN parameter of the VARCHAR2 datatype. Notice that no length is specified with the datatype. When creating parameters for procedures, do not specify a length for the parameter or an error will occur. The second parameter is an OUT parameter, which is passed back to the local PL/SQL module. The third parameter is an IN parameter, which is optional since a default value is specified. Line 3 declares a local variable for the stored procedure. The DECLARE clause is not used when named PL/SQL blocks, such as procedures and functions, are created. Lines 4 through 7 define the procedure body. The statement in line 4 sets the local variable to a value based on the parameters passed to the procedure. Line 6 sets the output parameter to the local variable. When the procedure is terminated, the value of the OUT parameter is passed back to the calling PL/SQL module.

6. Run the statement to create the stored procedure.

```
SQL>  /

Procedure created.
```

7. Load CHP13-4.sql into the SQL buffer. The PL/SQL module contained in the file runs the stored procedure created in the previous steps, demonstrating the use of parameters.

```
SQL> GET CHP13-4
  1  DECLARE
  2      X    VARCHAR2(30);
  3  BEGIN
  4      CHP13_3 ('HELLO WORLD',X);
  5      DBMS_OUTPUT.PUT_LINE(X);
  6      CHP13_3 (Y => X, X => 'HELLO WORLD', Z => 12);
  7      DBMS_OUTPUT.PUT_LINE(X);
  8* END;
```

Lines 1 and 2 contain the declarative section of the module. The variable declared in line 2 will receive the OUT parameter from the procedure when it is called. Line 4 passes two parameters to the CHP13_3 procedure using positional notation. PL/SQL assigns the values to the parameters based on their location in the parameter list. Since the third parameter in the procedure is optional, the default value will be used. Line 5 displays the results of the OUT parameter using the DBMS_OUTPUT.PUT_LINE procedure. Line 6 calls the same procedure using named notation. The name of the parameter is provided with the value allowing the parameters to be specified in any order. Line 7 displays the value passed back through the OUT parameter.

8. Run the module to display the output created by the procedure. The results of the operation are displayed in Figure 13-2.

Both calls to the stored procedure generate valid output. It doesn't matter whether position notation or named notation is used within your code, as long as the stored procedure can identify the values assigned to the parameters.

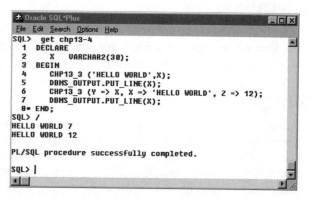

Figure 13-2 The results of the CHP13_3 stored procedure in SQL*Plus

How It Works

Stored procedures are created with the CREATE PROCEDURE statement. Steps 1 and 2 create a simple procedure which receives a parameter and displays it using DBMS_OUTPUT.PUT_LINE. Steps 3 and 4 run the stored procedure created in the first two steps and display its output. Steps 5 and 6 create a stored procedure with three parameters, one of which is assigned a default value. A parameter can be assigned a default value in the procedure specification, making it optional. Step 6 presents the two methods used to pass parameters to the stored procedure. The first call to the procedure uses positional arguments, which sets the parameter values based on their position in the list. The second call to the procedure uses named parameters, which specifies the parameter name with the value. Step 8 shows the output generated by a call to the stored procedure created in Steps 5 and 6.

Comments

Stored procedures allow your applications to perform business functions on the server. They can improve performance and reduce network traffic. Stored procedures promote code reuse by making a business function available to other applications. You should look at each PL/SQL procedure to determine whether it is a candidate for being stored on the database.

COMPLEXITY
INTERMEDIATE

13.2   How do I...
Create a stored function?

Problem

I want to create stored functions that can be used throughout our organization. Stored functions use data from the database and only need to return a result after performing the operation. How do I create a stored function?

Technique

Stored functions are very similar to stored procedures, except that a stored function returns a value and must be called as part of an expression. A function is a named PL/SQL block, which contains a declarative, an execution, and an exception section. For more information about the sections of a PL/SQL block, see How-To 12.1. The structure of a stored function is shown here:

```
CREATE [OR REPLACE] FUNCTION function_name (parameter list)
    AS
    Declarative section contains type, variable, and
    local subprogram declarations. (Note: There is
    no DECLARE statement.)
    BEGIN
```

Executable section which is run when the function is
executed. A RETURN statement must be contained to
return a value.
EXCEPTION
Optional exception section to handle errors that may
occur.
END;

A stored function can accept parameters like a stored procedure. For more
information on passing parameters, see the technique section of How-To 13.1. A stored
function must contain a RETURN statement to return a value back to the calling expression. A function can contain more than one RETURN statement, but only one can
be executed for each call to the function.

Steps

1. Run SQL*Plus and connect as the WAITE user account. Load CHP13-5.sql
into the SQL buffer. The CREATE FUNCTION statement contained in the
file receives a single parameter and returns a character string.

```
SQL> GET CHP13-5
  1  CREATE OR REPLACE FUNCTION
  2      CHP13_5 (X VARCHAR2) RETURN VARCHAR2 AS
  3  BEGIN
  4      RETURN X||' IS THE PARAMETER';
  5* END;
```

Lines 1 and 2 contain the function specification. Line 2 defines the name of
the function, its parameter, and the datatype of the value the function
returns. All functions must include a returned datatype, which must be
contained in the function specification. Lines 3 through 5 specify the body
of the function. Line 4 uses the RETURN statement to return the value of
the parameter concatenated with a text string. A RETURN statement must
be executed when the function is run. It is possible for a function to contain
more than one RETURN statement, but only one can be executed each time
the function is called.

2. Run the statement to create the stored function.

```
SQL> /
```

```
Function created.
```

Once the function is created, it can be used in expressions within PL/SQL
modules owned by the current user, or it can be used by others granted
EXECUTE privilege on the function.

3. Load CHP13-6.sql into the SQL buffer. The PL/SQL statement contained in
the file executes the stored function and displays the value returned.

```
SQL> GET CHP13-6
  1  DECLARE
```

continued on next page

continued from previous page

```
2        VALUE_RETURNED VARCHAR2(80);
3   BEGIN
4        VALUE_RETURNED := CHP13_5('HELLO WORLD');
5        DBMS_OUTPUT.PUT_LINE(VALUE_RETURNED);
6*  END;
```

Lines 1 and 2 contain the declarative section of the block. Line 2 declares a variable assigned the value returned by the function created in the previous steps. Line 4 calls the stored function, passing a string as a parameter and assigning its returned value to the variable created in line 2. Line 5 displays the value of the variable after the function is executed.

4. Set the SERVEROUTPUT system variable to ON and run the statement to display the results. Figure 13-3 shows the results of the operation in SQL*Plus.

When the PL/SQL block is executed, the stored function modifies the parameter passed and returns a value to the local variable. The output of the function is displayed by the DBMS_OUTPUT.PUT_LINE procedure.

How It Works

Stored functions are very similar to stored procedures because they execute a PL/SQL module on the server. Unlike stored procedures, stored functions return a value and must be used in an expression. A stored function can return simple datatypes or record variables. Steps 1 and 2 present a stored function that receives one parameter and returns a VARCHAR2 result. Steps 3 and 4 execute the function to display its operation. Steps 5 and 6 create a stored function returning a record variable from a stored function. The function executes a query and returns the record variable.

Comments

Stored functions can be used like built-in functions within PL/SQL modules and, in many cases, within SQL statements. Stored functions return a single value, and

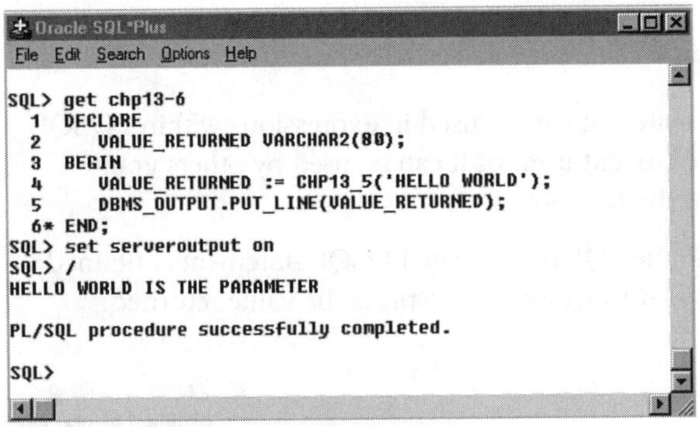

Figure 13-3 The results of a call to the
CHP13_5 stored function

unlike stored procedures, must be used in expressions. Although it is possible to return more than one value from a stored function by using OUT parameters, I do not recommend doing so because it creates code that's difficult to read and maintain. Under certain circumstances, a stored function can be used with SQL statements. How-To 13.9 presents this technique.

COMPLEXITY
BEGINNING

13.3 How do I...
Display compilation errors when creating a stored module?

Problem

After I create a stored procedure or function with compilation errors, I need to be able to view the errors. When I create the procedure or function, a message is returned that the procedure was created with compilation errors, but there is no information about the errors. How do I display compilation errors after creating a procedure?

Technique

Within SQL*Plus, the SHOW ERRORS command displays the errors caused by the last procedure or function created in the session. The USER_ERRORS data dictionary view also contains the compile errors and can be queried at any time. The description of the USER_ERRORS view is shown in Figure 13-4.

One line is contained in the view for each error generated by a module. The NAME column contains the name of the module where the error occurred. The LINE and POSITION columns identify the line number and position where the error occurred. The TEXT column provides a description of the error.

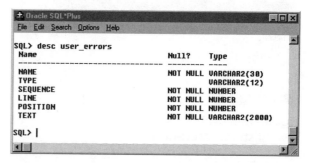

Figure 13-4 USER_ERRORS data dictionary view

Steps

1. Run SQL*Plus and connect as the WAITE user account. CHP13-7.sql, shown in Figure 13-5, creates a stored procedure with compilation errors.

The second line of the statement misspells the datatype of the variable. The invalid datatype will generate errors when the procedure is compiled. Run the file to create the stored procedure.

```
SQL>   START CHP13-7
```

Warning: Procedure created with compilation errors.

When a module is created containing compilation errors, a warning message is displayed in SQL*Plus. The SHOW ERRORS statement can be used in SQL*Plus to display the most recent errors, or the errors can be queried from the USER_ERRORS data dictionary view.

2. Run the SHOW ERRORS command in SQL*Plus to display the errors generated. Figure 13-6 shows the output of the command.

The error created by the misspelled keyword in line 2 generates two compilation errors. The error in line 2 created by the invalid datatype is displayed, and a second error occurs when the variable is used in line 4.

3. Load CHP13-8.sql into the SQL buffer. The file contains a query of the USER_ERRORS data dictionary view to display errors generated when the procedure was compiled.

```
SQL> GET CHP13-8
  1   SELECT
  2     TO_CHAR(LINE)||'/'||TO_CHAR(POSITION) LINE_POS,
  3     TEXT
  4   FROM
  5     USER_ERRORS
  6   WHERE
  7*    NAME = 'CHP13_7'
```

Figure 13-5 CHP13-7.sql creates an invalid stored procedure

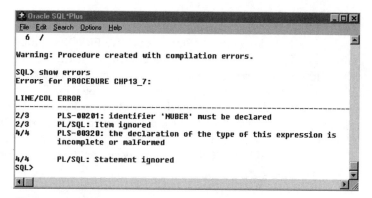

Figure 13-6 The output generated by the SHOW ERRORS statement

Line 2 concatenates the error's line number and position, displaying the column in the same format as the SHOW ERROR command. Line 2 displays the error text generated when the module was compiled. Line 5 specifies the USER_ERRORS data dictionary view as the source of the data. Lines 6 and 7 specify a WHERE clause, displaying the error generated by the sample stored procedure.

4. Run the query to display the errors. Figure 13-7 shows the results of the query in SQL*Plus.

The query displays the same errors as the SHOW ERRORS command. Unlike the SHOW ERRORS command, which only displays the last error generated, the USER_ERRORS data dictionary view contains errors generated by all unsuccessfully compiled modules.

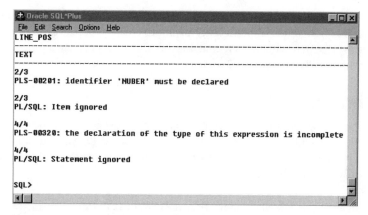

Figure 13-7 The results of the query to display errors

How It Works

When you are working in SQL*Plus, the SHOW ERRORS command displays the errors generated by the last module compiled in the current session. The USER_ERRORS data dictionary view contains the errors generated by all stored modules in the current user's schema. If the creation of a stored module generates no errors, there are no records in the view for the module. Step 1 creates a stored procedure containing an error. Step 2 shows the error contained in the module by running the SHOW ERRORS command in SQL*Plus. Steps 3 and 4 generate the same output by querying the USER_ERRORS view and specifying the sample stored procedure in the WHERE clause.

Comments

The SHOW ERRORS statement in SQL*Plus only works for the last module compiled in the session. If a SQL script is used to create stored modules, the command will not show all the errors generated. The USER_ERRORS view will show you the errors in the current version of the module, no matter when it was compiled.

COMPLEXITY
INTERMEDIATE

13.4 How do I...
Create a procedure or function within a PL/SQL module?

Problem

Within my PL/SQL module, there is repetitive code which could be better designed using procedures and functions. I want to create procedures and functions local to the PL/SQL module which contains them. How do I create a procedure or function within a PL/SQL module?

Technique

Procedures and functions can be created in the declarative section of a PL/SQL module and will be local to the module. The local PL/SQL module can be called anywhere in the module's executable section. The syntax used to create a local procedure is shown here:

```
DECLARE
    PROCEDURE procedure_name (parameter list) IS
        Declaritve Section
    BEGIN
        Executable Section
    EXCEPTION
```

```
        Exception Section
END;
```

A procedure or function created in the declarative section of a PL/SQL block has the same structure as other PL/SQL procedures and functions. They all contain a procedure specification, a declarative section, an executable section, and an exception section. Local functions and procedures can reference other local functions and procedures, as long as the module used was created before the calling module.

Steps

1. Run SQL*Plus and connect as the WAITE user account. Load CHP13-9.sql into the SQL buffer. The file contains a PL/SQL block which declares a function within the declarative section.

```
SQL> GET CHP13-9
  1   DECLARE
  2      FUNCTION HELLO RETURN VARCHAR2 IS
  3      BEGIN
  4          RETURN 'WORLD';
  5      END;
  6   BEGIN
  7      DBMS_OUTPUT.PUT_LINE(HELLO);
  8*  END;
```

Lines 1 through 5 contain the declarative section of the module. Lines 2 through 5 declare a function local to the block. Line 2 contains the function specification for the local function. Lines 3 through 5 contain the executable section of the local function. Line 4 returns the string WORLD any time the function is called. Lines 6 through 8 contain the executable section for the main PL/SQL block. Line 7 uses the local function within the DBMS_OUTPUT.PUT_LINE procedure to display the function output.

2. Set the SERVEROUTPUT system variable to ON and run the PL/SQL code.

```
SQL>  SET SERVEROUTPUT ON
SQL>  /

WORLD

PL/SQL procedure seccessfully completed.
```

The string returned by the local function is displayed by the DBMS_OUTPUT.PUT_LINE procedure. Since the local function always returns the string WORLD, it is displayed within SQL*Plus.

3. Load CHP13-10.sql into the SQL buffer. The PL/SQL block in the file contains a complicated function in the code's declarative section.

```
SQL> GET CHP13-10
  1   DECLARE
  2      FUNCTION SPELL_NUMBER (DEPT_NO IN NUMBER)
  3          RETURN VARCHAR2 IS
  4      TMP VARCHAR2(30);
```

continued on next page

continued from previous page

```
 5        BEGIN
 6          IF DEPT_NO >= 100 OR DEPT_NO < 1 THEN
 7             RETURN NULL;
 8          ELSE
 9           SELECT
10              TO_CHAR(TO_DATE(LPAD(TO_CHAR(DEPT_NO),4,'0'),'YYYY'),'YEAR')
11                INTO TMP
12             FROM
13                DUAL;
14             RETURN TMP;
15          END IF;
16        END;
17   BEGIN
18        DBMS_OUTPUT.PUT_LINE(SPELL_NUMBER(22));
19        DBMS_OUTPUT.PUT_LINE(SPELL_NUMBER(15));
20        DBMS_OUTPUT.PUT_LINE(SPELL_NUMBER(77));
21*  END;
```

Lines 2 through 16 define a function local to the PL/SQL block. Lines 2 and 3 specify the local function. The function receives a numeric parameter and returns a string. The purpose of the function is to convert a number between 1 and 99 to a written text representation. Line 4 declares the TMP variable of the local function. The variable holds the result of a DUAL table query using the TO_CHAR and TO_DATE functions to convert a numeric value to its written representation, shown in line 9. The conditional statement in line 6 returns a NULL value if the parameter is outside the acceptable range. Lines 17 through 21 contain the executable section for the main block. Lines 18 through 20 use the local function within the DBMS_OUTPUT.PUT_LINE procedure to display the output generated by the function.

4. Run the statement to display the output of the function. The results of the module are shown in Figure 13-8.

Each of the three values converted with the local function are displayed in SQL*Plus. The local function allowed the same set of statements to be

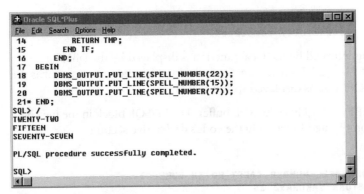

Figure 13-8 The output of the local function in SQL*Plus

executed again and again, without repeating the code or making it accessible to other PL/SQL modules.

5. Load CHP13-11.sql into the SQL buffer. The PL/SQL module within the file contains both a procedure and a function declared in the code's declarative section.

```
SQL> GET CHP13-11
  1  DECLARE
  2     FUNCTION HELLO RETURN VARCHAR2 IS
  3     BEGIN
  4         RETURN 'WORLD';
  5     END;
  6     PROCEDURE CALL_HELLO IS
  7     BEGIN
  8         DBMS_OUTPUT.PUT_LINE(HELLO);
  9     END;
 10  BEGIN
 11     CALL_HELLO;
 12* END;
```

The module demonstrates procedure calling functions within a PL/SQL module. Lines 2 through 5 create a local function returning the value WORLD when called. Lines 6 through 9 define a local procedure calling the function declared just before it. Since the function is declared before the procedure in the module, the function is visible to the procedure. If the order of the procedure and function were reversed, an error would occur. Lines 10 through 12 define the main body of the module, which calls the procedure defined in line 6, which in turn calls the function defined in line 2.

6. Run the statement to display the results of the nested procedure calls. Figure 13-9 shows the output of the module within SQL*Plus.

The output displayed in SQL*Plus was generated by a local procedure calling a local function. The visibility of local procedures and functions depends on the order in which they are declared in the module's declarative

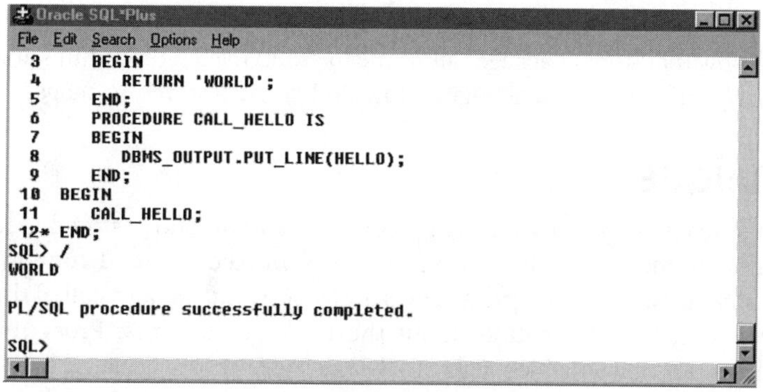

Figure 13-9 The results of the PL/SQL module in SQL*Plus

section. A local procedure or function can be used only if it has been declared first.

How It Works

Local procedures and functions can be defined in the declarations section of a PL/SQL module. The scope of the procedures is local to the module defining them. Steps 1 and 2 present a PL/SQL module that defines a local function within it. The function is called from the main body of the PL/SQL module. Steps 3 and 4 present a PL/SQL module containing a complete function. The function is called repeatedly from the module's main body to demonstrate how local procedures and functions create efficient code. Steps 5 and 6 present a PL/SQL module containing both a procedure and a function. The procedure created in the module calls the function created there. Since the function is declared in the code before the procedure, the function is visible to the procedure. The function cannot call the procedure, because the procedure is defined after the function.

Comments

Procedures and functions should always be used to make your code more modular. If there are sections of code within your PL/SQL module that run repeatedly, consider putting them in local procedures or functions. If they are modules that should be accessible to other applications, consider creating a stored object in the database.

COMPLEXITY
INTERMEDIATE

13.5 How do I...
Create a stored package?

Problem

I want to group related stored procedures and functions and let them share variables. I know that stored packages allow me to group related procedures and functions and have performance advantages. How do I create a stored package?

Technique

A *stored package* is a of related procedures and functions stored together and sharing common variables, as well as local procedures and functions. A package contains two separate parts. The *package specification*, also called the *package header*, contains information about the package contents. Procedures, functions, datatypes, and variables visible to the package user are declared in the package specification. The package specification does not contain any code, it only provides information about the available contents. The *package body* contains the code for the objects defined in the package specification and objects local to the package. The package specification and package body are compiled separately and stored in the data dictionary as two separate objects. The package body is optional and does not need to be created if the package specification does not contain any procedures or functions.

Steps

1. Run SQL*Plus and connect as the WAITE user account. Load CHP13-12.sql into the SQL buffer. The file contains the code to create a package specification.

```
SQL> GET CHP13-12
  1   CREATE OR REPLACE PACKAGE CHP13_12 AS
  2       PROCEDURE PROC1 (X NUMBER);
  3       FUNCTION FUN1 RETURN VARCHAR2;
  4       VAR1 NUMBER;
  5       VAR2 VARCHAR2(30);
  6       VAR3 BOOLEAN;
  7*  END CHP13_12;
```

Line 1 contains the keywords required to create the package specification. Lines 2 through 7 declare the procedures, functions, and variables visible to users of the package. Line 2 declares a procedure, and line 3 declares a function. Lines 4 through 6 declare package variables available to procedures and functions within the package, as well as to users of the package.

2. Run the code to create the package specification.

```
SQL> /

Package created.
```

Once the package is developed, it cannot be used until a package body is created. This is because the package body creates the procedures and functions declared in the package specification.

3. Load CHP13-13.sql into the SQL buffer. The file contains the code required to create the package body for the package developed in the previous step.

```
SQL> GET CHP13-13
  1   CREATE OR REPLACE PACKAGE BODY CHP13_12 AS
  2       PROCEDURE PROC1 (X NUMBER) AS
  3       BEGIN
  4           VAR1 := X;
  5       END;
  6       FUNCTION FUN1 RETURN VARCHAR2 AS
  7       BEGIN
  8           VAR2 := 'HELLO';
  9           RETURN VAR2||' '||TO_CHAR(VAR1);
 10       END;
 11*  END CHP13_12;
```

Line 1 presents the keywords required to create a package body. The procedures and function declared in the package specification must be contained in the package body, or errors will occur. Lines 2 through 5 create the procedure declared in the package specification. Line 4 references a package variable created in the package specification. Package variables are global throughout the package. Lines 6 through 10 create the function declared in the package specification. Line 11 ends the module creating the package body.

4. Run the code to create the package specification.

```
SQL>  /
```

Package body created.

The creation of the package body makes the package available to the current user or any account granted an EXECUTE privilege. When the EXECUTE privilege is granted on the package, the user can execute the procedures and functions, as well as access the global variables and datatypes.

5. Load CHP13-14.sql into the SQL buffer. The PL/SQL block in the file calls the procedures and functions in the stored package.

```
SQL> GET CHP13-14
  1  BEGIN
  2     CHP13_12.VAR3 := TRUE;
  3     CHP13_12.PROC1(1);
  4     DBMS_OUTPUT.PUT_LINE(CHP13_12.FUN1);
  5* END;
```

Line 2 assigns a value directly to a package variable. Variables defined in the package specification can be used by any account with EXECUTE privileges. Line 3 calls the package procedure, passing the required variable. Line 4 calls the package function within the DBMS_OUTPUT.PUT_LINE procedure, to display the output of the function in SQL*Plus.

6. Run the statement to display the results. The results are shown in Figure 13-10.

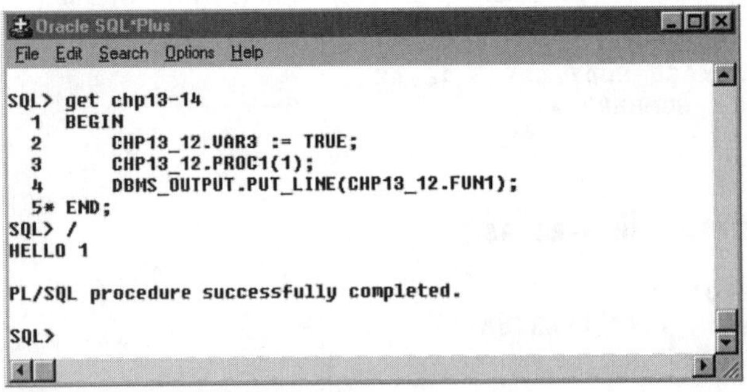

Figure 13-10 The results of executing the package procedure

The call to the package procedure assigns a value to a package variable, which the package function returns. This chain of events displays the parameter passed to the package procedure in SQL*Plus. A stored package allows you to share variables between modules and create global variables.

How It Works

Creating a stored package in PL/SQL requires two separate modules. The package specification defines which procedures, functions, datatypes, cursors, and variables are available to package users. The package body contains the code executed when the procedures and functions are called. Steps 1 and 2 present and create a package specification, which contains a procedure, function, and three variables. Variables defined in a package specification are global to the package and the session. If a package variable is set within a PL/SQL module, it retains its value until changed again or until the session is terminated. Steps 3 and 4 present and create the package body. Each of the procedures and functions declared in the package specification are created in the package body. Failure to do so would generate an error. The procedure and function both use the package variables created in the package specification. The procedure sets a package variable to a value and the function displays its value, showing how variables can be shared using packages. Steps 5 and 6 present a PL/SQL block that uses the stored package and executes it to display the package operation.

Comments

Stored packages let you group common procedures and functions and share variables between them. There are many benefits to packaging stored modules. Anytime you have related procedures that will most likely be run together, they should be grouped in a stored package. Once a stored package is accessed, the entire package is moved into the SGA and prepared to run. Stored packages can be used to create global variables shared between modules.

COMPLEXITY
BEGINNING

13.6 How do I...
View the source code of a stored module?

Problem

Once I have created a stored module, I need to be able to view its source code. Although I keep copies of the scripts that created the modules, I want to look in the data dictionary to be sure that the code is correct. How do I view the source code of a stored module?

Technique

The USER_SOURCE data dictionary view contains the source code of stored modules created by a user account. The description of the view is shown in Figure 13-11.

The view contains one line for each line of source code in the stored module. The TEXT column contains a line of code from the module. The LINE column represents the line number of the module. The NAME column represents the name of the stored object, and the TYPE column represents the type of stored module the code creates. The valid types are PROCEDURE, FUNCTION, PACKAGE, and PACKAGE BODY. In order to view the source code of the stored module, the TEXT column should be queried from the view ordered by the TYPE and LINE columns. The TYPE column must be included, since package specifications and package bodies have the same name.

Steps

1. Run SQL*Plus and connect as the WAITE user account. CHP13-15.sql, shown in Figure 13-12, creates a sample stored procedure which this technique illustrates.

Run the file to create the stored procedure.

```
SQL>   START CHP13-15

Procedure created.
```

2. Load CHP13-16.sql into the SQL buffer. The file contains a query of the USER_SOURCE data dictionary view to display the source code of the sample stored procedure.

```
SQL> GET CHP13-16
  1   SELECT
  2         TEXT
  3   FROM
```

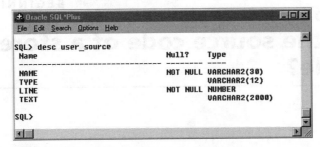

Figure 13-11 The USER_SOURCE data dictionary view

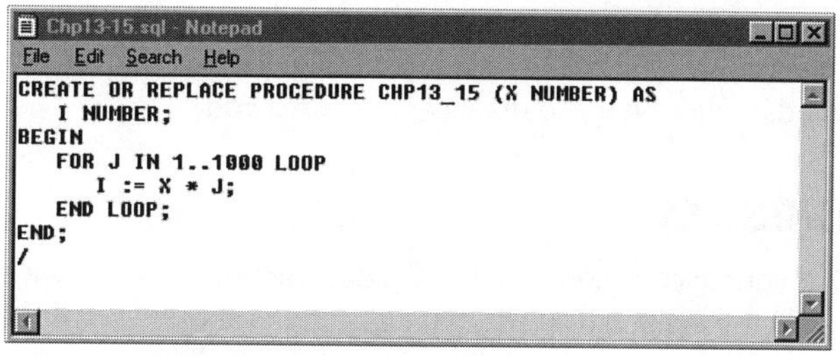

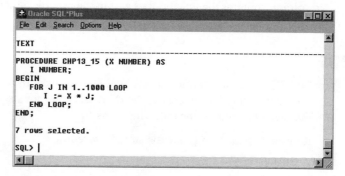

Figure 13-12 CHP13-15.sql creates a sample stored procedure

```
4        USER_SOURCE
5  WHERE
6        NAME = 'CHP13_15'
7* ORDER BY TYPE, LINE
```

Line 2 returns a single line of code for each record returned by the query. Line 4 specifies that the USER_SOURCE view is the data source. The WHERE clause in line 6 specifies that information about the sample stored procedure created in Step 1 will be returned. Line 7 organizes the results in the correct order for the stored procedure.

3. Run the query to display the results, shown in Figure 13-13.

The code contained in the sample stored procedure is displayed exactly as entered. The case of the characters and the code indentation is preserved in the USER_SOURCE data dictionary view.

How It Works

The USER_SOURCE data dictionary view contains the source code for the stored modules within a user account's schema. One row is contained for each line of code, and the code is contained in the TEXT column. The LINE column contains the line

Figure 13-13 The results of the query

number of the module and must be used in the ORDER BY clause to order the code correctly. Step 1 creates a sample table queried in later steps. Steps 2 and 3 query the data dictionary to display the source code.

Comments

The source code contained in the data dictionary will always be correct for the module being executed. If you have questions about the validity of the script files used to create the stored modules, query the data dictionary to compare the source code. How-To 13.7 presents a technique used to rebuild the DDL statements for creating stored modules.

COMPLEXITY
INTERMEDIATE

13.7 How do I...
Rebuild statements to create stored modules?

Problem

I need a technique to rebuild the CREATE statements that built the stored modules in my database. I need the capability of recreating a single module or all modules for a user account's schema. How do I rebuild statements for creating stored modules?

Technique

The USER_SOURCE data dictionary view contains the source code for all the modules in a user account's schema. Each record in the view represents a single line of source code in the stored module. The CREATE OR REPLACE keywords can be concatenated to the first line of the source code using the DECODE function. The LINE column contains the line number within the module, and the TEXT column contains the line of code.

Steps

1. Run SQL*Plus and connect as the WAITE user account. CHP13-17.sql, shown in Figure 13-14, creates the DDL statement for a sample procedure that will be rebuilt in the following steps.

Run the statement to create the stored procedure.

```
SQL> START CHP13-17

Procedure created.
```

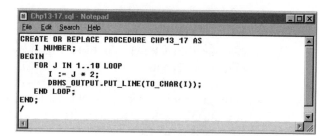

Figure 13-14 CHP13-17.sql creates the sample stored procedure used in How-To 13.7

2. Load CHP13-18.sql into the SQL buffer. The query contained in the file generates a CREATE OR REPLACE statement for a stored module.

```
SQL> GET CHP13-18
  1  SELECT
  2     DECODE(LINE,1,'CREATE OR REPLACE '||TEXT, TEXT)
  3  FROM
  4     USER_SOURCE
  5  WHERE
  6     NAME = '&MODULE_NAME'
  7* ORDER BY NAME, TYPE, LINE
```

Line 2 contains the DECODE function to concatenate the CREATE OR REPLACE keywords with the first line of source code. The first line of code is identified by a value of 1 in the LINE column. Line 4 identifies the USER_SOURCE data dictionary view as the source of the query. The WHERE clause contained in lines 5 and 6 uses a substitution variable that lets the user specify a module. The ORDER BY clause in line 7 ensures that the output of the source code is in the correct order. Including the TYPE column in the ORDER BY clause ensures that the order is correct for stored packages containing two parts.

3. Set the HEADING system variable to OFF to suppress the heading output and run the query. Supply CHP13_17 as the substitution variable, to return the statement that creates the sample procedure from Step 1. Figure 13-15 shows the results of the operation.

The CREATE OR REPLACE keywords are concatenated to the first line of the query to create a valid SQL statement.

4. Load CHP13-19.sql into the SQL buffer. The query contained in the file builds the statements needed to recreate all stored modules for a user's schema.

```
SQL> GET CHP13-19
  1  SELECT
  2     DECODE(LINE,1,'CREATE OR REPLACE '||TEXT, TEXT)
  3  FROM
```

continued on next page

continued from previous page

```
4        USER_SOURCE
5* ORDER BY NAME, TYPE, LINE
```

Line 2 concatenates the CREATE OR REPLACE keywords to the first line of each stored module. The use of the USER_SOURCE data dictionary view in line 4 and the absence of a WHERE clause returns the source code for all modules in the current user account's schema. The ORDER BY clause in line 5 ensures that the source code returned for each module is in order and that each module is separated.

5. Run the statement to display the results. Figure 13-16 shows the results of the operation.

The output shows the last two statements generated for a schema containing many stored modules. In order to save the statements to a file, execute the SPOOL command to write the output to a file.

How It Works

Step 1 creates a stored procedure and function queried from the data dictionary to rebuild the CREATE statements. Step 2 presents a query using the DECODE function to concatenate the CREATE OR REPLACE keywords to the beginning of the first line. Step 3 executes the query to generate a DDL statement for rebuilding the sample procedure. Step 5 presents a query creating the DDL statements needed to rebuild all the stored modules in the current user account's schema.

Comments

There will be times when you want to rebuild a stored module or lose the original source code in order to recreate the DDL statement. As we have done throughout this book, use the data dictionary with SQL*Plus to create DDL statements.

```
  7* ORDER BY NAME, TYPE, LINE
SQL> set heading off
SQL> set feedback off
SQL> /
Enter value for module_name: CHP13_17
old   6:    NAME = '&MODULE_NAME'
new   6:    NAME = 'CHP13_17'

CREATE OR REPLACE PROCEDURE CHP13_17 AS
   I NUMBER;
BEGIN
   FOR J IN 1..10 LOOP
      I := J * 2;
      DBMS_OUTPUT.PUT_LINE(TO_CHAR(I));
   END LOOP;
END;
SQL> |
```

Figure 13-15 The output of the query which rebuilds a stored procedure or function

```
+ Oracle SQL*Plus
File  Edit  Search  Options  Help
CREATE OR REPLACE PROCEDURE REM_FUN1 AS
    Y VARCHAR2(30);
BEGIN
    SELECT X INTO Y FROM DEPT22;
END;
CREATE OR REPLACE PROCEDURE REM_FUN2 AS
BEGIN
    RAISE_APPLICATION_ERROR(-20001,'This is an error');
END;
CREATE OR REPLACE FUNCTION TEST_FUNC (X NUMBER)
        RETURN VARCHAR2 AS
BEGIN
    RETURN TO_CHAR(X);
END;
SQL>
```

Figure 13-16 The output of the query that rebuilds all stored modules for a user account

COMPLEXITY
INTERMEDIATE

13.8 How do I...
Overload procedures and functions in packages?

Problem

I want to create procedures and functions with different parameter lists depending on their use. I know that within a stored package I can declare the same procedure or function many times, as long as the parameter lists are unique. How do I overload procedures and functions in packages?

Technique

PL/SQL allows two or more procedures or functions to have the same name within a package. Overloading is very useful in situations where you want a module to accept different parameter lists. When a package specification is created, the modules in the package are defined with their parameter lists. Each combination of module name and argument list must be unique within the package. The datatypes of the parameters make them unique. The name of the variable has no impact on the uniqueness of the parameter lists.

Steps

1. Run SQL*Plus and connect as the WAITE user account. Load CHP13-20.sql into the SQL buffer. The package specification in the file defines overloaded procedures.

```
SQL> GET CHP13-20
  1   CREATE OR REPLACE PACKAGE CHP13_20 AS
  2       PROCEDURE PROC1 (X NUMBER);
  3       PROCEDURE PROC1 (X VARCHAR2, Y NUMBER);
  4       PROCEDURE PROC1 (X VARCHAR2);
  5*  END CHP13_20;
```

Line 1 presents the keywords required to create a package specification. Lines 2 through 4 define the same function with three different parameter lists. When the package body is created, each of the procedure declarations listed in the package specification must be created. The datatypes of the parameters in the overloaded procedures must be unique in order for PL/SQL to identify the correct instance of the procedure to be used.

2. Run the statement to create the package header.

```
SQL> /
```

Package created.

After the package specification is created, each of the procedures must be created in the package body, or an error will occur.

3. Load CHP13-21.sql into the SQL buffer. The code created in the file creates the package body for the package developed in the previous step.

```
SQL> GET CHP13-21
  1   CREATE OR REPLACE PACKAGE BODY CHP13_20 AS
  2       PROCEDURE PROC1 (X NUMBER) AS
  3       BEGIN
  4           DBMS_OUTPUT.PUT_LINE('FIRST SPECIFICATION USED');
  5       END;
  6       PROCEDURE PROC1 (X VARCHAR2, Y NUMBER) AS
  7       BEGIN
  8           DBMS_OUTPUT.PUT_LINE('SECOND SPECIFICATION USED');
  9       END;
 10       PROCEDURE PROC1 (X VARCHAR2) AS
 11       BEGIN
 12           DBMS_OUTPUT.PUT_LINE('THIRD SPECIFICATION USED');
 13       END;
 14*  END CHP13_20;
```

Line 1 provides the keywords necessary to create or replace the package body. Lines 2 though 5 create the first of three versions of the overloaded procedure. Lines 6 through 9 create the second version of the procedure, and lines 10 through 13 create the third version. Each of the three procedure versions is displayed using the DBMS_OUTPUT package.

4. Run the statement to create the package body.

```
SQL>   /
```

Package created.

Once the package is created, the user can call the package procedures with any of the parameter lists specified. The instance of the procedure used depends upon the parameter list provided.

5. Load CHP13-22.sql into the SQL buffer. The PL/SQL module in the file calls the overloaded procedure with the three different parameter lists.

```
SQL> GET CHP13-22
  1  BEGIN
  2      CHP13_20.PROC1('X');
  3      CHP13_20.PROC1(1);
  4      CHP13_20.PROC1('X',1);
  5* END;
```

Line 2 calls the overloaded procedure passing a VARCHAR2 parameter, executing the third version of the procedure from the package. Line 3 calls the procedure passing a NUMBER parameter to the function, executing the first version. Line 4 passes a VARCHAR2 and a NUMBER parameter to the procedure, executing the second version of the procedure.

6. Run the PL/SQL code to display the results. Figure 13-17 shows the results of the three procedure calls in SQL*Plus.

When the procedure is called with the different parameter lists, different instances of the procedure are used, depending on the list. The DBMS_OUTPUT.PUT_LINE statement in each procedure version identifies the one used.

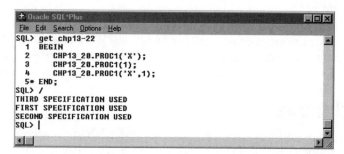

Figure 13-17 The results of the overloaded procedure calls in SQL*Plus

How It Works

Step 1 presents a package specification declaring three procedures with the same name but different parameter lists. The instance of procedure executed depends on the number and datatypes of the parameters. Step 3 presents the package body containing the overloaded procedures. Each procedure defined in the package specification must be created in the package body, or an error will occur. The DBMS_OUTPUT.PUT_LINE procedure displays a message from each procedure to identify the instance executed. Steps 5 and 6 call the procedures with different parameters, executing the different instances.

Comments

Overloading procedures and functions can simplify your applications by expanding the capabilities of a module. Overloaded modules are used throughout Oracle, although you might not notice. An example of an overloaded function is TO_CHAR, which receives a variety of parameters with different datatypes performing the same function.

COMPLEXITY
INTERMEDIATE

13.9 How do I...
Use a stored function in a SQL statement?

Problem

I have created a stored function that is passed columns from a query and parameters. I want to use the stored function in a SQL statement directly. I do not want to return the values from the query, and then call the function. Instead, I want to call the function as part of the query. How do I use a stored function in a SQL statement?

Technique

Ever since the release of PL/SQL version 2.1 (Oracle version 7.1), stored functions can be called during the execution of SQL statements with certain limitations. Programmer-created stored functions can be used like the functions presented in Chapter 10, but must meet certain conditions depending on how they are used. No stored function used in a SQL statement is allowed to modify data, and no procedures or functions called by the function can modify data. If the SQL statement is executed on a remote computer via a database link, the function cannot write to package variables. Only local functions used in the SELECT, SET, or VALUES clauses can write package variables. Parameters used in these functions cannot be OUT parameters or IN OUT parameters and must be defined as a database datatype. The database datatypes are CHAR, DATE, LONG, LONG RAW, NUMBER, ROWID, and VARCHAR2. PL/SQL datatypes such as BOOLEAN are not allowed as parameters or return types.

Steps

1. Run SQL*Plus and connect as the WAITE user account. CHP13-23.sql, shown in Figure 13-18, creates the table and stored function used throughout this How-To.

The sample table contains a text and numeric column and is populated with three records. The sample function receives two parameters and returns a string generated by modifying the parameters. Run the statement to create the sample objects.

```
SQL> START CHP13-23

Table created.

Function created.

1 row created.

1 row created.

1 row created.

Commit complete.
```

```
CREATE TABLE SAMPLE1323 (
    TEXT      VARCHAR2(20),
    LEN       NUMBER(5));

CREATE OR REPLACE FUNCTION CHP13_23 (T VARCHAR2, L NUMBER)
    RETURN VARCHAR2 AS
    TMP VARCHAR2(20);
BEGIN
    TMP := SUBSTR(T,1,L);
    RETURN TO_CHAR(L)||' '||TMP;
END;
/

INSERT INTO SAMPLE1323
    VALUES ('THIS IS A TEST', 5);

INSERT INTO SAMPLE1323
    VALUES ('OF A STORED FUNCTION', 10);

INSERT INTO SAMPLE1323
    VALUES ('WITHIN A QUERY',8);

COMMIT;
```

Figure 13-18 CHP13-23.sql creates the sample table and stored function used in How-To 13.9

2. Load CHP13-24.sql into the SQL buffer. The file contains a query which uses the stored function created in the previous step.

```
SQL> GET CHP13-24
  1  SELECT
  2      TEXT, LEN, CHP13_23(TEXT,LEN)
  3  FROM
  4*     SAMPLE1323
```

Line 2 returns the two columns contained in the sample table and stored function that uses the columns as parameters. The result of the function is displayed as a column in the query. Since the sample table contains three records, the function will execute three times. Each time the function is executed, the TEXT and LEN columns from the current record are used as parameters.

3. Run the statement to display the results.

```
SQL>  /

TEXT                          LEN CHP13_23(TEXT,LEN)
-------------------- --------- --------------------------------
THIS IS A TEST          5 5 THIS
OF A STORED FUNCTION         10 10 OF A STORE
WITHIN A QUERY                       8 8 WITHIN A
```

The CHP13_23 stored function is executed once for each record returned by the query. The columns returned by the query are used as function parameters to generate the third column. The datatype of the column displayed, is the datatype of the return value of the function.

How It Works

Ever since the release of PL/SQL 2.1, which is available with database version 7.1, stored functions can be used within SQL statements under certain conditions. When a function is used in a SELECT statement, it is executed once for each record the query returns. Step 1 creates a stored function called in the later steps by a SQL statement. The simple function returns a character string calculating a result based on the parameters passed to it. Steps 2 and 3 reference the stored function in a SQL statement. The output displayed in Step 3 shows the output of the function for each row the query returned.

Comments

Using stored functions within SQL statements lets you save steps in your operations. Columns returned by the query can be used as parameters for stored functions, to generate complex output from the query. Stored functions cannot be used in SQL statements if they modify data in the database.

CHAPTER 14
BUILT-IN PACKAGES

BUILT-IN PACKAGES

How do I...

Built-in packages are provided by Oracle to extend the functionality of the database. Oracle's modular approach allows new features to be added while maintaining compatibility with existing versions. Built-in packages contain functions and procedures that perform many tasks that would otherwise be impossible, or at least very difficult, to execute. With each new release, Oracle extends the functionality of the database by including new built-in packages. Many of the How-Tos presented in this chapter require PL/SQL versions 2.1, 2.2, or 2.3. The PL/SQL version required to perform each How-To is provided at the beginning of the How-To. The examples used throughout the chapter can be found in the \SAMPLES\CHAP14 directory of the accompanying CD.

14.1   Schedule programs within Oracle

It is very likely that within one or more of your applications, you need to perform some process at a regularly scheduled interval or need to schedule a program to be executed later. The DBMS_JOB package, available in PL/SQL version 2.2 and higher, allows you to schedule a single or recurring job. This How-To explores the use of the DBMS_JOB package to schedule programs within Oracle.

14.2   Execute dynamic SQL statements

The ability to execute dynamic SQL statements within PL/SQL greatly extends the tasks you can perform. The DBMS_SQL package, available in PL/SQL version 2.1 and higher, allows you to create, parse, and send a SQL statement to the database at runtime. This allows you to build SQL statements based on the results of actions or queries performed at runtime. This How-To presents the technique used to execute dynamic SQL statements.

14.3   Execute an action based on an event
in the database

It is sometimes necessary to perform an action when an event occurs in the database or to broadcast an event to other processes. The DBMS_ALERT package allows events to be recognized and notification of them to occur asynchronously within the database. This How-To explores using the DBMS_ALERT package within Oracle.

14.4   Send an Oracle*Mail message in PL/SQL

An Oracle*Mail message can be sent directly from a PL/SQL module using the DBMS_MAIL package. Oracle*Mail must be installed on the database in order for the package to appear in your database. This How-To presents the DBMS_MAIL package to send Oracle*Mail messages through PL/SQL.

14.5   Communicate between Oracle sessions

Messages can be sent between Oracle processes by using the DBMS_PIPE package. Named pipes referenced by one or more processes can be created in the database. This How-To presents the method used to pass messages between processes using DBMS_PIPE.

14.6   Read and write operating system files

The UTL_FILE package, available in PL/SQL version 2.3 and higher, allows you to read and write operating system files through PL/SQL. Files can be written on the server system by creating stored procedures or functions that use the UTL_FILE package. Files can be written on the client system by using the UTL_FILE package in client-side PL/SQL modules.

14.7   Use comma separated lists in PL/SQL

Comma separated lists can be moved in and out of PL/SQL tables using procedures in the DBMS_UTILITY package. The COMMA_TO_TABLE procedure converts a comma separated list into a PL/SQL table, and the TABLE_TO_COMMA procedure converts a PL/SQL table into a comma separated list. This How-To presents the method used to work with comma separated lists in PL/SQL.

COMPLEXITY
ADVANCED

14.1 How do I...
Schedule programs within Oracle?

COMPATIBILITY: PL/SQL VERSION 2.2

Problem

In our application, I have some processes that need to be run regularly to update data and perform calculations. In our client/server environment, it is very hard to schedule recurring jobs. When we run Unix as our server operating system we can schedule *cron* jobs that make the operating system schedule recurring programs, but we want our database applications to be operating system independent. How do I schedule programs within Oracle?

Technique

The DBMS_JOB package contains procedures to submit jobs for execution and manage batch processes. The DBMS_JOB package contains ten procedures used to manage the scheduling of jobs. Table 14-1 contains the procedures in the DBMS_JOB package.

PROCEDURE	DESCRIPTION
BROKEN	Terminates the scheduling of a job by marking the program as broken.
CHANGE	Allows the modification of one or more attributes of a job.
INTERVAL	Changes the interval that the job runs.
SUBMIT	Sends a job to the queue with a specified job number.
NEXT_DATE	Changes the date when a queued job is to be run.
REMOVE	Removes a job from the queue.
RUN	Executes a job immediately.
SUBMIT	Submits a job to the queue.
USER_EXPORT	Returns a job string associated with a job number.
WHAT	Changes the program on which the job is to run.

Table 14-1 Modules in the DBMS_JOB package

The SUBMIT procedure is used to send a job to the queue. Each job submitted to the queue is given a unique job number for identification. To remove a job from the queue, use the REMOVE procedure. If a job attempts to run and fails three times

```
SQL> desc user_jobs
 Name                            Null?    Type
 ------------------------------- -------- ----
 JOB                             NOT NULL NUMBER
 LOG_USER                        NOT NULL VARCHAR2(30)
 PRIV_USER                       NOT NULL VARCHAR2(30)
 SCHEMA_USER                     NOT NULL VARCHAR2(30)
 LAST_DATE                                DATE
 LAST_SEC                                 VARCHAR2(8)
 THIS_DATE                                DATE
 THIS_SEC                                 VARCHAR2(8)
 NEXT_DATE                       NOT NULL DATE
 NEXT_SEC                                 VARCHAR2(8)
 TOTAL_TIME                               NUMBER
 BROKEN                                   VARCHAR2(1)
 INTERVAL                        NOT NULL VARCHAR2(200)
 FAILURES                                 NUMBER
 WHAT                                     VARCHAR2(2000)
 CURRENT_SESSION_LABEL                    RAW MLSLABEL
 CLEARANCE_HI                             RAW MLSLABEL
 CLEARANCE_LO                             RAW MLSLABEL
 NLS_ENV                                  VARCHAR2(2000)
 MISC_ENV                                 RAW(32)

SQL> |
```

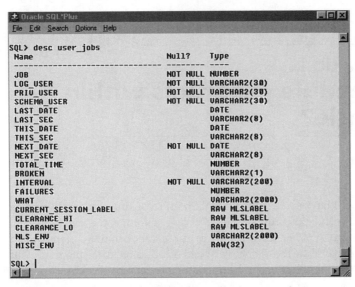

Figure 14-1 The USER_JOBS data dictionary view in SQL*Plus

in a row, it is marked as broken and stops running. The jobs currently in the queue can be viewed by querying the USER_JOBS data dictionary view shown in Figure 14-1.

Steps

1. Run SQL*Plus and connect as the WAITE user account. CHP14-1.sql, shown in Figure 14-2, creates the table and stored procedure used in this How-To. The stored procedure will be executed using the DBMS_JOB package and inserts a record into the table each time it runs.

```
CREATE TABLE LOG_TABLE (
     RUN_DATE    DATE);

CREATE OR REPLACE PROCEDURE LOG_PROC AS
BEGIN
   INSERT INTO LOG_TABLE
       VALUES (SYSDATE);
   COMMIT;
END;
/
```

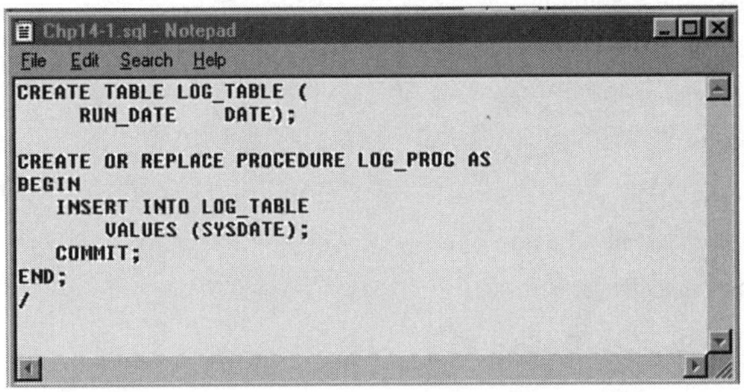

Figure 14-2 CHP14-1.sql creates the sample table and stored procedure used in How-To 14.1

The script creates a table containing a date column. The stored procedure created inserts a record with the date and time into the table each time it runs. Querying the sample table makes it easy to determine when the stored procedure last ran. Run the statement to create the sample table and stored procedure.

```
SQL>   START CHP14-1

Table created.

Procedure created.
```

2. Load CHP14-2.sql into the SQL buffer. The PL/SQL code contained in the file will schedule the stored procedure to run every other minute throughout the day.

```
SQL> GET CHP14-2
   1   DECLARE
   2       JOB_NUM INTEGER;
   3   BEGIN
   4       DBMS_JOB.SUBMIT (
   5               JOB_NUM,
   6               'LOG_PROC;',
   7               SYSDATE + 1/1440,
   8               'SYSDATE + 1/1440',
   9               FALSE);
  10       DBMS_OUTPUT.PUT_LINE('JOB NUMBER = '||TO_CHAR(JOB_NUM));
  11*  END;
```

Line 2 declares a variable to be passed the job number as an OUT parameter from the SUBMIT function. Lines 4 through 9 call the DBMS_JOB.SUBMIT procedure to schedule the procedure. The first parameter, shown in line 5, is an OUT parameter that returns the job number. The second parameter, shown in line 6, specifies the procedure scheduled to run. The third parameter, shown in line 7, is a date value including both the date and time. The value of the parameter is the current date and time, plus two minutes. If the value of the parameter is before SYSDATE, the job will never begin running. The fourth parameter, shown in line 8, is a VARCHAR2 parameter which specifies the scheduling algorithm used to set the procedure's later executions. Each time the job is executed, the scheduling algorithm provided in line 8 calculates the next time to run the job. If you want to schedule times less than a day apart, as line 8 does, add a fraction of a day. The last parameter, shown in line 9, specifies whether the procedure to be called should be re-parsed. Specifying FALSE makes Oracle trust that the stored procedure is valid. Line 10 displays the job number returned by the procedure by using the DBMS_OUTPUT package.

3. Set the SERVEROUTPUT system variable to ON to display the output from the PL/SQL module, and run the statement to schedule the job.

```
SQL>  SET SERVEROUTPUT ON
SQL>  /

JOB NUMBER = 1

PL/SQL procedure completed successfully.
```

4. Load CHP14-3.sql into the SQL buffer. The query contained in the file queries the USER_JOBS data dictionary view to show the scheduled jobs for the current user account.

```
SQL> GET CHP14-3
  1   SELECT
  2     JOB,
  3     TO_CHAR(NEXT_DATE,'MM/DD/YY HH24:MI:SS') NEXT_DATE,
  4     SUBSTR(WHAT,1,20) WHAT
  5   FROM
  6*    USER_JOBS
```

The JOB column specified in line 2 returns the job number of the scheduled job. The NEXT_DATE column specified in line 3 is formatted with the TO_CHAR function to display both the date and time portions of the date. The value contained in the NEXT_DATE column is the next date the procedure will be executed. The WHAT column shown in line 4 returns the name of the procedure to be executed.

5. Format the WHAT column in SQL*Plus with the COLUMN command and run the statement to perform the query.

```
SQL>  FORMAT WHAT FORMAT A30
SQL>  /

  JOB  NEXT_DATE           WHAT
-------- -------------------- --------------------------------
    1  05/14/96 11:30:22   LOG_PROC;
```

The stored procedure created in step 1 was scheduled by the PL/SQL module in step 3 and is displayed by the query. The value of the NEXT_DATE column depends on the date and time you scheduled the job.

6. Load CHP14-4.sql into the SQL buffer. The query contained in the file returns any records in the table created in step 1. Each time the scheduled job is run, a record is inserted into the table.

```
SQL> GET CHP14-4
  1   SELECT
  2     TO_CHAR(RUN_DATE,'MM/DD/YY HH24:MI:SS') RUN_DATE
  3   FROM
  4*    LOG_TABLE
```

Line 2 returns the RUN_DATE column formatted with the TO_CHAR function to display the date and time the procedure ran. The FROM clause in lines 3 and 4 specifies that the table created in step 1 is the source of data.

7. Run the statement to view records inserted into the table. The longer you wait before running the query, the more records will be contained in the table.

```
SQL>  /

RUN_DATE
-----------------
05/14/96 11:30:22
05/14/96 11:31:22
05/14/96 11:32:22
```

8. If the program is allowed to run over a long period of time, the table will grow very large. The REMOVE procedure is used to delete a job from the queue. Load CHP14-5.sql into the SQL buffer. The file contains PL/SQL code to remove the job scheduled. If the job number returned by the job created in step 2 is not the same as the number used in the REMOVE procedure, modify line 2 of the module and provide your job number as the parameter to the DBMS_JOB.REMOVE procedure.

```
SQL>  GET CHP14-5
  1   BEGIN
  2      DBMS_JOB.REMOVE(1);
  3*  END;
```

The REMOVE procedure receives the job number as its only parameter. The USER_JOBS view was used in Steps 4 and 5 to determine the job number.

9. Run the statement to remove the job.

```
SQL>  /

PL/SQL successfully completed.
```

Once the DBMS_JOB.REMOVE procedure has been executed, the job will no longer run. In order to start the job again, the SUBMIT function must be executed.

How It Works

The DBMS_JOB package contains a complete set of procedures for managing job scheduling within Oracle. The SUBMIT procedure is used to submit a job for execution either once, or repeatedly. After jobs have been scheduled, the REMOVE procedure is used to remove a scheduled job from the queue. Jobs scheduled for execution by the user connected to the database can be found in the USER_JOBS data dictionary view. Step 1 creates a sample table and stored procedure used in this How-To. The table contains a DATE field used to track the execution times of the sample stored procedure. The stored procedure inserts the system date and time into the table each time it runs. Steps 2 and 3 schedule the sample procedure to be executed every other minute, by specifying SYSDATE + 1/1440 as the execution interval time. Steps 4 and

5 query the USER_JOBS data dictionary view to display information about the job scheduled in the prior steps. Steps 6 and 7 query the sample table to view how often the scheduled job is running. The longer the job is allowed to run, the more records that will be created in the sample table. Steps 8 and 9 use the REMOVE procedure from the DBMS_JOB package to cancel execution of the scheduled job.

Comments

The DBMS_JOB package lets you schedule batch processes independent of the operating system. Whenever possible, it is best to have Oracle schedule jobs because the scheduling code is portable to any platform Oracle runs on. If you schedule batch processing within the operating system, your applications are no longer portable between operating systems.

COMPLEXITY
INTERMEDIATE

14.2 How do I...
Execute dynamic SQL statements?

COMPATIBILITY: PL/SQL VERSION 2.1

Problem

I do not always know the SQL statements that need to be executed in a PL/SQL procedure. The SQL statement is executed after some processing work is done to determine what action to take. Sometimes I use the results of a query in the SQL statements I want to process later. How do I execute dynamic SQL statements in PL/SQL?

Technique

Throughout this book we have used the data dictionary and SQL*Plus to create command files to execute a set of actions. The PL/SQL package DBMS_SQL performs the same type of operation. The DBMS_SQL package allows a SQL statement to be created, parsed, and executed dynamically at runtime. Table 14-2 shows the procedures and functions making up the DBMS_SQL package.

NAME	TYPE	DESCRIPTION
BIND_VARIABLE	Procedure	Binds a value to a host variable.
CLOSE_CURSOR	Procedure	Closes the specified cursor.
COLUMN_VALUE	Procedure	Retrieves a column value from a cursor into a variable.
DEFINE_COLUMN	Procedure	Defines a column in an existing cursor.
EXECUTE	Function	Executes the specified cursor.

NAME	TYPE	DESCRIPTION
EXECUTE_AND_FETCH	Function	Executes the specified cursor and fetches its rows.
FETCH_ROWS	Function	Fetches the rows from the specified cursor.
IS_OPEN	Function	Returns TRUE if the cursor is open, FALSE otherwise.
LAST_ERROR_POSITION	Function	Returns the location of the error in the SQL statement.
LAST_ROW_COUNT	Function	Returns the number of rows returned by the cursor.
LAST_ROW_ID	Function	Returns the ROWID of the last record fetched.
LAST_SQL_FUNCTION_CODE	Function	Returns the SQL Function code for the last statement.
OPEN_CURSOR	Function	Opens a cursor and returns its handle.
PARSE	Function	Parses the specified statement.
VARIABLE_VALUE	Procedure	Gets the value of a variable in a cursor.

Table 14-2 The modules in the DBMS_SQL package

When executing SQL statements with the DBMS_SQL package, the first step is to create a cursor with the OPEN_CURSOR function. The PARSE procedure is then used to parse the SQL statement and prepare it for execution. The EXECUTE function executes the cursor once it's been parsed. Column values from the cursor can be returned to the local PL/SQL module by binding local variables to the columns, using the DEFINE_COLUMN procedure, retrieving a record with the FETCH function, and using the COLUMN_VALUES procedure to move the values to the variable.

Steps

1. Run SQL*Plus and connect as the WAITE user account. Load CHP14-6.sql into the SQL buffer. The file contains PL/SQL code using the DBMS_SQL package to execute a dynamic SQL statement.

```
SQL> GET CHP14-6
  1   DECLARE
  2     TMP VARCHAR2(60);
  3     CURSOR_HANDLE INTEGER;
  4     CNT NUMBER;
  5     BEGIN
  6       TMP := 'SELECT ''X'' FROM DUAL';
  7       CURSOR_HANDLE := DBMS_SQL.OPEN_CURSOR;
  8       DBMS_SQL.PARSE(CURSOR_HANDLE, TMP, DBMS_SQL.V7);
  9       CNT := DBMS_SQL.EXECUTE(CURSOR_HANDLE);
 10       DBMS_SQL.CLOSE_CURSOR(CURSOR_HANDLE);
 11*   END;
```

Line 2 declares a variable containing a SQL statement to be executed. Line 3 declares a variable containing a handle for the cursor when it is created. Line 6 creates a SQL statement and puts it into the TMP variable. These lines could create any valid SQL statement to be executed dynamically.

Line 6 executes the OPEN_CURSOR function from the DBMS_SQL package to create a cursor and return its handle to the PL/SQL variable. Line 8 parses the statement to be executed using the PARSE procedure. The procedure is passed the cursor handle, the variable containing the SQL statement, and the DBMS_SQL.V7 constant. Line 9 uses the EXECUTE function from the DBMS_SQL package to execute the SQL statement and returns the number of rows processed if it is an INSERT, UPDATE, or DELETE statement. Line 10 closes the cursor.

2. Run the statement.

```
SQL>  /

PL/SQL procedure executed successfully.
```

3. If an exception is returned by the dynamic SQL statement, the exception must be handled in the PL/SQL code or an error will occur. Load CHP14-7.sql into the SQL buffer. The PL/SQL code creates a dynamic SQL statement containing an error.

```
SQL> GET CHP14-7
  1   DECLARE
  2    TMP VARCHAR2(60);
  3    CURSOR_HANDLE INTEGER;
  4    CNT NUMBER;
  5    BEGIN
  6       TMP := 'SELECT FROM DUAL';
  7       CURSOR_HANDLE := DBMS_SQL.OPEN_CURSOR;
  8       DBMS_SQL.PARSE(CURSOR_HANDLE, TMP, DBMS_SQL.V7);
  9       CNT := DBMS_SQL.EXECUTE(CURSOR_HANDLE);
 10       DBMS_SQL.CLOSE_CURSOR(CURSOR_HANDLE);
 11   EXCEPTION
 12     WHEN OTHERS THEN
 13          DBMS_OUTPUT.PUT_LINE(_ERROR OCCURED );
 14*  END;
```

Lines 11 through 13 handle any exceptions occurring with a WHEN OTHERS exception handler. Line 6 creates a SQL statement missing the FROM clause, causing an exception when parsed. Exceptions occurring in any of the DBMS_SQL package modules will be handled by the exception handler in the local PL/SQL block.

4. Run the statement to display the handling of the error.

```
SQL>  /

ERROR OCCURED
PL/SQL procedure executed successfully.
```

5. In order to return rows from a dynamic query, the columns must be passed to local variables in the procedure. Load CHP14-8.sql into the SQL buffer. The file contains PL/SQL code which performs a query and returns the results to the local PL/SQL block.

```
SQL> GET CHP14-8
  1   DECLARE
  2      TMP VARCHAR2(60);
  3      CURSOR_HANDLE INTEGER;
  4      COL1    NUMBER;
  5      COL2    VARCHAR2(80);
  6      CNT     NUMBER;
  7   BEGIN
  8      TMP := 'SELECT ROWNUM, VIEW_NAME FROM ALL_VIEWS';
  9      TMP := TMP||' WHERE ROWNUM <= 10';
 10      CURSOR_HANDLE := DBMS_SQL.OPEN_CURSOR;
 11      DBMS_SQL.PARSE(CURSOR_HANDLE, TMP, DBMS_SQL.V7);
 12      DBMS_SQL.DEFINE_COLUMN(CURSOR_HANDLE, 1, COL1);
 13      DBMS_SQL.DEFINE_COLUMN(CURSOR_HANDLE, 2, COL2, 80);
 14      CNT := DBMS_SQL.EXECUTE(CURSOR_HANDLE);
 15      LOOP
 16          IF DBMS_SQL.FETCH_ROWS(CURSOR_HANDLE) = 0 THEN
 17              EXIT;
 18          ELSE
 19              DBMS_SQL.COLUMN_VALUE(CURSOR_HANDLE, 1, COL1);
 20              DBMS_SQL.COLUMN_VALUE(CURSOR_HANDLE, 2, COL2);
 21              DBMS_OUTPUT.PUT_LINE(TO_CHAR(COL1)||' - '||COL2);
 22          END IF;
 23      END LOOP;
 24      DBMS_SQL.CLOSE_CURSOR(CURSOR_HANDLE);
 25* END;
```

The SQL statement created in lines 8 and 9 returns one NUMBER and one VARCHAR2 column. The variables used to retrieve the columns are declared in lines 4 and 5. Line 10 opens a cursor for the process, using the OPEN_CURSOR function. Line 11 parses the SQL statement using the PARSE procedure. Lines 12 and 13 use the DEFINE_COLUMN procedure to identify the variables which are the destination for the column values. Line 14 executes the statement and builds the cursor. The LOOP statement from lines 15 through 23 processes the rows of the cursor by executing the FETCH_ROWS function shown in line 16. If the function returns 0, there are no more records in the cursor and the loop is exited. The COLUMN_VALUE procedures in lines 19 and 20 are used to move the values from the record in the cursor to the variables in the PL/SQL code.

6. Run the statement to display the results.

```
SQL>  /
1 - ACCESSIBLE_TABLES
2 - ALL_CATALOG
3 - ALL_CLUSTERS
4 - ALL_CLUSTER_HASH_EXPRESSIONS
5 - ALL_COL_COMMENTS
6 - ALL_COL_GRANTS_MADE
7 - ALL_COL_GRANTS_RECD
8 - ALL_COL_PRIVS
9 - ALL_COL_PRIVS_MADE
10 - ALL_COL_PRIVS_RECD

PL/SQL procedure successfully completed.
```

How It Works

The DBMS_SQL package is used to execute dynamic SQL statements and return the results to the local PL/SQL code. The OPEN_CURSOR function is used to open a cursor and return its handle. The cursor handle is used in the PARSE procedure to parse the SQL statement passed to the function. The EXECUTE function is used to execute the SQL statement after it has been parsed. To return values from the cursor back to the local PL/SQL code, the DEFINE_COLUMN procedure identifies which local variable receives which column. The COLUMN_VALUE procedure is used to move the value from the cursor to the variable. When you are finished with the cursor, the CLOSE_CURSOR procedure is used to close the cursor. Steps 1 and 2 execute a SQL statement without returning values to the local PL/SQL code. The steps followed in the PL/SQL module are open cursor, parse, and execute. Steps 3 and 4 present exception handling routines in a PL/SQL module using dynamic SQL. When dynamic SQL is used, the local PL/SQL module is expected to handle any exceptions that occur. Steps 5 and 6 present a PL/SQL module returning column values from the SQL statement to the local module. The DEFINE_COLUMN procedure binds each of the columns of a local variable. The FETCH_ROWS procedure returns the record from the cursor into the local workspace. The COLUMN_VALUE procedure moves the values into the local PL/SQL module.

Comments

Dynamic SQL, available in PL/SQL 2.1 with RDBMS version 7.1, may be one of the most valuable advancements in Oracle for application developers. The ability to create SQL statements within PL/SQL, parse, and execute them at runtime adds a new dimension to application development. If you want to see an advanced example of dynamic SQL, look at How-Tos 7.3 and 7.4. The DBA_TOOLS package provided on the accompanying CD uses dynamic SQL to perform many database management tasks. If you have held off upgrading your database to version 7.1, dynamic SQL may be one of the most important reasons to upgrade.

COMPLEXITY
INTERMEDIATE

14.3 How do I...
Execute an action based on an event in the database?

COMPATIBILITY: PL/SQL VERSION 2.1

Problem

I want my application to be alerted when certain events take place in the database. I do not want to continuously query an object to determine if the event has occurred; I want to be notified by the database. How do I execute an action based on an event in the database?

Technique

The DBMS_ALERT package is used to alert a session when an event occurs in the database. Your session registers its interest in an alert, and the alert signals the session when the event occurs. Table 14-3 shows the modules contained in the DBMS_ALERT package.

NAME	TYPE	DESCRIPTION
REGISTER	Procedure	Registers that your session is interested in an alert.
REMOVE	Procedure	Notifies the database that your session is no longer interested in an alert.
REMOVEALL	Procedure	Removes your session from all alert registration lists.
SET_DEFAULTS	Procedure	Sets the time the package will wait when it begins a polling loop.
SIGNAL	Procedure	Signals that an alert has fired.
WAITANY	Procedure	Waits for any of the alerts which the session has registered.
WAITONE	Procedure	Waits for a signal from a specific alert.

Table 14-3 The DBMS_ALERT package

The SIGNAL procedure checks the list of sessions that registered an interest in the alert and sends a message to each. The REGISTER procedure is used by applications to express interest in an alert. Once an alert has been registered, the WAITONE procedure can be used to wait for a signal from a specific alert or the WAITANY procedure can be used to wait for a signal from any registered alert.

Steps

1. Run SQL*Plus and connect as the WAITE user account. This How-To requires two connections to the same database. This can be performed with two SQL*Plus 3.2 sessions in 32-bit environments, such as Windows NT or Windows 95, or can be performed using two computers connected to the same database. The first connection will register its interest in an alert and wait for the alert to fire. Load CHP14-9.sql into the SQL buffer.

```
SQL> GET CHP14-9
  1   DECLARE
  2      STATUS NUMBER;
  3      MESSAGE VARCHAR2(100);
  4   BEGIN
  5      DBMS_ALERT.REGISTER('WAITE_ALERT');
  6      DBMS_ALERT.WAITONE('WAITE_ALERT',MESSAGE,STATUS);
  7      IF STATUS = 1 THEN
  8          DBMS_OUTPUT.PUT_LINE('TIMEOUT OCCURED');
  9      ELSE
 10          DBMS_OUTPUT.PUT_LINE(MESSAGE);
 11      END IF;
 12*  END;
```

The STATUS variable declared in line 2 returns the status of the WAITONE procedure call to the module. The MESSAGE variable declared in line 3 returns the message sent by the session signaling the alert. Line 5 executes the REGISTER procedure to express interest in the WAITE_ALERT alert. Line 6 executes the WAITONE procedure, making the module wait for the alert to fire or the procedure to timeout. The first parameter defines the alert for which the procedure is waiting. The second parameter is an OUT parameter returning the message sent when the alert is signaled. The third parameter is also an OUT parameter returning the status of the procedure call. A value of 0 identifies that an alert was fired; a value of 1 identifies that the timeout occurred. Line 7 checks the status variable and displays the timeout message if it occurred or the alert message if fired.

2. Set the SERVEROUTPUT system variable to ON to display the output from the DBMS_OUTPUT package and execute the statement. When the statement is executed, it will *hang* until another session fires the alert. Figure 14-3 shows the operation in SQL*Plus before the alert is fired.

3. Establish another SQL*Plus session to the same database and connect as the WAITE user account. This session will be used to fire alerts to be received by the first session. Load CHP14-10.sql into the SQL buffer. The file contains a statement firing an alert.

```
SQL> GET CHP14-10
  1  BEGIN
  2      DBMS_ALERT.SIGNAL('WAITE_ALERT','ALERT HAS FIRED');
  3      COMMIT;
  4* END;
```

The statement in line 2 executes the SIGNAL procedure from the DBMS_ALERT package. The first parameter identifies the alert fired. The second parameter specifies a message sent to all processes receiving the alert. Line 3 executes a COMMIT statement to commit the transaction.

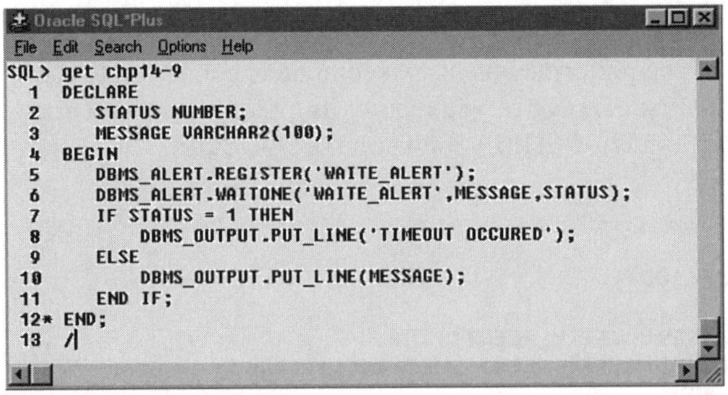

Figure 14-3 CHP14-9.sql waiting for an alert signal in SQL*Plus

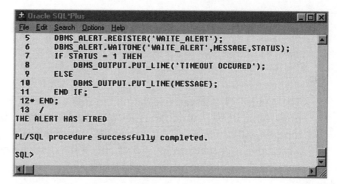

Figure 14-4 The results of the procedure
after the alert has fired

Since the DBMS_ALERT package uses tables and database triggers to provide its functionality, it requires a COMMIT to be executed before the alerts are fired.

4. Run the statement to fire the alert. Watch the first session when the statement is executed. The first session displays the message sent by the alert.

```
SQL>  /
```

```
PL/SQL procedure succcessfully completed.
```

Figure 14-4 shows the message displayed in the first session when the statement is executed in the second session.

5. Use the first session and load CHP14-11.sql into the SQL buffer. The PL/SQL statement in the file uses the WAITANY procedure to wait for more than one alert to fire.

```
SQL> GET CHP14-11
  1   DECLARE
  2      STATUS NUMBER;
  3      MESSAGE VARCHAR2(100);
  4      ALERT_NAME VARCHAR2(30);
  5   BEGIN
  6      DBMS_ALERT.REGISTER('ALERT_ONE');
  7      DBMS_ALERT.REGISTER('ALERT_TWO');
  8      DBMS_ALERT.REGISTER('CANCEL_ALERT');
  9      LOOP
 10      DBMS_ALERT.WAITONE(ALERT_NAME,MESSAGE,STATUS);
 11      IF STATUS = 1 THEN
 12          DBMS_OUTPUT.PUT_LINE('TIMEOUT OCCURED');
 13          EXIT;
 14      ELSE
 15          IF ALERT_NAME = 'CANCEL_ALERT' THEN
 16              EXIT;
 17          ELSE
```

continued on next page

continued from previous page

```
18              DBMS_OUTPUT.PUT_LINE(ALERT_NAME||': '||MESSAGE);
19          END IF;
20      END IF;
21      END LOOP;
22* END;
```

The ALERT_NAME variable defined in line 4 returns the name of the alert fired to the PL/SQL module. Lines 6 through 8 register three alerts that the module will listen for. CANCEL_ALERT terminates the module when the alert name is checked in line 15. If one of the other alerts is fired, the alert name and message are displayed by line 18.

6. Run the statement to begin waiting for the alerts to fire.

```
SQL>  /
```

7. Use the second session and execute CHP14-12.sql, watching the results the first session yields. CHP14-12.sql executes the SIGNAL procedure for firing alerts to be displayed by the first session. Figure 14-5 shows the operation performed in the second session. Figure 14-6 shows its results in the first session.

Figure 14-5 The execution of CHP14-12.sql in the second session to send alert signals

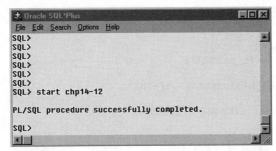

Figure 14-6 The results of CHP14-11.sql in the first session receiving alert signals

How It Works

The SIGNAL procedure of the DBMS_ALERT package is used to fire an alert on the database. Sessions that expressed an interest in the alert by executing the REGISTER function receive the alert when they execute the WAITONE or WAITANY procedures. The WAITONE procedure waits for a specific alert to fire. The WAITANY procedure waits for any of the registered alerts to fire. This How-To requires two SQL*Plus sessions connected to the same database. Steps 1 and 2 register interest in an alert and execute the WAITONE procedure to wait for it to fire. Steps 3 and 4 establish a second connection to the database and fire the alert by executing the SIGNAL procedure. When the alert is fired, the PL/SQL module in the first session displays the alert's message and terminates. Steps 5 and 6 register three alerts and execute the WAITANY procedure within a loop to receive alerts as they are fired. When a specific alert is fired, the module is terminated. Step 7 fires alerts from the second session to display the results in the first session.

Comments

The DBMS_ALERT package is very useful in sending messages between processes asynchronously. The DBMS_ALERT package uses tables and triggers requiring that commits be executed before the alert is fired. This can cause problems in development environments such as Developer 2000 which manages commits at the form level. If you do not commit the form, the alert will not fire. When using the package in your applications, keep in mind that the alerts you fire will not be received until a commit is performed.

COMPLEXITY

INTERMEDIATE

14.4 How do I...
Send an Oracle*Mail message in PL/SQL?

COMPATIBILITY: ORACLE*MAIL REQUIRED

Problem

I want to be able to send an Oracle*Mail message from within PL/SQL. I want to use Oracle*Mail within my applications to send e-mail when certain business operations are performed. How do I send an Oracle*Mail message in PL/SQL?

Technique

The DBMS_MAIL package allows you to send mail via Oracle*Mail from PL/SQL modules. This allows you to integrate electronic mail into your business applications.

In order to run the DBMS_MAIL package, the Oracle*Mail product must be installed on your system. The package contains the SEND procedure to send mail from within PL/SQL. The procedure call is shown here:

```
DBMS_MAIL.SEND(sender, list_of_recipients,
          list_of_copy_recipients,
          list_of_blind_copy_recipients,
          subject,
          reply_to,
          message_body);
```

When a list of recipients is specified as a parameter, the values can either be separated by spaces or commas. The body of the message sent with the DBMS_MAIL.SEND procedure can be up to 2,000 bytes long.

Steps

1. Run SQL*Plus and connect as the WAITE user account. Load CHP14-13.sql into the SQL buffer. The file contains a PL/SQL module which sends a mail message to an Oracle*Mail user.

```
SQL> GET CHP14-13
  1   BEGIN
  2       DBMS_MAIL.SEND('ehonour',
  3                          'mwaite, jsmith, rjones',
  4                          NULL,
  5                          NULL,
  6                          'Oracle Mail:',
  7                          NULL,
  8                          ' This message is send from within PL/SQL');
  9*  END;
```

Lines 2 through 8 execute the SEND procedure of the DBMS_MAIL package to send an Oracle*Mail message. The first parameter specified in line 2 identifies the user sending the mail message. If NULL is passed as the parameter, the current user account is employed. Line 3 presents the second parameter, which specifies the recipients of the message. The list of users can be space separated or comma separated. Line 4 presents the third parameter, which specifies the CC list of the message. The fourth parameter, shown in line 5, specifies the BCC (blind copy) list of the message. The fifth parameter, shown in line 6, contains the subject of the message. The sixth parameter, shown in line 7, contains the reply-to line of the message. The last parameter, shown in line 8, contains the body of the message.

2. Run the statement to send the message.

```
SQL>  /

PL/SQL procedure successfully completed.
```

How It Works

The DBMS_MAIL package can be used to send mail messages via Oracle*Mail. The system must have Oracle*Mail installed in order to use the package. The SEND procedure is the only module in the package and is used to send a mail message. Steps 1 and 2 present a PL/SQL module which sends an Oracle*Mail message using the DBMS_MAIL package.

Comments

The Oracle*Mail package is required to use the DBMS_MAIL package. If your application requirements need an interface between your database and a mail package, consider using Oracle*Mail with the DBMS_MAIL package.

COMPLEXITY
INTERMEDIATE

14.5 How do I...
Communicate between Oracle sessions?

COMPATIBILITY: PL/SQL VERSION 2.1

Problem

I need a method to allow Oracle processes to communicate. I want to be able to send a message and have the other process read it when it's ready. Each message will only be read by a single process. I do not want to use the DBMS_ALERT package presented in How-To 14.3, since it requires transactions to be committed. How do I communicate between Oracle sessions using a different method?

Technique

The DBMS_PIPE built-in package allows communication between processes through pipes. A user session can open a pipe and send data through it. Another session can read the information from the pipe. The DBMS_PIPE package contains ten modules, as shown in Table 14-4.

MODULE	TYPE	DESCRIPTION
CREATE_PIPE	Function	Creates a new pipe.
NEXT_ITEM_TYPE	Function	Returns the datatype of the next message in the buffer.
PACK_MESSAGE	Procedure	Puts an item into the message buffer.

continued on next page

continued from previous page

MODULE	TYPE	DESCRIPTION
PURGE	Procedure	Removes all data from a pipe.
RECEIVE_MESSAGE	Function	Receives a message from the pipe into the message buffer.
REMOVE_PIPE	Function	Removes a pipe.
RESET_BUFFER	Procedure	Clears the message buffer.
SEND_MESSAGE	Function	Sends the contents of the message buffer to a pipe.
UNIQUE_SESSION_NAME	Function	Returns a unique session identifier.
UNPACK_MESSAGE	Procedure	Unpacks the next message from the message buffer.

Table 14-4 DBMS_PIPE functions and procedures

Use the CREATE_PIPE function to create the named pipe. In PL/SQL version 2.2 and higher, a pipe can be public or private. A private pipe can only be used by sessions connected in the same user account as the pipe creator or by a user connected as SYSDBA or INTERNAL. A public pipe can be accessed by any user on the system and does not need to be created explicitly. The first time a pipe is used with the SEND_MESSAGE or RECEIVE_MESSAGE functions, it will be created automatically as a public pipe. To send a message through the pipe, first pack it in the local message buffer using the PACK_MESSAGE procedure and then send it using the SEND_MESSAGE function. When you no longer need the pipe, using the REMOVE_PIPE procedure removes it.

Steps

1. The example presented in this How-To requires two sessions connected to the same database. This can be performed with two SQL*Plus 3.2 sessions in 32-bit environments, such as Windows NT or Windows 95, or using two computers connected to the same database. Run SQL*Plus and connect as the WAITE user account for the first session. Load CHP14-14.sql into the SQL buffer. The statement contained in the file creates a new private pipe. This step requires PL/SQL version 2.2 or higher. If you are using PL/SQL 2.1, skip to Step 3.

```
SQL> GET CHP14-14
  1   DECLARE
  2      X NUMBER;
  3      PIPE_EXISTS EXCEPTION;
  4      PRAGMA EXCEPTION_INIT(PIPE_EXISTS,-23322);
  5   BEGIN
  6      X := DBMS_PIPE.CREATE_PIPE('WAITE_PIPE');
  7   EXCEPTION
  8      WHEN PIPE_EXISTS THEN
  9          DBMS_OUTPUT.PUT_LINE('PIPE WITH THIS NAME EXISTS');
 10*  END;
```

Line 2 declares a variable to handle the results of the CREATE_PIPE function. Line 3 declares an exception variable for handling the error that occurs when the pipe already exists. Line 4 declares a pragma to link the exceptions declared in line 3 with the Oracle error occurring when the pipe exists. Line 6 executes the CREATE_PIPE function to create a private pipe with the name WAITE_PIPE. No two pipes in the database can have the same name. A conflict will occur if another user has created a private pipe with the name specified. If a conflict occurs, the exception handler in lines 8 and 9 displays a message.

2. Run the statement to create a new private pipe.

```
SQL>  /
```

PL/SQL procedure successfully completed.

3. Load CHP14-15.sql into the SQL buffer. The statement in the file packs a message and puts it in the pipe.

```
SQL> GET CHP14-15
  1   DECLARE
  2      X NUMBER;
  3   BEGIN
  4      DBMS_PIPE.PACK_MESSAGE('THIS IS THE MESSAGE');
  5      X := DBMS_PIPE.SEND_MESSAGE('WAITE_PIPE');
  6*  END;
```

The variable declared in line 2 receives the value returned by the SEND_MESSAGE function. Line 4 uses the PACK_MESSAGE procedure to pack the message passed as a parameter, preparing it for delivery. Line 5 uses the SEND_MESSAGE function to send the message to the specified pipe.

4. Run the statement to pack and send the message to the pipe.

```
SQL>  /
```

PL/SQL procedure successfully completed.

5. Run SQL*Plus, creating a second connection to the database as the WAITE user account. Load CHP14-16.sql into the SQL buffer. The PL/SQL code within the file reads the message from the pipe created in the prior step and displays it on the screen.

```
SQL> GET CHP14-16
  1   DECLARE
  2      STATUS NUMBER;
  3      MESSAGE VARCHAR2(80);
  4   BEGIN
  5      STATUS := DBMS_PIPE.RECEIVE_MESSAGE('WAITE_PIPE');
  6   IF STATUS = 0 THEN
  7      DBMS_PIPE.UNPACK_MESSAGE(MESSAGE);
  8      DBMS_OUTPUT.PUT_LINE(MESSAGE);
```

continued on next page

continued from previous page

```
 9   ELSE
10       DBMS_OUTPUT.PUT_LINE('NO DATA FOUND IN PIPE');
11   END IF;
12*  END;
```

Line 2 declares a variable containing the status of the pipe when the
RECEIVE_MESSAGE function is executed. Line 3 declares the variable
receiving the message from the pipe. Line 5 executes the RECEIVE_
MESSAGE function to receive the next message from the specified pipe. If
the value returned is 0, the pipe contains a message. Line 7 uses the
UNPACK_MESSAGE procedure to retrieve the message from the buffer and
put it in a local variable. Line 8 displays the message using the PUT_LINE
procedure of the DBMS_OUTPUT package. If a message was not successfully received from the pipe, line 10 generates a message on the screen.

6. Set the SERVEROUTPUT system variable to ON and run the statement to
receive the message from the pipe. The results of the operation are shown
in Figure 14-7.

The message sent to the pipe by the first process is read, unpacked, and displayed within the second process.

7. Using the second process, load CHP14-17.sql into the SQL buffer. The
PL/SQL code in the file uses a loop to read messages from a public pipe
until a specific message is received.

```
SQL> GET CHP14-17
  1   DECLARE
  2       STATUS NUMBER(10);
  3       MESSAGE VARCHAR2(80);
  4   BEGIN
  5       LOOP
  6           STATUS := DBMS_PIPE.RECEIVE_MESSAGE('NEW_PIPE');
  7           IF STATUS = 0 THEN
  8               DBMS_PIPE.UNPACK_MESSAGE(MESSAGE);
  9               IF MESSAGE = 'STOP' THEN
 10                   DBMS_OUTPUT.PUT_LINE('DONE!');
 11                   EXIT;
 12               ELSE
 13                   DBMS_OUTPUT.PUT_LINE(MESSAGE);
 14               END IF;
 15           END IF;
 16       END LOOP;
 17*  END;
```

Line 2 declares the variable used to receive the status from the
RECEIVE_MESSAGE function. Line 3 declares the variable that receives the
message from the pipe. Lines 2 through 16 contain a loop that continues to
process messages until the message STOP is received. Line 6 uses the
RECEIVE_MESSAGE function to receive the next message from the
NEW_PIPE pipe. Since the pipe has not been created explicitly, it will be
created as a public pipe the first time it is read. Lines 9 through 11

Figure 14-7 A SQL*Plus session receiving a message from a pipe

terminate the module when the STOP message is received. If a different message is received, it is displayed by line 13.

8. Run the statement to execute the module. The module will appear to hang until the first message is sent to the pipe. Figure 14-8 shows SQL*Plus waiting for the first message.

9. Use the first session and load CHP14-18.sql into the SQL buffer. The PL/SQL code in the file sends ten messages to the public pipe to be displayed by the second session.

```
SQL> GET CHP14-18
  1  DECLARE
  2     X NUMBER;
  3  BEGIN
  4     FOR I IN 1..10 LOOP
  5         DBMS_PIPE.PACK_MESSAGE('THIS IS MESSAGE '||TO_CHAR(I));
  6         X := DBMS_PIPE.SEND_MESSAGE('NEW_PIPE');
  7     END LOOP;
  8     DBMS_PIPE.PACK_MESSAGE('STOP');
  9     X := DBMS_PIPE.SEND_MESSAGE('NEW_PIPE');
 10* END;
```

Lines 4 through 7 perform a loop ten times, using the PACK_MESSAGE procedure and SEND_MESSAGE function to send a message to the public pipe. Lines 8 and 9 send a STOP message to the second process through the pipe.

10. Run the statement while watching the second process. When the first process is executed, ten messages will be displayed in the second process before it terminates. Figure 14-9 shows the first process when executed, and Figure 14-10 shows the results in the second process.

The public pipe is used to communicate between the two processes. The actions in the first process cause results to be displayed in the second process.

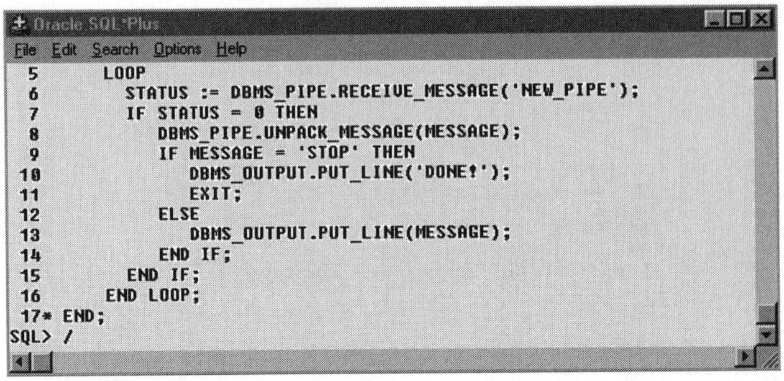

```
± Oracle SQL*Plus                                    _ □ ×
File  Edit  Search  Options  Help
  5      LOOP
  6         STATUS := DBMS_PIPE.RECEIVE_MESSAGE('NEW_PIPE');
  7         IF STATUS = 0 THEN
  8            DBMS_PIPE.UNPACK_MESSAGE(MESSAGE);
  9            IF MESSAGE = 'STOP' THEN
 10               DBMS_OUTPUT.PUT_LINE('DONE!');
 11               EXIT;
 12            ELSE
 13               DBMS_OUTPUT.PUT_LINE(MESSAGE);
 14            END IF;
 15         END IF;
 16      END LOOP;
 17* END;
SQL> /
```

Figure 14-8 Session two waiting for messages

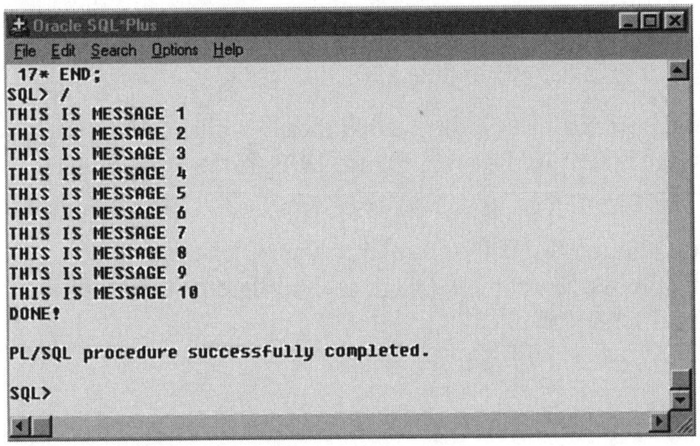

```
± Oracle SQL*Plus                                    _ □ ×
File  Edit  Search  Options  Help
 17* END;
SQL> /
THIS IS MESSAGE 1
THIS IS MESSAGE 2
THIS IS MESSAGE 3
THIS IS MESSAGE 4
THIS IS MESSAGE 5
THIS IS MESSAGE 6
THIS IS MESSAGE 7
THIS IS MESSAGE 8
THIS IS MESSAGE 9
THIS IS MESSAGE 10
DONE!

PL/SQL procedure successfully completed.

SQL>
```

Figure 14-9 The first process after it sends
messages through the pipe

```
± Oracle SQL*Plus                                    _ □ ×
File  Edit  Search  Options  Help
  3   BEGIN
  4      FOR I IN 1..10 LOOP
  5         DBMS_PIPE.PACK_MESSAGE('THIS IS MESSAGE '||TO_
  6         X := DBMS_PIPE.SEND_MESSAGE('NEW_PIPE');
  7      END LOOP;
  8      DBMS_PIPE.PACK_MESSAGE('STOP');
  9      X := DBMS_PIPE.SEND_MESSAGE('NEW_PIPE');
 10* END;
SQL> /

PL/SQL procedure successfully completed.

SQL> |
```

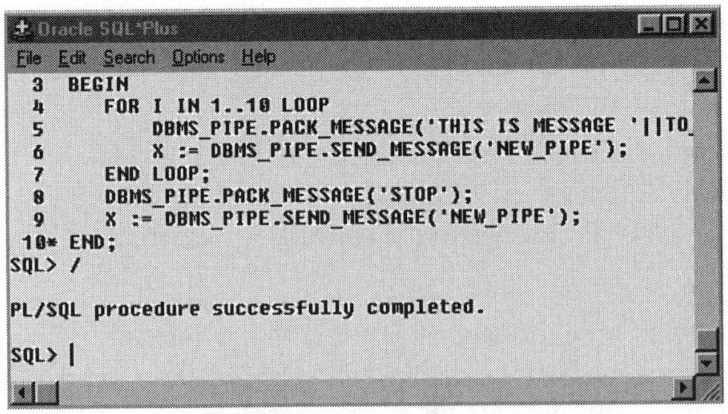

Figure 14-10 The second process receiving
messages through the pipe

11. From either session, load CHP14-19.sql into the SQL buffer. The PL/SQL code contained in the file removes the private pipes created in Step 1.

```
SQL> GET CHP14-19
  1  DECLARE
  2    X NUMBER;
  3  BEGIN
  4    X := DBMS_PIPE.REMOVE_PIPE('WAITE_PIPE');
  5* END;
```

Line 4 uses the REMOVE_PIPE function to remove the pipe specified. The variable declared in line 2 receives the results of the function. The function returns 0 if the pipe is removed successfully; otherwise, an error is raised. The NEW_PIPE pipe, which was created implicitly in step 7, is removed automatically when the pipe is emptied.

12. Run the statement to remove the pipe.

```
SQL>  /

PL/SQL procedure successfully completed.
```

How It Works

The DBMS_PIPE package can be used to communicate between processes. Named pipes that can be either public or private are created. Messages are packed with the PACK_MESSAGE procedure and sent to a pipe with the SEND_MESSAGE function. Messages are received with the RECEIVE_MESSAGE function and unpacked with the UNPACK_MESSAGE procedure. Steps 1 and 2 create a privately named pipe called WAITE_PIPE by executing the CREATE_PIPE function. Private pipes can only be accessed by processes connected in the same user account as the one that created the pipe. Steps 3 and 4 pack and send a message via the named pipe using the PACK_MESSAGE and SEND_MESSAGE procedures. Steps 5 and 6 employ a second SQL*Plus session to read the message from the pipe using the RECEIVE_MESSAGE and UNPACK_MESSAGE procedures. Steps 7 and 8 employ the second session to run a PL/SQL module using a loop to continuously check a public pipe for messages. When the message STOP is received, the module is terminated. Steps 9 and 10 execute a PL/SQL module sending ten messages to the named pipe followed by the STOP message. Steps 11 and 12 remove the pipe created in Step 1.

Comments

Pipes are an effective way to communicate between processes. Unlike the DBMS_ALERT package presented in How-To 14.4, a COMMIT statement does not need to be executed in order to send the message. When two processes need to communicate, the DBMP_PIPE package provides benefits over the DBMS_ALERT package. When many processes are interested in messages sent by another process, the DBMS_ALERT package is preferable.

COMPLEXITY
INTERMEDIATE

14.6 How do I...
Read and write operating system files?

COMPATIBILITY: PL/SQL VERSION 2.3

Problem

I need a method to read and write operating system files from within PL/SQL. I want to read and write files from within stored procedures and functions. I am running Oracle 7.3, which uses PL/SQL 2.3. How do I read and write operating system files?

Technique

The UTL_FILE built-in package is available with PL/SQL 2.3. The package allows you to both read and write operating system files. UTL_FILE modules can be called from within stored modules or client-side modules. Table 14-5 shows the modules that make up the UTL_FILE database package.

NAME	TYPE	DESCRIPTION
FCLOSE	Procedure	Closes the file specified.
FCLOSE_ALL	Procedure	Closes all open files.
FFLUSH	Procedure	Flushes all data from the buffer.
FOPEN	Function	Opens the specified file.
GET_LINE	Function	Gets the next line from the file.
IS_OPEN	Function	Returns TRUE if the file is currently open.
NEW_LINE	Procedure	Terminates current line and begins a new line.
PUT	Procedure	Puts text into the buffer.
PUT_LINE	Procedure	Puts a line of text into the buffer.
PUTF	Procedure	Puts formatted text into the buffer.

Table 14-5 The UTL_FILE database package

In order to read a file you first have to declare a file handle, which is used to reference the file in the other procedures. Next, you must open the file with a call to FOPEN. The file can be opened to read, write, or append. The PUT_LINE, PUT, and PUTF procedures are used to write data to the file. The file is closed using the FCLOSE procedure. The GET_LINE procedure is used to read a line of data and place it in a VARCHAR2 variable.

The locations of the accessible directories must be listed in the INIT.ORA file of the database. Only the exact directories listed in the INIT.ORA file are accessible. Sub-directories beneath an accessible directory are not automatically accessible.

Steps

1. Run SQL*Plus and connect as the WAITE user account. Load CHP14-20.sql into the SQL buffer. The file contains PL/SQL code to open a file and write a line to the end of it.

```
SQL> GET CHP14-20
  1   DECLARE
  2      FILE_HANDLE UTL_FILE.FILE_TYPE;
  3   BEGIN
  4      FILE_HANDLE := UTL_FILE.FOPEN('C:\','CHP14.TXT','A');
  5      UTL_FILE.PUT_LINE(FILE_HANDLE,'HELLO WORLD');
  6      UTL_FILE.FCLOSE(FILE_HANDLE);
  7*  END;
```

Line 2 declares a file handle variable of the type created in the UTL_FILE built-in package. A file handle must be declared any time you use the UTL_FILE modules. Line 4 uses the FOPEN function from the UTL_FILE package to open the file CHP14.TXT in the C:\ directory. The A parameter specifies that the file is opened in append mode. If a W is specified, the file is opened for writing. R opens the file for read. Line 5 uses the PUT_LINE procedure to write a full line of data to the file. Line 6 closes the file using the FCLOSE function.

2. Run the module to write the line of data.

```
SQL> /
```

```
PL/SQL procedure successfully completed.
```

3. Load CHP14-21.sql into the SQL buffer. The PL/SQL module in the file reads the line of data written in the previous step.

```
SQL> GET CHP14-21
  1   DECLARE
  2      DATA_LINE VARCHAR2(80);
  3      FILE_HANDLE UTL_FILE.FILE_TYPE;
  4   BEGIN
  5      FILE_HANDLE := UTL_FILE.FOPEN('C:\','CHP14.TXT','R');
  6      UTL_FILE.GET_LINE(FILE_HANDLE,DATA_LINE);
  7      DBMS_OUTPUT.PUT_LINE(DATA_LINE);
  8      UTL_FILE.FCLOSE(FILE_HANDLE);
```

continued on next page

continued from previous page

```
 9   EXCEPTION
10       WHEN NO_DATA_FOUND THEN
11           DBMS_OUTPUT.PUT_LINE('READ PAST EOF');
12           UTL_FILE.FCLOSE(FILE_HANDLE);
13*  END;
```

Line 2 declares a VARCHAR2 variable which receives the data when read from the file. Line 3 declares the file handle controlling access to the file. The datatype of the file handle is defined in the UTL_FILE package. Line 5 opens the file for read by using the FOPEN function and passing R as the second parameter. To open a file for append, an A is passed as the second parameter. To open a file for write, a W is passed. Line 6 uses the GET_LINE procedure to read the line from the file. If the file has reached the end, the exception handler beginning in line 10 will be executed. Line 7 uses the PUT_LINE procedure from the DBMS_OUTPUT package to display the line read from the file. Line 8 closes the file by executing the FCLOSE procedure.

4. Run the statement to display the results. Figure 14-11 shows the results of the operation in SQL*Plus.

How It Works

The UTL_FILE package is used to read and write operating system files. The FOPEN function is used to open a file. The PUT_LINE, PUT, and PUTF procedures are used to write data to a file. The GET_LINE procedure is used to read a line from a file. Steps 1 and 2 open an operating system file and write a single line to it. Steps 3 and 4 open the same file and read the line from it.

Comments

Reading and writing operating system files is very useful and expands the capabilities of PL/SQL. The UTL_FILE package is only available in PL/SQL 2.3 and above.

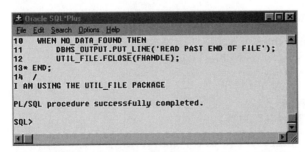

Figure 14-11 SQL*Plus displaying a line read from a file

COMPLEXITY
INTERMEDIATE

14.7 How do I...
Use comma separated lists in PL/SQL?

COMPATIBILITY: PL/SQL VERSION 2.1

Problem

I need a method to convert a comma separated list into a format I can easily use in PL/SQL. Some of our applications receive data in a comma separated format, and others are required to produce output in this format. Parsing character strings in PL/SQL can require a lot of code. How do I use PL/SQL built-in packages to use comma separated lists?

Technique

The DBMS_UTILITY package contains two procedures for working with comma separated lists. The COMMA_TO_TABLE procedure converts a comma separated list into a PL/SQL table. Once the list is in a PL/SQL table, it becomes easy to work with. The specification for the procedure is shown here:

```
DBMS_UTILITY.COMMA_TO_TABLE (list IN varchar2,
        tablen OUT binary_integer,
        tab OUT uncl_array);
```

The list parameter contains the comma separated list moved to the table by the procedure. The TABLEN parameter is an OUT parameter which returns the number of elements moved to the table. The TAB parameter returns the PL/SQL table containing the list to the calling module. The UNCL_ARRAY datatype is defined in the package and must be used in the procedure to declare the table variable. A variable can be defined as a datatype in a package by specifying the package name with the datatype. If you are working with a PL/SQL table and wish to move the values into a comma separated list, the TABLE_TO_COMMA procedure can be used. The specification for the procedure is shown here:

```
DBMS_UTILITY.TABLE_TO_COMMA (tab IN uncl_array,
        tablen OUT binary_integer,
        list OUT varchar2);
```

The TAB parameter specifies the table to be converted to a comma separated list. The TABLEN parameter is an OUT parameter returning the number of items moved to the list, and the LIST parameter returns the character string containing the comma separated list.

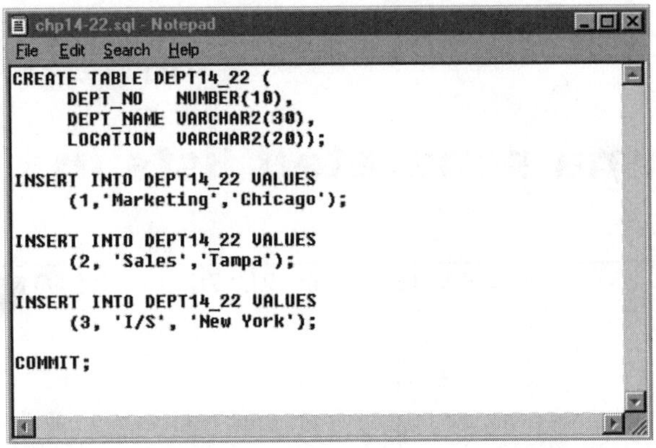

Figure 14-12 CHP14-22.sql creates a sample
table for How-To 14.7

Steps

1. Run SQL*Plus and connect as the WAITE user account. CHP14-22, shown
in Figure 14-12, creates the sample table and data used in the example. The
sample table contains three columns. The sample data will be converted to
a comma separated list using PL/SQL tables. Run the script to create the
sample table and its data.

```
SQL>   START CHP14-22

Table created.

1 row created.

1 row created.

1 row created.

Commit complete.
```

2. Load CHP14-23.sql into the SQL buffer. The PL/SQL code contained in the
file converts a comma separated list into a PL/SQL table and displays its
contents.

```
SQL> GET CHP14-23
  1   DECLARE
  2     MY_TABLE   DBMS_UTILITY.UNCL_ARRAY;
  3     CNT          BINARY_INTEGER;
  4     COMMA_STRING VARCHAR2(250);
  5   BEGIN
  6     COMMA_STRING := _Illinois,Iowa,Indiana,Kentucky,Maryland,Montana';
  7     DBMS_UTILITY.COMMA_TO_TABLE(COMMA_STRING,CNT,MY_TABLE);
  8     FOR I IN 1..CNT LOOP
```

```
 9        DBMS_OUTPUT.PUT_LINE(MY_TABLE(I));
10     END LOOP;
11* END;
```

Line 1 declares a variable of the UNCL_ARRAY datatype created in the DBMS_UTILITY package. In order to pass the table as a parameter to the COMMA_TO_TABLE procedure, it must be declared as this datatype. Line 2 declares a variable to be passed the number of elements processed in the list. Line 3 declares the variable containing the comma separated list. Line 6 moves a sample list into the COMMA_STRING variable. Line 7 calls the COMMA_TO_TABLE procedure. The first parameter contains the list to be processed. The last two parameters are both OUT parameters used to return values from the procedure. The CNT variable receives the number of elements processed, and the MT_TABLE variable contains the PL/SQL table. Lines 8 through 10 loop through each element in the table and display its values.

3. Set the SERVEROUTPUT system variable to ON and run the statement to display the results. Figure 14-13 shows the output of the operation within SQL*Plus.

Each element in the list is displayed as a separate line.

4. Load CHP14-24.sql into the SQL buffer. The PL/SQL code contained in the file reads records from the sample table, places the records in a PL/SQL table, and returns them as a comma separated list.

```
SQL> GET CHP14-24
  1   DECLARE
  2      CURSOR C1 IS
  3         SELECT DEPT_NO,
  4                DEPT_NAME,
  5                LOCATION
  6                FROM DEPT14_22;
  7   OUTPUT_TABLE DBMS_UTILITY.UNCL_ARRAY;
  8   CNT BINARY_INTEGER;
  9   OUTPUT_STRING VARCHAR2(80);
 10   COUNTER INTEGER := 0;
 11   BEGIN
 12      FOR I IN C1 LOOP
 13         OUTPUT_TABLE(COUNTER+1) := I.DEPT_NO;
 14         OUTPUT_TABLE(COUNTER+2) := I.DEPT_NAME;
 15         OUTPUT_TABLE(COUNTER+3) := I.LOCATION;
 16         COUNTER := COUNTER+3;
 17      END LOOP;
 18      DBMS_UTILITY.TABLE_TO_COMMA(OUTPUT_TABLE,CNT,OUTPUT_STRING);
 19      DBMS_OUTPUT.PUT_LINE(OUTPUT_STRING);
 20* END;
```

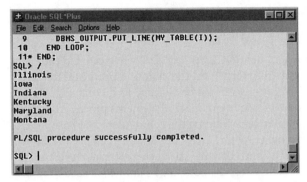

Figure 14-13 The results of a comma
separated list after being parsed

Lines 2 through 6 declare a cursor to query the sample table created in Step
1. Line 7 declares a variable of the UNCL_ARRAY datatype, defined in the
DBMS_UTILITY package. Line 8 declares a variable used as an OUT parameter and passes the number of elements processed by the procedure. Line
9 declares a variable used as an OUT parameter and returns the comma
separated list from the procedure. Line 10 declares a variable tracking the
current element in the PL/SQL table. The loop defined in lines 12 through
17 processes each record contained in the cursor. Lines 13 through 15
move the values in the columns next to the records in the PL/SQL table.
Line 16 increments the counter. Line 18 uses the TABLE_TO_COMMA
function to move the records in the PL/SQL table into the character string
as comma separated values. Line 19 displays the comma separated list to
the screen.

5. Run the statement to display the results. Figure 14-14 shows the results of
the PL/SQL module in SQL*Plus.

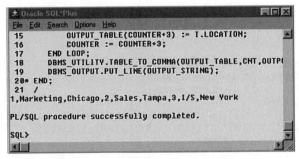

Figure 14-14 The comma separated list
created by the operation

How It Works

The TABLE_TO_COMMA and COMMA_TO_TABLE procedures in the DBMS_ UTILITY package can be used to work with comma separated lists in PL/SQL. The PL/SQL table used must be declared of the type UNCL_ARRAY, defined in the DBMS_UTILITY package. Step 1 creates a sample table with data used to demonstrate the procedures. Steps 2 and 3 present a PL/SQL module, which converts a comma separated list into a PL/SQL table using the COMMA_TO_TABLE procedure. Once the list is moved into the table, it can be manipulated easily within the PL/SQL code. Steps 4 and 5 present a PL/SQL module, which queries a database table and converts the results to a comma separated character string by using the TABLE_TO_COMMA procedure.

Comments

Working with comma separated lists can be difficult without the use of the DBMS_UTILITY package. You would have to use character functions and parse the comma separated list with PL/SQL code. The COMMA_TO_TABLE procedure is very useful for creating a PL/SQL table from a comma separated list. Since a PL/SQL table works like a one-dimensional array, it is perfect for handling lists.

CHAPTER 15
DATABASE TRIGGERS

DATABASE TRIGGERS

How do I...

Database triggers are stored procedures that execute when a table is modified. Triggers can be used to ensure that specific business rules related to a table are performed when records are inserted, updated, or deleted. Because database triggers are executed on the database and tied to the table, they will fire regardless of the application performing the operation. Creating database triggers helps ensure the integrity and consistency of data. Database triggers should not be used to enforce referential integrity or perform other actions where a specific tool was provided for that purpose. Like stored procedures and functions, database triggers are a fundamental part of application partitioning. Moving business rules from the application code to the database ensures that the business rules will be enforced and performance improved. Up to 12 database triggers can be created for each table. The examples presented in this chapter are found on the accompanying CD in the \SAMPLES\CHAP15 directory.

15.1   Create a database trigger

Database triggers ensure that an action is performed when a table is modified. They can be used to enforce business rules regardless of the source of the operation. This How-To demonstrates the creation of database triggers and the different types of triggers that can be created.

15.2   Use column values within database triggers

It is almost always necessary to use the column values from the table containing the trigger. The :NEW and :OLD column modifiers allow the column values to be used within a database trigger. If a statement within a trigger requires a value from the updated or new record, the :NEW modifier is used. If a statement requires the value of a column before it was modified, the OLD modifier is used. This How-To explores the use of column values within database triggers.

15.3   Manage data redundancy with database triggers

Designing your database in third normal form does not always yield the best overall performance. If you are performing data warehousing, creating summary information, or designing redundancy into your data model, database triggers can be used to ensure the integrity of the data. This How-To presents a method for managing data redundancy using database triggers.

15.4   Perform cascading deletes with database triggers

There will be situations when you will want to use database triggers to delete the data related to a record deleted from a table. If you want to delete a record referenced as the foreign key to a record in another table, the delete operation must be cascaded through the data model. This How-To presents the method for deleting related data using database triggers.

15.5   Disable and enable triggers

Database triggers will fire whenever a table is modified. You need to disable database triggers in order to perform management tasks or to perform batch operations. When a trigger is disabled, it will not fire when the triggering event occurs on the table. This How-To presents the method used to disable and enable triggers when necessary.

15.6   Rebuild CREATE TRIGGER statements

The CREATE TRIGGER statements used to create database triggers can be rebuilt using the data dictionary and SQL*Plus. This How-To presents the method and SQL scripts used to rebuild the CREATE TRIGGER statement for a specified trigger.

15.7 List information about triggers

Information about a trigger, including its name, status, owner, and triggering event, can be queried from the data dictionary through the USER_TRIGGERS and ALL_TRIGGERS data dictionary views. This How-To presents the method and queries used to display information about database triggers.

15.8 Use triggers to perform data replication

It is possible to use database triggers to replicate data from one database to another if your needs are fairly limited. If your data replication requirements only involve inserts and deletes, the method presented in this How-To may be more desirable than using snapshots, the data replication method presented in Chapter 11, Distributed Databases. If your requirements involve updating data or are more complex, snapshots will probably be a better method for data replication.

COMPLEXITY
INTERMEDIATE

15.1 How do I...
Create a database trigger?

Problem

I need to create database triggers on the tables used by my application. I want to use triggers to enforce business rules, manage redundancy, and perform cascading deletes. I want to create triggers that execute once when a statement is executed or for each row modified in the table. How do I create a database trigger on a table?

Technique

The CREATE TRIGGER statement is used to create a database trigger on a table. Each trigger is given a name and can be programmed to execute before or after an event on a table. Figure 15-1 shows the syntax of the CREATE TRIGGER statement.

The triggering events can be INSERT, UPDATE, or DELETE. Any combination of triggering events can be included in the same database trigger. The name of each trigger must be unique within its schema. The FOR EACH ROW option causes the trigger to fire once to each record created, modified, or deleted by the triggering statement. If the option is not included, the trigger will fire only once for each transaction. Only one trigger of each type can be created on a given table. Attempting to create more than one of the same type of trigger on the same table will generate a compile error. The possible triggers that can be created on a table are shown in Table 15-1.

```
CREATE [OR REPLACE] TRIGGER trigger_name          Keywords and
                                                  trigger_name

{BEFORE|AFTER} {INSERT|UPDATE [OF column,..]|DELETE} ON table_name    triggering
                                                                     event

[FOR EACH ROW]    Optional for Each
                  Row clause

[WHEN (condition)]    Optional WHEN
                      clause

trigger body     Required trigger
                 body
```

Figure 15-1 The syntax of the CREATE TRIGGER statement

NAME	FUNCTION
BEFORE INSERT	Fires once before an INSERT transaction
BEFORE INSERT FOR EACH ROW	Fires before each new record is created
AFTER INSERT	Fires once after an INSERT transaction
AFTER INSERT FOR EACH ROW	Fires after each new record is created
BEFORE UPDATE	Fires once before an UPDATE transaction
BEFORE UPDATE FOR EACH ROW	Fires before each record is updated
AFTER UPDATE	Fires once after an UPDATE transaction
AFTER UPDATE FOR EACH ROW	Fires after each record is updated
BEFORE DELETE	Fires once before a DELETE transaction
BEFORE DELETE FOR EACH ROW	Fires before each record is deleted
AFTER DELETE	Fires once after a DELETE transaction
AFTER DELETE FOR EACH ROW	Fires after each record is deleted

Table 15-1 Possible database triggers allowed on a given table

When working with row triggers, a WHEN clause can be used to restrict the records for which the trigger fires. The WHEN clause contains a boolean statement which, if evaluated to FALSE, suppresses the trigger for the given row.

Steps

1. Run SQL*Plus and connect as the WAITE user account. CHP15-1.sql, shown in Figure 15-2, creates a sample table displaying the triggers created in this How-To.

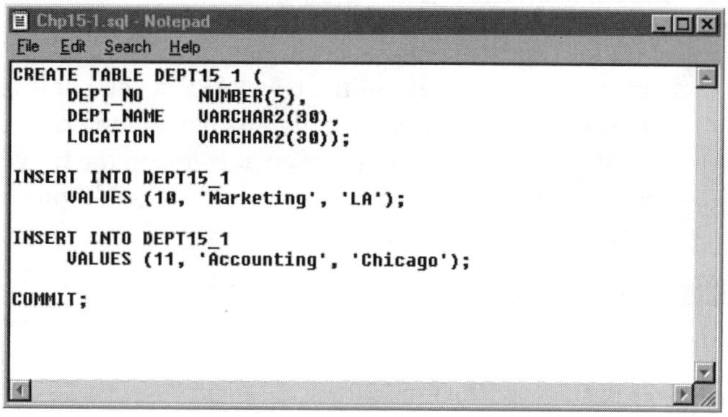
Chp15-1.sql - Notepad

```
CREATE TABLE DEPT15_1 (
     DEPT_NO      NUMBER(5),
     DEPT_NAME    VARCHAR2(30),
     LOCATION     VARCHAR2(30));

INSERT INTO DEPT15_1
     VALUES (10, 'Marketing', 'LA');

INSERT INTO DEPT15_1
     VALUES (11, 'Accounting', 'Chicago');

COMMIT;
```

Figure 15-2 CHP15-1.sql creates the sample table used in How-To 15.1

The sample table, DEPT152, is a simple table with three columns. In the steps that follow, triggers will be created on the table, and the capabilities of database triggers will be demonstrated. Run the file to create the sample table.

```
SQL>  START CHP15-1

Table created.

1 row created.

1 row created.

Commit complete.
```

2. Load CHP15-2.sql into the SQL buffer. The CREATE TRIGGER statement contained in the file creates a simple trigger that fires before each new record is created.

```
SQL>  GET CHP15-2
  1   CREATE OR REPLACE TRIGGER DEPT151_BIR
  2   BEFORE INSERT ON DEPT15_1
  3   FOR EACH ROW
  4   DECLARE
  5      X NUMBER(10);
  6   BEGIN
  7      DBMS_OUTPUT.PUT_LINE('BEFORE INSERT FIRED');
  8   END;
```

Line 1 presents the keywords required to create a trigger and gives the trigger a name. Line 2 specifies the triggering statement. The trigger will execute before records are inserted into the DEPT15_1 table. Line 3 specifies the FOR EACH ROW option which causes the trigger to fire once for each new row inserted into the table. The absence of this clause would make the trigger fire only once for each statement, no matter how many rows were created. Lines 4 and 5 present the syntax used to declare variables for database triggers, even though the variable created is not used. Unlike stored procedures, the DECLARE statement is used when creating database triggers. Lines 6 through 8 contain the executable portion of the stored procedure. The only executable line in the trigger displays a message that the trigger has fired, by using the PUT_LINE procedure of the DBMS_OUTPUT package.

3. Run the statement to create the database trigger.

```
SQL>  /
```

```
Trigger created.
```

The trigger is automatically enabled when created. Any new data added to the table after the trigger is created will make it fire. The next step creates a trigger that only fires when the data meets certain criteria.

4. Load CHP15-3.sql into the SQL buffer. The CREATE TRIGGER statement contained in the file creates a trigger that fires after new records are inserted into the table. It also includes a WHEN clause restricting when the trigger is fired.

```
SQL>  GET CHP15-3
  1    CREATE OR REPLACE TRIGGER DEPT151_AIR
  2    AFTER INSERT ON DEPT15_1
  3    FOR EACH ROW
  4    WHEN (NEW.DEPT_NO > 5)
  5    BEGIN
  6       DBMS_OUTPUT.PUT_LINE('AFTER INSERT TRIGGER FIRED');
  7    END;
```

Line 1 presents the keywords required to create the new trigger and gives it a name. Line 2 specifies the triggering event. The trigger will fire after new records are created. The FOR EACH ROW clause in line 3 ensures the trigger will fire once for each new row created. Line 4 specifies a WHEN clause making the trigger fire only when the DEPT_NO column of the new record is greater than 5. The expression in the WHEN clause must evaluate to a boolean TRUE or FALSE. Lines 5 through 7 contain the trigger body. The PUT_LINE procedure from the DBMS_OUTPUT package shown in line 6 will display a message when the trigger is fired.

5. Run the statement to create the database trigger.

```
SQL>  /
```

```
Trigger created.
```

There are now two triggers on the sample table. The first trigger will fire any time a new record is inserted into the table. The trigger just created will only fire when the DEPT_NO column is greater than 5 and after the record has been successfully inserted. The next step creates a trigger that fires when records in the table are updated.

6. Load CHP15-4.sql into the SQL buffer. The CREATE TRIGGER statement contained in the file creates a trigger which executes when a specific column in the sample table is changed.

```
SQL>  GET CHP15-4
  1   CREATE OR REPLACE TRIGGER DEPT151_BUR
  2   BEFORE UPDATE OF DEPT_NAME ON DEPT15_1
  3   FOR EACH ROW
  4   BEGIN
  5     DBMS_OUTPUT.PUT_LINE('BEFORE UPDATE TRIGGER FIRED');
  6   END;
```

Line 1 presents the required keywords and provides the name of the trigger. Trigger names must be unique within the schema. Since the CREATE OR REPLACE keywords are used, another trigger with the same name in the schema will be replaced, regardless of the table the trigger is on. Line 2 specifies the triggering statement. The trigger will fire whenever the DEPT_NAME column is updated and before the record is updated. If the OF DEPT_NAME clause is not on the trigger, the trigger fires when any columns are updated. The FOR EACH ROW clause in line 3 causes the trigger to execute once for each record updated. Lines 4 through 6 present a trigger body displaying a message when the trigger fires.

7. Run the statement to create the database trigger.

```
SQL>  /
```

```
Trigger created.
```

The next step creates a trigger that fires once for each delete operation performed on the table.

8. Load CHP15-5.sql into the SQL buffer. The CREATE TRIGGER statement contained in the file creates a trigger that executes after a DELETE statement has been executed.

```
SQL>  GET CHP15-5
  1   CREATE OR REPLACE TRIGGER DEPT151_AD
  2   AFTER DELETE ON DEPT15_1
  3   BEGIN
  4     DBMS_OUTPUT.PUT_LINE('AFTER DELETE TRIGGER FIRED');
  5   END;
```

Line 1 creates the trigger with the name DEPT151_AD. Line 2 specifies that the trigger will execute after a DELETE statement has been performed. The absence of a FOR EACH ROW clause means the statement will fire only once for each transaction, regardless of the number of rows deleted. Lines 3 through 5 contain the trigger body. The statement contained in line 4 displays a message when the trigger fires.

9. Run the statement to create the database trigger.

```
SQL>  /
```

Trigger created.

The sample table created in Step 1 now contains four database triggers. In the following steps, the data in the tables will be manipulated to make the triggers fire.

10. Load CHP15-6.sql into the SQL buffer. The INSERT statement contained in the file inserts a record into the sample table.

```
SQL>   GET CHP15-6
  1   INSERT INTO DEPT15_1
  2        VALUES (5, 'SALES', 'CHICAGO')
```

The INSERT statement creates a new record with a DEPT_NO value of 5. The BEFORE INSERT trigger will fire, but the AFTER INSERT statement will not, due to the WHEN clause contained in the statement.

11. Set the SERVEROUTPUT system variable to ON to display the output from the triggers within SQL*Plus. Run the statement to display the results of the operation. Figure 15-3 shows the results of the INSERT statement within SQL*Plus.

One message is displayed because only the BEFORE INSERT trigger fires. The WHEN clause in the AFTER INSERT trigger prevents it from firing, because the value of the DEPT_NO column is not greater than 5. The next step creates a record that does not prevent the AFTER INSERT trigger from firing.

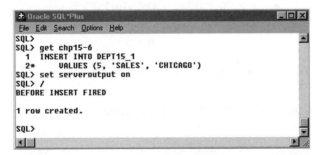

Figure 15-3 The results of the INSERT statement in SQL*Plus

12. Load CHP15-7.sql into the SQL buffer. The INSERT statement contained in the file creates a new record which has a DEPT_NO column greater than 5.

```
SQL>  GET CHP15-7
  1   INSERT INTO DEPT15_1
  2       VALUES (6, 'I/S', 'CHICAGO')
```

Because the record created will have a DEPT_NO column value greater than 5, both the BEFORE INSERT and AFTER INSERT triggers will fire.

13. Run the statement to display the results of the operation. Figure 15-4 shows the results in SQL*Plus.

Both the BEFORE INSERT and AFTER INSERT triggers are fired since the value of the DEPT_NO column does not prevent the AFTER INSERT trigger from firing. In the next step, an UPDATE statement will be used to fire the BEFORE UPDATE trigger.

14. Load CHP15-8.sql into the SQL buffer. The UPDATE statement contained in the file updates each of the records in the table.

```
SQL>  GET CHP15-8
  1   UPDATE DEPT15_1
  2       SET DEPT_NAME = 'NEW VALUE'
```

The UPDATE statement will make the BEFORE UPDATE trigger fire for each revised row, since the DEPT_NAME column is updated. The BEFORE UPDATE OF DEPT_NAME clause in the CREATE TRIGGER statement in Step 6 only lets the trigger fire when the DEPT_NAME column is modified. Modifying other columns without the DEPT_NAME column will not fire the trigger.

15. Run the statement to display the results of the operation. Figure 15-5 shows how the UPDATE statement causes the triggers to fire.

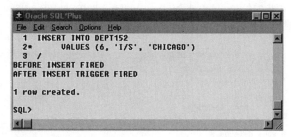

Figure 15-4 The results of the INSERT statement in SQL*Plus

```
Oracle SQL*Plus                                    _ □ ×
File  Edit  Search  Options  Help
SQL>
SQL> get chp15-8
  1  UPDATE DEPT15_1
  2*      SET DEPT_NAME = 'NEW VALUE'
SQL> /
BEFORE UPDATE TRIGGER FIRED
BEFORE UPDATE TRIGGER FIRED
BEFORE UPDATE TRIGGER FIRED
BEFORE UPDATE TRIGGER FIRED

4 rows updated.

SQL>
```

Figure 15-5 An UPDATE statement executed
on the table

Because four rows were updated by the statement, the BEFORE UPDATE
trigger was fired four times. Had the FOR EACH ROW clause not been
specified in the CREATE TRIGGER statement, the trigger would have fired
only once. In the next step, all records will be deleted to show the operation
of the AFTER DELETE trigger presented in Step 8.

16. Execute a DELETE statement to delete all the rows in the table. Figure 15-6
shows the operation and the output generated by the AFTER DELETE
trigger.

Because the AFTER DELETE trigger does not contain the FOR EACH ROW
option, the trigger was only executed once by the DELETE statement.

How It Works

The CREATE TRIGGER statement is used to create database triggers on a table. Up
to 12 triggers can be created on a single table. Table 15-1 shows the list of triggers
that can be created. Step 1 creates a sample table used throughout this How-To as
the table for the new triggers. Steps 2 and 3 create a BEFORE INSERT trigger

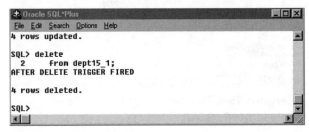

```
Oracle SQL*Plus                                    _ □ ×
File  Edit  Search  Options  Help
4 rows updated.

SQL> delete
  2      from dept15_1;
AFTER DELETE TRIGGER FIRED

4 rows deleted.

SQL>
```

Figure 15-6 A DELETE statement on
the sample table

containing the FOR EACH ROW option. The trigger executes once before each new row is created in the table. Steps 4 and 5 create an AFTER INSERT trigger, which includes a WHEN clause. The WHEN clause can only be used on triggers containing the FOR EACH ROW clause and restricts firing the trigger to rows satisfying a boolean condition. Steps 6 and 7 create a BEFORE UPDATE trigger, which fires only when certain columns are modified. Steps 8 and 9 create an AFTER DELETE statement, which only fires once for each transaction. The absence of the FOR EACH ROW clause causes the trigger to fire only once per transaction. The remaining steps demonstrate the execution of the database triggers by executing INSERT, UPDATE, and DELETE statements on the table.

Comments

Use triggers when you need to guarantee that certain actions are performed when tables are modified. Do not use triggers to perform operations that other Oracle features can execute. For example, referential integrity can be enforced through constraints and default values defined on the table. Avoid making your triggers too big. Triggers must be recompiled the first time they run or are pushed out of the shared pool. If a trigger becomes larger than 60 lines, call stored procedures to keep it small.

COMPLEXITY
INTERMEDIATE

15.2 How do I...
Use column values within database triggers?

Problem

When I create database triggers, I need to use the values of the columns in the records being inserted, updated, or deleted. There are many times when I need to use both the values of columns before and after the operation. How do I use column values within database triggers?

Technique

The :NEW and :OLD column modifiers access column values within a database trigger. The :NEW modifier provides the value the column will have after the operation is performed. You can access the value of the column before the operation is performed by specifying the :OLD qualifier.

Steps

1. Run SQL*Plus and connect as the WAITE user account. CHP15-9.sql, shown in Figure 15-7, creates the sample table used in this How-To.

The sample table created by the script contains three columns and has database triggers created in the steps that follow. A sample record is created so the :OLD modifier can be demonstrated with an existing record. Run the script to create the sample table and its sample record.

```
SQL>  START CHP15-9

Table created.

1 row created.

Commit complete.
```

2. Load CHP15-10.sql into the SQL buffer. The CREATE TRIGGER statement contained in the file creates a BEFORE UPDATE trigger referencing the new and old column values.

```
SQL>  GET CHP15-10
  1    CREATE OR REPLACE TRIGGER DEPT159_BUR
  2    BEFORE UPDATE ON DEPT15_9
  3    FOR EACH ROW
  4    BEGIN
  5       DBMS_OUTPUT.PUT_LINE('OLD DEPT_NO: '||TO_CHAR(:OLD.DEPT_NO));
  6       DBMS_OUTPUT.PUT_LINE('OLD DEPT_NAME: '||:OLD.DEPT_NAME);
  7       DBMS_OUTPUT.PUT_LINE('OLD LOCATION: '||:OLD.LOCATION);
  8       DBMS_OUTPUT.PUT_LINE('NEW DEPT_NO: '||TO_CHAR(:NEW.DEPT_NO));
  9       DBMS_OUTPUT.PUT_LINE('NEW DEPT_NAME: '||:NEW.DEPT_NAME);
 10       DBMS_OUTPUT.PUT_LINE('NEW LOCATION: '||:NEW.LOCATION);
 11    END;
```

```
 Chp15-9.sql - Notepad
 File  Edit  Search  Help
CREATE TABLE DEPT15_9 (
     DEPT_NO      NUMBER(5),
     DEPT_NAME    VARCHAR2(30),
     LOCATION     VARCHAR2(20));

INSERT INTO DEPT15_9
     VALUES (1, 'Marketing', 'Chicago');

COMMIT;
```

Figure 15-7 CHP15-9.sql creates the sample table used in How-To 15.2

The :NEW and :OLD qualifiers are used to reference the columns in the table. Line 1 presents the required keywords and specifies the name of the trigger. Lines 2 and 3 specify the triggering statement and FOR EACH ROW option. The trigger will fire any time a record in the table is updated. Line 5 through 10 use the :NEW and :OLD modifiers to display the values of the columns before and after the operation. Lines 5 through 7 display the values of the columns before the operation. Lines 8 through 10 show the values of the record after the operation.

3. Run the statement to create the database trigger.

```
SQL> /
```

```
Trigger created.
```

The next step will display the new and old values of the columns in the existing record by executing an update statement on the table.

4. Load CHP15-11.sql into the SQL buffer. The UPDATE statement contained in the file modifies the record in the sample table, firing the BEFORE UPDATE trigger.

```
SQL>  GET CHP15-11
   1    UPDATE DEPT15_9
   2       SET DEPT_NO = DEPT_NO * 2,
   3           DEPT_NAME = 'SALES'
```

The UPDATE statement modifies two of the three columns in the table. The new and old value of the third column will be the same.

5. Set the SERVEROUTPUT system variable to ON, and run the statement to display the results of the operation. Figure 15-8 displays the results of the operation within SQL*Plus.

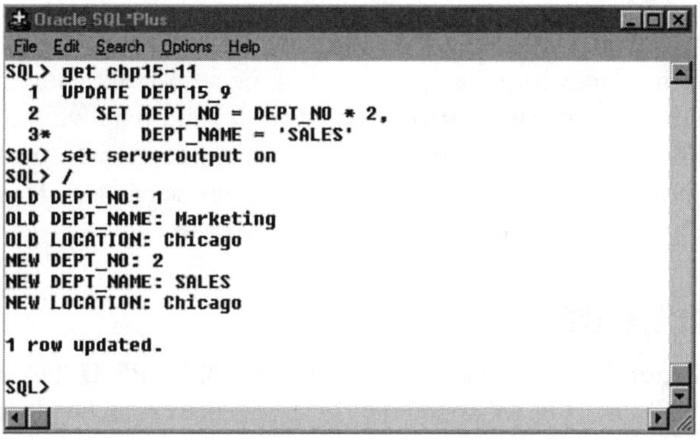

Figure 15-8 The results of the UPDATE statement in SQL*Plus

The output of the operation displays both the new and old values of the column. A new value was even available for the column not modified by the operation.

How It Works

The :NEW qualifier allows the trigger code to reference the new value of columns in the table. The :OLD qualifier provides access to the column values before the operation is performed. Step 1 creates a sample table and record used by the example trigger. Steps 2 and 3 create a BEFORE UPDATE trigger displaying the value of the columns in the table both before and after the update. Steps 4 and 5 execute an UPDATE statement on the table, causing the trigger to fire.

Comments

The :NEW and :OLD qualifiers are necessary to reference column values in triggers. Make sure you use the right value in your trigger. If you use a new value when you should have used an old value, you may see some invalid results.

COMPLEXITY
INTERMEDIATE

15.3   How do I...
Manage data redundancy with database triggers?

Problem

In order to improve the performance of analysis screens and reports, we have built redundancy into the data model. If the redundant data does not stay synchronized with the primary source of the data, invalid data will be displayed by the screens and reports. We cannot trust every application to manage the redundant data properly, so I want to do it through database triggers. How do I manage redundant data with triggers?

Technique

Redundant data can be managed by BEFORE UPDATE triggers specifying the FOR EACH ROW option. UPDATE statements can be placed in the triggers to update redundant data in all the locations required.

Steps

1. Run SQL*Plus and connect as the WAITE user account. CHP15-12.sql, shown in Figure 15-9, creates the sample tables used in the examples.

The script creates two tables. The CUST15_12 table is the primary source for customer data. The ORDER15_12 contains orders that customers place, and it contains redundant information. The two tables are joined by the CUST_NO column. If information is changed in the CUST15_12 table, it should be automatically updated in the ORDER15_12 table. The steps presented in this How-To will create a trigger to manage the redundant information. Run the file to create the sample objects.

```
SQL>   START CHP15-12

Table created.

Table created.

1 row created.

1 row created.

1 row created.

Commit complete.
```

```
Chp15-12.sql - Notepad
File  Edit  Search  Help
CREATE TABLE ORDER15_12 (
  ORDER_NO    NUMBER(10),
  CUST_NO     NUMBER(10),
  CUST_NAME   VARCHAR2(20),
  ADDRESS     VARCHAR2(20),
  CITY        VARCHAR2(10),
  STATE       VARCHAR2(2),
  ZIP         VARCHAR2(6));

CREATE TABLE CUST15_12 (
  CUST_NO     NUMBER(10),
  CUST_NAME   VARCHAR2(20),
  ADDRESS     VARCHAR2(20),
  CITY        VARCHAR2(10),
  STATE       VARCHAR2(2),
  ZIP         VARCHAR2(6));

INSERT INTO ORDER15_12 VALUES
  (1, 1, 'SMITH', '123 MAIN', 'CHICAGO', 'IL','60611');
INSERT INTO ORDER15_12 VALUES
  (2, 2, 'JONES', '345 WEST', 'CHICAGO', 'IL','60611');
INSERT INTO CUST15_12 VALUES
  (1, 'SMITH', '123 MAIN', 'CHICAGO', 'IL','60611');
COMMIT;
```

Figure 15-9 CHP15-12.sql creates the sample tables used in How-To 15.3

2. Load CHP15-13.sql into the SQL buffer. The CREATE TRIGGER statement in the file creates a BEFORE UPDATE trigger on the CUST15_12 table, which updates redundant data in the ORDER15_12 table when changes are made.

```
SQL> GET CHP15-13
  1   CREATE OR REPLACE TRIGGER BU_CUST1512
  2   BEFORE UPDATE ON CUST15_12
  3   FOR EACH ROW
  4   BEGIN
  5      UPDATE ORDER15_12 SET
  6          CUST_NO = :NEW.CUST_NO,
  7          CUST_NAME = :NEW.CUST_NAME,
  8          ADDRESS = :NEW.ADDRESS,
  9          CITY = :NEW.CITY,
 10          STATE = :NEW.STATE,
 11          ZIP = :NEW.ZIP
 12      WHERE
 13          CUST_NO = :OLD.CUST_NO;
 14   END;
```

Line 1 presents the keywords required to create the new trigger and names it BU_CUST1512. Lines 2 and 3 specify that the trigger fires before each row is updated in the CUST15_12 table created in Step 1. The FOR EACH ROW clause presented in Step 3 must exist in order to keep all records correct. If it were not included in the statement, the trigger would only fire once for each transaction, no matter how many records were updated. Lines 5 through 13 present an UPDATE statement which replaces the redundant data in the ORDER15_12 table with the new values in the CUST15_12 table.

3. Run the statement to create the trigger.

```
SQL>  /

Trigger created.
```

Any modifications to the CUST15_12 table will execute an UPDATE statement on the ORDER15_12 table. The next steps demonstrate operating the trigger by updating the sample record contained in the table.

4. Load CHP15-14.sql into the SQL buffer. The UPDATE statement contained in the file modifies the record in the CUST15_12 table, causing the trigger to fire.

```
SQL>  GET CHP15-14
  1   UPDATE CUST15_12
  2      SET CUST_NAME = 'New Company',
  3          ADDRESS = 'New Address'
  4   WHERE
  5      CUST_NO = 1
```

Line 1 presents the UPDATE keyword, which causes one or more records to be modified. Lines 2 and 3 specify that the CUST_NAME and ADDRESS columns will be updated. Lines 4 and 5 specify the WHERE clause, causing only one record to be updated by the statement.

5. Run the statement to execute the update and commit the transaction. The two columns modified in the CUST15_12 table will also be updated in the ORDER15_12 table.

```
SQL>  /

1 record updated.

SQL> COMMIT;

Commit complete.
```

Although the results of the operation only show one record updated, a second record was updated behind the scenes. The next step provides a query to show the redundant data modified by the operation.

6. Load CHP15-15.sql into the SQL buffer. The query contained in the file returns the redundant columns from the ORDER15_12 table.

```
SQL>   GET CHP15-15
   1    SELECT
   2         CUST_NAME,
   3         ADDRESS,
   4         CITY,
   5         STATE,
   6         ZIP
   7    FROM ORDER15_12
```

Lines 2 through 6 present the five columns returned by the query. Line 7 specifies the ORDER15_12 table and the source of the query.

7. Run the statement to return the records. Figure 15-10 shows the results of the query in SQL*Plus.

The first record returned by the query contains the new values for the CUST_NAME and ADDRESS columns. The record was updated by the BEFORE INSERT trigger contained in the CUST15_12 column.

How It Works

Redundant data can be managed by creating BEFORE UPDATE triggers on the primary source of the data. Step 1 creates two sample tables. The customer table serves as the primary source of information about customers. The order table contains orders placed by the customers and redundant information from the customer table. The

```
± Oracle SQL*Plus                                          _□×
File  Edit  Search  Options  Help
SQL> get chp15-15                                             ▲
  1  SELECT
  2      CUST_NAME,
  3      ADDRESS,
  4      CITY,
  5      STATE,
  6      ZIP
  7* FROM ORDER15_12
SQL> /

CUST_NAME              ADDRESS              CITY       ST ZIP
--------------------- --------------------- ---------- -- ------
New Company           New Address          CHICAGO    IL 60611
JONES                 345 WEST             CHICAGO    IL 60611

SQL>                                                         ▼
◄ ▐                                                        ► //
```

Figure 15-10 The results of the query

CUST_NO column is the foreign key on the order table and joins it to the customer table. Steps 2 and 3 create a BEFORE UPDATE trigger on the customer table (CUST15_12), which updates the redundant columns on the orders table (ORDER15_12) when the customer table is updated. Steps 4 and 5 update a record in the customer table, causing the BEFORE UPDATE trigger to modify the redundant data. Steps 6 and 7 query the orders table to view the changes made by the trigger.

Comments

If it is necessary to create redundant data in your data model, you should use database triggers. If you count on each application using the data to enforce redundancy, data integrity could be violated. Database triggers ensure the integrity of redundant data.

COMPLEXITY
INTERMEDIATE

15.4 How do I...
Perform cascading deletes with database triggers?

Problem

When our application deletes data in tables referenced by other tables, I want to ensure that data is deleted from all related locations. In order to ensure that the child records are deleted, I want to use database triggers. I know that when I use referential integrity constraints, I can make them cascade deletes automatically. However, in some cases

I do not want to use constraints, but still want to use cascade deletes. How do I perform cascading deletes using database triggers?

Technique

The BEFORE DELETE trigger can be used to delete child records referencing the record being deleted in the primary table. By placing DELETE statements in a BEFORE DELETE trigger, you can ensure that the child records are deleted. This technique cannot be used when foreign key constraints exist, but can be used to perform more complex logic relating to the cascading deletes.

Steps

1. Run SQL*Plus and connect as the WAITE user account. CHP15-16.sql, shown in Figure 15-11, creates the sample tables and data used in this How-To.

The script creates two sample tables for demonstrating cascading deletes. The CUST15_16 table contains customers of an organization. The ORDER15_16 table contains the orders placed by the customers. When a customer is deleted from the CUST15_16 table, all associated records in the ORDER15_16 table should also be deleted. Sample records are created in both tables to demonstrate the process. Run the script to create the sample tables and data.

```
CREATE TABLE ORDER15_16 (
    ORDER_NO    NUMBER(10),
    CUST_NO     NUMBER(10),
    CUST_NAME   VARCHAR2(20),
    ADDRESS     VARCHAR2(20),
    CITY        VARCHAR2(10),
    STATE       VARCHAR2(2),
    ZIP         VARCHAR2(6));

CREATE TABLE CUST15_16 (
    CUST_NO     NUMBER(10),
    CUST_NAME   VARCHAR2(20),
    ADDRESS     VARCHAR2(20),
    CITY        VARCHAR2(10),
    STATE       VARCHAR2(2),
    ZIP         VARCHAR2(6));

INSERT INTO ORDER15_16 VALUES
    (1, 1, 'SMITH', '123 MAIN', 'CHICAGO', 'IL','60611');
INSERT INTO ORDER15_16 VALUES
    (2, 2, 'JONES', '345 WEST', 'CHICAGO', 'IL','60611');
INSERT INTO CUST15_16 VALUES
    (1, 'SMITH', '123 MAIN', 'CHICAGO', 'IL','60611');
COMMIT;
```

Figure 15-11 CHP15-16.sql creates the sample tables used in How-To 15.4

```
SQL> START CHP15-16

Table created.

Table created.

1 row created.

1 row created.

1 row created.

Commit complete.
```

2. Load CHP15-17.sql into the SQL buffer. The CREATE TRIGGER statement contained in the file creates a BEFORE UPDATE trigger on the CUST15_16 table to delete child records referencing a deleted record.

```
SQL> GET CHP15-17
  1   CREATE OR REPLACE TRIGGER BD_CUST1516
  2   BEFORE DELETE ON CUST15_16
  3   FOR EACH ROW
  4   BEGIN
  5      DELETE FROM ORDER15_16
  6      WHERE
  7           CUST_NO = :OLD.CUST_NO;
  8   END;
```

Line 1 provides the required keywords to create or replace a trigger and specifies the trigger name. Line 2 specifies the triggering event that causes the trigger to fire before deletes are made on the CUST15_16 table. The FOR EACH ROW clause in line 3 ensures that all records are processed. Lines 4 through 8 contain the trigger body. Lines 5 through 8 provide a DELETE statement that removes child records from the ORDER15_16 table. The :OLD.CUST_NO column is used in the WHERE clause of the DELETE statement so the correct records are deleted.

3. Run the statement to create the trigger.

```
SQL>  /

Trigger created.
```

When records are deleted from the CUST15_16 table, the trigger can delete zero or more records from the ORDER15_16 table. In the next step, a record is deleted from the CUST15_16 table to demonstrate the trigger operation.

4. Load CHP15-18.sql into the SQL buffer. The DELETE statement contained in the file deletes a record in the CUST15_16 table, causing the trigger to fire and the cascading delete to occur.

```
SQL>   GET CHP15-18
  1    DELETE FROM
  2       CUST15_16
  3    WHERE CUST_NO = 1
```

The WHERE clause in line 3 specifies that all customers with a value of 1 in the CUST_NO column should be deleted by the statement. The BEFORE UPDATE trigger will also delete all ORDER15_16 tables with a value of 1 in the CUST_NO column.

5. Execute the statement to delete the record and commit the transaction.

```
SQL>   /
```

1 row deleted.

```
SQL>   COMMIT;
```

Commit complete.

Although the message provided shows one row deleted, it does not represent the records deleted by the BEFORE DELETE trigger. The next step queries the ORDER15_16 table to show whether the records were deleted.

6. Load CHP15-19.sql into the SQL buffer. The query contained in the file returns columns from the ORDER15_16 table.

```
SQL>   GET CHP15-19
  1    SELECT
  2       ORDER_NO,
  3       CUST_NO,
  4       CUST_NAME
  5    FROM
  6       ORDER15_16
```

Lines 2 through 4 specify the columns returned by the query. The absence of a WHERE clause allows all records from the ORDER15_16 table to be returned by the query.

7. Run the file to perform the queries. Figure 15-12 displays the records returned by the query.

The records returned by the query do not include any records in which the CUST_NO column is 1. The BEFORE DELETE trigger removed the records when the DELETE statement was executed by line 5.

How It Works

When referential integrity is not enforced through constraints, cascading deletes can be performed using BEFORE DELETE FOR EACH ROW triggers. Step 1 creates two sample tables. The CUST15_16 table contains the customers who purchase

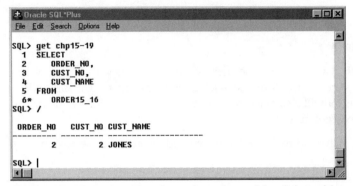

Figure 15-12 Statement querying the table deleted by
the database trigger

products from an organization. The ORDER15_16 table contains orders placed by
the customers. When a customer is deleted from the database, it is important to remove
all orders the customer placed. Steps 2 and 3 create a BEFORE DELETE trigger on
the CUST15_16 table, which deletes orders from the ORDER15_16 table for the customer being removed. Steps 4 and 5 demonstrate the execution of the trigger by deleting
a record from the CUST15_16 table. When the record is deleted, the BEFORE DELETE
trigger removes all orders for that particular customer from the ORDER15_16
table. Steps 6 and 7 query the ORDER15_16 table to show that the order record has
been removed.

Comments

Keep in mind that this technique does not work if referential integrity is enforced
through constraints. If you are using constraints, you can have the constraints perform deletes automatically. Beware of the effects of unintentional cascading of
updates and deletes. When cascading operations are performed on database tables,
it is possible for the database to perform more work than expected.

COMPLEXITY
INTERMEDIATE

15.5   How do I...
Disable and enable triggers?

Problem

When I perform batch processing and system management tasks on our database,
I need to disable triggers from firing. Many of our triggers modify data in one or more

tables. If I do not disable database triggers before performing these functions, they can fail. How do I disable and enable database triggers?

Technique

The ALTER TRIGGER statement is used to disable or enable a specified trigger. The DISABLE clause is used to disable a trigger, and the ENABLE clause is used to enable it. All triggers for a given table can be disabled or enabled together using the ALTER TABLE statement with the DISABLE ALL TRIGGERS or ENABLE ALL TRIGGERS clause.

Steps

1. Run SQL*Plus and connect as the WAITE user account. CHP15-20.sql, shown in Figure 15-13, creates a sample table and triggers used in this How-To.

The script creates a table with two triggers that will be disabled and enabled in the examples in this How-To. The DEPT15_20 table is created with a BEFORE INSERT trigger, BI_DEPT1520, and an AFTER INSERT trigger, AI_DEPT1520. Run the statement to create the objects.

```
SQL>  START CHP15-20

Table created.

Trigger created.

Trigger created.
```

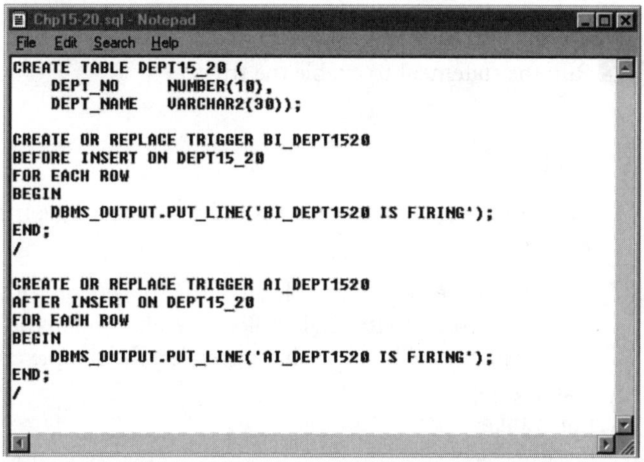


```
CREATE TABLE DEPT15_20 (
     DEPT_NO      NUMBER(10),
     DEPT_NAME    VARCHAR2(30));

CREATE OR REPLACE TRIGGER BI_DEPT1520
BEFORE INSERT ON DEPT15_20
FOR EACH ROW
BEGIN
     DBMS_OUTPUT.PUT_LINE('BI_DEPT1520 IS FIRING');
END;
/

CREATE OR REPLACE TRIGGER AI_DEPT1520
AFTER INSERT ON DEPT15_20
FOR EACH ROW
BEGIN
     DBMS_OUTPUT.PUT_LINE('AI_DEPT1520 IS FIRING');
END;
/
```

Figure 15-13 CHP15-20.sql creates the sample objects used in How-To 15.5

2. Load CHP15-21.sql into the SQL buffer. The file contains an ALTER TRIG-
GER statement to disable a specific trigger.

```
SQL>   GET CHP15-21
  1    ALTER TRIGGER
  2         BI_DEPT1520
  3    DISABLE
```

Line 1 presents the ALTER TRIGGER statement. The ALTER TRIGGER
statement can be used to disable a specific trigger. Line 2 provides the name
of the trigger to be disabled, and line 3 specifies the DISABLE clause to disable the trigger.

3. Run the statement to disable the trigger.

```
SQL> /
```

```
Trigger disabled.
```

When a record is inserted into the table, the BEFORE INSERT trigger will
not fire because it was disabled by the ALTER TRIGGER statement. When
you are done performing your management tasks, the trigger should be
enabled. The next step provides the technique to enable a specific trigger.

4. Load CHP15-22.sql into the SQL buffer. The file contains an ALTER TRIG-
GER statement to re-enable the trigger disabled in the previous step.

```
SQL>   GET CHP15-22
  1    ALTER TRIGGER
  2         BI_DEPT1520
  3    ENABLE
```

The format of the statement is the same as presented in Step 2. The only
difference is that line 3 specifies the ENABLE clause, which causes the trigger to be enabled.

5. Run the statement to enable the trigger.

```
SQL> /
```

```
Trigger enabled.
```

Once the trigger is enabled, it will fire whenever the triggering event
occurs.

6. It is often necessary to disable all of the triggers on a given table. Load
CHP15-23.sql into the SQL buffer. The file contains an ALTER TABLE statement which disables all of the triggers on the sample table.

```
SQL>   GET CHP15-23
  1    ALTER TABLE
  2         DEPT15_20
  3    DISABLE ALL TRIGGERS
```

Line 1 specifies the ALTER TABLE statement. Line 2 specifies the table to be altered. Line 3 presents the DISABLE ALL TRIGGERS clause, disabling all triggers on the specified table. Using this technique does not require that you know the names of the triggers on the table.

7. Run the statement to disable the triggers.

```
SQL>  /

Table altered.
```

Once you have completed your management tasks with the table, the triggers should be enabled. The next step presents the statement used to enable all the triggers on the table.

8. All the triggers on a table can be enabled using the ALTER TABLE statement. Load CHP15-24.sql into the SQL buffer. This file contains the statement to re-enable all the triggers disabled in the previous step.

```
SQL>  GET CHP15-24
   1   ALTER TABLE
   2       DEPT15_20
   3   ENABLE ALL TRIGGERS
```

The first two lines of the ALTER TABLE statement are identical to the statement provided in Step 6. Line 3 of the statement presents the ENABLE ALL TRIGGERS clause, enabling all triggers on the specified table.

9. Run the statement to enable the triggers.

```
SQL>  /

Table altered.
```

How It Works

The ALTER TABLE and ALTER TRIGGER statements disable and enable triggers. The ALTER TRIGGER statement is used to disable or enable a specific trigger by name. The ALTER TABLE statement with the ENABLE ALL TRIGGERS or DISABLE ALL TRIGGERS clause is used to enable or disable all triggers on the specified table. Step 1 creates a sample table and the two triggers used throughout this How-To. Steps 2 and 3 present the ALTER TRIGGER statement using the DISABLE clause to disable one of the sample triggers. The following two steps present the ENABLE clause, enabling the sample trigger. Steps 6 and 7 use the ALTER TABLE statement to disable all the triggers on the sample table. Steps 8 and 9 use the same statement with the ENABLE ALL TRIGGERS clause, enabling all the triggers on the sample table.

Comments

Database triggers ensure that a specific operation is performed when a table is modified. There will be times when you need to modify the data in a table but do not want the triggers to fire. The ALTER TABLE statement is the easiest way to disable and enable all of the triggers on a table. It does not require that you know the names of the triggers, or even how many exist.

COMPLEXITY
ADVANCED

15.6 How do I...
Rebuild CREATE TRIGGER statements?

Problem

I need to re-create the statements used to create some of the triggers in the database. I either lost the original files or entered the trigger directly into SQL*Plus without saving the CREATE TRIGGER statements. I know that throughout the book we have used the data dictionary and SQL*Plus to rebuild statements. How do I rebuild CREATE TRIGGER statements?

Technique

There are data dictionary views containing information about triggers. They are USER_TRIGGERS, ALL_TRIGGERS, and DBA_TRIGGERS. When you rebuild the CREATE TRIGGER statement for a trigger, you can connect to the database as the owner of the trigger and use the USER_TRIGGERS or ALL_TRIGGERS data dictionary view. The DBA_TRIGGERS view contains all views in the database and requires privileges in the DBA role. The description of the USER_TRIGGERS view is shown in Figure 15-14. The TRIGGER_BODY column contains the text of the trigger. The datatype of the column is LONG, so it will be slightly harder to work with. The TRIGGER_NAME, TRIGGER_TYPE, and TRIGGERING_EVENT columns will be concatenated with the trigger body in order to rebuild the statement.

Steps

1. Run SQL*Plus and connect as the WAITE user account. CHP15-25.sql, shown in Figure 15-15, creates the sample objects required by this How-To.

The script creates the DEPT15_25 table so the BI_DEPT1525 trigger can be created. The table will not be used in this How-To, but the CREATE TRIGGER statement will be rebuilt by the following steps. Run the file to create the objects.

```
SQL> desc user_triggers
 Name                            Null?    Type
 ------------------------------- -------- ----
 TRIGGER_NAME                    NOT NULL VARCHAR2(30)
 TRIGGER_TYPE                             VARCHAR2(16)
 TRIGGERING_EVENT                         VARCHAR2(26)
 TABLE_OWNER                     NOT NULL VARCHAR2(30)
 TABLE_NAME                      NOT NULL VARCHAR2(30)
 REFERENCING_NAMES                        VARCHAR2(87)
 WHEN_CLAUSE                              VARCHAR2(2000)
 STATUS                                   VARCHAR2(8)
 DESCRIPTION                              VARCHAR2(2000)
 TRIGGER_BODY                             LONG

SQL>
```

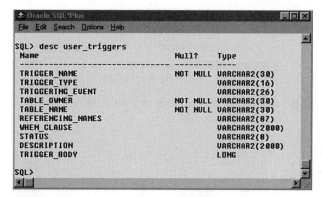

Figure 15-14 The USER_TRIGGERS data dictionary view

```
SQL>  START CHP15-25

Table created.

Trigger created.
```

In the next step, the trigger body will be queried from the ALL_TRIGGERS view.

2. Load CHP15-26.sql into the SQL buffer. The file contains a query of the ALL_TRIGGERS data dictionary view displaying the body of the trigger.

```
SQL>  GET CHP15-26
  1   SELECT
  2      TRIGGER_BODY
  3   FROM
  4      ALL_TRIGGERS
  5   WHERE
  6      TRIGGER_NAME = 'BI_DEPT1525'
```

```
CREATE TABLE DEPT15_25 (
    DEPT_NO     NUMBER(10),
    DEPT_NAME   VARCHAR2(30));

CREATE OR REPLACE TRIGGER BI_DEPT1525
BEFORE INSERT ON DEPT15_25
FOR EACH ROW
BEGIN
    DBMS_OUTPUT.PUT_LINE('BI_DEPT1525 IS FIRING');
END;
/
```

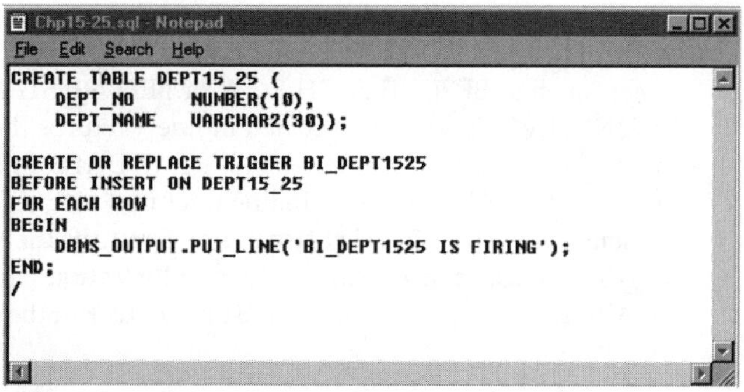

Figure 15-15 CHP15-25.sql creates the sample objects used in How-To 15.6

Line 2 specifies the TRIGGER_BODY column to be returned by the query. Line 4 specifies the ALL_TRIGGERS view and the source of the data, and line 6 specifies the name of the sample trigger. Since the TRIGGER_BODY column is of the LONG datatype, the LONG system variable must be set in the next step in order to display the column's entire value.

3. Set the LONG system variable to 2,000 to display all of the LONG column and run the statement.

```
SQL>   SET LONG 2000
SQL>   /

TRIGGER_BODY
----------------------------------------------------------------------
BEGIN
     NULL;
END;
```

The TRIGGER_BODY column contains the body of the trigger. Although the result of the query does not look like a CREATE TRIGGER statement, it provides a good start. The next step presents the other columns necessary to rebuild the statement.

4. Load CHP15-27.sql into the SQL buffer. The file contains a query of the other columns necessary to re-create the trigger.

```
SQL>   GET CHP15-27
   1   SELECT
   2      TRIGGER_NAME,
   3      TRIGGER_TYPE,
   4      TRIGGERING_EVENT,
   5      REFERENCING_NAMES,
   6      WHEN_CLAUSE
   7   FROM
   8      USER_TRIGGERS
   9   WHERE
  10      TRIGGER_NAME = 'BI_DEPT1525'
```

The TRIGGER_NAME column specified in line 2 returns the name of the trigger. The TRIGGER_TYPE column specified in line 3 returns the type of trigger, such as BEFORE EACH ROW or BEFORE STATEMENT. The TRIG-GERING_EVENT column specified in line 4 returns the type of event that causes the trigger to file, such as INSERT, UPDATE, or DELETE. The REF-ERENCING_NAMES column in line 6 returns a REFERENCING clause for the statement. The WHEN clause in line 5 returns the WHEN clause for the trigger if it exists. Since there is a lot of information returned by this query, the ARRAYSIZE system variable must be set to 1 in the next step to display all of it.

5. Set ARRAYSIZE to 1 and run the statement to display the results. The results of the operation are shown in Figure 15-16.

The values contained in the columns are not exactly what you need to rebuild a CREATE TRIGGER statement. The values of the query must be modified to build the statement. The next step uses Oracle functions to modify the values of the columns in order to create the trigger specification.

6. Load CHP15-28.sql into the SQL buffer. The file contains a query that returns the first part of the trigger specification.

```
SQL>  GET CHP15-28
  1   SELECT
  2     'CREATE OR REPLACE TRIGGER '||TRIGGER_NAME||
  3     ' '||SUBSTR(TRIGGER_TYPE,1,7)||
  4     ' '||TRIGGERING_EVENT||
  5     ' ON '||TABLE_OWNER||'.'||TABLE_NAME
  6   FROM
  7     USER_TRIGGERS
  8   WHERE
  9       TRIGGER_NAME = _BI_DEPT1525
```

Line 1 creates the CREATE OR REPLACE TRIGGER keywords and concatenates the trigger name to it. Line 3 uses the SUBSTR function to return only the first seven characters of the TRIGGER_TYPE column. The value returned will be either BEFORE or AFTER . Line 4 adds the TRIGGERING EVENT to the statement. Line 5 specifies the owner and name of the table. When this query is executed, it creates the first part of the trigger specification but may contain more information than the original statement in Step 1. This is because the query returns all the information that can be contained in the statement, even optional information. All the information will be displayed on a single line, so the LINESIZE system variable must be increased to display the entire line.

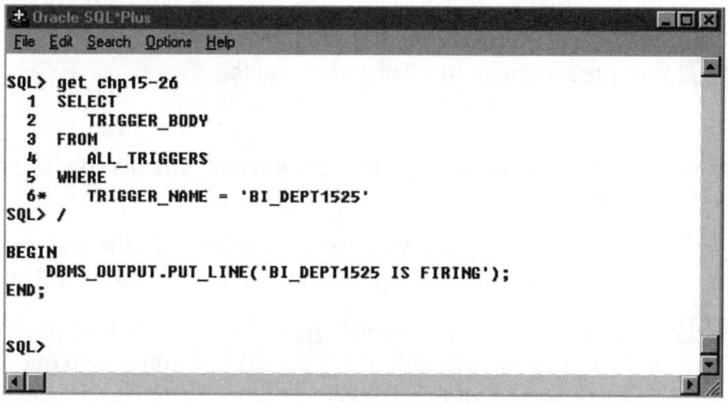

Figure 15-16 The results of the query of
USER_TRIGGERS

7. Set the HEADING system variable to OFF and the LINESIZE variable to 132. Run the statement to view the first part of the trigger specification.

```
SQL> SET HEADING OFF
SQL> SET LINESIZE 132
SQL> /

CREATE OR REPLACE TRIGGER BI_DEPT1525 BEFORE INSERT ON WAITE.DEPT15_25
```

The results of the query provide a very good start to the statement, but the FOR EACH ROW clause is not shown when it exists. In the next step, it will be included in the trigger specification.

8. Load CHP15-29.sql into the SQL buffer. The file contains a query returning the entire trigger specification, including the BEFORE EACH ROW clause if it exists.

```
SQL>   GET CHP15-29
  1    SELECT
  2      'CREATE OR REPLACE TRIGGER '||TRIGGER_NAME||
  3      ' '||SUBSTR(TRIGGER_TYPE,1,7)||
  4      ' '||TRIGGERING_EVENT||
  5      ' ON '||TABLE_OWNER||'.'||TABLE_NAME||' '||
  6      DECODE(INSTR(TRIGGER_TYPE,'STATEMENT'),0,' '||TRIGGER_TYPE)
  7    FROM
  8      USER_TRIGGERS
  9    WHERE
 10      TRIGGER_NAME = 'BI_DEPT1525'
```

Line 6 is added to the statement to display the BEFORE EACH ROW or AFTER EACH ROW clause if it exists. The INSTR function contained in line 6 returns the first location of the word STATEMENT in the TRIGGER_TYPE column. If the word does not exist in the column, a zero is returned and the DECODE function returns the trigger type; otherwise NULL is returned. This query now returns the entire trigger specification, except for the referencing clause. Since a referencing clause is rarely used, I chose not to include it in the statement.

9. Run the statement to display the results.

```
SQL> /

CREATE OR REPLACE TRIGGER BI_CHP1525 BEFORE INSERT ON WAITE.DEPT15_25 ⇐
BEFORE EACH ROW
```

The hardest part of the process is completed. In the next step, the trigger body is included to display the entire CREATE TRIGGER statement.

10. Load CHP15-30.sql into the SQL buffer. This file contains the final results of the operation. The TRIGGER_BODY column is also queried to display the code portion of the trigger.

```
SQL>  GET CHP15-30
  1   SELECT
  2     'CREATE OR REPLACE TRIGGER '||TRIGGER_NAME||
  3     ' '||SUBSTR(TRIGGER_TYPE,1,7)||
  4     ' '||TRIGGERING_EVENT||
  5     ' ON '||TABLE_OWNER||'.'||TABLE_NAME||' '||
  6     DECODE(INSTR(TRIGGER_TYPE,'STATEMENT'),0,' '||TRIGGER_TYPE),
  7     TRIGGER_BODY
  8   FROM
  9     USER_TRIGGERS
 10   WHERE
 11     TRIGGER_NAME = 'BI_DEPT1525'
```

Line 7 is added to return the body of the trigger. Since the column is of the LONG datatype, it cannot be concatenated to the statement and must be a separate column in the query.

11. Spool the output to a file using the SPOOL command and run the statement. Figure 15-17 displays the results of the operation.

Although the statement is not nicely formatted, it contains everything required to rebuild the CREATE TRIGGER statement.

How It Works

Throughout the book, we use SQL*Plus and the data dictionary to create a DDL statement. In this case, a CREATE TRIGGER statement is rebuilt. The ALL_TRIGGERS data dictionary view contains information about the triggers in the database. The columns in the view must be manipulated to be usable in a CREATE TRIGGER statement. Step 1 creates the sample table and trigger used throughout this How-To. Steps 2 and 3 display the TRIGGER_BODY column, which is a LONG column returning the code section of the trigger. Steps 4 and 5 present the other columns necessary

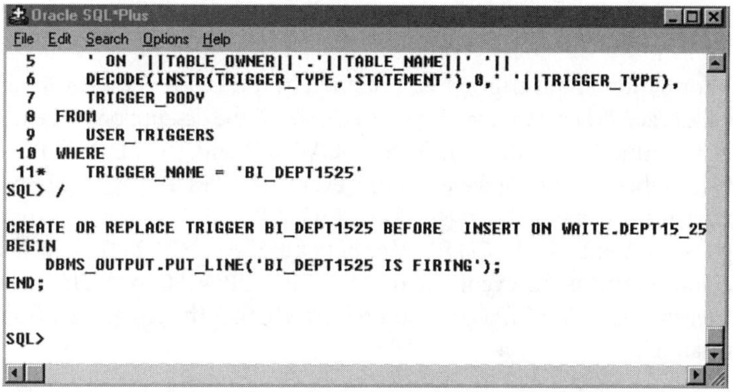

Figure 15-17 The output of CHP15-30 containing the rebuilt CREATE TRIGGER statement

to create the statement. These steps show that the data in the columns is not exactly in the format needed. Steps 6 and 7 create the first part of the trigger specification by concatenating the keywords from the statement to the values in the column. Steps 7 and 8 finish creating the trigger specification by adding the BEFORE EACH ROW or AFTER EACH ROW clauses if they exist. Steps 9 and 10 finish the process by adding the TRIGGER_BODY to the statement.

Comments

The process presented in this How-To can be used to rebuild CREATE TRIGGER statements when the original source code is no longer available. Rebuilding CREATE TRIGGER statements can be a necessary database management task. If you need to create all the triggers on a table or in the database, a simple modification to the WHERE clause of the query is all you need.

COMPLEXITY
BEGINNING

15.7 How do I...
List information about triggers?

Problem

I want to list information about the triggers in the database. I need to determine the trigger name, the table the trigger is on, and the status of the trigger. I know that we used the ALL_TRIGGERS data dictionary view in How-To 15.6, but would like to have a simple query presented giving me the required information. How do I list information about triggers?

Technique

Information about triggers is contained in the USER_TRIGGERS and ALL_TRIGGERS data dictionary views. Figure 15-14 shows the description of the USER_TRIGGERS view within SQL*Plus. The TABLE_OWNER and TABLE_NAME columns identify the table containing the triggering event. The TRIGGER_NAME column specified returns the name of the trigger. The TRIGGER_TYPE column returns the type of trigger, such as BEFORE EACH ROW or BEFORE STATEMENT. The TRIGGERING_EVENT column returns the event, such as INSERT, UPDATE, or DELETE, that causes the trigger to file. The STATUS column tells whether the trigger is currently enabled or disabled.

```
chp15-31.sql - Notepad                              _ □ X
File  Edit  Search  Help
CREATE TABLE DEPT15_31 (
    DEPT_NO      NUMBER(10),
    DEPT_NAME    VARCHAR2(30));

CREATE OR REPLACE TRIGGER BI_DEPT1531
BEFORE INSERT ON DEPT15_31
FOR EACH ROW
BEGIN
    DBMS_OUTPUT.PUT_LINE('BI_DEPT1531 IS FIRING');
END;
/

CREATE OR REPLACE TRIGGER AI_DEPT1531
AFTER INSERT ON DEPT15_31
FOR EACH ROW
BEGIN
    DBMS_OUTPUT.PUT_LINE('AI_DEPT1531 IS FIRING');
END;
/
```

Figure 15-18 CHP15-31 creates the sample table and triggers used in How-To 15.7

Steps

1. Run SQL*Plus and connect as the WAITE user account. CHP15-31.sql, shown in Figure 15-18, creates the sample table and triggers used in this How-To.

The DEPT15_31 table is created so two triggers can be created. The two triggers, BI_DEPT1531 and AI_DEPT1531, will demonstrate how a query to the data dictionary can provide you with valuable information about triggers. Run the statement to create the sample table and its database triggers.

```
SQL>   START CHP15-31

Table created.

Trigger created.

Trigger created.
```

2. Load CHP15-32.sql into the SQL buffer. The query contained in the file queries the USER_TRIGGERS table to display information about the triggers on the specified table.

```
SQL>   GET CHP15-32
  1    SELECT
  2        TRIGGER_NAME,
  3        TRIGGERING_EVENT,
  4        TRIGGER_TYPE,
  5        STATUS
  6    FROM
  7        USER_TRIGGERS
```

continued on next page

continued from previous page

```
8    WHERE
9        TABLE_NAME = '&TABLE_NAME'
```

3. Execute the COLUMN commands to format the columns and run the statement. Run the statement, and provide DEPT15_31 as the substitution variable. Figure 15-19 shows the results of the query for the sample table created in Step 1.

The query displays the two triggers created in step 1. The columns returned by the query show you the name of the trigger, when it fires, and its status. Including the TRIGGER_BODY column would also show you the code executed when the trigger fires.

How It Works

The USER_TRIGGERS and ALL_TRIGGERS data dictionary views contain information about the database triggers in the database. The TABLE_NAME column can be used in the WHERE clause of a query to either of the views for returning information about the views contained on a specific table. Step 1 creates the sample table and two sample triggers used to display the technique. Steps 2 and 3 execute a query of the USER_TRIGGERS data dictionary view to show information about the sample triggers.

Comments

A simple query to the USER_TRIGGERS data dictionary view will provide you with valuable information about the triggers on a table. If the triggers are not behaving the way you expect, query the data dictionary to verify that they are enabled, they fire when you want, and the code is valid for the operation.

```
± Oracle SQL*Plus                                    _ □ X
File  Edit  Search  Options  Help
SQL> get chp15-32
  1   SELECT
  2       TRIGGER_NAME,
  3       TRIGGERING_EVENT,
  4       TRIGGER_TYPE,
  5       STATUS
  6   FROM
  7       USER_TRIGGERS
  8   WHERE
  9*      TABLE_NAME = '&TABLE_NAME'
SQL> /
Enter value for table_name: DEPT15_31
old   9:     TABLE_NAME = '&TABLE_NAME'
new   9:     TABLE_NAME = 'DEPT15_31'

TRIGGER_NAME              TRIGGERING_EVENT      TRIGGER_TYPE
-----------------------   -----------------     ------------------
AI_DEPT1531               INSERT                AFTER EACH ROW
BI_DEPT1531               INSERT                BEFORE EACH ROW

SQL> |
```

Figure 15-19 The results of the query to the USER_TRIGGERS data dictionary view

COMPLEXITY
ADVANCED

15.8 How do I...
Use triggers to perform data replication?

Problem

I want to use database triggers to perform simple database replication. When a record is inserted into a table in one of my databases, I also want to insert the record in a remote database. Since database triggers fire when a specific action on a table occurs, I should be able to use triggers for data replication. How do I use triggers to perform data replication?

Technique

In order to use the technique presented in this How-To, the Oracle7 Procedural and Distributed options are required. A database link must be created to the remote database using the CREATE DATABASE LINK statement. For more information about creating database links, refer to Chapter 11. Once a database link has been established, an AFTER INSERT trigger can be created on the source table to insert each record into the remote database.

Steps

1. Run SQL*Plus and connect as the WAITE user account. CHP15-33.sql, shown in Figure 15-20, creates a database link referencing the local database and two tables.

The database link created in the script connects to the WAITE user account on the local database as a remote database. The DEPT_LOCAL table represents the source table on the local database. The DEPT_REMOTE table is located on the local database for demonstration purposes, but will be accessed through the database link as a remote table. Run the file to create the sample objects.

```
SQL>  START CHP15-33

Database link created.

Table created.

Table created.
```

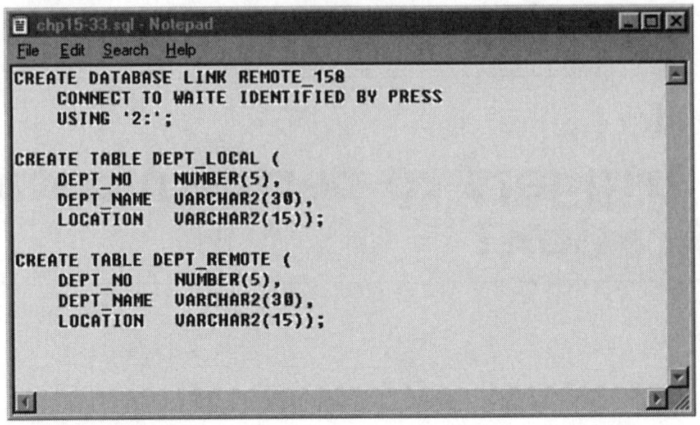

```
CREATE DATABASE LINK REMOTE_158
    CONNECT TO WAITE IDENTIFIED BY PRESS
    USING '2:';

CREATE TABLE DEPT_LOCAL (
    DEPT_NO     NUMBER(5),
    DEPT_NAME   VARCHAR2(30),
    LOCATION    VARCHAR2(15));

CREATE TABLE DEPT_REMOTE (
    DEPT_NO     NUMBER(5),
    DEPT_NAME   VARCHAR2(30),
    LOCATION    VARCHAR2(15));
```

Figure 15-20 CHP15-33.sql creates the sample database link and tables used in How-To 15.8

The database link and two tables adequately demonstrate a two-database system with identical tables on each.

2. Load CHP15-34.sql into the SQL buffer. The CREATE TRIGGER statement in the file creates an AFTER INSERT TRIGGER, replicating a record to the remote table.

```
SQL> GET CHP15-34
  1  CREATE OR REPLACE TRIGGER REPL_DEPT
  2  AFTER INSERT ON LOCAL15_33
  3  FOR EACH ROW
  4  BEGIN
  5      INSERT INTO REMOTE15_33@DBLINK15_33
  6      VALUES (:NEW.DEPT_NO, :NEW.DEPT_NAME, :NEW.LOCATION);
  7  END;
```

Line 1 provides the keywords required to create the trigger and names it REPL_DEPT. Line 2 provides the triggering event. It will fire after an insert on the LOCAL15_33 table. Line 3 provides the FOR EACH ROW clause to make the trigger fire once for each record inserted into the table. Lines 4 through 7 contain the trigger body. The INSERT statement contained in lines 5 and 6 uses the database link created in Step 1 to insert a duplicate record in the remote table.

3. Run the statement to create the database trigger.

```
SQL>  /

Trigger created.
```

The trigger created in this step ensures that new data is replicated in the remote table. In order to remove data deleted from the local table, the next step creates an AFTER DELETE trigger.

4. Load CHP15-35.sql into the SQL buffer. The CREATE TRIGGER statement contained in the file ensures that data deleted from the local table is also deleted from the remote table.

```
SQL> GET CHP15-35
  1  CREATE OR REPLACE TRIGGER DELETE_DEPT
  2  AFTER DELETE ON LOCAL15_33
  3  FOR EACH ROW
  4  BEGIN
  5     DELETE FROM REMOTE15_33@DBLINK15_33
  6        WHERE DEPT_NO = :OLD.DEPT_NO;
  7  END;
```

Line 1 provides the keywords required to create the trigger and names it DELETE_DEPT. Line 2 provides the triggering event. It will fire after a delete on the LOCAL15_33 table. Line 3 provides the FOR EACH ROW clause causing the trigger to fire once for each record deleted from the table. Lines 4 through 7 contain the trigger body. The DELETE statement contained in lines 5 and 6 uses the database link created in Step 1 to delete the corresponding record from the remote table.

5. Run the statement to create the database trigger.

```
SQL> /
```

```
Trigger created.
```

Now that the database triggers have been created to perform the replication tasks, the next step inserts a record into the local database. The AFTER INSERT trigger fires to create the same record in the remote table.

6. Load CHP15-36.sql into the SQL buffer. The INSERT statement contained in the file creates a new record in the local version of the table.

```
SQL>  GET CHP15-36
  1   INSERT INTO LOCAL15_33
  2      VALUES (1,'MARKETING','CHICAGO')
```

The INSERT statement creates a new record in the DEPT_LOCAL table containing the AFTER INSERT trigger.

7. Run the statement to create the new record and commit the transaction.

```
SQL> /
```

```
1 row created.
```

```
SQL>  COMMIT;
```

```
Commit complete.
```

Creating a new record in the local table should create a corresponding record in the remote table. In the next step, the remote table will be queried to view the record created.

8. Load CHP15-37.sql into the SQL buffer. The query contained in the file uses the database link created in Step 1 to reference the remote table.

```
SQL>   GET CHP15-37
  1    SELECT *
  2        FROM REMOTE15_33@DBLINK15_33
```

Line 2 includes the DBLINK15_33 database link with the table name to query the data from the remote database.

9. Run the query to display the data created in the remote database. Figure 15-21 shows the results of the query within SQL*Plus.

The record created in the local table was also created in the remote table by the database trigger. In the next step, the record is deleted from the local table, causing the corresponding record to be deleted from the remote database.

10. Load CHP15-38.sql into the SQL buffer. The DELETE statement created in the file removes the record from the local table, deleting it from the remote table.

```
SQL>   GET CHP15-38
  1    DELETE FROM
  2        LOCAL15_33
```

The DELETE statement fires the AFTER DELETE trigger for each row deleted by the statement. This will delete the corresponding records from the remote table.

11. Run the statement to delete the record from the local table and commit the transaction.

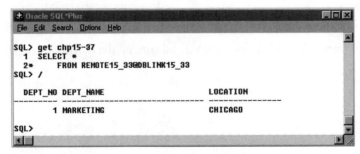

Figure 15-21 The results of a query to the remote database that shows the replicated data

```
SQL>  /

1 row deleted.

SQL>  commit;

Commit complete
```

Once the record is deleted from the local table, it is also deleted from the remote table by the AFTER DELETE trigger.

12. Query the remote table within SQL*Plus to display the records contained in the table. Figure 15-22 shows the query and its results.

Because the AFTER DELETE trigger ensures that the delete transaction occurs on both databases, there are no records in the remote table. The replication of the DELETE statements was successful.

How It Works

INSERT and DELETE statements can be easily replicated with the AFTER INSERT and AFTER DELETE triggers which modify data on the remote database using database links. Step 1 creates a sample database link and two sample tables used to demonstrate the process. Steps 2 and 3 create an AFTER INSERT trigger, which replicates all new records. An INSERT statement is used with a database link to create the records on the remote table. Steps 4 and 5 create an AFTER DELETE trigger which deletes the corresponding record from the remote table whenever a record is deleted from the local table. Steps 6 through 11 demonstrate the use of the triggers by inserting a record into the local table and viewing its corresponding record on the remote database. The record is deleted in a later step and automatically removed from the remote table.

Figure 15-22 A query of the remote table after the DELETE transaction

Comments

This technique is useful for performing simple replication tasks. It is also possible to create triggers to manage updates of records. However, as soon as you include updates in the process, it can become difficult to manage all of the possibilities. When it becomes too complex to manage replication through database triggers, you should explore the use of snapshots, presented in Chapter 11, Distributed Databases.

CHAPTER 16

APPLICATION TUNING

APPLICATION TUNING

How do I...

Application tuning within Oracle can be a confusing task. There is much disagreement in the industry over the best way to tune an application. There are many factors which can affect the performance of an application. They include normalization of the database, indexes on the tables, and the SQL statements themselves. Improving an application's performance is done by analyzing its execution, and taking steps to improve it. This chapter presents techniques for analyzing the execution path used by the optimizer and methods for improving performance by creating indexes, passing hints to the optimizer, and suppressing indexes. The examples presented in this chapter can be found on the accompanying CD in the \SAMPLES\CHAP16 directory.

16.1 Create an index on a table

Indexes can improve the performance of queries on a table and are created using the CREATE INDEX statement. When a query in Oracle7 returns less than 5 percent of the records in a table, an index may improve the performance of the query. This How-To presents the method used to create a new index on a table and explains when indexes are required.

16.2 Determine the indexes on a table

When tuning SQL statements, it is important to know the indexes on the table and the columns contained in each index. Information about indexes can be queried from the ALL_INDEXES and ALL_IND_COLUMNS data dictionary views. This How-To presents the method used to determine the indexes on a table and the columns contained in the index.

16.3 Analyze a query using Explain

The EXPLAIN PLAN statement can be used to analyze the execution path of SQL statements. The execution path defines the sequence of physical operations that Oracle goes through to execute the SQL statement. To achieve optimal performance, the number of physical operations should be kept as low as possible. This How-To explains the use of the EXPLAIN PLAN statement to analyze SQL statements.

16.4 Use SQL*Trace and TKPROF to analyze queries

SQL*Trace is similar to EXPLAIN PLAN because it analyzes the performance of SQL statements when they are executed, but also includes physical execution statistics such as rows returned, CPU time, elapsed time, and number of disk accesses. When SQL*Trace is run on the database, the execution of all SQL statements within an application can be analyzed and written to a trace file. The TKPROF utility is used to convert the trace file to a readable form. This How-To presents the use of SQL*Trace and TKPROF to analyze SQL statements.

16.5 Pass hints to the optimizer

In some cases, you will know more about the execution plan to be used with a SQL statement than the optimizer. If you want the optimizer to take a certain path when executing a statement, you can pass hints to it. This How-To presents the method for passing hints to the optimizer.

16.6 Suppress an index in a query

When a query returns more than 5 percent of the rows in a table or two or more indexes are contained on a single table, an index should suppressed. Indexes can be suppressed by modifying the WHERE clause of the query. This How-To presents the methods used to suppress an index when performing a query.

COMPLEXITY
INTERMEDIATE

16.1 How do I...
Create an index on a table?

Problem

I need to create an index on a table in order to improve the performance of certain queries on it. I need to know when an index should be created and how to create it. How do I create an index on a table?

Technique

It is important to determine when an index should be created based on the queries performed on the table. The generally accepted rule in Oracle7 is that an index should be used when the query returns less than 5 percent of the table. If more than 5 percent of the table is returned by the query, an index may not improve performance. In some situations, an index may improve performance when the query returns up to 20 percent of the rows from the table. If the size of the table is small, as in less than 8 database blocks or 250 records, an index should not be used regardless of the number of records the query returns. It is more efficient for Oracle to perform a full table scan to find the records on small tables than to incur the additional overhead of using an index. If the table contains many thousands of records, the need for indexes becomes necessary to avoid full table scans. Table 16-1 provides guidelines for creating indexes on tables.

SITUATION	CREATE INDEX?
The columns define a unique primary key.	YES, the index will enforce uniqueness.
The columns define a primary key and are used in the join condition of queries.	YES, to reduce the records read in a join.
The columns define a primary key and the table is smaller than 4 blocks or contains less than 250 records.	NO, unless the columns are used in table joins.
The columns define a foreign key that is often used to join to another table.	YES, because columns are used in joins.
The columns define a foreign key that is enforced through referential integrity.	YES, to improve the performance of validation.

continued on next page

continued from previous page

SITUATION	CREATE INDEX?
The columns are often used in the WHERE clause of a query which returns less than 5 percent of the rows.	YES, only if less than 5 percent of the rows are returned.

Table 16-1 Guidelines for creating indexes

Concatenated indexes are indexes containing more than one column. When multiple columns are always used together, concatenated indexes can make an index more efficient. The number of indexes created for a table depends on the queries performed on it. Each index requires space in the database and adds additional overhead to the INSERT statements and UPDATE statements modifying the indexed columns.

The CREATE INDEX statement is used to create an index on a table. The syntax of the CREATE INDEX statement is shown in Figure 16-1.

Steps

1. Run SQL*Plus and connect as the WAITE user account. CHP16-1.sql, shown in Figure 16-2, creates the sample table used throughout this How-To.

The sample table created in the file will have indexes developed in the following steps. Run the file to create the sample table.

```
SQL> START CHP16-1

Table created.
```

```
          CREATE INDEX Syntax


   CREATE[UNIQUE] INDEX index-name
        ON table-name (column-name, ..., column-name)
   [STORAGE(
        [INITIAL initial-extent-size]
        [TABLESPACE tablespace-name]
        [NEXT next-extent-size]
        [MINEXTENTS minimum-number-of-extents]
        [MAXEXTENTS maximum-number-of-extents])]
   [TABLESPACE tablespace-name]
   [PCTINCREASE pct-growth-rate]
```

Figure 16-1 The syntax of the CREATE INDEX statement

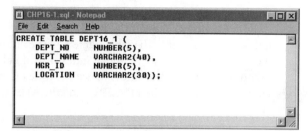

Figure 16-2 CHP16-1.sql creates the sample table used in How-To 16.1

2. Load CHP16-2.sql into the SQL buffer. The file contains a CREATE INDEX statement for building a unique index on the sample table.

```
SQL> GET CHP16-2
1   CREATE INDEX
2       IDX_DEPT16_2
3* ON DEPT16_1 (DEPT_NAME)
```

Line 1 presents the keywords required to create an index. Line 2 defines the name of the index. Index names must be unique within the schema. Line 3 specifies the name of the table and the columns contained in the index. The DEPT_NAME column is the only column indexed by this statement. To use multiple columns in the index, the column names must be separated by commas. Since no storage parameters or tablespaces were specified in the statement, the default tablespace for the connected user is the location of the index. The default storage parameters for that tablespace are used when the index is created.

3. Run the statement to create the index.

```
SQL>  /
```

```
Index created.
```

The index created in this step is a non-unique index. Duplicate values are allowed within the index. A unique index does not allow duplicate records to be created and can be used to enforce data uniqueness. The next step presents the statement used to create a unique index on a table.

4. Load CHP16-3.sql into the SQL buffer. The file contains a CREATE UNIQUE INDEX statement to build a unique index on the sample table.

```
SQL> GET CHP16-3
 1   CREATE UNIQUE INDEX
 2       IDX_DEPT16_3
 3* ON DEPT16_1 (DEPT_NO)
```

Line 1 presents the keywords required to create an index. The optional UNIQUE clause creates a unique index. Line 2 specifies the name of the index. Line 3 specifies the table name and the column to be indexed. Since the statement is creating a unique index, it will fail if duplicate values are found in the indexed columns. Once the index is created, only unique values will be allowed when INSERT and UPDATE statements modify the table.

5. Run the statement to create the unique index.

```
SQL>  /

Index created.
```

There are now two indexes on the sample table. Both indexes contain only a single column. In many cases, more than one column is part of a primary or foreign key. Plus, they are often used together in queries. The next step creates a concatenated index containing more than one column.

6. Load CHP16-4.sql into the SQL buffer. The file contains a CREATE INDEX statement to build a concatenated index on the sample table.

```
SQL> GET CHP16-4
  1   CREATE INDEX
  2       IDX_DEPT16_4
  3* ON DEPT16_1 (DEPT_NO, MGR_ID)
```

The keywords presented in line 1 do not include the UNIQUE clause creating a non-unique index. Line 2 specifies the name of the index, which must be unique within the schema. The table name and columns are defined in line 3. The multiple columns contained in the index are listed in order, separated by commas.

7. Run the statement to create the concatenated index.

```
SQL>  /

Index created.
```

So far, none of the indexes contained storage clauses or defined a specific tablespace. Indexes should be spread out over tablespaces to allow for concurrent reads and writes. The next step creates an index containing optional storage parameters.

8. Load CHP16-5.sql into the SQL buffer. The file contains a CREATE INDEX statement to build a concatenated index on the sample table with storage options.

```
SQL> GET CHP16-5
  1   CREATE INDEX
  2       IDX_DEPT16_5
  3  ON DEPT16_1 (DEPT_NO, LOCATION)
  4   STORAGE
```

```
5       (INITIAL 1M
6           NEXT 1M)
7* TABLESPACE SYSTEM
```

Line 1 provides the required keywords to create a non-unique index. Line 2 provides the name for the index. Line 3 specifies the name of the table and the list of columns to be indexed. Line 4 presents the STORAGE clause defining how the index will be created. The INITIAL clause in line 5 defines the first extent as 1 MB. The NEXT clause in line 6 defines the next extent created as 1 MB also. The TABLESPACE clause in line 7 specifies the location of the index as the SYSTEM tablespace.

9. Run the statement to create the index.

```
SQL> /
```

```
Index created.
```

To create the new index, a minimum of 1 MB of storage in the SYSTEM tablespace is required. The size of the INITIAL extent is the minimum amount of space required. If an index not needed is created, it is removed with the DROP INDEX statement. The next step removes the index created in this step.

10. Load CHP16-6.sql into the SQL buffer. The DROP INDEX statement contained in the file removes the index created in Steps 8 and 9.

```
SQL> GET CHP16-6
1   DROP INDEX
2*      IDX_DEPT16_5
```

Line 1 presents the keywords required to remove an index. Line 2 specifies the index to be dropped. When an index is dropped, it is removed from the data dictionary and the space it used is reclaimed by the database.

11. Run the statement to remove the index.

```
SQL> /
```

```
Index dropped.
```

Once the index has been dropped, it will no longer be used in any database operations.

How It Works

When you have determined that an index is required on a table, the CREATE INDEX statement is used to create it. An index can be either unique or non-unique and can contain one or more columns. The name of each index must be unique within the owner's schema, and two indexes on the same table cannot have identical column lists. Step 1 creates a sample table with indexes created in the remaining steps. Steps

2 and 3 create a non-unique index containing a single column. No storage clause or tablespace is specified, so the index is created in the default tablespace for the WAITE user account. Steps 4 and 5 create a unique index on the DEPT_NO column of the sample table. In order to create a unique index, the existing data in the table must be unique for the indexed columns. Steps 6 and 7 create a non-unique concatenated index containing two columns. When concatenated indexes are created, the order of the columns is important if both columns are not always specified. Steps 8 and 9 create an index specifying storage parameters and a tablespace. The INITIAL clause specifies the size of the first extent in the index and is the minimum amount of disk space the index requires. Steps 10 and 11 present the DROP INDEX statement to remove the index created in steps 8 and 9.

Comments

Indexes can dramatically improve the performance of your applications when used correctly, by eliminating full table scans within queries. If you create an index and find that the performance of a SQL statement has not improved, the techniques presented in How-To 16.4 and 16.5 can analyze the SQL statement to determine whether the index is actually being used.

COMPLEXITY
BEGINNING

16.2   How do I...
Determine the indexes on a table?

Problem

I need to determine which indexes are on a table and which columns in the table are indexed. When I create SQL statements, I want to be sure that they are executed in the most efficient way possible. How do I determine the indexes which exist on a table and the columns contained in the indexes?

Technique

The USER_INDEXES data dictionary view contains information about the indexes the user account owns. The USER_IND_COLUMNS data dictionary view contains the columns in an index. Figure 16-3 shows the description of the USER_IND_COLUMNS data dictionary view within SQL*Plus.

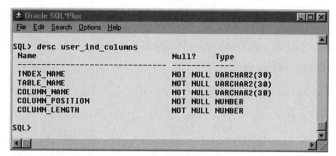

Figure 16-3 The USER_IND_COLUMNS data
dictionary view

The USER_IND_COLUMNS and the corresponding ALL_IND_COLUMNS view
are the ones most used by application developers. The TABLE_NAME and
TABLE_OWNER columns identify the table containing the index. The INDEX_NAME
column contains the name of the index, and the COLUMN_NAME column contains
the column indexed. The COLUMN_POSITION column is used to determine the
order of the columns within the index.

Steps

1. Run SQL*Plus and connect as the WAITE user account. CHP16-7.sql,
shown in Figure 16-4, creates a sample table with an index used in this
How-To.

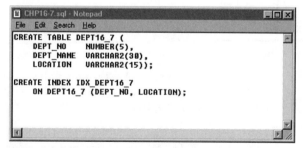

Figure 16-4 CHP16-7.sql creates the sample
table with an index used in How-To 16.2

The script creates a sample table and a sample index. The only purpose of the table is to contain the index described in the following steps. Run the file to create the sample objects.

```
SQL> START CHP16-7

Table created.

Index created.
```

Once the table and index are created, the data dictionary views can be queried to display the indexes on the table.

2. Load CHP16-8.sql into the SQL buffer. The file contains a query of the USER_INDEXES view to list the name of the indexes on a table.

```
SQL> GET CHP16-8
  1   SELECT
  2        INDEX_NAME
  3   FROM USER_INDEXES
  4   WHERE
  5*      TABLE_NAME = 'DEPT16_7'
```

Line 2 specifies the INDEX_NAME column to be returned by the query. Information such as the tablespace in which the index is located can also be queried. Line 3 specifies the USER_INDEXES view as the source of the data. Line 5 identifies that only indexes on the sample table will be returned by the query.

3. Run the query to display the results.

```
SQL>  /

INDEX_NAME
------------------
IDX_DEPT16_7
```

The index created in Step 1 is the only index returned by the query. If the WHERE clause was not contained in the query, all indexes in the user's schema would be displayed.

4. Load CHP16-9.sql into the SQL buffer. The file contains a query of the USER_IND_COLUMNS view to display the columns contained in the sample table's index.

```
SQL> GET CHP16-9
  1   SELECT
  2        INDEX_NAME,
  3        COLUMN_NAME
  4   FROM
  5        USER_IND_COLUMNS
  6   WHERE
  7        TABLE_NAME = 'DEPT16_7'
  8   ORDER BY
  9*      INDEX_NAME, COLUMN_POSITION
```

Lines 2 and 3 specify that the INDEX_NAME and COLUMN_NAME columns are returned by the query. Line 4 specifies that the data comes from the USER_IND_COLUMNS data dictionary view. The WHERE clause in lines 6 and 7 specifies that only data from the sample table is returned by the query. The ORDER BY clause in lines 8 and 9 orders the output correctly.

5. Run the statement to display the results. Figure 16-5 shows the results of the query in SQL*Plus.

The name of the sample index and each of the columns are returned by the query. This simple query makes it easy to determine the columns an index contains.

How It Works

The USER_INDEXES and ALL_INDEXES data dictionary views contain information about the structure of the database indexes. If you are looking for information about the location, extent size, and statistics on the indexes, these views are the ones to use. The USER_IND_COLUMNS and the ALL_IND_COLUMNS data dictionary views contain the columns in the indexes. Step 1 creates a sample table with an index, which is queried from the data dictionary in the following steps. Steps 2 and 3 query information about the index from the USER_INDEXES view. Steps 4 and 5 use the USER_IND_COLUMNS view to display the columns contained in the indexes.

Comments

When you are developing applications, you will find yourself querying the USER_IND_COLUMNS view any time a query runs slowly and makes you wonder about the indexes on a table. If you determine that the correct indexes do not exist

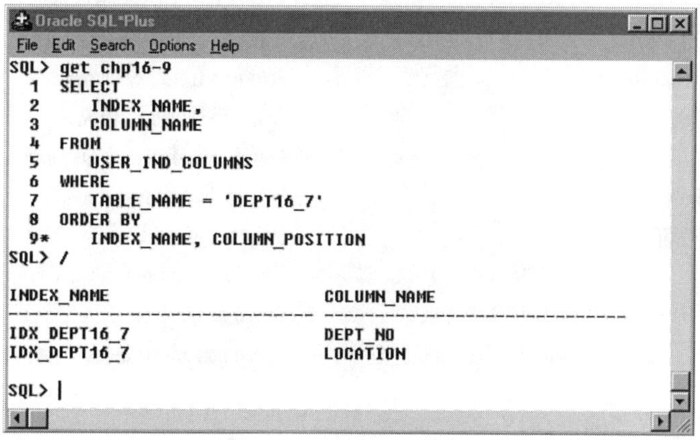

Figure 16-5 The results of the query within SQL*Plus

on the tables used in your queries, you can use the techniques presented in How-To 16.1 to create new ones.

COMPLEXITY
INTERMEDIATE

16.3 How do I...
Analyze a query using Explain?

Problem

I have a query I don't think is using the indexes it should. I want to use the EXPLAIN PLAN statement to analyze the query's execution path to determine if the proper indexes are being used. How do I analyze a query using Explain?

Technique

The EXPLAIN PLAN statement can be included with a SQL statement to determine its execution path. The *execution path* of a SQL statement is the order of physical operations the statement uses when executed. The EXPLAIN PLAN statement requires a table called PLAN_TABLE, which receives the data generated by EXPLAIN PLAN when executed. A script file is provided with the database to create the table. Although the name of the file is system dependent, it is probably called utilxplan.sql and found in the $ORACLE_HOME\rdbms72\admin directory. Once data is created with the EXPLAIN PLAN statement, PLAN_TABLE can be queried to analyze the execution path. The operations performed in the execution of the statement are shown in Table 16-2.

OPERATION	OPTION	DESCRIPTION
AND-EQUAL		Returns the intersection of multiple ROWIDs without duplicates.
CONNECT BY		Tree traversal using CONNECT BY.
CONCATENATION		Returns a UNION of all rows.
COUNTING		Counts the number of rows.
FILTER		Accepts and eliminates rows based on a WHERE clause condition.
FIRST ROW		Returns the first row of a query only.
FOR UPDATE		Locks the selected rows.
INDEX	DESCENDING	Uses a non-unique index and returns rows in descending order.
	UNIQUE RANGE SCAN	Uses a unique index to return one row.
	NON-UNIQUE RANGE SCAN	Uses a non-unique index to return rows.

OPERATION	OPTION	DESCRIPTION
INTERSECTION		Returns the intersection of rows without duplicates.
MERGE JOIN		Combines records from two sorted sets of rows.
	OUTER	Combines records from two sorted sets of rows and also includes outer join.
MINUS		Uses the MINUS function to subtract rows.
NESTED LOOPS		Compares two sets of rows and checks each row from one set with each row from the other.
	OUTER	Same as above, but includes outer join.
PROJECTION		Returns a subset of columns from a table.
REMOTE		Accesses data with database link.
	JOIN	Sorts rows to perform a MERGE JOIN.
	UNIQUE	Sorts rows to eliminate duplicates.
	ORDER BY	Sorts rows because of an ORDER BY clause.
TABLE ACCESS	FULL	Performs a full table scan.
	CLUSTER	Uses a cluster.
	HASH	Uses a hashing algorithm.
	ROWID	Accesses a table by ROWID.
UNION		Uses a UNION statement to combine queries.
VIEW		Performs retrieval from a view.

Table 16-2 The operations displayed by EXPLAIN PLAN

Steps

1. Run SQL*Plus and connect as the WAITE user account. The utlxplan.sql file found in the \rdbms72\admin directory under ORACLE_HOME must be executed before running Explain. The file creates the table required by the EXPLAIN PLAN statement. If the table PLAN_TABLE does not exist in your schema, run the file to create the required table.

```
SQL> start D:\orawin95\rdbms72\admin\utlxplan.sql

Table created.
```

Because my ORACLE_HOME directory is D:\ORAWIN95, I used it when I executed the command. You must use the correct directory for your installation. The operation creates a table called PLAN_TABLE. A description of the table is shown in Figure 16-6.

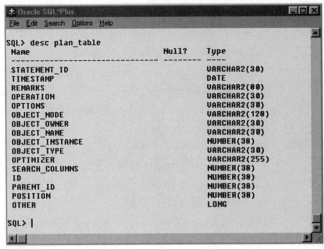

Figure 16-6 The description of PLAN_TABLE
within SQL*Plus

2. CHP16-10.sql, shown in Figure 16-7, creates the sample objects used in
this How-To.

Three tables and two indexes are created so that a fairly complex query can
be executed. Although no data is created in the tables, the execution path of
queries can still be determined. Run the statement to create the objects.

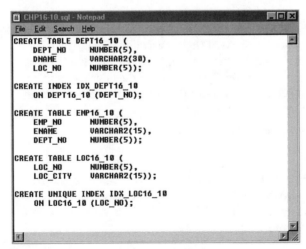

Figure 16-7 CHP16-10.sql creates the sample
objects used in How-To 16.3

```
SQL>   START CHP16-10

Table created.

Index created.

Table created.

Table created.

Index created.
```

3. Load CHP16-11.sql into the SQL buffer. The EXPLAIN PLAN statement in the file contains a query of the sample tables created in step 1.

```
SQL> GET CHP16-11
   1   EXPLAIN PLAN
   2   SET STATEMENT_ID = 'CHP16_11'
   3   INTO PLAN_TABLE FOR
   4   SELECT
   5     EMP16_10.ENAME,
   6     DEPT16_10.DNAME,
   7     LOC16_10.LOC_CITY
   8   FROM
   9     EMP16_10, DEPT16_10, LOC16_10
  10   WHERE
  11     EMP16_10.DEPT_NO = DEPT16_10.DEPT_NO AND
  12     DEPT16_10.LOC_NO = LOC16_10.LOC_NO
  13*  ORDER BY EMP16_10.ENAME
```

Line 1 specifies the EXPLAIN PLAN keyword generating explain information for the query. Line 2 gives the statement a name using the SET STATEMENT ID clause. The name given is used to identify the records created by the statement in PLAN_TABLE. Line 3 provides the name of the table receiving the data generated by the EXPLAIN PLAN statement. The PLAN_TABLE created in step 1 will receive the results of the analysis. Lines 4 through 13 provide a fairly complex query that joins three tables and contains an ORDER BY clause. The execution of this query will generate some good analysis results.

4. Run the statement to execute the query and create the analysis information.

```
SQL>   /

Explained.
```

The results of the query are not shown in SQL*Plus because the purpose of the EXPLAIN PLAN statement is not to display the results of the query, but to analyze its execution. In the next step, a query is presented displaying the information from PLAN_TABLE in an easy-to-read format.

5. Load CHP16-12.sql into the SQL buffer. The file contains a query provided in the *Oracle7 Server Utilities Guide*, which displays the Explain information in a tree format.

```
SQL> GET CHP16-12
  1   SELECT LPAD(' ', 2*(LEVEL-1))||OPERATION||' '||
  2       OPTIONS "QUERY PLAN" , OBJECT_NAME
  3        FROM PLAN_TABLE
  4   START WITH ID = 0 AND STATEMENT_ID = '&STATEMENT_ID'
  5   CONNECT BY PRIOR ID = PARENT_ID
  6*               AND STATEMENT_ID = STATEMENT_ID
```

The query traverses the tree-structured data created in PLAN_TABLE. Line 1 uses the LPAD function to indent the records returned, based on their level in the tree. The LEVEL pseudo-column contains the depth of the record within the tree structure. The OPERATION column contains the operation performed by the execution step. When present, the OPTIONS column contains the options of the operation. Line 2 provides an alias for the calculated column and returns the OBJECT column containing the database object the operation affects. Line 3 contains the FROM clause specifying PLAN_TABLE as the source of the data. The CONNECT BY PRIOR clause in lines 5 and 6, and the START WITH clause in line 4, are used to navigate a tree structure. The &STATEMENT_ID substitution variable contained in line 4 allows you to specify a statement to query. The STATEMENT_ID was generated by the SET STATEMENT_ID clause in line 2 of step 3.

6. Set the PAGESIZE system variable to 50 and format the columns using the COLUMN command. Execute the command to display the results, replacing the substitution variable with CHP16_11. The results of the operation are shown in Figure 16-8.

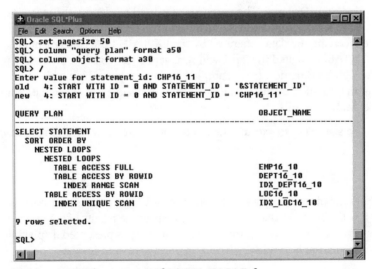

Figure 16-8 The query of PLAN_TABLE for the statement explained

The tree structure of the output shows the execution path the optimizer will use when the query is run. A line containing the statement INDEX RANGE SCAN identifies that a non-unique index is used and shows the index name. Lines containing the statement INDEX UNIQUE SCAN show that a unique index is used. TABLE ACCESS FULL shows a full table scan will be executed.

How It Works

The EXPLAIN PLAN statement analyzes the execution path of a SQL statement and puts the results in a table that can be queried. The PLAN_TABLE table is created by the utlxplan.sql file found in the \rdbms72\admin directory under ORACLE_HOME. Step 1 creates PLAN_TABLE by running the utlxplan.sql file. Step 2 creates three sample tables used in the query analyzed. Steps 3 and 4 execute an EXPLAIN PLAN statement with a fairly complex query in order to analyze the query. Steps 5 and 6 present a query of PLAN_TABLE, displaying the results of the analysis in a tree format.

Comments

The EXPLAIN PLAN statement is a good way to analyze problem SQL statements. If you have a statement that is not performing acceptably, use the EXPLAIN PLAN statement to determine the execution path of the query. This allows you to determine the order of the physical operations and see the indexes the statement is using. Since the query only performs an analysis and does not execute, you can analyze the results without waiting for the long-running query to execute.

COMPLEXITY

INTERMEDIATE

16.4   How do I...
Use SQL*Trace and TKPROF to analyze queries?

Problem

I want to use SQL*Trace to analyze the execution plan of SQL statements within my application. Since SQL*Trace analyzes all statements executed when it is turned on, I can use it to analyze the entire application as it runs. How do I use SQL*Trace and TKPROF to analyze queries?

Technique

SQL*Trace writes a file containing performance statistics of the SQL statements on the database. SQL*Trace generates a large number of statistics and can impact performance while running. In order to use the SQL*Trace facility, there are four database parameters in the INIT.ORA file you can set, one of which must be set. The parameters that may be set while using SQL*Trace are shown in Table 16-3.

PARAMETER	SETTING	DESCRIPTION
MAX_DUMP_SIZE	integer value	Specifies the largest physical size that a trace file can become.
SQL_TRACE	TRUE	When set to TRUE, SQL*Trace is enabled for all database users. FALSE is the default. If TRUE, SQL*Trace is executed for ALL statements on the database.
TIMED_STATISITICS	TRUE	REQUIRED. When set to TRUE, the database collects additional timing statistics that are important to SQL*Trace.
USER_DUMP_ DEST	directory on system	Specifies the location where the trace files will be written.

Table 16-3 Database parameters related to SQL*Trace

When the SQL_TRACE database parameter is set to TRUE, overall response time can degrade noticeably since a trace file is created for every statement executed. SQL*Trace can be executed on individual sessions without setting the SQL_TRACE parameter to TRUE. The ALTER SESSION SET SQL_TRACE TRUE statement generates a trace file for the current session. Within PL/SQL, the DBMS_SESSION.SET_SQL_TRACE procedure performs the same action. Once the trace file is written, the TKPROF utility is used to interpret it. TKPROF is run from the operating system command line. The syntax of the statement is shown here:

```
TKPROF tracefile outputfile [SORT = parameters] [PRINT = number]
[EXPLAIN = username/password]
```

The *trace file* is the file created by the database when SQL*Trace runs for a session. The *output file* is the file generated when the statement runs. The optional SORT statement lets you sort the output by any of the statistics collected by the trace. Table 16-4 contains the possible sort parameters.

PARAMETER	DESCRIPTION
EXECNT	Number of executes.
EXECPT	CPU time spent executing.
EXEELA	Elapsed time spent executing.
EXEPHR	Number of physical reads during execute.
EXECR	Number of consistent reads during execute.
EXECU	Number of current reads during execute.

PARAMETER	DESCRIPTION
EXEROW	Number of rows processed during execute.
FCHCNT	Number of fetches.
FCHCPU	CPU time spent fetching.
FCHELA	Elapsed time spent fetching.
FCHPH	Number of physical reads during fetch.
FCHCR	Number of consistent reads during fetch.
FCHCU	Number of current reads during fetch.
FCHROW	Number of rows fetched.
PRSCNT	Number of times parsed.
PRSCPU	CPU time spent parsing.
PRSELA	Elapsed time spent parsing.
PRSPHR	Number of physical reads during parse.
PRSCR	Number of consistent reads during parse.
PRSCU	Number of current reads during parse.

Table 16-4 TKPROF sort parameters

The PRINT parameter can be used to limit the number of statements contained in the output of TKPROF. This allows you to include only the worst performing statements in your report, using a sort parameter to specify an order and the print parameter to limit the output. The Explain parameter allows you to run the EXPLAIN PLAN statement on all the statements contained in the trace file. A user name and password must be provided with the parameter in order to connect to the database to run the statement.

Steps

1. Find and open the INIT.ORA file for your database. In the case of my Personal Oracle 7 for Windows 95 database, the file is found in the $ORACLE_HOME\Database directory. Add values for the MAX_DUMP_SIZE, TIMED_STATISTICS, and USER_DUMP_DEST parameters. Figure 16-9 shows the INIT.ORA file with these parameters set.

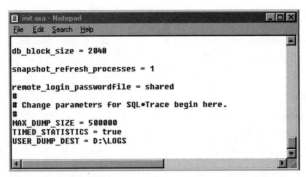

Figure 16-9 The INIT.ORA file configured to
run SQL*Trace

Do not set the SQL_TRACE parameter to TRUE unless you are the only
user of the database and want to run the SQL*Trace facility on all statements. Shut down and restart the database so the new parameters take
effect.

2. CHP16-13.sql, shown in Figure 16-10, creates three sample tables with
data which will be analyzed using the SQL*Trace facility.

Three tables and one index which will be queried with a fairly complex
query are created in this How-To. Three hundred rows of sample data are
created so that accurate statistics are generated.

```
CREATE TABLE DEPT16_13 (
    DEPT_NO     NUMBER(5),
    DNAME       VARCHAR2(30),
    LOC_NO      NUMBER(5));

CREATE TABLE EMP16_13 (
    EMP_NO      NUMBER(5),
    ENAME       VARCHAR2(15),
    DEPT_NO     NUMBER(5));

CREATE TABLE LOC16_13 (
    LOC_NO      NUMBER(5),
    LOC_CITY    VARCHAR2(15));

CREATE UNIQUE INDEX IDX_LOC16_13
    ON LOC16_13 (LOC_NO);
BEGIN
    FOR I IN 1..100 LOOP
        INSERT INTO DEPT16_13 VALUES (I,'DEPARTMENT '||TO_CHAR(I), 1)
        INSERT INTO EMP16_13 VALUES (I,'EMPLOYEE '||TO_CHAR(I), 1);
        INSERT INTO LOC16_13 VALUES (I,'LOCATION '||TO_CHAR(I));
    END LOOP;
END;
/
```

Figure 16-10 CHP16-13.sql creates the sample tables
with data used in How-To 16.4

```
SQL>   START CHP16-13

Table created.

Table created.

Table created.

Index created.

PL/SQL procedure executed successfully.

Commit complete.
```

3. Run SQL*Plus and connect as the WAITE user account. Load CHP16-14.sql into the SQL buffer. The file contains an ALTER SESSION command to invoke the SQL*Trace facility for the current session.

```
SQL>   GET CHP16-14
  1    ALTER SESSION
  2       SET SQL_TRACE TRUE
```

When the statement is executed, the SQL* Trace facility will create a trace file containing statistics about the execution of SQL statements.

4. Run the statement to enable the SQL*Trace facility for the current session.

```
SQL>   /

Session altered.
```

5. Load CHP16-15.sql into the SQL buffer. The query contained in the file is fairly complex and will generate good statistics.

```
SQL> GET CHP16-15
  1   SELECT
  2     EMP16_13.ENAME,
  3     DEPT16_13.DNAME,
  4     LOC16_13.LOC_CITY
  5   FROM
  6     EMP16_13, DEPT16_13, LOC16_13
  7   WHERE
  8     EMP16_13.DEPT_NO = DEPT16_13.DEPT_NO AND
  9     DEPT16_13.LOC_NO = LOC16_13.LOC_NO
 10* ORDER BY EMP16_13.ENAME
```

Lines 2 through 4 return the three columns the query returned. The three sample tables are specified in the FROM clause in line 6. The WHERE clause in lines 8 and 9 join the three tables. The ORDER BY clause in line 10 returns the data in the order specified.

6. Run the statement to execute the query.

```
SQL>   /
```

The query returns 100 rows and generates statistics in the trace file. The output of the query was not shown to conserve space.

7. Exit SQL*Plus and go to the operating system prompt. Find the trace file created by the previous session in the directory specified by the USER_DUMP_DEST database parameter, and execute the TKPROF command to create an output file.

```
TKPROF72 ORA36387.TRC OUTPUT.TXT EXPLAIN=WAITE/PRESS
```

Because my database is running Oracle version 7.2, I TKPROF72 is used to create the output file. The first command line parameter is the trace file generated by the session. Each trace file is given a unique name. The second command-line parameter is the output file created by the program. The EXPLAIN=WAITE/PRESS parameter is optional and executes the EXPLAIN PLAN statement for the queries in the trace file. The username and password are specified since the EXPLAIN PLAN statement must be run while connected to a database.

8. Open Windows Notepad and load the output file created in the previous step. Figure 16-11 shows the statistics portion of the trace file in Windows Notepad.

The PARSE row contains statistics for the parse steps performed by the SQL statements. The EXECUTE row shows statistics for the execute steps of the statements. If the statement is a data manipulation statement, the number of rows processed are shown. The FETCH row shows statistics for the fetch

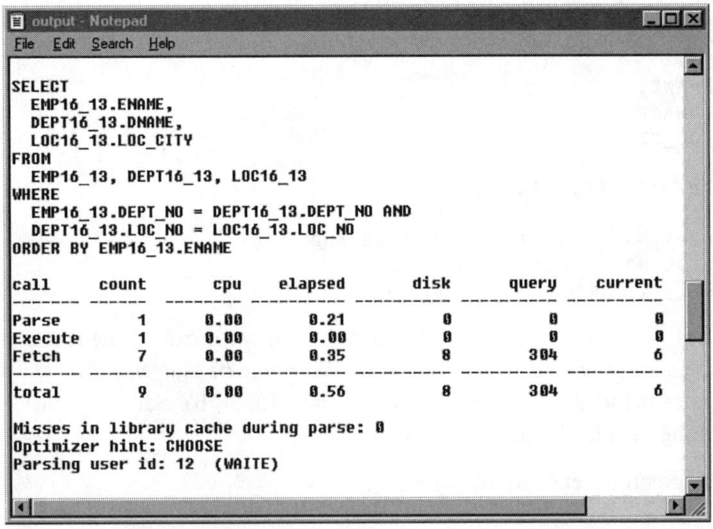

Figure 16-11 The statistics portion of the SQL*Trace output file

steps performed by the statement. The value shown for the SELECT statement is the number of rows processed. Table 16-5 shows the columns returned by the TKPROF utility in the statistics portion.

COLUMN	DESCRIPTION
count	The number of times a statement is executed or parsed. It also contains the number of times a fetch was executed to perform the operation.
cpu	CPU time for operations.
elap	Elapsed time for the operations.
phys	Physical blocks read from disk.
cr	The number of consistent reads required by the statement.
cur	The number of current reads required by the statement.
rows	The number of rows processed by a query.

Table 16-5 The columns displayed in the output of TKPROF

Figure 16-12 shows the Explain portion of the output file. The results displayed in the file are in the same format as in How-To 16.3.

In addition to the execution plan, the number of rows processed in each step is also displayed. In the 100-row query presented in this How-To, each step required the processing of 100 rows.

```
Misses in library cache during parse: 0
Optimizer hint: CHOOSE
Parsing user id: 12  (WAITE)

Rows     Execution Plan
-------  ---------------------------------------------------------------
      0  SELECT STATEMENT    HINT: CHOOSE
    100   SORT (ORDER BY)
    100    MERGE JOIN
    100     SORT (JOIN)
    100      NESTED LOOPS
    100       TABLE ACCESS (FULL) OF 'DEPT16_13'
    100       TABLE ACCESS (BY ROWID) OF 'LOC16_13'
    100        INDEX (UNIQUE SCAN) OF 'IDX_LOC16_13' (UNIQUE)
    100     SORT (JOIN)
    100      TABLE ACCESS (FULL) OF 'EMP16_13'
```

Figure 16-12 The Explain portion of the SQL*Trace output file

How It Works

The SQL*Trace facility is used to generate statistics about the SQL statements per-formed in a session. The TKPROF utility is used to translate the trace file generated by SQL*Trace into a readable format. The EXPLAIN PLAN statement can be exe-cuted with the TKPROF utility to analyze the statements executed by the session. Unlike the EXPLAN PLAN statement, which analyzes a single statement, SQL*Trace can be used to analyze all the statements executed by a session. Step 1 makes the modifications the INIT.ORA file needs to run SQL*Trace. The TIMED_STATISTICS parameter must be set to TRUE in order for SQL*Trace to generate accurate timing statistics. Step 2 restarts the database so the changes to the database parameters take effect. Step 3 creates three sample tables with indexes and sample data, queried later in the example. Steps 4 and 5 execute an ALTER SESSION statement to begin the SQL*Trace operation for the current session. Once the statement is executed, a trace file is generated for the session. Steps 6 and 7 execute a fairly complex query to demon-strate the trace facility. Step 8 runs the TKPROF utility from the operating system prompt to create an output file and analyze the output generated for the session. Step 9 opens the output file in Windows Notepad to display the results of the analysis.

Comments

A major advantage of the SQL*Trace facility over EXPLAIN PLAN is that it can ana-lyze all of the statements executed within the application. Do not set the SQL_TRACE INIT.ORA parameter to run a trace on the entire database unless you need to. Setting the SQL_TRACE parameter to TRUE can degrade performance of the database up to 30 percent. It is best to use the trace facility on one session at a time to minimize performance impact on the database.

COMPLEXITY
INTERMEDIATE

16.5   How do I...
Pass hints to the optimizer?

Problem

We are using cost-based optimization in our database. There are times when I know the data better than the optimizer and want to control how the database executes the statement. I know that hints can be passed to the optimizer to control how state-ments are executed. How do I pass hints to the optimizer?

Technique

Hints are passed to the optimizer inside of comments. When you pass a hint to the optimizer, it changes the execution plan of the statement. The syntax for a hint is /*+ hint */.

Table 16-6 contains the hints which can be passed to the optimizer.

HINT	DESCRIPTION
all_rows	Optimize the statement for best total throughput.
and_equal	Use index merging on the specified table.
cluster	Use a cluster scan.
cost	Use cost-based optimization.
first_row	Optimize the SQL statement for best response time.
full	Use a full table scan on the specified table.
hash	Use a hash search on the specified table.
index	Use the specified index on the specified table.
index_asc	Use the specified index in ascending order.
index_desc	Use the specified index in descending order.
ordered	Use the join sequence from the FROM clause.
rowid	Use the ROWID access method.
rule	Use rule-based optimization.
user_merge	Use sort-merge join techniques on the specified table.
use_nl	Use nested-loop join techniques on the specified table.

Table 16-6 Optimizer hints

After hints are provided to the optimizer, you can use SQL*Trace or EXPLAIN PLAN to determine how the execution of the statement is changed by the hint. The following steps present sample queries which pass hints to the optimizer.

Steps

1. Run SQL*Plus and connect as the WAITE user account. CHP16-16.sql, shown in Figure 16-13, creates sample tables used in this How-To.

```
chp16-16.sql - Notepad
File  Edit  Search  Help
CREATE TABLE DEPT16_16 (
      DEPT_NO       NUMBER(5),
      DNAME         VARCHAR2(30),
      LOC_NO        NUMBER(5));

CREATE TABLE EMP16_16 (
      EMP_NO        NUMBER(5),
      ENAME         VARCHAR2(15),
      DEPT_NO       NUMBER(5));
```

Figure 16-13 CHP16-16.sql creates the sample
tables used in How-To 16.5

Two sample tables are developed, allowing fairly complex queries that use
hints to be created. Run the file to create the sample tables.

```
SQL>   START CHP16-16

Table created.

Table created.
```

2. Load CHP16-17.sql into the SQL buffer. The file contains a query that
passes a hint to the optimizer.

```
SQL> GET CHP16-17
  1   SELECT /*+ rule */
  2       DNAME,
  3       ENAME
  4   FROM
  5       EMP16_16, DEPT16_16
  6   WHERE
  7*      EMP16_16.DEPT_NO = DEPT16_16.DEPT_NO
```

Line 1 specifies that rule-based optimization is used when the query is performed. The optimizer will not perform cost-based optimization for the
query. More than one hint can be passed to the optimizer. The next step
presents a query which passes two hints to the optimizer.

3. Load CHP16-18.sql into the SQL buffer. The file contains a query using full
table scans on both tables in the query.

```
SQL> GET CHP16-18
  1   SELECT
  2       DNAME,
  3       ENAME
  4   FROM
  5       EMP16_16,    /*+ full */
  6       DEPT16_16    /*+ full */
  7   WHERE
  8*      EMP16_16.DEPT_NO = DEPT16_16.DEPT_NO
```

Lines 5 and 6 both supply hints to the optimizer. The /*+full */ hint tells the optimizer to perform a full table scan on the table. In this example, a full table scan will be performed on both tables contained in the query.

How It Works

Hints can be passed to the optimizer within comments in a SQL statement. Hints are passed using the syntax /*+ hint */. One or more hints can be passed to the same SQL statement. Step 1 creates the two sample tables used throughout the example. Step 2 presents a query that passes a hint to the optimizer, causing the statement to use rule-based optimization. Step 3 presents a query that passes two hints to the optimizer, performing full table scans on both tables in the query, effectively suppressing all indexes.

Comments

If your database is running cost-based optimization and you want to run a specific query using rule-based optimization or control the way the query is executed, hints should be used. If multiple hints are provided that do not make sense together, unpredictable results may occur. For example, using the /*+rule */ hint to specify rule-based optimization and specifying an index in another hint do not work together.

COMPLEXITY

INTERMEDIATE

16.6   How do I...
Suppress an index in a query?

Problem

I know that one or more of the indexes will need to be suppressed in some of my queries. Within version 7 of the database, if an index returns too many of the rows, it should be suppressed. In other situations, the optimizer attempts to perform an index merge which is very slow. If I suppress one of the indexes, the index merge will not take place. How do I suppress the use of an index in a query?

Technique

The EXPLAIN PLAN and SQL*Trace facilities presented in How-To 16.3 and 16.4 allow you to analyze a SQL statement to determine the indexes used by the optimizer. If you have determined that an index should not be used in a SQL statement, it can be suppressed by changing the WHERE clause of the query. The optimizer will

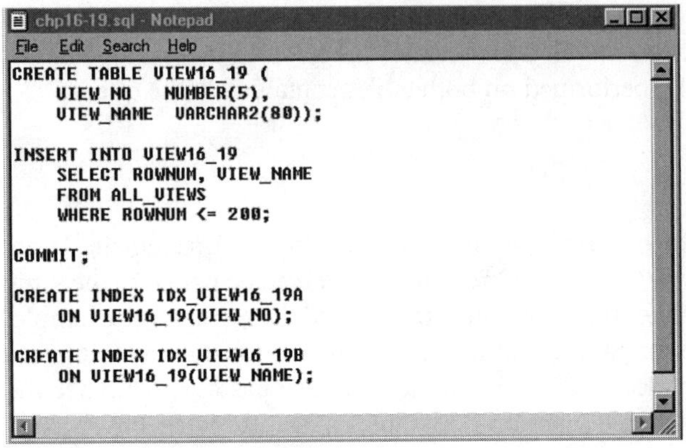


```
CREATE TABLE VIEW16_19 (
    VIEW_NO    NUMBER(5),
    VIEW_NAME  VARCHAR2(80));

INSERT INTO VIEW16_19
    SELECT ROWNUM, VIEW_NAME
    FROM ALL_VIEWS
    WHERE ROWNUM <= 200;

COMMIT;

CREATE INDEX IDX_VIEW16_19A
    ON VIEW16_19(VIEW_NO);

CREATE INDEX IDX_VIEW16_19B
    ON VIEW16_19(VIEW_NAME);
```

Figure 16-14 CHP16-19.sql creates the sample table used in How-To 16.6

not use an index if the columns contained in the index are modified in the WHERE clause in any way. Using a function on a column, adding 0 to a number column, or concatenating an empty string to a character column will suppress the index.

Steps

1. Run SQL*Plus and connect as the WAITE user account. CHP16-19.sql, shown in Figure 16-14, creates a sample table with an index.

The sample table contains three columns and has 200 records inserted into it. Two indexes are created, one that returns less than 1 percent of the records when used and another that returns 30 percent of the records. Run the statement to create the sample table, its records, and the indexes.

```
SQL>  START CHP16-19

Table created.

200 rows created.

Commit complete.

Index created.

Index created.
```

2. Load CHP16-20.sql into the SQL buffer. The query contained in the file queries a record and will suppress the use of the IDX_VIEW16_19A index.

```
SQL> GET CHP16-20
  1  SELECT
  2      VIEW_NAME
  3  FROM
  4      VIEW16_19
  5  WHERE
```

Line 6 specifies the WHERE clause of the query. Since an index was created on the VIEW_NO column it would normally be used, but the modification of the column suppresses the index. Adding 0 to a number column suppresses the index, but does not change the output of the query. Line 2 specifies that the VIEW_NAME column will be returned by the query, and line 4 specifies the source of the data as the table created in step 1.

3. Run the query to display its results.

```
SQL>  /

VIEW_NAME
------------------
ALL_CATALOG
```

The results of the query are the same as if the index were not suppressed. Since the table was relatively small, suppressing the index may improve performance. In the next step, the index on the character column will be suppressed in a query.

4. Load CHP16-21.sql into the SQL buffer. The query contained in the file queries a record and will suppress the use of the IDX_VIEW16_19B index.

```
SQL> GET CHP16-21
  1   SELECT
  2       VIEW_NAME
  3   FROM
  4       VIEW16_19
  5   WHERE
  6*      VIEW_NAME||'' = 'ALL_TABLES'
```

Line 6 suppresses the index that would normally be used by modifying the VIEW_NAME column in the query's WHERE clause.

How It Works

The optimizer will not use an index if one of its columns is modified in the WHERE clause in any way. Modifications can be made to the columns without changing the meaning of the clause. Adding 0 to a number or date column, or concatenating an empty string to a character column, suppresses the index on the column. Step 1 creates a sample table and two indexes. Steps 2 and 3 present a query suppressing an index by adding 0 to a number column in the WHERE clause. Step 4 presents a query suppressing an index on a character column by concatenating an empty string to it. In both queries presented, the results of the query are not changed by suppressing the index.

Comments

How-To 16.1 described the situation in which indexes should be used. If you have SQL statements which are not performing acceptably, run EXPLAIN PLAN or SQL*Trace to determine which indexes are used. If your SQL statements use indexes when they should not, they can be easily suppressed by modifying the WHERE clause of the query. This technique will work regardless of the optimization method used.

CHAPTER 17
DATABASE TUNING

DATABASE TUNING

How do I...

Tuning the database can be more of an art than a science. There is a large number of configurable parameters within the database that can be tuned to achieve maximum database performance. Making an application perform acceptably requires more than tuning SQL statements within it. There are several tuning issues that can dramatically affect the performance of your applications. This chapter presents several How-Tos designed to cover the more frequent database tuning problems.

Since this is not primarily a performance tuning book, not every topic related to database tuning is covered in this chapter. The files used in this chapter are found on the accompanying CD under the \SAMPLES\CHAP17 directory. Copy these files into your SQL*Plus working directory, or specify the complete path when executing the GET command within SQL*Plus. Refer to Appendix B for the SQL scripts related to database performance tuning that you can use in your everyday work.

17.1   Identify I/O contention and load balance

When there is contention among I/O devices, overall system performance can be adversely affected. Within the database, data is stored in multiple datafiles distributed across I/O devices. In most database servers, access can occur simultaneously to multiple disks. If one disk performs too much of the work while other disks sit idle, system performance is not maximized. This How-To covers the process for identifying I/O contention and load balance.

17.2   Stripe a tablespace across multiple devices

A tablespace can consist of multiple datafiles. These datafiles do not have to be located on the same device. If a tablespace is accessed heavily, you can improve performance by spreading (*striping*) the tablespace over multiple I/O devices to reduce contention. This How-To presents the method for creating a new tablespace spanning multiple devices and the method for adding datafiles to an existing tablespace.

17.3   Identify rollback segment contention

Oracle allows a user or application to undo uncommitted changes to the database. Whenever an operation has started but has not been committed, changed records are written to the rollback segments. If the database does not contain enough rollback segments for the system load, contention for rollback segments can reduce system performance. This How-To presents the method used to identify and correct rollback segment contention within the database.

17.4   Identify redo log contention

The redo logs record all changes made to objects within the database. The system must contain at least two redo logs. The active redo log is buffered in the System Global Area (SGA) to improve performance. If there is contention for redo log information in the SGA, performance can suffer. This How-To covers the process of identifying and correcting redo log contention.

17.5   Identify tablespace fragmentation

Fragmentation of the tablespaces within a system can reduce its performance. The more fragmented the extents within a tablespace become, the more work the database has when using the objects within the tablespace. This How-To covers the method used to identify tablespace fragmentation.

17.6   Determine sort area hit statistics

There are many database operations that require sorting. Each time an ORDER BY or a GROUP BY clause is specified within a SQL statement a sort occurs. Each user process is allocated an area in the SGA to sort data. If the sort area size is not large enough to execute the sort, the disk performs it. When a sort is performed in memory, it is much faster than if performed on disk. This How-To presents the method used to view the statistics of sorts performed on the system.

17.7   Query the current SGA values

In order to tune an Oracle database, it is necessary to know the current size of the SGA. If the SGA is too small, the operations within Oracle cannot be performed efficiently. If the SGA is too large, the operating system may not have enough memory to perform the operations required to run the computer efficiently. This How-To presents a method to determine the current SGA size by querying the data dictionary. It also presents the most common methods for changing the size of the SGA.

17.8   Identify the database buffer cache hit ratio

The database buffer cache contains the database blocks most recently read. When a database read is performed, Oracle returns the data block from the buffer cache if it exists. If the ratio of cache hits is less than 70 percent, you should consider increasing the size of the buffer cache if system memory permits. This How-To presents a method to determine the buffer cache hit ratio.

17.9   Determine the hit ratio in the shared pool

The shared pool contains the data dictionary cache and the SQL cache. If the shared pool is not large enough, the database may need to go to the disk for information which should be in memory. Information about users, tables, indexes, privileges, and other data dictionary objects is part of the data dictionary cache. The most recently parsed and executed SQL statements are located in the SQL cache. It is a relatively slow process to get dictionary cache and SQL cache information from the disk, and database performance can suffer greatly if the shared pool is not large enough. This How-To presents a method to determine the hit ratio of objects in the shared pool.

17.10   Query the INIT.ORA parameters

The INIT.ORA parameters currently being used by the database instance can be queried from the data dictionary. This allows you to view parameters from within SQL*Plus without opening the INIT.ORA file. It also allows you to view the value of a parameter even if it is not explicitly set in the INIT.ORA file. This How-To presents a method to query the INIT.ORA parameters from the data dictionary.

COMPLEXITY
ADVANCED

17.1 How do I...
Identify I/O contention and load balance?

Problem

I am trying to improve database performance. I want to determine whether there is I/O contention on the disks and whether the load on the physical disks is balanced. If the load is not balanced between the disks, I want to redistribute data to balance it. If there is excessive I/O contention, I will first redistribute the load, then consider adding more or faster I/O devices. How do I identify I/O contention and load imbalance?

Technique

The V$FILESTAT dynamic performance view contains statistics about the access of datafiles in the system. The V$DATAFILE view contains information about the datafiles in the database. The descriptions of the views are shown in Figure 17-1.

```
± Oracle SQL*Plus                                        _□×
File  Edit  Search  Options  Help
PL/SQL Release 2.2.2.3.1 - Production

SQL> desc v$filestat
 Name                              Null?     Type
 -------------------------------   -------   ----
 FILE#                                       NUMBER
 PHYRDS                                      NUMBER
 PHYWRTS                                     NUMBER
 PHYBLKRD                                    NUMBER
 PHYBLKWRT                                   NUMBER
 READTIM                                     NUMBER
 WRITETIM                                    NUMBER

SQL> desc v$datafile
 Name                              Null?     Type
 -------------------------------   -------   ----
 FILE#                                       NUMBER
 STATUS                                      VARCHAR2(7)
 ENABLED                                     VARCHAR2(10)
 CHECKPOINT_CHANGE#                          NUMBER
 BYTES                                       NUMBER
 CREATE_BYTES                                NUMBER
 NAME                                        VARCHAR2(257)

SQL> |
```

Figure 17-1 The V$FILESTAT and V$DATAFILE data dictionary views

The columns that are key to determining load balance are the PHYRDS and PHYWRTS columns from the V$FILESTAT view. PHYRDS contains the number of physical reads of the datafile, and PHYWRTS contains the number of physical writes to the datafile. If the number of physical reads and writes to a datafile is excessive compared to the other datafiles, the load is not balanced. If the TIMED_STATISTICS database parameter is set to TRUE, the READTIM and WRITETIM columns contain the average time in milliseconds required by a read or write to the datafile.

Steps

1. Run SQL*Plus and connect as the WAITE user account. Since the WAITE user account has been granted the DBA role, it is able to perform this process. Load CHP17-1.sql into the SQL buffer. The file contains a query of the V$DATAFILE and V$FILESTAT data dictionary views to determine the number of physical reads and physical writes on each datafile.

```
SQL>   GET CHP17-1
  1    SELECT
  2        DF.NAME,
  3        FS.PHYRDS READS,
  4        FS.PHYWRTS WRITES,
  5        (FS.READTIM / DECODE(FS.PHYRDS,0,-1,FS.PHYREADS)) READTIME,
  6        (FS.WRITETIM / DECODE(FS.PHYWRTS,0,-1,FS.PHYWRTS)) WRITETIME
  7    FROM
  8        V$DATAFILE DF,
  9        V$FILESTAT FS
 10    WHERE
 11        DF.FILE# = FS.FILE#
 11    ORDER BY
 12        DF.NAME
```

> **NOTE**
>
> If the TIMED_STATISTICS database parameter is not set to TRUE in the INIT.ORA file, the READTIM and WRITETIM columns will return 0. As part of your performance tuning operations, you should set this parameter to TRUE. Since the collection of statistics requires overhead, it should be set to FALSE whenever you do not need it.

Line 2 returns the name of the datafile from the V$DATAFILE view. Line 3 returns the number of physical reads on the file since the database was last started. Line 4 returns the number of physical writes to the datafile. Line 5 returns the average read time on the datafile in milliseconds. Line 6 returns the average write time to the datafile. Lines 8 and 9 specify the V$DATAFILE and V$FILESTAT data dictionary views as the source of the data. Line 11 specifies the join condition between the two views. The views are joined by the FILE# column identifying a unique file number for each datafile.

2. Execute a COLUMN command to format the columns, making the query more readable.

```
SQL>   COLUMN NAME FORMAT A35
SQL>
```

3. Execute the query. Figure 17-2 shows the results of the operation for my small Personal Oracle database.

The READS column shows the number of physical reads each datafile performed. The WRITES column shows the number of physical writes each datafile performed. If the number of reads and writes is excessive for any of the datafiles, the I/O load is not balanced. The datafiles making up the SYSTEM tablespace may normally have slightly higher I/O requirements. The READTIME column shows the average time in milliseconds a physical read required. The WRITETIME column shows the average time a physical write required. If the values in these columns are higher for a specific datafile, contention may be occurring. Keep in mind that some disks are faster than others and that you can expect a slower response time from slower disks.

How It Works

The V$FILESTAT dynamic performance view contains information about the number of physical reads and writes occurring on each disk and the time the operations required. By looking at the distribution of access to the datafiles, you can determine if a load is evenly distributed among the datafiles. By looking at the time required to perform the I/O operations, you can determine I/O contention. Step 1 presents a query of the V$FILESTAT and the V$DATAFILE views. The V$DATAFILE view is

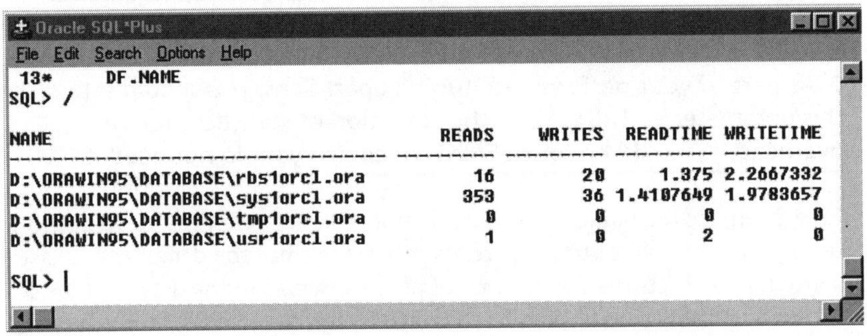

Figure 17-2 The results of the query

included in the query because the datafile name is not included in the V$FILESTAT view.

Comments

The methods presented in this How-To make it possible to identify I/O load imbalance and contention. Once you have identified that a problem exists, you should take action to correct it. One cause of load imbalance is not distributing your rollback segments between datafiles. If all of the rollback segments are in a single datafile, the datafile will be used for all data manipulation actions and some queries. Another cause of the problem is having all user accounts work on the same temporary tablespace. If several users perform operations requiring temporary data areas, they will all access the same datafile. How-To 17.2 presents a method to stripe a tablespace across devices. This allows a single tablespace to be accessed simultaneously over several I/O devices.

COMPLEXITY
ADVANCED

17.2   How do I...
Stripe a tablespace across multiple devices?

Problem

I have some very heavily used tablespaces that are causing contention on some of the disk devices. It does not make sense to move the objects out of the tablespace. I want to stripe the tablespace across devices to reduce contention. By having the same tablespace span multiple devices, simultaneous access of it will be much faster. How do I stripe a tablespace across multiple devices?

Technique

A tablespace can span multiple datafiles located on multiple devices. By distributing a tablespace over multiple physical devices, you speed I/O access by minimizing disk contention. You can stripe a tablespace when you initially create it, by specifying multiple datafiles in the CREATE TABLESPACE statement. You can add datafiles to an existing tablespace by using the ALTER TABLESPACE statement and creating new datafiles on a separate device.

Steps

1. Run SQL*Plus and connect as the WAITE user account. Load CHP17-2.sql into the SQL buffer. The file contains a CREATE TABLESPACE statement distributing a single tablespace over multiple devices. The format of this statement assumes you have three disk drives, C:, D:, and E:. If you do not have these drives, change the statement to reference valid disk drives on your system. Specify the filenames in the format required by your operating system.

```
SQL>   GET CHP17-2
  1    CREATE TABLESPACE WAITE_TBS
  2       DATAFILE 'C:\WAITE1.ORA' SIZE 1M,
  3                'D:\WAITE2.ORA' SIZE 1M,
  4                'E:\WAITE3.ORA' SIZE 1M
```

Line 1 identifies the statement with the CREATE TABLESPACE keyword and specifies the name of the tablespace as WAITE_TBS. Lines 2 through 4 specify the three datafiles making up the tablespace. The filename of the datafiles and the size are specified on each line.

2. Run the statement to create the tablespace.

```
SQL>   /
```

Tablespace created.

3. Load CHP17-3.sql into the SQL buffer. The file presents the technique used to add a datafile to an existing tablespace. The tablespace modified in this statement was created in steps 1 and 2. The new datafile can be located on a separate disk drive to balance the load of the I/O. This statement assumes that an E: drive exists on your system. If it does not, change the drive specification to a valid drive for your system.

```
SQL>   GET CHP17-3
  1    ALTER TABLESPACE WAITE_TBS
  2        ADD DATAFILE
  3        'E:\WAITE4.ORA' SIZE 1M
```

Line 1 identifies the statement as an ALTER TABLESPACE statement and specifies that the WAITE_TBS tablespace will be modified. Line 2 presents the keywords ADD DATAFILE to specify that a new datafile will be created. Line 3 specifies the datafile to be created and its size. The filename specification is operating system specific.

4. Run the statement to create the new datafile.

```
SQL>   /
```

Tablespace altered.

When a new datafile is created, the tablespace will begin using it as space is needed. Adding a new datafile to a nearly empty tablespace does not ensure that the load will be balanced across the files, since two tables will be added to the new datafile.

How It Works

Steps 1 and 2 create a new tablespace using the CREATE TABLESPACE statement and distribute the tablespace over three datafiles, each located on a separate disk drive. Steps 3 and 4 add a datafile to an existing tablespace using the ALTER TABLESPACE statement, including an ADD DATAFILE clause. Striping a tablespace does not ensure that all the datafiles will be used equally. A tablespace uses blocks in a datafile as needed.

Comments

The performance gains, which will be most dramatic on large database servers, only work if the datafiles created exist on separate physical devices. When you perform this How-To on your own computer, you may not have the disk drives specified in the statements. You can modify the statements to work on your computer. The method presented in this How-To is less reliable than creating new tablespaces on separate drives. By creating many tablespaces on multiple drives and placing objects in tablespaces depending on their drive location, you can control which objects exist on which physical drive.

COMPLEXITY
ADVANCED

17.3 How do I...
Identify rollback segment contention?

Problem

I want to improve the performance of my database and think I might have rollback segment contention. My applications are database intensive and perform many insert, update, and delete statements. Since every transaction that manipulates data uses the rollback segments, performance can suffer if there is contention. How do I identify rollback segment contention?

Technique

Any transaction that physically changes the database produces entries in the rollback segments. The rollback segments allow Oracle to undo changes made to the database that have not been committed. If a ROLLBACK statement is executed or a transaction is aborted before the commit, the rollback segment is used to reverse the operation on the database. Rollback segment contention occurs whenever two processes need to access the same segment block at the same time. The V$ROLLSTAT and V$ROLLNAME views can be used to identify rollback segment contention. The views are described in SQL*Plus in Figure 17-3.

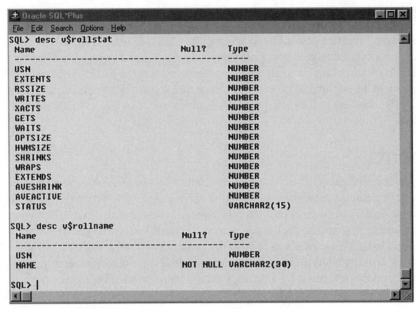

Figure 17-3 V$ROLLSTAT and V$ROLLNAME data
dictionary views

Statistical information about the rollback segments is contained in V$ROLLSTAT. The key columns for identifying contention are GETS and WAITS. GETS identifies the number of times the rollback segment was accessed. WAITS identifies the number of times a process waited for a block in a rollback segment. A ratio of GETS to WAITS of more than 2 percent identifies a contention issue. The V$ROLLNAME is included in the queries to provide the name of the rollback segment, since it is not included in the V$ROLLSTAT view.

Steps

1. Run SQL*Plus and connect as the WAITE user account. Load CHP17-4.sql into the SQL buffer. The file contains a query of the V$ROLLSTAT and V$ROLLNAME data dictionary views to identify rollback segment contention.

```
SQL>   GET CHP17-4
  1    SELECT
  2      RN.NAME,
  3      RS.GETS,
  4      RS.WAITS,
  5      (RS.WAITS / RS.GETS) * 100 RATIO
  6    FROM
  7      V$ROLLSTAT RS,
  8      V$ROLLNAME RN
  9    WHERE
 10      RS.USN = RN.USN
```

Line 2 returns the name of the rollback segment by returning the NAME column from the VSROLLNAME view. Line 3 returns the total number of rollback segment accesses by querying the GETS column from V$ROLLSTAT. Line 4 returns the number of times a process waited for a rollback segment. This information is contained in the WAITS column of the same view. Line 5 calculates the ratio of waits to accesses for the rollback segment. If the number is greater than 2, there is contention for the rollback segment.

2. Format the columns using the COLUMN command in SQL*Plus and run the statement. Figure 17-4 shows the results of the operation.

In the sample results on my Personal Oracle 7 database, there was very little contention for rollback segment blocks. If the ratio you get is over 2 percent, you should consider adding more rollback segments to your system.

How It Works

The query presented in step 1 allows you to analyze rollback segment contention. The V$ROLLSTAT view contains statistical information about each of the active rollback segments in the system. The V$ROLLNAME view provided the name of the rollback segment to make the query easier to read. The ratio of WAITS to GETS identifies rollback segment contention.

```
 Oracle SQL*Plus                                               _ □ ✕
File  Edit  Search  Options  Help
   7        V$ROLLSTAT RS,
   8        V$ROLLNAME RN
   9    WHERE
  10*       RS.USN = RN.USN
  11
SQL> /

NAME                                 GETS    WAITS     RATIO
-----------------------------------  ------  --------  --------
SYSTEM                                1202       0         0
RB1                                   1563       0         0
RB2                                   1563       0         0
RB3                                   1546       0         0
RB4                                   1557       0         0
RB5                                   1589       0         0

6 rows selected.

SQL>
```

Figure 17-4 The results of CHP17-4.sql in SQL*Plus

Comments

If the resulting ratio is greater than 2 percent, there is contention within a rollback segment. More rollback segments should be created with the CREATE ROLLBACK statement. By creating more rollback segments, you can reduce the chances that more than one process will attempt to use the same rollback segment blocks simultaneously. A good rule of thumb is one rollback segment for every four concurrent transactions. When determining the size of your rollback segments, you should analyze the type of transactions performed on the database. OLTP transactions write more data and need larger rollback segments. Decision support systems that perform many queries but do not write much data can use smaller rollback segments.

COMPLEXITY
ADVANCED

17.4 How do I...
Identify redo log contention?

Problem

Since there are many types of contention that can cause performance problems, I want to ensure that there is no contention in the SGA for the latches controlling the writing of redo log information. How do I identify and correct redo log contention?

Technique

Within the SGA, there is a buffer cache area containing redo information. The redo logs record all changes made to objects within the database. Since there is a considerable amount of information written to the redo logs, it is important to eliminate any possible contention. The redo information in the buffer cache is regulated by two latches. A *latch* is similar to a lock, except it locks information in memory. The *redo allocation* latch and the *redo copy* latch control access to the redo log cache and can be monitored through the V$LATCH view. The description of the V$LATCH view is shown in Figure 17-5.

There are two types of latch contentions to worry about: *immediate* and *wait*. A *wait* latch request will wait until the latch is free to continue processing. An *immediate* latch request will not wait and will continue processing. The calculation of wait contention uses the formula

```
Wait contention = (misses / (gets + misses)) * 100
```

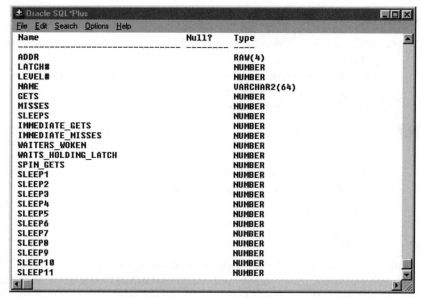

Figure 17-5 The V$LATCH view

The calculation of immediate contention uses the formula

```
Immediate contention =
(immediate_misses / (immediate_gets + immediate_misses))*100
```

If the value of either of the ratios is greater than 1, there will be contention for the latch and action should be taken.

Steps

1. Run SQL*Plus and connect as the SYS user account. Load CHP17-5.sql into the SQL buffer. The file contains a query of the V$LATCH data dictionary view to determine redo log contention.

```
SQL>    GET CHP17-5
  1     SELECT NAME,
  2       (IMMEDIATE_MISSES/
  3            DECODE((IMMEDIATE_GETS + IMMEDIATE_MISSES),0,-1,
  4                     (IMMEDIATE_GETS + IMMEDIATE_MISSES)))*100
  5           IMMEDIATE_CONTENTION,
  6       (MISSES / DECODE((GETS + MISSES),0,-1)) * 100
  7           WAIT_CONTENTION
  8     FROM
  9       V$LATCH
 10     WHERE
 11       NAME IN ('redo copy', 'redo allocation')
```

Lines 2 and 3 return the immediate contention for the latch by calculating the percentage of immediate misses occurring. The DECODE functions in lines 3 and 6 ensure that no divide by 0 errors occur. Line 5 provides an alias for the column. Line 6 returns the wait contention for the latch by calculating the percentage of misses. Line 6 provides an alias for the column. Line 11 declares that the latch name must be either REDO COPY or REDO ALLOCATION in order for the query to return it.

2. Run the query to view the results. Figure 17-6 contains the results of the query.

If either the IMMEDIATE_CONTENTION or WAIT_CONTENTION value is over 1 percent, contention is occurring for the latch.

How It Works

Steps 1 and 2 present a query that calculates immediate and wait contention for the two latches controlling redo cache information in the SGA. The V$LATCH contains information about the latches in the SGA. A latch is a lock within the SGA. If a lock is occurring when an access is made, there is contention. The IMMEDIATE_GETS and IMMEDIATE_MISSES columns contain statistics about immediate latch requests. The GETS and MISSES columns contain statistics about wait latch requests.

Comments

If contention occurs for the redo allocation latch, it can be alleviated by reducing the value of the LOG_SMALL_ENTRY_MAX_SIZE parameter in the INIT.ORA file. How-To 17.10 presents the process used to determine the current value of the parameter. If contention is occurring for the redo copy latch, it can be alleviated by increasing the value of the LOG_SIMULTANEOUS_COPIES parameter in the INIT.ORA parameter.

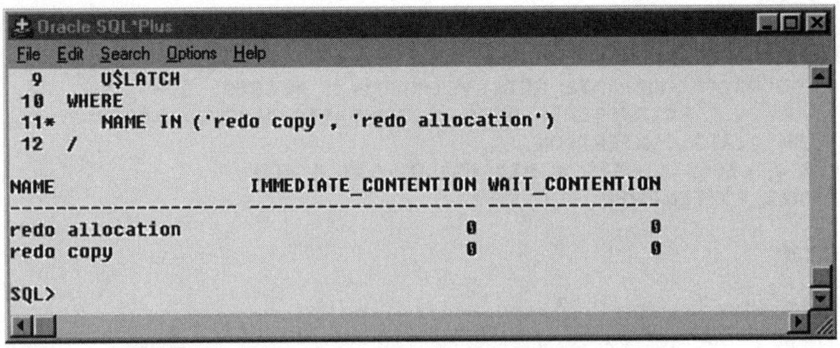

Figure 17-6 The results of CHP17-5.sql in SQL*Plus

COMPLEXITY
INTERMEDIATE

17.5 How do I...
Identify tablespace fragmentation?

Problem

Within our database, we have many database objects which get dropped and recreated. I know that this can cause fragmentation within tablespaces, making the database do more work when using the tablespace. How do I identify tablespace fragmentation?

Technique

The DBA_FREE_SPACE data dictionary view contains the extents within each tablespace that are not being used. If there aren't many free extents and they are large compared to the total amount of free space, then there is no fragmentation. Conversely, if there is a large number of free extents and they are relatively small, the tablespace will be fragmented. Figure 17-7 shows the description of the DBA_FREE_SPACE data dictionary view.

This How-To presents a query that determines the level of database fragmentation by counting the number of free extents and calculating the size of the largest extent and the total amount of free space in each tablespace.

Steps

1. Run SQL*Plus and connect as the WAITE user account. Load CHP17-6.sql into the SQL buffer. The file contains a query of the DBA_FREE_SPACE data dictionary view to determine tablespace fragmentation.

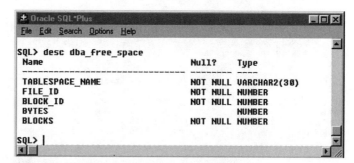

Figure 17-7 The DBA_FREE_SPACE data dictionary view

```
SQL>   GET CHP17-6
  1    SELECT
  2        TABLESPACE_NAME,
  3        SUM(BYTES),
  4        MAX(BYTES),
  5        COUNT(*)
  6    FROM
  7        DBA_FREE_SPACE
  8    GROUP BY TABLESPACE_NAME
  9    ORDER BY TABLESPACE_NAME
```

Line 2 returns the name of the tablespace. Line 3 calculates the number of free bytes in the tablespace. Line 4 calculates the largest free extent in the tablespace. Line 6 counts the number of free extents in the tablespace. Since the SUM, MAX, and COUNT functions are group functions and TABLESPACE_NAME is not, the GROUP BY clause in line 8 is required.

2. Run the statement. Figure 17-8 contains the results of the operation.

How It Works

Steps 1 and 2 present a query of the DBA_FREE_SPACE data dictionary view to analyze fragmentation of each tablespace. The query uses the COUNT function to determine the number of free extents. It uses the MAX function to determine the size of the largest extent and the SUM function to calculate the total amount of free space. The BYTES column is used to determine the size in bytes. It can be replaced with the BLOCKS column if you feel more comfortable working in blocks. Personally, I prefer bytes since it provides me with an easier point of reference.

Comments

To analyze the results, first compare the size of the maximum free extent with the total amount of free space. If the largest extent is a large percentage of the free space, fragmentation is probably not occurring. If the largest extent is a small percentage of the free space and there is a large number of free extents, then the tablespace is fragmented.

```
 9* ORDER BY TABLESPACE_NAME
10  /

TABLESPACE_NAME                  SUM(BYTES) MAX(BYTES)  COUNT(*)
-------------------------------- ---------- ----------  --------
ROLLBACK_DATA                       3500032    3500032         1
SYSTEM                              1148928    1054720         2
TEMPORARY_DATA                      2095104    2095104         1
USER_DATA                           2693120    2693120         1

SQL>
```

Figure 17-8 The results of CHP17-6.sql in SQL*Plus

COMPLEXITY
ADVANCED

17.6 How do I...
Determine sort area hit statistics?

Problem

As part of my performance tuning of our database, I need to analyze the hit statistics within the sort area. Since many operations require the performing of a sort, I want to be sure that as much as possible is performed in memory and not on disk. How do I determine sort area hit statistics?

Technique

When an operation requires sorting, such as a query with an ORDER BY or a GROUP BY clause, Oracle attempts to perform the operation in memory. If it cannot, it performs the sort to disk. Obviously, performing a sort in memory is much faster than performing it on disk. The V$SYSSTAT view contains system statistics. This view can be queried to determine sort statistics. Figure 17-9 shows the description of the V$SYSSTAT view within SQL*Plus.

If the number of disk sorts is very high, action should be taken to try reducing the number of sorts on disk and increasing the number of sorts in memory. This is done by modifying the SORT_AREA_SIZE and SORT_AREA_SIZE_RETAINED INIT.ORA parameters. Any time the sort requires more memory than is specified in the SORT_AREA_SIZE parameter, the sort will be performed on disk. Increasing the value of this parameter may increase the number of sorts occurring in memory.

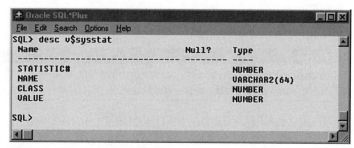

Figure 17-9 The V$SYSSTAT view

Steps

1. Run SQL*Plus and connect as the WAITE user account. Load CHP17-7.sql into the SQL buffer. The file contains a query of the V$SYSSTAT data dictionary view to determine the sorts performed on disk and the sorts performed in memory.

```
SQL>   GET CHP17-7
  1    SELECT
  2        NAME,
  3        VALUE
  4    FROM
  5        V$SYSSTAT
  6    WHERE
  7        NAME LIKE 'sort%'
```

Line 2 returns the name of the statistic from the V$SYSSTAT view. Line 3 returns the value of the statistic. Line 7 specifies that only sort statistics are returned by the query.

2. Run the statement to display the results. Figure 17-10 displays the results of the operation.

The query displays the number of memory sorts and the number of disk sorts as two separate lines. This query is very useful since it shows a count of the number of sorts performed. Many people prefer to view a ratio of memory sorts to total sorts. This ratio will be presented in the next step.

3. Load CHP17-8.sql into the SQL buffer. The file contains a query of the V$SYSSTAT view and calculates the ratio of memory sorts to total sorts.

```
SQL>   GET CHP17-8
  1    SELECT
  2        ( SUM(DECODE(NAME,'sorts (memory)',VALUE,0)) /
  3          (SUM(DECODE(NAME,'sorts (memory)',VALUE,0)) +
  4            SUM(DECODE(NAME,'sorts (disk)',VALUE,0)))) *100
  5            MEMORY_HIT_RATIO
  6    FROM
  7        V$SYSSTAT
  8    WHERE
  9        NAME LIKE 'sort%'
```

> **NOTE**
>
> A divide by zero error can occur running this SQL script if no sorts have been executed on the database.

Lines 2 through 4 use the SUM GROUP BY operator with the DECODE function to return multiple rows as a single calculation. The formula memory_hit_ratio = (memory sorts / (memory sorts + disk sorts)) * 100 is

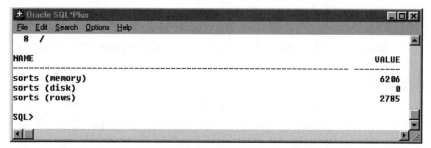

Figure 17-10 The results of CHP17-7.sql in SQL*Plus

calculated by the query. Line 6 provides an alias for the calculated column. Lines 8 and 9 contain a WHERE clause, which limits the number of records processed by the calculation but does not change the results. If these lines were missing, the same results would occur.

4. Run the statement to display the results. Figure 17-11 contains the output from the calculation on my Personal Oracle 7 database.

The MEMORY_HIT_RATIO value returned by the query gives you an indication if your sort area size is large enough. Unfortunately, it is difficult to tell what the impact of an increased sort area size will be. If the sorts performed by the system are very large, it may be impossible to create a sort area size large enough to sort the data in memory.

How It Works

The V$SYSSTAT view contains statistics needed to analyze sort performance. Steps 1 and 2 present a query which returns information about the number of disk sorts and memory sorts. Steps 3 and 4 present a query which calculates the percentage of sorts performed in memory. The data presented in steps 1 and 2 is useful because it shows how many sorting operations were performed. If the number is very low, it doesn't really matter where the sorts were performed since sorting is not a big operation on the database. If the number is very high and most of the sorts occur

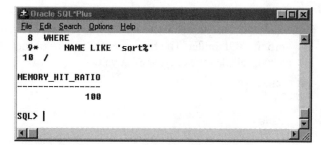

Figure 17-11 The results of CHP17-8.sql in SQL*Plus

on disk, changes may be necessary. The data presented in steps 3 and 4 lets you analyze the progress made when you change the database parameters. If you increase the sort area size and the percentage stays the same, you made no progress.

Comments

Do not rush to increase the SORT_AREA_SIZE parameter just because the percentage of memory sorts seems low. If the sorts performed in the database are very large, you will never be able to increase the SORT_AREA_SIZE parameter enough. Whenever you change the value of SORT_AREA_SIZE, you should generate some before and after statistics to determine if increasing the parameter increases the percentage of memory sorts. If you have increased the size as much as you can and the memory sort ratio has not increased, reduce the value of the SORT_AREA_SIZE parameter.

COMPLEXITY
INTERMEDIATE

17.7   How do I...
Query the current SGA values?

Problem

I want to query the current size of the SGA to determine how much it can be increased within the system. I know that I can use the SHOW SGA command in the server manager or calculate the size from the INIT.ORA parameters, but it would be easier to query it from the V$ tables. How do I query the current SGA values?

Technique

The V$SGA view contains the current SGA size values. It can be queried through SQL*Plus to show the size of the SGA. The V$SGA view contains two columns, NAME and VALUE. The NAME column contains the description of the values, and the VALUE column contains its value.

Steps

1. Run SQL*Plus and connect as the WAITE user account. Load CHP17-9.sql into the SQL buffer. The file contains a query of the V$SGA data dictionary view to display the current SGA values.

```
SQL>   GET CHP17-9
  1    SELECT *
  2    FROM
  3        V$SGA
```

2. Run the statement to view the current values of the SGA.

```
SQL>  /

NAME                          VALUE
--------------------    ----------
Fixed Size                    38296
Variable Size               3847332
Database Buffers             409600
Redo Buffers                   8192
```

How It Works

The V$SGA view is queried in Steps 1 and 2 to view the size of the different parts of the SGA. The size of the SGA does not change while the database is running. It is calculated based on the parameters in the INIT.ORA file. The V$SGA view only contains two columns, so it is very easy to query the size of the SGA.

Comments

The size of your SGA should be as large as possible without impacting the operating system memory requirement. A good rule of thumb is that the SGA should occupy 50 percent of system memory. If the size of your SGA is too small, database performance will suffer. If it is too large, the operating system may not have enough memory to perform efficiently. The DB_BLOCK_BUFFERS parameter in the INIT.ORA file has the largest effect on the size of the SGA. When the parameter is increased, expect the database buffers line to increase when you perform the query. The LOG_BUFFER parameter has a direct impact on the redo buffers line in the query.

COMPLEXITY
ADVANCED

17.8   How do I...
Identify database buffer cache hit ratio?

Problem

I need to identify how well database blocks are being cached in the SGA. If our buffer cache hit ratio is too low, we may benefit by adding more database block buffers to the SGA. I do not want to add database block buffers without analyzing the hit ratio, since it increases the SGA size and might use system memory required by the operating system. How do I identify the database buffer cache hit ratio?

Technique

Once again, the V$SYSSTAT dynamic performance view contains information important to tuning the database. The view contains three records which can determine the buffer cache hit ratio. The ratio of physical reads to total reads identifies what percentage of time a read must go to disk. A record with the NAME column equal to "physical reads" contains the number of physical reads made to the disk. Records with the NAME column equal to db block gets and consistent gets are added together for total number of accesses.

Steps

1. Run SQL*Plus and connect as the WAITE user account. Load CHP17-10.sql into the SQL buffer. The file contains a query of the V$SYSSTAT data dictionary view to determine the database buffer cache hit ratio.

```
SQL>   GET CHP17-10
  1    SELECT
  2      1 -   SUM(DECODE(NAME,'physical reads',VALUE,0)) /
  3          (SUM(DECODE(NAME,'db block gets',VALUE,0)) +
  4            SUM(DECODE(NAME,'consistent gets',VALUE,0)))
  5          HIT_RATIO
  6    FROM
  7      V$SYSSTAT
  8    WHERE
  9      NAME IN
 10        ('physical reads', 'db block gets', 'consistent gets')
```

Lines 2 through 4 calculate the hit ratio by applying the formula hit ratio = 1 - (physical reads / (db block gets + consistent gets)). The DECODE function and the SUM function return the three records the query would normally return as a single calculated row. Line 7 specifies the source of the data as the V$SYSSTAT view.

2. Run the query to display the results. Figure 17-12 contains the output of the operation.

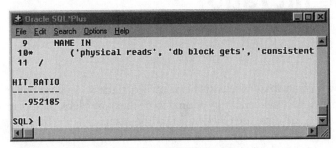

Figure 17-12 The results of CHP17-10.sql in SQL*Plus

If the buffer cache hit ratio is less than 70 percent, you should consider increasing the number of buffers by increasing the value of the DB_BLOCK_BUFFER parameter in the INIT.ORA parameter.

How It Works

Steps 1 and 2 present a query of the V$SYSSTAT view to calculate the hit ratio. The formula hit ratio = 1 - (physical reads / (db block gets + consistent gets)) is calculated within the query by using the SUM function with the DECODE function to return a single calculation from multiple rows.

Comments

If you establish that your buffer cache hit ratio is low, say less than 70 percent, you should determine if the size of the buffer cache can be safely increased. The size of the buffer cache has a direct impact on the size of your SGA. You should make your SGA as large as possible without hurting operating system performance. The number of block buffers should be as large as possible, but should not take away from memory required by the operation system.

COMPLEXITY
ADVANCED

17.9 How do I...
Determine the hit ratio in the shared pool?

Problem

As part of my performance tuning process, I want to make sure that the hit ratio in the shared pool is acceptable. Since the shared pool contains the dictionary cache and the SQL cache, performance can suffer greatly if it is not large enough. How do I determine the hit ratio in the shared pool?

Technique

The *shared pool* contains the data dictionary cache, which buffers information about tables, indexes, users, and other information. Every action on the database requires information from the data dictionary. If the information is not in the data dictionary cache, the database must get the information from disk. If the database is constantly going to disk for this information, performance will suffer dramatically. The shared pool also contains the SQL cache. The SQL cache contains previously executed queries, so they do not need to be reloaded and parsed if called again. If a SQL statement is executed repeatedly but cannot reside in the SQL cache because it is too small, performance will be slow. The V$LIBRARYCACHE view shown in Figure 17-13 contains information about the SQL cache. The V$ROWCACHE view shown in Figure 17-14 contains information about the data dictionary cache.

The important columns for identifying SQL cache hit statistics are the PINS and RELOADS columns from the V$LIBRARYCACHE view. The PINS column contains the number of times the database read the SQL cache looking for a statement. The RELOADS column contains the number of times SQL statements were loaded and parsed. The ratio of RELOADS to PINS determines the effectiveness of the SQL cache. If the ratio of RELOADS to PINS is more than 1 percent, the shared pool size should be increased by raising the value of the SHARED_POOL_SIZE parameter in the INIT.ORA file.

The important columns for determining effectiveness of the dictionary cache are the GETS and GETMISSES columns in the V$ROWCACHE view. The GET column shows how many times an attempt was made to find a data dictionary value in the dictionary cache. The GETMISSES column contains the number of times the value was not found in the cache. The ratio of GETMISSES to GETS determines the effectiveness of the dictionary cache. If the ratio is greater than 10 percent, the size of the shared pool should be increased.

Steps

1. Run SQL*Plus and connect as the WAITE user account. Load CHP17-11.sql into the SQL buffer. The file contains a query to analyze hits and misses to the SQL cache.

```
SQL>   GET CHP17-11
   1    SELECT
   2      SUM(PINS) PINS,
   3      SUM(RELOADS) RELOADS,
   4      (SUM(RELOADS) / (SUM(PINS))) * 100 RATIO
   5    FROM
   6      V$LIBRARYCACHE
```

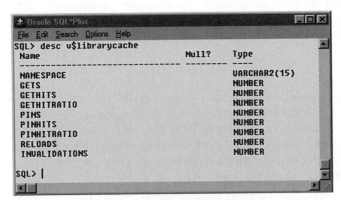

Figure 17-13 The V$LIBRARYCACHE view

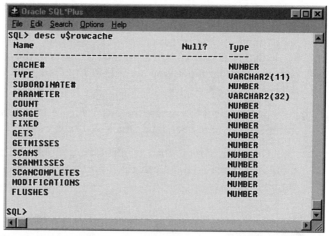

Figure 17-14 The V$ROWCACHE view

Line 2 returns the total number of hits to the SQL cache by using the SUM function on the PINS column. The PINS column contains the number of times a SQL statement was executed. The RELOADS column used in line 3 contains the number of times the statement was loaded and parsed from disk. Line 4 calculates the ratio of reloads to total executions.

2. Run the statement to view the results.

```
SQL> /

        PINS        RELOADS        RATIO
----------- ------------- -----------
      58776              5    .00850687
```

The sample data here shows that in over 58,776 reads to the SQL cache, only 5 misses occurred. This ratio is very good, but the number of executions is relatively small. Any RATIO value over 1 identifies a problem and requires increasing the size of the shared pool.

3. Load CHP17-12.sql into the SQL buffer. The file contains a query to analyze the data dictionary cache hit ratio by querying the V$ROWCACHE view.

```
SQL>  GET CHP17-12
  1   SELECT
  2     SUM(GETS) GETS,
  3     SUM(GETMISSES) MISSES,
  4     (SUM(GETMISSES) / SUM(GETS)) * 100 RATIO
  5   FROM
  6     V$ROWCACHE
```

Line 2 uses the SUM function on the GETS column to determine the total number of requests to the data dictionary cache. Line 3 calculates the number of times the row was not cached by using the GETMISSES column. Line 4 calculates the ratio of misses to total requests. If the miss ratio is over 10 percent, consider modifying the SHARED_POOL_SIZE parameter in the INIT.ORA file.

4. Run the statement to execute the query. Figure 17-15 shows the results of the operation on my Personal Oracle 7 database.

A RATIO value of more than 10 identifies a problem. The shared pool should be increased if the value is more than 10 over a significant number of transactions.

How It Works

There are two calculations required to determine whether the shared pool is large enough. Steps 1 and 2 present a query of the V$LIBRARYCACHE view to determine the amount of times a SQL statement was reloaded and parsed. Steps 3 and 4 present a query of the V$ROWCACHE view to determine the ratio of misses in the data dictionary cache to total reads. If the size of the shared pool is not large enough, it will be determined using these queries.

Comments

Any more than a 10 percent miss ratio in the data dictionary cache is reason enough to increase the size of the shared pool. Since every action on the database requires at least one read of the data dictionary, it is important the information is cached in the SGA. A miss ratio of more than 1 percent in the SQL cache buffer is another reason to increase the shared pool size. Since the values used in this process are calculated from the last time the database was started, it is important that

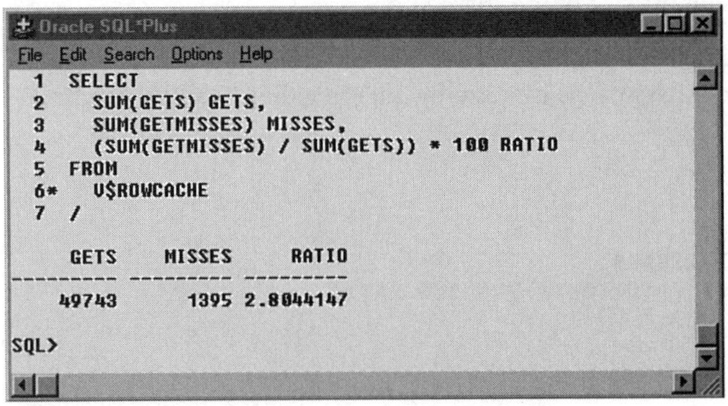

Figure 17-15 The results of CHP17-12.sql
in SQL*Plus

you allow the database sufficient time to calculate statistics. To modify the size of the shared pool, change the size of the SHARED_POOL_SIZE parameter in the INIT.ORA file.

COMPLEXITY
INTERMEDIATE

17.10 How do I...
Query the INIT.ORA parameters?

Problem

I am looking for a way to query the INIT.ORA parameters from the data dictionary. When using SQL*Plus to analyze database performance, I want to be able to query the current database parameters to see what changes are needed. I know I can look in the INIT.ORA file itself, but I want to view one or more specific values quickly. How do I query the INIT.ORA parameters?

Technique

The V$PARAMETER view contains the current INIT.ORA parameters. It can be queried to return the values needed. The description of the view is shown in Figure 17-16.

The NAME column returns the name of the parameter as referenced in the INIT.ORA file. The VALUE column returns the value of the parameter. The ISDEFAULT column is a text column that returns TRUE if the parameter contains the default value for the parameter, FALSE if it was set in the INIT.ORA file.

Steps

1. Run SQL*Plus and connect as the WAITE user account. Load CHP17-13.sql into the SQL buffer. The file contains a query of the V$PARAMETER view to show the current database parameters.

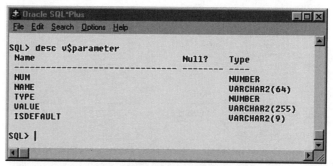

Figure 17-16 The V$PARAMETER view

```
SQL>   GET CHP17-13
  1    SELECT
  2       NAME,
  3       VALUE
  4    FROM
  5       V$PARAMETER
  6    ORDER BY NAME
```

The NAME column specified in line 2 returns the name of the INIT.ORA parameter. The VALUE column specified in line 3 returns the current value of the parameter.

2. Execute the SQL*Plus COLUMN command to format the two columns, making the output easier to read.

```
SQL>   COLUMN NAME FORMAT A20
SQL>   COLUMN VALUE FORMAT A40
SQL>
```

3. Run the statement to display the values of the INIT.ORA parameters. Figure 17-17 shows the results of the query in SQL*Plus.

The results of a query to the V$PARAMETER view can be very large. It is often best to limit the query with a WHERE clause.

4. There are many parameters which can be set through the INIT.ORA file. It is possible to view only the parameters not set in the INIT.ORA file. The ISDEFAULT column returns the value FALSE if the parameter is set through the INIT.ORA file, TRUE otherwise. Load CHP17-14.sql into the SQL buffer. The file contains a query returning the INIT.ORA parameters not set to the default value.

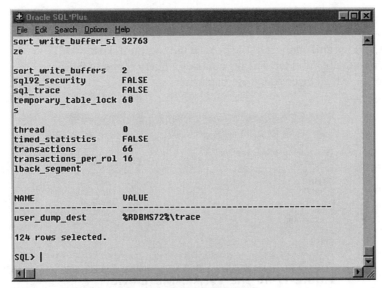

Figure 17-17 The results of CHP17-13.sql

```
SQL>   GET CHP17-14
  1    SELECT
  2       NAME,
  3       VALUE
  4    FROM
  5       V$PARAMETER
  6    WHERE ISDEFAULT = 'FALSE'
  7    ORDER BY NAME
```

Lines 2 and 3 return the NAME and VALUE columns by the query. The WHERE clause in line 6 returns only records in which the ISDEFAULT column is equal to FALSE.

5. Run the query to display the results.

```
SQL>   /

NAME                     VALUE
--------------------     ----------------------------------------
audit_trail              NONE
background_dump_dest      %RDBMS72%\trace
cache_size_threshold     20
compatible               7.2.0.0.0
control_files            D:\ORAWIN95\DATABASE\ctl1orcl.ora
cpu_count                1
db_block_buffers         200
db_block_size            2048
db_file_multiblock_
read_count               8

db_files                 20
db_name                  oracle
dml_locks                100
enqueue_resources        155
license_max_sessions     10
log_buffer               8192

NAME                     VALUE
--------------------     ----------------------------------------

max_dump_file_size       10240
mts_max_dispatchers      0
mts_max_servers          0
mts_servers              0
optimizer_mode           CHOOSE
processes                50
remote_login_
passwordfile             SHARED

sessions                 60
snapshot_refresh_
processes              1

NAME                     VALUE
--------------------     ----------------------------------------
sort_area_retained_
size                     65536
```

continued on next page

continued from previous page

```
transactions          66

user_dump_dest        %RDBMS72%\trace

26 rows selected.

SQL>
```

How It Works

The V$PARAMETER view contains the database parameters set by the INIT.ORA file when the database began. If a parameter was not set in the INIT.ORA file, the database uses its default value. The NAME column contains the name of the parameter, and the VALUE column contains its value. Step 1 presents a query returning all of the database parameters. Step 2 uses the COLUMN command to format the data. Step 3 displays sample output from the operation. Steps 4 and 5 present a query returning all the parameters set by the INIT.ORA file and not left as default. A simple modification to the query creates a query to return the value of a single database parameter.

Comments

Querying the V$PARAMETER view is sometimes faster than looking in the INIT.ORA file. It is very useful to quickly query one or more parameters through the view. Many database parameters may not be specified in the INIT.ORA file. If you have not specified a parameter, its default value is used by the database. This technique allows you to view the values of parameters you did not set.

CHAPTER 18
ORACLE OBJECTS FOR OLE

ORACLE OBJECTS FOR OLE

How do I...

Oracle Objects for OLE is an important product for developing Windows-based desktop applications with non-Oracle development languages. Oracle Objects allows OLE-compliant applications and programming languages like Microsoft Visual Basic and Microsoft Excel complete, high-speed access to Oracle databases. Oracle Objects for OLE consists of three products. The OLE automation server gives OLE-compliant applications access to the database through OLE automation. The Oracle data control is a Visual Basic custom control VBX which can be used as a replacement for the Visual Basic data control. The Oracle Objects class library provides Microsoft and Borland C++ applications direct access to the Oracle database. The examples in this chapter are found on the accompanying CD in the \SAMPLES\CHAP18 directory.

18.1   Connect to the database

In order to use any Oracle-based application, the user must connect to the database with a valid user account, password, and database name. Applications using Oracle Objects for OLE must be able to connect to the database. This How-To presents the method used to connect to the database using Oracle Objects for OLE.

18.2   Perform a query using Oracle Objects

Applications must be able to query records from the objects within the database. Within Visual Basic, a dynaset type recordset object can be created to hold the result set of a query. The OraDynaset object in Oracle Objects for OLE performs the same function. Records can be queried, inserted, updated, and deleted through the OraDynaset object. This How-To presents the method used to query records using Oracle Objects for OLE.

18.3   Navigate the records returned by a query

Once a query has been executed to create an OraDynaset object, the application can move through the recordset to process the records retrieved. The MOVE methods of the OraDynaset object are used to move through a record set. This How-To presents the methods used to move through an OraDynaset object.

18.4   Insert a record

Within most applications, it is necessary to create new records. The process of creating a new record is fundamental to building database applications. Records can be inserted into your Oracle database using the OraDynaset object. The process of creating new records is a covered in this How-To.

18.5   Update a record

Updating a record within an application is a necessary operation in database applications. It is not necessary to build and execute an UPDATE statement when modifying records with Oracle Objects. This How-To covers the method used to update a record using Oracle Objects.

18.6   Delete a record

A record can be deleted through the OraDynaset object in Oracle Objects for OLE. The DELETE statement used to delete a record is not necessary when deleting a record through Oracle Objects. This How-To covers the process used to delete a record using Oracle Objects.

18.7   Execute a stored procedure

One of the major strengths of Oracle is its ability to partition the application into client and server processing. The execution of stored procedures through Oracle Objects allows applications to perform processing on the server. This How-To presents the method used to execute a stored procedure or function and pass parameters.

18.8 Handle the LONG datatype

Columns containing the LONG or LONG RAW datatype must be handled differently in Oracle Objects than columns of other datatypes. Data in LONG columns must be moved to the database and retrieved from it in sections, since Oracle Objects can only move data in chunks smaller than 64KB. This How-To covers the topic of using LONG data with Oracle Objects.

18.9 Trap errors in Oracle Objects

Errors can occur any time an application is used. Oracle Objects provides the ability to trap database errors within your application. This How-To covers the topic of trapping errors within Oracle Objects for OLE.

COMPLEXITY
BEGINNING

18.1 How do I...
Connect to the database?

Problem

I want to use Oracle Objects for OLE in my Visual Basic 4.0 application. Since a user cannot execute any operations on the database until they connect to it, I need a method to connect to the database. How do I connect to a database using Oracle Objects for OLE?

Technique

The same method is used to connect to a database using Oracle Objects, no matter what product is used with it. Oracle Objects requires that two objects be created to access the database. The OraSession object manages connections to the database though the OraConnections collection, and it manages databases through the OraDatabases collection. An OraDatabase object must be created to manage the logon to the database. Within the event connecting to the database, the two objects must be created. In Visual Basic for Applications code, the statements look like this:

```
        Set OraSession = ⇐
CreateObject("OracleInProcServer.XOraSession")
        Set OraDatabase = ⇐
OraSession.DbOpenDatabase(database,user/passwd,0&)
```

Steps

1. Run Visual Basic. Create a new project and save it as CHP18-1.vbp. Use Form1 and create the objects and properties listed in Table 18-1. Save the form as CHP18-1.frm. If you wish to skip this step, you can open CHP18-1A.vbp from the accompanying CD. The final results of the project are contained in CHP18-1B.vbp. Figure 18-1 shows how the resulting form should look.

OBJECT	PROPERTY	SETTING
Form	Name	Form1
	Caption	"Database Logon Form"
TextBox	Nametxt	User
TextBox	Name	txtPassword
TextBox	Name	txtDatabase
Label	Name	Label1
	Autosize	True
	Caption	"User Name"
Label	Name	Label2
	Autosize	True
	Caption	"Password"
Label	Name	Label3
	Autosize	True
	Caption	"Database"
CommandButton	Name	cmdConnect
	Caption	"Connect"

Table 18-1 Objects and properties for Oracle Objects Logon form

The User Name field is used for entering the account of the user connecting to the database. The Password column is used to enter the password for the user account. The Database field is used to specify the database to which the user will connect. The Connect button is used to execute the connection to the database.

2. Add the following code to the Click event of the cmdConnect button. The cmdConnect button connects to the database as the user name specified in the textbox and creates the OraSession and OraDatabase objects. These objects are very important if the application does more than connect to the database.

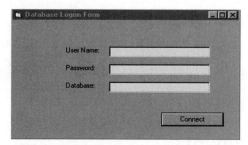

Figure 18-1 CHP18-1.vbp

```
'Declare the required objects.
Dim OraSession As Object
Dim OraDatabase As Object

'Create the OraSession object, using the VBA function CreateObject.

Set OraSession = CreateObject("OracleInProcServer.XOraSession")

'If the values are not provided by the user, exit the procedure.

If txtDatabase = "" Or txtUser = "" Or txtPassword = "" Then
     MsgBox "All Fields must be entered"
     Exit Sub
End If

'Create the Connection to the database. The three textboxes provide
'the values for the connection.

Set OraDatabase = OraSession.DbOpenDatabase(txtDatabase, txtUser & "/" _
                  & txtPassword, 0&)

'Display the username and database we are connected to.

MsgBox "Connected to " & OraDatabase.Connect & "@" & ⇐
OraDatabase.DatabaseName

End Sub
```

3. Run the Visual Basic project to display the results. Enter the WAITE username into the User Name field. Enter the password PRESS in the Password field. Enter the database name (2: for local databases) in the Database field. Choose the Connect button to connect to the database. A message box will be displayed on the screen when the connection is made. If an error occurs, check the user account, password, and database name within the code, and make sure Oracle Objects for OLE is installed on your system.

How It Works

When the user selects the Connect button, the OraSession object is created to reference the Oracle In-Process server. The dbOpenDatabase method of the object sets the OraDatabase object by connecting to the database with the user account and password specified. The OraSession and OraDatabase objects must be created in order to establish a connection to the database.

Comments

Within your applications, create global or public variables to contain the OraSession and OraDatabase objects. You will need to have access to these objects throughout your application in order to perform actions on the database. Create a logon screen in your applications to let your users supply a user name, password, and database name.

COMPLEXITY
BEGINNING

18.2 How do I...
Perform a query using Oracle Objects?

Problem

In my application, I want to perform queries of data within the Oracle database. I do not want to use a data control. I want to create a Dynaset or Recordset type object that I can control throughout my application. How do I query records using Oracle Objects?

Technique

The dbCreateDynaset method of the OraDatabase object is used to execute a query. The results of the query are contained in an OraDynaset type object. A connection must be established to the database using the process described in How-To 18.1 before a query can be executed. An OraDynaset object works like a dynaset type recordset in Visual Basic 4.0 and contains methods and properties that allow you to manipulate the dynaset.

Steps

1. Run SQL*Plus and connect as the WAITE user account. CHP18-1.sql, shown in Figure 18-2, creates the sample table used in this How-To.

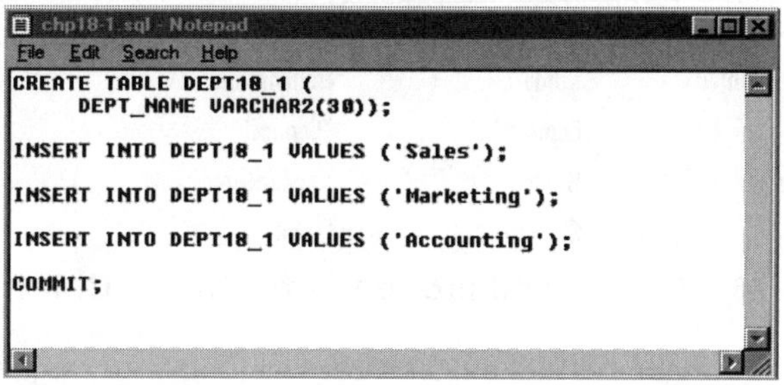

Figure 18-2 CHP18-1.sql creates the sample table used in How-To 18.2

A sample table is created by the script file and is populated with data. The Visual Basic form created in the this How-To will query the sample data. Run the statement to create the sample tables and data.

```
SQL> START CHP18-1

Table created.

1 row created.

1 row created.

1 row created.

Commit complete.
```

2. Run Visual Basic. Create a new project and save it as CHP18-2.vbp. Use Form1 and create the objects and properties listed in Table 18-2. Save the form as CHP18-2.frm. If you wish to skip this step, you can open CHP18-2A.vbp from the accompanying CD. The final results of the project are contained in CHP18-2B.vbp.

OBJECT	PROPERTY	SETTING
Form	Name	Form1
	Caption	"Oracle Objects Query"
ListBox	Name	lstQuery
Label	Name	Label1
	Autosize	True
	Caption	"Query Results"

continued on next page

continued from previous page

OBJECT	PROPERTY	SETTING
CommandButton	Name	cmdConnect
	Caption	"Connect"
CommandButton	Name	cmdExecute
	Caption	"Query"

Table 18-2 Objects and properties for Oracle Object Query form

Figure 18-3 shows how the resulting form should look.

Use the Connect button to connect to the database as the WAITE user account. The Query button is used to execute a query of the sample table created in step 1. The listbox is populated with the results of the query.

3. Add the following code to the declarations section of Form1. The OraDatabase and OraSession objects are declared as public variables so that they can be used throughout the form.

```
Option Explicit
Public OraDatabase As Object
Public OraSession As Object
```

4. Enter the following code as the Click event of the cmdConnect button. The cmdConnect button creates the OraSession and OraDatabase objects and connects to the database as the WAITE user account.

```
Private Sub cmdConnect_Click()
    Set OraSession = CreateObject("OracleInProcServer.XOraSession")
    Set OraDatabase = OraSession.DbOpenDatabase("2:", "waite/press", 0&)
    MsgBox "Connected to " & OraDatabase.Connect & "@" & _
                        OraDatabase.DatabaseName
End Sub
```

When the user is connected to the database, a message box is displayed advising the user of a successful connection. The OraSession and OraDatabase objects are created using the same method presented in How-To 18.1.

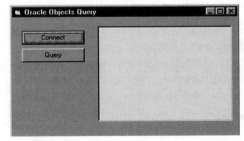

Figure 18-3 CHP18-2.vbp

5. Enter the following code as the Click event of the cmdExecute button. The cmdExecute button is used to execute a query and move the query results to the listbox.

```
Private Sub cmdExecute_Click()
Dim OraDynaset As Object
Dim SQL As String

    SQL = "SELECT DEPT_NAME FROM DEPT18_1 ORDER BY DEPT_NAME"
    Set OraDynaset = OraDatabase.DbCreateDynaset(SQL,&0)

    lstQuery.Clear
    If OraDynaset.RecordCount = 0 Then
        Exit Sub
    End If

    Do Until OraDynaset.EOF
        lstQuery.AddItem OraDynaset.Fields(0) & ""
        OraDynaset.dbMoveNext
    Loop

End Sub
```

A SQL statement is placed in the SQL variable and executed with the dbCreateDynaset method of the OraDatabase object. The RecordCount property of the OraDynaset object contains the number of records the query navigated through and returned. If the RecordCount property is 0 after the query has been executed, no records were returned. If the value of RecordCount property is 1, one or more records were returned. The EOF property of the OraDynaset object returns TRUE if the current record has navigated past the end of the query. The Do Until loop uses this property to determine the end of the recordset. The Do Until loop goes through each of the records the query returned, moving each one into the listbox.

6. Run the project to display the results. Select the Connect button to connect to the database as the WAITE user account. After a connection has been established, select the Query button to query the sample table and display the results.

How It Works

Step 1 creates the sample table and data used by the project. The user connects to the database by pressing the Connect button. This creates the OraSession and OraDatabase objects declared as public variables in the declarations section of the form. The user presses the Query button to execute the query and populate the listbox with the results. When the Query button is pressed, an OraDynaset object is created to execute the query and hold the results.

Comments

The techniques presented in this How-To are fundamental to using Oracle Objects for OLE. Connecting to the database and performing a query are actions required by any database application. Most of the code presented in this example can be migrated directly to Microsoft Excel to query records from Oracle into a spreadsheet.

COMPLEXITY
BEGINNING

18.3 How do I...
Navigate the records returned by a query?

Problem

Once I have created a dynaset type object with a query in Oracle Objects, I need to move through the records in the dynaset. In Visual Basic, methods are used to move through a dynaset type recordset, and Oracle Objects provides the same functionality. How do I move through a recordset in Oracle Objects for OLE?

Technique

The OraDynaset object has a set of methods used to navigate through the records returned by a query. The dbMoveFirst method moves the current record to the first record in the dynaset. The dbMoveLast record moves the current record to the last record in the dynaset. The dbMovePrevious and dbMoveNext methods move the current record backward or forward one record, respectively.

Steps

1. Run SQL*Plus and connect as the WAITE user account. CHP18-2.sql, shown in Figure 18-4, creates the sample table used in this How-To.

The script creates a sample table with four records navigated by the example program. Run the file to create the sample table and its data.

```
SQL> START CHP18-2

Table created.

1 row created.

1 row created.

1 row created.

1 row created.

Commit complete.
```

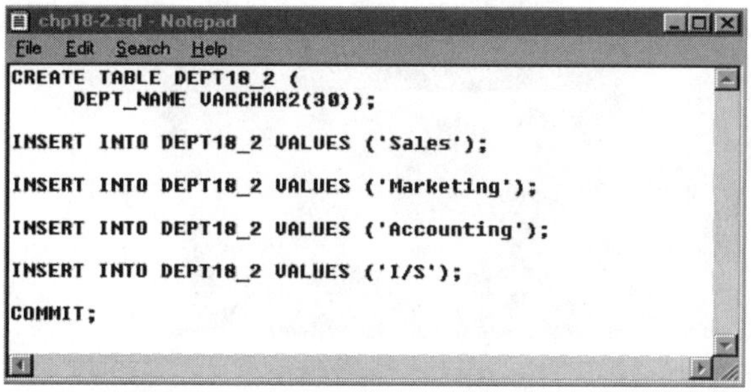

Figure 18-4 CHP18-2.sql creates the sample table used in How-To 18.3

2. Run Visual Basic. Create a new project and save it as CHP18-3.VBP. Use Form1 and create the objects and properties listed in Table 18-3. Save the form as CHP18-3.frm. If you wish to skip this step, you can open CHP18-3A.vbp from the accompanying CD. The final results of the project are contained in CHP18-3B.vbp.

OBJECT	PROPERTY	SETTING
Form	Name	Form1
	Caption	"Oracle Objects Navigation"
TextItem	Name	txtDept
Label	Name	Label1
	Autosize	True
	Caption	"Department:"
CommandButton	Name	cmdConnect
	Caption	"Connect"
CommandButton	Name	cmdQuery
	Caption	"Query"
CommandButton	Name	cmdFirst
	Caption	"First Record"
CommandButton	Name	cmdPrev
	Caption	"Previous Record"
CommandButton	Name	cmdNext
	Caption	"Next Record"
CommandButton	Name	cmdLast
	Caption	"Last Record

Table 18-3 Oracle Objects Record Navigation Demo

Figure 18-5 shows how the resulting form should look.

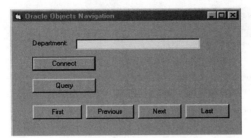

Figure 18-5 The resulting form

The Department field is used to display the current record in the Dynaset object. The Connect button is used to connect to the database as the WAITE user account. The Query button is used to execute a query of the sample table created in step 1 and display the first record. The First Record, Previous Record, Next Record, and Last Record buttons navigate the records the query returned.

3. Add the following code to the declarations section of Form1. The OraDatabase and OraSession objects are declared as public variables in the declarations section of the form. This makes the objects available through-out the form. The OraDynaset object contains the results of the query and must be available throughout the form.

```
Option Explicit
Public OraDatabase As Object
Public OraSession As Object
Public OraDynaset As Object
Public RecordCount As Integer
Public CurrentRecord As Integer
```

The RecordCount variable is used to hold the number of records the query returns. The CurrentRecord variable is used to maintain the location of the current record within the query and ensure that the user does not navigate past the file's beginning or end.

4. Enter the following code as the Click event of the cmdConnect button. The cmdConnect button creates the OraSession and OraDatabase objects and connects to the database as the WAITE user account. For more information about connecting to the database, refer to How-To 18.1.

```
Private Sub cmdConnect_Click()
    Set OraSession = CreateObject("OracleInProcServer.XOraSession")
    Set OraDatabase = OraSession.DbOpenDatabase("2:", "waite/press", 0&)
    MsgBox "Connected to " & OraDatabase.Connect & "@" & _
                    OraDatabase.DatabaseName
End Sub
```

5. Enter the following code as the Click event of the cmdQuery button. The cmdQuery button executes a query of the sample table created in step 1 and sets the RecordCount variable to the number of records the query returned. The OraDynaset object created contains the navigation methods for moving through the dynaset.

```
Private Sub cmdQuery_Click()

    Dim SQL As String
    SQL = "SELECT DEPT_NAME FROM DEPT18_2 ORDER BY DEPT_NAME"
    Set OraDynaset = OraDatabase.DbCreateDynaset(SQL,&0)

    OraDynaset.dbMoveLast
    OraDynaset.dbMoveFirst
    RecordCount = OraDynaset.RecordCount
    If RecordCount > 0 Then
        CurrentRecord = 0
        txtDept = OraDynaset.Fields(0).Value
    End If

End Sub
```

The SQL variable is declared and set to the SQL statement being executed. Using a string variable to contain the SQL statement lets you build dynamic SQL statements at runtime. The DbCreateDynaset method of the OraDatabase object creates an OraDynaset object and executes the query. The dbMoveLast and dbMoveFirst methods from the OraDynaset object navigate the dynaset, ensuring the RecordCound property is accurate. The value of the first field in the first record is moved into the txtDept field.

6. Enter the following code as the Click event of the cmdFirst button. The cmdFirst button moves the current record to the first record in the dynaset.

```
Private Sub cmdFirst_Click()

    If RecordCount = 0 Then
        Exit Sub
    End If
    OraDynaset.dbMoveFirst
    CurrentRecord = 0
    txtDept = OraDynaset.Fields(0).Value

End Sub
```

If the value of the RecordCount variable is 0, then the query has not been executed and the procedure is exited. The dbMoveFirst property of the OraDynaset object moves the current record to the first record in the dynaset. The CurrentRecord variable is set to 0, since the current record is now the first. The value of the txtDept field is set to the value of the first column in the first record.

7. Enter the following code as the Click event of the cmdLast_Click button. The cmdLast_Click button moves the current record to the end of the query and displays the value of the last record.

```
Private Sub cmdLast_Click()
    If RecordCount = 0 Then
        Exit Sub
    End If
    OraDynaset.dbMoveLast
    CurrentRecord = RecordCount - 1
    txtDept = OraDynaset.Fields(0).Value
End Sub
```

If the value of the RecordCount variable is 0, then the query has not been executed and the procedure is exited. The dbMoveLast method of the OraDynaset object moves the current record to the first record in the dynaset. The CurrentRecord variable is set to RecordCount - 1, representing the last record in the query. The value of the txtDept field is set to the value of the first column in the last record.

8. Enter the following code as the Click event of the cmdNext button. The cmdNext button moves the current record forward by one if the end of the query has not been reached.

```
Private Sub cmdNext_Click()
    If RecordCount = 0 Then
        Exit Sub
    End If
    If CurrentRecord < RecordCount - 1 Then
        OraDynaset.dbMoveNext
        CurrentRecord = CurrentRecord + 1
        txtDept = OraDynaset.Fields(0).Value
    End If
End Sub
```

If the RecordCount variable is 0, then the query has not been executed and the procedure is exited. If the value of the CurrentRecord variable is less than the end of the file, the dbMoveNext method of the OraDynaset object is used to move forward one record. The CurrentRecord variable is incremented by 1, and the txtDept field is set to the value of the first column of the new record.

9. Enter the following code as the Click event of the cmdPrev button. The cmdPrev button is used to move the current record back one record if the current one is not at the beginning of the query.

```
Private Sub cmdPrev_Click()
    If RecordCount = 0 Then
        Exit Sub
    End If
```

```
        If CurrentRecord > 0 Then
        OraDynaset.dbMovePrevious
        CurrentRecord = CurrentRecord - 1
        txtDept = OraDynaset.Fields(0).Value
        End If
End Sub
```

If the value of the RecordCount variable is 0, then the query has not been executed and the procedure is exited. If the value of the CurrentRecord variable is greater than 0, the dbMovePrevious method of the OraDynaset object moves backward one record. The CurrentRecord variable is decremented by 1, and the txtDept field is set to the value of the first column of the new record.

10. Run the project to display the results. Connect to the database by selecting the Connect button. A message will appear announcing a successful connection. Execute the sample table's query by selecting the Query button. After the query has been executed, you can use the navigation buttons to move through the query results.

How It Works

Step 1 creates a sample table used throughout the How-To and populates it with data. The Connect button created in Step 4 connects the user to the database. The Query button created in Step 5 executes a query of the sample table, populating the OraDynaset object. The First button created in Step 6 uses the dbMoveFirst method of the OraDynaset object to move to the first record. The Click event for the Last button created in Step 7 uses the dbMoveLast method to move to the last record. The Click event for the Next button created in Step 8 uses the dbMoveNext method to move to the next record. The Click event in the Previous button created in step 9 uses the dbMovePrevious method to move to the previous record. The four navigational buttons let you navigate through the records in the OraDynaset object.

Comments

The Move records in the OraDynaset objects make it easy to navigate through the records in a record set. You must keep track of your location in the record set since an error will occur if you try navigating to an invalid record. The EOF property returns TRUE if the end of file has been reached.

COMPLEXITY
BEGINNING

18.4 How do I...
Insert a record?

Problem

My applications need to create new records in a table. In SQL*Plus, I use the INSERT statement to add new records to a table. I do not want to build and execute SQL statements to add new records. I know that the OraDynaset object works very much like a dynaset type recordset in Visual Basic. How do I insert a new record into a table using the OraDynaset object?

Technique

A record can be created through the dbDynaset object. The dbAddNew method creates a new record in the table referenced by the dynaset. The dbUpdate method commits the new record to the database after the values have been moved into the fields. The OraDynaset object must be created with an updatable query referencing the table to which the new records will be added. The query does not need to return the rows in the table, but must reference a valid table.

Steps

1. Run SQL*Plus and connect as the WAITE user account. CHP18-3.sql, shown in Figure 18-6, creates the sample table used in this How-To.

The script creates a sample table used to demonstrate the process for inserting records through Oracle Objects. For simplicity, the table contains a single column. Run the file to create the sample table.

```
SQL> START CHP18-3

Table created.
```

2. Run Visual Basic. Create a new project and save it as CHP18-4.vbp. Use Form1 and create the objects and properties listed in Table 18-4. Save the

Figure 18-6 CHP18-3.sql creates the sample table used in How-To 18.4

form as CHP18-4.frm. If you wish to skip this step, open CHP18-3A.vbp from the accompanying CD. The final results of the project are found in CHP18-3B.vbp.

OBJECT	PROPERTY	SETTING
Form	Name	Form1
	Caption	"Oracle Objects Insert"
TextItem	Name	txtValue
Label	Name	Label1
	Autosize	True
	Caption	"Value:"
CommandButton	Name	cmdConnect
	Caption	"Connect"
CommandButton	Name	cmdSave
	Caption	"Insert Record

Table 18-4 Oracle Objects Insert Record Demo

Figure 18-7 shows how the resulting form should look.

The Connect button is used to connect to the database as the WAITE user account. After connecting to the database, a value can be entered into the Value field and saved by selecting the Insert Record button.

3. Add the following code to the declarations section of Form1. The OraDatabase and OraSession objects are declared as public variables in the declaration section of the form. This makes the objects available throughout the form.

```
Option Explicit
Public OraDatabase As Object
Public OraSession As Object
```

4. Enter the following code as the Click event of the cmdConnect button. The cmdConnect button creates the OraSession and OraDatabase objects and connects to the database as the WAITE user account.

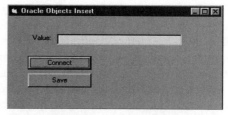

Figure 18-7 The Oracle Objects Insert Record form

```
Private Sub cmdConnect_Click()
    Set OraSession = CreateObject("OracleInProcServer.XOraSession")
    Set OraDatabase = OraSession.DbOpenDatabase("2:", "waite/press", 0&)
    MsgBox "Connected to " & OraDatabase.Connect & "@" & _
           OraDatabase.DatabaseName
End Sub
```

5. Enter the following code as the Click event of the cmdSave button. The cmdSave button inserts the value contained in the Value field into the sample table and clears the field.

```
Private Sub cmdSave_Click()
Dim OraDynaset As Object
Dim SQL As String

    SQL = "SELECT DEPT_NAME FROM DEPT18_3 WHERE 1 = 0"
    Set OraDynaset = OraDatabase.DbCreateDynaset(SQL,&0)

    OraDynaset.dbAddNew
    OraDynaset.Fields(0).Value = txtValue
    OraDynaset.dbUpdate
    MsgBox "Record Inserted"
    txtValue = ""
End Sub
```

An OraDynaset object is used to insert records with Oracle Objects. An object variable is declared to hold the dynaset that inserts the record. A query is executed for the dynaset using the dbCreateDynaset method of the OraDatabase object. The query returns no rows, but sets up the dynaset so that a record can be created. The dbAddNew method of the OraDynaset object creates a new record in the table. Once the AddNew method has been executed, the values of the fields can be set to the new values. The dbUpdate method is used to commit the transaction to the database after the field values have been specified.

6. Run the project to display the results. Connect to the database by selecting the Connect button. Type a value into the text field and select the Insert Record button to create a new record. A message box announcing your success is displayed.

How It Works

The dbAddNew method of the OraDynaset object prepares the dynaset to create a new record. It sets the fields the dynaset references to the values of the new record. The dbUpdate method commits the new record to the database. Step 1 creates the sample table which will have records inserted in it. Step 4 creates the code to connect to the database as the WAITE user account with the method presented in How-To 18.1. Step 5 creates the code to insert records into the sample table. The procedure creates an OraDynaset object that queries the sample table created in Step 1. The query used to create the dynaset does not return any rows, but creates a dynaset that can insert records. The dbAddNew method is executed on the dynaset, preparing it to add a new record. The field contained in the dynaset is set to the value in the textbox, and the record is committed using the DbUpdate method.

Comments

Users of Visual Basic will find the method presented in this How-To very easy. For developers used to Developer 2000 or other programming languages, it may be more confusing. Although this method is not difficult, you may have to work with it a few times before getting comfortable.

COMPLEXITY
BEGINNING

18.5 How do I...
Update a record?

Problem

After I query a record using an OraDynaset object, I need to make modifications to it and commit the changes to the database. How do I update a record using Oracle Objects for OLE?

Technique

The dbEdit method of the OraDynaset object puts the current record into edit mode. The current record is locked so other users cannot access the record the application is changing. After modifications are made to the record, the dbUpdate method is used to commit the changes to the database and unlock it. The record being updated must be queried into a dynaset object before it can be modified.

Steps

1. Run SQL*Plus and connect as the WAITE user account. CHP18-4.sql, shown in Figure 18-8, creates the sample table used in this How-To.

```
chp18-4.sql - Notepad
File  Edit  Search  Help
CREATE TABLE DEPT18_4 (
        DEPT_NAME VARCHAR2(30));

INSERT INTO DEPT18_4 VALUES ('Sales');

INSERT INTO DEPT18_4 VALUES ('Marketing');

INSERT INTO DEPT18_4 VALUES ('Accounting');

INSERT INTO DEPT18_4 VALUES ('I/S');

COMMIT;
```

Figure 18-8 CHP18-4.sql creates the sample table used in How-To 18.5

The script creates a sample table with four records that can be updated by the project. Run the file to create the sample table and data.

```
SQL> START CHP18-4

Table created.

1 row created.

1 row created.

1 row created.

1 row created.

Commit complete.
```

2. Run Visual Basic. Create a new project and save it as CHP18-5.vbp. Use Form1 and create the objects and properties listed in Table 18-5. Save the form as CHP18-5.frm. If you wish to skip this step, you can open CHP18-5A.vbp from the accompanying CD-ROM. The final results of the project are contained in CHP18-5B.vbp.

OBJECT	PROPERTY	SETTING
Form	Name	Form1
	Caption	"Oracle Objects Update"
TextItem	Name	txtValue
Label	Name	Label1
	Autosize	True
	Caption	"Value:"
CommandButton	Name	cmdConnect
	Caption	"Connect"
CommandButton	Name	cmdSave
	Caption	"Update Record"
CommandButton	Name	cmdNext
	Caption	"Next Record"
CommandButton	Name	cmdPrev
	Caption	"Previous"
CommandButton	Name	cmdQuery
	Caption	"Query"

Table 18-5 Oracle Objects Update demo

Figure 18-9 shows how the resulting form should look.

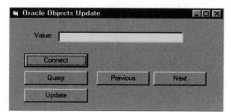

Figure 18-9 Object Update
demo form

3. Add the following code to the declarations section of Form1. The
OraDatabase, OraSession, and OraDynaset objects are declared as public
variables in the declarations section of the form so they can be referenced
throughout the form.

```
Option Explicit
Public OraDatabase As Object
Public OraSession As Object
Public OraDynaset As Object
Public RecordCount As Integer
Public CurrentRecord As Integer
```

The OraDynaset variable contains the dynaset that has the records to be
updated. The RecordCount variable contains the number of records in the
dynaset. The CurrentRecord variable contains the location of the current
record in the dynaset.

4. Enter the following code as the Click event of the cmdConnect button. The
cmdConnect button connects to the Oracle database and the WAITE user
account and creates the OraSession and OraDatabase objects.

```
Private Sub cmdConnect_Click()
    Set OraSession = CreateObject("OracleInProcServer.XOraSession")
    Set OraDatabase = OraSession.DbOpenDatabase("2:", "waite/press", 0&)
    MsgBox "Connected to " & OraDatabase.Connect & "a" & _
                OraDatabase.DatabaseName
End Sub
```

5. Enter the following code as the Click event of the cmdQuery button. The
cmdQuery button executes a query of the sample table created in step 1
and builds the OraDynaset object. Once the query has been executed, the
records can be modified.

```
Private Sub cmbQuery_Click()

    Dim SQL As String
    SQL = "SELECT DEPT_NAME FROM DEPT18_4"
    Set OraDynaset = OraDatabase.DbCreateDynaset(SQL,&0)
    If OraDynaset.RecordCount = 0 Then
```

continued on next page

continued from previous page

```
        MsgBox "No data found"
        CurrentRecord = 0
    Else
        txtValue = OraDynaset.Fields(0)
        CurrentRecord = 1
        OraDynaset.dbMoveLast
        OraDynaset.dbMoveFirst
        RecordCount = OraDynaset.RecordCount
    End If

End Sub
```

The DbCreateDynaset method is used to execute the query contained in the SQL variable and to create the OraDynaset object. If no records are returned, a message box is displayed. If one or more records are retrieved, the number of records returned by the query is placed in the RecordCount variable. The value of the first record is placed in the txtValue textbox.

6. Enter the following code as the Click event of the cmdNext button. The cmdNext button moves the current record to the next record. If no query has been executed, the Click event performs no action. If the user is at the end of the list, a message box is displayed.

```
Private Sub cmdNext_Click()

    If RecordCount = 0 Then
        Exit Sub
    End If
    If CurrentRecord < RecordCount Then
        OraDynaset.dbMoveNext
        txtValue = OraDynaset.Fields(0)
        CurrentRecord = CurrentRecord + 1
    Else
        MsgBox "End Of Table"
    End If

End Sub
```

If the query has not been executed or no records were returned by it, the value of the RecordCount variable will be 0 and the procedure exited. If the current record is not at the end of the dynaset, the dbMoveNext method of the OraDynaset object is executed and the new value is displayed. If the record is at the end of the dynaset, a message box is displayed.

7. Enter the following code as the Click event of the cmdPrev button. The cmdPrev button moves the current record back one. If no query has been executed, the button performs no action. If the user is at the first record in the list, a message box is displayed.

```
Private Sub cmdPrev_Click()

    If RecordCount = 0 Then
        Exit Sub
    End If
    If CurrentRecord > 0 Then
        OraDynaset.dbMovePrevious
        txtValue = OraDynaset.Fields(0)
        CurrentRecord = CurrentRecord -1
    Else
        MsgBox "At first record"
    End If

End Sub
```

If the query has not been executed or no records have been returned by it, the procedure is exited. If the current record is not the first record in the dynaset, the dbMovePrevious method of the OraDynaset object is executed and the new value is displayed. If the current record is the first record, a message box is displayed.

8. Enter the following code as the Click event of the cmdSave button. The cmdSave button moves the value in the text item into the current record and saves the record. If no query has been executed, the button performs no action.

```
Private Sub cmdSave_Click()

    If RecordCount = 0 Then
        Exit Sub
    End If
    OraDynaset.dbEdit
    OraDynaset.Fields(0).Value = txtValue
    OraDynaset.dbUpdate
    MsgBox "Record Updated"

End Sub
```

If no query has been executed or there were no records returned by the query, the procedure is exited. The dbEdit method of the OraDynaset object is executed to lock the current record. This method must be executed before the values in the fields can be modified. The value of the field is then modified to the value in the textbox. The dbUpdate method commits the record to the database and unlocks the record.

9. Run the project to display the results. Select the Connect button to connect to the database as the WAITE user account. Select the Query button to query the sample table and populate the dynaset. Use the navigation buttons to move through the queried results. Change a value in the textbox and select the Update Record button to save the changes to the database.

How It Works

The project presented in this How-To queries data from a sample table created in Step 1 and updates the data. Step 4 creates the code used to connect to the database as the WAITE user account. The technique used is shown in How-To 18.1. Step 5 creates the Click event in the cmdQuery button, which queries the sample table and creates the OraDynaset object. Steps 6 and 7 create navigational procedures, letting the user move through the records to choose one for updating. The method used in Steps 6 and 7 is presented in How-To 18.3. Step 8 creates the code used to update the record in the table. The dbEdit method locks the current record and lets it be updated. After the fields in the current record have been set to their new values, the dbUpdate method is executed to commit the changes to the database.

Comments

The method presented in this How-To is very useful for changing records that have been queried into a OraDynaset object. If you plan to update a record that does not need to be queried first, it may be easier to create an UPDATE statement and execute it using the DbUpdateSQL method from the OraDatabase object. This method does not require that the record be queried first.

COMPLEXITY
BEGINNING

18.6   How do I...
Delete a record?

Problem

Within my application, it is necessary to delete records from a table. I want to delete records retrieved as part of a query and now in an OraDynaset object. I do not want to create a DELETE statement to remove the records. How do I delete a record in Oracle Objects?

Technique

The dbDelete method of the OraDynaset object is used to delete the current record in the dynaset. A record must be queried into the dynaset before it can be deleted. The dbDelete method deletes the record immediately and commits the transaction.

Steps

1. Run SQL*Plus and connect as the WAITE user account. CHP18-5.sql, shown in Figure 18-10, creates the sample table and data used in this How-To.

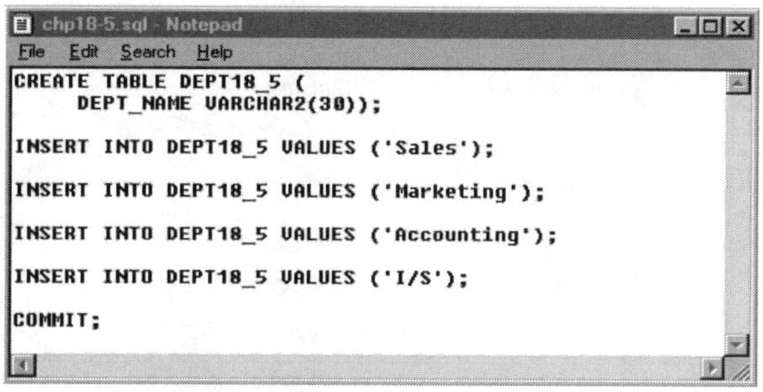


```
CREATE TABLE DEPT18_5 (
    DEPT_NAME VARCHAR2(30));

INSERT INTO DEPT18_5 VALUES ('Sales');

INSERT INTO DEPT18_5 VALUES ('Marketing');

INSERT INTO DEPT18_5 VALUES ('Accounting');

INSERT INTO DEPT18_5 VALUES ('I/S');

COMMIT;
```

Figure 18-10 CHP18-5.sql to create the sample table and data used in How-To 18.6

The script creates a sample table and four records which can be deleted by the sample project. Run the file to create the sample table and data.

```
SQL> START CHP18-5

Table created.

1 row created.

1 row created.

1 row created.

1 row created.

Commit complete.
```

2. Run Visual Basic. Create a new project and save it as CHP18-6.vbp. Use Form1 and create the objects and properties listed in Table 18-6. Save the form as CHP18-6.frm. If you wish to skip this step, open CHP18-6A.vbp from the accompanying CD-ROM. The final results of the project are found in CHP18-6B.vbp.

OBJECT	PROPERTY	SETTING
Form	Name	Form1
	Caption	"Oracle Objects Delete"
TextItem	Name	txtValue
Label	Name	Label1
	Autosize	True
	Caption	"Value:"
CommandButton	Name	cmdConnect
	Caption	"Connect"

continued on next page

continued from previous page

OBJECT	PROPERTY	SETTING
CommandButton	Name	cmdSave
	Caption	"Delete Record"
CommandButton	Name	cmdNext
	Caption	"Next Record"
CommandButton	Name	cmdPrev
	Caption	"Previous"
CommandButton	Name	cmdQuery
	Caption	"Query"

Table 18-6 Oracle Objects Delete Demo

Figure 18-11 shows how the resulting form should look.

3. Add the following code to the declarations section of Form1. The OraDatabase, OraSession, and OraDynaset objects are declared as public variables in the declaration section of the form so they can be referenced throughout the form.

```
Option Explicit
Public OraDatabase As Object
Public OraSession As Object
Public OraDynaset As Object
Public RecordCount As Integer
Public CurrentRecord As Integer
```

The OraDynaset variable contains the dynaset with updatable records. The RecordCount variable contains the number of records in the dynaset. The CurrentRecord variable contains the location of the current record in the dynaset, preventing movement past the beginning or end of it.

4. Enter the following code as the Click event of the cmdConnect button. The cmdConnect button connects to the database as the WAITE user account and creates the OraSession and OraDatabase objects.

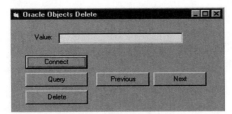

Figure 18-11 Object Delete
Demo form

```
Private Sub cmdConnect_Click()
   Set OraSession = CreateObject("OracleInProcServer.XOraSession")
   Set OraDatabase = OraSession.DbOpenDatabase("2:", "waite/press", 0&)
   MsgBox "Connected to " & OraDatabase.Connect & "a" & _
OraDatabase.DatabaseName
End Sub
```

5. Enter the following code as the Click event of the cmdQuery button. The
cmdQuery button executes a query of the sample table created in Step 1
and creates the OraDynaset object.

```
Private Sub cmdQuery_Click()

   Dim SQL As String
   SQL = "SELECT DEPT_NAME FROM DEPT18_5"
   Set OraDynaset = OraDatabase.DbCreateDynaset(SQL,&0)
   If OraDynaset.RecordCount = 0 Then
      MsgBox "No data found"
      CurrentRecord = 0
   Else
      txtValue = OraDynaset.Fields(0)
      CurrentRecord = 1
      OraDynaset.dbMoveLast
      OraDynaset.dbMoveFirst
      RecordCount = OraDynaset.RecordCount
   End If

End Sub
```

The dbCreateDynaset method of the OraDatabase object is used to execute
the query contained in the SQL variable. If the query returns records, the
value of the first record is displayed in the txtValue textbox, and the number of records returned by the query is placed in the RecordCount variable.

6. Enter the following code as the Click event of the cmdNext button. The
cmdNext button moves the current record to the next record. If no query
has been executed, the Click event performs no action. If the user is at the
end of the list of records, a message box is displayed.

```
Private Sub cmdNext_Click()

   If RecordCount = 0 Then
      Exit Sub
   End If
   If CurrentRecord < RecordCount Then
      OraDynaset.dbMoveNext
      txtValue = OraDynaset.Fields(0)
      CurrentRecord = CurrentRecord + 1
   Else
      MsgBox "End Of Table"
   End If

End Sub
```

If no query has been executed or the query returned no rows, the value of the RecordCount variable will be 0 and the procedure exited. If the current record is not at the end of the list, the dbMoveNext method of the OraDynaset object is used to move the current record forward one. If the current record is at the end of the list, a message box is displayed.

7. Enter the following code as the Click event of the cmdPrev button. The cmdPrev button moves the current record back one. If no query has been executed, the button performs no action. If the user is at the first record in the list, a message box is displayed.

```
Private Sub cmdPrev_Click()

    If CurrentRecord = 0 Then
        Exit Sub
    End If
    If CurrentRecord > 1 Then
        OraDynaset.dbMovePrevious
        txtValue = OraDynaset.Fields(0)
        CurrentRecord = CurrentRecord -1
    Else
        MsgBox "At first record"
    End If

End Sub
```

If the value of the RecordCount variable is 0, the procedure exited. If the current record is not at the beginning of the list, the dbMovePrevious method of the OraDynaset object is used to move the current record back one. If the current record is at the beginning of the list, a message box is displayed.

8. Enter the following code as the Click event of the cmdSave button. The cmdSave button deletes the current record in the dynaset and clears the value from the textbox.

```
Private Sub cmdSave_Click()
    If RecordCount = 0 Then
        Exit Sub
    End If
    OraDynaset.dbDelete
    MsgBox "Record Deleted"
    txtValue = ""
    RecordCount = RecordCount - 1
End Sub
```

If the value of the RecordCount variable is 0, the procedure is exited. The dbDelete method of the OraDynaset object is used to delete the current record from a dynaset and commit the transaction. Once the record is deleted, a message box is displayed and the txtValue field cleared.

9. Run the project to display the results. Connect to the database as the WAITE user account by selecting the Connect button. Select the Query button to execute a query of the sample table created in step 1. Use the navigation buttons to move through the records returned by the query. To delete a record, select the Delete button.

How It Works

The dbDelete method of the OraDynaset object is used to delete a record contained in a dynaset. The dbDelete method deletes the current record. Step 1 creates a sample table with data that can be deleted by the project. Step 4 creates the code for connecting to the database, using the method presented in How-To 18.1. Step 5 creates a procedure to query the sample table created in Step 1 and creates the OraDynaset object. Steps 6 and 7 create the code for two navigation buttons, letting you move through the recordset to find a record to delete. Step 8 creates the code that deletes the record. The dbDelete method of the OraDynaset object deletes the current record.

Comments

If the record you plan to delete has not been queried into an OraDynaset object, it may be easier to build and execute a DELETE statement using the DdExecuteSQL method in the OraDynaset object. This method does not require you to query the deleted record first, and it executes much faster. The method presented in this How-To is preferable when the record is already contained in an existing dynaset.

COMPLEXITY
INTERMEDIATE

18.7 How do I...
Execute a stored procedure?

Problem

My application makes frequent use of stored objects. The application uses stored procedures and functions created both within it and from built-in packages. Since parameters are passed to objects and functions return values, I need to pass parameters through Oracle Objects. How do I execute a stored object using Oracle Objects for OLE?

Technique

The dbExecuteSQL method of the OraDatabase object allows PL/SQL code to be executed. The PL/SQL code can contain any valid PL/SQL statements, including calls to stored procedures, functions, and packages. Parameters can be passed to and returned by the PL/SQL code through the Parameters collection of the OraDatabase object. The Add method of the collection is used to create a new parameter and set its value. The Remove method is used to delete an existing parameter. Parameters can be referenced from within the PL/SQL statement by prefixing the parameter name with a colon (:). The Value property of the parameter can be used to return the value to the Visual Basic procedure after the dbExecuteSQL method has been executed.

Steps

1. Run SQL*Plus and connect as the WAITE user account. CHP18-6.sql, shown in Figure 18-12, creates the stored function used in this How-To.

The stored function created in the script receives a parameter and returns a value that's a simple modification of it. Run the file to create the sample stored function.

```
SQL>   START CHP9-6
```

```
Function created.
```

2. Run Visual Basic. Create a new project and save it as CHP18-7.vbp. Use Form1 and create the objects and properties listed in Table 18-7. Save the form as CHP18-7.frm. If you want to skip this step, you can open CHP18-7A.vbp. The final results of the example are contained in CHP18-7B.vbp.

OBJECT	PROPERTY	SETTING
Form	Name	Form1
	Caption	"Stored Procedure Demo"
TextItem	Name	txtInput
TextItem	Name	txtResults
Label	Name	Label1
	Autosize	True
	Caption	"Results:"
Label	Name	Label2
	Autosize	True
	Caption	"Input"
CommandButton	Name	cmdConnect
	Caption	"Connect"
CommandButton	Name	cmdExecute
	Caption	"Execute"

Table 18-7 Oracle Objects Stored Procedure Demo

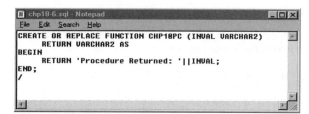

Figure 18-12 CHP18-6.sql creates the stored function used in How-To 18.7

Figure 18-13 shows how the resulting form should look.

3. Add the following code to the declarations section of Form1. The OraDatabase and OraSession objects are created as public variables to be used throughout the project.

```
Option Explicit
Public OraDatabase As Object
Public OraSession As Object
```

4. Enter the following code as the Click event of the cmdConnect button. The cmdClick button connects to the Oracle database as the WAITE user account and creates the OraSession and OraDatabase objects. For more information about connecting to the database, refer to How-To 18.1.

```
Private Sub cmdConnect_Click()
    Set OraSession = CreateObject("OracleInProcServer.XOraSession")
    Set OraDatabase = OraSession.DbOpenDatabase("2:", "waite/press", O&)
    MsgBox "Connected to " & OraDatabase.Connect & "@" & _
OraDatabase.DatabaseName
End Sub
```

5. Enter the following code as the Click event of the cmdExecute button. The cmdExecute button passes a parameter to the stored function created in Step 1 and returns a value to the code displayed in a textbox on the form.

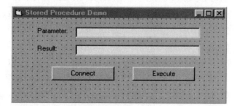

Figure 18-13 Oracle Objects Stored Procedure Demo

```
Private Sub cmdExecute_Click()

OraDatabase.Parameters.Add "INVAL", txtInput, 1
OraDatabase.Parameters("INVAL").ServerType = 1

OraDatabase.Parameters.Add "OUTVAL", 0, 2
OraDatabase.Parameters("OUTVAL").ServerType = 2

OraDatabase.DbExecuteSQL ("Begin :OUTVAL:= CHP18PC(:INVAL); end;")
txtResults = OraDatabase.Parameters("OUTVAL").Value
OraDatabase.Parameters.Remove "INVAL"
OraDatabase.Parameters.Remove "OUTVAL"
End Sub
```

The Add method of the Parameters collection in the OraDatabase object is used to create a new database parameter which can be passed to the PL/SQL code. Setting the ServerType property of a Parameter collection to 1 defines it as an input parameter. A value of 2 specifies the parameter as an output parameter. The INVAL parameter is created to pass a value into the function. The OUTVAL parameter is defined to pass a value out of the PL/SQL statement, back to the Visual Basic procedure. The dbExecuteSql method is used to execute a PL/SQL statement. Any valid PL/SQL statement can be executed. The parameters used within the PL/SQL code are identified with a colon (:) preceding the parameter name. The txtResults textbox is set to the value of the OUTVAL parameter, and the parameters are removed by executing the Remove method of the parameters collection.

6. Run the project to display the results. Connect to the database as the WAITE user account by selecting the Connect button. Enter a value into the Input field and select the Execute button. The results returned by the stored function will be displayed in the Results field.

How It Works

The dbExecuteSQL method in the OraDatabase object is used to execute a PL/SQL statement. The PL/SQL code may contain stored procedures or functions. The Parameters collection in the OraDatabase object contains the database parameters used to pass parameters to and from PL/SQL code. Step 1 creates a stored function which is passed a parameter and returns the parameter with a simple modification. Step 2 creates a procedure to connect to the database, as shown in How-To 18.1. Step 3 creates a procedure which passes the value contained in a textbox to the stored function and displays the resulting value in another textbox. The Add method of the Parameters collection in the OraDatabase object creates two parameters. The first parameter is used to pass a value to the stored function. The second parameter is used to retrieve the results of the operation. The dbExecuteSQL method is passed the PL/SQL block containing a call to the stored procedure created in step 1. The parameters used in the PL/SQL code are identified as parameters with a colon (:).

Comments

The ability to partition applications into client side and server side processing is one of the major strengths of the Oracle database. Whenever possible, stored procedures and functions should be used to process data on the server. The procedures and functions contained in built-in packages can also be executed through Oracle Objects. Refer to Chapter 14 for many of the techniques that can be performed using built-in packages.

COMPLEXITY
ADVANCED

18.8 How do I...
Handle the LONG datatype?

Problem

The LONG datatype has caused problems whenever used in our applications. When I use Oracle Objects, I need a method to insert and query values contained in a LONG column. How do handle the LONG datatype in Oracle Objects?

Technique

Oracle Objects can only move chunks of data from LONG columns 64KB at a time. Since it is possible to have LONG data larger than 64KB, the data must be moved in and out of the columns in sections. The dbGetChunk method, which is part of the OraField object, retrieves a section of a LONG column from the record. The dbAppendChunk method, which is also part of the OraField object, appends data to a LONG column. A Do Until loop can be used to process the value in the field until the entire value has either been read from the column or put into the column.

Steps

1. Run Visual Basic. Create a new project and save it as CHP18-8.vbp. Use Form1 and create the objects and properties listed in Table 18-8. Save the form as CHP18-8.frm. If you want to skip this step, you can open CHP18-8A.vbp. To view the final results of the project, open CHP18-8B.vbp.

OBJECT	PROPERTY	SETTING
Form	Name	Form1
	Caption	"Long Datatype Demo"
TextItem	Name	txtViewName

continued on next page

continued from previous page

OBJECT	PROPERTY	SETTING
TextItem	Name	txtViewQuery
Label	Name	Label1
	Autosize	True
	Caption	"View Name:"
Label	Name	Label2
	Autosize	True
	Caption	"View Query"
CommandButton	Name	cmdConnect
	Caption	"Connect"
CommandButton	Name	cmdExecute
	Caption	"Execute"

Table 18-8 Oracle Objects Long Data Demo

Figure 18-14 shows how the resulting form should look.

The View Name field is used to accept the name of a data dictionary view. The View Query text item is used to display the query that makes up the entered view. Since the VIEW_NAME column of the ALL_VIEWS data dictionary view is of the LONG datatype, it must be displayed using the techniques shown in this How-To. Prior to executing the query, you must connect to the database by selecting the Connect button.

2. Add the following code to the declarations section of Form1. The OraDatabase and OraSession objects are created as public variables so they are visible throughout the form.

```
Option Explicit
Public OraDatabase As Object
Public OraSession As Object
```

3. Enter the following code as the Click event of the cmdConnect button. The cmdConnect button connects to the Oracle database as the WAITE user account and creates the OraSession and OraDatabase objects.

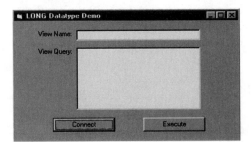

Figure 18-14 Oracle Object Long
Data Demo

```
Private Sub cmdConnect_Click()
    Set OraSession = CreateObject("OracleInProcServer.XOraSession")
    Set OraDatabase = OraSession.DbOpenDatabase("2:", "waite/press", 0&)
    MsgBox "Connected to " & OraDatabase.Connect & "@" & _
OraDatabase.DatabaseName
End Sub
```

4. Enter the following code as the Click event of the cmdExecute button. The cmdExecute button executes two queries, displaying the query that makes up the view. The method of field processing used to query a column of the LONG datatype cannot be executed on a complex view. To get around this limitation, the base tables making up the ALL_VIEWS data dictionary views are used.

```
Private Sub cmdExecute_Click()
Dim OraDynaset As Object
Dim SQL As String
Dim ChunkSize As Long
Dim CurChunk As String
Dim CurSize As Integer
Dim I As Integer

    ChunkSize = 1024
    SQL = "SELECT OBJ# FROM SYS.OBJ$ WHERE NAME = UPPER('" & txtViewName ⇐
& "')"
    Set OraDynaset = OraDatabase.DbCreateDynaset(SQL, &O0)
    If OraDynaset.RecordCount = 0 Then
        MsgBox "Invalid View"
        Exit Sub
    End If
    I = OraDynaset.Fields(0).Value

    SQL = "SELECT TEXT FROM SYS.VIEW$ WHERE OBJ# = " & CStr(I)
    Set OraDynaset = OraDatabase.DbCreateDynaset(SQL, &O0)

    txtViewQuery = ""
    If OraDynaset.RecordCount = 0 Then
        MsgBox "Invalid View"
        Exit Sub
    Else
        I = 0
        Do
            CurChunk = OraDynaset.Fields(0).DbGetChunk(I * ChunkSize, ⇐
ChunkSize)
            CurSize = Len(CurChunk)
            txtViewQuery = txtViewQuery & CurChunk
            I = I + 1
        Loop Until CurSize < ChunkSize
    End If
End Sub
```

The first query returns the OBJ# column from the SYS.OBJ$ data dictionary table for the entered view name. The OBJ# column contains a unique number representing the object. The second query uses the value from the first query to return the TEXT column from the SYS.VIEW$ table. If the

RecordCount property from either of the queries is 0, the view name is not valid and a message box is displayed. If the view is valid, the dbGetChunk method of the field object is used to return a section of the LONG column. The Do Until loop is used to return sections of the column until the entire column has been retrieved and displayed in the textbox.

5. Run the project to display the results. Select the Connect button to connect to the database as the WAITE user account. Enter the name of a view in the View Name field, such as DBA_OBJECTS, and select the Execute button to display the query results.

How It Works

The Connect button uses the technique presented in How-To 18.1 to connect to the database as the WAITE user account. The Execute button queries a data dictionary table containing a LONG column, moving the data into the Results field. The dbGetChunk method is used to process sections of the column data until the entire column has been retrieved. The procedure presented in Step 4 performs the processing of the LONG data. The dbGetChunk method is executed within a Do Until loop until the entire value has been retrieved from the column.

Comments

The dbGetChunk method cannot be used on a query to which the ROWID is not available. Since the ROWID is not available on complex views, the method could not be used directly against the ALL_VIEWS data dictionary view in this How-To. Unless LONG columns are absolutely required by your application, it is better to avoid using them.

COMPLEXITY
INTERMEDIATE

18.9   How do I...
Trap errors in Oracle Objects?

Problem

In my Visual Basic applications, I have developed error handling routines. If a database error occurs, I need a method for trapping it and displaying the Oracle error message. I would like to see the actual error code and message returned by the database. How do I trap errors in Oracle Objects?

Technique

The LastServerErr and LastServerErrText properties are available from the OraSession and OraDatabase objects. These properties in the OraSession object return errors occurring in connections. The properties in the OraDatabase object return errors related to cursors and stored procedures. If an Oracle error has not occurred, the LastSeverErr property is 0. An Oracle error executes the error handling routine in your application. This allows Oracle errors to be checked in your application's error handling routines.

Steps

1. Run SQL*Plus and connect as the WAITE user account. CHP18-7.sql, shown in Figure 18-15, creates the sample table used in this How-To.

The script creates a sample table with a record. The table is used to generate errors trapped by the error handling code in this How-To. Run the file to create the sample table and data.

```
SQL> START CHP18-7

Table created.

1 row created.

Commit complete.
```

2. Run Visual Basic. Create a new project and save it as CHP18-9.vbp. Use Form1 and create the objects and properties listed in Table 18-9. Save the form as CHP18-9.frm. To skip this step, open CHP18-9A.vbp from the accompanying CD-ROM. The final results of the project are contained in CHP18-9B.vbp.

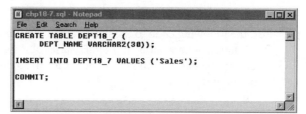

Figure 18-15 CHP18-7.sql creates the sample table used in How-To 18.15

OBJECT	PROPERTY	SETTING
Form	Name	Form1
	Caption	"Oracle Objects Error Trapping"
TextItem	Name	txtValue
Label	Name	Label1
	Autosize	True
	Caption	"Value:"
CommandButton	Name	cmdConnect
	Caption	"Connect"
CommandButton	Name	cmdConErr
	Caption	"Connect Error"
CommandButton	Name	cmdQuery
	Caption	"Query"
CommandButton	Name	cmdQryErr
	Caption	"Query Error"
CommandButton	Name	cmdInsert
	Caption	"Insert Error"

Table 18-9 Oracle Objects Error Demo

Figure 18-16 shows how the resulting form should look.

The Connect button is used to perform a valid connection to the database as the WAITE user account. This must be done prior to selecting the Query, Query Error, or Insert Error buttons. The Connect Error button attempts an invalid connection to the database by specifying a nonexistent user account. The Query Error button attempts a query containing a syntax error. The Insert Error button attempts to insert a record into the sample table, which is too large for the size of the column.

3. Add the following code to the declarations section of Form1. The OraDatabase, OraSession, and OraDynaset objects are declared as public objects in the declaration section of the form, so they can be referenced throughout it.

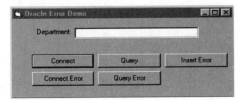

Figure 18-16 Error Trapping
Demo form

```
Option Explicit
Public OraDatabase As Object
Public OraSession As Object
Public OraDynaset As Object
```

4. Enter the following code as the Click event of a cmdConnect_Click button.
The cmdConnect button connects to the Oracle database using the process
described in How-To 18.1 and creates the OraSession and OraDatabase
objects.

```
Private Sub cmdConnect_Click()
    Set OraSession = CreateObject("OracleInProcServer.XOraSession")
    Set OraDatabase = OraSession.DbOpenDatabase("2:", "waite/press", 0&)
    MsgBox "Connected to " & OraDatabase.Connect & "@" & _
OraDatabase.DatabaseName
End Sub
```

5. Enter the following code as the Click event of the cmdConErr button. The
cmdConErr button attempts to connect to the database using an invalid
user name.

```
Private Sub cmdConErr_Click()

On Error GoTo errhandler

    Set OraSession = CreateObject("OracleInProcServer.XOraSession")
    Set OraDatabase = OraSession.DbOpenDatabase("2:", "w/press", 0&)

    MsgBox "Connected to " & OraDatabase.Connect & "@" & _
        OraDatabase.DatabaseName
    Exit Sub

errhandler:
 'Since we are checking for a connection error the OraSession
 'object is used to check and display the error message.
 If OraSession.LastServerErr <> 0 Then
  MsgBox OraSession.LastServerErrText
 Else
  MsgBox "Visual Basic Error:" & Err & " " & Error(Err)
 End If

 Exit Sub

End Sub
```

The error handler created in the procedure checks the LastServerErr property of the OraSession object. Since a valid connection to the database has
not occurred, the OraDatabase object cannot be checked. The
LastServerErrText property contains the text of the Oracle error that last
occurred.

6. Enter the following code as the Click event of the cmdQuery button. The
cmdQuery button performs a valid query on the database without error
handling code. If you execute this code without first establishing a valid

connection to the database, you will see how errors should not be handled
using Oracle Objects.

```
Private Sub cmdQuery_Click()

    Dim SQL As String
    SQL = "SELECT DEPT_NAME FROM DEPT18_7"
    Set OraDynaset = OraDatabase.DbCreateDynaset(SQL,&0)
    If OraDynaset.RecordCount = 0 Then
        MsgBox "No data found"
    Else
        txtValue = OraDynaset.Fields(0)
End If

End Sub
```

7. Enter the following code as the Click event of the cmdQryErr button. The
cmdQryErr button attempts to execute a query of the sample table containing a syntax error.

```
Private Sub cmdQryErr_Click()

On Error GoTo errproc2

    Dim SQL As String
    SQL = "SELECT DEPT_NAME DEPT18_7"
    Set OraDynaset = OraDatabase.DbCreateDynaset(SQL, &00)
    If OraDynaset.RecordCount = 0 Then
        MsgBox "No data found"
    Else
        txtValue = OraDynaset.Fields(0)
    End If

errproc2:

  If OraDatabase.LastServerErr <> 0 Then
   MsgBox OraDatabase.LastServerErrText
  Else
   MsgBox "Visual Basic Error:" & Err & " " & Error(Err)
  End If

End Sub
```

The error handler errproc2 checks the LastServerErr property of the
OraDatabase object to determine if the error handler was called because of
an Oracle error. If it was, the LastServerErrText property contains the
description of the error that occurred. Since the SQL statement executed in
this event is missing a FROM clause, executing this procedure will display
an Oracle error message.

8. Enter the following code as the Click event of the cmdInsert button. The
cmdInsert button attempts to insert a record into the sample table with a
value that's too long for the column.

```
Private Sub cmdInsert_Click()

On Error GoTo errproc3

   Dim SQL As String
   SQL = "SELECT DEPT_NAME FROM DEPT18_7 WHERE 1 = 0"
   Set OraDynaset = OraDatabase.DbCreateDynaset(SQL, &00)

   OraDynaset.dbAddNew
   OraDynaset.Fields(0).Value = "XXXXXXXXXXXXXXXXXXXXXXXXXXXXXXXXX"
   OraDynaset.dbUpdate

errproc3:

  If OraDatabase.LastServerErr <> 0 Then
   MsgBox OraDatabase.LastServerErrText
  Else
   MsgBox "Visual Basic Error:" & Err & " " & Error(Err)
  End If

  Exit Sub
End Sub
```

The error handling routine for the cmdInsert_Click procedure checks the LastServerErr property of the OraDatabase object. To cause an error, the procedure attempts to fill the DEPT_NAME column with a value longer than the column size. The error handler checks the LastServerErr property to ensure the error is an Oracle one and displays the LastServerErrText property.

9. Run the project to display the results. Select the Connect Error button to display the error occurring when an invalid user name or password is supplied during a connection. Select the Connect button to make a valid connection to the database. Once a valid connection has been established, select the Query Error button to display an error occurring when an invalid query is attempted. Select the Insert Error button to display the error occurring when an inserted value is too long for the destination column.

How It Works

When an Oracle error occurs in a Visual Basic application, the error handling routine created in the procedure is executed. The LastServerErr and LastServerErrMsg properties contain the last Oracle error that occurred. If the value of the LastServerErr property is 0, no Oracle error occured. Both properties are available in the OraSession and OraDatabase objects. Step 5 uses the properties from the OraSession object in its error handling code. The logon attempted in the procedure specifies an invalid user name and password, causing an error to occur. Step 6 creates a procedure using the LastServerErr and LastServerErrMsg properties from the OraDatabase object. The query attempted in the procedure is missing a FROM clause, causing an error to occur. Step 7 creates a procedure using the same properties from the OraDatabase object to display the error that occurs when an inserted value is too long for its column.

Comments

Error handling code should be created for all operations using Oracle Objects within an application. Errors may occur no matter how well your code is developed. In any place you handle Visual Basic errors, you should include code for dealing with possible Oracle errors.

CHAPTER 19

BUILDING WEB APPLICATIONS WITH ORACLE WEBSERVER

19

BUILDING WEB APPLICATIONS WITH ORACLE WEBSERVER

How do I...

The Oracle WebServer supports the creation of HTML documents using stored procedures. The Oracle WebServer Developer's Toolkit is a set of stored packages that simplifies the creation of Web documents by reducing the need to understand HTML programming. The Oracle Web Listener and the Oracle Web Agent process requests from users on any Web browser, handle the connection to the server, and transmit the HTML documents back to the browser. The examples presented in this chapter require that Oracle WebServer be installed on your system and can be found on the accompanying CD in the \SAMPLES\CHAP19 directory.

A document presented by the server can be generated dynamically by a stored procedure in the database. Creating a Web document can be as easy as creating a stored procedure using the Developer's Toolkit packages. Since the documents are generated by stored procedures, they can be data driven and updated automatically as data changes. Since the HTML code is contained within the database, the maintenance issues associated with managing HTML files are simplified.

19.1   Generate a dynamic Web document

One of the basic features of the Oracle WebServer is its ability to create dynamic Web pages. A Web document can be generated by stored procedures you create. When a request is made of a dynamic Web document, the Oracle Web Agent executes the corresponding stored procedure and returns the resulting HTML to the browser. This How-To presents the basic techniques used to generate a dynamic Web page.

19.2   Generate a page with dynamic content

Because a Web page is created by a stored procedure, a page can contain content generated dynamically. The results of functions, PL/SQL operations, and queries can be presented within Web documents. This How-To presents an example of dynamic content within a Web page.

19.3   Return the results of a query to a Web document

When developing business applications for the Web, it will be necessary to display the results of a query within a Web page. The Developer's Toolkit packages and cursors within PL/SQL make displaying query results an easy task. This How-To presents the technique used to display the results of a query within a Web document.

19.4   Create a link to another page

Hypertext links, called *anchors*, are used to link Web pages. Creating anchors is fundamental to building intuitive, easy-to-use Web applications. This How-To presents anchors and the methods used to create them with the Oracle Web Developer's Toolkit.

19.5   Format and highlight text in my Web documents?

Several text styles are available within HTML to emphasize text and make your Web applications more visually appealing. Text can be displayed in a variety of heading formats and in boldface, italics, underlined, or monospaced fonts. This How-To presents the techniques used to format text in Web documents.

19.6   Use lists in my Web documents

Lists can be created within Web pages by generating the HTML list processing tags. An ordered list automatically generates line numbers when displayed. An unordered list contains bullets that look different depending on the browser. This How-To presents the methods used to generate lists within HTML documents and create nested lists.

19.7 Use images in my Web documents

Images are the key to making your Web applications visually interesting. Images can be the difference between a boring Web document and an exciting one. This How-To presents the technique used to include images in Web documents.

19.8 Create an HTML form

HTML forms allow users of a Web application to interface with the application and the database. An HTML form lets the user enter information which can be processed by the Oracle database. When a form is submitted within an Oracle WebServer application, the items on the form are passed to another stored procedure as parameters. This How-To presents the technique used to create HTML forms within Oracle WebServer.

19.9 Use HTML tables in my Web documents

HTML tables can be used to organize data by rows and columns. When you query data from Oracle, you will probably want to format the data using HTML tables. Tables allow you to present a wide range of content and can include other HTML tags. This How-To presents the techniques used to create HTML tables within the WebServer Developer's Toolkit procedures.

19.10 Access and use CGI environment variables

Common Gateway Interface (CGI) environment variables provide important information about the person browsing your Web page and his or her environment. The Oracle WebServer allows you to access and use CGI variables in your Web application through the GET_CGI_ENV function in the OWA_UTIL package. This How-To covers the process of retrieving CGI variables and using them in your documents.

19.11 Create a password field in a form

A password field within a form lets you enter data into a field that doesn't display the characters as they are entered. When the form is submitted, the entered password data is passed as a normal VARCHAR2 parameter to the stored procedure being processed. This How-To presents the method for creating a password field within an HTML document.

COMPLEXITY
BEGINNING

19.1 How do I...
Generate a dynamic Web document?

Problem

I want to create a Web page using Oracle's WebServer. I want to store the contents of the Web page in the database, but I do not want to manage HTML files. How do I generate a dynamic Web page with Oracle?

Technique

Web pages created by the Oracle WebServer are dynamic by nature. The Oracle Web Listener waits for requests to process. When a request is made of a document, the Oracle Web Agent executes the corresponding stored procedure and returns the results to the browser. Three packages contained in the Web Developer's Toolkit process Web requests. The HTP package contains a set of procedures which print text and HTML tags to the browser. The HTF package contains functions which correspond to each of the HTP procedures. The functions return VARCHAR2 results that can be used within the PL/SQL code. The OWA_UTIL package contains utility procedures and functions that let you manage the environment. The basic HTP package procedures needed to generate a dynamic Web page are listed in Table 19-1.

PROCEDURE	DESCRIPTION
htp.print	Prints a text string to the browser.
htp.p	Same as HTP.PRINT.
htp.prn	Same as HTP.PRINT but does not put a new line at the end of the string.
htp.prints	Prints a text string to the browser and replaces all occurrences of the '<', '>', '"', and '&' characters with the corresponding escape sequences so they can be displayed literally in the browser.
htp.ps	Same as HTP.PRINTS.

Table 19-1 Print procedures

Steps

1. Run SQL*Plus and connect as the WWW_USER account. The WWW_USER account is a default account created when WebServer is installed. Load CHP19-1.sql into the SQL buffer. The file contains a procedure generating a static text message within the browser when executed.

```
SQL>  GET CHP19-1
  1    CREATE OR REPLACE PROCEDURE CHP19_1 AS
  2    BEGIN
  3       HTP.PRINT('<TITLE>CHP19-1.sql</TITLE>');
  4       HTP.PRINT('MY FIRST ORACLE WEB PAGE');
  5    END;
```

Line 1 presents the keywords required to create a stored procedure and specify its name. When the procedure name is referenced within a user's URL, the procedure is executed by the Web Agent. Lines 2 through 5 contain the procedure body. Lines 3 and 4 use the HTP.PRINT procedure to send static text to the browser. Line 3 sends the HTML <TITLE> and </TITLE> tags as part of the string for creating the document title. The HTP.PRINT procedure is useful because it lets you send HTML tags as part of your text. If you want to send the tags as literal strings, use the HTP.PRINTS procedure, otherwise the browser will process the tags as HTML commands.

2. Run the statement to create the procedure.

`SQL> /`

Procedure created.

The URL developed by creating the stored procedure is http://localhost:80/ows-bin/owa/chp19_1. The server name localhost represents the server on the computer you are using. All examples in this chapter assume you are working on the server. If you are not, replace localhost with your server name or IP address. The :80 represents the default listener port number created when WebServer was installed. The ows-bin component of the URL tells the server to use the default service for the listener, and the owa component tells the Web Listener that the Web Agent must handle the request.

3. Load a browser. Open the URL created when the stored procedure was generated. For a default installation within Windows NT, the URL is http://localhost:80/ows-bin/owa/chp19_1. Figure 19-1 shows the results of the Web page within Oracle PowerBrowser.

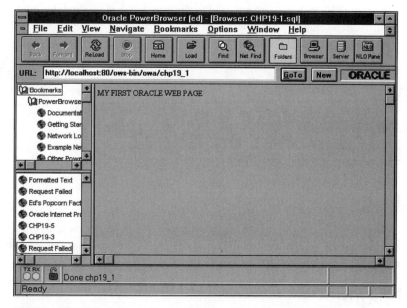

Figure 19-1 http://localhost:80/ows-bin/owa/chp19_1 as the output of CHP19_1

The simple Web page generates a single line of output to a file. In the other How-Tos in this chapter, this technique is expanded to generate complex documents and forms.

How It Works

A stored procedure created in a database schema is referenced by the Web Agent service and executed using a Web browser. When the stored procedure is executed, the print procedure within the HTP package sends information to the browser. Text sent to the browser using the HTP.PRINT procedure may contain HTML tags to format the document, or the document may be formatted using other procedures from the HTP package. Steps 1 and 2 create a procedure which passes a simple line of text to the browser. Step 3 executes the stored procedure and displays the dynamic document within Oracle PowerBrowser.

Comments

The ability to create dynamic Web documents brings the power of the Web to business applications. It would be almost impossible to create complex business applications without being able to create Web documents dynamically. The Web document created in this How-To shows the bare minimum capabilities of the Oracle WebServer. The techniques presented in the remainder of this chapter explore more sophisticated Oracle capabilities.

COMPLEXITY

BEGINNING

19.2 How do I...
Generate a page with dynamic content?

Problem

I want to generate dynamic content within my Web page. I want to display the date and time of the visit, as well as the number of hits made to the page. How do I generate a page with dynamic content?

Technique

Web pages developed with Oracle WebServer are generated by stored procedures. Since stored procedures have access to Oracle's many features, a Web page can be easily generated with dynamic content. A Web document can contain the results of Oracle pseudo-columns, PL/SQL operations, and queries. Conditional logic and looping operations within PL/SQL allow sophisticated Web documents containing dynamic content to be created.

Steps

1. Run SQL*Plus and connect as the WWW_USER account. Run CHP19-2.sql to create a sequence enabling the Web page to track the number of users reading the page.

```
SQL> START CHP19-2

Sequence created.
```

The HIT_COUNT sequence created in the script starts with 1 and increments by 1 each time it is read. The next step creates a stored procedure which references the sequence.

2. Load CHP19-3.sql into the SQL buffer. The file contains a procedure which generates a Web document with dynamic content. The Web page uses the SYSDATE pseudo-column to display the date and time. It also displays the number of hits maintained by the HIT_COUNT sequence.

```
SQL> GET CHP19-3
  1    CREATE OR REPLACE PROCEDURE CHP19_3 AS
  2    COUNTER NUMBER;
  3    BEGIN
  4       SELECT
  5          HIT_COUNT.NEXTVAL INTO COUNTER
  6       FROM DUAL;
  7       HTP.HTMLOPEN;
  8       HTP.PRINT('<TITLE>CHP19-3</TITLE>');
  9       HTP.PRINT('<H1>Dynamic Web Page</H1>');
 10       HTP.PRINT('The system date and time is '||
 11             TO_CHAR(SYSDATE,'MM/DD/YY HH:MI PM')||'<p>');
 12       HTP.PRINT('YOU ARE VISITOR NUMBER: '||
 13             TO_CHAR(COUNTER));
 14       HTP.HTMLCLOSE;
 15*   END;
```

Line 1 specifies the required keywords for creating a stored procedure and names it. Line 2 declares a numeric variable named COUNTER, which is used within the stored procedure to hold the value of the sequence created in Step 1. Lines 3 through 15 contain the procedure body. The query in lines 4 through 6 returns the next value from the HIT_COUNT sequence and puts it in the COUNTER variable. Line 7 begins generating the HTML document by calling the HTP.HTMLOPEN procedure to generate the <HTML> tag. Line 8 uses the HTP.PRINT procedure, printing a text string to the browser containing the <TITLE> and </TITLE> tags in order to create a document title. Line 9 uses the HTP.PRINT procedure to print a heading line to the browser. The <H1> and </H1> tags are provided to define the heading line. Line 10 uses the SYSDATE pseudo-column within the

HTP.PRINT procedure to print the current date and time within the document. The HTP.PRINT procedure in lines 12 and 13 prints a piece of static text with the COUNTER variable. The HTP.HTMLCLOSE procedure in line 14 prints the </HTML> tag to close the document.

3. Run the statement to create the stored procedure.

SQL> /

Procedure created.

Once the stored procedure is created, it can be referenced by any Web browser as the /ows-bin/owa/chp19_3 document on the server.

4. Load a browser and query the page created in the previous step. Figure 19-2 shows the results of the query within Oracle PowerBrowser.

The current date and time, along with the hit count, is displayed in the HTML document. Each time the page is displayed, the hit count will be incremented and a new date and time displayed. The content of the page is dynamic, based on the number of times the page has been called and the current system date.

How It Works

A Web document is started by the <HTML> tag and terminated by the </HTML> tag. The HTP.HTMLOPEN and HTP.HTMLCLOSE procedures can be used to

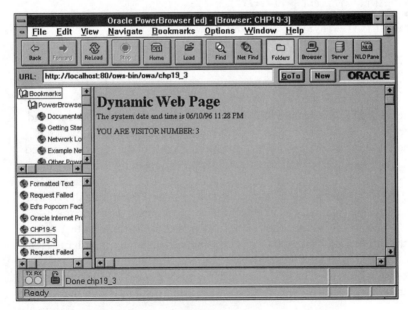

Figure 19-2 The results of the Web page

generate the tags. The HTP.PRINT procedure sends text to the browser, which may contain text to be displayed and HTML tags. Since the HTP.PRINT procedure can be passed any text string as a parameter, PL/SQL functions and pseudo-columns can be passed. Step 1 creates a sequence used to keep track of the number of hits the document receives. Steps 2 and 3 create a stored procedure using the SYSDATE pseudo-column and the sequence created in Step 1 to generate dynamic content. How-To 19.3 takes this process one step further by generating the content of a Web document from a query.

Comments

Once you have started developing Web documents with the Developer's Toolkit, you will find that almost all of the documents you create contain dynamic content. Tasks that might be difficult using other Web products are very easy within Oracle, because of the way the Developer's Toolkit is integrated into PL/SQL and the database.

COMPLEXITY
INTERMEDIATE

19.3 How do I...
Return the results of a query to a Web document?

Problem

I want to use Oracle Web technology to display query results to users. By displaying the results of database queries within Web documents, I would provide an easy way to generate reports and analysis information to our users. Many of the people who want this type of information don't need large applications and already have Web browsers. How do I return the results of a query to a Web page?

Technique

Queries can be returned to PL/SQL modules and stored procedures by using cursors. Using the HTP package, a query can be executed by a stored procedure and the results can be displayed to the document. The combination of PL/SQL and the Developer's Toolkit makes it easy to display the results of queries within Web documents.

Steps

1. Run SQL*Plus and connect as the WWW_USER account. CHP19-4.sql, shown in Figure 19-3, creates the sample table used in this How-To.

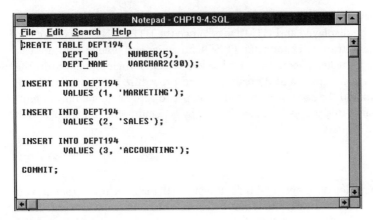

Figure 19-3 CHP19-4.sql creates the table used
in How-To 19.3

The sample table created by the script contains the departments within an organization and is populated with sample records. The table is used in the following steps to display the query capabilities of PL/SQL and the Oracle WebServer. Run the file to create the sample table and data.

```
SQL>   START CHP19-4

Table created.

1 row created.

1 row created.

1 row created.

Commit complete.
```

2. Load CHP19-5.sql into the SQL buffer. The procedure contained in the file queries the DEPT194 table created in Step 1 and displays the results of the query using the Developer's Toolkit packages.

```
SQL> GET CHP19-5
  1   CREATE OR REPLACE PROCEDURE CHP19_5 AS
  2   CURSOR C1 IS
  3      SELECT
  4          DEPT_NO,
  5          DEPT_NAME
  6      FROM DEPT194
  7      ORDER BY DEPT_NO;
  8   BEGIN
  9      HTP.HTMLOPEN;
 10      HTP.HTITLE('Ed''s Internet and Chicago Style Pizza');
 11      HTP.PARAGRAPH;
 12      HTP.BOLD('Department Listing:');
 13      HTP.PARAGRAPH;
```

```
14        HTP.ULISTOPEN;
15        FOR I IN C1 LOOP
16            HTP.PRINT(TO_CHAR(I.DEPT_NO)||' - '||I.DEPT_NAME);
17            HTP.BR;
18        END LOOP;
19        HTP.ULISTCLOSE;
20        HTP.HTMLCLOSE;
21* END;
```

Line 1 presents the keywords required to create a stored procedure and names the procedure. The cursor declared in lines 2 through 7 creates a query which is executed within the procedure body. Once the cursor is generated, the rows can be formatted and displayed within the document. Lines 8 through 21 contain the procedure body. The HTP.HTMLOPEN procedure in line 9 and the HTP.HTMLCLOSE procedure in line 20 begin and end the document, respectively. Line 10 uses the HTP.HTITLE procedure to create the title tags, <TITLE> and </TITLE>, and heading tags, <H1> and </H1>, establishing a title and a heading for the document. The parameter passed to the procedure is used as both the title and the heading. Table 19-2 contains the HTP package procedures used for formatting headings within the Web Developer's Toolkit. Lines 14 and 19 begin and end an unordered list by using the HTP.ULISTOPEN and HTP.ULISTCLOSE procedures. How-To 19.6 presents techniques for using lists within a document. Lines 15 through 18 loop through each item returned by the query and print its value to the document using the HTP.PRINT procedure. Table 19-2 contains the heading-related HTP procedure.

PROCEDURE	DESCRIPTION
htp.title	Prints the title specified with the <TITLE> and </TITLE> tags.
htp.htitle	Creates both title tags and heading tags for the specified string.
htp.base	Prints a tag that records the URL of the current document.

Table 19-2 Heading-related procedures

3. Run the statement to create the procedure.

```
SQL>   /
```

```
Procedure created.
```

Once the procedure is created, it can be referenced by using any browser to call /ows-bin/owa/chp19_5 from the server.

4. Load a browser and open the URL http://localhost:80/ows-bin/owa/chp19_5 to display the document created in the previous step. Figure 19-4 shows the page in the Oracle PowerBrowser.

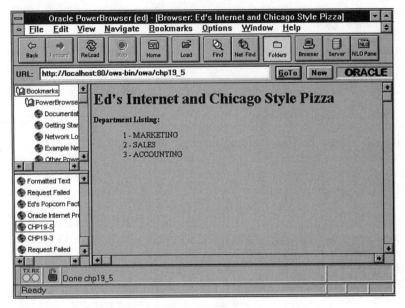

Figure 19-4 The results in the browser

The three records contained in the sample table created in Step 1 are displayed in the document. The header created by the HTP.HTITLE procedure is displayed as a top level heading.

5. Make the selection within your browser to view the source of the document. This will show how the Oracle procedures are translated to HTML tags and static text. Figure 19-5 shows the source created for the document.

The source code of the document looks like standard HTML code that can be read from a file. The procedures contained in the HTP package generate the HTML tags passed to the browser as if read from a file.

How It Works

A cursor within PL/SQL is used to execute a query and return its results to the PL/SQL code. The results of a query can be displayed within a Web document by processing a cursor and displaying its contents using the HTP.PRINT procedure or other HTP procedures. Step 1 creates a sample table with data queried in the Web document. Steps 2 and 3 develop a stored procedure that creates and processes a cursor to display the results of a query within a Web document. Step 4 executes the procedure from within a browser to display the query results. Step 5 presents the HTML code generated from the results of the query.

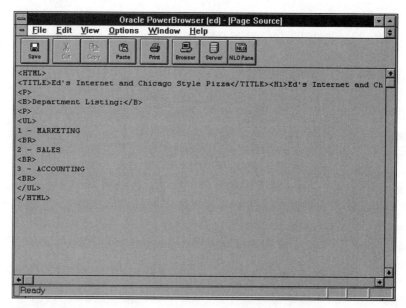

Figure 19-5 The source code of the document

Comments

The technique presented in this How-To is critical to developing business applications which use the Oracle database. Since Web documents are created in stored procedures, you should refer to Chapter 13, Procedures, Functions, and Packages, for more information on creating stored procedures.

COMPLEXITY
BEGINNING

19.4 How do I...
Create a link to another page?

Problem

I need to create Web applications containing more than one page. In order to develop an application that's easy to navigate and intuitive to the user, I need to create links to other Web documents. How do I create a link to another page?

Technique

A link to another page is called an *anchor*. Within HTML, anchors are created by the <A HREF="url"> and </A> tags. The Developer's Toolkit provides the HTP.ANCHOR procedure that develops the tags for creating a link. A URL and a text string must be provided in order to create the proper tags. Table 19-3 contains the HTP procedures related to creating the document body.

PROCEDURE	DESCRIPTION
htp.anchor	Creates an anchor that links to another document.
htp.br	Creates a linefeed within the document.
htp.line	Creates a line by generating the <HR> tag.
htp.hr	Same as HTP.LINE.
htp.nl	Same as HTP.BR.
htp.header	Creates the tag required to generate a heading. Valid heading levels are from 1 to 6.
htp.mailto	Creates an anchor with a mailto address.
htp.img	Creates the tags required to load an image.
htp.para	Starts a new paragraph by generating the <P> tag.
htp.paragraph	Same as HTP.PARA.
htp.address	Creates the <ADDRESS> tag, allowing you to specify address lines for your document.
htp.comment	Creates comments within the HTML sent to the browser.
htp.preOpen	Creates the tag to begin an area of preformatted text within the document.
htp.preClose	Creates the tag to end a preformatted text area.

Table 19-3 Body-related procedures

Steps

1. Run SQL*Plus and connect as the WWW_USER account. Load CHP19-6.sql into the SQL buffer. The stored procedure contained in the file creates an anchor within a Web document, which calls another dynamic Web document.

```
SQL> GET CHP19-6
  1   CREATE OR REPLACE PROCEDURE CHP19_6 AS
  2   BEGIN
  3       HTP.HTMLOPEN;
  4       HTP.HTITLE('Ed''s Popcorn Factory');
  5       HTP.PARAGRAPH;
  6       HTP.PRINT('Here at Ed''s Popcorn Factory we are happy ');
  7       HTP.PRINT('to offer a variety of popcorn flavors ');
  8       HTP.PRINT('Choose the ');
  9       HTP.ANCHOR('http:/ows-bin/owa/chp19_7', 'Popcorn Link');
 10       HTP.PRINT('to display our wonderful popcorn selections.');
 11       HTP.HTMLCLOSE;
 12*  END;
```

Line 1 contains the required keywords to create the stored procedure and name it. Lines 2 through 12 contain the procedure body. The HTP.HTMLOPEN and HTP.HTMLCLOSE procedures contained in lines 3 and 11 begin and end the HTML document, respectively. Line 4 contains the HTP.HTITLE procedure for creating the title and heading of the document. The HTP.PARAGRAPH procedure contained in line 5 generates the <P> tag to create a new paragraph. Lines 6 through 8 use the HTP.PRINT procedure to generate static text for the document. Line 9 uses the HTP.ANCHOR procedure to create a hypertext link to the page represented by the CHP19_7 procedure developed in the following steps. Line 10 prints the static text following the hypertext link.

2. Run the statement to create the procedure.

```
SQL>  /

Procedure created.
```

Once the procedure is created, it can be called from any browser by using the URL http://localhost:80/ows-bin/owa/chp19_6, even though choosing the hypertext link contained in the document will fail until the referenced procedure is created.

3. Load CHP19-7.sql into the SQL buffer. The stored procedure contained in the file creates the document called by the anchor in the previous document.

```
SQL> GET CHP19-7
  1   CREATE OR REPLACE PROCEDURE CHP19_7 AS
  2   BEGIN
  3       HTP.HTMLOPEN;
  4       HTP.HTITLE('Popcorn Listing');
  5       HTP.PARAGRAPH;
  6       HTP.ULISTOPEN;
  7       HTP.PRINT('Caramel<BR>');
  8       HTP.PRINT('Chocolate<BR>');
  9       HTP.PRINT('Regular<BR>');
 10       HTP.ULISTCLOSE;
 11       HTP.BR;
 12       HTP.ANCHOR('http:/ows-bin/owa/chp19_6','Back to Main Page');
 13       HTP.HTMLCLOSE;
 14*  END;
```

Line 1 contains the keywords required to create the stored procedure and name it. Lines 2 through 14 contain the procedure body. Lines 3 through 13 begin and end the document by generating the <HTML> and </HTML> tags, respectively. The HTP.HTITLE procedure in line 3 supplies the tags for the document title and header. Line 5 uses the HTP.PARAGRAPH procedure to generate the <P> tag to create a new paragraph. Lines 6 and 10 use the HTP.ULISTOPEN and HTP.ULISTCLOSE procedures to contain an unordered list. The list is used to make the document more visually appealing. The HTP.PRINT procedure in lines 7 through 9 supplies the items in the list without bullets. The HTP.BR procedure contained in line 11 generates the <BR> tag, causing a line break. The HTP.ANCHOR procedure in line 12 generates an anchor referencing the original document.

4. Run the statement to create the procedure.

```
SQL>    /
```

Procedure created.

Creating the procedure lets you call it directly from a browser or another document. The next step uses the original document to call the new document.

5. Load a browser and open the URL http://localhost:80/ows-bin/ows/chp19_6. Figure 19-6 shows the document in PowerBrowser.

The hypertext link is displayed by a colored line which you can click on to select. Notice that the link is contained in a sentence and does not break its format. Select the Popcorn Link to display the results of the hypertext link. Figure 19-7 shows the document in PowerBrowser.

Calling the linked page from the original document generates the same results as calling it directly.

How It Works

An anchor is created in a document by the <A HREF="URL"> tag and ends with an </A> tag. The text between the tags is highlighted and calls the URL specified in the first tag when selected. The HTP.ANCHOR procedure simplifies the creation of

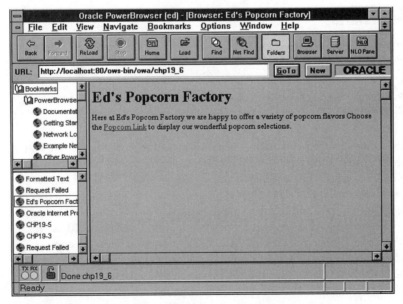

Figure 19-6 A document containing a hypertext link in PowerBrowser

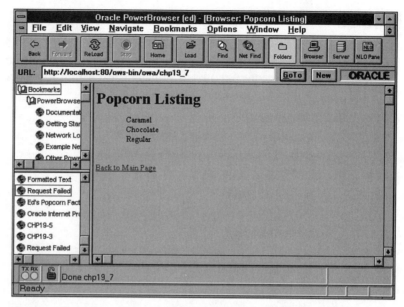

Figure 19-7 The document called by the hypertext link

the tags by generating the tags and text. Steps 1 and 2 create a stored procedure which uses HTP.ANCHOR to build a link to the procedure developed in Steps 3 and 4. The second procedure also contains a link back to the original document. Step 5 displays the use of the linked documents within Oracle's PowerBrowser.

Comments

You will not be able to avoid using links within your Web applications, and you should not even try. Creating links to pages on your server or others is the key to making your Web applications intuitive and well-organized.

COMPLEXITY
BEGINNING

19.5   How do I...
Format and highlight text in my Web documents?

Problem

Within my Web documents, I want to format text and highlight text for emphasis. I want to create headings at different levels, boldface and italic type, and print code listings in a monospaced font. I also want to center text on the page. How do I format and highlight text in my Web documents?

Technique

HTML provides tags allowing you to format text in a variety of ways. The Developer's Toolkit provides procedures which generate these tags in your documents. Table 19-4 shows the HTP procedures related to formatting text within your documents.

PROCEDURE	DESCRIPTION
htp.cite	Specifies a citation, usually in italics.
htp.code	Specifies a code example, usually in monospace font.
htp.emphasis	Shows emphasis, usually in italics.
htp.em	Same as htp.emphasis.
htp.keyboard	Used to specify text as it was typed by a user, usually in monospace font.
htp.kbd	Same as htp.keyboard.
htp.strong	Specifies text needing strong emphasis, usually in bold.
htp.variable	Specifies text as a variable string, usually in italics.
htp.bold	Specifies text as bold.
htp.italic	Specifies text as italic.
htp.teletype	Specifies text as fixed typewriter font.

Table 19-4 Format-related procedures

HTP.BOLD and HTP.ITALIC are the most frequently used text formatting procedures. The HTP.BOLD procedure prints text in a boldfaced font. The HTP.ITALIC prints italicized text. The HTP.CODE procedure is used to print text in a monospaced font.

Steps

1. Run SQL*Plus and connect as the WWW_USER account. Load CHP19-8.sql into the SQL buffer. The procedure contained in the file creates a document demonstrating a variety of text formats.

```
SQL>   GET CHP19-8
  1    CREATE OR REPLACE PROCEDURE CHP19_8 AS
  2    BEGIN
  3       HTP.HTMLOPEN;
  4       HTP.HTITLE('Top Level Heading );
  5       HTP.PRINT('CENTER>Centered Text</CENTER>');
  6       HTP.PRINT('H2>Second Level Heading</H2><BR>');
  7       HTP.PRINT('H3>Third Level Heading</H3><BR>');
  8       HTP.PRINT('H4>Fourth Level Heading</H4><BR>');
  9       HTP.PRINT('H5>Fifth Level Heading</H5><BR>');
 10       HTP.PRINT('H6>Third Level Heading</H6><BR>');
 11       HTP.BOLD('This Line is Bold faced );
 12       HTP.BR;
```

```
13      HTP.ITALIC('This Line is italic');
14      HTP.BR;
15      HTP.CODE('This is how sample code is printed');
16      HTP.BR;
17      HTP.PRINT('<U>This Line is underlined.</U>');
18      HTP.BR;
19      HTP.EMPHASIS('This is how text is printed with emphasis');
20      HTP.HTMLCLOSE;
21* END;
```

Line 1 specifies the keywords required to create the procedure and name it. Lines 2 through 21 contain the body of the stored procedure. The HTP.HTMLOPEN and HTP.HTMLCLOSE procedures in lines 3 and 20 create the <HTML> and </HTML> tags to begin and end the HTML document, respectively. The HTP.HTITLE procedure contained in line 4 serves two purposes: it creates the <TITLE> and </TITLE> tags to specify the document title, and it creates the <H1> and </H1> tags to create the page header. Line 5 presents the <CENTER> and </CENTER> tags for centering a string of text within the HTP.PRINT procedure. Lines 6 through 10 present the tags used to format five more levels of headings within a document. Since there are no procedures created for this purpose, the HTP.PRINT procedure must be used with the tags to create the effect. Line 11 presents the HTP.BOLD procedure to generate the tags for making the text boldfaced. The HTP.BR procedure in lines 12, 14, 16, and 18 creates a <BR> tag that generates a linefeed within the document. The HTP.ITALIC procedure in line 13 generates the tags needed for italic text. The HTP.CODE procedure in line 15 creates a monospaced code listing. The HTP.EMPHASIS procedure in line 17 creates the tables for generating text with emphasis.

2. Run the statement to create the procedure.

```
SQL>   /
```

Procedure created.

Creating the procedure makes the /ows-bin/owa/chp19_8 page available on the server. The procedure executes anytime a reference is made to the URL to display the formatted text.

3. Load a browser and open the URL http://localhost:80/ows-bin/owa/chp19_8. Figure 19-8 shows the results within PowerBrowser.

How It Works

Text can be easily highlighted and formatted with HTML tags. The formatting procedures contained in the Developer's Toolkit can be used to create the format tags. Text can be printed in boldface by using the HTP.BOLD procedure, italics by using the HTP.ITALICS procedure, and in a monospaced font by using the HTP.CODE

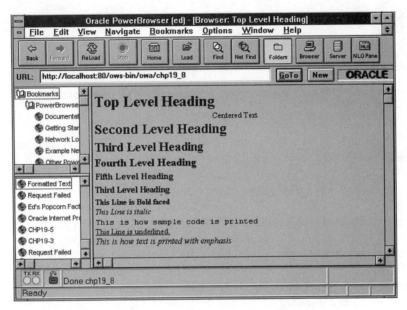

Figure 19-8 The document containing formatted text

procedure. The HTP.HEADER procedure creates six levels of headings. Steps 1 and 2 create a stored procedure displaying a variety of text-formatting options within a Web document. Step 3 displays the document showing the results of the formatting procedures.

Comments

Without highlighting text and using different font styles, your Web documents will look very plain and won't be visually pleasing to the reader. Whether you use the procedures contained in the Developer's Toolkit or manually provide the tags in your documents, you should use text formatting to emphasize important ideas.

COMPLEXITY
INTERMEDIATE

19.6   How do I...
Use lists in my Web documents?

Problem

I want to use lists in my documents to better format data. Lists in HTML allow me to create bullets or number the list items automatically. When I am returning records from a query, HTML lists will present the data in a better format. How do I create lists within my HTML documents?

Technique

HTML contains three types of lists that can be used within your documents. An ordered list automatically generates line numbers for the list elements. The <OL> tag begins an ordered list and is terminated by the </OL> tag. Each element is created by the <LI> tag. An unordered list generates bullets for the list item. The look of the bullets depends on the browser used. In most browsers, nesting unordered lists creates different bullets for each list level. An unordered list is started with the <UL> tag and ended by the </UL> tag. A definition list presents a term and its definition. It is started with the <DL> tag and ended with the </DL> tag. A definition term is created with the <DT> tag, and the definition is created by the <DD> tag.

Each of the tags can be generated by procedures in the HTP package of the Developer's Toolkit. Table 19-5 shows the procedures related to lists in the HTP package.

PROCEDURE	DESCRIPTION
htp.listHeader	Creates a header for any type of list.
htp.listItem	Generates a list item for an ordered or unordered list.
htp.ulistOpen	Opens an unordered list.
htp.ulistClose	Closes an unordered list. Must be used with HTP.ULISTOPEN.
htp.olistOpen	Opens an ordered list.
htp.olistClose	Closes an ordered list. Must be used with HTL.OLISTOPEN.
htp.dlistOpen	Opens a definition list.
htp.dlistClose	Closes a definition list. Must be used with HTP.DLISTOPEN.
htp.dlistDef	Creates a definition in a definition list.
htp.dlistTerm	Creates a term in a definition list.

Table 19-5 List-related procedures

Steps

1. Run SQL*Plus and connect as the WWW_USER user account. Load CHP19-9.sql into the SQL buffer. The stored procedure contained in the file creates a document demonstrating ordered and unordered lists.

```
SQL> GET CHP19-9
  1   CREATE OR REPLACE PROCEDURE CHP19_9 AS
  2   BEGIN
  3      HTP.HTMLOPEN;
  4      HTP.LISTHEADER('This is an ordered list');
  5      HTP.OLISTOPEN;
  6      HTP.LISTITEM('Item 1');
```

continued on next page

continued from previous page

```
 7        HTP.LISTITEM('Item 2');
 8        HTP.LISTITEM('Item 3');
 9        HTP.OLISTCLOSE;
10        HTP.LISTHEADER('This is an unordered list');
11        HTP.ULISTOPEN;
12        HTP.LISTITEM('Unordered Item 1');
13        HTP.LISTITEM('Unordered Item 2');
14        HTP.LISTITEM('Unordered Item 3');
15        HTP.ULISTCLOSE;
16        HTP.HTMLCLOSE;
17* END;
```

Line 1 supplies the required keywords for creating the stored procedure and gives the procedure its name. Lines 2 through 17 contain the procedure body. Lines 3 and 16 begin and end the document by supplying the <HTML> and </HTML> tags, respectively. Line 4 uses the HTP.LISTHEADER procedure to give the first list a title. The HTP.OLISTOPEN and HTP.OLISTCLOSE procedures in lines 5 and 9 define the boundaries of the ordered list. Each list item created with the HTP.LISTITEM procedure between the HTP.OLISTOPEN and HTP.OLISTCLOSE procedures creates items in the ordered list. Line 10 uses the HTP.LISTHEADER procedure to create the heading for the second list. The HTP.ULISTOPEN and HTP.ULISTCLOSE procedures in line 11 and 14 create the boundaries of the unordered list. Lines 12 through 14 create the list items for the list with the HTP.LISTITEM procedure.

2. Run the statement to create the stored procedure.

```
SQL>   /
```

```
Procedure created.
```

Once the procedure is created, it can be called by referencing the http://localhost:80/ows-bin/owa/chp19_9 URL. When the document is displayed, the ordered and unordered lists are displayed.

3. Load your browser and open the http://localhost:80/ows-bin/owa/chp19_9 URL. Figure 19-9 shows the results within a Netscape browser.

The ordered list and the unordered list in the document display the list items in the order they were created. Line numbers are generated by the ordered list, and bullets are generated by the unordered list. Lists can be nested within other lists. The next step creates a stored procedure containing nested lists.

4. In SQL*Plus, load CHP19-10.sql. The file contains the statement to create a stored procedure containing a nested list.

```
SQL> GET CHP19-10
  1   CREATE OR REPLACE PROCEDURE CHP19_10 AS
  2   BEGIN
  3       HTP.HTMLOPEN;
```

```
 4       HTP.LISTHEADER('This is a nested list');
 5       HTP.ULISTOPEN;
 6       HTP.LISTITEM('Item 1');
 7       HTP.LISTITEM('Item 2');
 8       HTP.ULISTOPEN;
 9       HTP.LISTITEM('Item A');
10       HTP.ULISTOPEN;
11       HTP.LISTITEM('Item A1');
12       HTP.LISTITEM('Item A2');
13       HTP.LISTITEM('Item A3');
14       HTP.ULISTCLOSE;
15       HTP.LISTITEM('Item B');
16       HTP.LISTITEM('Item C');
17       HTP.ULISTCLOSE;
18       HTP.LISTITEM('Item 3');
19       HTP.ULISTCLOSE;
20       HTP.HTMLCLOSE;
21*  END;
```

Line 1 specifies the keywords required to create the stored procedure and
name it. Lines 2 through 21 contain the procedure body. Lines 3 and 20 use
the HTP.HTMLOPEN and HTP.HTMLCLOSE procedures to begin and end
the HTML document, respectively. The HTP.LISTHEADER procedure contained in line 4 provides the title for the nested lists. Three lists are
contained in the document, all of which are unordered lists beginning with
HTP.ULISTOPEN and ending with HTP.ULISTCLOSE. The outermost list
begins in line 5 and ends in line 19. Nested lists span lines 10 through 14
and lines 8 through 17. The HTP.LISTITEM procedure is used to supply
items for all the lists.

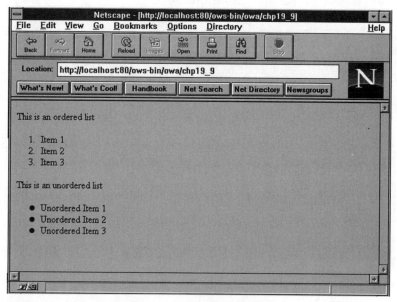

Figure 19-9 The URL demonstrating HTML lists

5. Run the statement to create the procedure.

`SQL>    /`

Procedure created.

The procedure can be executed from within a browser by referencing the
http://localhost:80/ows-bin/owa/chp19_10 URL.

6. From your browser, display the page created in the previous steps. Figure
19-10 shows the results of the procedure within a Netscape browser.

Each level of the nested lists are represented by a different type of bullet
and indented. If your navigator does not support multiple bullets, each
level will use the same type of bullet.

How It Works

This How-To presents ordered and unordered lists created with the HTP.ULISTOPEN
and HTP.OLISTOPEN procedures and terminated with the HTP.ULISTCLOSE and
HTP.OLISTCLOSE procedures. The HTP.LISTITEM procedure creates list items for
both types of lists. Steps 1 and 2 create a document displaying ordered and
unordered lists. Step 3 uses the Netscape Navigator to display the results of the page.
Steps 4 and 5 create a stored procedure generating a document using nested lists.
Step 6 shows that nested lists are indented and represented by different bullets.

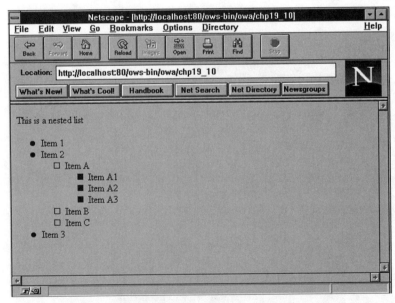

Figure 19-10 Nested lists within the Netscape browser

Comments

A trick can be used to indent lines in a document by creating the tags for an unordered list, but not creating any list items. Each list displayed after the <UL> tag will be indented to its particular list level. HTML lists are a good way to format data displayed in your documents.

COMPLEXITY
BEGINNING

19.7 How do I...
Use images in my Web documents?

Problem

I want my Web documents to contain images that make them look like the pages I see on the Internet. Without images, my documents won't have any flash and my applications will look boring. How do I use images in my Web documents?

Technique

The <IMG SRC="url"> tag is used to include an image in a Web document. The HTP.IMAGE procedure from the Developer's Toolkit simplifies creating the tag within your dynamic documents.

Steps

1. Run SQL*Plus and connect as the WWW_USER account. Load CHP19-11.sql into the SQL buffer. The stored procedure contained in the file displays the image provided as part of the WebServer administration screen.

```
SQL> GET CHP19-11
  1   CREATE OR REPLACE PROCEDURE CHP19_11 AS
  2   BEGIN
  3       HTP.HTMLOPEN;
  4       HTP.PRINT('Using Graphics');
  5       HTP.IMG('http:/ows-img/ows.gif');
  6       HTP.HTMLCLOSE;
  7*  END;
```

Line 1 specifies the keywords required to create the stored procedure and name it. Lines 2 through 7 contain the procedure body. Lines 2 and 6 begin and end the document with the HTP.HTMLOPEN and HTP.HTMLCLOSE procedures. Line 4 prints a simple message at the top of the form. Line 5 uses the HTP.IMG procedure to display the image. The parameter passed to the procedure must be a valid URL referencing an image.

2. Run the statement to create the procedure.

```
SQL>  /
```

Procedure created.

Once the procedure is created, it can be executed by calling the http://
localhost:80/ows-bin/owa/chp19_11 URL. The image provided by the
WebServer administration form will be displayed by the procedure.

3. Load a browser and retrieve the http://localhost:80/ows-bin/owa/chp19_11
URL. Figure 19-11 displays the results of the document in Oracle
PowerBrowser.

The document loads the graphic image represented by the URL in the
HTP.IMG procedure. A document can contain any number of images, but
you should take bandwidth issues into account when including graphics
within your documents.

How It Works

The <IMG SRC="URL"> tag displays a graphic image within a Web document. The
HTP.IMG procedure from the Developer's Toolkit generates the tag with the prop-
er options. Steps 1 and 2 create a stored procedure using HTP.IMG to display an image.
Step 3 shows the results of the procedure within Oracle PowerBrowser.

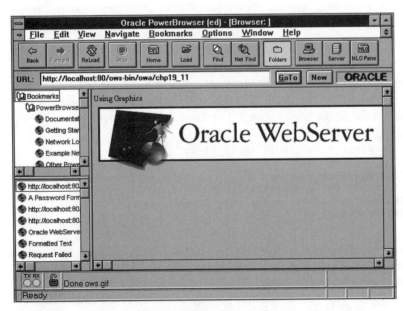

Figure 19-11 A document containing an image
in Oracle PowerBrowser

Comments

It is difficult to imagine Web documents without images. To make your documents more visually appealing, you should use graphics whenever possible. If you are running an internal Intranet application, bandwidth may not be an issue. If you are publishing Web documents for the Internet, the slow speeds at which graphics are loaded may make your documents unreadable if you include too many.

COMPLEXITY
ADVANCED

19.8 How do I...
Create an HTML form?

Problem

In order to create sophisticated Web applications, I need to include forms in my documents. I want to use the forms to insert new data into the database and pass information to the database to perform queries. How do I create an HTML form?

Technique

A complete set of procedures for creating HTML forms is provided by the Developer's Toolkit. When an HTML form is submitted to the Web Agent, a second stored procedure is called to process it. Each item on the form is passed to the second procedure as a parameter. Table 19-6 shows the form procedures within the HTP package.

PROCEDURE	DESCRIPTION
htp.formopen	Prints the tag that starts the form
htp.formclose	Prints the tag that ends the form
htp.formcheckbox	Inserts a checkbox into the form
htp.formhidden	Sends the content of the field to the browser, although it is not visible to the user
htp.formimage	Creates an image field that submits the form and returns the x and y location of where on the image the user clicked
htp.formpassword	Creates a field where user's input is not readable as it is typed
htp.formradio	Creates a radio button in the form
htp.formreset	Creates a reset button that clears all the fields of the form when clicked
htp.formsubmit	Creates a submit button that submits the form when clicked
htp.formtext	Creates a field for a single line of text
htp.formselectopen	Begins a select list that allows the user to select alternatives

continued on next page

continued from previous page

htp.formselectoption	Represents one choice in a select list
htp.formselectclose	Ends a select list
htp.formtextarea	Creates a text area that allows the user to create multiple lines of text
htp.formtextareaopen	Creates a text area that allows you to specify default values
htp.formtextareaclose	Ends a text area field

Table 19-6 Form-related procedures

The HTP.FORMOPEN procedure is used to begin a new form. The name of the processing procedure must be passed to the procedure as a parameter. The HTP.FORMCLOSE procedure ends the definition of the form. Within the form definition, a variety of HTP procedures can be used to create text items, check boxes, radio buttons, text areas, and selection lists.

Steps

1. Run SQL*Plus and connect using the WWW_USER account. CHP19-12.sql, shown in Figure 19-12, creates a sample table that receives the data entered into the form this How-To creates.

The EMP199 table created in the script will receive data entered into an HTML form. Run the script to create the sample file.

```
SQL>  START CHP19-12
```

```
Table created.
```

2. Load CHP19-13.sql into the SQL buffer. The stored procedure contained in the file creates a form allowing data entry.

```
SQL> GET CHP19-13
  1   CREATE OR REPLACE PROCEDURE CHP19_13 AS
  2   BEGIN
  3      HTP.HTMLOPEN;
  4      HTP.HTITLE('Employee input form');
  5      HTP.FORMOPEN('CHP19_14');
  6      HTP.PREOPEN;
  7      HTP.P('LAST_NAME: '|| HTF.FORMTEXT('LAST_NAME'));
  8      HTP.P('FIRST_NAME: '|| HTF.FORMTEXT('FIRST_NAME'));
  9      HTP.PRECLOSE;
 10      HTP.PARAGRAPH;
 11      HTP.FORMSUBMIT;
 12      HTP.FORMCLOSE;
 13*  END;
```

Line 1 specifies the keywords required to create a new procedure named CHP19_15. Lines 2 through 13 contain the procedure body. The HTP. HTITLE procedure in line 3 gives the HTML document a name by generating the <TITLE> and </TITLE> tags. The HTP.FORMOPEN procedure in line 4 begins the area of the HTML document containing the form and supplying the name of the processingprocedure. Line 5 uses the HTP.PREOPEN

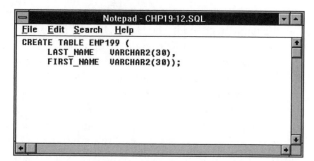

Figure 19-12 CHP19-12.sql creates the sample table used in How-To 19.7

procedure to begin a preformatted text area. Lines 6 and 7 use the HTP.P procedure to print to the document and the HTF.FORMTEXT function to create text fields, respectively. The names of the fields specified in the procedures are the parameters passed to the processing procedure. The HTP.PRECLOSE procedure in line 8 ends the formatted text beginning on line 5. The HTP.PARAGRAPH procedure in line 9 begins a new paragraph in the document by generating the <P> tag. The HTP.FORMSUBMIT procedure in line 10 creates a submit button which processes the form when clicked. The HTP.FORMCLOSE procedure in line 11 ends the declaration of the form.

3. Run the statement to create the procedure.

```
SQL>   /
```

Procedure created.

The form can be displayed calling the http://localhost:80/ows-bin/owa/ chp19_15. Although the form can be displayed at this point, it cannot be submitted until the processing procedure is created, as shown in the following steps.

4. Load CHP19-14.sql into the SQL buffer. The stored procedure contained in the file processes the form created in the previous steps.

```
SQL> GET CHP19-14
  1   CREATE OR REPLACE PROCEDURE CHP19_14 (
  2             LAST_NAME   VARCHAR2 := NULL,
  3             FIRST_NAME  VARCHAR2 := NULL) AS
  4   BEGIN
  5      INSERT INTO EMP199
  6             VALUES (LAST_NAME, FIRST_NAME);
  7      HTP.HTITLE('SUBMISSION COMPLETE');
  8      HTP.P('LAST NAME: <B>'||LAST_NAME||'</B><BR>');
  9      HTP.P('FIRST NAME: <B>'||FIRST_NAME||'</B><BR>');
 10* END;
```

Line 1 specifies the keywords for creating a stored procedure and gives it the name declared in the HTP.FORMOPEN procedure in the calling document. This procedure executes when the Submit button is clicked on the calling document. The two text fields from the calling document are specified as the procedure parameters. Lines 1 through 3 contain the procedure specification. All parameters on the processing procedure must be optional and must default to NULL. Lines 4 through 10 contain the procedure body. The INSERT statement on lines 4 and 5 creates a new record in the table using the form's values. Lines 7 though 9 use the HTP.P procedure to display a submission message to the user when the record is created.

5. Run the statement to create the procedure.

```
SQL>  /
```

Procedure created.

Although the procedure can be called directly as a URL, it will not perform any useful function unless called from the form created in Steps 2 and 3 . The next step demonstrates using the form.

6. Run a browser and load the http://localhost:80/ows-bin/owa/chp19_14 URL. Figure 19-13 shows the form within the Netscape browser.

Enter values into the two fields on the form and select the Submit button to process it. Figure 19-14 shows the results displayed after the fields are entered and the form submitted.

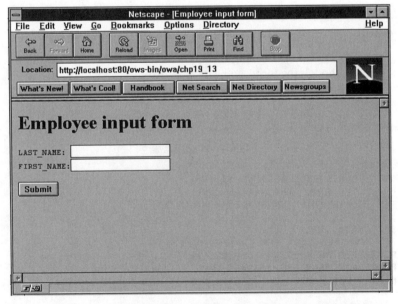

Figure 19-13 A simple data entry form in Netscape Navigator

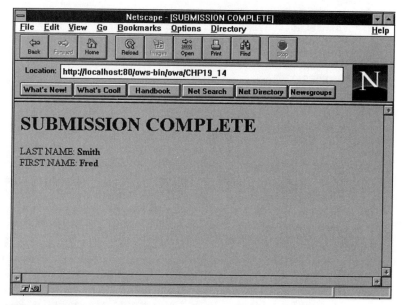

Figure 19-14 The submission message generated by processing the form

In addition to displaying the information entered into the form, the values are inserted into the EMP199 table created in Step 1. The simple form created in the earlier steps does not display the numerous controls an HTML form can contain. The following steps create a more complex form using many of the available controls.

7. Load CHP19-15.sql into the SQL buffer. The stored procedure contained in the file creates a complex form which includes text fields, radio buttons, a checkbox, and a selection list.

```
SQL> GET CHP19-15
  1    CREATE OR REPLACE PROCEDURE CHP19_15 AS
  2    BEGIN
  3      HTP.HTMLOPEN;
  4      HTP.HTITLE('Employee Identification Form');
  5      HTP.LINE;
  6      HTP.FORMOPEN('CHP19_16');
  7      HTP.PREOPEN;
  8      HTP.P('Last Name: '|| HTF.FORMTEXT('LAST_NAME')||' '||
  9                     'First Name:'|| HTF.FORMTEXT('FIRST_NAME'));
 10      HTP.P('Sex: ');
 11      HTP.P('     Male:    '||HTF.FORMRADIO('SEX','M'));
 12      HTP.P('     Female: '||HTF.FORMRADIO('SEX','F'));
 13      HTP.FORMSELECTOPEN('Department', 'Department:');
 14      HTP.FORMSELECTOPTION('Marketing');
 15      HTP.FORMSELECTOPTION('Sales');
 16      HTP.FORMSELECTOPTION('I/S');
```

continued on next page

continued from previous page

```
17      HTP.FORMSELECTOPTION('Accounting');
18      HTP.FORMSELECTCLOSE;
19      HTP.P('Exempt: '||HTF.FORMCHECKBOX('Exempt'));
20      HTP.PRECLOSE;
21      HTP.PARAGRAPH;
22      HTP.FORMRESET;
23      HTP.FORMSUBMIT;
24      HTP.FORMCLOSE;
25      HTP.LINE;
26      HTP.HTMLCLOSE;
27* END;
```

Line 1 specifies the keywords required to create the stored procedure and names it. Lines 2 through 27 contain the body of the stored procedure. Lines 3 and 26 begin and end the HTML document with the HTP. HTMLOPEN and HTP.HTMLCLOSE procedures, respectively. Line 5 uses the HTP.LINE procedure to generate an <HR> tag for displaying a line. Line 6 begins a form with the HTP.FORMOPEN procedure. The parameter passed to the HTP.FORMOPEN procedure specifies the name of the procedure receiving the input form data when the form is submitted. Line 7 uses the HTP.PREOPEN procedure to begin a section of pre-formatted text within the document. Lines 8 and 9 use the HTP.PRINT procedure containing the HTF.FORMTEXT function to create two text fields. Lines 11 and 12 create two radio buttons using the HTP.FORMRADIO procedure. By specifying the same name for the two radio buttons, the browser knows the buttons occupy the same radio group. Lines 13 through 18 create a drop-down listbox containing the elements created by the HTP.FORMSELECTOPTION procedure. The selection list is created with the HTP.FORMSELECTOPEN procedure and ended with the HTP.FORMSELECTCLOSE procedure. The HTF.FORMCHECKBOX function contained in the HTP.PRINT procedure in line 19 creates a checkbox. The values generated by a checkbox are ON or OFF. Line 21 uses the HTP.RESET procedure to create a reset button which clears the form when selected. The HTP.SUBMIT procedure in line 22 creates a submit button which processes the form when selected. The HTP.FORMCLOSE procedure in line 24 ends the form area.

8. Run the statement to create the procedure.

```
SQL>   /
```

```
Procedure created.
```

Creating the procedure lets you call the /ows-bin/owa/chp19_15 page from any browser. The CHP19_16 procedure referenced by HTP.FORMOPEN must be created in order to process the form. The next step creates the stored procedure to process the form.

9. Load CHP19-16.sql into the SQL buffer. The procedure within the file processes the form created in the previous step and displays the values entered into the items.

```
SQL> GET CHP19-16
  1   CREATE OR REPLACE PROCEDURE CHP19_16 (
  2               LAST_NAME   VARCHAR2 := NULL,
  3               FIRST_NAME   VARCHAR2 := NULL,
  4               SEX VARCHAR2 := NULL,
  5               DEPARTMENT VARCHAR2 := NULL,
  6               EXEMPT VARCHAR2 := NULL) AS
  7   BEGIN
  8     HTP.HTMLOPEN;
  9     HTP.HTITLE('SUBMISSION COMPLETE');
 10     HTP.P('LAST NAME: <B>'||LAST_NAME||'</B><BR>');
 11     HTP.P('FIRST NAME: <B>'||FIRST_NAME||'</B><BR>');
 12     HTP.P('SEX : <B>'||SEX||'</B><BR>_);
 13     HTP.P('DEPARTMENT: <B>'||DEPARTMENT||'</B><BR>');
 14     HTP.P('EXEMPT: <B>'||EXEMPT||'</B><BR>');
 15     HTP.HTMLCLOSE;
 16*  END;
```

Lines 1 through 6 contain the specification for the stored procedure. The calling document represents each of the form variables it contains. The order of the parameters is unimportant because the Web Agent reorders them at runtime. Lines 7 through 16 contain the procedure body. Lines 8 and 15 begin and end the document by specifying the HTP.HTMLOPEN and HTP.HTMLCLOSE procedures, respectively. Line 9 uses the HTP. HTITLE procedure to generate the tags for the document's title and heading. Lines 9 through 14 use the HTP.P procedure to print the parameters passed from the calling document. The <B> tag is included in the parameter to print the values in boldfaced text. The <BR> tag is included to generate a linefeed.

10. Run the statement to create the procedure.

```
SQL>  /
```

Procedure created.

11. Run a browser and load the http://localhost:80/ows-bin/owa/chp19_15 URL. Figure 19-15 shows the form displayed by the Netscape browser.

Enter a first and last name into the text fields, select a value from the radio buttons and listbox, and check the checkbox. If you want to clear information entered, you can select the Reset button. Submit the form by selecting the Submit button. Figure 19-16 shows the Web document displayed when the form is submitted.

Each of the values from the calling form are displayed by the processing form. Notice that the value of the EXEMPT checkbox is ON, not TRUE or FALSE. The <B> tags passed to the HTP.PRINT procedure display the textbox values in boldface.

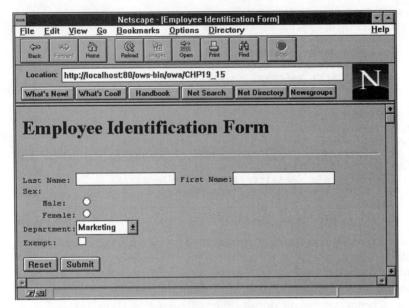

Figure 19-15 The employee identification form

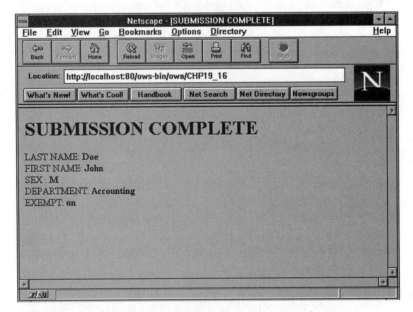

Figure 19-16 The results of submitting the employee
identification form

How It Works

In order to create a form using Oracle WebServer, two stored procedures are required. The initial procedure lets the user enter values into the form, and the second procedure receives these values as parameters and processes the form. A form begins with the <FORM METHOD="post" ACTION=processing procedure> tag and ends with the </FORM> tag. Between the tags, form elements and other HTML tags are defined. Text fields, radio buttons, selection lists, checkboxes, and text areas can all be defined within a form. Step 1 creates a table that receives the data entered into a form. Steps 2 and 3 create a stored procedure that generates a simple form to enter a name. When the form is submitted, the procedure created in steps 4 and 5 inserts the data into the sample table and displays the values of the field in a document. Step 6 shows the operation of the simple form within a browser. Steps 7 and 8 create a stored procedure generating a form with many of the objects an HTML form uses. The form contains text boxes, radio buttons, a checkbox, and a selection list. The stored procedure created in steps 9 and 10 processes the data from the calling form by displaying the values within a document. Step 11 shows the operation of the complex form.

Comments

Forms enable you to generate sophisticated Web applications. The method used by the Oracle WebServer to process forms simplifies this technique. In developing your Web applications, you will find that Oracle has made the process of creating HTML forms as easy as possible.

COMPLEXITY
INTERMEDIATE

19.9   How do I...
Use HTML tables in my Web documents?

Problem

I want to use HTML tables to display information that should appear in row/column format. When I use a browser capable of displaying tables, I notice they greatly enhance the look of Web documents. How do I use HTML tables in my page?

Technique

Tables are created within an HTML document by generating table-related tags in the document. The <TABLE> tag begins a table and can be generated by the HTP.TABLEOPEN procedure. Table 19-7 shows the Developer's Toolkit procedures related to the creation of tables.

PROCEDURE	DESCRIPTION
htp.tableopen	Begins the creation of a table
htp.tableclose	End the table specification
htp.tablecaption	Creates a caption for the table
htp.tablerowopen	Starts the processing of row information
htp.tablerowclose	Ends the processing of row information
htp.tableheader	Creates column headers for the table
htp.tabledata	Creates a column data element

Table 19-7 Table-related procedures

Each row of the table is created beginning with the HTP.TABLEROWOPEN procedure, creating elements with the HTP.TABLEDATA procedure, and ending with the HTP.TABLEROWCLOSE procedure. A caption can be created for the table by using the HTP.TABLECAPTION procedure. Column headings can be created just like a row, or the HTP.TABLEHEADER procedure can be used. If the HTP. TABLEHEADER procedure is used, the column headings will look slightly bolder.

Steps

1. Run SQL*Plus and connect as the WWW_USER account. CHP19-17.sql, shown in Figure 19-17, creates the sample table used in this How-To.

The SALES199 table contains regional sales information for a sample company. Four sample records to be queried into an HTML table in a later step are created. Run the file to create the sample table and its data.

```
SQL>  START CHP19-17

Table created.

1 row created.

1 row created.

1 row created.

1 row created.

Commit complete.
```

2. Load CHP19-18.sql into the SQL buffer. The stored procedure contained in the file demonstrates the use of HTML tables within a document. A simple table is presented by the procedure, displaying static data.

```
SQL> GET CHP19-18
  1   CREATE OR REPLACE PROCEDURE CHP19_18 AS
  2   BEGIN
  3     HTP.HTMLOPEN;
  4     HTP.P('<CENTER>');
  5     HTP.TABLEOPEN('BORDER');
```

```
 6    HTP.TABLECAPTION('Regional Sales', 'CENTER');
 7    HTP.TABLEROWOPEN;
 8    HTP.TABLEDATA;
 9    HTP.TABLEDATA('Jan');
10    HTP.TABLEDATA('Feb');
11    HTP.TABLEDATA('Mar');
12    HTP.TABLEDATA('Apr');
13    HTP.TABLEDATA('May');
14    HTP.TABLEDATA('Jun');
15    HTP.TABLEROWCLOSE;
16    HTP.TABLEROWOPEN;
17    HTP.TABLEDATA('New York');
18    HTP.TABLEDATA('1', 'CENTER');
19    HTP.TABLEDATA('39','CENTER');
20    HTP.TABLEDATA('82','CENTER');
21    HTP.TABLEDATA('22','CENTER');
22    HTP.TABLEDATA('2','CENTER');
23    HTP.TABLEDATA('12','CENTER');
24    HTP.TABLEROWCLOSE;
25    HTP.TABLEROWOPEN;
26    HTP.TABLEDATA('Chicago');
27    HTP.TABLEDATA('4', 'CENTER');
28    HTP.TABLEDATA('9','CENTER');
29    HTP.TABLEDATA('27','CENTER');
30    HTP.TABLEDATA('21','CENTER');
31    HTP.TABLEDATA('4','CENTER');
32    HTP.TABLEDATA('11','CENTER');
33    HTP.TABLEROWCLOSE;
34    HTP.TABLECLOSE;
35    HTP.P('</CENTER>');
36    HTP.HTMLCLOSE;
37*   END;
```

Line 1 specifies the keywords for creating the stored procedure and names it. Lines 2 through 37 contain the trigger body. The HTP.HTMLOPEN and HTP.HTMLCLOSE procedures in lines 3 and 36 provide the tags to begin

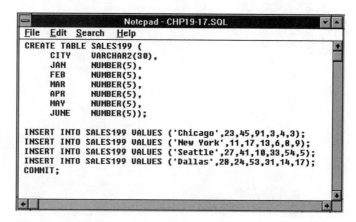

Figure 19-17 CHP19-17.sql creates the sample table used in How-To 19.8

and end the document, respectively. The HTP.P procedure is used in line 4 to print the <CENTER> tag which centers the table. The HTP.TABLEOPEN procedure in line 5 begins the table specification. The BORDER parameter displays a border around the table and between the rows and columns. The HTP.TABLECAPTION procedure in line 6 creates a caption for the table. Each row in the table is started with the HTP.TABLEROWOPEN procedure and ended with the HTP.TABLEROWCLOSE procedure. Each cell in the row is created with the HTP.TABLEDATA procedure. Lines 7 through 15 create the headings for the columns by treating them as rows. Lines 16 through 24 and 25 through 33 create two rows in the table. The HTP.TABLECLOSE procedure in line 34 ends the creation of the table.

3. Run the statement to create the procedure.

```
SQL>   /
```

Procedure created.

The document can be displayed by any browser by calling the http://localhost:80/ows-bin/owa/chp19_18 URL.

4. Load your browser and display the http:/localhost:80/ows-bin/owa/chp19_18 URL. The document is displayed in Figure 19-18 within Netscape Navigator.

When the table is generated in the document, it contains three rows and seven columns. The first row contains the column headings, and the next

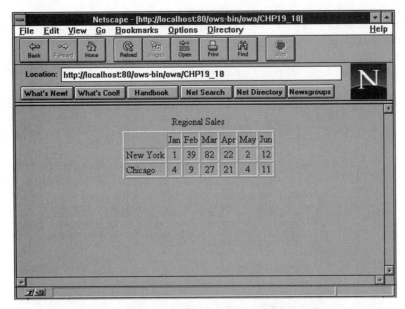

Figure 19-18 The http://localhost:80/ows-bin/owa/chp19_18 URL showing an HTML table

two rows contain data. The data presented in this example is static data programmed into the procedure. The next step creates a procedure that builds an HTML table based on the results of a query.

5. From within SQL*Plus, load CHP19-19.sql into the SQL buffer. The procedure contained in the file queries the sample table created in Step 1 and creates an HTML table with the results.

```
SQL> GET CHP19-19
   1   CREATE OR REPLACE PROCEDURE CHP19_19 AS
   2   CURSOR C1 IS
   3       SELECT
   4                   CITY, JAN, FEB, MAR, APR, MAY, JUNE
   5       FROM
   6                   SALES199
   7       ORDER BY CITY;
   8   BEGIN
   9     HTP.HTMLOPEN;
  10     HTP.P('<CENTER>');
  11     HTP.TABLEOPEN('BORDER');
  12     HTP.TABLECAPTION('Regional Sales','CENTER');
  13     HTP.TABLEROWOPEN;
  14     HTP.TABLEDATA;
  15     HTP.TABLEDATA('Jan');
  16     HTP.TABLEDATA('Feb');
  17     HTP.TABLEDATA('Mar');
  18     HTP.TABLEDATA('Apr');
  19     HTP.TABLEDATA('May');
  20     HTP.TABLEDATA('Jun');
  21     HTP.TABLEROWCLOSE;
  22     FOR I IN C1 LOOP
  23         HTP.TABLEROWOPEN;
  24         HTP.TABLEDATA(I.CITY);
  25         HTP.TABLEDATA(TO_CHAR(I.JAN),'CENTER');
  26         HTP.TABLEDATA(TO_CHAR(I.FEB),'CENTER');
  27         HTP.TABLEDATA(TO_CHAR(I.MAR),'CENTER');
  28         HTP.TABLEDATA(TO_CHAR(I.APR),'CENTER');
  29         HTP.TABLEDATA(TO_CHAR(I.MAY),'CENTER');
  30         HTP.TABLEDATA(TO_CHAR(I.JUNE),'CENTER');
  31         HTP.TABLEROWCLOSE;
  32     END LOOP;
  33     HTP.TABLECLOSE;
  34     HTP.P('</CENTER>');
  35     HTP.HTMLCLOSE;
  36*  END;
```

Line 1 specifies the keywords required to create the stored procedure and name it. Lines 2 through 7 create a cursor which queries the sample table created in Step 1. The cursor is executed within the procedure body and the rows displayed in a table. Lines 8 through 36 contain the procedure body. Lines 9 and 35 use the HTP.HTMLOPEN and HTP.HTMLCLOSE procedures to begin and end the document, respectively. Line 10 centers the table by printing the <CENTER> tag, using the HTP.PRINT procedure. Line 11 begins the creation of the table using the HTP.TABLEOPEN procedure.

Lines 13 through 21 develop the column headings by creating a row containing the headings. Lines 22 through 32 use a FOR loop to move through each record returned by the query. A row is created for each record returned by the query by using the HTP.TABLEROWOPEN, HTP.TABLE-DATA, and HTP.TABLEROWCLOSE procedures. The table is closed in line 33 with the HTP.TABLECLOSE procedure.

6. Run the statement to create the procedure.

```
SQL>  /
```

```
Procedure created.
```

When the URL represented by the stored procedure is called, a query is executed on the sample table to dynamically create the HTML table.

7. From within your browser, display the http://localhost:80/ows-bin/owa/chp19_19 URL. Figure 19-19 shows the page within Netscape.

Each of the four records in the sample table generates a row in the HTML table. The column headings are created as a row in the table. The HTP.TABLEHEADER procedure could be used to create the column headings.

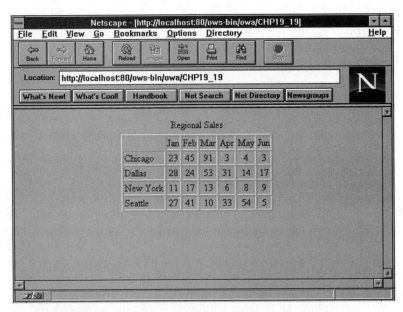

Figure 19-19 The results of the dynamically created HTML table

How It Works

Tables within HTML are created by the <TABLE> tag and terminated by the </TABLE> tag. Between the two tags, other tags create the format of the table. In order to put a border around the table and between the columns and rows, the BORDER attribute is supplied with the <TABLE> tag. The HTP.TABLEOPEN procedure generates the <TABLE> tag, and the HTP.TABLECLOSE procedure generates the </TABLE> tag. Within a table, the <TR> and </TR> tags enclose the rows contained in the table. They can be generated with the HTP.TABLEROWOPEN and HTP.TABLEROWCLOSE procedures. Table data is contained within the <TD> and </TD> tags. The HTP.TABLEDATA procedure generates both these tags containing a string. The <CAPTION> and </CAPTION> tags contain a caption for the table. These tags can be generated by the HTP.TABLECAPTION procedure.

Step 1 creates a sample table which is the source of data in a later step. Steps 2 and 3 demonstrate the capabilities of tables by creating a document containing a table with static text. Step 4 displays the simple table using a browser. Steps 4 and 5 create an HTML table which receives its data from a database query. The sample table created in Step 1 is queried by a cursor in the stored procedure. When the query is executed, each row of it is created as a row in the HTML table.

Comments

HTML tables are an appealing way to display row and column information. In your applications, you may find yourself often displaying the results of queries. HTML tables are a good method for presenting data from queries, since a query contains rows and columns.

COMPLEXITY
ADVANCED

19.10 How do I...
Access and use CGI environment variables?

Problem

I need to retrieve and use CGI environment variables in my application. Information like the IP address of the remote host making the request is necessary in developing sophisticated applications. How do I access and use CGI environment variables in my Web applications?

Technique

All CGI environment variables that are part of the Common Gateway Interface 1.1 specification are passed from the Oracle Web Listener to the Web Agent. All relevant environment variables are available through PL/SQL. The GET_CGI_ENV function from the OWA_UTIL package allows you to access CGI environment variables. The procedures and functions provided by the OWA_UTIL package are shown in Table 19-8.

PROCEDURE	DESCRIPTION
owa_util.get_cgi_env	Returns the value of the specified CGI variable
owa_util.get_owa_service_path	Prints the currently active service path and its virtual path
owa_util.print_cgi_env	Prints all of the CGI variables made available to the PL/SQL module
owa_util.signature	Allows the developer to create a signature line for the document
owa_util.showpage	Allows the user to display the output from a procedure call to SQL*Plus, SQL*DBA, or Server Manager
owa_util.showsource	Prints the source of the specified PL/SQL module
owa_util.tableprint	Prints an Oracle table as a preformatted HTML table

Table 19-8 Functions contained in the OWA_UTIL package

The OWA_UTIL.GET_CGI_ENV function returns the value of the CGI variable that is passed in as a parameter.

Steps

1. Run SQL*Plus and connect as the WWW_USER account. Load CHP19-20.sql into the SQL buffer. The stored procedure contained in the file displays the available CGI environment variables.

```
SQL> GET CHP19-20
  1  CREATE OR REPLACE PROCEDURE CHP19_20 AS
  2    X VARCHAR2(80);
  3  BEGIN
  4    HTP.PRINT('<TITLE>CHP19_20</TITLE>');
  5    HTP.PRINT('<H2>CGI Environment Variables</H2>');
  6    X := OWA_UTIL.GET_CGI_ENV('AUTH_TYPE');
  7    HTP.PRINT('AUTH_TYPE = '||X||'<br>');
  8    X := OWA_UTIL.GET_CGI_ENV('GATEWAY_INTERFACE');
  9    HTP.PRINT('GATEWAY_INTERFACE = '||X||'<br>');
 10    X := OWA_UTIL.GET_CGI_ENV('HTTP_USER_AGENT');
 11    HTP.PRINT('HTTP_USER_AGENT = '||X||'<br>');
 12    X := OWA_UTIL.GET_CGI_ENV('PATH_INFO');
 13    HTP.PRINT('PATH_INFO = '||X||'<br>');
 14    X := OWA_UTIL.GET_CGI_ENV('PATH_TRANSLATED');
 15    HTP.PRINT('PATH_TRANSLATED = '||X||'<br>');
 16    X := OWA_UTIL.GET_CGI_ENV('REMOTE_HOST');
 17    HTP.PRINT('REMOTE_HOST = '||X||'<br>');
```

```
18     X := OWA_UTIL.GET_CGI_ENV('REMOTE_ADDR');
19     HTP.PRINT('REMOTE_ADDR = '||X||'<br>');
20     X := OWA_UTIL.GET_CGI_ENV('REMOTE_USER');
21     HTP.PRINT('REMOTE_USER = '||X||'<br>');
22     X := OWA_UTIL.GET_CGI_ENV('REMOTE_IDENT');
23     HTP.PRINT('REMOTE_IDENT = '||X||'<br>');
24     X := OWA_UTIL.GET_CGI_ENV('SERVER_PROTOCOL');
25     HTP.PRINT('SERVER_PROTOCOL = '||X||'<br>');
26     X := OWA_UTIL.GET_CGI_ENV('SERVER_SOFTWARE');
27     HTP.PRINT('SERVER_SOFTWARE = '||X||'<br>');
28     X := OWA_UTIL.GET_CGI_ENV('SERVER_NAME');
29     HTP.PRINT('SERVER_NAME = '||X||'<br>');
30     X := OWA_UTIL.GET_CGI_ENV('SERVER_PORT');
31     HTP.PRINT('SERVER_PORT = '||X||'<br>');
32     X := OWA_UTIL.GET_CGI_ENV('SCRIPT_NAME');
33     HTP.PRINT('SCRIPT_NAME = '||X||'<br>');
34*  END;
```

Line 1 specifies the keywords required to create the stored procedure. Line 2 declares a variable used to hold the CGI variables as they are returned to the PL/SQL code. Lines 3 through 34 contain the procedure body. Line 6 is representative of most lines in the stored procedure. The OWA_UTIL.GET_CGI_ENV function is used to return the value of a CGI environment. The HTP.PRINT procedure is used to print a line to the browser.

2. Run the statement to create the stored procedure.

```
SQL>  /
```

```
Procedure created.
```

When the page is displayed, the CGI variables are retrieved from the server by the OWA_UTIL procedures and displayed within the document.

3. Load your browser and browse the URL created by the stored procedure. Figure 19-20 shows the results of the operation.

How It Works

The GET_CGI_ENV function from the OWA_UTIL package returns the value of the specified CGI variable to the PL/SQL function. The PRINT procedure in the HTP package is used to print text or HTML commands to the browser. Steps 1 and 2 create a stored procedure using the OWA_UTIL.GET_CGI_ENV to retrieve the values of each available CGI environment variable. Step 3 displays the page within a browser.

Comments

CGI variables will provide you with information required to create complex Web documents and applications. The OWA_UTIL package gives you easy access to these

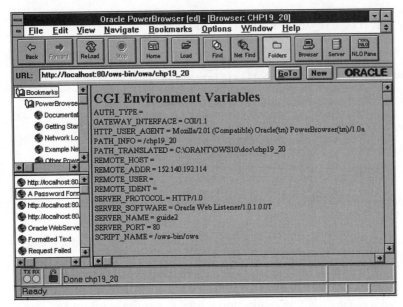

Figure 19-20 The results of the operation displaying the CGI environment variables

variables for use within yourapplications. Other OWA_UTIL procedures allow you to control the environment and display debugging information.

COMPLEXITY
INTERMEDIATE

19.11 How do I...
Create a password field in a form?

Problem

I need to create fields in my Web pages in which the user enters a password. When the user enters the password, I don't want it to be readable by people looking at the document. How do I create a password field on a page?

Technique

The HTP.FORMPASSWORD procedure is used to create a password field within a form. The HTF.FORMPASSWORD function can be used within the HTP.PRINT procedure to create the password field. The field has the characteristics of a password field, because it isn't readable when the text is entered.

Steps

1. Run SQL*Plus and connect as the WWW_USER account. Load CHP19-21.sql into the SQL buffer. The stored procedure created in the file creates a form containing a password field.

```
SQL> GET CHP19-21
  1   CREATE OR REPLACE PROCEDURE CHP19_21 AS
  2   BEGIN
  3      HTP.HTMLOPEN;
  4      HTP.HTITLE('A Password Form');
  5      HTP.FORMOPEN('CHP19_22');
  6      HTP.PREOPEN;
  7      HTP.P('USER NAME: '|| HTF.FORMTEXT('USER_NAME'));
  8      HTP.P('PASSWORD: '|| HTF.FORMPASSWORD('PASSWORD'));
  9      HTP.PRECLOSE;
 10      HTP.PARAGRAPH;
 11      HTP.FORMSUBMIT;
 12      HTP.FORMCLOSE;
 13      HTP.HTMLCLOSE;
 14*  END;
```

Line 1 contains the keywords required to create the stored procedure and provide its name. Lines 2 through 14 contain the procedure body. Lines 3 and 13 use the HTP.HTMLOPEN and HTP.HTMLCLOSE procedures to begin and end the HTML document. Lines 5 and 12 use the HTP. FORMOPEN and HTP.FORMCLOSE procedures to begin and end the form. The HTP.FORMOPEN procedure contains the name of the procedure executed when the form is submitted as a parameter. Lines 6 and 9 define a preformatted text area by calling the HTP.PREOPEN and HTP.PRECLOSE procedures. Lines 7 and 8 use the HTP.P procedure to print text to the document. Line 7 uses the HTF.FORMTEXT function to create a standard text field. The HTF.FORMPASSWORD function is used in line 8 to create a password field.

2. Run the statement to create the procedure.

```
SQL>  /
```

```
Procedure created.
```

Once the procedure is created, the document can be called by any browser by specifying http://localhost:80/ows-bin/owa/chp19_21 as the URL. The HTP.FORMOPEN procedure in line 5 references the CHP19_22 stored procedure to process the form when the submit button is selected. The next step creates the stored procedure which receives the form when it is submitted.

3. Load CHP19-22.sql into the SQL buffer. The stored procedure contained in the file receives the fields from the calling page and prints the values within a document. When the password value is passed to the stored procedure, it can be displayed as normal text.

```
SQL> GET CHP19-22
  1   CREATE OR REPLACE PROCEDURE CHP19_22 (
  2              USER_NAME  VARCHAR2 := NULL,
  3              PASSWORD   VARCHAR2 := NULL) AS
  4   BEGIN
  5      HTP.HTMLOPEN;
  6      HTP.HTITLE('SUBMISSION COMPLETE');
  7      HTP.P('USER NAME IS: <B>'||USER_NAME||'</B>');
  8      HTP.BR;
  9      HTP.P('PASSWORD IS: <B>'||PASSWORD||'</B>');
 10      HTP.BR;
 11      HTP.HTMLCLOSE;
 12*  END;
```

Lines 1 through 3 contain the procedure specification for the stored procedure. The USER_NAME and PASSWORD parameters contained in lines 2 and 3 are passed by the calling document. Lines 4 through 10 contain the procedure body. The HTP.HTMLOPEN and HTP.HTMLCLOSE procedures in lines 5 and 9 begin and end the document. Line 6 uses the HTP.HTITLE procedure to create the title and heading of the document. Lines 7 and 8 display the user name and password entered into the calling form.

4. Run the statement to create the procedure.

```
SQL>  /
```

Procedure created.

Although the procedure can be called by specifying its name in the URL, no data will be displayed unless it is called from the other page.

5. Run your browser and load http://localhost:80/ows-bin/owa/chp19_22 as the URL. Figure 19-21 shows the form created in Steps 1 and 2 within the browser.

Enter WAITE as the user name and PRESS as the password. When the password is entered, you will see it displayed as asterisks. Select the Submit button to process the form. Figure 19-22 shows the results of the form when it is submitted.

Even though the password is not readable when entered, it is passed to the processing procedure as a normal VARCHAR2 parameter. The password is displayed by the processing document in a normal format.

How It Works

The HTP.FORMPASSWORD procedure and HTF.FORMPASSWORD function create the HTML tags for developing a password field in a form. Step 1 creates a stored procedure which generates an HTML document containing a form. Within the form, a password field is created by using the HTP.PRINT and HTF.FORMPASSWORD

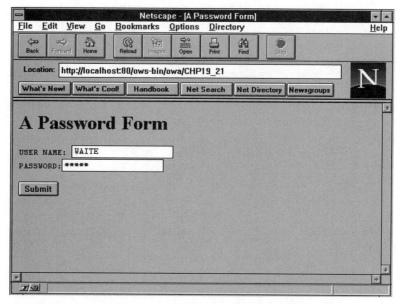

Figure 19-21 A form containing a password field

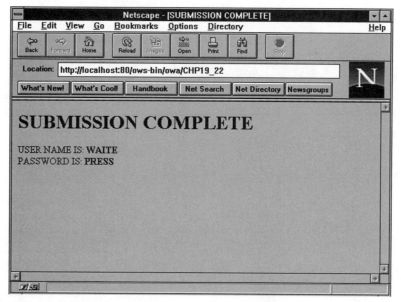

Figure 19-22 The values passed to the processing procedure

functions. Step 3 creates a stored procedure which is passed to the fields from the calling document as parameters and displays them in the document.

Comments

Anytime you have form fields which should be hidden from onlookers, use a password field. The HTF.FORMPASSWORD function is provided by the Oracle WebServer Developer's Toolkit to make the creation of password fields easier.

CHAPTER 20
ADMINISTERING WEBSERVER

20

ADMINISTERING WEBSERVER

How do I...

In order to use the Oracle WebServer effectively, it is necessary to perform some basic administration tasks. The Oracle WebServer contains three major components, two of which are administered through Web documents presented by the WebServer. The Oracle Web Listener listens on a port and determines whether the request should be read from the file system or passed to the Oracle Web Agent to execute a stored procedure. The Web Agent controls connections to the database and the execution of the stored procedures through services. Both the Oracle Web Listener and Oracle Web Agent are administered through Web documents using any browser. This chapter presents the common administration tasks required when developing applications using the Oracle WebServer. The sample files used in this chapter are found on the accompanying CD-ROM in the \SAMPLES\CHAP20 directory.

20.1   Start up and shut down the Oracle Web Listener

Each Web listener listens to a port address to process Web requests. As part of your system maintenance tasks, you will need to start and stop Web listeners. This How-To presents the method used to start and stop Oracle Web Listeners using the administration Web documents.

20.2   Create a new service

A service controls how a user connects to the database when executing dynamic Web documents. Since dynamic Web documents are stored procedures, the user must connect to the database in order to execute them. When you create multiple applications using the same WebServer, you will need to create new services for each separate application. This How-To presents the method used to create a new service.

20.3   Create an error page for the Web Agent

Whenever the Web Agent encounters an error, a message is provided to inform the user of the error. Each Web service can have its own error document to provide a customized error message. This How-To presents the method used for defining the error page used by a service.

20.4   Display errors encountered by the Web Agent

Whenever errors are encountered by the Web Agent, they are logged to an error file. The error log file provides useful information when debugging your Web applications. This How-To presents the method used to find and display the error log file created for each service.

20.5   Create a new Web listener

If you want to partition your applications using multiple Web listeners, you will need to create a new Web listener specifying the listener name, the port on which it listens, and the parameters used to control the listener. This How-To presents the technique used to create a new Web listener.

20.6   Use a single copy of the Developer's Toolkit with multiple services

Each user account referenced by a service must have access to the Developer's Toolkit packages in order to generate documents. When a new service is created in the Web Agent Administration screen, you have the option of creating the Developer's Toolkit packages for the user account the service uses. Creating a copy of the Developer's Toolkit packages for each user account can be an unnecessary waste of space. This How-To presents the method for sharing a single set of Developer's Toolkit packages for multiple services.

COMPLEXITY
BEGINNING

20.1 How do I...
Start up and shut down the Oracle Web Listener?

Problem

I want to start and stop the Oracle Web Listener. When I create a new service or perform other system administration tasks, I need to stop and start the Web listener. How do I start up and shut down the Oracle Web Listener?

Technique

Oracle WebServer administration is performed using any browser. When the Oracle WebServer is installed, a listener is created to handle WebServer administration. Executing the default page for the administration port lets you launch the WebServer administration screen. For the default installation, referencing the http://localhost:9999/ URL launches the administration Web documents. The Oracle Web Listener administration screen is launched from the Oracle WebServer administration screen and is used to start and stop a listener.

Steps

1. Load a Web browser and connect to the default page of the administration service. In most cases, the administration listener is found on the 9999 port and is launched by referencing the http://localhost:9999/ URL. Figure 20-1 shows the Oracle WebServer home page displayed in Netscape Navigator.

Most WebServer administration tasks are performed from within the browser using the administration documents. Page down in the document until you find the Oracle WebServer Administration link. This document is used to administer the components of the Oracle WebServer.

2. Select the Oracle WebServer Administration link to display the WebServer Administration document. From this page, you can perform WebServer administration tasks. Figure 20-2 shows the Oracle WebServer Administration page.

Starting and stopping listeners is performed in the Oracle Web Agent administration document selected as a link from this document.

Figure 20-1 Netscape Navigator and the WebServer home page

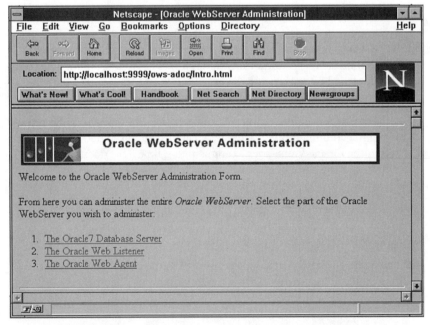

Figure 20-2 The Oracle WebServer Administration page

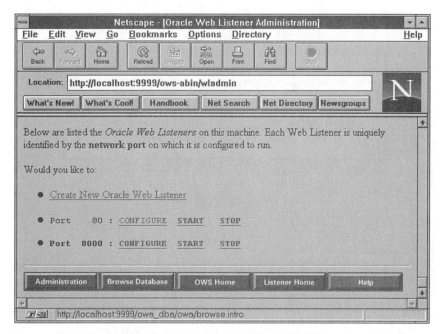

Figure 20-3 The Oracle Web Listener Administration page

3. Select the Oracle Web Agent link from the WebServer Administration page. The Oracle Web Listener Administration document is displayed. The document allows you to create and maintain Oracle Web listeners. Figure 20-3 shows the Oracle Web Listener Administration page.

To stop a listener, choose the STOP link corresponding to the listener. To start the listener, choose the START link for the listener. A message will be displayed in the resulting document when a listener is started or stopped. Figure 20-4 shows the message displayed when the listener is stopped.

How It Works

Oracle WebServer administration tasks are performed by using a Web browser and using the administration listener. The Oracle Web Listener Administration screen is used to start, stop, and configure listeners. The Oracle WebServer home page is launched by selecting the default service for the administration listener, usually on port 9999. The Oracle Web Listener Administration screen is used to start, stop, and configure a Web listener. Step 1 launches a browser and displays the WebServer default document for the administration listener. Step 2 displays the WebServer Administration screen launched from the default document. The Web Agent Administration screen is launched in Step 3, and a Web listener is stopped from the screen by selecting the STOP link for the listener.

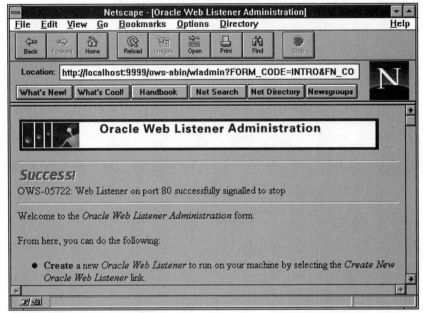

Figure 20-4 The document displayed when the listener is successfully stopped

Comments

In your WebServer administration tasks, you will need to start, stop, and configure Web listeners. The Oracle WebServer makes it easy to perform these tasks by presenting management tools as Web documents. As you get used to using these tools, you will find it easy to administer Oracle WebServer.

COMPLEXITY
INTERMEDIATE

20.2 How do I...
Create a new service?

Problem

I want to create a new service controlling which Web pages and data a user has access to. If I only have one service defined, then all users will connect to the same database account. Since I want to have different applications that are Web-based, I need to create multiple services to manage object privileges. How do I create a new service?

Technique

A new service is created using the Web Agent Administration document, which is part of the Oracle WebServer administration screens. A new user account can be created when developing a service, or an existing user account can be assigned to the service. The Developer's Toolkit packages can be installed in the user account's schema when the service is created or modified. Once a new service is developed, a directory entry must be created using the Web Listener Administration document to make a virtual directory reference the service. The default Web document for the administrative listener, which is usually port 9999, contains a link to the WebServer Administration documents.

Steps

1. Load a Web browser and connect to the default page of the administrative service. If you are working on the computer containing the server, the URL is probably http://localhost:9999/. Most WebServer administration tasks are performed within Web documents on the WebServer host. When you page down through the default document, you will be presented with a variety of options. Figure 20-5 shows the menu selections available in the default WebServer page.

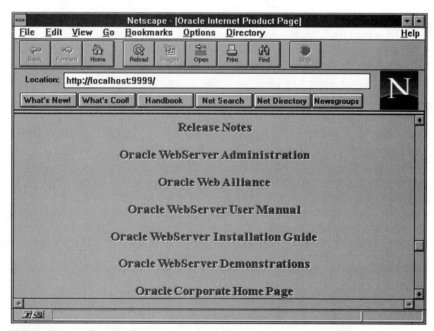

Figure 20-5 The WebServer page administration options

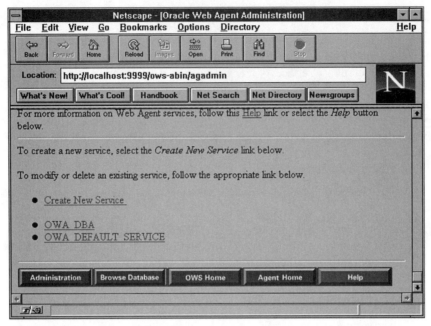

Figure 20-6 The Oracle Web Agent Administration document

2. Select the Oracle WebServer Administration link to display the administration page. You can perform WebServer administration tasks from this document. A new service is created in the Oracle Web Agent Administration screens displayed through the Oracle Web Agent link.

3. Select the Oracle Web Agent option from the WebServer Administration page. The Oracle Web Agent Administration page is displayed, allowing you to create and maintain services. Services control how the user is connected to the database when dynamic Web pages are accessed. Figure 20-6 shows the Oracle Web Agent Administration page.

4. Select the Create New Service link to begin the process of creating a new service. The service creation document used to create a new service will be displayed. Figure 20-7 shows the Service Creation document.

Enter the values contained in Table 20-1 into the fields on the form to create a new service named WAITE.

FIELD	VALUE
OWA Service	WAITE
OWA Database User	WAITE
OWA User Password	PRESS

FIELD	VALUE
Confirm Password	PRESS
ORACLE_HOME	C:\ORANT
ORACLE_SID	ORCL
SQL*Net V2 Service	
Authorized Ports	80
Log File Directory	C:\ORANT\OWS10\log
HTML Error Page	
NLS Language	
Create OWA Database User	unchecked
Change OWA Database User Password	unchecked
Install WebServer Developer's Toolkit PL/SQL	checked
DBA User Name	SYSTEM
Password	MANAGER

Table 20-1 Entries used to create a new service

The OWA Service field specifies the name of the service to be created. The OWA Database User field contains the name of the user account the service employs to connect to the database. If the user account does not exist, it can be created in the process. The Identified By field specifies how the

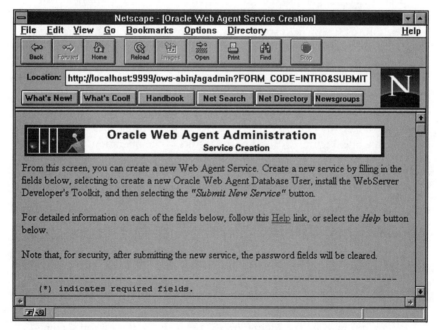

Figure 20-7 The Web Agent Service Creation document

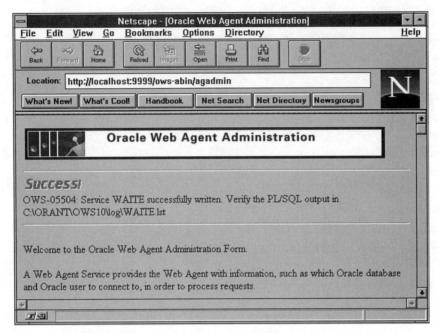

Figure 20-8 The Success Page after creating a service

password is supplied to the database. The ORACLE_HOME field will default to the current value of ORACLE_HOME for the default database. The ORACLE_SID field specifies the system identifier of the database to which the user connects. The SQL*Net V2 Service specifies the database to connect to if the Web Agent is located on a different machine. If the Web Agent is on the same computer as the database, use the ORACLE_SID field instead. The Authorized Ports fields specifies the Web listener network ports on which the service will listen. Choose the Submit New Service button to create the new service. The process of creating the new service may take a while. Figure 20-8 shows the results of the operation.

5. Load the WebServer Administration screen by loading http://localhost:9999/ ows-odoc/intro.html, and select the Oracle Web Listener option. Once a service is created, a virtual directory translating a directory entry in a URL to a service name must be created for the Web listener. Figure 20-9 shows the Oracle Web Listener page.

Since the new service is defined to listen on port 80, the listener using port 80 must be configured.

6. Choose the CONFIGURE link for the port 80 Web Agent. The Oracle Web Agent Advanced Server configuration form used to configure the many Web Agent options appears. Figure 20-10 shows the configuration screen.

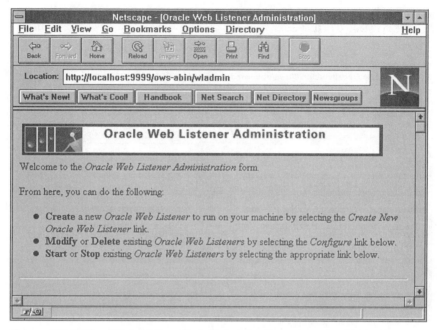

Figure 20-9 The Web Listener Administration document

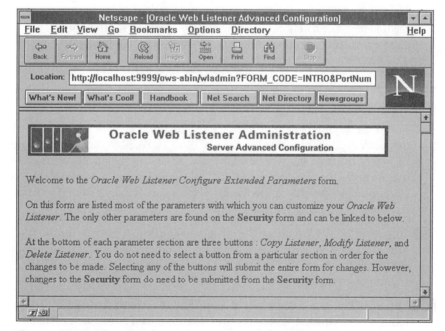

Figure 20-10 The Oracle Web Agent Advanced Server Configuration screen

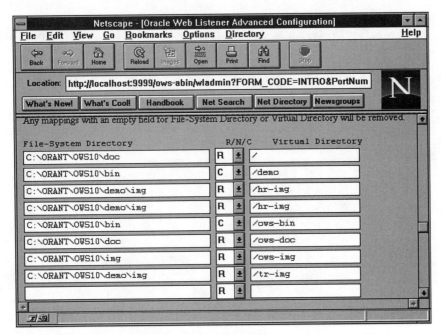

Figure 20-11 The directory mapping section

Move to the directory mapping section of the document by paging through the document or by choosing the Directory Mapping shortcut link. The directory mapping section of the document is shown in Figure 20-11.

Add the following line of the directory mapping to the list of virtual directories.

```
C:\ORANT\OWS10\bin        C        /waite
```

This causes a URL beginning with the /waite directory to be executed by the Oracle Web Agent contained in the C:\ORANT\OWS\bin directory. Without this entry, the user will receive a URL not found error when attempting to use the new service. Select the MODIFY LISTENER button to apply the changes. Once the changes to the listener are successfully made, it must be restarted for the changes to take effect.

7. Stop and start the listener so the changes take effect. Return to the http://localhost:9999/ows-abin/wladmin document and select STOP to stop the port 80 listener. After the listener has been stopped, select START to restart the listener.

8. Run SQL*Plus and connect as the WAITE user account. Load CHP20-1.sql into the SQL buffer. The stored procedure contained in the file generates a dynamic Web page that tests the new service.

```
SQL>   GET CHP20-1
  1    CREATE OR REPLACE PROCEDURE CHP20_1 AS
  2    BEGIN
  3       HTP.HTMLOPEN;
  4       HTP.HTITLE(_PROCEDURE EXECUTED );
  5       HTP.HTMLCLOSE;
  6    END;
```

Line 1 specifies the required keywords to create the stored procedure and give it a name. Lines 2 through 6 contain the procedure body. Lines 3 and 5 open and close the document by generating <HTML> and </HTML> tags. The HTP.HTITLE procedure in line 4 generates the tags required to create a title and display a heading.

9. Run the statement to create the procedure.

```
SQL>   /
```

Procedure created.

Once the procedure is created, it can be executed by the service to generate the document. The /waite virtual directory contains the name of the service and tells the Web Agent to process the procedure using the Waite service.

10. From within your browser, load the http://localhost:80/waite/owa/chp20_1 document. The /waite directory in the URL specifies that the Waite service is used to execute the procedure. Figure 20-12 shows the document in a browser.

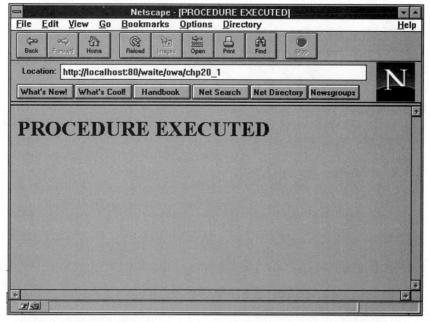

Figure 20-12 The test document within the Netscape browser

The stored procedure was created in the WAITE user account's schema. An attempt to reference the document with the default service will fail, because the procedure does not exist in that user account's schema.

How It Works

A new service allows you to have separate applications use different user accounts in the database. Services are created and maintained through the Web Agent Administration documents using the administration listener. Once a service is created, the Web listener must be modified to include the virtual directories for referencing the service. The Web Listener administration documents are used to maintain Web listeners. Step 1 displays the default document for the administration listener by browsing the http://localhost:9999/ URL. Step 2 displays the WebServer Administration document by choosing the appropriate link from the default document. The WebServer Administration document allows you to access the maintenance documents for the three major components of the Oracle WebServer. Step 3 displays the Oracle Web Agent Administration document by selecting it from the previous document. Step 4 displays the Web Agent Service Creation document used to create a new service and enters the values required. Once the new service is created, Step 5 displays the Web Listener Administration document allowing the required changes to be made to the Oracle Web Listener. Step 6 configures the listener on port 80 to include the virtual directory for the new service. When the listener receives a request for a document in the virtual directory, it will know to use the new service. Step 7 restarts the Web listener so the new changes take effect. Steps 8 through 10 demonstrate the new service by creating a simple dynamic document in the WAITE user account and displaying it in a browser.

Comments

Every application should not connect to the same user account in the database. If you are using WebServer for more than one application, you will want to create at least one service for each application. Since the server controls which user account connects to the database, it also controls which objects in the database the user can access. If you must create multiple services, refer to How-To 20.6 for an important technique that saves database space.

COMPLEXITY
INTERMEDIATE

20.3 How do I...
Create an error page for the Web Agent?

Problem

When the Web Agent encounters an error processing a document, I want to present the users with a custom error page for each service. Since different services are used by different groups of people within the organization, I want to create a different error page for each application. How do I create an error page to handle Web Agent errors?

Technique

The Oracle WebServer lets you create customized error pages for each service. Each service can contain only one error page, and its location is managed by the Web Agent Administration screen. Anytime the Web Agent encounters an error while executing or finding a stored procedure, the error page for the service is displayed and the error logged to a file. The error page displayed is a standard HTML file stored on the file system containing links to other Web documents.

Steps

1. Copy ERROR.html from the \SAMPLES\CHAP20 directory on the accompanying CD-ROM to the C:\ORANT\OWS10 directory. The file contains an error document to be displayed anytime a Web Agent error is encountered.

2. Load a browser and retrieve the default document for the administrator service by referencing the http://localhost:9999/ URL. Page down through the document until the options linking to other documents are displayed.

3. Select the Oracle WebServer Administration link to display the WebServer Administration form used to administer Oracle WebServer.

4. Choose The Oracle Web Agent link to display the Web Agent Administration screen used to maintain services. Page down through the document until you reach the end displaying the names of the existing services and the Create New Service options.

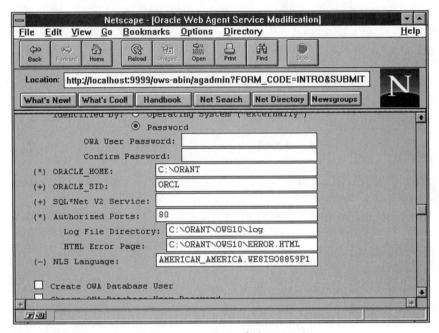

Figure 20-13 The parameter section of the service modification document

5. Select the OWA_DEFAULT_SERVICE link to modify the default service for the listener. Enter the full pathname of the HTML document into the HTML Error Page: field. Figure 20-13 shows the page with an entry for the sample document.

Once the error document is entered, select the MODIFY SERVER button to process the change. If the directory does not exist, the changes will fail. A success document is displayed once the changes are successfully made. In the next step, an invalid document is referenced, causing the error document to be displayed.

6. Enter an invalid dynamic page for the default service to display the error document. Figure 20-14 shows the error document displayed within the browser.

The error document referenced in the service's administration screen is displayed when an invalid dynamic document is referenced. Since the virtual directory in the URL identified the document as a dynamic document, the error was handled by the Web Agent.

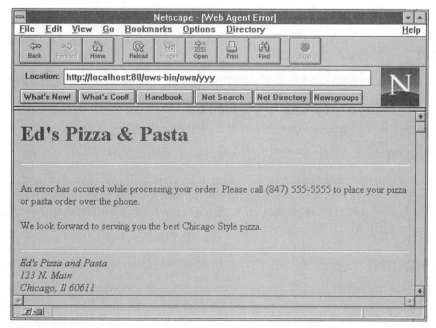

Figure 20-14 The error document generated by the Web Agent

How It Works

An error page can be created for each service with the Oracle Web Agent Administration document. Anytime the Web Agent encounters an error processing a request, the error document defined for the service is displayed. The error document is contained in a file on the file system, and only one error page can be defined per service. Step 1 copies a sample error document from the accompanying CD-ROM to a directory on the file system. Steps 2 through 4 navigate through the administration documents until the OWA_DEFAULT_SERVICE is modified by the Web Agent Administration document. Step 5 defines an error document for the default service by specifying its location in the Error Page: field and selecting the MODIFY DOCUMENT button. Step 6 generates an error to display the document by attempting to reference an invalid document.

Comments

A custom error document should be created for each service so that an informational message is displayed when an error occurs. The document should either contain information the user needs to resolve the problem or links to other documents.

20.4 How do I...
Display errors encountered by the Web Agent?

Problem

When errors occur within the PL/SQL procedures generating Web documents, I need to display the errors. When an error occurs, the user sees the error page for the service but is unable to give me any information about them. How do I display errors encountered by the Web Agent?

Technique

Each service writes errors to its own file in the \OWS10\LOGS directory under ORACLE_HOME. The name of the error log file is service_name.ERR. Each time an error occurs, information is appended to the end of the file. The log file can be displayed or printed to show detailed information about the errors which occurred for the service.

Steps

1. Open Windows Notepad and choose File|Open to open a file. The C:\ORANT\OWS10\LOGS directory contains log files from a default installation.

2. Open the OWA_DEFAULT_SERVER.err file to display the errors which occurred in the default service. Figure 20-15 shows the error log file displayed in Windows Notepad.

The three errors shown in Figure 20-15 occurred due to execution problems with a stored procedure. Each time the errors occurred, the error document for the service was displayed. The information within the error log file is helpful for correcting the problem.

How It Works

Each error occurring during the execution of a procedure by the Web Agent is logged in an error file for the service. The file contains detailed information about the error. If the error is a PL/SQL error, it contains the Oracle error generated by the module. If the Web Agent is processing a form, all of the parameters passed to the processing procedure are displayed in the file. Step 1 opens the error file from the default service contained in the C:\ORANT\OWS10\LOGS directory, showing the errors that occurred.

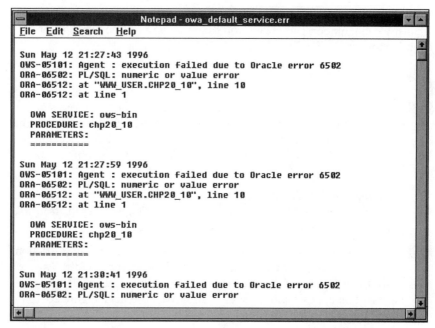

Figure 20-15 A Web Agent error log file in Windows Notepad

Comments

If you develop complex applications using many forms and stored procedures, you may need to view the error log to debug the application. The error log file gives you important information for debugging your application.

COMPLEXITY
INTERMEDIATE

20.5 How do I...
Create a new Web listener?

Problem

I want to create a new Web listener that listens for requests on a different port. I want to keep certain Web applications totally separate, and to do this, I want them to be processed by different Web listeners. How do I create a new Web listener?

Technique

A new Web listener is created using the Web Listener Administration screen. When you create a new listener, you must name it, assign a port number to listen on, and specify an administration and root directory. After the listener is created, there are many configuration parameters you can modify in order to change the listener's behavior.

Steps

1. Load your Web browser and open the default page for the administration service by specifying the http://localhost:9999/ URL. The 9999 port is the listener port for the administration user account for default installations. Choose the WebServer Administration link to enter the administration screen.

From this screen, you can choose to perform Oracle database administration tasks, Web listener tasks, and Web Agent tasks. In order to create a new Web listener, the Web Listener link is chosen.

2. Choose the Web Listener link from the Oracle WebServer Administration screen to display the Oracle Web Listener Administration screen. Page down to the bottom of the screen where the Create New Oracle Web Listener link appears with a list of existing Web listeners. Figure 20-16 shows this area of the page in Netscape Navigator.

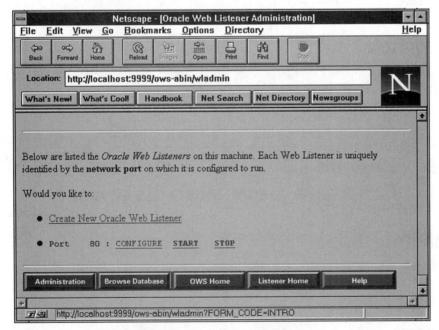

Figure 20-16 The Web Listener Administration screen

From this area of the page, you can choose to create a new Web listener or configure, start, or stop an existing one.

3. Choose the Create New Oracle Web Listener link to display the Oracle Web Listener Administration Server Creation screen shown in Figure 20-17.

Four fields are required to create a new listener. Fill in the form with the values specified in Table 20-2 to create a new listener for the 8000 port.

FIELD	VALUE
Host Name	Waite
Port Number	8000
Configuration Directory	C:\ORANT\OWS10\admin
Web Listener "/" Directory	C:\ORANT\OWS10\doc

Table 20-2 New listener configuration parameters

The Host Name field specifies the name of the listener. The port number field specifies the port which the listener listens on. The range of available ports are 0 to 65535. Any port number below 1024 requires super user privileges to be created. The directories specified for the configuration, Web

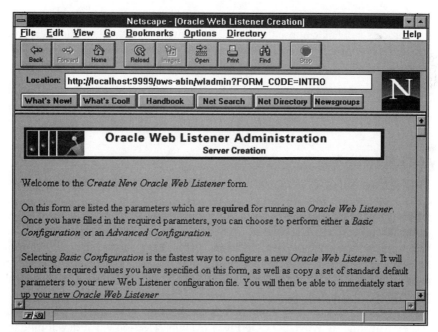

Figure 20-17 The Oracle Web Listener Administration Server Creation screen

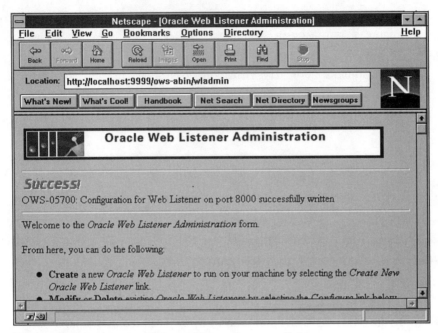

Figure 20-18 A successful creation of a new listener

listener configuration, and root directories must exist, or the creation process will fail. Choose the BASIC CONFIGURATION button to create the listener. Once the listener is created, a success message will be display like the one shown in Figure 20-18.

You may choose the ADVANCED CONFIGURATION button when creating the new listener to configure all the available parameters.

How It Works

A new listener process can be created using the administration documents developed by the installation process. The port 9999 is the administration listener process by default. Selecting the default page for the administration listener allows you to perform administration tasks. A new listener process is created through the Web Agent Administration screen. To begin creating a new listener, choose the Create New Web Listener link. Each listener process must be given a unique name and port number. When the BASIC CONFIGURATION selection is chosen, most of the default parameters are generated for the new service. Any of the parameters can be modified by choosing CONFIGURE from the Web Listener Administration screen, or initially created using the ADVANCED CONFIGURATION selection when developing the listener.

Comments

You can create a new Web listener to handle applications which need a completely different configuration from the default applications. When you create a new listener, you need to create at least one new service to handle requests for dynamic documents. Many of the advanced configuration parameters are very confusing. If you do not have a strong understanding of Web services and the CGI specification, you are better off choosing the basic configuration.

COMPLEXITY
INTERMEDIATE

20.6 How do I...
Use a single copy of the Developer's Toolkit with multiple services?

Problem

I want to use multiple services within my WebServer installation, but I do not want to have a copy of the Developer's Toolkit for each one. When a new service is formed, it asks to create the Developer's Toolkit packages in the user account represented by it. The four packages created are very large, and I do not want to waste space by having one copy for each service. How do I use a single copy of the Developer's Toolkit with multiple services?

Technique

The Developer's Toolkit can be installed in one user's schema, and privileges can be granted on the packages to all user accounts referenced by the services. There are four packages which contain the procedures and functions of the Developer's Toolkit. They are HTP, HTF, OWA, and OWA_UTIL. Granting the EXECUTE privilege on these packages to a user account and creating private synonyms to reference them is the same as creating a new copy of the packages. If the Toolkit is already installed in a user account's schema, it can be replaced by synonyms without impacting your existing applications.

Steps

1. Ensure that the Developer's Toolkit is installed in at least one user's schema. When the Oracle WebServer is first installed, the WWW_USER user account containing the Developer's Toolkit packages is created.

2. Run SQL*Plus and connect as a user account that you want to have access to the packages. For demonstration purposes, connect as the WAITE user account. If the packages exist in the user account's schema, you will first have to remove them. CHP20-2.sql, shown in Figure 20-19, drops the packages from the current user's schema if they exist.

A DROP PACKAGE statement is contained in the script for each of the four packages making up the Developer's Toolkit. Run the file to remove the packages.

```
SQL>   START CHP20-2

Package Dropped.

Package Dropped.

Package Dropped.

Package Dropped.
```

3. Once the packages are removed, they must be replaced by synonyms with the same name. CHP20-3.sql, shown in Figure 20-20, creates private synonyms for each of the packages.

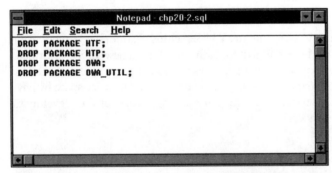

Figure 20-19 CHP20-2.sql removes the Developer's Toolkit packages from the current schema

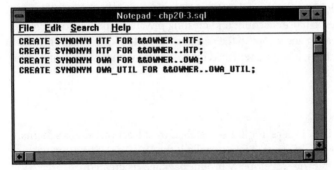

Figure 20-20 CHP20-3.sql creates private synonyms to reference the shared packages

The &&OWNER substitution variable identifies the owner of the shared set of packages. Run the file providing WWW_USER as the &&OWNER substitution variable.

```
SQL>  START CHP20-3

Enter value for owner: WWW_USER
old   1: CREATE SYNONYM HTF FOR &&OWNER..HTF
new   1: CREATE SYNONYM HTF FOR WWW_USER.HTF

Synonym created.

old   1: CREATE SYNONYM HTP FOR &&OWNER..HTP
new   1: CREATE SYNONYM HTP FOR WWW_USER.HTP

Synonym created.

old   1: CREATE SYNONYM OWA FOR &&OWNER..OWA
new   1: CREATE SYNONYM OWA FOR WWW_USER.OWA

Synonym created.

old   1: CREATE SYNONYM OWA_UTIL FOR &&OWNER..OWA_UTIL
new   1: CREATE SYNONYM OWA_UTIL FOR WWW_USER.OWA_UTIL

Synonym created.
```

Although the synonyms referencing the shared packages are created, EXECUTE privileges must be granted to the user account so it can run the procedures and functions contained in the packages.

4. Connect to the owner of the packages. In most cases, the WWW_USER account is the owner created when Oracle WebServer is installed. CHP20-4.sql, shown in Figure 20-21, grants the EXECUTE privilege on the packages to a user account.

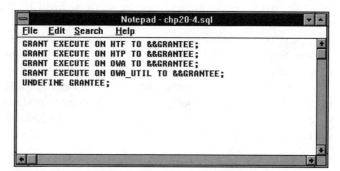

Figure 20-21 CHP20-4.sql grants EXECUTE privileges on the Developer's Toolkit packages to a user account

The &&GRANTEE substitution variable identifies the user account receiving the privileges. Run the file providing the WAITE user account for the substitution variables.

```
SQL>   START CHP20-4
Enter value for grantee: WAITE
old    1: GRANT EXECUTE ON HTF TO &&GRANTEE
new    1: GRANT EXECUTE ON HTF TO WAITE

Grant succeeded.

old    1: GRANT EXECUTE ON HTP TO &&GRANTEE
new    1: GRANT EXECUTE ON HTP TO WAITE

Grant succeeded.

old    1: GRANT EXECUTE ON OWA TO &&GRANTEE
new    1: GRANT EXECUTE ON OWA TO WAITE

Grant succeeded.

old    1: GRANT EXECUTE ON OWA_UTIL TO &&GRANTEE
new    1: GRANT EXECUTE ON OWA_UTIL TO WAITE

Grant succeeded.
```

By granting EXECUTE privileges to the user account in this step and creating private synonyms in the previous one, the user account can execute all the procedures and functions that are part of the Developer's Toolkit packages.

How It Works

The Developer's Toolkit packages can be installed in a single user account and shared by other user accounts represented by services. EXECUTE privileges must be granted on the four packages to each user account that needs them. Synonyms must be created for each of the packages to reference the shared packages in the owner's schema. Step 2 presents a SQL script for removing the Developer's Toolkit packages from a user account. Before the shared packages can be used, copies must be removed from the user account's schema. Step 3 presents a SQL script to create private synonyms for each package, in order to reference the shared set of packages in the owner's schema. Step 4 presents a SQL script which grants EXECUTE privileges on the four packages to a user account.

Comments

If you will be using multiple services with your Web applications, you should use this technique. The Developer's Toolkit packages are very large, and you should not maintain multiple copies of them in your environment. If you are using the procedures displaying source code or accessing tables directly, one exception would be the OWA_UTIL package. Since a stored procedure executes as its owner, certain OWA_UTIL procedures will provide invalid information because the wrong user account will be used.

HANDLING ERROR MESSAGES

This appendix covers common error messages that may occur when working with Oracle. Many of the error messages returned by Oracle do not adequately describe the error and the solution to the problem. Each error covered in this appendix contains the reasons the error occurs and the action taken to correct it.

ORA-00054: resource busy and acquire with NOWAIT specified

Problem

The resource you attempted to lock with a LOCK table or a SELECT FOR UPDATE statement is busy. In your statement, you specified the NOWAIT option. Had NOWAIT not been specified, the statement would wait for the resource to become available.

Solution

You can try the operation later. If you are the only user account working with the resource, it is possible you have another session locking the table. It you terminated a session performing an operation on the resource, the lock may not have been cleared.

ORA-00901: invalid CREATE command

Problem

In your statement, you attempted to create an object that is not valid. It is easy to type CREATE instead of GRANT or some other command. It is possible you misspelled the object you were attempting to create. Misspelling an object or using CREATE instead of the right statement will cause this error.

Example

It is easy to misspell the object you are attempting to create. Misspelling the object name will generate the error.

Incorrect:: `CREATE TABEL X (Y NUMBER);`
Correct: `CREATE TABLE X (Y NUMBER);`

Trying to CREATE something which should be GRANTed will also generate this error.

Incorrect: `CREATE ALL ON DEPT TO PUBLIC;`
Correct: `GRANT ALL ON DEPT TO PUBLIC;`

Solution

Look closely at the statement. You probably misspelled the object you are trying to create or used the wrong command. If the type of object you are trying to create is not valid, this error will occur.

ORA-00910: specified length too long for its datatype

Problem

The length you specified for a datatype in a CREATE TABLE or ALTER TABLE statement is invalid. This error will occur when an invalid length is specified for a character column. The maximum length for a VARCHAR2 datatype is 2,000.

Example

The character column defined in a CREATE TABLE statement must be of a valid length. If the length specified is not valid, the error will occur.

Incorrect: `CREATE TABLE TEST (G VARCHAR2(3000));`
Correct: `CREATE TABLE TEST (G VARCHAR2(2000));`

Solution

Analyze each of the columns in your CREATE TABLE or ALTER TABLE statement to ensure that the length specified for each of the columns is valid.

ORA-00913: too many values

Problem

Your statement requires that the number of values specified is equal to the number of values required. This error can occur in an INSERT statement in which you specify more values than there are columns. The error can also occur in sub-queries that are part of a WHERE or HAVING clause.

Example

In an INSERT statement, the number of values provided must be the same as the number of columns in the column list. This error will occur if more columns are provided than the column list contains.

```
Incorrect:   INSERT INTO DEPT (DEPT_NO, DEPT_NAME) VALUES (1,'TEST',32);
Correct:     INSERT INTO DEPT (DEPT_NO, DEPT_NAME) VALUES (1,'TEST');
Correct:     INSERT INTO DEPT (DEPT_NO, DEPT_NAME, MGR_ID)
                                        VALUES (1,'TEST',32);
```

Within a sub-query for an UPDATE statement, the number of values returned by the sub-query must equal the number of columns being updated. In both incorrect statements, the number of columns returned by the sub-query exceeds the number expected.

```
Incorrect:   UPDATE DEPT SET DEPT_NO = (SELECT DEPT_NO, DNAME FROM TEMP);
Correct:     UPDATE DEPT SET DEPT_NO = (SELECT DEPT_NO FROM TEMP);

Incorrect:   UPDATE DEPT SET (DEPT_NO, DEPT_NAME) =
                                        (SELECT DEPT_NO, DEPT_NAME,
MGR_ID FROM TEMP);
Correct:     UPDATE DEPT SET (DEPT_NO, DEPT_NAME) =
                                        (SELECT DEPT_NO, DEPT_NAME
FROM TEMP);
```

The error can also occur in the WHERE clause of a statement. If a sub-query is used in a WHERE clause, it must equal the number of columns expected.

```
Incorrect:   SELECT DEPT_NAME FROM DEPT
                                WHERE DEPT_NO IN (SELECT DEPT_NO,
MGR_ID FROM DEPT_LIST);
Correct:     SELECT DEPT_NAME FROM DEPT
                                WHERE DEPT_NO IN (SELECT DEPT_NO FROM
DEPT_LIST);
```

Solution

If your statement is an INSERT statement, count the number of columns specified in the column list and match it with the number of columns provided in the VALUES clause or the query. For statements with sub-queries, match the number of columns expected by the sub-query with the number actually returned.

ORA-00918: column ambiguously defined

Problem

Within a query that contains at least two tables, columns with the same name occur in more than one table. If a column that exists in more than one table is specified anywhere in the statement, it must be prefixed with the table name or this error will occur.

Example

In this example, the MGR_NO column exists in both tables used in the query. The column must be prefixed with the table name or alias if used in the query.

Incorrect: SELECT MGR_NO FROM DEPT, EMP
                        WHERE DEPT.EMP_NO = EMP.EMP_NO;
Correct: SELECT DEPT.MGR_NO FROM DEPT, EMP
                        WHERE DEPT.EMP_NO = EMP.EMP_NO;

The error will occur if the duplicate column name is found anywhere in the statement. In this example, a duplicate column name is found in the WHERE clause.

Incorrect: SELECT DEPT.MGR_NO FROM DEPT, EMP
                        WHERE DEPT.EMP_NO = EMP_NO;
Correct: SELECT DEPT.MGR_NO FROM DEPT, EMP
                        WHERE DEPT.EMP_NO = EMP.EMP_NO;

Solution

It is good practice to specify the table name with the column name throughout the statement. It can be easy to lose track of column names and define columns ambiguously. Look through your code for columns that may be duplicates. If it is not obvious, specify a table name for all columns. This will quickly correct the problem.

ORA-00932: inconsistent datatypes

Problem

You are attempting to perform an operation on two columns of different datatypes. The error occurs frequently when you attempt to use character functions with LONG columns. Whenever possible, Oracle performs type conversions to make the operation successful.

Example

The error will occur if you attempt to add a character to a date column. Since Oracle cannot perform this operation, the error occurs.

Incorrect: SELECT DATEFLD + 'X' FROM TABLENAME;

Correct: `SELECT DATEFLD + 1 FROM TABLENAME;`

The error will occur if you attempt any character functions on a LONG column.

Incorrect: `SELECT SUBSTR(LONGCOL,1,20) FROM TABLENAME;`
Incorrect: `SELECT LONGCOL||CHARCOL FROM TABLENAME;`

Solution

Analyze the expressions in your statement. Use functions such as TO_CHAR, TO_NUMBER, and TO_DATE to ensure the datatypes are consistent across the statement.

ORA-00934: group function is not allowed here

Problem

You are attempting to use a group function in a WHERE clause. Group functions such as MAX, MIN, COUNT, and AVG cannot be used in a WHERE clause. The HAVING clause can be used to achieve the desired effect. You cannot use group functions as the join condition of a WHERE clause.

Example

Attempting to use a group function in a WHERE clause will cause this error. The error can be removed by moving the group function into the HAVING clause. The following example queries items where the highest price is greater than 25.

Incorrect: `SELECT ITEM_NO, MAX(PRICE)`
                        `FROM ITEMS WHERE`
                        `MAX(PRICE) > 25`
               `GROUP BY ITEM_NO;`
Correct: `SELECT ITEM_NO, MAX(PRICE)`
                        `FROM ITEMS`
               `GROUP BY ITEM_NO`
               `HAVING MAX(PRICE) > 25;`

Solution

Search for group functions in the WHERE clause. Remove the function from the WHERE clause and add a HAVING clause to achieve the same result.

ORA-00936: missing expression

Problem

You are missing part of the expression expected by Oracle. In a SELECT statement, you may be missing the column list. If you are using math operators, you may be missing part of the operator. These errors are usually caused by incorrectly typing the statement.

Example

Within a SELECT statement, the columns must be listed. If they are not, the error will occur.

Incorrect: `SELECT FROM DEPT;`
Correct: `SELECT DEPT_NO FROM DEPT;`

In a math expression, the entire expression must be entered correctly. If any part of the expression is missing, this error will occur.

Incorrect: `SELECT NUMFLD + FROM TABLENAME;`
Correct: `SELECT NUMFLD + 1 FROM TABLENAME;`

Solution

Errors of this type are usually obvious. Analyze your statement looking for a malformed expression. Pay close attention to the select list and math operations.

ORA-00937: not a single-group group function

Problem

Your select list contains both group functions and single value functions, and you have not specified a GROUP BY clause. If your select list uses functions like AVG, COUNT, MAX, MIN, SUM, or STDDEV, along with value columns, a GROUP BY clause must exist or this error will occur.

Example

This example shows a single value column as part of the same select list as a GROUP BY function. Since no GROUP BY clause is specified, the error occurs.

Incorrect: `SELECT DEPT_NO, COUNT(*) FROM DEPT;`
Correct: `SELECT DEPT_NO, COUNT(*) FROM DEPT GROUP BY DEPT_NO;`

Solution

Create a GROUP BY clause in your statement and list all of the nongroup expressions after the GROUP BY keywords.

ORA-00938: not enough arguments for a function

Problem

You are attempting to call a function that requires more arguments than you specified. If you do not specify enough arguments, this error will occur.

Solution

Review each of the function calls in the code segment where the error exists to verify the number of parameters the function requires. The ALL_SOURCE data dictionary view can be used to view the source that created the function.

ORA-00942: table or view does not exist

Problem

One or more of the tables you are using in your statement does not exist, or you do not have privileges on the object. You may be referencing an object through a synonym that's no longer valid, or you may have spelled the object name wrong. If you are referencing an object in another schema on which you have no privileges, this error will occur.

Solution

Check the spelling of the object name. If you have spelled it correctly, verify that you have privileges on the object by using the ALL_TAB_PRIVS data dictionary view. If you are referencing a synonym, verify that the underlying object exists and you have privileges for it. You can check the ALL_SYNONYMS data dictionary view to verify the object the synonym references.

ORA-00947: not enough values?

Problem

In an INSERT statement, Oracle expects more values than you supplied. This can happen often if you do not specify column names in your INSERT statement. Make sure your VALUES clause contains the correct number of columns for the table.

Example

The error will occur if the table contains more columns than you specify and you do not list columns to be inserted. In this example, the table contains three columns.

```
Incorrect:    INSERT INTO TABLENAME VALUES (1,2);
Incorrect:    INSERT INTO TABLENAME
                    SELECT FLD1, FLD2 FROM OTHERTABLE;
Correct:      INSERT INTO TABLENAME VALUES (1,2,3);
Correct:      INSERT INTO TABLENAME
                    SELECT FLD1, FLD2, FLD3 FROM OTHERTABLE;
```

The error can also occur when column names are specified and the wrong number of columns are still specified.

```
Incorrect:    INSERT INTO TABLENAME (FLD1, FLD2) VALUES (1);
Incorrect:    INSERT INTO TABLENAME (FLD1, FLD2)
                                    SELECT FLD1 FROM OTHERTABLE;
Correct:      INSERT INTO TABLENAME (FLD1, FLD2) VALUES (1,2);
Correct:      INSERT INTO TABLENAME (FLD1, FLD2)
                                    SELECT FLD1, FLD2 FROM

OTHERTABLE;
```

Solution

Always specify column names when using an INSERT statement. If you do not specify column names and columns are added later, this error will occur. Look through your code for INSERT statements. Match the VALUES clause with the column list for the INSERT statement or the column list for the table.

ORA-00979: not a GROUP BY expression

Problem

Within your query, you are using a GROUP BY expression such as SUM, COUNT, MIN, or MAX. One or more of the columns in your query are not group expressions. If a column is included in a query with group functions, it must be listed in the GROUP BY clause of the SELECT statement. If you specify a column that's not a GROUP BY expression with columns that are and do not list the column in a GROUP BY clause, this error will occur.

Example

In this example, the DEPT_NO column is included in the select list with the COUNT GROUP BY function. If a GROUP BY clause is not included, the error will occur.

```
Incorrect:    SELECT DEPT_NO, COUNT(*) FROM DEPT;
Correct:      SELECT DEPT_NO, COUNT(*) FROM DEPT
                                    GROUP BY DEPT_NO;
```

If there are multiple columns which are not GROUP BY expressions, each must be listed in the GROUP BY clause.

Incorrect:
```
SELECT DEPT_NO, MGR_NO, COUNT(*) FROM DEPT
                               GROUP BY DEPT_NO;
```
Correct:
```
SELECT DEPT_NO, MGR_NO, COUNT(*) FROM DEPT
                               GROUP BY DEPT_NO, MGR_NO;
```

Solution

This is a very common error when using GROUP BY expressions. It can also be very hard to find when your queries become complex. Be sure to list all of your non-GROUP BY columns in a GROUP BY clause. Any time you use a combination of GROUP BY and non-GROUP BY columns in a single query, you must remember the GROUP BY clause or this error will occur.

ORA-00980: synonym translation no longer valid

Problem

You are attempting to use a synonym which does not reference a valid object. If you remove the object referenced by a synonym and attempt to reference the synonym, this error will occur.

Solution

How-To 7.3 presents a method to determine the object a synonym references. How-To 7-4 presents a method to delete all invalid synonyms from a user's schema. Delete the synonym and re-create it referencing the valid object.

ORA-01031: insufficient privileges

Problem

You are attempting an operation for which you do not have privileges. If you are attempting a data manipulation operation on an object you have only SELECT privileges on, this error will occur.

Solution

You can check your privileges on a table by using the USER_TAB_PRIVS data dictionary view. If you do not have privileges on an object, contact the database administrator to receive the privileges required.

ORA-01400: primary key or mandatory (NOT NULL) column is missing during insert

Problem

You have attempted to insert a record into a table with one or more mandatory NOT NULL columns missing. Every column with a NOT NULL constraint must be provided when a record is inserted.

Solution

Review the INSERT statement to ensure all mandatory columns have been provided. The SQL*Plus DESCRIBE command can be used to view which columns are required during the INSERT.

ORA-01401: inserted value too large for column

Problem

One or more of the values specified by an INSERT or UPDATE statement is larger than the column allows. The maximum width for a column is specified when the column is created.

Solution

Review the statement, looking for the column value which is too large for the column. Users can query the size of the columns from the ALL_TAB_COLUMNS data dictionary view or use the DESCRIBE command in SQL*Plus. If you find the data is valid for the record, the length of the column can be made larger using the ALTER TABLE statement with a MODIFY clause. Ensure your application does not allow users to enter values larger than the column can handle. This is a common error in Developer 2000 applications when the default column length is used in text items.

ORA-01452: cannot create unique index; duplicate keys found

Problem

When attempting to create a unique index on a table, Oracle found duplicate keys. A unique index can only be created when there are no duplicate key fields. Creating a primary key on a table also requires the key fields to be unique.

Solution

How-To 8-6 presents a method for deleting duplicate rows from a table. If the column list specified in the CREATE UNIQUE INDEX statement contains duplicate rows, change the statement to CREATE INDEX to create a non-unique index.

ORA-01830: date format picture ends before converting entire input string

Problem

You are using a date string which is not in the default format of Oracle dates. If you attempt to insert a value into a date field and the format is longer than the default format, this error will occur.

Example

The following statement causes an error because the date column is specified in the format DD-MON-YYYY. The default format for Oracle dates is DD-MON-YY. The column must either be specified in the default format or formatted with the TO_DATE function.

```
Incorrect:   INSERT INTO TABLENAME (DTEFLD) VALUES ('01-JAN-1996');
Correct:     INSERT INTO TABLENAME (DATEFLD) VALUES ('01-JAN-96');
Correct:     INSERT INTO TABLENAME (DATEFLD)
                 VALUES (TO_DATE('01-JAN-1996','DD-MON-YYYY'));
```

The same error can occur in an UPDATE statement if a date column specified a value in the wrong date format.

```
Incorrect:   UPDATE TABLENAME SET DTEFLD = '01-JAN-1996';
Correct:     UPDATE TABLENAME SET DTEFLD = '01-JAN-96';
Correct:     UPDATE TABLENAME SET DTEFLD = TO_DATE('01-JAN-1996', ⇐
'DD-MON-YYYY');
```

The error can also occur when date strings are used in the WHERE clause of a statement.

```
Incorrect:   SELECT * FROM TABLENAME WHERE DTEFLD = '01-JAN-1996';
Correct:     SELECT * FROM TABLENAME WHERE DTEFLD = '01-JAN-96';
Correct:     SELECT * FROM TABLENAME
                 WHERE DTEFLD = TO_DATE('01-JAN-1996', ⇐
'DD-MON-YY');
```

Solution

Search your statement for date strings. Anywhere a column of the date datatype is set to a constant is a candidate for this error. Look for date columns and date constants. If you want to specify a date constant using a non-default format, use the TO_DATE function to specify the format of the date.

ORA-01840: input value not long enough for date format

Problem

You are using a date string which is not in the default format of Oracle dates. If you attempt to insert a value into a date field and the format is shorter than the default format, this error will occur.

Example

The following statement causes an error because the date constant is missing the year portion. In order to correct the problem, either specify the date in the default format or use the TO_DATE function to identify the date format.

Incorrect: INSERT INTO TABLENAME (DTEFLD) VALUES ('01-JAN');
Correct: INSERT INTO TABLENAME (DTEFLD) VALUES ('01-JAN-96');
Correct: INSERT INTO TABLENAME (DTEFLD) VALUES TO_DATE('01-JAN', ⇐
'DD-MON');

The same error can occur when a format string is specified with the TO_DATE function.

Incorrect: UPDATE TABLENAME SET DTEFLD = TO_DATE('01/01/9','MM/DD/YY');
Correct: UPDATE TABLENAME SET DTEFLD = TO_DATE('01/01/96','MM/DD/YY');

Solution

Search your statement for date strings. Anywhere a column of the date datatype is set to a constant is a candidate for this error. Look for date columns and date constants. If you want to specify a date constant using a non-default format, use the TO_DATE function to specify the format of the date. When using the TO_DATE function, make sure the format mask specifies the format of the date string.

TOOLS ON THE ACCOMPANYING CD-ROM

The CD-ROM accompanying this book includes, among other things, free 90-day trial versions of several Oracle products. These products enable you to follow the examples in the book, even if you do not currently have access to Oracle products. Oracle trial software contained on the CD-ROM includes

- Personal Oracle7 for Windows
- Personal Oracle7 for Windows 95
- Oracle WebServer for Solaris
- Oracle WebServer for Windows NT
- Oracle Power Browser for Windows 3.1, Windows NT, and Windows 95

If you are interested in other Oracle trial software currently available, visit Oracle's Web site at *http://www.oracle.com*.

In addition to the Oracle products, the CD-ROM contains an HTML to Oracle WebServer conversion utility that I developed called Kava 1.0. I am working on many other utilities and will make them available on my Web site, *http:// www.sdcnet.com*. These are free for you to download.

Each product contained on the CD-ROM must be installed individually. There is a README.TXT file in the root directory of the CD-ROM, which will alert you to any updates made at the last minute. Table B-1 shows the location of all directories on the CD-ROM.

DIRECTORY	CONTENTS
KAVA10	Kava HTML to WebServer conversion utility
ORACLE	
PO7WIN	Personal Oracle7 for Windows 3.1
INSTALL	Installation directory for Personal Oracle7 for Windows 3.1
PO7WIN95	Personal Oracle7 for Windows 95
INSTALL	Installation directory for Personal Oracle7 for Windows 95
WEBSOL	Oracle WebServer for Solaris
INSTALL	Installation directory for Oracle WebServer for Solaris
WEBNT	Oracle WebServer for Windows NT
INSTALL	Installation directory for Oracle WebServer for Windows NT
POWERBR	Oracle Power Browser for Windows 3.1, Windows NT, and Windows 95
INSTALL	Installation directory for Oracle Power Browser
SOURCE	
CHAP01	Example code - Chapter 1
CHAP02	Example code - Chapter 2
CHAP03	Example code - Chapter 3
CHAP04	Example code - Chapter 4
CHAP05	Example code - Chapter 5
CHAP06	Example code - Chapter 6
CHAP07	Example code - Chapter 7
CHAP08	Example code - Chapter 8
CHAP09	Example code - Chapter 9
CHAP10	Example code - Chapter 10
CHAP11	Example code - Chapter 11
CHAP12	Example code - Chapter 12
CHAP13	Example code - Chapter 13
CHAP14	Example code - Chapter 14
CHAP15	Example code - Chapter 15
CHAP16	Example code - Chapter 16
CHAP17	Example code - Chapter 17
CHAP18	Example code - Chapter 18
CHAP19	Example code - Chapter 19
CHAP20	Example code - Chapter 20

Table B-1 CD-ROM directory listing

Each product is installed from its installation directory by running SETUP.EXE. The appropriate installation program will run for the product you are installing. You should exit any other programs before running the installation programs. The system requirements for the Oracle software are listed here.

System Requirements—Personal Oracle7 for Windows

- An IBM, COMPAQ, or 100% compatible PC, based on 80486 or Pentium CPU
- 16 MB RAM
- At least 50 MB free hard disk space
- Microsoft Windows 3.1 or Windows for Workgroups 3.1
- Win32s

System Requirements—Personal Oracle7 for Windows 95

- An IBM, COMPAQ, or 100% compatible PC, based on 80486 or Pentium CPU
- 16 MB RAM
- Between 40 MB and 80 MB free hard disk space, depending on options installed
- Microsoft Windows 95

NOTE

This product does not run on Windows NT.

System Requirements—Oracle WebServer for Solaris

- SPARC processor
- 64 MB of RAM
- 200 MB of hard disk space
- 64 MB of swap space
- CD-ROM in the RockRidge format
- Solaris 2.4 with X Window, and Motif or Open Windows
- Any Web browser that supports tables and forms

System Requirements—Oracle WebServer for Windows NT

- A minimum of 16 MB of RAM; 32MB recommended
- 65 MB of free hard disk space

- A compatible network interface card (NIC) for networked operation
- Microsoft Windows NT Workstation V3.51 or Microsoft Windows NT Server V3.51

System Requirements—Oracle Power Browser

- An IBM, COMPAQ, or 100% compatible PC with 80386SX, 80386 processor or higher
- 12 MB RAM
- 7 MB of free disk space
- Microsoft Windows V3.11, NT, or Windows 95

INDEX

Symbols

%ROWTYPE attribute, 429-431
%TYPE attribute, 429-431
(%) pattern matching operator
(&) ampersand, database links, 370-372
(+) addition operator, 332-334
(-) subtraction operator, 332-334

A

ACCEPT command, 31
accessing
  ad hoc query tools, restricting, 102-104
  CGI environmental variables for Web applications, 697-700

achieving array functionality in tables, 432-434
active user accounts, determining, 62-63
ad hoc query tools, access, restricting, 102-104
ADD CONSTRAINT clause, 141
ADD PRIMARY KEY clause, 144-145
adding statements in SQL buffer, 8
ADD_MONTHS function, 334
administering object privileges in Web pages, 712-720
alerts, databases notification, 482-487
  DBMS_ALERT package, 482-487
ALL_COL_COMMENTS data dictionary, 120-123
ALL_COL_COMMENTS view, 118-119
ad-hoc query tools, restricting, 102-104
ALL_INDEXESdata dictionary, 559
ALL_SEQUENCES view, 192-193
ALL_SNAPSHOTS view, 385-389
ALL_SYNONYMS data dictionary, 206-213

F

fast refresh, defined, 383
FEEDBACK system variable, 36
FETCH statement, 424-428
files
    logging, SQL script progress, 33-35
    operating system, writing, 496-498
    query results, saving, 20-22
    saving SQL statements, 6-8
    UTL_FILE package, 496-498
first letter, strings, capitalizing, 345-347
FLUSH system variable, modifyiing, 23
FOR loop, 413-416
FOR UPDATE clause, 310-312
FORCE option, CREATE VIEW
    statement, 177-178
format masks
    J, 347-349
    JSP, 348-349
formatting
    checks, numbers as words, 347-349
    dates, 323-328
    reports in SQL*Plus, 24-30
    text on Web pages, 673-675
    time, 323-328
formatting commands, 30
forms (HTML),
    creating, 683-691
    HTP.FORMCLOSE procedure,
      684-691
    HTP.FORMOPEN procedure, 684-691
free extent, 137-139
functions
    ADD_MONTHS, 334
    CHARTTOROWID, 307-309

functions (*continued*)
    CONCAT, 342-344
    COUNT, 279-282
    CREATE FUNCTION statement,
      445-446
    CREATE PIPE, 490, 495
    CYCLE, 198
    DECODE, 133-137, 168-170,
      304-306
    DECRYPT, 101
    ENCRYPT, 101
    INITCAP , 345-347
    INSTR, 353-356
    LOWER, 356-357
    MAX, 139
    MONTHS_BETWEEN, 334
    NOCYCLE, 198
    NVL, 335-338
    OPEN_CURSOR, 166-167
    REPLACE, 353-356
    stored, creating, 444-446
    SUBSTR, 350-352
    SUM, 139
    TEST_CHECK, 167
    TO_CHAR, 324-330, 339-341
    TO_DATE, 225-228, 328
    TRANSLATE, 98-101
    UPPER, 356-357

G - H

generating Web pages
dynamic content, 662-664
Oracle WebServer, 659-661
GET command, loading, 19
GRANT statement, CREATE SESSION
privilege, 58-61
granting privileges to user accounts,
58-61
GRANT SESSION privilege, 60-61
group functions, returning records,
315-318
GROUP BY clause, 263-266
grouping data in logical groups, 263-266
handling
exceptions in PL/SQL, 404-409
LONG datatype (Oracle Objects),
645-648
user-defined errors in stored
procedures, 419-421
HAVING clause, 315-318
highlighting text in Web pages, 673-675
hints, optimizers, passing, 572-575
hit ratio, shared pools, calculating,
603-606
HTML (Hypertext Markup Language)
forms, creating, 683-691
IMG tag, 681-683
TABLE tag, 691-697
tables, displaying, 691-697
tags, lists, 676-679
HTP package
document body procedures, 669
form-related procedures, 674, 683
list-related procedures, 677

HTP package (*continued*)
Oracle WebServer, 660-661
print procedures, 660
table-related procedures, 691-697
HTP.ANCHOR procedure, 671-672
HTP.FORMCLOSE procedure, 684-691
HTP.FORMOPEN procedure, 684-691
HTP.FORMPASSWORD procedure,
700-704
HTP.HTMLCLOSE procedure, dynamic
Web pages, 663-665
HTP.HTMLOPEN procedure, dynamic
Web pages, 663-665

I - J - K

I/O contention
identifying, 584-586
V$DATAFILE view, 584-586
IDENTIFIED clause, 54
IDENTIFIED BY clause, passwords, 56
identifying
cache hit ratio in database buffers,
601-602
I/O contention in databases, 584-586
redo log contention, 592-594
rollback segment contention in data-
bases, 589-592
tablespace fragmentation, 595
IF...THEN...ELSE logic, performing with
DECODE function, 304-306
IF...THEN...ELSE statement, 410-412
images
IMGtag, 681-683
Web pages, implementing, 681-683
IMG tag, 681-683

S

T

779

Books have a substantial influence on the destruction of the forests of the Earth. For example, it takes 17 trees to produce one ton of paper. A first printing of 30,000 copies of a typical 480-page book consumes 108,000 pounds of paper, which will require 918 trees!

Waite Group Press™ is against the clear-cutting of forests and supports reforestation of the Pacific Northwest of the United States and Canada, where most of this paper comes from. As a publisher with several hundred thousand books sold each year, we feel an obligation to give back to the planet. We will therefore support organizations that seek to preserve the forests of planet Earth.

Message from the
Publisher

WELCOME TO OUR NERVOUS SYSTEM

Some people say that the World Wide Web is a graphical extension of the information superhighway, just a network of humans and machines sending each other long lists of the equivalent of digital junk mail.

I think it is much more than that. To me, the Web is nothing less than the nervous system of the entire planet—not just a collection of computer brains connected together, but more like a billion silicon neurons entangled and recirculating electro-chemical signals of information and data, each contributing to the birth of another CPU and another Web site.

Think of each person's hard disk connected at once to every other hard disk on earth, driven by human navigators searching like Columbus for the New World. Seen this way the Web is more of a super entity, a growing, living thing, controlled by the universal human will to expand, to be more. Yet, unlike a purposeful business plan with rigid rules, the Web expands in a nonlinear, unpredictable, creative way that echoes natural evolution.

We created our Web site not just to extend the reach of our computer book products but to be part of this synaptic neural network, to experience, like a nerve in the body, the flow of ideas and then to pass those ideas up the food chain of the mind. Your mind. Even more, we wanted to pump some of our own creative juices into this rich wine of technology.

TASTE OUR DIGITAL WINE

And so we ask you to taste our wine by visiting the body of our business. Begin by understanding the metaphor we have created for our Web site—a universal learning center, situated in outer space in the form of a space station. A place where you can journey to study any topic from the convenience of your own screen. Right now we are focusing on computer topics, but the stars are the limit on the Web.

If you are interested in discussing this Web site or finding out more about the Waite Group, please send me e-mail with your comments, and I will be happy to respond. Being a programmer myself, I love to talk about technology and find out what our readers are looking for.

Sincerely,

Mitchell Waite

Mitchell Waite, C.E.O. and Publisher

200 Tamal Plaza
Corte Madera, CA 94925
415-924-2575
415-924-2576 fax

Web site:
http://www.waite.com/waite

CREATING THE HIGHEST QUALITY COMPUTER BOOKS IN THE INDUSTRY

Waite Group Press

Come Visit
WAITE.COM
Waite Group Press
World Wide Web Site

Now find all the latest information on Waite Group books at our new Web site, **http://www.waite.com/waite.** You'll find an online catalog where you can examine and order any title, review upcoming books, and send e-mail to our authors and editors. Our FTP site has all you need to update your book: the latest program listings, errata sheets, most recent versions of Fractint, POV Ray, Polyray, DMorph, and all the programs featured in our books. So download, talk to us, ask questions, on **http://www.waite.com/waite.**

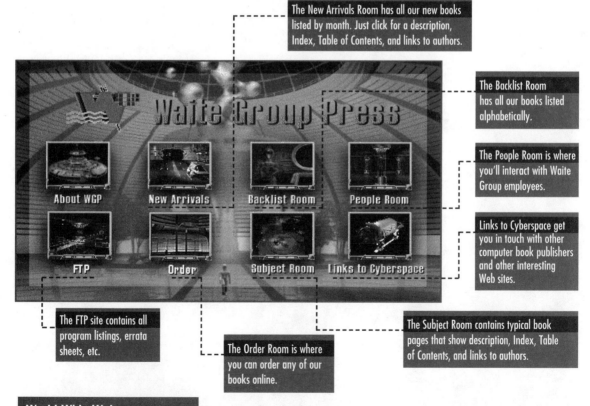

The New Arrivals Room has all our new books listed by month. Just click for a description, Index, Table of Contents, and links to authors.

The Backlist Room has all our books listed alphabetically.

The People Room is where you'll interact with Waite Group employees.

Links to Cyberspace get you in touch with other computer book publishers and other interesting Web sites.

The FTP site contains all program listings, errata sheets, etc.

The Order Room is where you can order any of our books online.

The Subject Room contains typical book pages that show description, Index, Table of Contents, and links to authors.

World Wide Web:

COME SURF OUR TURF—THE WAITE GROUP WEB

http://www.waite.com/waite
Gopher: gopher.waite.com
FTP: ftp.waite.com

LIMITED WARRANTY

The following warranties shall be effective for 90 days from the date of purchase: (i) The Waite Group, Inc. warrants the enclosed disk to be free of defects in materials and workmanship under normal use; and (ii) The Waite Group, Inc. warrants that the programs, unless modified by the purchaser, will substantially perform the functions described in the documentation provided by The Waite Group, Inc. when operated on the designated hardware and operating system. The Waite Group, Inc. does not warrant that the programs will meet purchaser's requirements or that operation of a program will be uninterrupted or error-free. The program warranty does not cover any program that has been altered or changed in any way by anyone other than The Waite Group, Inc. The Waite Group, Inc. is not responsible for problems caused by changes in the operating characteristics of computer hardware or computer operating systems that are made after the release of the programs, nor for problems in the interaction of the programs with each other or other software.

THESE WARRANTIES ARE EXCLUSIVE AND IN LIEU OF ALL OTHER WARRANTIES OF MERCHANTABILITY OR FITNESS FOR A PARTICULAR PURPOSE OR OF ANY OTHER WARRANTY, WHETHER EXPRESSED OR IMPLIED.

EXCLUSIVE REMEDY

The Waite Group, Inc., will replace any defective disk without charge if the defective disk is returned to The Waite Group, Inc. within 90 days from date of purchase.

This is Purchaser's sole and exclusive remedy for any breach of warranty or claim for contract, tort, or damages.

LIMITATION OF LIABILITY

THE WAITE GROUP, INC. AND THE AUTHORS OF THE PROGRAMS SHALL NOT IN ANY CASE BE LIABLE FOR SPECIAL, INCIDENTAL, CONSEQUENTIAL, INDIRECT, OR OTHER SIMILAR DAMAGES ARISING FROM ANY BREACH OF THESE WARRANTIES EVEN IF THE WAITE GROUP, INC. OR ITS AGENT HAS BEEN ADVISED OF THE POSSIBILITY OF SUCH DAMAGES.

THE LIABILITY FOR DAMAGES OF THE WAITE GROUP, INC. AND THE AUTHORS OF THE PROGRAMS UNDER THIS AGREEMENT SHALL IN NO EVENT EXCEED THE PURCHASE PRICE PAID.

COMPLETE AGREEMENT

This Agreement constitutes the complete agreement between The Waite Group, Inc. and the authors of the programs, and you, the purchaser.

Some states do not allow the exclusion or limitation of implied warranties or liability for incidental or consequential damages, so the above exclusions or limitations may not apply to you. This limited warranty gives you specific legal rights; you may have others, which vary from state to state.

SATISFACTION REPORT CARD

Please fill out this card if you wish to know of future updates to *Oracle How-To,* or to receive our catalog.

First Name: _____ **Last Name:** _____

Street Address: _____

City: _____ **State:** _____ **Zip:** _____

E-Mail Address _____

Daytime Telephone: (____) _____

Date product was acquired: Month _____ **Day** _____ **Year** _____ **Your Occupation:** _____

Overall, how would you rate *Oracle How-To?*
- ☐ Excellent ☐ Very Good ☐ Good
- ☐ Fair ☐ Below Average ☐ Poor

What did you like MOST about this book? _____
_____
_____

What did you like LEAST about this book? _____
_____
_____

Please describe any problems you may have encountered with installing or using the disk: _____
_____

How did you use this book (problem-solver, tutorial, reference...)?
_____

What is your level of computer expertise?
- ☐ New ☐ Dabbler ☐ Hacker
- ☐ Power User ☐ Programmer ☐ Experienced Professional

What computer languages are you familiar with? _____
_____

Please describe your computer hardware:
Computer _____ Hard disk _____
5.25" disk drives _____ 3.5" disk drives _____
Video card _____ Monitor _____
Printer _____ Peripherals _____
Sound Board _____ CD-ROM_____

Where did you buy this book?
- ☐ Bookstore (name): _____
- ☐ Discount store (name): _____
- ☐ Computer store (name): _____
- ☐ Catalog (name): _____
- ☐ Direct from WGP ☐ Other _____

What price did you pay for this book? _____

What influenced your purchase of this book?
- ☐ Recommendation ☐ Advertisement
- ☐ Magazine review ☐ Store display
- ☐ Mailing ☐ Book's format
- ☐ Reputation of Waite Group Press ☐ Other

How many computer books do you buy each year? _____

How many other Waite Group books do you own? _____

What is your favorite Waite Group book? _____
_____

Is there any program or subject you would like to see Waite Group Press cover in a similar approach? _____
_____

Additional comments? _____
_____
_____

Please send to: **Waite Group Press**
200 Tamal Plaza
Corte Madera, CA 94925

☐ **Check here for a free Waite Group catalog**